IN VINO VERITAS

IN VINO VERITAS

Edited by

OSWYN MURRAY AND
MANUELA TECUŞAN

British School at Rome, London, in Association with American Academy at Rome, Swedish
Institute at Rome, Istituto Universitario Orientale Napoli, and Università di Salerno

1995

ISBN 0 904152 27 8

Jacket illustration: The 'stork-vase' from the Mola di Monte Gelato
(Drawn by S.J. Ashley; courtesy of Dr T.W. Potter and the Trustees of the British Museum)

The inscription, published by Oswyn Murray, Peter Parsons, Tim Potter and Paul Roberts in *Papers of the British School at Rome* 59 (1991), reads: 'I am called a friend of friends: when you drink you will understand that I do not deceive'.

Typeset by Alden Multimedia, Northampton
and printed by The Alden Press, Oxford
Jacket design by Three's Company, 18 Henley Avenue, Oxford OX4 4DJ

CONTENTS

WINE AND SOCIETY IN ETRURIA AND ITALY

WINE AND SOCIETY IN REPUBLICAN AND IMPERIAL ROME

LIST OF FIGURES

LIST OF FIGURES

To Chapter 5:

To Chapter 9:

PREFACE

This volume is the record of a four day international conference on wine and society in the ancient world, held in Rome from 19th to 22nd March, 1991. The occasion was initiated by Oswyn Murray as Balsdon Fellow at the British School, and was in part a sequel to two earlier colloquia, the first held in Oxford in September 1984 (published in *Sympotica: a Symposium on the* Symposion, edited by Oswyn Murray (Oxford, 1990)), and the second held at McMaster University in September 1989 (published as *Dining in a Classical Context*, edited by William J. Slater (Ann Arbor, 1991)). On this occasion however we sought to broaden our theme to cover, not just Greece and Rome, but other cultures where alcohol played a major role, like Egypt, the Near East and Etruria.

The theme of the conference was the place of wine in ritual, culture and society. In the ancient world, wine was an article of value and the focus for a series of social and religious rituals. It served often to express and even to create forms of social stratification, and to structure communities through shared religious and other rituals. Around these activities there developed a complex art, expressing the values of the court or the drinking group and serving its needs through decorated objects. There also developed around the consumption of wine a conception of pleasure, which included song, dance, music and sexual desire, and which has left its mark in the literatures of many ancient cultures. These rituals of conviviality often evolved through cross-fertilization from one culture to another. In this conference we sought to explore a variety of leading themes within the chosen cultures of the ancient world — the relationship between conviviality and social structure (royal pleasures, honour and rank in feasting, the Männerbund, social equality, the development of societies under the impact of new drinking customs); the relationship between wine and religion (gods and myths of wine, religious rituals, the place of wine in the festival context); the relationship between culture and wine (art, literature and the arts of pleasure). In other words we concentrated our attention on wine as a social and cultural phenomenon, and as an essential characteristic of the ancient mentality. We were not primarily concerned with economic aspects of the production and distribution of wine; for this reason a number of fringe cultures which were deeply affected by the reception of Mediterranean products and customs, like the Scythians and the Gauls, were passed over. Encyclopedic or systematic completeness is anyway impossible: there is perhaps no definitive study to be written, and the theme is so limitless that (properly conceived) there can be no end to the deipnosophistic activity, as we may perhaps demonstrate on future occasions. But we hope at least that on this occasion we have enlarged and enriched our understanding of the various senses in which for the different ancient cultures *in vino est veritas*.

The conference was jointly organized and funded by the British School, the American Academy, the Swedish Institute, the Istituto Universitario Orientale di Napoli, and the Università di Salerno. The responsible organizing committee comprised

Oswyn Murray (British School), Bruno D'Agostino (Naples), Carl Nylander (Swedisn Institute), Angela Pontrandolfo (Salerno), Michael Putnam (American Academy), and Carlo Zaccagnini (Bologna). The central Secretariat was at the British School. Each day was organized around three sessions, each with two invited speakers, two morning sessions and one evening session. Papers were by invitation only, but there was ample time for discussion. Each institution in Rome had primary responsibility for one day. The first day on 'Alcohol in Near Eastern Cultures' was organized by Carl Nylander and Carlo Zaccagnini, and held at the Swedish Institute; the second day on 'Wine in Greek Culture', was organized by Oswyn Murray, the third day on 'Wine and Society in Etruria and Italy' by Bruno D'Agostino and Angela Pontrandolfo; both were held at the British School. The fourth day on 'Wine and Society in Republican and Imperial Rome' was the responsibility of Michael Putnam, and was held in the American Academy.

The organizers wish to thank our large and enthusiastic audiences, the speakers and the participants in the discussions (of which only a small fraction are here presented as formal *interventi*). We should also like to thank the chairmen who were, apart from the organizers: Mario Liverani (Rome), L.E. Rossi (Rome), Giovanni Colonna (Rome), Mauro Cristofani (Rome), Agnès Rouveret (Paris), Amanda Claridge (British School), Nicholas Purcell (Oxford). We thank too the directors of the British and American institutes, Richard Hodges and Joseph Connors, for enthusiastically supporting our venture, and the heads of all the schools involved for underwriting the costs of accommodation and administration. Direct financial support was gratefully received from the British Academy, the British School and especially the University of Salerno. We also thank the staff of the various institutes, and especially the British School (who provided the catering for three days) for their magnificent hospitality to ourselves and our guests.

An event of this nature, involving so many institutions and so many scholars, in which the nominal organizer was normally resident in a different country, must have a hidden secret. The practical details and the coordination were provided by two individuals, who are responsible for this conference being a model of convivial efficiency. The first is Amanda Claridge, then Assistant Director of the British School, who oversaw every practical aspect of the event. The second is Jane Leitch, then personal assistant to the Director and now of the British Academy, who provided the real organization of the whole conference. To both we offer heartfelt thanks. The proceedings have been prepared for publication by Oswyn Murray and Manuela Tecuşan. The costs of publication have been borne by the American Academy, the British School, the Swedish Institute, the M. Aylwin Cotton Foundation, and the Jowett Copyright Trust.

To all those who have helped at each stage the editors and organizers are deeply grateful. We hope that, apart from the scientific interest of the conference and its proceedings, it may stand as an example of international and interdisciplinary cooperation, and will especially encourage the various institutions in the most intellectually alive of all capital cities to collaborate in similar projects in the future.

NOTE ON ABBREVIATIONS

For periodical titles the abbreviations given in *L'Année Philologique* have been used, supplemented when necessary by those given in the *American Journal of Archaeology*. For classical authors and works, the abbreviations given in *The Oxford Classical Dictionary* have been used primarily. However, for the convenience of the reader the details for journals and standard works relevant to this volume are given below.

Journals

AA	*Archäologischer Anzeiger*
AAntHung	*Acta Antiqua Academiae Scientiarum Hungaricae*
AAWM	*Abhandlungen der Akademie der Wissenschaften in Mainz, Geistes- und Sozialwissenschaftliche Klasse*
ACD	*Acta classica universitatis scientiarum Debreceniensis*
AEHE (V^e sect.)	*Annuaire de l'École pratique des hautes études, V^e sect., sciences religieuses*
AION(archeol)	*Annali dell'istituto universitario orientale di Napoli. Dipartimento di studi del mondo classico e del mediterraneo antico. Sezione di archeologia e storia antica*
AJA	*American Journal of Archaeology*
AK	*Antike Kunst*
Annales (ESC)	*Annales: économies, sociétés, civilisations*
AR	*Archaeological Reports (Society of Hellenic Studies/British School at Athens)*
ArchDelt	Ἀρχαιολογικὸν Δελτίον
ArchEph	Ἀρχαιολογικὴ Ἐφημερίς
ARID	*Analecta Romana Instituti Danici*
ArtB	*The Art Bulletin*
ASNP	*Annali della scuola normale superiore di Pisa. Classe di lettere e filosofia*
AU	*Der Altsprachliche Unterricht: Arbeitshefte zu seiner Wissenschaftlichen Begründung und Praktischen Gestalt*
AW	*Antike Welt*
AZ	*Archäologische Zeitung*
BaM	*Baghdader Mitteilungen*
BASO	*Bulletin of the American Schools of Oriental Research in Jerusalem and Baghdad*
BCH	*Bulletin de correspondance hellénique*
BEFAR	*Bibliothèque de l'École française d'Athènes et de Rome*
BJ	*Bonner Jahrbücher des Rheinischen Landesmuseums in Bonn und des Vereins von Altertumsfreunden im Rheinlande*
BO	*Bibliotheca Orientalis*
CArch	*Cahiers archéologiques: fin de l'antiquité et moyen âge*
CJ	*The Classical Journal*

CQ	*Classical Quarterly*
CRAI	*Comptes rendus de l'Académie des Inscriptions et Belles-Lettres*
CW	*The Classical World*
DArch	*Dialoghi di archeologia*
EMC	*Échos du monde classique (Classical Views)*
ErIsr	*Eretz-Israel*
G&R	*Greece and Rome*
GIF	*Giornale italiano di filologia*
GRBS	*Greek, Roman and Byzantine Studies*
HSPh	*Harvard Studies in Classical Philology*
IA	*Iranica antiqua*
JbAC	*Jahrbuch für Antike und Christentum*
JBerlM	*Jahrbuch der Berliner Museen*
JBL	*Journal of Biblical Literature*
JDAI	*Jahrbuch des Deutschen Archäologischen Instituts*
JHS	*Journal of Hellenic Studies*
JMainz	*Jahrbuch. Akademie der Wissenschaften und der Literatur [Mainz]*
JNES	*Journal of Near Eastern Studies*
JÖAI	*Jahreshefte der Österreichischen Archäologischen Instituts, Wien*
JRA	*Journal of Roman Archaeology*
JRS	*Journal of Roman Studies*
MD	*Materiali e discussioni per l'analisi dei testi classici*
MDAI(A)	*Mitteilungen des Deutschen Archäologischen Instituts (Athen. Abt.)*
MDAI(R)	*Mitteilungen des Deutschen Archäologischen Instituts (Röm. Abt.)*
MDIK	*Mitteilungen des Deutschen Archäologisches Instituts, Abteilung Kairo*
MEFR	*Mélanges d'archéologie et d'histoire de l'École française de Rome*
MEFRA	*Mélanges d'archéologie et d'histoire de l'École française de Rome. Antiquité.*
MH	*Museum Helveticum: revue suisse pour l'étude de l'antiquité classique*
MonAL	*Monumenti antichi*
NSA	*Notizie degli scavi di antichità*
OAth	*Opuscula Atheniensia*
ORom	*Opuscula Romana: acta Inst. Rom. Regni Sueciae*
P&P	*Past and Present: a Journal of Historical Studies*
PBSR	*Papers of the British School at Rome*
PP	*La parola del passato*
PSN	*Petronian Society Newsletter*
QUCC	*Quaderni urbinati di cultura classica*
RA	*Revue archéologique*
RAAN	*Rendiconti dell'accademia di archeologia, lettere e belle arti di Napoli*
RAssyr	*Revue d'assyriologie et d'archéologie orientale*
REA	*Revue des études anciennes*
REL	*Revue des études latines*
RhM	*Rheinisches Museum*
RHR	*Revue de l'histoire des religions*
RPh	*Revue de philologie de littérature et d'histoire anciennes*
SE	*Studi etruschi*

SIFC	*Studi italiani di filologia classica*
SMSR	*Studi e materiali di storia delle religioni*
StudClas	*Studii Clasice (Bucureşti)*
TAPhA	*Transactions and Proceedings of the American Philological Association*
UF	*Ugarit-Forschungen*
WS	*Wiener Studien: Zeitschrift für Klassische Philologie und Patristik*
YClS	*Yale Classical Studies*
ZATW	*Zeitschrift für die Alttestamentliche Wissenschaft*
ZPE	*Zeitschrift für Papyrologie und Epigraphik*

Standard works

ABV	J.D. Beazley, *Attic Black-figure Vase-painters* (Oxford, 1956)
ANET	J.B. Pritchard (ed.), *Ancient Near-Eastern Texts Relating to the Old Testament* (Princeton, 1950; third edition 1969)
ARV	J.D. Beazley, *Attic Red-figure Vase-painters* (first edition, Oxford 1942; second edition, Oxford 1963)
CIL	*Corpus Inscriptionum Latinarum* (1863-)
CLE	F. Bücheler (ed.), *Carmina Latina Epigraphica* (1895-1926)
CVA	*Corpus Vasorum Antiquorum* (1925-)
CVP	D.A. Amyx, *Corinthian Vase-painting of the Archaic Period* (Berkeley, 1988)
Dar.-Sag.	Ch. Daremberg and E. Saglio, *Dictionnaire des antiquités grecques et romaines d'après les textes et les monuments* (Paris, 1877-1919)
FGrH	F. Jacoby, *Fragmente der Griechischen Historiker* (1923-69)
HE	A.S.F. Gow and D.L. Page (eds), *Hellenistic Epigrams* (Cambridge, 1965)
I. Histriae	*Inscriptiones Daciae et Scythiae Minoris Antiquae, series altera: Inscriptiones Scythiae Minoris Graecae et Latinae, vol. I: Inscriptiones Histriae et Viciniae* (Bucarest, 1983)
I. Priene	F. Hiller von Gaertringen (ed.), *Inschriften von Priene* (Berlin, 1906)
I. Stratonikeia	M. Çetin Şahin (ed.), *Die Inschriften von Stratonikeia* (Bonn, 1981-90)
ID	F. Durrbach, *Inscriptions de Délos* (Paris, 1926-37)
IG	*Inscriptiones Graecae* (1873-)
ILLRP	H. Degrassi, *Inscriptiones latinae liberae rei publicae* (Rome, 1957-63)
ILS	H. Dessau, *Inscriptiones Latinae Selectae* (Berlin, 1892-1916)
K.-A.	R. Kassel and C. Austin (eds), *Poetae Comici Graeci* (Berlin, 1893-; cf. *PCG*)
Kock	T. Kock, *Comicorum Atticorum Fragmenta* (Leipzig, 1880-8)
Kühn	C.G. Kühn, *Medicorum Graecorum Opera* (Leipzig, 1821-33)
LIMC	*Lexicon Iconographicum Mythologiae Classicae* (Zurich and Munich, 1974-)
Paralipomena	J.D. Beazley, *Paralipomena* (Oxford, 1971)
PCG	R. Kassel and C. Austin (eds), *Poetae Comici Graeci* (Berlin, 1893-; cf. K.-A.)
P.Hal.	*Dikaiomata: Auszüge aus Alexandrinischen Gesetzen und Verordnungen in einem Papyrus des Philologischen Seminars der Universität Halle, herausgegeben von der Graeca Halensis* (Berlin, 1913)
PIR^2	E. Groag and A. Stein (eds), *Prosopographia Imperii Romani Saeculi I, II, III* (second edition) (Berlin, 1933-)

PLondon   F.G. Kenyon and H.I. Bell (eds), *Greek Papyri in the British Museum* (London, 1893-1907)
PMG   D.L. Page (ed.), *Poetae Melici Graeci* (Oxford, 1962)
POxy.   B.P. Grenfell and A.S. Hunt (eds), *The Oxyryhnchus Papyri* (London, 1898-)
Pyr.   K. Sethe, *Die Altägyptischen Pyramidentexte* (Leipzig, 1908-22)
RE   Pauly-Wissowa, *Real-Encyclopädie der Klassischen Altertumswissenschaft*
SVF   H. von Arnim, *Stoicorum Veterum Fragmenta* (Leipzig, 1903-24)

INTRODUCTION

1

Histories of Pleasure

OSWYN MURRAY

Fortius est vinum: fortior est rex: fortiores sunt mulieres, super omnia autem vincit veritas.

Now when Darius reigned, he made a great feast unto all his subjects, and unto all his household, and unto all the princes of Media and Persia, and to all the governors and captains and lieutenants that were under him, from India unto Ethiopia, of an hundred twenty and seven provinces. And when they had eaten and drunken, and being satisfied were gone home, then Darius the king went into his bedchamber, and slept, and soon after awaked. Then three young men, that were of the guard that kept the king's body, spake one to another: Let every one of us speak a sentence: he that shall overcome, and whose sentence shall seem wiser than the others, unto him shall the king Darius give great gifts, and great things in token of victory: as, to be clothed in purple, to drink in gold, and to sleep upon gold, and a chariot with bridles of gold, and an headtire of fine linen, and a chain about his neck: and he shall sit next to Darius because of his wisdom, and shall be called Darius his cousin. And then every one wrote his sentence, sealed it, and laid it under king Darius his pillow; and said that, when the king is risen, some will give him the writings; and of whose side the king and the three Princes of Persia shall judge that his sentence is the wisest, to him shall the victory be given, as was appointed.

The first wrote, Wine is the strongest. The second wrote, The king is strongest. The third wrote, Women are strongest: but above all things truth beareth away the victory.

First Book of Esdras (Authorized Translation)

The story of the Three Pages appears only in the Greek version of the rebuilding of Jerusalem; it was well known to Josephus and the early Fathers, and survived the condemnation of Saint Jerome to become a standard topic for medieval *disputationes*, where it must have disturbed the meditations of many a lusty young monk studying Saint Thomas Aquinas, *Quaestiones Quodlibetales* 14.1. Apart from the somewhat implausible ending which has been added to the sentence of the last Page, the story displays the typical features of the court novel of the Persian period, and surely reflects the same popular folk traditions that are found elsewhere, for instance in the Books of Judith, Tobit and Esther: whether the original was composed in Greek or Aramaic, it belongs to a Hellenistic koine of the storytelling art.[1] In approaching the theme *In vino veritas* from so many different cultures, we can scarcely do better than remind ourselves of the words of the first Page:

---

[1] The best general discussion of this story remains C.C. Torrey, *Ezra Studies* (Chicago, 1910), 37-61. He argued that the original was in Aramaic not Greek (20-5), and plausibly connected the name of the king's concubine, Apama (4.29) with Apama, daughter of Artabazus, given in marriage by Alexander the Great to Ptolemy, later king of Egypt (Arr. *Anab.* vii. 4.6; Plut. *Eumenes* 1). It was however R. Laqueur, 'Ephoros', *Hermes* 46 (1911), 161-206, in particular note on pp. 168-72, who first pointed out that truth was a later addition to the story, and who established that the original order had been king, wine,

Viri quam praevalet vinum: O ye men, how exceeding strong is wine! It causeth all men to err that drink it: it maketh the mind of the king and of the fatherless child to be all one; of the bondman and of the freeman, of the poor man and of the rich: it turneth also every thought into jollity and mirth, so that a man remembereth neither sorrow nor debt: and it maketh every heart rich, so that a man remembereth neither king nor governor; and it maketh to speak all things by talents: and when they are in their cups, they forget their love both to friends and brethren, and a little after draw out swords: but when they are from the wine, they remember not what they have done. O ye men, is not wine the strongest, that enforceth to do thus?

The general tone of this praise of wine should give us pause for thought. Wine is seen as the antithesis of social organization: confronted by its power, all men are equal; the social order disintegrates, the constraints of reality are loosened: even the bonds of group companionship turn to conflict. Wine is a savage release, which dissolves the structures of society. It operates in antithesis to the power of the king, and in a way analogous to the power ascribed to women, who through sexual desire subvert the male order. But whereas women (as in the story of Esther) offer an alternative power structure based on manipulation of the existing system, wine is truly anarchic. The order is subverted, 'but when they are from the wine, they remember not what they have done'.

This anarchic quality of wine, this tendency towards anomie, is perhaps the truth that will be revealed in the course of our discussions; yet it is a quality which we as cultural historians find most disturbing. Many of us have tended, I think, to investigate the role of wine in society and literature from a social point of view. We accept that alcohol is a drug which may have antisocial aspects when abused; but these we leave to the doctors and the sociologists.[2] We find ourselves more in sympathy with the anthropologists, who assert the positive value of wine: 'It is a striking pattern that most non-anthropological writers who deal with alcohol tend to focus primarily on various problems that they consider derive from its use, whereas most anthropologists tend to focus more on the use' (Heath, 'A decade...', p. 36).

Among historians there is indeed an increasing tendency to emphasize the socializing aspects of alcohol. For them the truth in wine is a social truth. Unlike most drugs, alcohol does not isolate the individual in a private world; it is normally consumed in a social context: its characteristic physiological effect of reducing inhibitory social

---

woman; medieval versions of the story often revert to this more piquant triad (E. Lommatzsch, 'Die stärkste Dinge', *JMainz* (1961), 236-8). W. Rudolph, 'Der Wettstreit der Leibwächter des Darius 3 Esr. 3.1-5.6', *ZATW* 61 (1945-8), 176-90 argued for a Greek original. The closest parallel yet adduced is indeed Greek, the story of the three Samian girls at the Festival of Adonis from Diphilus, *Theseus* (Ath. 451B) where the three strongest things are iron, blacksmith, penis, since each conquers the other in succession; this shows that the folk motif was already naturalized in the Greek world in the fourth century, whatever the origin of the particular version in First Book of Esdras. For a longer Ethiopian catena containing the same elements, see Laqueur, p. 172 note. There is a general literary discussion by J.L. Crenshaw, 'The contest of Darius' guards', in B.O. Long (ed.), *Images of Man and God: Old Testament Stories in Literary Focus* (Sheffield, 1981), 74-88. I owe the observation on Aquinas to Liberato Santorio of University College, Dublin.

[2] For this difference in approach see D.B. Heath, 'A decade of development in the anthropological study of alcohol use: 1970-1980', in M. Douglas (ed.), *Constructive Drinking: Perspectives on Drink from Anthropology* (Cambridge, 1987), 16-69. For the increasing emphasis on the problematization of alcohol during the nineteenth century see D. Nourisson, *Le buveur du XIXe siècle* (Paris, 1990).

barriers is seen not as leading to anomie, but as helping to create a sense of togetherness, of group bonding: 'In most societies, drinking is essentially a social act and, as such, it is embedded in a context of values, attitudes, and other norms (*ibid.* p. 46). We thus interpret the rituals concerned with alcohol in a functionalist sense, as serving to establish group relations, or creating a religious atmosphere, or as offering a release from social tensions. We emphasize the *usefulness* of alcohol, even when we qualify that usefulness as usefulness for relaxation — as when the warrior group, in leisure moments, prepares itself for future conflicts through the pleasures of the male drinking group.[3]

And yet there remains the fact of the potentiality for anomie, the power of Dionysus to disrupt society, to send his devotees mad — that is to offer not an alternative order, but the alternative of disorder. There remains also the fact that 'whatever the problems that sometimes result from drinking, the act of drinking is usually viewed as a pleasant and sociable one' (*ibid.* p. 31): even before the arrival of madness, however the historian may regard all this activity, drinking is not perceived by the drinkers as being itself useful, but as simply pleasurable.

My aim in what follows is not to contradict the functionalist view of alcohol, but rather to explore a range of possible theories which would situate our investigations in the general context of the problem of the history of pleasure. For I feel that our doubts are part of a wider problem concerned with the autonomy of pleasure as a factor in history. The focus of a history of pleasure is those activities which are engaged in primarily because they cause physical or mental sensations of pleasure, and only incidentally, if at all, because they may have a usefulness to society. Thus for instance we would count sexual activity and the pleasures of food and drink as basic pleasures. But we should also include in the history of pleasure many other more complex human activities which are engaged in primarily for pleasure, such as sport, hunting, reading, the appreciation of art, or thinking, provided that these activities are undertaken mainly for their own sake, that is for the pleasure of the person who engages in them, rather than for social reasons. Thus visiting art galleries is a pleasure, while owning works of art may perhaps be more a socially determined status symbol, and making them involves an economic and social relationship of patronage.[4] Contemplation, the *bios theoretikos* in the Greek sense, is a pleasure,[5] while in the Christian sense of contemplation of God it is a moral duty, and in the modern sense of 'research' it is a social activity, to be measured in terms of productivity and output. It will be seen that I follow Epicurus and Freud in thinking that there is a close relationship between pleasure and culture: for if there exists a separate area of discourse which can be described as cultural history, its distinguishing characteristic is surely that it concerns itself with that which is independently pleasurable, rather than with that which can be reduced to the concept of the useful.

This independence of culture is of course a fragile independence, and one which worries the practitioners of the dominant schools of history, whose theories are based on the primacy of power relations or economic laws; for they wish to subsume all human

---

[3] Cf. O. Murray, 'War and the Symposium', in W.J. Slater (ed.), *Dining in a Classical Context* (Ann Arbor, 1991), 83-103; P. Schmitt Pantel, *La cité au banquet* (Paris, 1992).

[4] Cf. H.S. Becker, *Art Worlds* (Chicago, 1982).

[5] What Burckhardt called 'the contemplative mode', Veblen 'idle curiosity', and Foucault simply 'curiosity'; for Aristotle see A.J.P. Kenny, *Aristotle on the Perfect Life* (Oxford, 1992), esp. chs 7-8.

activities within their hierarchy of categories. Yet it seems to me clear that pleasures exist independently of any social function they may possess, and cannot be wholly reduced to these functions. In such diverse areas as literature, art, music or sport, man has invented a range of activities which are practised for their own sake and for the pleasures they bring; these pleasures may often begin from physical sensations, but they cannot be explained purely in terms of behavioural psychology; for such attempts scarcely do justice to the complexity of the activity, or to its development over time. They may be related to other aspects of human history, to economic forces or power relations; but again a history of art in terms of the forms of patronage or of literature in terms of social use, although clearly revealing an important aspect of the social history of a period, seem ultimately to miss the point of the activity, which is to give pleasure.

The economists have a way of describing this problem. The laws of economics may establish the proper outcome of an economically rational choice, but the agent will often opt for an alternative, apparently non-rational course of action. This is explained by the claim that the value of any object or course of action is determined, not by any abstract measure, but by the subjective 'Utility' or desiredness attributed to it by the agent.[6] The concept of 'Utility', whatever its historical origin, is indeed curiously named, for it represents not so much the use*ful*, as the use*less*: it is the reason why I choose a *cornetto* rather than a *panino* for breakfast, preferring pleasure to profit and health; it is the reason why I prefer the life of scholarship to the money-making life. It is an explanation of that part of human behaviour which would otherwise fall outside the laws of economics.

Laws of history also possess their 'Utility Factor'; for they deal in an absolute sense only with the necessities of history, with those extreme situations where choice is limited. Most of us live most of the time in an easier clime where individual choice leads to collective chance, and where the complexity of the resulting structures defies analysis according to historical laws. And it is clear that within that complexity there resides an unresolved but human attention to the non-necessary, to pleasure for its own sake.

Let me explain this by presenting a series of attempts to offer a theoretical explanation of the role of pleasure in history. In my brief comments I do not wish to suggest that these attempts are wrong, for like all historical theories they are merely theories, ways of organizing the material into forms of explanation and hierarchies of subordination: each is likely to have its use in particular circumstances, whatever we may think of it as a general theory. I do not in fact wish to offer a theory of the history of pleasure (*l'histoire du plaisir*), still less a history of pleasures (*l'histoire des plaisirs*), but rather to discuss the different histories of pleasure (*les histoires du plaisir*). At least, whether or not you agree with my comments, I shall have presented at the start of our discussions a variety of possible ways of ordering the truth of the phenomena we are investigating.

The problem is to make the history of pleasure more than mere description. There is of course a place for the chronological catalogue of activity, in which the lack of causal explanation is represented as the consequence of fashion, the necessity of change. A history of style in clothing, or of a particular sport, almost presupposes a history without

---

[6] See R.D. Collison Black *s.v.* 'utility', in J. Eatwell, M. Millgate and P. Newman (eds), *The New Palgrave, A Dictionary of Economics*, Vol. 4 (London, 1987), 776-9.

causal links, or one in which the causal links are subordinate to the mere phenomenon of change; even a history of literature or painting can be written in terms of technical schools, as a diadochal succession, where such causal links as exist are not intrinsic, but relate to phenomena outside the activity, in society in general. Paul Veyne has indeed elevated such 'sub-lunary' randomness to the status of a theory in itself: history is about that which cannot be explained, *l'inventaire des différences*.[7] But most of us wish for a history which is more than mere description; the problem is to develop a concept of causation which is appropriate to the arbitrary, and a theory of history which finds a place for such non-functional but apparently necessary human activities as sport, literature and art.

It seems to me that the theories at present available fall into two main groups. On the one hand there are those theories which seek to explain the function of pleasure in its relationship to the traditional forces of history, and which therefore subordinate it to the structures of political power, to economics or to religious forms. On the other hand there are those theories which regard pleasure or culture as an independent phenomenon with its own historical laws.

Perhaps the most coherent explanation of pleasure in terms of economic theory remains that of Thorstein Veblen in his work *The Theory of the Leisure Class* (New York, 1899).[8] According to him any social hierarchy generates leisure, and it is part of the function of an aristocracy to identify itself through display. Some forms of display, such as military training, are socially useful; but in the majority of cases it is not the activity in itself, but the display, which has social value, in creating envy, competition, and a sense of hierarchical order. We should not therefore ask of any activity of the leisure class, 'what is its use?' but, 'how does it serve to distinguish the leisure class from those without leisure?'. It follows that the less useful the activity, the more it is removed from economic or social rationality, the more effective it is as a mark of class distinction. Sport is not a training for health or war, but, as a Phaeacian nobleman points out to Odysseus, the prerogative of the privileged: 'You look like one who travels with a well-benched ship, a master of sailors that are merchantmen, a man mindful of his cargo, watching his route and the gains he has snatched: you look no athlete.' (*Od.* viii. 159-64).

Inevitably in a competitive aristocratic world, the uselessness of an activity is not enough; it must also be positively wasteful and publicly displayed as such. Variety or

---

[7] *Comment on écrit l'histoire: essai d'épistémologie* (Paris, 1971 (second edition 1978)); *L'inventaire des différences* (Paris, 1976). For critiques of the successive phases of Veyne's ideas, see reviews by R. Aron, *Annales (ESC)* 26 (1971), 1319-54; J. Andreau, P. Schmitt, A. Schnapp and F. Hartog, *Annales (ESC)* 33 (1978), 307-30; my introduction to P. Veyne, *Bread and Circuses* (London, 1990), vii-xxiii; M.A. Katz, review of *Did the Greeks Believe in their Myths?*, *History and Theory* 31 (1992), 65-81.

[8] On Veblen (1857-1929) see the classic biography of J. Dorfman, *Thorstein Veblen and his America* (New York, 1934 (seventh edition 1967)), and the introduction to J. Dorfman, *Thorstein Veblen: Essays Reviews and Reports: Previously Uncollected Writings* (Clifton, 1973), 5-326. There is important new biographical material in R. Tilman, *Thorstein Veblen and his Critics, 1891-1963* (Princeton, 1992), ch. 1; although this book claims to be concerned only with Veblen on political economy and social theory, it contains much of interest about critics of his theories on culture and aesthetics. See also the introduction of C. Wright Mills to the reprint of *The Theory of the Leisure Class* (London, 1970), which is the edition I quote. But the most fundamental analysis of the cultural aspect of Veblen remains T.W. Adorno's brilliant essay of 1941, 'Veblen's attack on culture', *Studies in Philosophy and Social Science* 9 (1941), 389-413; German version in *Gesammelte Schriften 10.2: Kulturkritik und Gesellschaft I* (Frankfurt, 1977), 72-96.

fashion has its origins in the need for continuous display; value is related to the unnecessary labour that has gone into the acquisition, manufacture or decoration of those objects which are intended for display, not use. In addition, the complexity and the difficulty of the activity serve to demonstrate the extent of leisure required to achieve such standards of skill:

> The ability to use and to understand certain of the dead languages of southern Europe is not only gratifying to the person who finds occasion to parade his accomplishments in this respect, but the evidence of such knowledge serves at the same time to recommend any savant to his audience, both lay and learned. It is currently expected that a certain number of years shall have been spent in acquiring this substantially useless information, and its absence creates a presumption of hasty and precarious learning, as well as of a vulgar practicality that is equally obnoxious to the conventional standards of sound scholarship and intellectual force.
>
> (Veblen, *op. cit.* p. 255)

Conspicuous consumption and conspicuous waste are the characteristic signs of an élite. The ultimate form of display lies in public destruction unaccompanied by pleasure or use, in the rituals of the potlatch or modern warfare.

The feast in one of its aspects as a social phenomenon fits easily into such an analysis. For the feast is in essence the use of an agricultural surplus for non-necessary ends. If it can be institutionalized as a public activity belonging to a certain class it will become a prerogative of privilege, regardless of the elements of usefulness which may also be involved. Thus some aspects of the warrior feast may promote military virtues, just as some elements in the monastic *mensa* may promote the contemplative life; but these occasions are essentially moments of rest and of the public display of that felicity which is due to those groups who labour on behalf of the community in the non-necessary activities which mark them out as an élite. Such practices are not confined to aristocracies: in the monarchic societies of the Near East, the ultimate felicity of the king is portrayed in representations of his feasting alone, as a symbolic image of the fortune of his people; and honour in the Persian Empire is apportioned by the king to his nobles in the form of rations for feasting.[9]

Wine too serves as an obvious mark in the leisure structures of an élite of this type. Again it can have (as Plato argued in the *Laws*) a use in the proving of courage and in the creation of a group mentality. Yet the activity of drinking is in itself, not a preparation for war, but an activity of a warrior class at leisure. In ancient Greece I would argue that an important aspect of the *symposion* is its origin in the privileges of a military class.[10] Elsewhere even more clearly the introduction of wine and the customs associated with the drinking of wine into cultures like those of Italy and southern Gaul was accompanied by the use of these customs as a symbol of social differentiation for an

---

[9] On the role of rations in the creation of the Old Persian hierarchy, see R.T. Hallock, 'The evidence of the Persepolis tablets', in I. Gershevitch (ed.), *Cambridge History of Iran* ii (1985), ch. 11; D.M. Lewis, 'The king's dinner (Polyaenus iv, 3, 32)', in H. Sancisi-Weerdenburg and A. Kuhrt (eds), *Achaemenid History II: The Greek Sources* (Leiden, 1987), 79-87; and 'The Persepolis fortification texts', in H. Sancisi-Weerdenburg and A. Kuhrt (eds), *Achaemenid History IV: Core and Periphery* (Leiden, 1990), 1-10.

[10] See esp. my paper cited in n. 3, with P. Schmitt Pantel's important critique, *La cité au banquet* (above, n. 3), 45-52.

aristocracy which was in the process of formation.[11] The luxurious lifestyle was a symbol of superiority in Veblen's sense of conspicuous consumption, rather than the strictly necessary attribute of a gentilicial nobility: 'Drunkenness and the other pathological consequences of the free use of stimulants therefore tend in their turn to become honorific, as being a mark, at the second remove, of the superior status of those who are able to afford the indulgence.' (Veblen, *op. cit.* p. 62).

The strength of Veblen's approach surely lies in its ability to illuminate the role of culture in the formation and maintenance of élites. It frees us from the need to relate the leisure activities of such groups to their specific social function: all élites have this need for badges of office and styles of life. It also enables us to justify the progressive complication of leisure activities, as part of the intrinsic need for change in a competitive situation. But I do not think it helps much in the understanding of the specific character of the culture produced by a particular élite. And it does not illuminate the psychology of the participating group: the pleasures they engage in remain arbitrary ones, serving only to set them apart from the rest of society.

A second type of general theory seems to lie behind a variety of modern writings, especially on the feast. In the ancient world the feast is closely related to occasions of religious worship, in that the sacrifice is distributed to the worshippers, and serves as the basis for a common meal. This meal can be exclusive, used to distinguish a special group of priests or devotees; but it is also often inclusive, uniting the community, which consists of all those taking part in the occasion, often on a basis of equality. In the civic religion of the Greek *polis*, the festival meal is an occasion when all worshippers share equally, and affirm their identity as a community; it may also be an occasion when men and gods share a common feast.[12] The use of wine in this ritual context seems to have special significance, for it raises man to a new level of consciousness, and enables him to partake in the pleasures of the gods — as Euripides' Cyclops says:

> O joy unmixed! heaven seems brought low to earth and mingled with it!
> I see the throne of Zeus and the whole heavenly gathering of the gods!

> (*Cyc.* 577-80).

These attitudes are not confined to civic occasions; they are also characteristic of closed religious groups, such as the Pythagoreans who chose to identify themselves as different by means of complex food taboos and communal meals. The pleasures of wine and the sympotic life were regarded as a privilege which was available to initiates of the

---

[11] For the wine trade to Etruria and the west, see M.A. Rizzo, *Le anfore di trasporto e il commercio etrusco arcaico I: complessi tombali dall'Etruria meridionale* (Rome, 1990); P.S. Wells, *Culture Contact and Culture Change* (Cambridge, 1980); B. Cunliffe, *Greeks, Romans and Barbarians: Spheres of Interaction* (London, 1988), ch. 2; and the documents from Ampurias (*ZPE* 68 (1987), 119-27; 72 (1988), 100-2; 77 (1989), 36-8) and the Languedoc (*CRAI* 1988, 526-36). On the development of an aristocratic style of life, see A. Rathje, 'The adoption of the Homeric banquet in central Italy in the Orientalizing period', in O. Murray (ed.), *Sympotica: a Symposium on the* Symposion (Oxford, 1990), 279-88, and in this volume; M. Torelli, 'Banchetto e simposio nell'Italia arcaica: qualche nota', in O. Longo and P. Scarpi (eds), *Homo Edens* (Verona, 1989), 301-7.

[12] M. Detienne and J.-P. Vernant, *La cuisine du sacrifice en pays grec* (Paris, 1979); C. Grottanelli and N.F. Parise (eds), *Sacrificio e società nel mondo antico* (Rome, 1988); Schmitt Pantel, *La cité au banquet* (above, n. 3).

Mysteries after death, when they would share in the life of the immortal heroes; and heroic cult in the ancient world was itself a specific focus for occasions of eating and drinking.[13] The role of pleasure in religious experience is an aspect of ancient religions which has been neglected by modern historians brought up in the Platonic and Christian tradition: the notion that man can achieve the same happiness as the gods through physical pleasures has been lost in that long process of renunciation of the flesh and of the separation between the spiritual and the temporal world. It is surely true that in the ancient world gods and men were united in their pleasures, and divided only by the time-span allotted for their enjoyment. Yet even in the classical period the assertion of a direct equivalence between men and gods in this respect is reserved for less solemn occasions and for less august, more human and less 'divine', gods. The idea that men and gods may share pleasures in the religious feast does not imply a belief that human pleasures are themselves divine.

A third analysis of the role of pleasure in history is related to the importance given by Freud to the instinct of pleasure in human psychology: 'we have no hesitation in asserting that the course taken by mental events is automatically regulated by the pleasure principle' (*Beyond the Pleasure Principle* (London, 1961), 1).[14] Pleasure is the basic human instinct; but 'under the influence of the ego's instincts of self-preservation, the pleasure principle is replaced by the reality principle', the willingness to postpone pleasure. This repression is a phenomenon imposed on the individual by his relation to society; it may involve the socialization of pleasure, its manipulation for social ends determined consciously or unconsciously as useful, or it may involve the internalization of pleasure in the imagination, the region which 'was expressly exempted from the demands of reality-testing and was set apart for the purpose of fulfilling wishes which were difficult to carry out' (*Civilization and its Discontents* (London, 1963), 17). Freud recognizes that alcohol plays a special part in this process, enabling man to overcome his superego:

> The service rendered by intoxicating media in the struggle for happiness and in keeping misery at a distance is so highly prized as a benefit that individuals and peoples alike have given them an established place in the economics of their libido. We owe to such media not merely the immediate yield of pleasure, but also a greatly desired degree of independence from the external world. For one knows that, with the help of this 'drowner of cares' one can at any time withdraw from the pressure of reality and find refuge in a world of one's own with better conditions of sensibility.
>
> (*Civilization and its Discontents*, 15)

More generally the existence of a variety of pleasures in history is related to the explanation of culture as sublimation of the pleasure principle, and to the development of the creative consciousness of the individual in the same process.

---

[13] See O. Murray, 'Death and the symposion', *AION(archeol)* 10 (1988), 239-57; C. Grottanelli in this volume.

[14] For the purpose of this paper I return to the original ideas of Freud, though well aware that they have been developed and complicated in the work of the Frankfurt school, notably by T.W. Adorno and H. Marcuse. Their theories are chiefly concerned with the problems of modern society, rather than historical analysis: a useful introduction can be found in A. Elliott, *Social Theory and Psycoanalysis: Self and Society from Freud to Kristeva* (Oxford, 1992).

It seems to me that this theory of Freud's lies behind the enterprise of Michel Foucault, proclaimed especially in the first volume of his *History of Sexuality* and elsewhere, with his attempt to view the problematization of the basic drives of man by society as a form of social control. The force now comes entirely from the outside: the problematization of sexuality is not an autonomous decision of the individual to postpone his pleasures, but a demand by society imposed with the intention of controlling the individual and using his energies for social ends. It is characteristic for this form of social control that it accepts an element of the arbitrary: it is as important that there should be rules to problematize the sex drive as that these rules should be rational. And ultimately the sublimation of these rules will create a moral code and an aesthetics of existence, as it becomes 'an element for reflection, material for stylisation'.[15]

I find myself in great sympathy with such theories of the role of pleasure in history, because they assert the basic importance of the pleasure principle; it becomes the foundation for that long civilizing process which Norbert Elias has described: it enables us to relate the primitive and the civilized in a process of development towards the triumph of the superego and its discontents. The insight of Freud in particular into cultural history seems to me an important one, which should not become lost in the debates about his psychology of the individual. But I am dissatisfied on two counts, particularly with the version presented by Foucault.

Firstly, it seems to me that the theory of the problematization of basic drives by a hostile society is an external interpretation, not one which would be generally accepted by members of the many ancient societies which regarded pleasure as a goal attainable by social means. Secondly, this analysis seems to imply the ultimate subordination of pleasure to power in human history. The purpose of Foucault's *History of Sexuality* may originally have been to liberate modern man from his social constraints; but it is less easy to see how a history of, for instance, table manners or drinking customs would respond to this treatment: the *symposion* is ritualized, but not problematized in its approach to pleasure. Many rituals involving food and drink may indeed come into existence in order to enhance pleasure, for not all socialization is problematization. The element of the arbitrary has taken over.

The theories I have discussed so far have in common the feature that they wish to explain the relationship between pleasure and those serious concerns of society which the historian has identified as primary — such as the power structures, the economy, or religion. Too often the analysis results in the subordination of pleasure and culture to these other forms. Let us therefore turn to those theories which have attempted to establish the autonomy of culture and of pleasure.

It was Jacob Burckhardt who explicitly asserted the independence of Culture in relation to the other forces in history, the State and Religion (to which we would now add the Economy):

---

[15] *Histoire de la sexualité: 1. La volonté de savoir* (Paris, 1976 (English trans. 1978)). For the development from this viewpoint to the rather different programme of the later Foucault, see esp. the introduction to *2. L'usage des plaisirs* (Paris, 1984 (English trans. 1985)), from p. 30 of which my quotation comes. On the change in Foucault's views during this decade the biography of D. Eribon, *Michel Foucault* (Paris, 1989 (English trans. 1991)) is very helpful; see also the excellent exposition of C. O'Farrell, *Foucault, Historian or Philosopher?* (London, 1989).

The three powers are supremely heterogeneous to each other and cannot be co-ordinated, and even if we were to co-ordinate the two constants, State and Religion, Culture would still be something essentially different ... Culture ... is the sum of all that has *spontaneously* arisen for the advancement of material life and as an expression of spiritual and moral life — all social intercourse, technologies, arts, literatures and sciences. It is the realm of the variable, free, not necessarily universal, of all that cannot lay claim to compulsive authority.

(Reflections on History, 34)

This claim of the autonomy of the cultural order explicitly rejects the notion of a theory of culture, which is essentially 'the realm of the variable' and of the spontaneous. Burckhardt therefore regarded culture as an infinitely varied phenomenon created by the accumulation of individual acts of free will. The time and place in which such creation occurred were important social constraints, but not causal determinants; he emphasized also especially contact between cultures, and the susceptibility of high cultures to renaissances. He emphasized too the importance of competition in the creation of culture. All these elements will surely come into our discussions; and it is worth remembering that Burckhardt was the first to take seriously the role of the *symposion* in the formation of Greek culture. But ultimately Burckhardt's emphasis on freedom in the development of cultural forms is only distinguished from the descriptive 'sub-lunary' world of Paul Veyne by Burckhardt's greater insight into the individual patterns of culture: like Veyne, Burckhardt deliberately rejects the notion of a general theory.[16]

Two disciples seem to me to offer such theories. The first is Johan Huizinga, who in *Homo Ludens* (1938) universalized Burckhardt's concern with the agonistic spirit to produce a theory of culture as play: civilization 'does not come *from* play like a babe detaching itself from the womb: it arises in and as play and never leaves it'.[17] Of course Huizinga's book intentionally instantiates his own theory: both book and theory are themselves elements in the game of culture, and it is easy not to take them seriously. But Huizinga is in a sense merely drawing out the logic inherent in the universe demarcated by Burckhardt: the freedom and spontaneity claimed by Burckhardt are seen as ordered by the disinterested pursuit of rules, repetition, competition and by the willing acceptance of chance. Play is an arbitrary and self-created order distinct from 'ordinary life', limited in time and place, with specific rules which may be different from those which hold elsewhere: it implicitly contrasts a real world with a world of pleasure; but, like the Latin language, it regards the world of artificial order, not reality, as the basis of society: *otium* is logically prior to *negotium*. So pleasure, the artificial order, explains

[16] *Weltgeschichtliche Betrachtungen* (1905) (English trans., *Reflections on History* (London, 1943)); the original text of these lectures was edited by P. Ganz, *Über das Studium der Geschichte* (Munich, 1982). On this aspect of Burckhardt, see the classic book of K. Löwith, *Jacob Burckhardt* (Lucerne, 1936/Stuttgart, 1984 (Italian trans. 1991)), ch. iv; A. Momigliano, 'Introduction to the *Griechische Kulturgeschichte* by Jacob Burckhardt', *Essays in Ancient and Modern Historiography* (Oxford, 1977), 295-305. For Burckhardt's recognition of the importance of the *symposion*, see *Griechische Kulturgeschichte* iv.9 (Berlin, 1902), 'Der hellenische Mensch in seiner zeitlichen Entwicklung'.

[17] My quotation is from the paperback edition of the English translation (London, 1970), p. 198; see also 'The task of cultural history' (1926) in *Men and Ideas* (London, 1960), 17-76. Against the attacks by conventional historians, see R. Anchor, 'History and play: Johan Huizinga and his critics', *History and Theory* 17 (1978), 63-93.

society, the official order; the claim of the autonomy of culture is revealed as a claim to make culture the foundation of the social order.

It seems to me that this theory offers one of the most satisfactory ways of analysing the Greek *symposion*, which in its developed form saw itself as a world apart, separate from the external world of the *polis*: its aim was pleasure, its rituals were rules designed to enhance pleasure by complicating it; many of its customs were distinct from and in opposition to the conventions of society.[18] The element of contest was dominant in drinking, in games, in poetry and speech; the challenge and competitive tests of loyalty could lead even to sacrilege and murder. Originating perhaps in the genuine social needs of the *polis*, it could end by becoming an alternative to the *polis*.

But as a general theory, the concept of culture as play has obvious limitations; more persuasive is the suggestion of Ernst Gombrich that we should concentrate on one aspect of this picture, the sense of order: this he sees as an innate psychological drive, which can be observed even at the level of animal behaviour.[19] Pleasure in the creation of order is responsible for the elaboration of rules and patterns, for the desire both to create a world of habit and regularity, and also for the need to complicate it. Pattern making is a characteristic of primitive and peasant art, and the discovery of meaningful patterns is the basis of even representational art as a set of visual stimuli to mental interpretation.

The explanation of culture as the creation of ritual and pattern has again some similarities with Norbert Elias's attempt to demonstrate the progress of civilization through the history of manners; but it avoids his mistake of assuming a linear development through time, in which western man is progressing towards a code of civility embodied in the European bourgeoisie.[20] The conception of culture as founded in the instinct for order and the pleasure derived from it, once again emphasizes the delight in ritualization and rules which is to be found flourishing paradoxically in the potentially disordered society devoted to the truth of wine.

It has often been pointed out that such conceptions of the autonomy of culture are essentially aristocratic, concerned with high culture. In themselves they establish a problematization of pleasure for its own sake, which enables society to make use of pleasure as an ordered alternative to the more serious structures of communal life. Another group of theories would specifically see pleasure as being in opposition to the social order. The oppression of natural instincts within any society engenders distinctive forms of revolt, in which violence and disorder are genuinely popular elements whose strength is related to the extent of economic or religious oppression exercised by authority. Under the influence of Bakhtin's studies of popular humour, parody, obscenity and the vituperation of authority have come to seem a necessary part of the ritual of the carnival, reluctantly sanctioned and ineffectively policed by Church and state because of their inability totally to suppress a true manifestation of popular

---

[18] L.E. Rossi, 'Il simposio greco arcaico come spettacolo a se stesso', *Spettacoli conviviali dall'antichità classica alle corti italiane dell'400: Atti del VII convegno di studio* (Viterbo, 1983), 41-50; E. Pellizer, 'Outlines of a morphology of symptotic entertainment', in Murray (ed.), *Sympotica* (above, n. 11), 177-84.

[19] E.H. Gombrich, *The Sense of Order* (Oxford, 1979).

[20] *The Civilizing Process I. The History of Manners* (Oxford, 1978); *II. State Formation and Civilization* (Oxford, 1982). See S. Mennell and N. Elias, *Civilization and the Human Self-Image* (Oxford, 1989).

culture.[21] Occasionally, as at Romans in 1579-80, such a carnival occasion could indeed become a popular rising, without losing its carnival character.[22]

The ancient world is familiar with similar occasions of licence; like the carnival they tend to take place at a specific point in the religious calendar, the New Year, the opening of the new wine, the vintage, or festivals of particular gods like Dionysus.[23] As such they are licensed or tolerated by the authorities; the occasions of suppression are rare, although there are certain parallels between the suppression of the Bacchanalia by the Roman senate in 186 BC and the carnival at Romans described by Ladurie.[24] Modern scholars often characterize such festivals as rituals of reversal, in which society permits the overturning of the established order in order to restore it, in a symbolic assertion of the contingent rightness of the existing system; sometimes such festivals are also connected to foundation myths, as a form of charter myth, a re-enactment of the original creation of the political order. They are also often related to particular oppressed groups such as women (in festivals like the Lenaia, the Agrionia and the Adonia) and slaves (in the Saturnalia).[25] As in the Middle Ages, these popular carnivalesque influences enter literature through specific occasions of performance: ritualized abuse, sexual language and parody of political and religious institutions are an intrinsic part of the performance of comedy at the Dionysia, just as they were in the medieval festival of fools.[26]

This interpretation emphasizes certain important facts about these carnivalesque occasions. They are determined by a religious calendar, and therefore licensed in some sense by authority; they are popular manifestations in which cultural forms are either ridiculed or swept away in favour of a popular form of anomie which involves activities freed from all social inhibitions; often these include both extremes of physical violence and sexual freedom. And of course wine and drunkenness were an essential factor in the necessary release of inhibitions.

Although such occasions are important in the ancient world, we need to distinguish carefully between the drunkenness and sexual license practised here in a popular milieu,

[21] M. Bakhtin, *Problems of Dostoevsky's Poetics* (Manchester, 1984), ch. 4; idem, *Rabelais and his World* (Indiana, 1984).

[22] The literature on the carnival is vast; I mention only J. Caro Baroja, *El Carnaval* (Madrid, 1965) (Italian trans. *Il Carnevale* (Genoa, 1989)); C. Gaignebet, *Le Carneval* (Paris, 1974); E. Le Roy Ladurie, *Le Carneval de Romans* (Paris, 1979).

[23] There is still room for a scholarly study of Dionysus, despite the varied evocations of W.F. Otto, *Dionysos, Mythos und Kultus* (Frankfurt, 1933 (English trans. 1965)); H. Jeanmaire, *Dionysos: Histoire du culte de Bacchus* (Paris, 1951); W. Kerenyi, *Dionysos: Urbild des Unzerstörbaren Lebens* (Munich, 1976 (English trans. 1976)); M. Detienne, *Dionysos mis à mort* (Paris, 1977 (English trans. 1979)); idem, *Dionysos à ciel ouvert* (Paris, 1986 (English trans. 1989)); M. Daraki, *Dionysos* (Paris, 1985). For a modern survey see W. Burkert, *Griechische Religion der Archaischen und Klassischen Epoche* (Stuttgart, 1977 (English trans. 1985)), III 2.10.

[24] J.-M. Pailler, *Bacchanalia: la répression de 186 av. J.-C. à Rome et en Italie: vestiges, images, tradition* (Rome, 1988).

[25] For rituals of reversal, see W. Burkert, 'Jason, Hypsipyle and new fire at Lemnos', *CQ* 20 (1970), 1-16. Typical festivals of disorder, apart from the various Dionysia, are the Anthesteria, Lenaia, Agrionia, and Adonia in Greece, the Saturnalia in Rome.

[26] H. Cox, *The Feast of Fools* (Harvard, 1969); P.G. Schmidt, 'The quotation in Goliardic poetry: the Feast of Fools and the Goliardic *strophe cum auctoritate*', in P. Godman and O. Murray (eds), *Latin Poetry and the Classical Tradition* (Oxford, 1990), 39-55. Compare J. Henderson, *The Maculate Muse: Obscene Language in Attic Comedy*, second edition (Oxford, 1991); W. Rösler, 'Michail Bachtin und die Karnevalskultur im antiken Griechenland', *Quaderni Urbinati* 23 (1986), 25-44.

and the quite different occasions for such license which existed in the élite culture. The various types of disorder and inversion practised in the context of the Greek *symposion* and its derivatives in other cultures involve both drunken revelry and explicit sexual activity, but the ethos is that of the right to pleasure. The *komos* and the Roman orgy are not popular occasions; they belong to aristocracies which used wine to enhance the life of pleasure which was a symbol of its *truphe* or *otium*. In these aristocratic occasions no calendar is involved, no anxious control by the authorities; the display of power in drunken processions through the streets, assaults and damage to property, are a sign not of being oppressed but of arrogance.

This example perhaps shows how important it is to distinguish similar behaviour by different social classes. The drunkenness of an Alcibiades or a Nero does not have the same roots as the drunkenness of Philocleon in Aristophanes's *Wasps*.[27] But it also points to an important similarity in the need to break the rules: every society has its concept of sin, and it seems that every society has the need to disapprove of pleasure in some way, indeed that pleasure has the need to be disapproved of as part of its definition; and of course, as sophistication increases, the breaking of taboos in turn brings an enhancement of pleasure. Legislation for the control of pleasure is a rich theme in the ancient and the modern world; the relationship between morality and pleasure is a constant in human history, which will ensure that there will always be those who deny any connection between wine and truth.

Yet even that ancient man most obsessed with his own sinfulness could find a positive message in drunkenness. Saint Augustine records his abject state as a brilliant young professor of rhetoric one day in Milan in AD 385:

> I gaped after honours, gains, marriage, and thou mockedst me ... That same day, when I was pre-
> paring an oration in praise of the Emperor, in which I would say many lies, and be applauded for
> my lies by men of letters, while my heart panted after these cares and seethed with the feverishness
> of these consuming thoughts, walking along one of the streets of Milan, I noticed a poor beggar,
> already drunk I think, and joking and happy. ... That state which he had achieved for a few coins
> begged from someone, I was plotting after by many a troublesome turning and winding path —
> namely to attain the happiness of temporal felicity ... But even then there was a great distance
> between us; for he was truly the more happy man, not so much because he was drenched in laugh-
> ter, while my bowels were being twisted with cares; but also because he had obtained his wine by
> wishing someone good luck, while I was seeking an empty pride through lies.
>
> (*Confessions* vi. 6)

Among historians of pleasure only Epicurus has tried to produce a theory of history which would regard pleasure as a wholly positive force, and I do confess I have a strong inclination to regard him as the greatest historian of culture. For surely the purpose of history is the creation of culture, and he was right to see pleasure as the motive force in that process. The description of the progress of civilization in book v of Lucretius is the great manifesto for a history of pleasure as it should be:[28]

---

[27] See my article, 'The affair of the Mysteries: democracy and the drinking group', in Murray (ed.), *Sympotica* (above, n. 11), 149-61.
[28] For the tradition behind this passage see esp. T. Cole, *Democritus and the Sources of Greek Anthropology* (*American Philological Association Monograph*) (Hartford, Conn., 1967).

Ships and tillage, walls laws arms roads dress and all such like things, all the prizes, all the elegancies too of life without exception, poems pictures and the chiselling of fine-wrought statues, all these things practice together with the acquired knowledge of the untiring mind taught men by slow degrees as they advanced on the way step by step. Thus time by degrees brings each several thing forth before men's eyes and reason raises it up into the shores of light; for men saw one notion after another shine clear in their minds, until by their arts they reached the highest summit.

namque alid ex alio clarescere corde videbant,
artibus ad summum donec venere cacumen.

(v. 456-7)

A modern Epicurean theory of history has yet to be written, but it will not be a neutral one: like most theories of history it is likely to be prescriptive rather than descriptive. Until it arrives, we can perhaps remain content with the variety of histories of pleasure which we already possess, and which reveal how many senses we may attach to the theme, *In vino veritas.*

* * *

'Intervento' by Antonio La Penna

L'introduzione del collega Oswyn Murray è ricca di problemi tanto importanti quanto attraenti; ci apre un ampio terreno fecondo ed affascinante e ad esplorarlo indica molte prospettive suggerite dalla sociologia e dall'antropologia più recente. Da questa apertura eclettica bisognerà poi approdare a trattazioni coerenti e rigorose nel metodo e nei risultati, ma in partenza la massima apertura è consigliabile. Su tutta la ricchissima riflessione di Murray occorrerà meditare con calma; per ora non saprei esprimere nessun dissenso rilevante se non sulla conclusione, dove egli ci esorta, per esplorare e interpretare la storia del piacere, ad una teoria epicurea della storia.

Naturalmente il piacere incomincia dalla soddisfazione dei bisogni materiali; ma il piacere che qui è in questione va molto al di là, sino ad assumere un valore autonomo, come nel gioco e nelle varie arti; uno dei casi più chiari è quello del piacere erotico: alla radice è la soddisfazione di un bisogno naturale e assolve la funzione procreativa e riproduttiva, ma né le complicate figure erotiche né l'amore cantato dai poeti restano molto attaccati a questa radice. Ora io temo che Epicuro ben poco possa aiutarci ad una storia dei piaceri quale emerge dall'introduzione di Murray. È vero, sì, che per Epicuro il fine dell'uomo è il piacere; ma il piacere sommo coincide con l'atarassia, e l'atarassia comporta *la riduzione dei bisogni ad un minimo di bisogni naturali,* un minimo che si pone al di sopra della soglia fissata dai cinici, ma che certamente esclude la massima parte dei piaceri che noi dovremmo prendere in considerazione. Come quasi tutta la filosofia antica, anche quella epicurea porta ad un'etica anticonsumistica. Nella storia della civiltà umana tracciata, con grande originalità, da Democrito e da Epicuro la molla del progresso è il bisogno di soddisfare le necessità naturali, da cui nasce il senso dell'utilità; la soddisfazione di un bisogno naturale è, ripeto, piacere, ma non per caso nella storia epicurea della civiltà si parla di *chreia (usus)* piuttosto che di *hedone (voluptas).* È inutile che io esponga cose ben note. È ovvio che, nel lavoro prospettato, Epicuro non può essere lasciato da parte; ma io fermerei l'attenzione piuttosto su quella letteratura antica, non abbondante, che, al di fuori dell'area filosofica, legittima, per lo più implicitamente, talora anche esplicitamente, l'incremento dei consumi e il lusso.

'Intervento' by Christopher Lord: Art Value and Exchange Value in the Mycenean Palace Culture

Your remarks about the inherent uselessness of objects which conform to aristocratic tastes lead my thoughts back to a chapter of Moses Finley on the function of treasure in the Mycenean palace culture (actually part of chapter 3, 'Wealth and labour', of *The World of Odysseus*). Do not the treasure objects he discusses — bowls, tripods, and other pieces of elaborately worked metal — correspond precisely to your description of apparently useless and yet highly prized artefacts? If so, perhaps it will be possible to find some deeper significance in their cunning if impractical designs.

It seems that the ritualized offering and acceptance of treasure objects gradually superseded the sacking of cities as the principal means of metal exchange in bronze age Greece. Perhaps this more businesslike approach could be connected with improvements in the techniques of metalworking, as well as with the political utility of such ritualized contacts between cities in a society increasingly concerned with alliances and diplomacy, rather than straightforwardly with battle. At any rate, the magnificent gesture of handing over this or that gold plate or set of bronze spears seems to have been a prototype of the modern cash transaction: it is interesting to note, though, in this connection, that nothing was immediately given in return: all that was required was a readiness to make a similar gesture at some point in the future. It is difficult to resist the interpretation of this activity as a kind of prehistoric credit scheme, the function of the credit extended being mainly to involve both 'lender' and 'borrower' in a ritual of mutual trust. Returning to the objects themselves, might it not be apposite to remark that their decorations may well have had the important function of identifying them as potential exchange objects, in other words, as pieces of treasure? The modern goldsmith works with gold and diamonds, not because these materials are beautiful, but because they are expensive, and therefore desirable to his customers; his bronze age counterpart surely worked under similar constraints. To pursue the analogy a little further, we can observe that the market value of, say, a Cartier brooch is somewhat higher than that of its raw materials: the same was probably true of the beaten gold artefacts from Grave Circle A at Mycenae. Their value as exchange objects must have depended to some extent on their elaboration: to apply a slightly different terminology, their artistic value and their exchange value were interdependent (if not actually interchangeable). Perhaps their very uselessness made them more appropriate repositories for both types of value: indeed, leaving aside the question of artistic value for a moment, the movement from a barter system of exchange to a system involving money of some kind might be seen to consist exactly in an agreement to attach exchange value to some set of objects devoid of practical utility.

The artistic value, then, of the decoration of treasure objects seems, according to this tentative analysis, to have consisted both in their identification as treasure, and perhaps also in the fixing of their market value within a primitive system of exchange; and thus we will do best to seek a modern equivalent of this decoration, not in the arbitrary working of the Cartier brooch, but in the tasteful and yet informative engravings which adorn the coins and banknotes exchanged all over the world today.

ALCOHOL IN NEAR EASTERN CULTURE

2

Le Vin dans une Civilisation de la Bière: la Mésopotamie

JEAN BOTTÉRO

Je crains de devoir ma présence ici à une pure condescendance de votre part. J'ignore pourquoi vous vous êtes refusés à tenir compte, en ma faveur, de l'avertissement pourtant net que vous avait adressé, il y a quelque dix-huit siècles, l'obscur Jules l'Africain, en expliquant, dans ses *Kestoi*,[1] que Dionysos, dieu du vin, en colère contre les Babyloniens à cause de leur entêtement à ne boire que de la bière,[2] n'avait pas voulu demeurer chez eux et leur apprendre à cultiver la vigne et à faire le vin. C'est, hélas, parfaitement vrai, même s'il m'est pénible de le confesser devant un aréopage de résolus oenophiles, réunis en colloque à la gloire antique du vin. Mais puisque vous m'avez bel et bien invité à représenter ici (je ne dis pas: à défendre!) ces vieux buveurs de bière de Babylone, mieux vaut mettre cartes sur table et vous présenter d'abord, franchement, en deux mots, ce qui était sans contredit une 'civilisation de la bière', quitte à vous expliquer ensuite quel rôle a pû y tenir le vin.[3] Même accessoire, un tel rôle n'était pas tout à fait négligeable, d'autant que, comme c'est la règle dans les affaires humaines, les choses n'ont jamais été simples, et que la situation a pu se modifier plus ou moins, selon les temps, et surtout les lieux.

La civilisation mésopotamienne est née entre le quatrième et le tout début du troisième millénaires, au plus tard.[4] Elle est venue au monde — la précision a son importance — dans la partie méridionale de la Mésopotamie: en gros, entre Baghdad et le Golfe persique. Et elle est issue de la confluence de plusieurs cultures. D'abord celle — et beaucoup plus vraisemblablement: celles — des premiers occupants du

---

[1] *Cestes* i. 19.21-22 (pp. 172-3 de J.R. Vieillefond, *Les Cestes de Julius Africanus* (Paris, 1970)). Je remercie vivement Mme B. Leclecq de m'avoir indiqué et trouvé cet ouvrage.

[2] Dans le texte en question, Jules l'Africain s'en prend aussi aux Egyptiens, aux Pannoniens et aux Celtes, qui usent tous seulement de boissons à base d'orge, respectivement *zython*, *camum* et *cervoise*. Pour le nom de *sikéra* qu'il donne à bière babylonienne, voir plus loin, n. 22.

[3] Sur les boissons en usage en Mésopotamie ancienne, voir en particulier H.F. Lutz, *Viticulture and Brewing in the Ancient Orient* (Leipzig-New York, 1922); et l'article '*Getränke*' (en français), au tome III du *Reallexikon der Assyriologie* (Berlin, 1957-8), 302-6. Pour la bière, en particulier: L.F. Hartman et A.L. Oppenheim, *On Beer and Brewing Techniques in Ancient Mesopotamia* (Baltimore, 1950); et W. Röllig, *Das Bier im Alten Mesopotamien* (Berlin, 1970).

[4] On peut, à ce sujet, voir J. Bottéro, 'Sumériens et "Accadiens" en Mésopotamie ancienne', dans *Modes de contacts et processus de transformation dans les sociétés anciennes. Actes du colloque de Cortone 1981* (Pisa-Rome, 1983), 7-8.

territoire. Ils y sont arrivés à partir du sixième millénaire, descendus des piémonts du Nord et de l'Est et s'avançant vers le Sud à mesure que s'asséchait l'ancien lit unique d'un énorme fleuve qui avait d'abord tout recouvert, pour se réduire, en fin de compte, aux deux cours d'eau séparés et plus modestes: Tigre et Euphrate, donnant de la sorte au pays sa configuration 'historique'. Ces antiques populations, dont il ne nous reste plus que des vestiges archéologiques, copieux, mais peu loquaces et trop souvent ambigus, et quelques reliques linguistiques, plutôt mystérieuses, ont apporté chacune sa quote part (à nos yeux le plus souvent indiscernable) à l'édification d'une culture commune. Mais, pour nous, la masse principale des données qui ont fait la civilisation mésopotamienne, est imputable à deux groupes ethniques d'origines, de cultures et de langues fort différentes et irréductibles, que nous connaissons et identifions mieux parce qu'elles ont été, à la fois, les dernières venues, les plus actives et les mieux attestées.

Ce sont, d'une part, les Sumériens, arrivés on ne sait d'où, mais sans doute du Sud-Est, par la côte iranienne du Golfe persique, au cours du quatrième millénaire, au plus tard.[5] D'un autre côté, des Sémites, que, par convention, nous appelons (eux et leur langue) Akkadiens, et qui sont venus, peut-être plus anciennement encore, par le couloir du Moyen Euphrate, depuis le Nord-Ouest: les franges septentrionales du Grand Désert syro-arabe. C'est principalement leur symbiose séculaire en Basse Mésopotamie qui, sur un fond de culture(s) préhistorique(s), a donné le jour à la civilisation mésopotamienne, laquelle ne devait s'éteindre, après 3.000 ans d'histoire, qu'aux alentours de notre ère. Originale, riche, inventive et puissante, longtemps très supérieure à toutes les cultures modestes qui l'environnaient, elle ne les a pas seulement fécondées, avec largesse, de ses trouvailles en tous genres, mais elle en a créé de plus ou moins profondément dépendantes, çà et là, autour d'elle, et principalement vers le Nord (Assyrie) et le Nord-Ouest (Ebla, Mari, Emar ...).

Nous la connaissons mieux depuis le premier tiers du troisième millénaire, parce qu'alors le système d'écriture que, la première au monde, semble-t-il, elle s'était inventé, depuis 3200 à peu près, d'abord comme simple aide-mémoire, s'est assez vite précisé et rendu capable de noter le langage parlé comme tel:[6] le sumérien, pendant une grande partie du troisième millénaire, puis, surtout après la disparition des Sumériens, 'phagocytés' par les Sémites, ethniquement plus nombreux et plus forts, l'akkadien. Il nous reste donc, sur ces 3.000 ans, en ces deux langues, quelque chose comme un demi-million de documents, la plupart en forme de plaquettes d'argile sur lesquelles on avait imprimé, avant de les sécher ou de les cuire, les caractères, dits 'cunéiformes', de l'écriture en question. Cet imposant dossier couvre (inégalement, cela va sans dire), non seulement tous les temps, mais à peu près tous les secteurs de la vie: personnelle, sociale, économique, militaire, politique (locale et internationale), intellectuelle et religieuse. Nous sommes donc en mesure de nous en faire une idée assez juste, alimentation et boisson comprises. Ce qui ne veut pas dire que nous en savons tout ...

En Mésopotamie, comme partout au monde, existence et mode de vie étaient obligatoirement commandés par les impératifs premiers des conditions géographiques et

[5]Un autre opinion, fortement infirmée, à mon sens, par le 'Mythe des Sept Sages' (J. Bottéro et S.N. Kramer, *Lorsque les dieux faisaient l'homme* (Paris, 1989), 198-9) compte les Sumériens entre les plus anciens occupants du pays.

[6]J. Bottéro, *Mésopotamie: l'écriture, la raison et les dieux* (Paris, 1987), 89-90.

écologiques. La partie méridionale du pays n'était rien d'autre qu'un ancien lit de fleuve, une large vallée limoneuse: plat pays de terre argileuse, désséchée en surface, mais potentiellement très fertile, sans pierres, sans autres produits minéraux que, çà et là, du bitume, et où ne venaient volontiers que des roseaux et du palmier-dattier, sous un climat une bonne partie de l'année torride, avec peu de précipitations, plutôt hivernales. Un tel pays eût été invivable, sinon pour quelques poignées d'ascétiques Bédouins, si ses habitants ne s'étaient donné pour tâche première de l'irriguer de toutes parts, en y traçant, pour rejoindre les lits des deux fleuves et amener l'eau presque partout, un extraordinaire réseau de canaux de toute importance. Ainsi rendu au maximum cultivable — à la réserve d'une assez large frange de steppes, abandonnées aux herbages plus ou moins spontanés et merveilleusement propres à l'élevage du menu-bétail (vocation traditionnelle des Sémites les plus vieux connus) — on s'y est d'emblée adonné à ce à quoi il était le mieux adapté: la culture céréalière en grand, qui semble y avoir été inaugurée très tôt, dès avant la prédominance suméro-akkadienne. Cette agriculture généralisée a dû se trouver très vite structurée sur un plan collectif, seule la production des autres denrées traditionnelles (légumes et fruits, comme, d'autre part, la chasse et la pêche) se trouvant plus ou moins abandonnée à l'initiative individuelle.

Les larges surplus, lainiers et céréaliers, laissés par un pareil système de travail d'un sol aussi fécond, ont rapidement fait surgir dans le pays, non seulement une puissance économique et politique alors et longtemps unique au Proche Orient, mais le besoin d'une vie plus à l'aise et mieux fournie, ainsi que les moyens d'en compléter ce que le sol ne fournissait pas, en recourant, par l'échange, le commerce, l'importation, mais aussi la razzia et la guerre, à l'exploitation des contrées environnantes accessibles.

Les céréales fournissaient donc, forcément, la base traditionnelle de l'alimentation: le pain, autour duquel s'est développée très tôt toute une constellation de techniques, qui, par certains de leurs produits et de leurs procédés (céréales maltées et conservées, avec, ou sans, assaisonnements divers), menaient tout droit à la préparation de liquides, non seulement infusés, mais fermentés, voire alcooliques, et notamment à la bière.[7] A partir du moment où s'est fait sentir le besoin, ou l'envie, d'une boisson plus nourricière et plus goûteuse que l'eau, plus capiteuse et plus forte que le lait, en d'autres termes, d'autant plus plaisante que sa consommation pouvait aisément monter à la tête et égayer le coeur, on ne devait guère la chercher et la trouver ailleurs. Les propres conditions de leur écologie native et de leur activité principale de production, déterminaient donc et condamnaient, pour ainsi parler, les créateurs et les sujets de la civilisation mésopotamienne à fabriquer et à consommer la bière. Il y a du reste des chances que la mise au point et la préparation de ce breuvage aient été inaugurées par les anciens occupants du Bas-pays, avant les Suméro-akkadiens: presque tout le vocabulaire sumérien de la brasserie, sinon le propre nom de la 'bière' (kash), ne s'explique point par cette langue, ni par le sémitique, et doit, en conséquence, lui avoir été transmis d'un idiome et d'une culture différents et antérieurs.[8]

[7]Voir notamment A. Maurizio, *Die Geschichte Unserer Pflanzennahrung von den Urzeiten bis zur Gegenwart* (Berlin, 1927-70), 370-1; *Die Geschichte der Gegorenen Getränke* (Berlin, 1933/1982), 110-11, et *passim*.

[8]M. Civil, 'A Hymn to the Beer Goddess', dans *Studies Presented to A.Leo Oppenheim* (Chicago, 1964), 67-8, 85.

Certes, comme je l'ai suggéré, il existait, connues et appréciées dans le pays, depuis le début et de tout temps, d'autres boissons courantes, voire fermentées et alcooliques, à base notamment de fruits divers, et en particulier de dattes.[9] Mais dès les débuts de l'histoire, et, sans changer jamais par la suite, au long des millénaires, la bière a occupé le rang du breuvage le plus prisé, le plus produit et le plus consommé, le plus enraciné dans les usages et dans les goûts, le plus créateur d'habitudes nouvelles, le plus populaire: c'était véritablement, si l'on peut s'exprimer ainsi, la boisson 'nationale'. Toutes nos sources, de toutes les époques, accusent à l'envi ce rôle de premier plan dans le régime alimentaire.

Je n'en rapporterai ici que deux ou trois traits, suffisamment persuasifs. Dans l'*Epopée de Gilgamesh*, lorsque le sauvage Enkidu, qui vivait jusque là, dans le désert, d'herbages et de lait, apprivoisé par la Courtisane, est d'abord amené par elle dans une bergerie — première étape vers la vie hautement civilisée de la ville — elle l'encourage à s'initier à l'existence véritablement 'humaine' de l' 'homme cultivé' (*awîlu*), et premièrement à manger et à boire ce que lui offrent les bergers, et dont il se détourne d'emblée avec méfiance: le pain et la bière:

> Mange du pain, Enkidu (lui dit-elle):
> C'est ce qu'il faut pour vivre!
> Bois de la bière:
> C'est l'usage du pays![10]

Pour invoquer un second témoignage, pris d'un tout autre secteur: dans la *Grande encyclopédie* mésopotamienne, que nous appelons par son *incipit*: *URra = hubullu*,[11] dont les premières ébauches remontent très haut et dont le texte classique est d'avant la fin du deuxième millénaire, ouvrage qui, en 24 tablettes et une dizaine de milliers de rubriques, enregistrait et classait par les noms, sur deux colonnes (sumérien à gauche; akkadien en face), tout ce que l'on avait pu recenser dans l'ordre de la nature et de la culture propres au pays, les savants compilateurs avaient réservé à la bière — dans le contexte de l'alimentation, à la XXIIIe tablette — quelque chose comme 200 entrées, dont près de la moitié pour en définir présentations et variétés, le reste se rapportant aux techniques de la brasserie.[12]

Enfin, autre indice notable de l'importance de ce breuvage aux yeux de tous dans le pays: depuis, au plus tard, les débuts du troisième millénaire, on avait fait de la bière le domaine propre de deux divinités, qui la représentaient et l'incarnaient — comme c'était le cas des céréales, du menu-bétail, et de quelques autres éléments culturels fondamentaux. L'une était Sirish; l'autre, féminine: Ninkasi.[13] Leurs origines, leur histoire ancienne, non moins que leurs rapports mutuels antiques nous

---

[9]Article *'Getränke'* (ci-dessus, n. 3), 302-3.

[10]Version paléo-babylonienne, tablette dite de Philadelphie: 92s (J. Bottéro, *L'Epopée de Gilgamesh* (Paris, 1992)).

[11]Bottéro, *Mésopotamie* (ci-dessus, n. 6), 45-6.

[12]Hartman et Oppenheim, *On Beer and Brewing Techniques* (ci-dessus, n. 3), 22-3; et B. Landsberger, *Materials for the Sumerian Lexicon* XI (1974), 69-70 notamment.

[13]Röllig, *Das Bier im Alten Mesopotamien* (ci-dessus, n. 3), 65; et Civil, 'A Hymn to the Beer Goddess' (ci-dessus, n. 8), 74-5.

échappent: les théologiens avaient plus tard résolu le problème de leur coexistence en faisant du premier, tantôt l'époux, tantôt le fils de la seconde, solution qui supposerait une antériorité, ou une préponderance ancienne de Ninkasi. Ainsi au premier rang des breuvages et définissant, couramment, *a potiori*, avec le 'pain', le domaine entier de l'alimentation,[14] quel était le rôle social de la bière dans cette vieille civilisation?

Il s'exerçait, pour l'essentiel, sur deux plans. D'abord *à table*, puisque c'était un breuvage, premièrement destiné à compléter et accompagner la nourriture. L'an passé, à l'occasion du colloque sur 'La boisson dans le Proche Orient ancien', j'avais tenté de réfléchir sur la signification du repas, et surtout du repas festif: du banquet, en Mésopotamie. Je ne vais pas reprendre à présent ce que j'en avais développé, mais au moins en résumer l'essentiel, qui se trouve ici tout à fait en place. On semble donc, dans ce vieux pays, avoir eu très tôt, et toujours gardé, le vif sentiment que, *les vivres* donnant, ou, ce qui revient au même, entretenant *la vie*, s'assimiler et consommer *les mêmes vivres*, c'était faire passer en soi, ou conforter, *la même vie*: d'où l'importance du repas et surtout du repas en commun, du festin plus solennel, du banquet, qui réunissait un certain nombre de ce que nous appelons toujours les *convives*. Il était, non seulement l'occasion, mais le moyen d'affirmer et de confirmer la solidarité 'existentielle' et vitale de ces convives: solidarité de la famille et des concitoyens. Voilà pourquoi de tels festins accompagnaient régulièrement et consacraient, en quelque sorte, les tournants de la vie, tant familiale que politique: établissement des grands échanges de ce que l'on appelle les 'biens nobles', indispensables à la vie (personnes et terres), pour les particuliers; importantes décisions à prendre par les autorités pour l'organisation et l'avenir de la communauté. La bière y tenait, et peut-être plus encore dans ces derniers cas, une place d'autant plus centrale que, non seulement on ne pouvait s'en passer pour accompagner les nourritures solides, mais que, par sa nature propre et son caractère alcoolisé, elle mettait le coeur en joie, sinon en goguette, et favorisait enthousiasme, générosité et élan d'entente et d'unisson indispensables à de telles réunions. Je ne cite qu'un document tiré d'un de ces 'romans théologiques' que sont, en somme, les mythes, et qui constituent très souvent notre documentation la plus riche, la plus sûre et la plus parlante touchant la vie et la pensée de leurs auteurs, à défaut de rien nous apprendre sur celles de leurs objets.

Dans l'*Epopée de la Création*,[15] au moment où il s'agit, pour les dieux, d'investir un champion capable de les garder des mortelles menaces que fait peser sur eux leur mère originelle Tiamat, leur chef à tous les convoque en assemblée plénière. Et il arrivent

Tenir conciliabules et (dans ce but) prendre place au banquet,
Manger leur pain, boire leur bière
Et arrêter ainsi le destin[16]

de leur champion, le jeune dieu Marduk, à qui il vont déléguer les pouvoirs nécessaires pour lui faciliter la tâche. Et le texte continue, confondant la consommation collective de la nourriture et de la boisson avec ses effets euphoriques, propices à l'échange des vues et à la prise unanime des décisions:

[14]*akalu u shikâru*, mot à mot 'pain et bière' = aliments et boisson (on disait aussi, dans le même sens, *akalu u mû*: 'pain et eau'): voir *Chicago Assyrian Dictionary*, A/1 (1964), 239-40.
[15]Bottéro, *Lorsque les dieux faisaient l'homme* (ci-dessus, n. 5), 602-3.
[16]*Ibid.* p. 619: lignes 8-9.

Tous les grands Dieux ...,
Entrés devant leur Souverain, furent remplis de joie
Et s'embrassèrent l'un l'autre, en leur Assemblée plénière.
Ils tinrent donc conciliabules et prirent place au Banquet:
Ils mangèrent leur pain et ils burent leur bière.
Du doux breuvage capiteux ils remplirent leurs chalumeaux-à-boire.[17]
Humant ainsi la boisson enivrante,
Ils se sentaient le corps détendu:
Sans le moindre souci, leur âme était en allégresse![18]

On ne peut pas mieux souligner l'importance de la consommation de la bière dans la vie sociale, et même politique.

Mais si les qualités excitantes que ce liquide devait à son alcoolisation avaient, on vient de le percevoir, leurs avantages, elles avaient aussi leurs inconvénients, non seulement *à table*, mais *hors table*. Un autre mythe[19] raconte comment le dieu Enki, créateur et détenteur des secrets de la haute civilisation, ayant invité à un festin la déesse Inanna venue lui rendre visite et, au cours du repas, levé un peu trop le coude, avait assez perdu la tête pour faire cadeau d'un seul coup, avec la générosité emphatique des ivrognes, de tous ses trésors à Inanna, laquelle les avait aussitôt emportés chez elle et mis en lieu sûr, alors que lui, reprenant ses esprits, cherchait en vain à tout récupérer.[20]

Il arrivait aussi que l'on bût de la bière, non plus en mangeant, mais pour le seul plaisir de boire, jusqu'à l'ébriété plus ou moins complète. Nos textes, toujours réservés, et comme pudiques, sur cet article comme sur celui de l'amour,[21] ne nous évoquent pas souvent, et pas beaucoup, cette faiblesse. Une chose du moins est certaine: c'est que le caractère grisant de la bière était souligné dans son nom même, en akkadien: *shikâru*,[22] de la racine *SHKR* qui, en sémitique, marque précisément l'ébriété. La bière était donc tenue pour la boisson-enivrante par excellence. Nos documents, je le répète, sont avares de détails touchant les effets d'une propriété aussi fortement soulignée par la nomenclature. Mais je puis au moins, par la bande, en suggérer l'essentiel.

Il y a notamment l'existence de ce qu'au cours de la première moitié du deuxième millénaire on appelait, dans le pays, la 'maison de la cabaretière' — donnant ainsi la priorité à ce rôle féminin, sans doute parce que la préparation de la bière, rôle principal du 'cabaretier' d'après son nom,[23] avait d'abord relevé de l'économie domestique, et par conséquent de la femme.[24] C'était à la fois le centre d'un débit de boisson, d'un commerce de détail et de carrefour, et l'estaminet, le cabaret, comme nous disions, sans doute même une des ces maisons ouvertes à tous que, dans notre manière sournoise de

---

[17]Voir ci-dessous, n. 25.

[18]Bottéro, *Lorsque les dieux faisaient l'homme* (ci-dessus, n. 5), 624: 130-7.

[19]*Ibid.* pp. 230-1.

[20]*Ibid.* pp. 231-2, ii: 5ss., et pp. 236-7, v: 40ss.

[21]J. Bottéro, 'L'amour à Babylone', *L'Histoire* (1984), n° 63, 9-10.

[22]C'est le propre nom, transcrit en grec, qu'utilise Jules l'Africain dans le passage cité plus haut (nn. 1 et 2): *sikéra*.

[23]*sâbû* (dont le féminin est *sâbîtu*): voir *Chicago Assyrian Dictionary*, S (1984), 5-6.

[24]Pour la 'cabaretière' et sa 'maison', voir *ibid.* pp. 8-9. Après l'époque paléo-babylonienne (première moitié du deuxième millénaire), on ne parle plus que de la 'maison du cabaretier' (*ibid.* p. 9), comme si l'homme, dans cette activité et ce commerce, avait pris le pas sur la femme.

parler, nous appelons 'closes', et où nous avons lieu de penser qu'il se passait bien des choses peu convenables autour de ce qui constituait la finalité essentielle du lieu: la consommation de la bière. Il y a en effet des chances qu'on y doive localiser les scènes reproduites sur des plaquettes d'argile, où l'on voit des convives réunis autour d'une jarre et aspirant dévotement la bière qu'elle contenait, au moyen de 'chalumeaux-à-boire' filtrants, qui en écartaient la lie et les impuretés.[25] Parfois, pendant qu'ils sirotent ainsi, une des buveuses, ou un des buveurs, debout, sont sodomisés par un autre personnage. C'était donc, en somme, autour de l'usage, facilement immodéré, de la boisson capiteuse, une maison vouée 'au plaisir', comme le dit tout net une lettre de Mari.[26] Mais ce plaisir, indispensable pour oublier les contraintes sociales et personnelles; canaliser et comme sublimer les révoltes; aider, en somme, à prendre la vie du bon côté, pouvait aisément, vu la difficulté de se contrôler sous l'emprise de l'alcool, aller beaucoup trop loin et déboucher sur le désordre: d'où la rigueur du *'Code' de Hammurabi*, qui, d'une part, condamne au bûcher la dévote béguine (*nadîtu*), de haut lignage, qui aurait seulement franchi le seuil de cette 'maison de la cabaretière',[27] et, d'autre part, en menace la tenancière de mort, pour peu qu'elle tolère chez elle des malfaiteurs rassemblés aux fins d'y tramer quelque mauvais coup.[28]

On voit que le rôle social de la bière pouvait sans difficulté devenir carrément antisocial. Mais pour ne point laisser sous cette impression gênante et suggérer au moins ce qui était déjà le comble du plaisir noble de boire, à savoir l'enthousiasme littéraire pour la boisson, voici, traduite presque entière, l'unique 'chanson-à-boire' que nous ayons jusqu'ici retrouvée dans notre vaste documentation. Elle est en langue sumérienne et doit avoir été écrite au tournant du troisième au deuxième millénaires:

O Cuve-à-bière, Cuve-à-bière![29]
Cuve-à-bière qui béatifies l'âme!
Hanap qui mets le coeur en joie!
Gobelet si indispensable!
Jarre remplie de bière!
Tous ces récipients dressés sur leur piédestal!
Que votre dieu-patron vous bénisse!
Ce qui vous réjouira, nous réjouira aussi,
A merveille!
Oui! notre âme est heureuse et notre coeur en joie!
Je vais mander brasseurs et échansons,
Pour nous servir des flots de bière à la ronde!
Quel plaisir! Quel délice!
A la humer béatement,
à entonner dans la liesse cette noble liqueur,
Le coeur joyeux et l'âme radieuse![30]

[25]L'un de ces reliefs est reproduit à la p. 9 de l'article de *L'Histoire*, ci-dessus, n. 21.
[26]G. Dossin, *Archives royales de Mari, 1: Correspondance de Shamshi-Addu* (Paris, 1950), 70-1, n° 28, ll. 17-18.
[27]A. Finet, *Le Code de Hammurabi* (Paris, 1983), 75: § 110.
[28]*Ibid.* § 109.
[29]Il s'agit de la cuve de fermentation, instrument essentiel de la brasserie. Les vers suivants interpellent tous les vases dans lesquels on entreposait ou consommait la bière.
[30]Civil, 'A Hymn to the Beer Goddess' (ci-dessus, n. 8), 73-4.

J'avais prévenu que, vu l'état de la question, je serais obligé de m'étendre d'abord quelque peu sur la bière. Il est peut-être temps d'en revenir au principal: Jules l'Africain a-t'il dit la vérité, et les Babyloniens n'étaient-ils que d'incorrigibles buveurs de ce liquide, totalement abandonnés de Dionysos? Ou bien ce dernier avait-il, malgré tout, fait quelque chose en leur faveur? Leur avait-il transmis le breuvage dont il était le patron surnaturel? En d'autres termes, cette 'civilisation de la bière' s'il en fut, avait-elle ménagé une place au vin, et laquelle?

La situation n'est pas simple. Tenons-nous-en surtout, et d'abord, au lieu propre et au cadre natif de cette civilisation, à ce que l'on appelle volontiers la Babylonie.

Tout d'abord, c'est un fait que dès le début du troisième millénaire figure dans le catalogue des caractères picto- et idéographiques de l'écriture locale, non encore cunéiformisée,[31] un signe figurant la présentation linéaire la plus ancienne de celui qui sera entendu plus tard comme désignant la vigne et le vin. On ne l'y relève, il est vrai, pas plus de quatre ou cinq fois dans la masse assez considérable (quelque 4.000)[32] de tablettes archaïques, ce qui n'encourage guère à imputer au produit qu'il représente une véritable notoriété. Il était alors clairement composé d'un caractère dont le sens est alors inconnu, en sumérien, et qui se lisait quelque chose comme *TIN*, superposé à celui du 'bois', qui s'articulait *GISH*. On devait donc déjà le lire, comme on fera plus tard, *GISH.TIN* ou *GESH.TIN* (graphie décomposée qui se rencontre, çà et là, au deuxième millénaire notamment), et l'entendre 'le bois/l'arbre/l'arbuste de ...'.[33]

Une difficulté vient du fait qu'en Mésopotamie le même signe, dont je viens de parler, et le même mot (en sumérien *GESHTIN*; en akkadien *karânu*) s'entendaient aussi bien de *la plante*: la vigne, et de *ses fruits*: les raisins, que du *breuvage* que l'on en tirait: le vin. Sans le contexte, et c'est le cas des tablettes archaïques, indéchiffrables du fait que le système de notation alors utilisé ne dépassait point la mnémotechnie,[34] il est donc impossible de décider si, en Babylonie, dès ce temps reculé, le vin était connu; seule la présence de la vigne, et par conséquent du raisin, est certaine.

Que cette plante y ait été *importée*, c'est indiscutable, puisqu'aussi bien, dans un pays originellement immergé, tout, sauf la terre et le sous-sol, avait été introduit du dehors. Il y a quelque chance qu'une pareille importation ait été le fait de la partie sémitique de la population, arrivée précisément d'une contrée — le Haut-pays et la Syrie — vouée depuis toujours, nous le savons,[35] à la culture intense de la vigne, en vue de la production du vin. C'est sans doute pourquoi ces 'Akkadiens' ont gardé à la vigne le nom de *karânu*, répondant à la racine *KRM* qui la désigne dans toutes les langues du groupe sémitique. Pour le souligner en passant, cette même racine a donné en akkadien le terme de *kurunnu*, passé en sumérien sous la forme *KURUN* (idéographié, du reste, à

---

[31]Bottéro, *Mésopotamie* (ci-dessus, n. 6), 95-6.

[32]Aux 656 documents publiés d'abord par A. Falkenstein (*Archaische Texte aus Uruk* (Berlin, 1936)), se seraient ajoutés, depuis, quelque 3.400 pièces, selon M.W. Green et H.J. Nissen (edd.), *Zeichenliste der Archaische Texte aus Uruk* (Berlin, 1987), 13.

[33]Plus tard, le signe *TIN* sera utilisé pour désigner la 'vie'; mais on n'est pas assuré qu'il ait eu d'emblée cette valeur. On ne saurait donc poser à coup sûr que les vieux Mésopotamiens auraient donné à la vigne le nom de 'bois/arbre de vie', même si ce binôme avait insisté seulement sur l'excellence et le prix qu'on attribuait à cette plante et à ses fruits.

[34]Bottéro, *Mésopotamie* (ci-dessus, n. 6), 98-9.

[35]Lutz, *Viticulture and Brewing* (ci-dessus, n. 3), 22-3.

l'image de *GESH.TIN*, par le binôme *KASH.TIN*: 'bière de ...'), pour désigner une boisson alcoolisée voisine de la bière et peut-être préparée plus ou moins à la manière du vin, ou comparable au vin, dont nous ne savons pas de quoi elle était faite. En akkadien également, je le répète, *karânu* — comme *GESHTIN* sumérien — s'entendait aussi bien de la vigne, de ses fruits: les raisins, et de leur produit principal: le vin.[36] *Înu*, apparenté à *woinos*/*uinum* préindoeuropéen, et connu en hébreu sous la forme *yayîn*, n'est jusqu'à ce jour attesté qu'une fois, enregistré dans une sorte de dictionnaire récent.[37]

Que les Sémites (ou d'autres? car il ne s'agit là, après tout, que d'une forte vraisemblance) aient introduit la vigne en Basse Mésopotamie dès les débuts de l'histoire, c'est donc un fait. Mais c'est un fait, aussi, qu'ils n'ont réussi à y implanter, ni sa culture en grand, ni les techniques de la vinification. Sans doute était-il difficile d'y changer un régime profondément ancré, depuis longtemps, dans la vie et la propre nature du pays, et qui tournait résolument les habitants vers la culture généralisée des céréales. La vigne semble donc y avoir été volontiers plantée (comme certains reliefs, notamment assyriens, la représenteront plus tard)[38] par quelques pieds et tonnelles, parmi les autres arbres fruitiers des 'jardins', dûment irrigués, ombreux et agréables, bien clos, que les particuliers se ménageaient hors la ville, pour leur profit alimentaire, mais aussi pour leur détente, leur repos, voire leur exercices amoureux dans les conditions les plus plaisantes de secret, de calme et de poésie.[39] Les fruits qu'elle portait, et qu'on appréciait grandement, frais ou séchés (on les appelait alors *muzîqu*),[40] devaient plus volontiers être consommés comme tels, parmi les autres produits de l'arboriculture.

Dans ces conditions, pas davantage que la viticulture, la vinification n'a jamais dû être autre chose, en Babylonie, qu'affaire privée. Aujourd'hui encore — si je m'en rapporte à mes derniers souvenirs d'Iraq, en 1979 — à Baghdad notamment, c'était une tradition d'acheter (ou de cueillir, si l'on possédait quelques ceps) une certaine quantité de raisin, de l'écraser, et de le laisser fermenter, en le sucrant volontiers (même trop!), pour en préparer une petite provision d'un vin dont on était fier. J'en ai goûté plus d'une fois, assez cependant pour me rendre compte qu'il n'est pas question, pour le juger, de faire appel aux critères qui sont les nôtres pour nos crus. Il est vrai que cette réserve aurait valu tout autant pour les vins d'autrefois. Le vin lui-même, au moins dans la partie méridionale du pays, a donc toutes chances, quand il y est attesté sûrement et en quantité, d'avoir été un produit toujours importé. Dans la première mention explicite qui en est faite, au cours d'une inscription commémorative, le souverain de Lagash vers 2340, *Uru-inim*/*ka-gina*, le laisse entendre fort clairement, quand il déclare avoir 'construit un cellier' (faute de vocabulaire spécialisé — et pour cause! — il désigne cette construction par le terme propre à la 'réserve de bière'), 'dans lequel, depuis la montagne, on apportait du vin par grands vases'.[41] La 'montagne', la 'région montagneuse', c'était le Nord et le Nord-Ouest du pays, la Syrie, ou peut-être déjà la

---

[36]*Chicago Assyrian Dictionary*, K (1971), 203-4.

[37]W. von Soden, *Akkadisches Handwörterbuch* (Wiesbaden, 1965), 383b: *înu* II.

[38]Ainsi dans *L'Histoire* (ci-dessus, n. 21), n° 65, pp. 58-9.

[39]Voir notamment S.N. Kramer, *Le mariage sacré* (Paris, 1983), 196.

[40]*Chicago Assyrian Dictionary*, M/2 (1977), 322-3, où l'on voit, aux textes cités, qu'on les prisait fort.

[41]E. Sollberger et J.R. Kupper, *Inscriptions royales sumériennes et akkadiennes* (Paris, 1971), 78: IC11 (I:1-II:7).

Mésopotamie septentrionale, contrées traditionnellement vouées à la culture de la vigne et à la production du vin. Ce dernier apparaît ainsi, en Babylonie tout au moins, comme un produit étranger. On lui donnera même, quelque fois, par une périphrase éloquente, le nom de 'bière de la montagne' (*shikâr shadî*).[42]

Pour illustrer son trafic, qui suivait plus volontiers la voie fluviale, et le commerce de redistribution auquel les arrivages donnaient lieu, voici deux extraits de lettres d'affaires. Elles ont pour auteur un négociant des alentours de 1750 avant notre ère, un certain Bêlânu, et pour destinataire un de ses commis: Ahûni, chargé par lui d'aller acheter du vin, soit sur les lieux de production, d'où il l'expédiait par bateau avec d'autres marchandises, soit aux quais d'arrivée, en la ville de Sippar, à 50 km au Nord de Babylone. Dans la première lettre, Bêlânu mande à Ahûni: 'Les bateaux (frêtés, chargés et expédiés par toi) sont arrivés ici (à Sippar) en fin de parcours. Mais pourquoi n'as-tu pas acheté et ne m'as-tu pas envoyé de bon vin? Envoie-m'en, et (pour l'apporter) viens me trouver en personne dans les dix jours!'[43] Dans la seconde: 'Il est arrivé à Sippar un bateau chargé de vin. Achète-m'en pour dix sicles[44] et, dès demain, (pour me l'apporter) viens me rejoindre à Babylone'.[45] Nous ignorons le prix du vin, à cette époque, en Babylonie: il devait être notablement plus cher qu'à Mari, à 350 km en amont, sur l'Euphrate, où il paraît s'être vendu un sicle les vingt litres.[46] Nous ne savons donc pas bien quelle quantité Ahûni pouvait s'en procurer: de 200 à 300 litres, probablement, volume modeste, en somme, pour une marchandise que Bêlânu devait ultérieurement détailler et qui reviendrait encore plus cher à ses acquéreurs.

Importé, le vin était donc coûteux: il représentait un produit de luxe, plutôt rare, mal accessible — sinon inaccessible — aux gens de la rue, et réservé à la haute classe: le roi et son entourage, d'une part; les dieux, de l'autre. On le met en effet régulièrement en rapports avec ces divers personnages.[47] Qu'il ait été hautement prisé et recherché — comme tout ce qui est rare et dispendieux — de ceux qui en avaient les moyens, s'entend, la chose ne fait pas le moindre doute: nous le sentons déjà aux épithètes dont on l'ornait volontiers: 'bon', 'succulent', 'très doux' ...[48] et au rapprochement qui en était souvent fait avec le 'miel', autre produit de luxe, également importé du Nord/Nord-Ouest.[49]

Pour avancer qu'il était, depuis très anciennement, estimé une denrée d'importance culturelle première, nous ne saurions toutefois arguer du fait que, comme à la bière, on lui avait assigné deux divinités tutélaires. Car — leur nom les trahit — celles-ci, surtout à haute époque, devaient avoir pour domaine, non pas le vin, mais la vigne: la vigne

---

[42]*Chicago Assyrian Dictionary*, K, 205-6: d; et 203, *passim*.

[43]R. Frankena, *Briefe aus dem Berliner Museum* (Leiden, 1974), 34-5, n° 52: 12-13.

[44]Soit environ 80 gr. (d'argent, s'entend): valeur, à l'époque, d'à peu près 1.500/1.800 litres de grains.

[45]G. Dossin, *Lettres de la Première Dynastie babylonienne* (Paris, 1933-4), pl. cx, n° 133: 6-7.

[46]Voir J.M. Durand, *Archives royales de Mari* 21 (1983), 104-5, et A. Finet, 'Le vin à Mari', *Archiv für Orientforschung* 25 (1974), 122-3.

[47]*Chicago Assyrian Dictionary*, K, 203-4: *passim*.

[48]*Ibid.*

[49]Ainsi, dans un chant en l'honneur d'une déesse, cette comparaison: 'La célébrer est plus doux que le miel et le vin' (*Cuneiform Texts ... in the British Museum* (London, 1902), XV, pl. 1, i:4).

avec ses raisins, que l'on prisait assez pour l'avoir ainsi reliée au monde surnaturel. La déesse Geshtin-anna, en sumérien, c'était la 'Vigne céleste', et je dois dire du reste que, dans ce qu'il nous reste de son dossier, ses rapports immédiats avec cette plante ou ses fruits n'apparaissent guère.[50] Quant au dieu Nin-gish-zida: 'Patron du bois authentique', dont les rapports avec Geshtin-anna nous échappent, il ne semble pas, non plus, avoir été lié le moins du monde au vin: bien plutôt à la vigne.[51] On vient de déchiffrer un morceau de mythe qui le montre libéré de l'Enfer, dans lequel il était descendu ou tombé, on ne sait trop pourquoi ni comment; mais, sitôt reparu sur terre, il se mettait à 'verser des larmes de couleur rouge-sombre', allusion manifeste à la vigne sortie de terre pour porter ses raisins.[52] Même les auteurs de la *Grande encyclopédie* mentionnée ci-devant, à en juger par ce qu'il nous en reste, n'ont réservé au vin qu'une quinzaine de rubriques:[53] une misère, au regard des 200 assignées à la bière.

On rencontre, certes, le vin un peu partout: introduit, non seulement aux festins des mortels, mais à la table des dieux, dans les 'repas' qu'on leur servait en manière de culte liturgique.[54] Il figure aussi, mais pas très souvent,[55] dans les rituels et les manipulations du culte d'exorcisme, et jusque dans les recettes de médecine et de pharmacopée, en qualité d'excipient.[56] Mais, où qu'il paraisse, ce n'est jamais qu'après la bière, en second, en retrait, nulle part à la première place et dans le rôle de protagoniste. Comparé à elle, il fait penser, de loin, à ce que représente l'alcool dans notre civilisation du vin: un supplément agréable, apprécié, soumis à la mode, plus dispendieux et d'autant recherché, mais pas du tout tenu pour essentiel, produit de luxe et que n'importe qui ne peut pas se permettre.

A tout ce que j'ai dit plus haut des fonctions sociales de la bière, je ne puis rien ajouter qui soit particulier au vin. Comme si ce dernier, dans les plaisirs de la table et du boire, dans les bienfaits de la 'convivialité', dans les euphories de l'ivresse, non moins que dans ses excès, n'avait été qu'un brillant second, compagnon de la bière, mais sans la remplacer jamais. La Babylonie, tout au moins, est restée jusqu'au bout fidèle à sa 'civilisation de la bière'.

En disant: 'la Babylonie, tout au moins' et 'jusqu'au bout', j'introduis dans le débat des nuances possibles de lieu et de temps. Il est clair, tout d'abord, du moins à en juger sur pièces, que le vin s'est trouvé, à mesure, de plus en plus fréquemment utilisé pour breuvage, tant des hommes que des dieux. Pour le dire en passant, je ne pense pas qu'il faille accorder un grand poids, en le généralisant, au texte fameux de Quinte-Curce, dans lequel, parlant, au premier siècle de notre ère, des débauches d'Alexandre à Babylone, il accuse 'les Babyloniens' de 's'abandonner au vin, jusqu'à l'ébriété et tout ce qui s'ensuit'.[57] Non seulement l'époque dont il parle est tardive (330 av. J.-C.), et,

---

[50] *Reallexikon der Assyriologie*, III, 299-300.

[51] W.G. Lambert, 'A new Babylonian descent to the Netherworld', dans T. Abush, J. Huehnergard et P. Steinkeller (edd.), *Lingering over Words* (Atlanta, 1990), 295-6.

[52] *Ibid.* pp. 291-2.

[53] En réalité, il n'en subsiste rien dans nos témoins retrouvés, et lacunaires, de la XXIIIe tablette de l'ouvrage; seuls les antécédents sumériens nous en donnent une idée: voir Landsberger, *Materials for the Sumerian Lexicon* (ci-dessus, n. 12), 125-6, n° 15: 1-2; 135, n° 1, col. xii: 35-6; 158, n° 15: 418-19.

[54] *Chicago Assyrian Dictionary*, K, 204: b.

[55] *Ibid.*

[56] *Ibid.* p. 205: c.

[57] *Histoires* v. 37.

comme je viens de le dire, le vin s'était déjà fait adopter davantage dans le pays, surtout par la haute classe qui, beaucoup plus aisément que le populaire, pouvait se laisser prendre à son goût et sa mode, le préférant, en particulier — et ce serait le cas ici — pour les beuveries et ripailles (comme nous pouvons préférer le cognac); mais personne n'a jamais célébré le souci d'exactitude historique de l'auteur de la *Vie d'Alexandre*. Il n'en est donc pas moins clair qu'à ma connaissance, en tous cas, la bière a toujours prédominé en Babylonie, comme boisson véritablement populaire, 'nationale' et universelle, le vin n'ayant jamais représenté qu'une sorte de supplément raffiné et luxueux, même si la mode et le goût l'ont fait, çà et là, apprécier davantage. Encore plusieurs siècles après notre ère, toujours en Babylonie, le breuvage principal, c'était toujours la bière, comme on le discerne fort bien dans les archives des communautés juives de ce pays.[58] Un Rabbi Johanan y avançait même que c'était à leur accoutumance à la bière que les Babyloniens devaient d'avoir été préservés de la lèpre ...[59]

Si l'on prend les choses, non plus dans l'ordre du temps, mais du lieu, la situation a pu changer quelque peu dans les deux ou trois principaux territoires voisins de la Babylonie et conquis depuis le troisième millénaire à sa civilisation, mais beaucoup plus sémitisés et géographiquement attenants aux grands centres de viticulture et de vinification: l'Assyrie, Mari et, entre autres, Emar, que nous connaissons beaucoup mieux.[60]

A Emar, au cours de la seconde moitié du deuxième millénaire, dans les rituels et autres usages, le vin apparaît beaucoup plus fréquemment qu'à Babylone.[61] A Mari, quelques siècles plus tôt, alors que la bière se trouve à peine mentionnée, le vin est d'usage quotidien et courant:[62] il est même distribué aux travailleurs et au peuple, et fait l'effet de la boisson usuelle. Mais il reste un produit importé — même si l'on peut supposer quelques centres de production, sur culture locale plus intensive de la vigne, ce qui n'est du reste pas prouvé. Et un signe que, sur le plan culturel tout au moins, la bière gardait sa prépondérance, c'est qu'à en croire nos relevés quotidiens fort nombreux de la table royale, le souverain, à ses repas, buvait seulement de la bière, une bière particulière, il est vrai (on l'appelait *alappânu*), mais ce n'était pas du vin.[63] Et dans la langue de Mari, comme en Mésopotamie propre, l'alimentation était toujours définie par 'le pain et la bière'.[64]

---

[58]Rabbi J. Newman, *The Agricultural Life of the Jews in Babylonia, between the Years 200 CE and 500 CE* (New Haven, 1932), 93-4 et 107-8.

[59]*Ibid.* p. 107.

[60]Je laisse de côté Ebla, dont la documentation, encore incomplètement publiée, n'est pas de ma compétence.

[61]Non seulement on en importe du vin à Mari (G. Dossin, J. Bottéro, M. Birot, M. Lurton Burke, J.-R. Kupper et A. Finet, *Archives royales de Mari*, 13: *Textes divers* (Paris, 1964), 128-9, n° 126: 5-6), mais le vin y joue, par exemple, un rôle majeur dans les rituels — la bière aussi, du reste: ainsi D. Arnaud, *Emar* 6 (3) (1986), 329: 4 (et 8); 330: 12; 331: 26-7, etc.; 342: 30', 45', 53' etc.

[62]Finet, 'Le vin à Mari', 122, et Durand, *Archives royales de Mari*, 21, 104-5 (ci-dessus, n. 46).

[63]*Chicago Assyrian Dictionary*, A/1, 335-6.

[64]Ainsi Ch.F. Jean, *Archives royales de Mari*, 2: *Lettres diverses* (Paris, 1950), 154, n° 82: 11 et 22; G. Dossin, *Archives royales de Mari*, 10: *Correspondance féminine* (Paris, 1978), 172-3, n° 116: 14. Pour l'expression elle-même, voir ci-dessus, n. 14.

L'autre domaine adjacent à la Babylonie, c'était la partie Nord du pays, que nous appelons l'Assyrie, quelque peu à part (y compris sur le plan linguistique, puisque le dialecte assyrien différait assez du babylonien) de la Babylonie, même si elle y a été intégrée à plus d'une reprise, avant de succomber finalement devant elle. Ici aussi, le vin a manifestement plus d'importance et se consomme toujours davantage: le roi en boit, et en fait boire;[65] il s'en fait même des réserves.[66] On connaît et l'on apprécie des crus particuliers, plus ou moins estimés et fameux: ceux de Tupliash, d'Inzalla, de Sûhu, etc.[67] Sont même signalés des cas d'ivrognerie populaire au vin.[68] Mais la bière n'a pas disparu, et si le vin a quelque peu entamé sa suprématie, elle est toujours la première des boissons, traditionnelle depuis la nuit des temps. Dans le fameux pantagruélique repas de 69.574 couverts, offert, vers 870 av. J.-C., au peuple de sa capitale renovée, par le roi assyrien Assur-nasir-apal II (883-859), et dont une stèle commémorative nous a conservé, non le menu, hélas, mais la formidable énumération des denrées consommées, le vin figure pour 10.000 jarres (quelque chose comme 100.000 litres), mais la bière aussi, et pour autant![69] Elle n'a pas cédé!

Même dans les territoires plus soumis à la vigne et au vin, la vieille civilisation mésopotamienne est demeurée jusqu'au bout obstinément fidèle à ses céréales, et foncièrement centrée sur sa bière. Jules l'Africain avait donc raison: Dionysos ne s'y sentait pas chez lui!

* * *

'Intervento' by Christopher Lord: Le sexe de la boisson

D'abord, il faut dire que la situation que vous avez décrite en Mésopotamie me semble d'une certaine manière analogue à celle qui se trouve actuellement en Angleterre: une société de vieille tradition de production et de consommation de la bière se transforme peu à peu en société d'importation du vin.

Mais après ça, et plus sérieusement peut-être, je voudrais vous proposer une hypothèse un peu fragile: une hypothèse au sujet du *sexe* de la boisson. Vous avez expliqué que la bière était traditionellement préparée par les femmes, à la maison, comme une partie de la cuisine de tous les jours, alors que le vin a toujours été importé, et cela veut dire aussi acheté, bien entendu: je suppose que cette activité d'importation et de commerce a été dirigée exclusivement par les hommes.

Si tout cela est vrai, on pourrait peut-être suggérer l'interprétation suivante: une société antérieure, basée sur la culture des céréales, avec toute l'activité alimentaire et alcoolique dirigée et contrôlée par les femmes, a été transformée par l'innovation masculine de l'achat du vin étranger. L'étendue d'une telle transformation serait très

---

[65]S. Parpola, *Letters from Assyrian Scholars to the Kings Esarhaddon and Assurbanipal*, I (Neukirchen-Vluyn, 1970), 32-3, n° 51: rev. 3-4.

[66]R.H. Pfeiffer, *State Letters of Assyria* (New Haven, 1935), 106, n° 139: 11-12.

[67]*Reallexikon der Assyriologie*, III (voir n. 3), 305.

[68]Pfeiffer, *State Letters of Assyria* (ci-dessus, n. 66), 139, n° 191.

[69]D.J. Wiseman, 'A new stela of Aššur-nasir-pal II', *Iraq* 14 (1952), 34-5: 115-16.

difficile à analyser, mais peut-être il ne serait pas tout-à-fait impossible de faire quelques premiers pas vers une explication de sa nature.

Dans le français de nos jours, on parle de la bière et du vin — la bière féminine et le vin masculin. Quelle est l'archéologie de cette distinction? Est-ce qu'on pourrait trouver ou construire une distinction similaire dans la civilisation de la Mésopotamie antique? Les arguments pour ou contre cette hypothèse pourraient être étymologiques, ou bien mythologiques, mais en voilà l'idée centrale: la fémininité de la bière, et la masculinité du vin.

3

The *Symposion* in Ancient Mesopotamia: Archaeological Evidence

JULIAN EDGEWORTH READE

There are elaborate and simple pleasures, interlocked. The subject discussed in this paper is at first sight a relatively simple pleasure, one of those to which all labours tend. After any achievement, whether it be a battle won, a book written, or a day's work finished, those who are free to do so will sometimes relax almost as if relaxation were the prime aim of their endeavours. In reality it is just one of the rewards, a short-term one but none the less pleasurable, and its intensity is or often seems to be sharpened by consumption of a psychotropic drug such as alcohol and by the companionship of friends or sexual partners.

This to my mind is the reason for social drinking, the background to the *symposion*. There is scope for a ceremonial framework in which to drink, and for additional features: gossip; intrigue; peer-group solidarity; the encounter therapy suggested by Rösler elsewhere in this volume; the intellectual pleasures of the *symposia* adduced by writers such as Plato and Lowes Dickinson; the sense of fulfilment said to be achieved in comparable religious ceremonies that involve drugs. Social drinking may indeed be associated with these other things, but our preliminary hypothesis has to be the plain one, that alcohol was used as a drug, warm, encouraging, deceptive, to enhance the pleasures of relaxation.

Scenes of communal drinking are a recognized theme in the art of ancient Mesopotamia. Containers and other objects used by people drinking or by those serving them are among the commonest archaeological finds. The main problem is how far such evidence can take us in interpreting Mesopotamian social practice, and whether it can be correlated with the kind of event known in the Mediterranean world as the *symposion*.

My first question, however, is a technical one, and concerns the difference between the grape wine which is the liquid to which the papers in this volume are devoted, and other alcoholic drinks. These latter are potentially relevant because we are considering not the quality of specific vineyards and vintages, but cruder characteristics of wine, which are liable to be the main reasons for its consumption, namely its alcoholic content and consequent effects on perception and behaviour. While individuals may react differently to particular beverages, these are essential characteristics which wine shares with beer made from barley and with other fermented drinks such as palm wine. One can even enter an English pub and buy a drink known as barley wine. The technology that goes to making these things is well understood by many people, and need not be discussed here. Texts tell us that drinks were made in ancient Mesopotamia from grapes, barley, dates and other substances, and that the drinkers sometimes became drunk; the *Chicago Assyrian Dictionary*, s.v. *karanu* ('wine'), *shikaru* ('beer'), hence *shakaru* ('become inebriated') and cognate words, is most informative on these matters.

It then seems possible that archaeology or iconography may tell us what was being consumed at one time or another, and whether there was, between different kinds of drink, a distinction which we would find helpful in understanding the status of grape wine. For a European such as myself, a distinction between beer and wine is manifest. It divides the north from the south, the German from the Latin. In my own country, England, there is often a social distinction: wine for the urbane, beer for everyone else. There are economic considerations behind the distinction, as there will have been in the ancient Near East. There beer was a staple food throughout agricultural societies, apportioned to workers among their rations as a matter of course. Wine will have been more readily available in areas such as north Mesopotamia, where vines were cultivated in the foothills, than in south Mesopotamia. So there is a presumption in favour of wine having greater social punch, but it is doubtful whether this status can be demonstrated.

There is a class of sieve-like and comparable objects that were used to filter liquids. Many examples were collected by Moorey (1980), who identified them as belonging to 'wine-sets'. Some examples date from the mid third millennium BC, in the Early Dynastic period of Sumerian civilization, coming from the Royal Tombs of Ur in south Mesopotamia. They may be made out of precious materials such as gold and silver, and appear to have been in regular use; they are associated with spouted jars and beakers, which appear together in at least one drinking scene of the period (Fig. 1,b), and were probably used to filter wine. This suggestion may be supported by reference to an Egyptian illustration of the mid second millennium BC, which shows a liquid served through comparable sieves (Desroches-Noblecourt 1963: 205, fig. 126; see also Lesko 1977): my Egyptological colleagues assure me that this is wine. Sets of vessels, including sieves, are known from later sites within the Egyptian sphere of influence (Fig. 2), and by the Achaemenid period they appear to have become standard components of a gentleman's equipment in the tomb and presumably in life beforehand.

Beer may have been filtered in a different way, drunk through straws or metal tubes with filters at the base. Evidence for this practice has been assembled recently by Maeir and Garfinkel (1992). Such tubes are attested at Ur, and illustrations of the period show people drinking through them (Fig. 1,a). There is a scattering of examples from many Near Eastern sites over the next two millennia. Xenophon in *Anabasis* iv. 5 refers to men in eastern Turkey drinking in this fashion, and a modern illustration of the technique comes from a book about the Moi people of Vietnam (Riesen 1957: plate section after p. 112).

It seems, then, that grape wine was sometimes filtered before drinking by being poured out through a sieve, and that other fermented drinks were sometimes filtered by being sucked up from one, but the distinction is clearly far from safe. Besides the likelihood that sieves were also used for non-alcoholic drinks, it may be that some alcoholic drinks did not require filtering at all, or not immediately before consumption. For instance, an Assyrian carving represents drink served direct from a large bowl, very probably a mixing-bowl (see below, Fig. 9). In the circumstances, unless analysis of

a

b

FIG. 1. Impression of a Sumerian cylinder-seal, *c.* 2600 BC (WA 121545) *(Courtesy of the Trustees of the British Museum)*

FIG. 2. Bronze wine-set from Tell es-Sai'diyeh, Jordan, *c.* 1200 BC *(Courtesy of the excavator, J.N. Tubb)*

organic residues is available (for example, Badler *et al.* 1990), or there is clear textual evidence of the kind discussed elsewhere in this volume by Bottéro, I would hesitate to differentiate wine from beer either in ancient illustrations or in the archaeological record.

Symposia (often probably feasts) are among the standard themes of the representational art of ancient Mesopotamia. This tradition of narrative art emerged before 3000 BC and we have an abundance of Sumerian examples from the mid third millennium. They appear mainly on objects dedicated in temples, in wall-decoration of various kinds, on inlaid items of furniture, and on cylinder-seals. The range of themes is wide. Besides largely decorative motifs such as animal contests, there are portrayals of gods and of magical and probably some mythical figures. Many show a ruler performing his official duties, the ways in which he protected the interests of his city and his gods: so there are scenes of worship, warfare, and the construction of sacred buildings. Individuals other than rulers also appear. In the *symposion* scenes it is often far from clear who is being represented.

Within the *symposion* scenes, which have been largely brought together by Selz (1983), there is considerable variety. They include men only, often a ruler, or men and women, seated and drinking, sometimes holding fans. They drink from beakers or through tubes. Servants attend to them. Musicians are often present. Sometimes there are animals and supplies of food apparently being brought to the *symposion*, and occasionally, though the small scale of cylinder-seals makes it hard to be sure, the people may be envisaged as eating too rather than merely drinking. Occasionally one *symposion* composition may be linked to another. A fine example, part of the inlaid decoration on the so-called Standard of Ur, an object of uncertain shape and function, shows a procession of people bringing supplies to the ruler, who is seated with others drinking to the sound of music (Figs 3 and 4); on the other side of this object there is a scene of military victory which might be regarded as preceding the *symposion*, and therefore linked to it thematically. On another object, a wall-plaque, what is probably a scene of drinking adjoins a pair of figures making love (Selz 1983: Taf. IX). On the many cylinder-seals there is a range of themes besides drinking, but the associations are seldom clear-cut. Another relationship is that between the figures in drinking scenes and the statues of themselves that individuals dedicated in temples: the statues often look as if they are participating in a *symposion*, holding beakers or fans (for examples, Spycket 1981: figs 37 and 43).

On this and suchlike evidence, with invocation of appropriate ancient texts, various proposals have been made concerning the significance of the *symposion* scene; they are well collected by Dentzer (1982: 21-6). For instance, one idea is that it shows a feast connected with a sacred marriage which is consummated by humans personifying divinities; another is that it shows a feast involving communion with dead ancestors. Obviously such religious ceremonies will have involved celebrations of which a *symposion* or feast was part. Similarly, however, the rituals involved in the completion of civic projects, and other activities, will have included feasting and celebrations, and so of course will successful wars. In the Ur graves there was a clear tendency for cylinder-seals showing *symposia* to belong to individuals of high status (Rathje 1977). At a material level, once the opportunity for leisure has been established in society, then the *symposion* or feast is a normal natural activity. Its suitability as a theme for publicity through

Fig. 3. The Standard of Ur, *c.* 2600 BC — detail of a *symposion* or feast (WA 121201) *(Courtesy of the Trustees of the British Museum)*

Fig. 4. The Standard of Ur, *c.* 2600 BC — detail of a *symposion* or feast (WA 121201) *(Courtesy of the Trustees of the British Museum)*

artistic representation, extolling the grandeur of kingship, may be accentuated if it is also an act of conspicuous consumption or generosity.

In the circumstances it is not sensible to ascribe one grand interpretation to all the various *symposion* scenes. A more modest approach is to interpret each one in its own context, starting from the presumption that they do not necessarily mean more than they appear to. If then we look at Sumerian literature, stories that are somewhat later in date but probably derive from versions current in the mid third millennium, then we observe that the *symposion* is indeed accepted social practice. Moreover, since Sumerian gods seem to have behaved as humans, we can deduce from their behaviour on such occasions how people in reality reacted to alcohol and judged its effects (Leick 1991: 191, *s.v.* 'drunkenness').

In one story the god Enki, renowned for his wisdom, is at a feast after the creation of mankind. He and the goddesss Ninmah become tipsy and decide to compete in the creation of further beings. The results all have physical disabilities of one kind or another. A second story recounts how the same god Enki entertains the goddess Inanna with beer and wine. Intoxicated, he hands over to her, one by one, the arts of civilization which she then successfully removes to her own city of Uruk. This negative image of the results of overindulgence is comparable with that in the Old Testament, from Noah's disgrace onwards, and in the Hittite myths of Turkey, an area where the grape and probably wilder Dionysiac revelries were at home. Yet it is balanced, in various texts, by references to the sensations of well-being that alcohol induces. In the early second millennium BC, popular art was still illustrating the relationships between alcohol and music, and between alcohol and sexual activity (Fig. 5). There is every reason to suppose that such stories and illustrations reflect the social pleasures of drinking and companionship, but I doubt whether the evidence can be pressed further.

In one group of illustrations, of the late third and early second millennia BC, that may at first sight seem to have something to do with drinking and *symposia*, kings or gods are shown holding or receiving small jars or other containers. These may perhaps be interpreted, however, as symbolizing divine authority, with the vessels containing for instance not wine but the oil through which omens were read (Winter 1986). Other illustrations of various dates show men pouring libations of some kind of liquid, and texts indicate that this could be water, wine, or beer, but the scenes have no direct relevance to human *symposia* (Danmanville 1955). Scenes of individuals drinking or feasting are not uncommon on seals, but again have no direct or demonstrable relevance to *symposia* (for example, Homès-Fredericq 1989). The other liquid one sees poured out in enormous quantities by Mesopotamian magic figures with flowing vases is almost certainly water (for example, Spycket 1981: figs 154-5).

An odd characteristic of Mesopotamian narrative art, in so far as it survives for us, is that the best represented periods are the Sumerian, in the mid third millennium BC, and the Neo-Assyrian in the ninth to seventh centuries. It is not that there is nothing in the intervening periods — there is enough to show that it continued to exist — but there is not much. Nevertheless, the themes of Sumerian and Neo-Assyrian art are much the same as one another. This partly reflects the continuity of Near Eastern civilization and royal requirements, and partly also, in all probability, artistic continuity that was maintained on perishable objects such as furnishings and textiles which were being manufactured even when political or economic problems prevented the creation

FIG. 5. Babylonian terracotta showing relationship between alcohol and sexual activity, *c.* 1800 BC (WA 116731) *(Courtesy of the Trustees of the British Museum)*

of monumental court art. So, for example, on an ivory from Palestine of the late second millennium BC (Dentzer 1982: pl. 5, fig. 28), we see the theme of a victory followed by drinking which calls back the Sumerian inlays of the Standard of Ur at the same time as it looks forward to the wall-panels of Ashurbanipal.

In north Mesopotamia the theme of communal drinking or feasting reappears twice on a monument known as the White Obelisk, probably carved about 1050 BC: the contexts imply that both events were religious celebrations (Fig. 6). A scene on a wall-panel of about 860 BC, in which the Assyrian king is represented drinking while seated at the head of a room, served by courtiers and protected by magical figures, is ambivalent (Fig. 7). Though I have argued that this room was genuinely used for banquets, while Brandes has maintained that it had a religious function, the case cannot be proved either way and the two views are not necessarily incompatible (for references, see Reade 1980: 85). On the other hand an Assyrian ivory furniture panel, again of the ninth century, shows the king and other members of his court seated and drinking together (Fig. 8); this looks like social drinking, since other such ivories present typical themes of Assyrian narrative art, notably warfare and tribute, much as the Standard of Ur had done 1,800 years previously, without positive religious connotations. Certainly every decent Assyrian house had at least one large room suitable for entertainments of this nature.

This presentation of communal drinking as a basically secular social activity is repeated in the palace of the Assyrian king Sargon II, built about 710 BC. His palace

FIG. 6. Assyrian king at a feast, *c.* 1050 BC (WA 118807, detail) *(Courtesy of the Trustees of the British Museum)*

FIG. 7. Assyrian king drinking, *c.* 860 BC (WA 124564-6) *(Courtesy of the Trustees of the British Museum)*

FIG. 8. Assyrian ivory showing the king seated and
drinking with members of
his court, probably about
850 BC *(Courtesy of the British
School of Archaeology in Iraq)*

incorporates an elaborate scheme of decoration, in the form of carved wall-panels whose component themes can be related to the architectural plan and interpreted consistently. For instance, in several places the scenes on the walls represent or reflect the kinds of activity which went on nearby or which might have been regarded as suitable viewing for likely visitors. This applies also to the *symposion* or banquet sequences, which are present in two rooms, in both of which they comprise the upper of two registers of narrative composition. The better preserved of them is above a group of campaign scenes, in a reception room on the more private side of the building, where courtiers may well have eaten and drunk; it shows wine being brought from the mixing bowl, musicians, and men raising their drinking vessels (Figs 9-13). The other comparable sequence is above a group of hunting scenes in a small room which was only accessible from a relatively public reception room and which might have been suitable for occasions when the king received important visitors in private. No religious content has been identified in either of these two *symposion* sequences. They appear to show celebrations after success in war and sport, and to offer a straightforward view into the Assyrian court and the convivial atmosphere in which men discussed matters of common interest.

In the scenes cited so far the drinkers, if not standing, are seated on chairs or stools. It is also possible to drink while lying outstretched on a couch with raised end, an item of furniture that was to be associated with *symposia* in the classical world and one which may seem to imply a greater degree of ceremonial commitment to the process of drinking wine in the company of a few friends. The Assyrians did employ couches: they are present in several illustrations of life on campaign during the ninth to seventh

FIG. 9. Assyrian celebration, *c.* 710 BC: attendants bringing wine *(From Botta and Flandin 1849, pl. 64)*

FIG. 10. Assyrian celebration, *c.* 710 BC: musicians *(From Botta and Flandin 1849, pl. 65)*

FIG. 11. Assyrian celebration, *c.* 710 BC: officials drinking *(From Botta and Flandin 1849, pl. 66)*

FIG. 12. Assyrian celebration, *c.* 710 BC: officials drinking *(From Botta and Flandin 1849, pl. 67)*

FIG. 13. Assyrian celebration, *c.* 710 BC: officials drinking *(From Botta and Flandin 1849, pl. 76)*

centuries (Fig. 14), and the remains of a couch have been found in an Assyrian barrack (Fig. 15). One scene (Fig. 16) shows an officer in his tent, seated at table on a stool, while a couch is being prepared nearby, as if for sleep; this might suggest that the couch was only a variety of bed, a refined alternative to bedding laid on the ground. My own experience, however, is that people in camp are inclined to use their tents to entertain friends, and this tendency could even have been partly responsible in Assyria for promoting the couch from the bedroom to the living room. The prime explanation,

FIG. 14. Scene in an Assyrian camp, including a couch, *c.* 645-640 BC (WA, Or. Dr. V, 26) *(Courtesy of the Trustees of the British Museum)*

FIG. 15. Remains of a couch in position, Nimrud *(Courtesy of the British School of Archaeology in Iraq)*

however, should probably be that the Assyrians adopted social use of the couch, like much else, from the recently conquered Levantine states where the couch was at home (Dentzer 1982: 553) and whose ruling classes were devoted to the arts of indolence and luxury.

One standard theme of Assyrian palace decoration is the illustration of sets of furniture, sometimes including chairs, couches and equipment for serving and drinking wine, that had been donated by foreign rulers or captured from them (Figs 17 and 18). The clearest examples of sets that include couches are in groups of booty from south Mesopotamia around 640-620 BC (Figs 19-22). Sometimes the groups of furniture, or specific items such as thrones or sunshades, will have acquired symbolic value as markers of high status; but they were also used in practice. Probably, from prehistory, all those who could afford to do so had regularly possessed furniture sets suitable for relaxed drinking and entertainment. From 900 to 600 BC, a period of economic growth and prosperity in much of the civilized world, from the Mediterranean to Iran, these appurtenances were widely used by respectable people, while fringe barbarians quickly

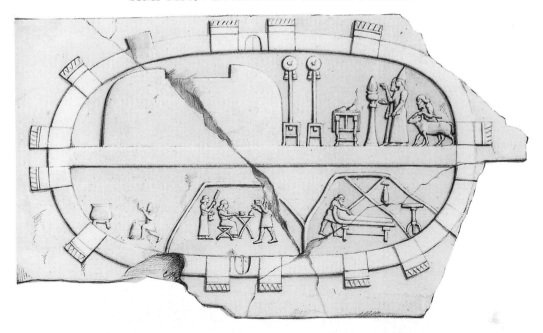

FIG. 16. Scene in an Assyrian camp, showing couch being prepared *c.* 730 BC (WA, Or. Dr. I, 14) *(Courtesy of the Trustees of the British Museum)*

FIG. 17. Levantine furniture, *c.* 880-860 BC (WA 118800) *(Courtesy of the Trustees of the British Museum)*

learnt to appreciate them. Some drinkers, but not all, adopted, or felt entitled to adopt, the couch as part of the set.

The best illustration of an Assyrian couch in use, indeed with the king himself as protagonist reclining upon it, is the one in Ashurbanipal's famous feast or picnic scene of about 645-640 BC (Fig. 23). The composition may be regarded as a precursor of those that appear later in the Mediterranean, for instance in the painted funerary groups of Turkey and Tuscany. There is a satisfying degree of artistic continuity, and the Assyrian scene has frequently been cited in this connection. Its relaxed atmosphere may seem to be echoed in what we imagine of Phoenician drinking clubs and Greek *symposia*. Alternatively, Ashurbanipal's picnic has been interpreted as showing a formal ceremony. Before considering these possibilities, however, I need to digress briefly.

FIG. 18. Furniture, including a couch, tables, a pail and a ruler's parasol, captured by the Assyrians, probably in Phoenicia, *c.* 700 BC (WA, Or. Dr. VI, 4) *(Courtesy of the Trustees of the British Museum)*

FIG. 19. Weapons and a set of furniture, including a couch, tables, a small incense-burner and a range of vessels, captured from a ruler in southern Babylonia, *c.* 640-620 BC (WA 124955-6) *(Courtesy of the Trustees of the British Museum)*

FIG. 20. Weapons and a set of furniture, comprising a
couch, table and vessels, captured from a ruler in southern
Babylonia, *c.* 640-620 BC (WA 124782) *(Courtesy of the
Trustees of the British Museum)*

While in early Mesopotamia the drinking scenes displayed in art did not necessarily
have any clear link with the traditional practice of offering food and drink to the dead,
the situation in Egypt was different (Dentzer 1982: 26-30). From the Old Kingdom
onwards, there were grave *stelai* carved with representations of the dead man receiving
offerings of food and drink. They were supplemented by the scenes of festivity that
appeared on the walls of Egyptian tombs, delineating the delights of past or future life.
When, from the mid second millennium BC on, in the Amarna Period and later, there
was extensive interchange of ideas and objects throughout the Middle East, including
Egypt, the idea of monumental funerary art seems to be one that spread from Egypt
eastward. The traditional drinking scenes of Syrian and Mesopotamian art were liable
to be employed in a fresh funerary context, representing offerings of food to the dead
(for example, Dentzer 1982: 44-5).

This is part of the background to Barnett's proposal (1985) that the Ashurbanipal
picnic scene represents an Assyrian version of the Levantine *marzeah*. This latter is a
ceremony in which, as described by the prophet Amos, the perfumed celebrants lie on
ivory beds and eat and drink wine to the sound of music. There are suggestions of ritual

FIG. 21. Weapons and a set of furniture, comprising a couch, table
and vessels, captured from a ruler in southern Babylonia, *c.* 640-620
BC (WA 124825) *(Courtesy of the Trustees of the British Museum)*

marriage, consonant with the presence of Ashurbanipal's queen at the foot of the couch,
and of the involvement of dead ancestors in the feasting. The idea has a superficial
appeal. There is no doubt but that by the seventh century, when this panel was carved,
Assyria was deeply influenced by the culture of the western provinces of the empire,
where the *marzeah* is attested. For instance, Assyrian kings explicitly record their
adoption of a Syro-Hittite architectural unit, probably a free-standing building with
columned portico (Reade 1979: 22). Yet the *marzeah* parallel cannot stand.

The context of the Ashurbanipal picnic scene has been discussed at length by
Albenda (1977), and her analysis is largely correct. The room in which it was carved was

FIG. 22. A cartload of furniture, including a couch, tables and vessels, captured from a ruler in southern Babylonia, *c.* 640-62O BC (WA 124953-4) *(Courtesy of the Trustees of the British Museum)*

FIG. 23. Ashurbanipal picnicking with the queen, *c.* 645-640 BC (WA 124920) *(Courtesy of the Trustees of the British Museum)*

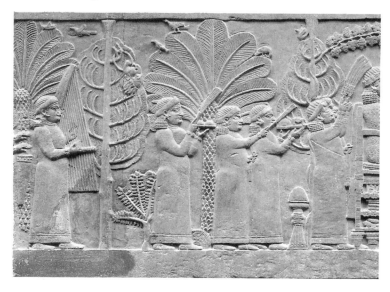

FIG. 24. Women attending Ashurbanipal's picnic, *c.* 645-640 BC (WA 124920) *(Courtesy of the Trustees of the British Museum)*

a private one, overlooking a postern gate in a corner of the king's palace at Nineveh. In the room there were wall-panels showing three themes: lion-hunts, military victories, and the feast. These are standard themes used in royal art from the Sumerian period onwards. The feast itself happens in an enclosure surrounded by temporary screens, evidently a royal garden. The king reclines on a couch, with the queen seated beside him, and the people closest to him, bringing food or playing music, are all women (Fig. 24). There are eunuchs or courtiers and guards a little further away, but this is a relatively domestic occasion, quite different from a male *symposion* or the feasts of Sargon's palace.

There is an additional facet to the picnic scene, as it is also a triumph, an epitome of the king's achievements, many of which were simultaneously illustrated on the other walls around. Thus captured kings are forced to bring supplies for the table; the head of a dead opponent hangs from a tree; and, if Albenda is right, trophies from Egypt and Babylon are on display. The king's horse is present, an allusion to his successes in the hunt. The presence of the queen could be seen almost as a personification of fertility. The lush landscape background may further allude to the king's success, which he was pleased to record elsewhere, in ensuring the divine approval necessary for rain and abundant harvests. A vine trellis overhanging the couch is a feature that was to have specifically royal connotations in later art (Dentzer 1982: 68). The composition also includes one priest whose purpose is unclear; there were so many priests about the Assyrian court, however, ensuring proper magical procedures, that his presence need not impose a restricted religious purpose on the scene.

We are faced then with a compendium of classic imperial motifs, a sophisticated version of the kind of decoration which otherwise appears, in official Near Eastern art, in groups of complementary compositions. The picnic scene may represent a special occasion, or an idealized version of a special occasion, or a generalized version of what was liable to happen, in pleasant weather, when the king left his palace through a postern gate to relax with his wife in his garden. It is possible that alternative versions of this or similar compositions were visible in other Assyrian palaces and in other media. For instance, provincial palaces sometimes had painted wall decoration, a likely source of ideas for subsequent rulers such as Iranian chiefs and ultimately for the designers of Pasargadae and Persepolis. Motifs could also be copied on textiles and small luxury objects, things which were suitable for distribution as prestige gifts or which were sold through the Phoenician trading networks associated in Greek legend with the name of Cadmus. So the central elements of the picnic composition hardly needed reinvention. Safe in the market-place, they could survive the fall of Nineveh and re-emerge like so much else Assyrian in Achaemenid, Greek and Etruscan art. Once the couch had been popularized as an item of furniture, the motif could have been adopted or adapted by any artist illustrating a scene in which couches were used. We should not read too much symbolism into such similarities.

It seems then that the drinking scenes of Mesopotamia do not present us with any wealth of unmistakable parallels to anticipate the intellectual pleasures, gang loyalties and ritual undercurrents of Greek *symposia*. Yet every large house had its reception room, and the equipment necessary to drink in comfort and elegance came to be common in the possession of private individuals. The angry prophets of the Old Testament make it plain how popular social drinking was in the Levant, while the Assyrian carvings illustrate it as normal practice at court. It is difficult to avoid concluding that the wines drunk in cosmopolitan Nineveh contributed to conversations as varied as most of those heard in Athens.[1]

REFERENCES

Albenda, P. (1977) Landscape bas-reliefs in the *bit-hilani* of Ashurbanipal. *BASO* 224: 49-72; 225: 29-48.

Badler, V.R., McGovern, M.E. and Michel, R.H. (1990) Drink and be merry! Infrared spectroscopy and ancient Near Eastern wine, in W.R. Biers and P.E. McGovern (eds), *Organic Contents of Ancient Vessels: Materials Analysis and Archaeological Investigation* (*MASCA Research Papers in Science and Archaeology* 7): 25-36. Philadelphia.

Barnett, R.D. (1985) Assurbanipal's feast. *ErIsr* 18: 1-6.

Botta, P.E. and Flandin, E. (1849) *Monument de Ninive*, I. Paris.

Danmanville, J. (1955) La libation en Mésopotamie. *RAssyr* 49.2: 57-68.

Dentzer, J.-M. (1982) *Le motif du banquet couché dans le proche-orient et le monde grec du VIIe au IVe siècle avant J.-C.* Rome-Paris.

Desroches-Noblecourt, C. (1963) *Tutankhamen: Life and Death of a Pharoah*. London.

Homès-Fredericq, D. (1989) Cylindre néo-assyrien inédit avec représentation de banquet, in M. Lebeau and P. Talon (eds), *Reflets des deux fleuves* (*Mélanges Finet — Supplementa ad Akkadica* VI): 55-9.

Leick, G. (1991) *A Dictionary of Ancient Near Eastern Mythology*. London-New York.

[1] I am indebted to Carl Nylander, who first suggested that I should write on this theme and whose stimulating conversation, during the Rome conference, suggested a number of improvements to the paper originally given.

Unless described otherwise, my illustrations appear by courtesy of the Trustees of the British Museum. The abbreviation WA refers to material in the Western Asiatic Department of the Museum.

Lesko, L.H. (1977) *King Tut's Wine Cellar*. Berkeley.

Maeir, A.M. and Garfinkel, Y. (1992) Bone and metal straw-tip beer-strainers from the ancient Near East. *Levant* 24: 218-23.

Moorey, P.R.S. (1980) Metal wine-sets in the ancient Near East. *IA* 15: 182-97.

Rathje, W.L. (1977) New tricks for old seals, in M. Gibson and R.D. Biggs (eds), *Seals and Sealing in the Ancient Near East* (*Bibliotheca Mesopotamica* 6): 25-32. Malibu.

Reade, J.E. (1979) Assyrian architectural decoration: techniques and subject-matter. *BaM* 10: 17-49.

Reade, J.E. (1980) The architectural context of Assyrian sculpture. *BaM* 11: 76-87.

Riesen, R. (1957) *Jungle Mission*. London.

Selz, G. (1983) *Die Bankettszene: Entwicklung eines "Überzeitlichen" Bildmotivs in Mesopotamien von der Frühdynastischen bis zur Akkad-Zeit* (*Freiburger Altorientalische Studien* 11). Wiesbaden.

Spycket, A. (1981) *La statuaire du Proche-orient ancien*. Leiden.

Winter, I.J. (1986) The king and the cup: iconography of the royal presentation scene on Ur III seals, in M. Kelly-Buccellati (ed.), *Insight through Images: Studies in Honor of Edith Porada* (*Bibliotheca Mesopotamica* 21): 253-68. Malibu.

4

Il Vino nell'Antico Egitto

GABRIELLA SCANDONE MATTHIAE

Secondo la felice espressione utilizzata da Jean Bottéro per definire i gusti potori degli abitanti dell'antica Mesopotamia, anche la cultura dell'Egitto faraonico può definirsi *civilisation de la bière*: la bevanda ottenuta dall'orzo, infatti, era tanto popolare nella terra del Nilo, che la combinazione dei due termini pane-birra, *ta-heneket*, designava l'offerta funeraria per antonomasia, quella che il faraone concedeva ad Osiride, e ad alcuni altri dèi legati al mondo dell'oltretomba, affinché costoro, poi, la ridistribuissero ai defunti.[1] È vero che insieme a pane e birra erano poi elencati altri elementi di prima necessità per gli abitanti del Paese d'Occidente, come carni di bovini e di volatili, unguenti e stoffe per abbigliamento: ma il 'nutrimento' per eccellenza dell'Egiziano medio era pur sempre il pane, accompagnato di un buon boccale di fresca birra dorata.

Accanto alla bevanda nazionale, il vino occupava però uno spazio non indifferente: si cercherà qui di tracciare una rapida storia del vino nell'Egitto di età faraonica classica (ossia fino all'occupazione persiana del 525 a.C.), sia dal punto di vista della produzione e del consumo, sia da quello della simbologia celata dietro l'uso rituale di questo liquido, particolarmente gradito agli dèi ed ai sovrani.

Il vino, in egiziano *irp*,[2] è, come ognuno sa, il prodotto della fermentazione del succo del frutto della vite, l'uva, in egiziano *iarrt*.[3] I più antichi resti di uva coltivata rinvenuti in Egitto risalgono al periodo preistorico di el-Omari (seconda metà del quinto millennio a.C.); poiché la pianta della vite selvatica non appartiene alla flora egiziana indigena, è probabile che in Egitto siano state importate dalla regione siro-palestinese delle viti già domesticate.[4] Non tutto il paese, a causa del clima, era adatto alla coltivazione intensiva della vite: infatti, essa veniva piantata soprattutto nella regione del Delta e nelle oasi.[5] Niente escludeva, però, che i giardini dei grandi personaggi del Sud fossero abbelliti da pergolati, cui venivano dedicate cure particolari.

Sin dall'Antico Regno, pitture e rilievi tombali ci consentono di capire che le viti venivano collocate nel centro dei frutteti, separate dagli altri alberi mediante un muro e

---

[1]N.J. Darby, P. Ghalioungui e L. Grivetti, *Food: The Gift of Osiris* II (Londra, 1977), 532-3.

[2]Cfr. *Wörterbuch des Ägyptischen Sprache* I (Berlino, 1961), 115.

[3]*Ibid.* p. 32.

[4]Cfr. *Lexikon der Ägyptologie* (Wiesbaden, 1986) VI, *s.v.* 'Wein', col. 1169.

[5]Darby, Ghalioungui e Grivetti, *Food* (sopra, n. 1), 597-607. Sono cui elencati quattordici vini del Basso Egitto, tre vini dell'Alto Egitto, cinque vini delle oasi e due vini del territorio confinario Egitto-Libia. Gli autori rilevano, però, che tali indicazioni provengono per lo più da testi greci dell'inizio dell'era cristiana e quindi non sono strettamente applicabili all'epoca faraonica.

sollevate su pertiche a formare pergolati. Al momento della vendemmia, i grappoli raccolti venivano posti in canestri e portati al torchio per la pigiatura: il torchio consisteva in una grande vasca di pietra, terracotta o legno, sopra la quale si trovava un'impalcatura da cui pendevano delle corde; ad esse si aggrappavano i pigiatori, che pestavano con i piedi i grappoli, per non scivolare. Il succo così ottenuto raggiungeva, per mezzo di un canaletto di scarico, un grande recipiente sottostante; sopra il canaletto di scarico spesso vegliava benevola un'immagine di Renenutet, dea-serpente delle messi e dei raccolti.[6]

Un altro sistema per ottenere il mosto era la spremitura dei grappoli, o forse meglio delle vinacce e di quanto rimaneva nella vasca dopo la pigiatura con i piedi, collocati entro un sacco, che poi veniva fortemente attorto da più persone, mentre il succo colava in un recipiente predisposto all'uopo.[7] Dai recipienti di raccolta il mosto era poi travasato in anfore dalla morfologia caratteristica: collo abbastanza largo, corpo espanso, due anse laterali che andavano dalla spalla alla pancia, fondo appuntito.[8] Nelle anfore avveniva la fermentazione, che mutava il mosto in vino: poiché il processo doveva svolgersi nell'oscurità, i recipienti, collocati nei ripostigli, venivano accurata-mente chiusi con pezzi di tela, o di cuoio, con coperchi, con tappi ottenuti attorcendo vegetali; le chiusure erano poi ricoperte di fango del Nilo, e infine sigillate. Per consentire la fuoruscita del diossido di carbonio formatosi durante la fermentazione, si praticavano dei fori nel collo delle anfore, i quali venivano richiusi quando il processo di trasformazione era compiuto.[9] Il vino egiziano è sempre di color rosso; per trovare menzione di vini bianchi bisogna giungere al periodo greco-romano.

Passando a considerare il consumo del vino in Egitto, possiamo innanzitutto osservare che esso, a differenza della onnipresente birra, era particolarmente gradito e riservato al faraone e ai grandi personaggi della nazione. Già all'epoca della I dinastia (*ca* 2950 a.C.) dalle tombe di sovrani e di appartenenti alla famiglia reale nelle necropoli di Abido e di Saqqara provengono anfore vinarie, riconoscibili dalla caratteristica forma panciuta.[10] Dall'epoca del re Agib (metà della I dinastia) il palazzo reale comprendeva un 'tesoro' ove veniva conservato il vino; un funzionario del re Qaa (fine della I dinastia) portava il titolo di 'soprintendente alla stanza del vino'.[11] Nella lista offertoria funebre

---

[6]Scene di vendemmia e di pigiatura sono raccolte in L. Klebs, *Die Reliefs des Alten Reiches (2980-2475 v.Chr.)* (Heidelberg, 1915), 56-7 (dalla tomba di Ptahhotep); *eadem, Die Reliefs und Malereien des Mittleren Reiches (VII-XVII Dynastie ca 2475-1580 v.Chr.)* (Heidelberg, 1922), 79-82 (con la conservazione del vino in anfore sigillate); *eadem, Die Reliefs und Malereien des Neuen Reiches (XVIII-XX Dynastie, ca 1580-1100 v.Chr.)* (Heidelberg, 1934), 51-61.

[7]Altre raffigurazioni di vendemmia e, in particolare, di spremitura mediante il sacco attorto in Darby, Ghalioungui e Grivetti, *Food* (sopra, n. 1), fig. 14: 1-10.

[8]Cfr. *Lexikon der Ägyptologie* VI, *s.v.* 'Weinkrug', coll. 1182-6.

[9]Si veda il coperchio di una delle anfore vinarie di Tutankhamon con foro nella sigillatura poi richiuso con un grumo di argilla: Darby, Ghalioungui e Grivetti, *Food* (sopra, n. 1), fig. 14.9. Nella tomba del giovane sovrano erano conservate ben 36 anfore vinarie.

[10]Il nome egiziano di questi recipienti era *mnt*. Sulle sigillature cfr. P. Kaplony, *Die Inschriften der Ägyptischen Frühzeit* I (Wiesbaden, 1963), 50-4; W.B. Emery, *Hor-Aha* (Cairo, 1939), 19, fig. 10.

[11]Kaplony, *Die Inschriften der Ägyptischen Frühzeit* (sopra, n. 10), III, Taf. 59 n. 213; W.M.F. Petrie, *The Royal Tombs of the First Dynasty* I (Londra, 1900), pl. XXX. In quest'epoca la bevanda era associata al dio Horus: cfr. Darby, Ghalioungui e Grivetti, *Food* (sopra, n. 1), 555-6.

classica, a partire dalla V dinastia (2465-2325 a.C. circa) sono elencati ben sei tipi di vino: del Basso Egitto, della Mareotide, dell'Occidente, di Nebesheh, di Sile e delle Paludi.[12] Le iscrizioni sulle anfore vinarie del Nuovo Regno recano: l'anno di produzione, il luogo di provenienza, il nome del possessore (ossia dell'istituzione che possedeva il vigneto), il nome del capo vendemmiatore;[13] sui coperchi, invece, era scritta la categoria cui il vino contenuto nel recipiente apparteneva; buono, due volte buono, tre volte buono, dolce.[14] Anche in quest'epoca i luoghi di provenienza si trovano soprattutto sul ramo occidentale del Delta del Nilo e talora nelle oasi; ma anche a Menfi.

Il vino veniva consumato per lo più in occasione di importanti banchetti: lo contenevano grandi anfore, spesso decorate con foglie di vite, che venivano collocate su tavoli, oppure entro portavasi posati sul suolo, ed erano mantenute fresche da servi che agitavano ventagli, ovvero mediante una copertura di rami e fronde. I servitori versavano da esse il vino entro piccoli recipienti privi di manico o in piccole brocche con manico, da cui venivano poi serviti gli ospiti. Non sappiamo se in Egitto si mescolassero vino e acqua, come era uso nel Vicino Oriente e in Grecia. Gli ospiti bevevano in coppe piatte o con breve piedino ed anche in bicchieri, spesso di materiali pregiati quali oro e argento, e talora raggiungevano stati di forte ubriachezza, come possiamo vedere in dipinti, soprattutto del Nuovo Regno.[15] Nei rilievi di Amarna, Amenophis IV — Ekhnaton e la sua famiglia sono raffigurati in atto di bere vino:[16] come si è già detto, si trattava di una bevanda costosa e raffinata, per sovrani e nobili, tanto è vero che, ad esempio, gli operai di Deir el Medina, addetti allo scavo ed alla decorazione delle tombe regali, non ricevevano razioni di vino; l'esercito invece, che normalmente beveva birra, veniva talora provvisto della regale bevanda, in particolare modo gli ufficiali.

Oltre ad essere la bevanda dei faraoni, il vino era in Egitto anche quella degli dèi: esso ricopriva quindi, negli atti del culto, un suo ruolo. I Testi delle Piramidi, della fine dell'Antico Regno, collocano nel cielo i vigneti degli dèi.[17] Anche i beati nell'Aldilà bevevano il nobile liquido, privilegio divino e reale: all'ingresso della Dat il defunto veniva asperso con vino e latte.

Come si è detto precedentemente, il vino occupava una posizione assai importante negli elenchi delle offerte funerarie; anch'esso, come tutto ciò che si presentava agli dèi per gratificarli, era identificato all''occhio di Horus', l'offerta per eccellenza.[18]

Una divinità che gradiva particolarmente libazioni della rossa bevanda era Hathor, signora delle feste, dei divertimenti e dell'ebbrezza: il vino consumato in

[12]W. Barta, *Die Altägyptische Opferliste* (Berlino, 1963), 62; il 'vino delle paludi' è menzionato solo a partire dalla VI dinastia.

[13]I principali gruppi di anfore vinarie del Nuovo Regno sono stati rinvenuti a Malgata, ad el-Amarna e nel Ramesseo.

[14]Darby, Ghalioungui e Grivetti, *Food* (sopra, n. 1), 567.

[15]Darby, Ghalioungui e Grivetti, *Food* (sopra, n. 1), fig. 14.3. Si veda anche la voce '*Trunkenheit*' del *Lexikon der Ägyptologie* VI, coll. 773-7.

[16]K. Lange e M. Hirmer, *Ägypten* (Monaco, 1955), Taf. 83.

[17]Il vino è menzionato abbastanza di frequente nei *Testi delle Piramidi*: 1112d, 816c, 1511b, 1723a-b, 130c, 92b-94b.

[18]*Pyr.* 926. In epoca tarda è detto talora 'Occhio verde di Horus', nel senso di 'Occhio fresco, vivo': cfr. *Lexikon der Ägyptologie* VI, *s.v.* '*Wein*', n. 109.

occasione di solennità a lei dedicate era apportatore di gioia, mentre quello bevuto in occasione di feste delle dee-leonesse Tefnut e Sekhmet era carico di simbolismo ostile, perché era considerato il sangue dei nemici delle due colleriche e feroci divinità.[19]

Il sovrano nei templi ed i privati nel segreto delle loro tombe usavano offrire agli dèi il vino entro caratteristici recipienti sferici con breve orlo chiamati *mnw*; una delle iconografie reali più tipiche è costituita dalla figura del sovrano, inginocchiato o stante, che presenta alla divinità due vasi *mnw* colmi di vino, uno in ciascuna mano.[20] Nel rituale della veglia presso il cadavere di Osiride, il dio morto riceveva un libazione di vino misto a latte.[21]

In Egitto, tuttavia, anche se considerato bevanda nobile, il vino non venne esaltato e divinizzato come in Grecia. Gli scrittori greci classici (Erodoto e Plutarco)[22] affermano che Osiride, da essi assimilato a Dioniso in quanto dio della vegetazione e oggetto di un particolare tipo di culto, fu l'inventore della viticoltura e quindi del vino: una simile notizia non compare nei testi egiziani, anche se, certo, dalla lettura di essi si ha la sensazione di uno stretto legame tra il dio e la vite, poiché costui, già nel Testi delle Piramidi, è detto 'Signore del vino durante la festa Wag' e 'Signore del vino durante l'inondazione'.[23] Il motivo è duplice: il carattere agrario di Osiride, signore della vegetazione che muore e risorge, e l'identificazione del dio con Orione, il cui sorgere segnava l'inizio della vendemmia. Anche alcune rappresentazioni figurative racchiudono il medesimo concetto: la splendida vite che ricopre gran parte delle pareti della tomba di Sennefer, del Nuovo Regno, ha le radici davanti a un'immagine di Osiride[24] e in un'illustrazione di un Libro dei Morti una vite ricopre un baldacchino sotto cui è Osiride in trono.[25]

Non solo Osiride, però, ma anche altre divinità erano considerate in Egitto legate al vino ed alla vite: si riteneva la bevanda originaria del Nun, l'Oceano Primordiale che circondava la Terra, figlia del Cielo, Sangue di Ra, Lacrima di Horus. Abbiamo già accennato al ruolo di Hathor come 'Signora dell'Ebbrezza': nella sua 'festa dell'ebbrezza', che si celebrava a Dendara nel ventesimo giorno del primo mese della stagione di *akht*, ossia dell'Inondazione, il suo ritorno dalla lontana Nubia veniva festeggiato vuotando una grande quantità di vasi *mnw*. Anche Iside era talora chiamata

---

[19]Epiteti caratteristici della dea erano quelli di 'Signora dell'ebbrezza' e 'Signora della brocca da vina'; cfr. la voce '*Hathor*' del *Lexikon der Ägyptologie*. Anche Thot di Pnubs era detto 'Signore del vino, che beve molto', forse in ricordo del ruolo da lui sostenuto nel mito del Ritorno dell'Occhio del Sole.

[20]Ramses II offre vino a Ra-Harakhty: Darby, Ghalioungui e Grivetti, *Food* (sopra, n. 1), fig. 14.12 (dal Ramesseo).

[21]H. Junker, *Die Stundewachen in den Osirismysterien* (*Denkschriften der Akademie der Wissenschaften in Wien*) (Wien, 1910), 54, 82.

[22]Incomprensibilmente, Erodoto e Plutarco danno sul consumo del vino nell'Egitto faraonico notizie inattendibili: il primo (ii. 77) nega l'uso della bevanda nel paese del Nilo, mentre il secondo afferma che essa venne in uso solo durante la XXVI dinastia e precisamente ad opera del faraone Psammetico: cfr. G. Piccaluga, 'Plutarco "de Is" 6. Il vino nella religione dell'antico Egitto', *SMSR* 37 (1966), 47-60. Erodoto, però, si contraddice quando cita vari episodi egiziani di consumo del vino (ii. 60, 121, 133, 168), e quando identifica Osiride a Dioniso.

[23]*Pyr.* 819, 1524.

[24]R. Gundlach *et al.*, *Sennefer. Die Grabkammer des Burgmeister von Theben* (Magonza, 1986), tavole alle pp. 25-7, 38-9, 58, 64, 70.

[25]E. Hornung, *Das Totenbuch der Ägypter* (Zurigo, 1990), Fig. 87.

'Signora del vino' e Shesemu, personificazione divinizzata del Torchio, in un passo dei Testi delle Piramidi offre vino al re defunto.[26]

Nei rituali templari, benché non si faccia menzione nei testi di offerte di vino durante il rituale giornaliero che comprendeva il risveglio, la toilette e i pasti della divinità, è molto probabile che la bevanda facesse parte del menu quotidiano mediante il quale il dio si sostentava: infatti, un testo tardo di Edfu allude all'offerta di vino in occasione della cosiddetta cerimonia della 'apertura della faccia', cioè al momento in cui, di primo mattino, veniva aperto il *naos* che ospitava il simulacro divino.[27] Si sa inoltre che il vino veniva offerto durante la festa del dio Min,[28] al dio Amon particolarmente in occasione della cerimonia dell'incoronazione reale e della festa *sed*, che ogni 30 anni di regno rinnovava le energie indebolite del sovrano,[29] nonché quando si celebrava la Festa della Valle: in quest'ultima solennità, destinata a rafforzare il legame tra mondo dei vivi e mondo dei morti, i parenti offrivano vino sulle tombe dei propri cari defunti.[30] In generale, però, ogni divinità poteva ricevere libagioni di vino e nessuna ne rimaneva esclusa.

Concludendo, quindi, questa breve notizia sul vino dell'Egitto faraonico, possiamo senz'altro affermare che il suo consumo era abbastanza diffuso, ma riservato agli dèi, ai sovrani ed ai grandi dignitari del regno. Bevanda nobile ed aristocratica, dunque, a differenza della modesta birra che anche il contadino ed il bracciante potevano permettersi come accompagnamento al proprio semplice pasto, formato per lo più di pane e verdure, il vino allietava i banchetti dei re e delle persone facoltose, accanto alle diverse varietà di pani, di carni, di frutta e di dolci che gli antichi Egiziani vollero riprodurre nelle pitture e nei rilievi delle proprie sepolture, con la speranza di poter condurre nell'Aldilà una vita altrettanto gradevole di quella trascorsa sulla terra, dopo che apposite formule avessero magicamente animato le immagini, perfette in ogni particolare.

[26]*Pyr.* 1552a.

[27]Cfr. *Lexikon des Ägyptologie* VI, s.v. 'Weinopfer', col. 1187.

[28]Il vino veniva offerto nel corso della processione detta *prt* ('uscita'); C.J. Bleeker, *Die Geburt eines Gottes* (Leiden, 1956), Fig. 17.

[29]In occasione della festa *sed* venivano preparati tipi speciali di vini, come ci fanno comprendere alcune impronte di sigilli sui coperchi delle anfore vinarie da Malgata: 'vino buonissimo per la festa *sed*', 'vino per offerte per la festa *sed*', 'vino per la festa *sed*'. Cfr. W.C. Hayes, 'Inscriptions from the palace of Amenhotep III. II. The jar sealings', *JNES* 10 (1951), 157, fig. 25A-D.

[30]S. Schott, *Das Schöne Fest vom Wüstentale, Festbrauche einer Totenstadt* (Magonza, 1952), 840-2.

5

Wine and Death — East and West

CRISTIANO GROTTANELLI

To the memory of Arnaldo Momigliano, author of *Alien Wisdom*, who helped younger scholars.

THE PROBLEM

Before going into my chosen field, I must quote our organizer and symposiarch, Oswyn Murray, on wine and death. In 1983 he presented a paper in Stockholm and in Gjöteborg — as a guest of our generous Swedish hosts! — and in that paper, published in Naples in 1988,[1] he stated that 'there existed in the Greek world a polarity ... between the world of the *symposion* and the world of the dead'. Let me state immediately that a similar polarity exists in other social contexts — including, of course, the ones I shall briefly discuss here. My problem here is the existence of some specific connections between the two opposite poles; more precisely, the existence and the meaning of connections between wine and death described by Greek and Latin authors, mostly Hellenistic or later, and ascribed by those authors to Orientals — especially to Egyptians and to Syrians.

THE 'EGYPTIAN' DEAD *SYMPOTES*

I shall begin by quoting Lucian of Samosata (*c.* 120-80 AD), surely the most witty, and probably also the most nasty, of Greek moralists, who wrote something on wine and volumes on death. In his *De Luctu*, a short text that, since Helm's *Lukian und Menipp* (Leipzig-Berlin, 1906), is commonly defined as a cynic diatribe on current funerary customs,[2] he commented thus on the different ways in which different cultures treated dead bodies:

> Up to that point, up to the wailing, the same stupid custom prevails everywhere; but in what follows, the burial, they have apportioned out among themselves, nation by nation, the different modes. The Greek burns (*sc.* corpses) the Persian buries, the Indian encases in glass, the Scythian

---

[1] O. Murray, 'Death and the Symposion', *AION(archeol)* 10 (1988), 234-57.
[2] In studying Lucian's *De Luctu* I have used V. Andò, *Luciano*, Il lutto (Palermo, 1984), with its useful commentary and bibliography.

eats, the Egyptian salts. And the latter — I have seen it myself! — after drying the dead man makes him his guest during meals as well as during *symposia*. Many a time too, when an Egyptian wants money, his (dead) brother or his (dead) father help him out of his straits by becoming security (for him) at the critical juncture.

(Lucian, De Luctu ch. 21)

It is interesting to note that, in saying more about Egyptian customs than about those of the other nations he quotes, Lucian states explicitly that he has actually seen the dried or salted dead used as companions during the *deipnon* (*syndeipnon*) or during the *symposion* (*sympoten*). It would be pleasant to take this statement seriously, and to remind ourselves that Pflaum has convincingly shown Lucian to have been an important official in Roman Egypt, *archistator praefecti Aegypti* (and thus an exceptionally successful Syrian from Commagene whose brilliant career is the more striking if we consider he was not even a Roman citizen).[3]

But is this really a case of what Clifford Geertz would call 'being there'?[4] One is induced to doubt if one considers that the Egyptian home with its dead guests (embalmed, of course, rather than salted or dried) is a fairly widespread topos. We find it, about 200 years before Lucian's time, in Cicero's *Tusculan Disputations* i. 44.108 (written 45 BC, published 44 BC), and in a context that is most strikingly similar to the passage in Lucian's *De Luctu* we have just quoted:

> The Egyptians embalm their dead and keep them in the house; the Persians even smear them with wax before burial, that the bodies may last for as long a time as possible; it is the custom of the Magi not to bury the bodies of their dead unless they have been first mangled by beasts; in Hyrcania the populace support dogs for the benefit of the community, while the nobles keep them for family use: it is, as we know, a famous breed of dogs, but in spite of the cost, each householder procures animals in proportion to his means, to mangle him, and that they consider the best mode of burial.

(Cic. Tusc. i. 44.108)

After the Persian custom Cicero lists a *Magorum mos* (letting dead bodies be torn by wild beasts) and a similar treatment of corpses in Hyrcania. But on the different ways of treating the dead among different nations Cicero and Lucian had both been preceded by Teles, the Cynic philosopher of the fourth century BC, who had written in his Περὶ ξένης: '... we hesitate to look at, or to touch, the dead, while they (*sc.* the Egyptians) make mummies of them and keep them in the house as something handsome, and accept dead men as security. So opposed is their way to ours' (*Teletis Reliquiae*, ed. O. Hense, p. 31, 1.9; cf. Stob. *Flor.* iii. 40.8).

Though the relationship between Teles and Lucian seems assured, there is no reason to imagine that both these authors depend upon Bion of Borysthenes, as A.M. Harmon suggests.[5] Probably both Teles and Bion were important models for Lucian, but Lucian had a more ancient and authoritative source for his 'Egyptian' scene. In the first century AD the Egyptian *sympotes* and his coffin reappear in Silius Italicus (*c.* 35-100 AD), *Punica* xiii. 474-6, where we find that 'the Egyptians enclose their dead, standing in

---

[3]H.G. Pflaum, 'Lucien de Samosate, archistator praefecti Aegypti', *MEFRA* 71 (1959), 281-6.
[4]C. Geertz, *Works and Lives. The Anthropologist as Author* (Stanford, 1988).
[5]A.M. Harmon, *Lucian*, IV (Cambridge-London, 1925 (reprinted 1969)), 128, n. 1.

an upright position, in a coffin of stone, and worship them; and they admit a bloodless spectre to their banquets'.

And in the same century or in the first decades of the following century Plutarch mentions the custom twice:

> We may be sure that the likeness of a corpse which, as it is exhibited to them is carried around in a chest, is not a reminder of what happened to Osiris, as some assume; but it is to urge them, as they contemplate it, to use and to enjoy the present, since all very soon must be what it is now and this is their purpose in introducing it into the midst of merry-making.
>
> (Plut. *De Is. et Os.* 17)

> The Egyptian corpse, which is brought to *symposia* and shown (around), (in order) to invite those present to remember that soon they shall be like it, though it is unpleasant and untimely, is of some use, if it invites them, rather than to drink and to enjoy themselves, to mutual friendship and affection, and to refrain from prolonging with troubles a life that is in itself so short.
>
> (Plut. *Conv. sept. sap.* ch. 2)

So three topoi on Egyptian mummies lasted for at least six centuries, from Teles to Lucian: (1) Egyptians keep the bodies of their dead relatives in their homes; (2) they treat them as companions in their *deipna* and *symposia*;[6] (3) they use them as security. As is well known, these three topoi are at least one century older than the earliest date we have quoted so far, for they go back to Herodotus.

The first topos is implied by the other two, but both the use of dead relatives as security and the presence of corpses during the banquets of the rich are mentioned by the Father of History in his famous Second Book, dedicated to the description of Egyptian customs:

> During the reign of this king (*i.e.* Asuchis), as they told me, money did not pass readily from hand to hand in Egypt; and therefore a law was made that a man might borrow on the security of his father's dead body; and the law also provided that the lender should have a lien on the whole burial-vault of the borrower and that the penalty for the giver of the security, should he fail to repay the debt, should be that he might neither himself be buried at death nor bury any deceased of his kin either in that tomb of his fathers or in any other.
>
> (Hdt. ii. 136)

Clearly the other accounts of corpses used as security by Egyptians are to be explained as shortened and actualized versions of this Herodotean passage about the reign of king Asuchis; in turn the Herodotean *logos* may be the result of an Egyptian tale about hard times when *khremata* were not easily available. The relationship we can reconstruct between the oldest and the later versions of this topos does not differ much, in my opinion, from the relationship that should be imagined between the accounts of dead *sympotai* we have quoted above and the account we find in Herodotus:

> At rich men's banquets, after the *deipnon*, a man carries round a wooden image of a corpse in a coffin, painted and carved in exact imitation, a cubit or two cubits long. This he shows to each of the *sympotai*, saying: 'Drink and make merry, and look at this; for such shall you be when you are dead'. Such is the custom in their *symposia*.
>
> (Hdt. ii. 78)

---

[6]On this topos see K. Dunbabin, 'Sic erimus cuncti ... The skeleton in Graeco-Roman art', *JDAI* 101 (1986), 208-12.

If we compare this Herodotean passage with Lucian's *De Luctu* 21 on Egyptian *symposia*, we shall note not only that the later text is probably a shortened version of the same topos, but also that in Lucian's text real corpses take over the role attributed by Herodotus to a wooden imitation of a corpse in its coffin. I would suggest that this is the consequence of a contamination between Herodotus's account of the use of dead relatives as security and his description of Egyptian *symposia*: the wooden corpse has become a real one for reasons of simplicity and symmetry. During a sympotic discussion after I presented a shorter version of this paper, my British classicist friends encouraged me to interpret Lucian's *De Luctu* 21 as a somewhat indirect (even perverse) but clear quotation of Herodotus ii. 78, where the clause may be seen, paradoxically, as an ironic Herodotean *sphragis*. Thus fortified, I even dare to point out that, in Herodotus's account of Egyptian banquets (ii. 78), drying and salting (*taricheuo*) occur, as they do in *De Luctu* 21: only in Herodotus these verbs are not, as in Lucian, meant to express the treatment of the dead *sympotes*, but ways of preparing small birds and fish for the *deipnon* and *symposion* during which the wooden corpse is displayed. This may well be a further playful Lucianic 'quotation' whereby the dead Egyptian is treated like fish or fowl. Finally, I must point out that, as Herodotus puts it, '(the Egyptians) use a wine made of barley, for they have no vines in their own country' (ii. 77).

The Egyptian 'wine made of barley' is beer, of course: and on beer in connection with wine we have learnt important things from our friend Bottéro. Herodotus's Greek has no word for beer, and this fact allows me to treat the topos here under the title 'Wine and Death'.

My comparative treatment of Herodotus ii. 78 (and ii. 136) and *De Luctu* 21 could still be expanded upon. But what seems most important here is the fact that the later text is a *shortened* version of the Herodotean. Now, what has been left out by Lucian in his rendering of the topos is precisely what is most interesting to us — indeed, what seems to me the very core of the Herodotean passage — the *carpe diem* that goes with the corpse. In Herodotus, the gruesome exhibition makes sense; in Lucian's *De Luctu*, as in the versions of Teles, of Cicero, and of Silius Italicus, it is only a further example of human folly.

In his treatment of the topos, however, Plutarch seems to return to the Herodotean interest in the moral meaning of the strange Egyptian behaviour. It would be more precise to say that Plutarch *adds* to Herodotus's treatment of this problem, for he presents us not with one, but *two* ethical messages which can be deduced from the display of the dead *sympotes* by Egyptian drinkers.[7] The first message is presented very simply in *De Iside et Osiride* 17: the εἴδωλον ἀνθρώπου carried around during banquets is meant to urge banqueters 'to use and to enjoy the present'. The second message is compared to — and preferred to — the first in the Second Chapter of the *Convivium septem sapientium*: Plutarch states that such a sight should invite to friendship, to mutual *agape* and to a philosophical attitude to life rather than to 'drink and make merry'. Clearly, the first message is Herodotus's original interpretation of the Egyptian custom, while the second message is a (Stoic?) afterthought. Plutarch's ideological stance would

---

[7]For Herodotus and Plutarch on Egypt see S. Donadoni, 'Erodoto, Plutarco e l'Egitto', *Belfagor* 2 (1942), 203-8 (now republished in *Cultura dell'antico Egitto* (Rome, 1986)).

not permit him to stop at Herodotus's *carpe diem*; a more sober and solemn *memento mori* was required.

PACUVIUS AND THE SYRIAN *FUNEBRIA EPULA*

About a hundred years before Lucian, Seneca, who died in 65 AD, wrote much about death from the very different standpoint of Stoic philosophy.[8] In one of the *Epistulae Morales* addressed to young Lucilius (written from 61 to 65 AD) he urged Lucilius to regulate each day as if it closed the series of his days, as if it rounded off and completed his life. As an example of such behaviour he quoted a strange Syrian custom adopted by a famous and powerful Roman:

> Pacuvius, who by long occupancy made Syria his own [Pacuvius was Aelius Lamia's *legatus*, then succeeded him as a governor of Syria and retained that office for many years], used to hold a burial sacrifice or *parentatio* in his own honour, with wine and the usual funerary feast, and then he would have himself carried from the dining-room to his chamber, while the debauched young men of his entourage applauded and sang in Greek to a musical accompaniment: 'He has lived his life, he has lived his life.' Thus Pacuvius had himself carried out to burial every day. Let us, however, do from a good motive what he used to do from a debased motive; let us go to our sleep with joy and gladness; let us say: 'I have lived; the course which Fortune set out for me is finished' [a quotation from Virgil's *Aeneid* iv. 653].[9] And if the god is pleased to add another day, we should welcome it with glad hearts. That man is happiest, and is secure in his own possession of himself, who can wait the morrow without apprehension. When a man has said: 'I have lived!', every morning he arises he receives a bonus.
>
> (Sen. *Ep.* i. 12)

The situation described here by Seneca should be compared to the situation I had imagined — but only to reject it — for Lucian's text on the Egyptian dead *sympotes*: in the *Epistle*, a Roman magistrate is shown learning Syrian habits in Syria, while in Lucian's *De Luctu* 21 a supposed Syrian official of the Roman administration of Egypt presents himself as observing and describing Egyptian customs. The fact that the possible comparison is probably a result of Lucian's imagination, and thus merely fictitious, does not make it any less interesting, I hope. Of course, the scenes described are really rather different: in Lucian's text a dead body is displayed during *deipna* and *symposia*, while in Seneca's a powerful man pretends to celebrate his own funerary ritual and his body is treated like a corpse at the end of the wine banquet. But what is most important in the present context is the fact that Seneca's description of an oriental scene is presented in a philosophical context which gives it a precise moral meaning; and that the meaning is related to the meaning given by Herodotus to his Egyptian scene with the dead *sympotes*.

So we should note that, while we have seen that the *carpe diem* message conveyed most explicitly by the Herodotean text about the corpse as a *sympotes* in Egypt failed to survive in some later versions of that topos, on the other hand a slightly different Syrian,

---

[8]For Seneca's ideas on death (some Stoic, some not) see R. Hoven, *Stoïcisme et Stoïciens face au problème de l'Au-Delà* (Paris, 1971), 107-26.

[9]The quotation in question refers, meaningfully, to Dido's suicide: it is before putting an end to her life that the Carthaginian queen pronounces these words. An implicit reference to (Stoic) suicide in this passage of Seneca's *Epistle* is thus very probable.

rather than Egyptian, scene conveyed a similar message centuries later, in the writings of Seneca. But the situation is still more complex, for Seneca's attitude to the Syrian ritual daily enacted by Pacuvius may be compared to Plutarch's treatment of the Egyptian topos of the corpse as a *sympotes*. We have seen that Plutarch offered two different interpretations of Herodotus's Egyptian scene, and we have called the two interpretations *carpe diem* and *memento mori*. Likewise Seneca uses, on the one hand, the strange Syrian custom attributed to the 'orientalizing' Pacuvius as a positive example of the right attitude to take in regard to death; on the other hand he consistently treats it as strange, and explicitly states that Pacuvius himself behaved as he did *e mala conscientia*, that is, both with the wrong attitude and for a bad reason, while Seneca and Lucilius must behave in a similar way but *bona conscientia*.

In Seneca's *Epistle* the Syrian ritual repeated daily by Pacuvius is the symbol not of one, but of two different moral attitudes to death. It means both (as it did to Pacuvius) that life should be enjoyed in the company of *exoleti* because death may come any day, and (as it must have meant to Seneca and Lucilius) that, precisely because any day may be the last, life must be taken seriously and lived virtuously. It points thus both to a light-hearted *carpe diem* and to a severe *memento mori*. Obviously the first attitude, not the second, corresponds to the message that goes with the mummy in Herodotus's Egyptian banquet.

We are thus confronted with two sympotic scenes, one presented as Egyptian, the other as Syrian, in Greek and Latin texts, and with two moral messages arising from the combination of wine and death in those two scenes. At this point the obvious question is, how 'oriental' (how Egyptian, how Syrian) are the scenes, and how 'oriental' (Egyptian or Syrian) are the messages? This is the question to which I shall devote the remainder of the present paper.

THE TWO THEMES IN THEIR GRAECO-ROMAN CONTEXT

Let me point out immediately that the *carpe diem* message we found in Herodotus and recognized in Pacuvius's *conscientia* in celebrating his own *Totenmahl* is a genuinely Greek cultural trait, often expressed, as Oswyn Murray has shown in the article I quoted at the beginning, by way of the opposition between death and the *symposion*.[10] One of the clearest expressions of such a message is to be found in the poetry of Theognis of Megara, who lived in the sixth century BC.[11] The long history of the *carpe diem* theme, both in Greek and in Latin, may not even be summarized in the short space available here. The same is true of the *memento mori*. It is, however, between the first century BC and the second century AD that both themes become specially widespread in the cultural production of the ancient Mediterranean and are most often expressed by variations on the relationship between death and the *symposion*. As we have seen, it is precisely during

---

[10] See n. 1 above.

[11] Murray translates Theog. 973-8 thus: 'Nobody, when the earth once covers him and he descends to the darkness, the abode of Persephone, can rejoice in hearing either the lyre or the flute-player, or be gladdened by the gifts of Dionysos. Knowing this, I follow my heart's desire while my limbs are yet nimble and I bear my head unshaken'.

these three centuries that the 'Egyptian' theme of the corpse as a *sympotes* is most often attested; and, as Katherine Dunbabin has shown in her important article (above, n. 6), the popularity of this theme is surely connected with the contemporary success of the representation of banqueting skeletons in Graeco-Roman art. Pacuvius's imitation of a Syrian ritual, described and discussed by Seneca, also belongs to this period.

During the same centuries, and in the tradition of Greek sympotic poetry, poets sang of wine and death both in Greek and in Latin. Here I shall quote Martial, who published his *Epigrammata*, mostly in Rome, during the last two decades of the first century AD. Martial sang of wine and death together, in two separate epigrams.[12] In ii. 54 he celebrates a banqueting hall called *mica* ('crumb', 'bit', 'morsel'):

> *Mica vocor: quid sim cernis, cenatio parva:*
> *Ex me Caesareum prospicis esse tholum.*
> *Frange toros, pete vina, rosas cape, tinguere nardo:*
> *Ipse iubet mortis te meminisse deus.*

I am called *mica*; what I am, you see, a small banqueting room; from me you look — see — upon Caesar's dome. Crush the couches, call for wine, take up roses, anoint yourself with nard; the god himself bids you to remember death.

(Martial ii. 54)

The banqueting hall called *mica* is generally supposed to have been built by the emperor Domitian, and to have had a view of the Mausoleum Augusti, Augustus's monumental funerary tholos, which stood for about 650 years south of the Porta Flaminia, the north gate of Rome, and not far from the banks of the Tiber. If this identification is correct (but there is at least another possible one), then the banqueters, who drank wine and were perfumed with nard and crowned with roses, could see the tholos and were reminded by *divus* Augustus himself (*ipse ... deus*) of his, and thus of their own, death. A different development is given to the same association in v. 64:

> *Sextantes, Calliste, duos infunde Falerni,*
> *Tusuper aestivas, Alcime, solve nives,*
> *Pinguescat nimio madidus mihi crinis amomo,*
> *Assenturque rosis tempora subtilibus.*
> *Tam vicina iubent nos vivere Mausolea,*
> *Cum doceant ipsos posse perire deos.*

Pour in, Callistus, two double-measures of Falernian: and you, Alcimus, dissolve upon them the summer's snow; let my dripping locks be rich with over-bounteous amomus, and my temples droop between the knitted roses. The tombs, so near, bid us live, for they teach us that the very gods can die.

(Martial v. 64)

Here the plural *Mausolea* refers (also) to the funerary monument of Augustus: Martial sees it while drinking in his own house on the Quirinal, or in the banqueting hall presented in ii. 54. Its nearness reminds the drinkers that even gods (i.e. even 'divine'

---

[12]I have used the Loeb translation and notes by W.A. Ker (Cambridge-London, 1919), as well as A. Carbonetto's useful bibliography (*Marziale*, Epigrammi (Milan, 1979), xiii-xxii). On aspects of the two epigrams discussed here I have seen F. Sauter, *Der Römischen Kaiserkult bei Martial und Statius* (Stuttgart, 1934). G. Friedrich, 'Zu Seneca und Martial', *Hermes* 51 (1916), 233-60, is disappointing.

emperors) can die, and thus urges them to enjoy life: *iubent ... vivere*. The sympotic scene, as in ii. 54, is rapidly sketched by referring to three ingredients: Falernian, perfumed ointments (*amomum* here rather than *nardum*) and rose garlands. As we shall note in the following pages, all three may also point to death; and the same is true of the fourth element, found in ii. 54: *torus*, the couch.

In both epigrams, Martial's message is of the *carpe diem* type, even if the last line of ii. 54, *ipse iubet morti te meminisse deus*, is a *memento mori*. Of course, this message is more faithful to the sympotic tradition; but sombre and sober *memento mori* themes are not at all uncommon in the poetry of the more Stoic Latin authors. For instance, a *memento mori* use of the wine-and-death association is to be found in Persius's *Third Satire*,[13] that text is especially useful in the present context because it depicts a scene that may be compared to Seneca's description of Pacuvius's Syrian behaviour. For in arguing against debauchery Persius, who died three years before Seneca's suicide, shows that it can be fatal, and describes a young wine drinker suddenly turned into a perfumed corpse:

> 'Please examine me', the rake says to a physician; 'something unknown trembles in my breast and a heavy breath comes out of my mouth. Oh do examine me, please!' This he says to the physician, and he is ordered to rest; but after three nights, when he notices that his blood flows (normally) in his veins once more, of course he sends someone to a more wealthy home with an empty half-bottle, to ask for some sweet Sorrento wine in order to drink it before his bath. 'You look pale, my dear!' a friend says to him; 'It's nothing!' 'Look out, however, for your skin is yellow and swollen'. 'You are paler than I am; don't try to tutor me. I've buried my tutor long ago: it maybe your turn to be buried, now!' 'All right; go on living as you like: I'll keep quiet'. Swollen with crapulence, he lowers his white belly into the *balneum* water while a heavy sulphureous breath comes out of his throat; but in drinking wine a sudden tremor shakes him and makes his cup of *calda* fall from his hands: uncovered, his teeth rattle and greasy morsels are vomited out of his open lips. Soon the sound of trumpets is heard, candles are lighted, and finally our hero lies in beatitude, tidily arranged upon a high couch and smeared with oily *amomum*, his rigid limbs pointing to the house door. And new-made citizens carry him away on their shoulders, their freedmen's *pilei* on their heads.[14]

(Pers. *Sat.* iii. ll. 88-106)

The most striking part of this satire is the description of the young rake's death *inter vina*, in the *balneum* but surely not far from the *triclinium*, and of the funeral, with the body carried away on its high couch by the dead man's slaves, freed by him on his death-bed and transformed *ipso facto* into grateful *liberti* with their characteristic head-wear. Instead of the mock funeral presented by Seneca in his description of Pacuvius's habits, we have here a real funeral: Pacuvius is carried *a cena*, from the dining-hall, *in cubiculum*, to his bedroom, while Persius's rake is carried out of the house, through the door to which his legs, stiffened by *rigor mortis*, point as he lies *compositus alto lecto*. Pacuvius's Syrian ritual, daily repeated, sanctioned the happy continuity of a life of pleasures; in Persius's *Third Satire* the funerary ritual puts an end to a crapulous life. In order to understand both texts, a scene depicted upon a slightly earlier funerary monument of central Italy is more

---

[13]On Persius and Stoic philosophy Ch. Burnier, *Le rôle des satires de Perse dans le développement du néo-stoïcisme* (La Chaux-de-Fonds, 1909), is still useful.

[14]On this passage see E. Pasoli, 'Persio e il bagno durante il banchetto (Sat. iii 98-106); tecnica imitativa ed espressionismo', *Scritti in onore di A. Scolari* (Verona, 1976), 23-233, and A. La Penna's introduction to *Persio, Satire* (Milan, 1979), 55-7.

useful than any detailed commentary. In a relief from Amiternum, L'Aquila, dated to the first half of the first century BC, now in the local Museo Nazionale, the funeral of a person of high rank involves mourners, wailers (*preficae*), players of various musical instruments including horn-blowers, and a litter carried by eight bearers. Upon the litter is a couch with a small table beside it, and on the couch a human figure reclines in the typical position of a banqueter (Figs 1 and 2). This position seems to indicate that the corpse has either been embalmed or substituted by a facsimile of some kind. Behind the reclining human figure the starry heavens and the sickle moon appear, decorating what seems to be a cloth canopy. In presenting the relief, Ranuccio Bianchi Bandinelli[15] noted that Amiternum was the birthplace of Cicero's friend Nigidius Figulus, who was responsible for the introduction of oriental astronomy to Rome precisely at the time of the funerary relief; and, whether this correspondence is significant or not, surely the heavenly setting of the reclining banqueter has some eschatological meaning. But the other aspects of the funeral on the Amiternum relief seem both less controversial and more important in the present context. They provide a useful illustration for Pacuvius's *exoleti* and the *sumphonia* sung while *ferebatur a cena*, as well as for the funeral of Persius's anonymous rake, with its *tubae* and its *lectum*.

To understand our Latin texts, funerary inscriptions are even more useful than the funerary relief from Amiternum. We have seen how Martial declared that the funerary tholos of Augustus, or the *Mausolea*, reminded him and his guests of death, while also ordering him and them to live: *iubent ... vivere ... cum doceant ... posse ... perire*. This is precisely what many funerary inscriptions of different times, both Latin and Greek, 'say' from the tombstones as they 'speak' to the passers-by. I. Kajanto[16] has dealt with these

Fig. 1. Relief from Amiternum, showing the funeral of a person of high rank (Museo Nazionale di L'Aquila) *(Courtesy of the Deutsches Archäologisches Institut Rom, neg. no. 85-1276)*

---

[15]R. Bianchi Bandinelli, *Roma. L'arte romana nel centro del potere* (Milan, 1969), 58-60 and figs 60 and 61.

[16]I. Kajanto, 'Balnea uina uenus', in I. Bifanur (ed.), *Hommages à M. Renard*, II (Paris, 1969), 357-67. On reclining skeletons holding drinking vessels or otherwise shown to be banqueting on funerary monuments, see Dunbabin, 'Sic erimus cuncti' (above, n. 6), 237-47.

Fig. 2. Detail of the relief from Amiternum, showing the litter and the deceased on a couch (Museo Nazionale di L'Aquila) *(Courtesy of the Deutsches Archäologisches Institut Rom, neg. no. 85-1278)*

messages (very rich in variations upon the *carpe diem* theme) in a brief and clever article. Here I quote his first two examples: a Greek one from Syria and a Latin one from Spain:[17]

'Greetings! Enjoy the pleasures of life! For Hades is for us the end of our empty vain efforts';

'Live joyfully, since you are alive: life is a gift that lasts for a short time: it starts, then slowly grows, and finally ends, imperceptibly'.

In many such epitaphs the message of the dead consists of praise of stark sexuality. The prototype of such epitaphs (and of the corresponding epigrams) was the so-called epitaph of Sardanapallus, attributed in Greek tradition to the legendary Assyrian king, notorious for his loose way of life, who was said to have burned himself to death after his army had risen against him, and to have ordered a maxim to be inscribed as his epitaph. There are many versions of that maxim: Kajanto gives us what he suggests was the

[17]From Syria: W. Peek, *Griechische Vers-Inschriften*, I (Berlin, 1967), no. 1957 (from Seleukeia); from Spain: *CLE* no. 245 (from Tarraco).

earliest version known, attributed to Callisthenes, who died in 327 BC.[18] I quote it here: 'Eat, drink, have sex, for all else is worthless'.

The rationalizing explanation offered by Kajanto — and, before him, by many others — for the origin of this Greek tradition is probably worthless; and the tradition itself is important because it connects the theme of oriental *truphe* with that of the *carpe diem* message conveyed by an epitaph. In this kind of epitaph, the pleasures of life are often listed, and the list is a short one: eating, drinking wine, sex, and the joys of the *balneum*. Often the praise of such pleasures goes together with a negative attitude to expectations for the afterlife; as Kajanto shows, this is not necessarily true. The fact that attention to the pleasures of this life can coexist in epitaphs with the hope of some kind of happy immortality is proved by many inscriptions; and among them is the following epigram from Ostia,[19] chiselled on the gravestone of C. Domitius Primus:

'In this tomb I lie, the famous Primus. I fared on oysters, and often I drank Falernum. Baths, wine and Venus, year after year, accompanied me to my old age. If I could do as much, let the earth be light on my bones. But in the world of the *Manes* a phoenix awaits me, and makes ready to renew itself together with me'.

The sequence *balnea vina Venus* appears often in epitaphs as a synthetic list of earthly pleasures. In the epitaph of Ti. Claudius Secundus,[20] probably a freedman of the Claudian emperors, inscribed on his tomb in Rome, the same clause is given a double meaning, so that the inscription conveys an ambiguous message:

Balnea vina Venus corrumpunt corpora nostra/ set vitam faciunt b(alnae) v(ina) v(enus)

'Baths, wine and sex corrupt our bodies; but baths, wine and sex also make up our lives'.

The idea that pleasures kill, and in particular that wine and baths harm bodies, is perfectly expressed and agrees very well with the moral lesson taught by the plight of Persius's young rake in the *Third Satire*, from which I have quoted at length. This idea coexists with the apparently contradictory one that wine, baths and sex are life. That a bath after a rich banquet with wine and food can be deadly is confirmed by the final episode in the *Cena Trimalchionis* of the *Satyricon*: we shall return to this novel shortly.[21] Here I only wish to quote an Italian proverb that is very popular today and exactly echoes Secundus's epitaph. It goes: '*Bacco tabacco e Venere riducon l'uomo in cenere*'.

SOME 'ORIENTAL' CONNECTIONS OF THE TWO THEMES

In his *Epistle* xii, Seneca quoted Virgil in order to comment upon a custom which he presented as Syrian. We have shown this combination to be quite acceptable, for the very simple reason that both the 'Egyptian' scene of the dead *sympotes* and the strange *parentalia* celebrated with wine by Pacuvius at the end of each day and presented as Syrian were perfectly integrated in the context of contemporary (and also of more

---

[18] *Suda* 122.
[19] *CLE* no. 1318.
[20] *Ibid.* no. 1499 (from Rome).
[21] See below, 'Wine and Death in the *Satyricon*'.

ancient, or traditional) Greek and Latin associations of death and wine.[22] Though they are said to be 'oriental', our two themes are in no way foreign to the cultural context which transmits them to us while playing with their possible meanings. Yet a well-known Latin poetic text associates what could be an 'oriental' figure with a drinking scene of a *carpe diem* variety; and another more famous Latin prose text may be interpreted as indicating that both the exhibition of a corpse during banquets and the mock funeral of a rich host at the end of a meal are 'oriental' customs. Let us examine both texts to see how they can help us to answer our questions.

COPA SURISCA

The poetic text in question, called *Copa*, belongs to the *Appendix Vergiliana*; it was not composed by Virgil, but contains a few verses clearly imitating (or rather, taken from) the works of that poet. It celebrates the peaceful joys of wine-drinking alfresco, as presented in the pressing invitation of a sexy innkeeper to the passer-by:

> The inn-keeper Surisca, her head bound in a Greek kerchief, trained as she is to sway her tremulous limbs to the notes of her castanets, tipsily dances in wanton wise within her smoky tavern, shaking against her elbow her noisy reeds: 'What is the use', she cries out, 'of staying outside, weary with the summer's dust, instead of reclining on a drinking couch? Here are garden nooks and arbours, mixing-cups, roses, flutes, lyres, and cool bowers with shady canes'.
>
> (*Copa* 1-8)

After the description of an inviting landscape, with the paraphernalia of wine-drinking and the shady protection of a vine to ward off the summer heat, the poem suddenly swerves towards the final scene — an unexpected visitor has the last cue:

> If you are wise, lay down now and steep yourself in a huge summer glass bowl, or in fresh crystal cups, if you like. Come, rest your wearied frame beneath the shade of vines, and entwine your heavy head in a garland of roses, sweetly snatching kisses from a tender girl's lips. Ah! Away with old-time sternness! Why should you keep the fragrant garlands for thankless ashes? Would you want to have those limbs of yours covered with a tombstone crowned with flowers? Set forth the wine and dice! Away with him who cares about tomorrow! Death plucks your ear and cries: Live; I come!
>
> (*Copa* 29-38)

In Martial's two *Epigrammata* which I have previously quoted, it was the funerary monument of Augustus (or, more generally, the Roman *Mausolea*) that ordered (*iubet* ii. 54.4, *iubent* v. 64.5) the drinking party either to remember death (*mortis te meminisse* ii. 4.4) and therefore to enjoy the pleasures of life, or, more simply, to 'live' (*vivere*). Here, it is Death himself who appears and says: 'Live (*vivite*), I come!'. The *carpe diem* message is clear, and expressed also by the ambiguous meaning of rose garlands (to be used for drinking, and not for covering tombstones). But what makes this text important in the present context is the fact that *vina* and *Venus* are offered by the inviting innkeeper *Surisca*. The name *Surisca* is surely a proper name, typical of a slave-woman and originally meaning 'the small Syrian woman', 'the Syrian girl', but we may not be sure

---

[22]This is shown admirably by K. Dunbabin in the article quoted above (n. 6), though Dunbabin accepts an Egyptian origin for the motifs she studies.

that it was not considered to be still meaningful, and to refer to the innkeeper's nationality or origin. In any case, *Copa Surisca* resembles the expression *Caupona ... Syra*, meaning 'the Syrian innkeeper', of Lucilius fr. iii. 128 Marx; and Lucilius's Syrian innkeeper proves that such a profession could be attributed to a woman (probably a slave-woman) from Syria at the time of Scipio Aemilianus, more than a century before the date of the pseudo-Virgilian *Copa*.[23]

Even if she is a Syrian woman, however, the *copa* need not be seen as the messenger, or even as a representative, of an exotic culture. Though her *Graeca ... mitella* points to the Eastern Roman provinces, still the music, the dance, the wine-drinking and the *carpe diem* message she stands for were perfectly integrated aspects of Roman culture at the beginning of the Christian era. It is to another Latin text of roughly the same period that we must turn in order to find behaviour which may be compared with the 'Egyptian' and with the 'Syrian' customs discussed here.

WINE AND DEATH IN THE *SATYRICON*

I refer, of course, to the *Satyricon*, written around the middle of the first century AD by a contemporary of Seneca and of Persius — and more precisely to the *Cena Trimalchionis*. As Katherine Dunbabin has shown in the article I have so often quoted, the *cena* offered by the rich *libertus* Trimalchio to the protagonist of the novel and to a group of other guests, which ended in a general alcoholic orgy, contains two episodes which can be compared respectively to the motif of the dead Egyptian *sympotes* and to the 'Syrian' behaviour attributed by Seneca to Pacuvius.

The first episode is placed at the very beginning of the meal. After the hors d'oeuvres, Trimalchio has the hands of his guests washed with wine by two long-haired Ethiopian slaves, and then:

> Carefully sealed wine bottles were immediately brought, their necks labelled: ALERNIAN. CONSUL OPIMIUS. ONE HUNDRED YEARS OLD. While we were examining the labels, Trimalchio clapped his hands and said with a sigh: 'Wine has a longer life than poor little man. So let's wet our whistles. Wine is life. I'm giving you real Opimian. I didn't put out such good stuff yesterday, though the company was much better class'. Naturally we drank and missed no opportunity of admiring his elegant hospitality. In the middle of this a slave brought in a silver skeleton, put together in such a way that its joints and backbone could be pulled out and twisted in all directions. After he had flung it about on the table once or twice, its flexible joints falling into various postures, Trimalchio recited: 'Alas, poor us, man is a nothing, We'll be like this, when Death takes us away, so let us live, as long as things are good'.
>
> (Petronius, *Satyricon* xv. 34)

This reminder of death while drinking Falernum is the other side of the coin represented by the funerary inscription of C. Domitius Primus (*CLE* no. 1318; *CIL* XIV, 914) quoted above and stating that the dead man *potabi(t) saepe Falernum*; but the silver *larva* is a slightly modified version of the 'Egyptian' *skeleton* shown to banqueters.

As for the second episode to be considered here, it is placed symmetrically, towards the opposite end of the *cena* (xv. 77). The meal is over, the 'second tables' have been

---

[23]For this parallel see C. Marchesi, *Storia della letteratura latina*, I (Milan-Messina, 1959), 258-9 and n. 3, p. 258.

brought in, and everybody is already drunk. At this point, Trimalchio becomes thoughtful and sententious:

'Believe me: have a penny, and you're worth a penny. You get something, you'll be thought something. Like your friend Trimalchio: first a frog, now a king. Meantime, Stichus, bring out the shroud and the things I want to be buried in. Bring some perfumed oil [for embalming], too, and a sample from that jar of wine I want my bones washed in'. Stichus did not delay over it, but brought his white shroud and his *praetexta* into the *triclinium* [...] Trimalchio told us to examine them to see if they were made of good wool. Then he said with a smile: 'Now you, Stichus, see no mice or moths get at those — otherwise I'll burn you alive. I want to be buried in style, so the whole town will bless my soul'. He opened a bottle of nard on the spot, rubbed some on all of us and said: 'I hope this'll be as nice when I'm dead as when I'm alive'. The wine he had poured into a big decanter and said: 'I want you to pretend you've been invited to my wake [*ad parentalia mea*]'.

The thing was becoming absolutely sickening, when Trimalchio, showing the effects of his disgusting drunkenness, had a fresh entertainment brought into the *triclinium*, some cornet players. Propped up on a lot of cushions, he stretched out along the edge of the couch and said: 'Pretend I'm dead and say something nice'. The cornet players struck out a funerary march [*funebri strepitu*]. One man in particular, the slave of his undertaker (who was the most respectable person present) blew so loudly that he raised the neighbourhood. As a result, the fire brigade, thinking Trimalchio's house was on fire, suddenly broke down the front door and began kicking up their own sort of din with their water and axes. Seizing this perfect chance, we gave Agamemnon the slip and escaped as rapidly as if there really were a fire.

(Petronius, *Satyricon* xv. 77)

The resemblance between each of these two scenes from the *Satyricon* and the corresponding scenes we have discussed above (Egyptian dead *sympotes*, Pacuvius's 'Syrian' custom) need not be stressed. In order to understand the fake *parentalia* at the end of Trimalchio's *cena*, it seems to me useful to turn to the death of the crapulous banqueter in Persius's *Third Satire*, and to the ensuing description of his corpse. Trimalchio *extendit se super torum extremum* with his pile of cushions, when he pretended to be dead, and the *cornicines* played their instruments; Persius's anonymous rake dies *inter vina*; later he is *alto compositus lecto*, and the *tubae* begin to play. The relief from Amiternum I have shown above (Figs 1 and 2) is also a useful illustration.

As for the message conveyed by the two scenes of the *Cena Trimalchionis*, it is clearly *carpe diem*, though not devoid of bitterness and of sadness. The message is most clearly expressed during the episode with the skeleton: Trimalchio says, *vinum vita est, vivam dum licet esse bene*: a good correspondence is found in the *Copa* (Death himself says *Vivite, venio*), in Martial's *Epigrammata*, discussed above, and in the expressions *vive, vivite* or *vivite felices* so often found in funerary inscriptions, and also discussed above.

Now, the same general message is conveyed by other episodes in the *Cena Trimalchionis* and the two scenes discussed here are only two among many aspects of a general picture presented by the *Cena Trimalchionis* and centred precisely on the combination of wine and death.[24] At the same time, they stand out because each corresponds to a specific topos, described by Greek and Latin authors respectively as Egyptian and as Syrian. But what does their presence and function in the *Satyricon* tell us about their supposed 'oriental' origin?

---

[24]See A.D. Leeman, 'Morte e scambio nel romanzo picaresco di Petronio', *GIF* 20 (1967) (*In Memoriam Entii Marmorale* I), 146-57; D. Gagliardi, 'Il tema della morte nella "cena" petroniana', *Orpheus* 10 (1989), 13-25; R.M. Newton, 'Trimalchio's bath', *CJ* 77 (1981-2), 315-19.

In my opinion the answer to this question is twofold. First of all, the fact that a banquet scene placed in southern Italy may contain the two episodes without explicitly connecting them to Egyptian or to Syrian customs is meaningful in itself, and becomes more meaningful still if we consider that, both in literature and in the visual arts of Italy and of the Roman West around the beginning of the Christian Era, parallels to these scenes are frequent — as we have seen.

On the other hand, the scenes we are discussing are presented by the author of the *Satyricon* as strange and even as disgusting (I quote only the expression *ibat res ad summam nauseam*, which we have found in xv. 78), and attributed by him to a class of rich and vulgar freedmen.

To this we should add that the freedmen in question (and most specifically Trimalchio and his friend Habinnas whom we have just met), and like them some of their slaves, are not only vulgar and low-born, and therefore disgusting in their habits, but also oriental. Trimalchio himself declares that he comes from Asia; Habinnas from Cappadocia; Trimalchio's name probably means something like 'three times kingly' and is half Semitic;[25] though Luigi Pepe[26] has convincingly disproved it, Habinnas also, because of his name and because of a proverb he quotes, has been thought by some scholars to be a Cappadocian Jew.[27]

This circumstance may lend some credibility to the hypothesis of an oriental origin, not of the 'wine and death' theme and of its many variations, but of the two specific motifs, the skeleton displayed during a banquet and the mock *parentalia* of the host at the end of a copious meal accompanied by wine. The first of these customs is considered a probable import from Hellenistic Egypt by Katherine Dunbabin in the article I have quoted so often.

Though I wish to stress the fact that this is a hypothesis, I must also add that another series of texts of comparable date could be seen as reinforcing the hypothesis. It is thus necessary to examine these texts.

THE *DEIPNON* AT BETHANY

We have just seen that in *Satyricon* xv. 78 Trimalchio anoints each of his guests with perfumed oil from the *ampulla nardi* he is keeping for his own funeral. Surely that *nardum* was meant to be used for anointing (embalming) his corpse: we have found the practice ridiculed in Lucian's *De Luctu* (25) as well as in Persius's *Third Satire* where the *beatulus* is *compositus lecto crassisque lutatus amomis*. We have also seen that Trimalchio's behaviour in xv. 78 was described as disgusting; and I shall add that a different but equally shameful use of precious ointments (here not *nardum* but more in general *unguentum*) is described elsewhere in the *Satyricon*:

[25]Recently: J. Balkenstein, 'Trimalchio, een naam mit een betekenis?', *Hermeneus* 43 (1971), 12-17, and the short summary of the article in *PSN* 2.2 (December 1971), 1. On the possible implications of Trimalchio's name, P. Vidal-Naquet, *Flavius Josèphe ou du bon usage de la trahison* (Paris, 1977), ch. 1.
[26]L. Pepe, *Studi petroniani* (Naples, 1957), 75-82.
[27]T.H. Gaster, 'The name Habinna', *CW* 48 (1955), 53; and E. Flores, 'Un ebreo cappadoce nella Cena Trimalchionis', *RAAN* 38 (1963), 45-69.

I blush to say what happened next. Boys with their hair down their backs came round with perfumed ointment in a silver bowl and rubbed it on our feet as we lay there, but first they wrapped our legs and ankles in wreaths of flowers. Some of the same stuff was dropped into the decanter and the lamp.

(Petronius, *Satyricon* xv. 70)

If we combine this awful behaviour (anointing the feet of the guests with *unguentum*) with Trimalchio's nauseous rubbing of *nardum* kept for his burial on each of his guests in xv. 78, we have the use of precious nard, intended for a burial, for anointing the feet of guests. And this 'combined' treatment corresponds precisely to what happened to Jesus during a famous *deipnon* in Bethany, according to all four canonic gospels. I quote only the version found in the Gospel According to St John (12.1-8); but one should see also Matthew 26.6-13, Mark 14.3-9 and Luke 7.35-60.

Six days before the Passover, Jesus came to Bethany, where Lazarus lived, whom he had raised from the dead. There they invited him to a *deipnon*, and Martha served, and Lazarus was one of those who reclined with him [συνανακείμενον]. Mary took a *litra* of nard, very costly, and anointed Jesus's feet and wiped them with her hair: and the house was filled with the smell of the ointment. Then one of the disciples, Judas Iscariot, Simon's son, the one who would betray him, asked: 'Why was not this ointment sold for three hundred denarii, and the money given to the poor?' [...] Jesus answered: 'Let her keep the ointment for the day of my burial [ἀφὲς αὐτήν, ἵνα εἰς τὴν ἡμέραν τοῦ ἐπιταφισμοῦ μου τηρήσῃ αὐτό]. For the poor you shall always have with you; but me you shall not always have.'

(John 12.1-8)

The correspondence between this scene and the two aspects of Trimalchio's *cena* represented by the two scenes I have quoted is precise. In both the *Satyricon* and the Gospels the play with the double function and thus with the ambiguous symbolic value of *unguentum* (or more specifically of *nardum*) is more elaborate and detailed than in Martial's famous joke on the hospitality of Fabullus:

Unguentum, fateor, bonum dedisti,
Convivis here, sed nihil scidisti.
Res salsa est bene olere et esurire.
Qui non cenat et unguitur, Fabulle,
Hic vere mihi mortuus videtur.

Yesterday you gave a good *unguentum* to your guests, I will admit as much, but you carved nothing. It's strange indeed to smell so good while being so starved and thirsty! He who dines not and is anointed, o Fabullus, he seems to me a dead man.

(Martial iii. 12)

Instead of Martial's comic metaphor, Trimalchio's *cena* and the *deipnon* of Bethany contain very serious, even poignantly dramatic ritualized behaviour: it is only in the author's judgement that the ritual enacted in *Satyricon* xv. 70 and 78 is both disgusting and comical. Is this behaviour 'Syro-Palestinian'? It is difficult to say much on this topic on the basis of the *deipnon* in Bethany, for we know too little about the composition, and thus about the real background, of the Gospel narratives.[28] Unless we can understand

[28]On the possible meaning and context of this episode, see C. Grottanelli, 'Adonis e i profumi dei re siriani', in *Adonis. Relazioni del colloquio in Roma, 22-23 maggio 1981* (Rome, 1984), 46-54.

whether the *deipnon* in Bethany is a genuine Palestinian banquet — and I don't think we can — it is impossible to use it as evidence of the 'oriental' quality of the banqueting habits of Trimalchio and his friends. With these observations I think we have concluded our search for 'oriental' traits in the Graeco-Latin evidence for our two wine-and-death topoi. We should now turn to whatever direct evidence we have from Egypt and from the Syro-Palestinian world.

DEATH AND WINE IN EGYPT, SYRIA AND PALESTINE

DEATH AND WINE IN EGYPT: *CARPE DIEM* AND *MEMENTO MORI*

In the 1985 article I have so often quoted, Katherine Dunbabin seemed inclined to believe in the authenticity of Herodotus's story of the Egyptian dead *sympotes*, and very cautiously advanced the hypothesis of an Alexandrian, and ultimately Egyptian, origin of the motif of the skeleton at the banquet. The suggestive archaeological documentation she presented — and in particular two small wooden skeleton-like human bodies from the Egyptian Museums of Hanover and Berlin — is, however, in no way decisive, for we are not really able to reconstruct the function served by those objects, and the way in which they were used.[29] It is correct to state, with the Italian Egyptologists I consulted,[30] that there is no secure Egyptian evidence of the custom described by Herodotus and the later Greek and Latin sources I have quoted, though some of the innumerable mummy-shaped artefacts of ancient Egypt could correspond to Herodotus's description. As for the possible use of some such artefacts in the way described by Herodotus, the verdict of the specialists does not seem very favourable.

On the other hand, a *carpe diem* message not unlike the message conveyed by the corpse in the Egyptian banquet of Herodotus and Plutarch may indeed be found in ancient Egyptian texts — or perhaps I should say in one particular Egyptian text — though it is actually the reverse of the canonical and generalized Egyptian attitude to matters of death and life.

The text in question, entitled 'the song that is from the tomb of King Antef, which is before the harper' (that is, written on the wall of the tomb in question, by the picture of a harper), attested by papyrus Harris 500 in the British Museum, has recently been translated as follows:

> (6.2) The song that is from the tomb of King Antef the justified which is before the harper:
> 1.   Flourishing is this noble:
> 2.   Good is the fate,
> 3.   Good is the injury.
> 4.   A generation passes on.
> 5.   Another (6.4) remains,
> 6.   since the time of the ancestors.
> 7.   The gods who came into being long ago
> 8.   rest in their sepulchres.

---

[29]For those objects see the data and the discussion offered by Dunbabin, 'Sic erimus cuncti' (above, n. 6), 208-12, fig. 20, and notes 90 and 91, pp. 209-10.

[30]Profs S. Donadoni and C. Roccati: I thank them warmly.

9.	Revivified (6.5) nobles as well
10.	are buried in their sepulchres.
11.	Those who built tombs — they have no (burial) places.
12.	Look (6.6) what has become of them!
13.	Now I have heard the words of Imhotep and Djedef-Hor
14.	that are so much quoted as (6.7) their sayings
15.	Look at their (burial) places!
16.	Their walls have crumbled — they have no (burial) places,
17.	like those who have never come into existence (6.8).
18.	There is no one who returns from there
19.	to tell their condition,
20.	to tell their needs,
21.	and thus to heal our hearts;
22.	before we hasten (6.9) to the place they went to.
23.	Be hale!
24.	while your heart is directed towards self-forgetfulness
25.	which performs the funerary rituals for you.
26.	Follow your heart while you exist.
27.	(6.10) Put myrrh on your head.
28.	Dress in fine linen.
29.	Anoint yourself with true wonders (6.11) from the god's property.
30.	Increase your pleasures greatly.
31.	Let not your heart be weary.
32.	Follow your heart and your pleasure.
33.	(6.12) Carry out your concerns (?) on earth.
34.	Let not your heart be injured,
35.	Until there comes your day of lamentation —
36.	And the Weary (7.1) of Heart cannot hear their wailing;
37.	Weeping cannot save a man from the Netherworld.
38.	Refrain: (7.2) Spend a pleasant day!
39.	Weary not of it!
40.	No one can make his property go with him.
41.	There is no one who goes (7.3) who will return.[31]

There is a series of such *Harpers' Songs*, assigned various dates by the specialists, as well as a series of later songs of a similar type, known to Egyptologists as 'orchestra songs'.[32] All of the harper's songs and most of the Middle Kingdom and Eighteenth Dynasty 'orchestra songs', M.V. Fox noted,[33] contain some explicit reference to the master of the tomb, to which they are appended or referred, as dead, so that in their present composition they are mortuary songs and function within the mortuary cult, whose purpose was to revive the dead and provide for their eternal welfare. In such songs, the same author adds, the purpose of the merry-making advice in a mortuary setting is to declare that the deceased's state is such that he is (still) able to enjoy himself. In line with the dominant Egyptian afterlife ideology, the deceased is seen as being revitalized, so that he has his faculties with him and is eternally provided with the requisites for pleasure. The reader is taught that one can enjoy oneself for eternity.

In the *Antef* song, Fox argues, 'themes and patterns of Middle Kingdom and Eighteenth Dynasty entertainment songs are taken up and given meanings different

---

[31]I quote here the translation by M.V. Fox, 'A study of *Antef*, *Orientalia* 26 (1978), 403-7.
[32]*Ibid.* pp. 396-7.
[33]*Ibid.* p. 397.

from those they had in other songs of the genre. Its basic statement is diametrically opposed to that of other entertainment songs. *Antef* is a reversed beatitude. The *Antef* poet speaks within the tradition of the entertainment beatitude, not as an outsider but as a singer who is expected to declare and help actualize eternal plenitude and security for the deceased. The reversal of this expected reassurance is an attack on belief by one expected to reinforce that belief and for that reason must have been profoundly shocking to the Egyptian reader (...) The later polemics against *Antef* testify to the power and persistence of the shock waves sent forth from this song.'[34]

In this part of his essay, Fox expresses with especial clarity and strength an opinion which is common among Egyptologists, that the specific meaning of the *carpe diem* theme in the *Harper's Song* of papyrus Harris 500, attributed to king Antef, is unique, and a reaction against the general Egyptian attitude. But on two other important problems the specialists disagree, and I have no way of deciding whom to follow. First of all, no agreement has been reached on the function and nature of these songs, despite the efforts of scholars such as Lichtheim, Brunner, Assmann, Lüddekens, and Fox.[35] According to some (among them, as we have seen, Fox), the songs are exclusively funerary, while others suggest that, though the whole documentation is funerary, the songs may have been sung also during the banquets of the living, and may thus be taken as related to the Herodotean description. Secondly, the date of *Antef* is debated: kings bearing the name Antef existed both immediately before, and immediately after, the Twelfth Dynasty (in both cases, in an age of profound crisis); on the other hand, some scholars favour a date more in accordance with the date of the papyrus, which is admittedly much later. M.V. Fox may be right in suggesting a date in the El Amarna period (also a period of profound crisis!) and in comparing the attribution of the song to king Antef's tomb to the biblical attribution of the Book of Ecclesiastes to king Solomon.

However these two problems are solved, we may state that in Egyptian literature the joys of banqueting (with food, alcoholic drinks and perfumed ointments) and more specifically drunkenness, are connected with death in two opposite ways, one of which is more ancient and more frequent — indeed, almost canonical — while the other is recent and rare. The first way consists of attributing enjoyment, and drunkenness in particular, to the deceased in a (special) afterlife; the second way consists of denying there is anything of the kind after death, and of stressing the brevity of earthly pleasures in a *carpe diem* key. I shall quote only two examples, one for each type. My first example is from Tomb no. 21 in Thebes (Middle Kingdom) where we find an inscription inviting the deceased to get drunk: 'By your ka! Drink, be merrily drunk, make a holiday! Do not ever cease to enjoy yourself in your pleasant house (=tomb)!'[36] My second example is

---

[34]*Ibid.* p. 417.

[35]M. Lichtheim, 'The songs of the harpers', *JNES* 4 (1945), 178-212 and pls I-VII; E.F. Wente, 'The Egyptian "Make Merry" songs reconsidered', *JNES* 21 (1962), 118-28 and pls XVI-XIX; H. Brunner, 'Wiederum di Ägyptische "Make Merry" Lieder', *JNES* 25 (1966), 130-1; J. Assmann's ('Fest des Augenblicks - Verheißung der Dauer. Die Kontoresse der ägyptischen Harfnerlieder') and E. Lüddekens's ('Zum Demotischen Gedicht vom Harfner') contributions to the discussion were published in the volume *Fragen an die Altägyptische Literatur. Studien zur Gedenken an Eberhard Otto* (Wiesbaden, 1977), 55-84 and 318-26 respectively. This bibliography is already in Dunbabin, 'Sic erimus cuncti' (above, n. 6), 209, n. 87.

[36]This tomb (see pls XXV-XXVI of N. de G. Davies, *Five Theban Tombs* (London, 1913)) is briefly discussed by M. Lichtheim (at p. 183) in her article cited in the previous note.

from Tomb no. l67 in Thebes (New Kingdom), where one reads: 'He who loved to be drunk / is now in a land without (even) water to drink'.[37]

I repeat that we have no evidence of the fact that the second type of connection between wine and death was expressed in ways similar to those described by Herodotus and by Plutarch; but most probably, as shown by inscriptions such as those of Petosiris and of Taimhotep, that topos became less rare in the later centuries.[38] And it seems quite plausible that during the Ptolemaic and Roman periods Greek songs such as this one from Oxyrhynchus, from Heitsch's edition of Greek poetic fragments,[39] may have been composed in Egypt and influenced by local *carpe diem* themes:

> Spring, winter, summer: these are forever.
> The sun sets, night receives its portion,
> Seek not to find the sun's or the water's sources, but to find sources for buying perfume and garlands.
> ... Play me a pipe!
> When you see a man dead, or pass a mute gravestone,
> you see everyman's mirror. That's what he expected.
> ... Blessed was Midas, and thrice blessed was Cinyras;
> But who of them reached Hades with more than an obol?
> Play me a pipe!

(M.L. West, 'Near Eastern material ...' p. 131)

This translation by M.L. West[40] gives the song a peculiar ballad-like twist; but the themes are still very clearly expressed, and in the verse about the super-rich Midas and Cinyras reaching Hades with an obol one may still recognize the concept expressed by v. 40 of the *Antef* song: 'No one can make his property go with him. In spite of this, there is no compelling reason to think of a historical derivation of the later song from the repertory of the earlier composition'.[41]

Of course, no historical derivation is necessary to explain why a theme not unlike the one we have identified as *memento mori* is present in a series of Egyptian texts of the

---

[37]E. Luddekens, 'Untersuchungen uber religiöse Gehalt, Sprache und Form der ägyptischen Totenklage', *MDIK* 11 (1943), 81-5. See the treatment of this text in S. Donadoni, *La letteratura egizia* (Milan, 1967), 216-17.

[38]Petosiris: G. Lefebvre, *Le tombeau de Petosiris*, 3 vols (Cairo, 1923-4); E. Otto, *Die Biographischen Inschriften der Ägyptische Spätzeit* (Leiden, 1954) (for a general discussion of this type of text); Donadoni, *La letteratura egizia* (above, n. 37), 262-4; E. Bresciani, *Letteratura e poesia dell'antico Egitto*, second edition (Turin, 1990), 663-7. Taimhotep: The *stela* containing the inscription is now in the British Museum (no. 147); see A. Erman, 'Zwei Grabsteine griechischer Zeit', in G. West (ed.), *Festschrift Eduard Sachau* (Berlin, 1915), 107; Otto, *Die Biographischen Inschriften der Ägyptische Spätzeit*, 123 and Inscription no. 57, pp. 190-4; Bresciani, *Letteratura e poesia dell'antico Egitto*, 669-71 (a partial translation).

[39]E. Heitsch, *Die Griechischen Dichterfragments der Römischen Kaiserzeit* (Göttingen, 1961), 39-40 (*POxy*. 15 (1922), no. 1795, col. ii).

[40]M.L. West, 'Near Eastern material in Hellenistic and Roman literature', *HSPh* 73 (1969), 128-33. Such a sceptical attitude to the afterlife became more frequent in later Egypt; see the epitaph quoted and discussed by S. Donadoni, *La religione dell'antico Egitto. Testi* (Bari, 1959), 531-3 (also translated by S. Schott, *Altägyptische Liebeslieder* (Zürich, 1950), 144-5).

[41]The problem of the historical derivation must of course be kept separate from the problem of the general cultural 'climate' which was expressed by these texts: for this see Donadoni's comment in *La religione dell'antico Egitto* (above, n. 40), 531.

New Kingdom. Here I shall quote only the description of a young man who drinks wine instead of learning to be a scribe:[42]

> Ah, if only you knew how horrible wine is, and stopped with your *shedeh*, and refrained from setting your heart upon the (wine) jug, and if only you could forget the *telek*!
>
> But they teach you to sing to the accompaniment of flutes, to trill with the sound of pipes, to warble like a Syrian to the sound of the *kinnor*, to sing with the *nechekh*. You sit in the (drinking) house, and women of pleasure are all around you. Your *ishetpenu* garland is round your neck, and you use your own belly as a drum. You sit next to the girl, and you are anointed with precious ointments. You slip, and you perfume yourself with dung.
>
> (Text no. 18, in R.A. Caminos, *Late Egyptian Miscellanies*, 182-8)

These Egyptian exercise books point first of all to the fact that a specific way of drinking wine with women of pleasure in a public cabaret was considered to be a Syrian custom during the New Kingdom, and involved singing to the sound of Syrian musical instruments like the *kinnor*. At the same time, these texts show that such a lifestyle is frowned upon; and the *memento mori* message conveyed by them is just as clear as the message contained in Persius's *Third Satire*. Indeed, the young, unruly scribe presented by the description I have just quoted is as foolish as the rake in ll. 88-106 of that *Satire*; and, like the poet speaking in the first person in ll. 44-51 of the Latin text, he prefers wine and play to work in the classroom.

While Persius shows us his debauched rake dying *inter vina*, we are not told that the young scribe dies because he drinks. Yet we do read that he slips, falls and pollutes himself with excrement. The contrast between perfumed ointment and dung is extremely clear, as is the meaning of the fall; but what makes the passage specially eloquent is the fact that in ancient Egyptian culture, as shown most recently by J. Zandee,[43] the dead — or at least those dead who were not protected by ad hoc spells — were believed to waddle in, or even to eat and drink, faeces and urine. Clearly, when the Egyptian rake is dead drunk, he dies, at least symbolically, *inter vina*.

I repeat that no relationship of historical derivation is necessary to explain the similarities between this passage of the Late Egyptian Miscellanies and Persius's *Third Satire*: the opposition between schoolwork and play (including food, wine, sex and perfume or bathing) and the even simpler connection between debauchery and a bad end can well have been discovered more than once in ancient literate societies. But the correspondence is even more striking if we do not account for it by imagining a precise 'genetic' relationship between the texts we compare; and, in the light of the comparison between Persius's *Third Satire* and the Ramesside papyri with their *memento mori* message, and the similar comparison we have drawn between *Antef* and the *carpe diem* spirit of a Greek papyrus from Egypt, it appears even less specific, and less necessarily to be explained by a historical relationship of derivation. If confronted with an Egyptian

---

[42]See Donadoni, *La letteratura egizia* (above, n. 37), 174-5. I have used the English translation by R.A. Caminos, *Late-Egyptian Miscellanies* (London, 1954), 182-8 (Text no. 18: Rebuke addressed to a dissipated scribe). See also Papyrus Sallier I.9.9. = Papyrus Anastasi IV.11.8 = Papyrus Anastasi IV.16.1-2, published by A.H. Gardiner in *Late Egyptian Miscellanies* (Brussels, 1937), 47.

[43]J. Zandee, 'Egyptian funerary ritual: coffin texts, Spell 173', *BO* 41 (1984), 5-33. See also S.B.A. Mercer, *The Pyramid Texts* (New York, 1952) (127c, 441a, 718a); R.G. Faulkner, *The Ancient Egyptian Coffin Texts* (Westminster, 1973) (Spells nos. 184-97); P. Barguet, *Le Livre des Morts* (Paris, 1967), 44, 147, 190.

mummy, Greeks and Romans had their own *carpe diem* (or *memento mori*) explanations to offer, and they had little need to learn local combinations of wine and death.

DEATH AND WINE: TRACES OF THE THEME IN SYRIA AND PALESTINE

Syria and Palestine have not been as generous as ancient Egypt in terms of literary (or artistic) treasures bequeathed to posterity; and this makes the search for wine-and-death combinations in the cultures of those societies less fruitful. The Bible must be exploited very warily,[44] for it is a most specific collection of texts, hardly typical of the ancient literary culture of the area. It offers many *memento mori* themes, and a few *carpe diem* flashes, but of a peculiar type. Thus, in Ecclesiastes 2.3 we find: 'I have decided within myself to gladden my own flesh with wine' (cf. Ben Sira 4.46); but a few verses later we read that this, just like any other attitude, is vanity.

The most explicit instance of a *carpe diem* theme is presented by the Bible in a specific context which transforms the *carpe diem* into a *memento mori* of the utmost gravity. In Isaiah 22 we find a terrible warning addressed by Yahweh, through the prophet, to the wicked inhabitants of Jerusalem. The city, Yahweh says, shall be besieged and taken, and its inhabitants killed. Though they have been forewarned, the city-dwellers ignore the divine command to mourn: instead of 'crying and lamenting, shaving their heads and donning sack-cloth', they give way to 'joy and gladness, slaying oxen, and killing sheep, eating flesh, and drinking wine', and as they do so they exclaim: *akol we ato ki mahar namut*, 'feast and drink, for tomorrow we die!' (22.13). This exclamation, almost identical to the *motto* attributed by Herodotus to his banqueting Egyptians, is the *carpe diem* of the guilty people of Jerusalem: instead of mourning, they feast, and Yahweh shall cause them to perish, so that their *mahar namut* ('tomorrow we die') is truer than they think.

Thus reinterpreted and transformed, the ancient topoi can be used only very indirectly to reconstruct the traditional cultures of Syria and Palestine and the role played in that tradition by wine-and-death themes. On the other hand, evidence other than the Bible is rare and often cryptic. There is, however, a text not too distant in time from the Ramesside papyri, about the debauched young scribes, which we have examined above: this was written in the Syrian city of Ugarit and seems to contain a counterpart of some of the narrative topoi, and possibly also the *memento mori* message, of those Egyptian texts. The tablet in question (*KTU* 1.114) was written in the cuneiform 'alphabet' of Ugarit and contains a recipe against a hangover (oil and various drugs) on the obverse and the story of a banquet offered to the other gods by the supreme deity Ilu on the reverse.[45] In the narrative text Ilu gets drunk. To show you how this happens I quote the Ugaritic text in my own tentative translation:

---

[44]On wine in the Bible I have learnt a lot from Jack Sasson's presentation 'Imagining the intoxicated in Hebrew literature', at the conference *Storia e cultura del bere nelle antiche società orientali, Rome, 17-19 mai 1990*, organized by Lucio Milano. The paper is to be published in the proceedings of that conference.

[45]The text can be consulted in the transcription (with vocalization) of D. Pardee, *Les textes paramytho-logiques de la 24ème campagne (1961). Ras-Shamra-Ougarit*, IV (Paris, 1988), 13-74.

I	Ilu offers a banquet in his house,
II	prepares a meal inside (2) his palace.
III	He invites the gods to the apportioning.
IV	The gods eat (3) and drink.
V	They drink wine until they are sated,
VI	(4) liquor until they are drunk.

Later on the drinking continues after the meal and Ilu gets awfully drunk:

XIX	(15) Ilu sits enthroned in his marzihu.
XX	(16) Ilu drinks wine until he is sated,
XXI	liquor until he is drunk.
XXII	(17) Ilu goes to his house,
XXIII	he moves (18) towards his court.
XXIV	Tukamuna (19) and Sunama hold him up,
XXV	Habi pushes him from behind (?).
XXVI	(20) The lord-of-the-horns-and-tail,
XXVII	waddles (21) in his own faeces and urine.
XXVIII	Ilu falls down as dead.
XXIX	(22) Ilu (is) like those who descend to the Netherworld.

So in this Ugaritic text the supreme god gets so drunk that he can hardly stand; two of his children hold him up, and in spite of this he falls. Most translators do not agree with my rendering of lines 19-21, because they do not accept the idea that it is Ilu himself who waddles in urine and dung after having defecated and urinated. But all agree on the fact that Ilu's fall is compared to death, not only because he becomes limp like a corpse (line 21, verse **XXVIII**), but also because he is explicitly compared to those who go down to the Netherworld: *yaridima arsi* in line 22 (verse **XXIX**) means just this, as confirmed by the identical biblical Hebrew expression and by the Akkadian *ana irsiti urid* used by the goddess Ishtar herself to indicate her own descent to the Netherworld. Moreover, the comparison between being drunk and being dead is also indicated, indirectly but clearly, by the fact that the ideal son, as described by other poetic texts from Ugarit, is the one who takes care of his father when he is drunk and after he is dead, by protecting him, dead or alive, from dirt.[46] This is precisely what Tukamuna and Sunama do to Ilu, so that many scholars have seen this element as an important aspect of the strange text *KTU* 1.114.

As readers may have gathered, the text *KTU* 1.114 has its own problems, and this is not the right occasion for dwelling on them.[47] What is important here is the fact that a text from Syria, composed within a chronological distance of 100 years at most from the Egyptian texts on the horrors of Syrian wine-drinking, ended up by showing that wine could kill. For in this Ugaritic poem wine kills — symbolically and temporarily, but explicitly — not only a god, but the father and chief of all gods, Ilu. The remedy for a hangover which is written on the other side of the tablet is thus guaranteed and

---

[46]See J.F. Healey, 'The *pietas* of an ideal son in Ugarit', *UF* 11 (1979), 353-6.

[47]For my own personal opinion on these problems see C. Grottanelli, 'Ancora sull'ebbrezza del dio El (*KTU* 1.114)', *Vicino Oriente* 7 (1988), 13-74; and now also 'Carne e vino: misura e dismisura', in P. Scarpi (ed.), *Homo Edens. II. Storie del Vino* (Milan, 1991), 151-66.

sanctioned by the very description of the divine precedent; and at the same time the patient is both reassured and admonished.

Even though it seems 'natural' (and has been dismissed as such even by a prominent member of my audience when I presented this paper in the Swedish Academy in Rome), the scene presented by the description of El's banquet in *KTU* 1.114 is no mere story of a fall. It is the conclusion of a formal wine banquet offered by a divine 'patriarch' to his people, and ending with the transportation of the dead-drunk host to his private apartment. This scene has often been compared to what happened to Noah in Genesis 9.1-29; and some years ago I compared it to ll. 13-34 of Theocritus's *Seventeeth Idyll*, which features Herakles who sits on an iron throne on Olympus and banquets with the gods, gets drunk on nectar and is literally carried to his beloved wife's alcove by his two descendants Alexander and Ptolemy.[48] A gloss explains that Herakles is so drunk he is no longer able to move his feet (μηκέτι κινεῖν τοὺς πόδας).[49] In both the Ugaritic and the Theocritean scene, ebriety is stronger than a god.

Whether or not a historical relationship exists between the scene in *KTU* 1.114 and Theocritus's description of Herakles's Olympic *défaillance*, both scenes show a drunken reveller being carried from the drinking quarters to the sleeping quarters. It is only in the Ugaritic text, however, that the fall of the drunkard is described, and presented, as similar to death. This aspect of the scene recalls Seneca's rendering of Pacuvius's Syrian habit of being carried to his *cubiculum* after the *cena*, for, as Ilu is said to fall to the ground like the dead who go down to the Netherworld, Pacuvius celebrates his own *parentalia* at the end of the banquet, and his guests pretend that he is dead and sing a dirge for him.

There is a very faint possibility that this similarity between Pacuvius's ritual and the Ugaritic myth in *KTU* 1.114 reflects the permanence of an ancient Syrian tradition. More probably, the resemblance stems simply from a similar play with drunkenness and death, at the respectable chronological distance of about 1,200 years. But certainly the wine-drinking culture of ancient Syria and Palestine seems endowed with an amazing continuity, precisely during the long period in question, that is roughly between the middle of the second millennium BC and the Hellenistic and Roman times. And one of the elements of this continuity is the wine-drinking institution called in Hebrew *marzeah* — a society of consumers possibly indicated, in the Ugaritic text *KTU* 1.114, by Ilu's *marzihu*. The *mrzh* institution is attested in Ugarit, in Phoenician texts, in the Bible, in the Aramaic texts from Elephantine in Egypt, among the Nabataeans and in the city of Palmyra; most recently a papyrus has been discovered with a text, possibly authentic, in a North-West Semitic language of southern Palestine, also mentioning a *mrzh*: it should be dated to the eighth or seventh century BC.[50] The Bible presents the *marzeah* as a band of drunkards; the 'house of the *marzeah*' is also associated with funeral banquets. Rabbinic sources also frown upon the *marzeah*. Greek translations of Semitic texts render *mrzh* as *thiasos* or *symposion*.

---

[48]C. Grottanelli, 'La prova del buon figlio', *Religioni e Civiltà* 3 (1983) (*Studi in memoria di A. Brelich*), 217-34.

[49]Fr. Dübner, *Scholia in Theocritum* (Paris, 1849), 165.

[50]I quote only the most intelligent article: J. Greenfield, 'The marzeah as a social institution', *AAntHung* 22 (1974), 450-5. For the recent discovery of a papyrus mentioning a *mrzh*: P. Bordereuil and D. Pardee, 'Le papyrus du *marzeah*', *Semitica* 38 (1990) (*Hommages à M. Szycer* I), 49-68, pls VII-X.

The great antiquity and the great continuity of Syrian and Palestinian traditions of wine drinking surely implied a rich wine-culture, if not a rich wine-literature. Yet Pacuvius's *parentalia* remain rather isolated, because the Biblical attitude to wine and to *carpe diem* ended up by winning over a considerable proportion of the local scribes and poets and other *literati* were just as thoroughly hellenized a few centuries later. It is from archaeological discoveries such as Ugarit (and possibly Ebla) that we can hope to recover some fragments of the ancient wine-wisdom of these cultures.

A TENTATIVE CONCLUSION

Let me summarize and try to offer a tentative conclusion, if not a definitive answer, to my search for the possible 'oriental' connections of Greek and Roman wine-and-death themes. I have shown that some specific forms of behaviour symbolically connecting death to wine-drinking, and implying evaluations of lifestyles, are presented by Greek and Latin authors as typical of the cultures of Egypt and Syria. I have found that the 'oriental' quality of such behaviours is never confirmed by actual Egyptian or Syrian documentation. But I have also shown that the ascription of such customs, and of the corresponding conceptions, to the Eastern neighbours of the Greeks and Romans was no mere Western fantasy about exotic peoples and their manners. In particular, both a *carpe diem* philosophy and its opposite, a strongly critical attitude to hedonism of the type I have indicated above with the motto *memento mori*, are present in different forms in the literary legacy of Egypt and of the Syro-Palestinian world.

To this I must add two more concluding observations. First, I wish to stress the fact that not all cultural similarities must — or indeed can — be explained as the result of contact or influence. I started by quoting Oswyn Murray's discussion of the Greek polarity between the world of merry, sociable wine-drinking and the dark world of death. I hope that these pages of mine have shown that this polarity, and with it many other symbolic contrasts or associations, are not only Greek, but generally Mediterranean — or, indeed, generally human.

Secondly, I wish to dedicate a page or two to the possibility of cultural influence moving in the opposite direction: not from East to West, but from Greece, for instance, to Palestine or to Egypt. To do so I shall quote from a text which is present only in some biblical canons, and significantly not included in the Hebrew canon: the so-called Wisdom of Solomon. Of this book we have only a Greek text; and it was probably written directly in Greek by a pious and wise Jew of the first century BC, possibly in Alexandria.[51] This text, attributed to king Solomon just like the *Harper's Song* discussed above was attributed to king Antef, contains an *Antef*-like *carpe diem* section, which exploits all the typically Greek paraphernalia of the *symposion*, including even rose garlands:

---

[51]On the Greek inspiration of the Wisdom of Solomon see already S. Lange, 'The Wisdom of Solomon and Plato', *JBL* 55 (1936), 293-302; more recently J.M. Reese, *Hellenistic Influence on the Book of Wisdom and its Consequences* (Rome, 1970).

Our life is short and miserable, and there is no remedy to man's end, nor is it known that anyone has escaped from Hades. We are born by mere chance, and after (death) it shall be as if we had never been. Smoke is the breath from our nostrils, and speech is a mere sparkle of fire, caused by the movement of our hearts. When this sparkle is extinguished, the body becomes ashes and the spirit is dispersed like light air. With time our name shall be forgotten, and nobody will remember our deeds. Our life passes like the shadow of a cloud, and dissolves like fog pursued by sun-rays, defeated by the heat of the sun. Our life is like the passing of a shadow, nor is there a returning after our end, and, once it is sealed, nobody comes back. So, come, let us enjoy the pleasures of the present, and let us hurry up and use what there is, with the ardour of our youth. Let us fill ourselves up with precious wine and perfumes, and let us not waste any of the flowers of Spring. Let us crown ourselves with roses, before they fade. Let no-one be absent from the feast, and let us leave signs of our joy everywhere, for this is our destiny and our heritage.

(Wisdom of Solomon 2.2-9)

Words such as these were shocking to those Egyptians who read *Antef*; to Greeks they were familiar. In this Jewish text, they are the words attributed to those evil-doers whose doom is announced in the following part of the book. The line immediately following the last one quoted here features the nihilists inviting their fellows to 'oppress the just man who is poor' and to waste no pity on widows and old men. The Greek picture of the *symposion* is thus exalted by a band of wicked men, in line with the message of Isaiah 22.13, where *carpe diem* is the motto of the impious and foolish Jerusalem. For this Jewish contemporary of Cicero, as for Seneca when he was confronted with Pacuvius's nightly ritual, *carpe diem* themes may be envisaged only in relation to a *memento mori* message. Cultural influence, when it does exist, is never a simple phenomenon, for cultures take what they can transform, and reject the rest — often violently.[52]

* * *

'Intervento' by Antonio La Penna

Il Dott. Grottanelli, con padronanza invidiabile di culture e letterature varie, dall'oriente all'occidente, ci ha offerto una ricca serie di passi riguardanti l'uso del vino in connessione col pensiero della morte; una riflessione su questo florilegio non è superflua.

Io credo che solo poche connessioni fissate dal Dott. Grottanelli siano convincenti. Non è certo discutibile, giacché l'attesta Seneca stesso, la provenienza siriaca dei

[52]I am grateful to the conference members who discussed with me various aspects of this paper; in particular to E.L. Bowie and to J. Griffin, who encouraged me in my distrust of Lucian. Readers will very easily realize how much this study owes to K. Dunbabin's article quoted in footnote 6: here I wish to express my admiration and gratitude to her once more. Giorgio Brugnoli, Lucio Milano and Pauline Schmitt Pantel have critically read my typescript. In translating Greek and Latin texts, I have availed myself more or less freely of English (Loeb) translations, in particular by the following scholars: for Lucian, A.M. Harmon; for Silius Italicus, J.D. Duff; for Plutarch, P.A. Clement; for Herodotus, A.D. Godley; for Seneca, R.M. Gummere; for Martial, W.C.A. Ker; for Persius, G.G. Ramsay; for the *Copa*, H. Rushton Fairclough; for the *Satyricon*, I have used the lively Penguin translation of J.P. Sullivan. And finally I thank Oswyn Murray for inviting me to his symposium and for his generosity with offprints and advice.

funerali di se stesso che un certo Pacuvio ogni giorno celebrava dopo un banchetto funebre: il personaggio si divertiva a fare la caricatura di un costume conosciuto in Siria. Ma l'invito della *copa Surisca* al viandante, nel noto carme dell'*Appendix Vergiliana*, perché si fermi alla taverna e si goda la vita ricordandosi che la Morte è sempre pronta a sopraggiungere, non ha niente di specificamente siriaco: è un motivo che conosciamo bene da Orazio e da tanta altra letteratura. Strano, poi, mi sembra il ricorso al passo della terza satira di Persio: qui si tratta dei funerali di un ricco personaggio morto improvvisamente durante una crapula: funerali solenni, data la posizione sociale del personaggio, ma che non hanno niente a che fare con la Siria; funerali reali per un morto, non per un vivo.

Dal rito di Pacuvio è diverso quello di Trimalcione in Petronio 34, cioè il rito dello scheletro d'argento portato in giro durante il convito per ricordare la morte ed invitare a godersi la vita; il confronto con Erodoto ii. 78, dove lo scheletro è di legno, è noto dai commenti; l'origine egiziana si può ritenere probabile. Legittimo, naturalmente, e anch'esso noto, è l'accostamento del funerale di Trimalcione vivo, con cui si chiude il racconto della cena, al funerale di Pacuvio. Il costume siriaco e il costume egiziano sono diversi e, credo, indipendenti fra loro.

Non mi pare che si possa ricavare niente dall'accostamento del passo di Petronio (70) con quello del Vangelo di Giovanni (12, 1-8) e quello di un papiro egiziano: se ne deduce solo l'uso, in oriente e in occidente, di unguenti nel lavare il corpo, o parti del corpo (come i piedi), di vivi e anche di morti.

. La connessione dell'esortazione a godere di vita fugace con l'ammonimento che la morte può sopraggiungere da un momento all'altro e che dopo la morte o non c'è nulla o c'è un oltretomba squallido, è motivo molto diffuso nella letteratura egiziana prima che nei lirici greci e in Orazio: un ampio florilegio ne diede P. Gilbert ('Horace et l'Egypte. Aux sources du *carpe diem*, *Latomus* 5 (1946) (*Mél. M.-A. Kugener*), 61-74), che suppose anche una dipendenza diretta o indiretta di Orazio dalla cultura egiziana. Ipotesi non necessaria e poco persuasiva: credo che passi possano indicarsi anche in letteratura cinese, persiana, araba: solo coincidenze verbali significative potrebbero indurci a supporre derivazione. I florilegi del Gilbert e del Grottanelli confermano la grande diffusione del motivo, nato indipendentemente in culture varie.

Reply by Cristiano Grottanelli

Il Professore La Penna è dunque d'accordo con me (o io sono d'accordo con lui: scegliete voi) sul fatto che le somiglianze che ho rilevato fra varie associazioni del vino con la morte in diversi contesti antichi non sono quasi mai frutto di un influsso diretto, o di una reale conoscenza di pratiche e idee orientali in Occidente. Io forse sono stato ancor più drastico di lui, perché ho proposto che un caso di contatto reale fosse quello relativo allo scheletro portato in giro nel banchetto, ma poi ho anche proposto che, dopo Erodoto, questo tema fosse diventato un topos diffuso; anzi, proprio un topos erodoteo.

Se dunque per 'connessioni' il Professore La Penna intende 'rapporti di derivazione', la sua posizione è più ottimistica della mia. Restano però: (1) le attribuzioni, da parte di fonti 'occidentali', di specifiche associazioni vita-morte a personaggi o ambienti 'orientali'; (2) le concordanze, o le somiglianze più o meno strette, fra idee o pratiche relative alla morte e al vino che *non* si spiegano con influssi o intercambi culturali. Sono proprio questi i casi che più mi sembravano interessanti, e ad essi ho dedicato gran parte della mia relazione. Spero di averne 'ricavato' qualcosa — in altri termini, mi auguro che non 'ricavare' un rapporto diretto di derivazione fra due fenomeni culturali sia cosa diversa da 'non ricavare niente'.

WINE IN GREEK CULTURE

6

Rite Cultuel et Rituel Social: à propos des Manières de Boire le Vin dans les Cités Grecques

PAULINE SCHMITT PANTEL

En faisant une recherche sur les banquets publics grecs je n'ai guère rencontré la question de la consommation du vin dans les cités grecques. Je voudrais d'abord m'arrêter sur ce fait qui peut paraître étrange quand on connait l'importance joué par le *symposion* dans la vie sociale grecque. Puis j'élargirai l'enquète en rappelant la place du vin dans les rites cultuels et en montrant que la juxtaposition des deux termes du titre de cet article (rite cultuel et rituel social) n'est pas la marque d'une séparation mais bien celle d'une symbiose entre les manières de boire antique. Enfin, en écho à ce que propose Oswyn Murray comme ligne de réflexion pour le colloque, je m'interrogerai sur le statut du plaisir procuré par ces mêmes activités et sur les difficultés de l'analyse d'une société 'holiste' comme la société grecque antique.

VIN ET BANQUETS PUBLICS

Partons de deux constatations. La première, les Grecs vivant en cités organisent de grands repas publics et non de grandes beuveries. La seconde, dans ces repas la part de la boisson en général et du vin en particulier est rarement spécifiée.

Les inscriptions grecques, surtout celles d'époques hellénistique et romaine, qui rapportent la tenue de banquets publics mentionnent rarement le vin alors qu'elles précisent très souvent la qualité et le nombre des animaux sacrifiés qui vont permettre le repas de viande. Il y a bien sûr quelques exceptions. A Eresos, au premier siècle apr. J.-C., le bienfaiteur fournit une amphore (*keramion*) de vin, ce qui est peu pour un repas auquel prend part toute la population de la cité mais bien en accord avec les autres quantités de denrées.[1] Un décret de Coressos du troisième siècle av. J.-C. indique que l'on doit fournir du vin pour le banquet, sans donner d'indications de quantité.[2] A

---

[1] *IG* XII, *Suppl.* 124, l. 15. Voir P. Schmitt Pantel, *La cité au banquet. Histoire des repas publics dans les cités grecques* (Rome-Paris, 1992).
[2] *IG* XII 5, 647, l. 11.

Akraiphia l'évergète Epaminondas au premier siècle apr. J.-C. distribue pour la fête à venir un *hemitea* de vin par personne, soit un 'half-jug' selon J.H. Oliver.[3] Et le même évergète donne encore après un repas un vase de vin vieux par *triclinium*, indication sur la bonne qualité du vin.[4] Autre source de renseignements: les comptes de Délos font apparaître le vin dans les achats nécessaires à la tenue des banquets des Posideia et des Eileithyia.[5] Ils donnent l'origine et la quantité du vin bu. L'origine est double: vin de Cnide et vin de Cos, le premier est de qualité, semble-t-il supérieure.[6] Ces exemples et quelques autres ne forment pas un ensemble documentaire comparable à celui que nous possédons pour connaître la première partie du banquet public, celle du repas proprement dit où l'on consomme la viande des sacrifices. Une pratique toutefois mérite d'être rappelée, celle du *glukismos*, à mi chemin entre le repas et la beuverie.

LE *GLUKISMOS*

Sur le chemin qui monte de la cité de Stratonicée au sanctuaire de Panamara et que gravissent les pélerins lors des Komyria, les prêtres Tib. Flavius Théophanès d'une part,[7] Jason et Statilia de l'autre,[8] offrent du vin doux (*glukus*) et du vin afin de permettre à la foule de se reposer et de se désaltérer. Ce ne sont pas de véritables distributions comme celles qui sont faites ensuite dans le Komyrion et l'Heraion. Le vin doux et le vin sont offerts en dehors du repas qui a lieu dans le sanctuaire, et sans doute avant lui. Deux autres termes désignent une pratique semblable: *glukizein*, verbe qui signifie 'donner du vin doux' ou 'faire une collation de vin doux'[9] et *glukismos* que l'on traduit de préférence par 'collation de vin doux'. Ce terme indique qu'il n'y a pas eu seulement distribution de vin mais dégustation sur place avec peut-être quelque accompagnement alimentaire.

Les deux mots *glukismos* et *glukus* apparaissent peu souvent dans les inscriptions en regard des termes classiques désignant un banquet.[10] Ils recouvrent une pratique particulière et ne sont en aucun cas interchangeables avec d'autres noms du banquet,

---

[3]*IG* VII 2712, ll. 65-6; J.H. Oliver, 'Epaminondas of Acraephia', *GRBS* 12 (1971), 221-37 (note à la ligne 66).

[4]*IG* VII 2712, l. 81.

[5]Ph. Bruneau, *Recherches sur les cultes de Délos à l'époque hellénistique et à l'époque impériale* (Paris, 1970), 261ss.

[6]Vin de Cnide: *ID* 440, l. 62; 445, l. 4; 452, l. 9; 461, l. 51; 464, l. 4. Vin de Cos: *ID* 406, l. 74; 440, l. 66; 445, ll. 9-10; 464, ll. 9-10. Sur la qualité des vins voir A. Jardé, Dar.-Sag., *s.v.* '*vinum*'; F. Salviat, 'Le vin de Thasos, amphores, vin et sources écrites', dans J.Y. Empereur et Y. Garlan (edd.), *Recherches sur les amphores grecques* (*BCH* Suppl. XIII) (Paris, 1986), 145-96; A. Tchernia, *Le vin de l'Italie romaine* (Paris, 1986).

[7]*I. Stratonikeia* 203, ll. 22-4.

[8]*I. Stratonikeia* 205, ll. 36-7.

[9]C'est ainsi que traduit L. Robert qui a traité plusieurs fois de cette question: *Etudes anatoliennes* (Paris, 1937), 38; 'Sur des inscriptions d'Ephèse', *RPh* 41 (1967), 7-84 (voir p. 17); 'Sur quelques fragments de décrets à Istros', *StudClas* 10 (1968), 77-85; 'Sur des inscriptions d'Athènes et de la Grèce centrale', *ArchEph* (1969), 1-58 (voir p. 35); J. Robert et L. Robert, *Bulletin épigraphique* (1940), 85; (1958), 336; (1968), 444.

[10]M.C. Amouretti, 'Vin, vinaigre, piquette dans l'antiquité', dans *Le vin des historiens* (Suze la Rousse, 1990), 75-87, parle du γλευκός (moût ou vin nouveau), mais il semble bien que l'on doive distinguer γλευκός de γλυκύς, vin sucré, vin doux.

contrairement à ce que l'on a souvent écrit. Ils ne sont pas non plus porteurs d'une nuance qualitative que l'on traduirait par 'repas fin', 'régal'. Dans les textes le *glukismos* est toujours distinct du *deipnon*. Il se place à un moment précis de la journée lors de fêtes complexes, ou apparaît dans des types d'activités où un banquet n'est pas prévu ou pas possible.

L'inscription d'Akraiphia par exemple énumère les générosités d'Epaminondas. Il ne cessa de donner des distributions de viande, des petits déjeuners, des collations de vin doux, des dîners.[11] Les *glukismoi* sont distincts des repas et sont cités entre les déjeuners (*arista*) et les dîners (*deipna*), ce qui est peut-être une indication sur le moment de leur tenue dans la journée. A Eresos l'évergète offre plusieurs fois une collation de vin doux aux mêmes catégories de personnes.[12] Elle a lieu lors des fêtes, après un sacrifice, mais le *glukismos* ne peut pas être assimilé au festin, lui-même mentionné deux fois dans le texte.[13] Dans la même journée ont lieu une collation et un repas. Comme le banquet se tient en général en fin d'après-midi, le *glukismos* serait un goûter qui permettrait aux gens venus tôt à la fête pour prendre part au sacrifice d'attendre le repas du soir.[14]

Les exemples de Priène à la fin du deuxième et début du premier siècle av. J.-C. confirment ce schéma. Dans les trois décrets honorifiques pour Moschion, Hérodès et Kratès, le jour de fête se déroule de la même façon.[15] L. Robert le décrit ainsi: 'la journée s'est ouverte pour tous, citoyens et étrangers, par un goûter (*glukismos*) dans la maison de l'évergète. Puis s'est formée la procession pour conduire les victimes aux dieux poliades. Puis l'on prononce des voeux solennels pour la prospérité de toute la ville; on sacrifiera ensuite et les chairs seront consommées en un grand banquet'.[16] Le *glukismos* est, là encore, distinct du *deipnon*, il a lieu plus tôt dans la journée, son caractère frugal est évident puisque Hérodès et Kratès peuvent l'organiser dans leur propre maison alors qu'ils ont invité tout le monde. Cette foule ne va pas s'installer pour se mettre à table, mais boire du vin doux et peut-être grignoter quelques galettes avant de prendre part aux activités de la fête.

D'autres exemples encore illustrent le caractère spécifique du *glukismos*. A Kymé en Eolide, en 130 av. J.-C., Archippé à l'occasion de la dédicace du *bouleuterion* dont elle a financé la construction, décide d'offrir du vin doux aux citoyens et aux autres habitants de la cité dans le *bouleuterion*, alors qu'elle donne une somme d'argent pour le sacrifice et le banquet.[17] Elle fit de même lors de la dédicace des statues honorifiques élevées devant le *bouleuterion*. La collation a lieu dans un endroit, le *bouleuterion*, qui n'est pas spécialement aménagé pour les repas et où l'on ne dispose pas d'un espace comparable à celui d'une agora ou d'un théâtre nécessaire au déploiement du banquet. Dans la même cité, Kléanax au tournant de notre ère a aussi offert du vin doux.[18] A Istros enfin, à la fin du second siècle av. J.-C., un évergète a fait une distribution d'huile lors de la

[11]*IG* VII 2712, ll. 67-8.

[12]*IG* XII, *Suppl.* 124, ll. 3-4, 6 et 10; J. Robert et L. Robert, *Bulletin épigraphique* (1940), 85.

[13]*IG* XII, *Suppl.* 124, ll. 8 et 15.

[14]*Glukizein* est employé dans une autre inscription d'Eresos, *IG* XII, *Suppl.* 528.

[15]*I. Priene* 108, 109, 111.

[16]Robert, *Etudes anatoliennes* (ci-dessus, n. 9), 38.

[17]H. Engelmann, *Die Inschriften von Kyme* 13 (Bonn, 1976), II A, ll. 27-30.

[18]R. Hodot, 'Décret de Kymé en l'honneur du prytane Kléanax', *The Getty Museum Journal* 10 (1982).

fête des Hermaia et offert une collation de vin doux.[19] Le banquet a lieu à un autre moment de la journée et on y distribue du vin.

Tous ces exemples montrent que lors d'une fête qui dure toute une journée, le *glukismos* est distinct du repas et a lieu avant lui. Mais la consommation de vin doux prend place aussi au cours de festivités où normalement il n'y a pas de repas, par exemple, lors des concours.

Le second jour de la fête, pendant que les *paides* sont en train de concourir après avoir été introduits au théâtre, Sotélès, à Pagai, au premier siècle av. J.-C., fait donner un *glukismos* à tous, et également aux femmes et aux étrangers.[20] Le premier jour au contraire il avait envoyé du vin pour le repas. Lors des spectacles des concours à Akraiphia, Epaminondas donne une collation de vin doux à tous les spectateurs au théâtre.[21] A la même occasion il fait lancer des friandises. Les deux pratiques avaient sans doute le même but: faire prendre patience aux gens lors de spectacles qui pouvaient durer toute la journée et qui ne pouvaient être interrompus par un repas véritable. Selon Philochore d'ailleurs, offrir du vin doux et apporter des desserts se fait dans tout concours.[22] Un vainqueur aux concours panhelléniques, Polémaios de Colophon, a, quant à lui introduit les couronnes dans sa patrie et offert des sacrifices et des collations de vin doux.[23]

Les occasions de *glukismos* furent certainement plus nombreuses que ne le laissent penser ces quelques textes. Ce n'était pas une pratique exceptionnelle due au hasard de la générosité inventive de tel ou tel bienfaiteur. A Priène cette coutume apparaît trois fois dans le même contexte, l'entrée en charge dans une magistrature, et à trois dates assez différentes pour que l'on puisse parler d'une certaine pérennité.[24] A Istros la distinction honorifique de la remise d'une couronne est accordée pour chaque année 'lors du *glukismos*', preuve que la collation est habituelle dans certaines circonstances et en particulier lors des fêtes du gymnase que sont les Hermaia.[25] A Eresos la tenue du *glukismos* se répète quatre fois, grâce au même évergète il est vrai, mais à l'occasion de fêtes différentes.[26] De plus ces inscriptions viennent d'aires géographiques diverses, il est impossible d'isoler une région particulière pour l'emploi de ce terme et donc pour cette forme de festivité. Il faut donc souligner l'importance de cet autre mode de convivialité, moins bien connu, à mi-chemin entre le banquet et la beuverie.

L'*OINOPOSION*

Les Grecs ne connaissent pas les *symposia* (au sens précis de beuveries) publics. J'entends par là qu'ils n'organisent pas dans le cadre de l'ensemble de la cité des réunions

---

[19]*I. Histriae* 59. Corrigé par Robert, 'Sur quelques fragments de décrets à Istros' (ci-dessus, n. 9).

[20]*IG* VII 190, ll. 25-6.

[21]*IG* VII 2712, ll. 75-6. Cf. Robert, 'Sur des inscriptions d'Athènes' (ci-dessus, n. 9), 34-9.

[22]Philochore, dans Ath. xi. 464-5.

[23]Décret inédit de Colophon dont un passage est cité par L. Robert, *RPh* 41 (1967), 17; et 'Les juges étrangers dans la cité grecque', dans E. von Caemmerer (ed.), *XENION. Festschrift für P.I. Zepos* (1973), 765-82.

[24]*I. Priene* 108, 109, 111.

[25]ἐπὶ τοῦ γλυκισμοῦ: sur l'emploi de ἐπί + génitif quand il s'agit de la proclamation d'une fête, voir les exemples donnés par Robert, 'Sur quelques fragments de décrets à Istros' (ci-dessus, n. 9), 79 et 80.

[26]*IG* XII, *Suppl.* 124.

uniquement faites pour boire. Et on ne peut pas dire que la pratique connue à l'époque romaine de l'*oinoposion* ('la beuverie' ou mieux 'le pot' au sens où l'on dit en français: 'aller prendre un pot') brise cette règle. En effet l'*oinoposion* est connu dans des villages de Bithynie au deuxième siècle apr. J.-C. où il a un caractère communautaire et public comme l'a montré L. Robert.[27] A Ishaniye en Bithynie des listes de libéralités lors d'une fête mentionnent toujours l'*oinoposion*.[28] Ce 'pot' est parfois accompagné d'un concert. Ailleurs l'*oinoposiarchès* était vraisemblablement le titre de celui qui faisait les frais du 'pot', un dignitaire du village dont les habitants se réunissaient pour ce type de réjouissance.[29] Mais l'exemple de la Bithynie nous plonge dans un monde différent de celui des cités grecques, aux frontières du monde des non grecs. Or c'est, on le sait, un trait récurrent de la description par les Grecs du monde barbare que de présenter ces peuples souvent rassemblés par des beuveries, les Scythes comme les Perses en sont des exemples connus. Ce faisant les textes grecs insistent sur l'étrangeté de tels comportements, voire sur le mauvais usage fait de la boisson. Nous ne sommes pas forcément dans le domaine d'une description réaliste des moeurs des non Grecs, mais peut-être dans la construction d'un discours qui en retour nous fait comprendre à quel point la beuverie publique est étrangère au monde grec.

A ces très rares mentions de 'pots' publics, il faudrait ajouter les distributions de vin faites à la fin des repas et qui, à l'égal des distributions d'aliments et d'argent, permettaient de continuer ailleurs la fête. Mais il ne s'agit pas dans ces cas de l'organisation d'une beuverie publique.

Que les sources épigraphiques parlent peu de la boisson ne signifie pas que les Grecs ne buvaient pas de vin lors des banquets publics. Au contraire, cette consommation allait tellement de soit qu'il était inutile de la mentionner. Lors d'un banquet public on mangeait les viandes du sacrifice accompagnées de céréales, puis l'on buvait selon le schéma habituel des deux temps successifs de tout banquet grec. Ce silence en revanche signifie que le moment de la boisson en commun n'était pas valorisé de la même manière dans les banquets publics que dans les banquets privés et que les Grecs n'ont jamais organisé leur convivialité publique autour de la seule boisson prise en commun. Le statut de la consommation du vin en dehors des banquets publics nous aidera peut-être à comprendre ce fait.

Si l'on fait l'inventaire des occasions de boire du vin qu'avaient les Grecs, on trouve la boisson solitaire, l'absorption de vin à un moment précis d'un rite cultuel complexe, le *symposion* soit le 'boire ensemble' deuxième temps de tout repas privé grec. La boisson solitaire échappe à notre propos.[30] Je m'arrête un instant sur la place du vin dans les rites religieux, plus pour poser des questions que pour proposer des pistes nouvelles.

---

[27]L. Robert, 'Voyages épigraphiques en Asie Mineure', *RPh* 15 (1943), 170-201.

[28]F.K. Dörner, *Inschriften und Denkmäler aus Bithynien* (Berlin, 1941), 57ss., nn° 31, 32, 33.

[29]Ainsi à Nicée, G. Mendel, 'Inscriptions de Bithynie', *BCH* 24 (1900), 385, n° 1, l. 12. A Gölbazar, 'Inscriptions de Bithynie', *BCH* 24 (1900), 407, n° 90, l. 11. A Nicomédie et A. Zingerle, 'Oinoposiarches', *JÖAI* 6 (1903), 122.

[30]Voir P. Villard, *Recherches sur l'ivresse chez les Grecs* (Thèse d'Etat, Université d'Aix en Provence, 1988).

VIN ET RITE CULTUEL

L'utilisation du vin dans le rite cultuel est constante sous la forme de la libation qui accompagne la prière comme le sacrifice, l'offrande comme le serment. C'est un geste religieux quotidien.[31] En revanche le fait de boire du vin en l'honneur d'une divinité au cours d'un rite cultuel est relativement rare. Pour Dionysos on célèbre à Athènes la fête des Anthestéries au début du printemps.[32] Son déroulement qui est bien connu donne lieu à la consommation rituelle de vin.

Le premier jour ou Pithoigia les *pithoi* contenant le vin depuis l'automne sont ouverts. Chaque récoltant athénien apporte un *pithos* au sanctuaire du marais, le Limnaion, fait une libation de son contenu et goûte le vin. Le second jour, jour des *Choês*, l'archonte roi préside un concours de buveurs au Limnaion ou au Thesmotheteion. Chaque participant doit au signal avaler le plus vite possible le contenu d'une cruche (*chous*). Le vainqueur reçoit une couronne de feuillage et peut-être une outre de vin. Ce jour là en dehors de ce concours, tout athénien pouvait boire le contenu de son *chous*, y compris les enfants qui recevaient à cette occasion des *chous* miniatures. Quand on sait que la capacité normale du *chous* est d'environ douze coupes, on peut imaginer le degré d'ébriété atteint dans la population adulte. C'est à vrai dire la seule fête en l'honneur de Dionysos à Athènes où boire du vin faisait partie d'un temps du rituel nettement séparé de la pratique du *symposion*. En effet lors des Dionysies aux champs la procession comprenait outre le *phallos*, une outre de vin et un concours, l'*askoliasmos*, qui consistait à se tenir debout sur une outre préalablement enduite d'huile.[33] Mais on ne parle pas de consommation de vin dans le rituel. Lors des Grandes Dionysies on buvait du vin lors du banquet final, on sait que Hérode Atticus offrit du vin à cette occasion à l'époque romaine, mais le processus est celui de la distribution étudiée précédemment.[34] Enfin lors de la fête des *Haloa*, fête de Déméter à laquelle Dionysos était associé, on buvait, semble-t-il, beaucoup de vin mais il est impossible de savoir si le vin était bu dans le rite lui-même ou lors des banquets qui terminaient cette fête comme les autres.[35] Le vin est seulement dit être présent en abondance sur les tables, à un moment du rituel où les femmes sont seules, les hommes s'étant retirés.

En dehors d'Athènes, si l'on faisait une enquète exhaustive dans les textes littéraires et les lois sacrées, on trouverait sans doute quelques autres mentions de vin bu à un moment précis d'un rite plus complexe et en dehors du *symposion*, mais ces mentions sont très rares au regard de la masse de références concernant l'utilisation du vin pour les libations.

[31]Sur les libations: E. Simon, *Opfernde Götter* (Berlin, 1953) et l'article de F. Lissarrague dans ce livre.

[32]Sur les Anthestéries, voir L. Deubner, *Attische Feste* (Berlin, 1966), 93-123.

[33]Sur les Dionysies rurales, *ibid.* pp. 134-8.

[34]Philostr. *VS* ii. 15. Hérode Atticus, lors des Dionysies, offrit à boire au Céramique aux habitants de la ville et aux étrangers, allongés sur des jonchées de lierre.

[35]Sur les *Haloa*, Deubner, *Attische Feste* (ci-dessus, n. 32), 60ss. Une scholie à Lucien (Sch. Lucian 279, 24 Rabe) décrit la fête et souligne l. 20: ἐνταῦθα οἶνός τε πολὺς πρόκειται. Sur les femmes et le vin, voir P. Villard, 'Femmes au symposion', dans F. Thélamon (ed.), *Sociabilité, pouvoir et société* (Rouen, 1987), 106-10; M.-C. Villanueva-Puig, 'La ménade, la vigne et le vin', *REA* 90 (1988), 35-64 (avec une bibliographie sur ce thème); F. Frontisi-Ducroux, 'Qu'est-ce qui fait courir les Ménades?', dans D. Fournier et S. D'Onofrio (edd.), *Le ferment divin* (Paris, 1991), 147-66.

Une autre piste de recherches pourrait être l'archéologie. Mais l'archéologie qui s'est, pour le thème qui nous retient ici, surtout interessée à l'étude des salles de banquets, est très décevante quand on cherche à préciser les occasions rituelles de boire.[36] Parfois les archéologues baptisent leurs salles de banquets 'salles de *symposion*' laissant entendre que la pratique concernait surtout le 'boire ensemble', mais ces appellations se révèlent fallacieuses. Ainsi au Cabirion près de Thèbes, les structures rondes et rectangulaires retrouvées ont été baptisées 'salles de *symposion*'.[37] Mais les restes trouvés dans ces pièces: morceaux d'os, cendres, indiquent clairement que l'on mangeait là les viandes du sacrifice.[38] Les preuves archéologiques de la consommation de vin existent bien sûr aussi: restes de la vaisselle du *symposion* en particulier, mais ceci n'est que la confirmation du déroulement habituel du banquet avec les deux temps successifs de la nourriture et de la boisson.

Une autre sorte de documents archéologiques serait interessante à interroger dans la perspective d'une recherche sur la place de la consommation du vin dans le rite cultuel: les consécrations, les objets donnés en offrandes au dieu. Cette idée m'est venu en étudiant le cas du sanctuaire du Cabirion déjà cité pour lequel nous disposons d'un nombre important d'objets votifs et en particulier de toute une série de vases étroitement liés à la manipulation du vin et à sa consommation: *skyphoi* et *kantharoi*.[39] Je laisse de côté la question non élucidée du sens à donner aux scènes représentées sur cette vaisselle très exceptionnelle. Je me demande seulement s'il n'y aurait pas un certain rapport entre ce type massif d'offrande et un rituel, pour nous inconnu, touchant à la manipulation et la consommation du vin. Interrogeant des amis archéologues sur ce point, leur réponse fut négative. Il semblerait que d'une manière générale on ne puisse pas sérieusement établir de rapports entre les offrandes faites à une divinité et la fonction de cette même divinité (les offrandes seraient en quelque sorte interchangeables) et à plus forte raison que l'on puisse faire des rapprochements entre les offrandes et un rituel particulier perpétré pour une divinité. Je ne suis pas totalement convaincue par cette réponse. Il me semble plutôt que ce type de question est très rarement posé lors de l'étude du matériel archéologique et qu'il mériterait de l'être. Il y a peu de temps on ne cherchait pas systématiquement les bâtiments servant aux banquets dans les sanctuaires: depuis qu'on les cherche, les salles de banquets fleurissent un peu partout. Plus récemment encore les archéologues ne portaient pas une grande attention aux cendres et débris d'ossements animaux autour des temples, les prendre en charge permet pourtant depuis peu de préciser la place des repas rituels dans de très nombreux

---

[36]Voir la bibliographie sur les salles de banquet dans O. Murray, *Sympotica: a Symposium on the* Symposion (Oxford, 1990).

[37]Ainsi W. Heyder et A. Mallwitz, *Die Bauten im Kabirenheiligtum bei Theben* (Berlin, 1978), parlent de 'maison de *symposion*' pour les *tholoi* découvertes dans le sanctuaire. Mais dans un compte rendu de ce livre dans *Gnomon* 54 (1982), 56-63, F.A. Cooper a bien montré que ces *tholoi* étaient des salles de banquet où l'on mangeait assis. Voir aussi F.A. Cooper et S. Morris, 'Dining in round buildings', dans Murray (ed.), *Sympotica* (ci-dessus, n. 36), 66-85.

[38]Sur les restes au Cabirion voir J. Boessneck, *Die Tierknochenfunde aus dem Kabirenheiligtum bei Theben* (Berlin, 1973).

[39]K. Braun et T.E. Haevernick, *Bemalte Keramik und Glas aus dem Kabirenheiligtum bei Theben* (Berlin, 1981); U. Heimberg, *Die Keramik des Kabirions* (Berlin, 1982).

sanctuaires.[40] Les recherches archéologiques sur les banquets illustrent parfaitement ce truisme: on ne trouve que ce que l'on cherche, une synthèse sur les restes archéologiques dans les sanctuaires de la vaisselle liée à la consommation de vin d'une part, et de sa place dans les offrandes de l'autre permettrait peut-être de préciser la place de la consommation du vin dans les rituels.

Une autre voie de recherches consiste à interroger les images peintes sur les vases, à se servir de l'iconographie très riche du vin pour tenter de répondre à la question de la place de la consommation du vin dans un rite cultuel, en dehors du *symposion*.[41] Toutefois des recherches récentes font douter qu'il soit possible d'obtenir, en ce domaine de l'iconographie comme en d'autres, une réponse univoque. En effet, comme vient de le montrer F. Frontisi à propos de l'ensemble des vases dits des Lénéennes, il est impossible de donner un nom précis aux scènes de manipulation rituelle de vin sur les vases attiques.[42] Certes tout se passe autour de l'effigie de Dionysos (un dieu-masque accroché à un pilier) et le rituel est sans aucun doute adressé à ce dieu. Mais bien que l'érudition depuis plus d'un siècle ait cherché à préciser de quel rituel il était question et se soit allégrement divisée entre partisans de la fête des Lénéennes et de celle des Anthestéries, F. Frontisi renvoie dos à dos les deux partis et démontre que les images ne permettent pas de trancher entre les deux fêtes car tel n'est pas leur propos. Leur rapport à la réalité n'est pas direct et il est vain de les prendre pour des documents illustrant tel culte. Elles indiquent seulement que le service du vin, puisage et distribution, fait partie d'un ensemble de pratiques rituelles qui ont lieu autour de l'effigie de Dionysos. Que les femmes y jouent un rôle dominant mais non exclusif et que la consommation du vin n'apparaît pas: les images dissocient les rites autour du dieu-masque où l'on ne consomme pas de vin, des rites du *symposion* autour du cratère où les buveurs sont présents.

Ainsi ni les textes, ni l'archéologie, ni les images ne permettent, dans l'état actuel des recherches, de dire que la consommation du vin avait une place régulière dans le rite cultuel. Ce geste apparaît très exceptionnel, même dans le culte de Dionysos. Pour préciser ce point j'esquisserai un parallèle. Au sacrifice sanglant correspond la libation de vin, offrande de l'animal et offrande du vin aux dieux. A la consommation des *splanchna*, ces parties des viscères nobles qui sont grillées et mangées immédiatement après le sacrifice par les participants, il ne semble pas correspondre de geste de boire. Excepté dans les cas très précis d'un rituel en l'honneur de Dionysos inventeur du vin (par la grappe de raisin et par l'art de cultiver la vigne et de fabriquer le vin) comme lors des Anthestéries. Dans ce cas là boire le vin, voire s'enivrer avec le vin nouveau, c'est reconnaître dans le produit culturel la marque du dieu. L'absorption de vin dans le rite cultuel a une fonction symbolique précise en rapport avec la fonction du dieu alors célébré. De même dans les rites cultuels concernant les divinités qui ont apporté aux

---

[40]Voir par exemple la mise au point de M.H. Jameson, 'Sacrifice and animal husbandry in classical Greece', dans C. Whittaker (ed.), *Pastoral Economies in Classical Antiquity* (Cambridge, 1988). Et pour une époque plus ancienne plusieurs articles dans R. Hägg, N. Marinatos et G.C. Nordquist (edd.), *Early Greek Cult Practice* (Stockholm, 1988).

[41]Sur le vin dans le *symposion* voir F. Lissarrague, *Un flot d'images: une esthétique du banquet grec* (Paris, 1987).

[42]F. Frontisi-Ducroux, *Le dieu-masque* (Paris, 1991).

humains les céréales et leur culture, on absorbe un mélange de ces céréales. On boit rituellement le vin comme on mange rituellement la bouillie de céréales dans les fêtes qui accompagnent la consécration des prémices des récoltes: vin nouveau, fruits de la terre.

La place limitée du vin dans les rites cultuels est celle du vin comme produit. Mais, chacun le sait, Dionysos n'a pas seulement apporté avec lui un produit, il a appris aux hommes comment en user, et ce faisant, autour du mélange dans le cratère et de la répartition, il a introduit une des formes du lien social. C'est sous cet aspect là, le vin comme partage, que le vin est omniprésent dans le rite.[43]

Le cortège même en l'honneur de Dionysos est composé des comastes tout juste sortis du *symposion*. Et le *symposion*, deuxième partie du banquet grec, n'est pas une beuverie tout à fait ordinaire mais la consommation ritualisée du vin sous le regard de Dionysos et d'autres divinités invoquées lors des libations. Dire que la consommation du vin lors du *symposion* est ritualisée signifie à la fois qu'elle fait l'objet d'un cérémonial particulier, bien connu et souvent décrit, et qu'elle marque l'adhésion à une croyance: le bon usage du vin est un don de Dionysos et tout ce qui suit sa consommation est envoyé par le dieu. En ce sens la consommation du vin dans le *symposion* est une des marques du culte rendu à Dionysos.[44] Ce rituel social est-il un rite cultuel? A-t-on le droit de mettre sur le même plan le fait de boire du vin lors du *symposion* qui fait suite au repas pris dans un cadre public et plus souvent privé à partir de l'époque classique, au vin bu lors du concours des buveurs de la journée des cruches en plein coeur d'une fête religieuse publique organisée sous l'autorité de l'archonte roi? Le rapport au sacré est-il le même?

Comme l'a souvent rappelé J.-P. Vernant, 'il y a des formes et des degrés divers de sacré plus qu'une polarité sacré profane. L'insertion du religieux dans la vie sociale à ses divers étages, ses liens avec l'individu, sa vie, sa survie, ne prêtent pas à une délimitation précise du domaine de la religion'.[45] Des formes diverses de sacré: comme dans le cas du sacrifice et de ses suites alimentaires, nous pouvons aborder l'étude de la consommation du vin 'sous deux angles, sous deux aspects, pour nous différents mais qui n'en faisaient qu'un pour les Grecs. D'une part comme fête solennelle où les dieux invités sont présents, d'autre part comme' préparation de la boisson 'selon des règles qui rendent licites et même pieuses' la consommation du vin.[46] Ces différentes formes d'expression du sacré ne sont pas forcément hiérarchisées. Elles sont plutôt complémentaires, et, dans le cas du vin, mettent l'accent sur le vin comme produit cultivé que l'on goûte dans les cultes où Dionysos est l'inventeur de cette boisson et le vin comme usage social que l'on partage et que l'on boit en célébrant Dionysos initiateur du lien social qu'est la *philia*. Ainsi boire du vin est tout à la fois un rite cultuel et un rituel social, mais n'est-ce pas le propre de bien des pratiques grecques et de leurs représentations de lier de façon étroite des valeurs que nos propres sociétés ont disjointes?

---

[43]Voir Lissarrague, *Un flot d'images* (ci-dessus, n. 41).

[44]Voir plusieurs articles dans des recueils d'articles récents: F. Berti (ed.), *Dionysos, mito e mistero* (*Atti del convegno internazionale Comacchio 3-5 novembre 1989*) (Comacchio, 1991); P. Scarpi (ed.), *Storie del vino. Homo edens* II (Milan, 1991); D. Fournier et S. D'Onofrio (edd.), *Le ferment divin* (Paris, 1991).

[45]J.-P. Vernant, 'Religion grecque, religions antiques', dans J.-P. Vernant, *Religions, histoires, raisons* (Paris, 1979), 11.

[46]*Ibid.* p. 21. Je cite la phrase de J.-P. Vernant en remplaçant la nourriture carnée par le vin.

La présence constante dans le temps, dans l'espace, à tous les niveaux de la vie sociale, de comportements qui tirent une partie de leur sens de leur insertion dans la sphère du sacré est une donnée absolument incontournable de la société grecque antique et pose un problème pour l'interprétation globale de ce type de société. Je ne dis pas cela pour raviver la querelle entre les partisans du 'tout religieux' et les autres, mais, bien au contraire, pour admettre avec ceux qui trouvent que l'on exagère parfois la part du sacré dans toutes les pratiques grecques, que le sacré a une part, mais qu'elle n'explique pas tout. Comme le suggère Oswyn Murray, le rapport au sacré entretenu par la consommation de vin ne suffit pas à expliquer le plaisir pris à boire par exemple.[47] Certes, mais le plaisir pris à boire, une fois promu au rang de facteur explicatif, ne doit pas étouffer la dimension sacrée de l'acte de boire. Le problème n'est sans doute pas de choisir à quelle explication on doit accorder le primat: explication sociale, explication religieuse, explication culturelle (le plaisir comme moteur de l'histoire). Il est préférable de considérer la société antique comme un organe totalisant, comme une société holiste (ou holistique) et de réfléchir dans une autre logique que celle de la concurrence entre ces facteurs.

PLAISIRS SOCIAUX

Avant de reprendre ce point je voudrais prolonger la suggestion faite par Oswyn Murray, celle de nous tourner plus résolument vers une histoire culturelle qui donnerait en particulier toute son importance au principe de plaisir et en ferait un facteur déterminant dans l'histoire des sociétés antiques. Je le ferai d'autant plus volontiers qu'en écrivant l'histoire des banquets publics grecs j'ai donné une vision somme toute assez austère et désincarnée de ce qui avait été un des grands plaisirs des cités grecques. De ce point de vue là je ne séparerai pas le plaisir de manger de celui de boire, même si le thème du colloque nous y invite. C'est, plus particulièrement, la réflexion sur les ressorts de l'évergétisme qui m'a conduite à m'interroger sur le rôle du plaisir dans cette société.[48] En effet cherchant le pourquoi des dons de banquets par les évergètes de façon si constante et si dispendieuse pendant des siècles, j'avais été frappée de ce que les historiens modernes, à l'exception de Paul Veyne et de ses 'rois de la fête', n'avaient pas voulu entendre une des raisons de la permanence de telles évergésies.[49] Ils mettaient ces invitations au banquet sur le compte de l'absence de véritable sens politique des évergètes, comme autant de signes annonciateurs du déclin de leur pouvoir. Ils refusaient ce faisant de reconnaître un rôle déterminant à la dimension de la joie, de la liesse, du plaisir partagé, de l'oubli momentané d'une condition de vie quotidienne difficile, proche de la pauvreté.

En ce moment je ne parle pas bien sûr des cercles de riches Grecs pour lesquels le *symposion* était un plaisir quotidien de la vie privée et qui, sans doute, problématisaient le

---

[47]O. Murray, ci-dessus, Ch. 1.
[48]Schmitt Pantel, *La cité au banquet* (ci-dessus, n. 1), 408ss.
[49]P. Veyne, *Le pain et le cirque* (Paris, 1976).

plaisir de façon différente, mais je m'interesse à la masse des habitants des cités. C'est le plaisir pris au banquet qui leur faisait réclamer des banquets aux évergètes, qui leur faisait voter des décrets louangeurs pour leurs hôtes d'un jour, qui les faisait reconnaître les vertus politiques des dispensateurs de festins. C'est admettre que le plaisir, un certain plaisir dont on peut mesurer les effets sur le corps social en terme de groupe, et non celui d'individus pour lequel les sources ne sont pas les mêmes et dont je ne saurais rien dire, est un des critères qu'utilise une société, aussi bien dans le choix d'individus la dirigeant, que dans le choix de pratiques dispendieuses ayant des conséquences sur l'économie des cités. Mais le plaisir de manger, de boire, de se réjouir collectivement, est à l'évidence, tel que je le décris, subordonné à une fonction sociale. Cela ne veut pas dire qu'il n'existe pas en soi, mais cela signifie qu'en tant qu'historienne je le saisis au moment, et seulement au moment, où il acquiert une efficacité dans la vie sociale, quand le peuple dit 'merci' à l'évergète par un décret honorifique, merci à Epaminondas pour le banquet qu'il a donné.[50]

Cela ne me semble pas du tout en contradiction avec ce qu'Oswyn Murray écrivait dans 'Sympotic history': '*Even if we admit the autonomy of pleasure, we must nevertheless accept that pleasures exist within a social context, and will be subject to manipulation and development for social ends*'.[51] Peut-être a-t-il un peu radicalisé son point de vue depuis en affirmant dès l'ouverture de ce colloque: '*Yet it seems to me clear that pleasures exist independently of any social function they may possess, and cannot be wholly reduced to such functions*',[52] et en précisant que l'on n'explique pas le but de l'art et de la littérature, qui est de donner du plaisir, en mettant en avant leur fonction sociale à différents niveaux. L'ambition d'Oswyn Murray est dès lors nettement théorique: '*But most of us wish for a history which is more than mere description; the problem is to develop a concept of causation which is appropriate to the arbitrary, and a theory of history which finds a place for such non-functional but apparently necessary human activities, as sport, literature and art*'.[53]

Pour ma part, et pour poursuivre la réflexion proposée par Oswyn Murray, je dirais plutôt ceci: la dimension de plaisir est une parmi d'autres, mais elle n'est ni la seule (c'est une évidence), ni l'explication en dernière instance, c'est à dire la plus importante, des manières de boire. Non qu'il faille lui préférer à tout prix une autre explication: sociale, économique, religieuse, mais parce qu'un type de société comme celui du monde grec antique ne permet pas de séparer nettement le plaisir de boire du sentiment d'être en accord avec les dieux, de l'appartenance à une communauté sociale, de repères politiques. Autrement dit il me paraît difficile, voire même inutile, de vouloir introduire une hiérarchie des explications en ce domaine, à moins que celle-ci n'ait été explicitée par les Grecs eux-même. Il ne s'agit pas d'un refus de prendre parti entre ceux qui subordonnent le plaisir aux forces traditionnelles de l'histoire et ceux qui considèrent le plaisir comme possédant une fonction autonome. Mais de déplacer la question, non dans une perspective générale des histoires du plaisir mais dans le cadre de la civilisation grecque, et non pas pour toutes les formes de plaisir mais pour les

---

[50]*IG* VII 2712.
[51]O. Murray, 'Sympotic history', dans Murray (ed.), *Sympotica* (ci-dessus, n. 36), 5.
[52]Murray, ci-dessus, p. 6.
[53]Ci-dessus, p. 7.

plaisirs de table. Je reviens ainsi à ce que j'esquissais plus haut: l'idée d'une société où 'la logique rituelle est la logique du tout'.

Faisons un détour par l'anthropologie. Serge Tcherkézoff remarquait récemment que 'l'étude de la religion et du rituel n'avait guère trouvé d'assises stables autour d'une méthodologie qui serait largement acceptée'[54] (contrairement à l'anthropologie de la parenté, des systèmes politiques et économiques, des techniques). Et que pour de nombreuses sociétés (dont la société africaine des Nyamwezi qu'il étudiait) le sacré n'est pas un domaine circonscrit que l'on déduirait du profane, mais un apport constant à la valeur, c'est à dire au tout de la société. Ceci est tout à fait conforme à ce que l'on souligne depuis longtemps à propos de la société grecque et ne paraîtra pas très neuf aux hellénistes. Mais les conséquences qu'en tire cet ethnologue sont intéressantes: il suggère d'appliquer à l'étude de telles sociétés une logique nouvelle d'analyse. C'est ce que je voudrais seulement retenir et proposer un regard qui insisterait plus sur la manière dont les différentes composantes de la vie grecque se structurent que sur leur antagonisme supposé.

Il apparaît clairement qu'il n'y a pas un seul, un unique modèle de la manière grecque de boire, mais des modèles qui se distinguent et se répondent, et que c'est dans leur articulation que naît la spécificité du monde grec. De même je dirais volontiers qu'il n'y a pas un système explicatif dominant qui permettrait de rendre compte de l'importance des manières de boire dans le monde antique, parce que cette société déborde et brouille constamment les grilles de lecture modernes et qu'elle oblige à tenir ensemble des éléments disparates d'explication. Aussi je ne prendrais pas pour un pis aller l'étape dans laquelle nous sommes qui consiste à écrire *des* histoires du plaisir (*histories of pleasure*), mais bien pour une chance. Car c'est leur articulation qui interesse au premier chef l'historien, quel que soit le nom dont il baptise le domaine de l'histoire qu'il entend étudier et qu'il espère comprendre.

* * *

'Intervento' by Antonio La Penna

Non intendo discutere, anche perché non ho la competenza necessaria, l'illustrazione che la Signora Schmitt ha data del simposio come rito sociale nella *polis* greca e dell'uso che vi si faceva del vino: la trattazione mi pare seriamente documentata, convincente, attraente. I miei dubbi riguardano l'interpretazione generale della società e della cultura greca arcaica in cui la trattazione della Signora Schmitt si colloca, che è poi l'interpretazione oggi prevalente nella scuola antropologica francese da cui la Signora proviene. Nella prima metà del nostro secolo in Germania e in Italia fu vivo l'interesse per la nascita dell'individuo nella cultura arcaica greca, nascita che segnava un distacco, se non una contrapposizione, rispetto all'organismo sociale e culturale della *polis*: in questa prospettiva furono interpretati, in parte, Archiloco, Saffo, Anacreonte. Mi rendo

---

[54]S. Tcherkézoff, 'Logique rituelle, logique du tout. L'exemple des jumeaux nyamwezi (Tanzanie)', *L'Homme* 100 (1986), 91-117.

conto che il rischio di interpretazioni modernizzanti non fu sempre evitato; probabilmente la visione complessiva era unilaterale. Ma probabilmente unilaterale è anche la visione che riconduce tutto all'organismo sociale della *polis*: sicuramente vi fu un uso rituale del simposio e del vino, ma vi sarà stato anche un uso più laico, più privato, più libero. Il piacere del vino in Anacreonte, come l'*eros* di Saffo, non rientrerà tutto in una vita collettiva regolata da riti. Io temo che la visione francese odierna della cultura greca risenta troppo della sociologia di Fustel de Coulanges e di Durkheim, in cui la vita sociale è completamente integrata nell'organismo della società; nella *polis* greca emerse anche un gusto individuale della vita, che sfuggì al tessuto dell'integrazione o lo lacerò. Credo che anche di questo gusto si debba tener conto per capire il piacere del vino, l'uso del vino come droga contro gli affanni; non è detto che Orazio leggesse i suoi lirici greci in modo molto più arbitrario del nostro. Insomma io temo che vi sia un abuso del concetto di integrazione sociale. La mia osservazione è consapevolmente generica; mi rendo conto che andrebbe sviluppata adeguatamente in altra sede.

7

Wine and Truth in the Greek *Symposion*

WOLFGANG RÖSLER

That there is a particular relationship between wine and truth is a central idea of the Greek *symposion*. The earliest evidence can be found in fragment 366 V. of Alcaeus. It is the beginning of a poem:

οἶνος, ὦ φίλε παῖ, καὶ ἀλάθεα.

We do not know how this song continued. Three hundred years later we find a reminiscence in Theocritus's *Carmen* 29, in which he starts the poem off with the same words. But it would be inconsiderate to deduce from this poem — the lament of an *eromenos* about being disappointed by his *erastes* — how Alcaeus proceeded. It is possible that Theocritus intended an intertextual joke, conceiving his poem as a contrast to Alcaeus's song. οἶνος καὶ ἀλάθεα — thus or in slightly different words — either became a proverb,[1] or was already one before. Both possibilities are plausible: either that Alcaeus himself is quoting an already existing proverb[2] or that the proverb owes its origin to this very poem.

But what does 'wine and truth' mean? Usually it is understood as a variant of οἶνος γὰρ ἀνθρώπω δίοπτρον ('wine is a means for seeing through a man'), which is another fragment of Alcaeus (333 V.).[3] This concept can also be found elsewhere. Wine shows the real thought (*noos*) of a man, as we can read in the *Corpus Theognideum* (500) and similarly in an elegy by Ion of Chios (fr. 26.12 W. = 1.12 G.-P.). Aeschylus refers to wine as *katoptron* ('mirror') of *noos* (fr. 393 R.), thus echoing Alcaeus's words. At the end of the first book of Plato's *Laws* (649A-650B) this concept is worked out in detail.[4] The starting-point of the argument is the psychic state caused by wine: in drinking wine one enjoys a feeling of boundless freedom and strength. This feeling can be compared to states like anger, love, craving for gain, and so forth. The feature they have in common is a certain kind of intoxication, which affects temperance and self-control. In order to

---

[1] In Alcaeus's fragment the word ἀλάθεα seems to be used as an adjective, not as a noun (Page 1955: 312); in such a manner it is interpreted by Theocritus (*Carmen* 29.2). The later, 'normalized' version is οἶνος καὶ ἀλήθεια. The evidence is collected by Gow (1952) on Theocritus 29.1 and Voigt (1971) *ad locum.*

[2] Cf. fr. 360 V.

[3] Snell (1961), 33-4 ('The truth he means is that wine unveils the real mind of companions in the *symposion*: it reveals who is the genuine and trustworthy friend'); Trumpf (1973), 141-2; Lissarrague (1987), 12-13 (= *idem* (1990), 8-9).

[4] Cf. Tecuşan (1990), 245ff.

get to know another's true character, one must drink with him. This kind of examination, Plato concludes, surpasses any other in its simplicity, security and promptness.

But is that all that is to be said about the relationship between wine and truth? I think that there is another aspect, and that it is this aspect in particular which came to the mind of a Greek when speaking of 'wine and truth'. Recent investigations have clarified the meaning of ἀληθές and ἀλήθεια in early Greek.[5] Three aspects have to be emphasized. First of all the words ἀληθές and ἀλήθεια refer to a person who speaks (that is, somebody *tells* the truth). Thus οἶνος καὶ ἀλάθεα cannot simply mean that the effect of drinking wine is that one person's character lies exposed to another's perception. In the second place, to tell the truth (in the sense of *alethes* and *aletheia*) implies consciousness and intentionality. οἶνος καὶ ἀλάθεα, then, cannot mean, either, that wine makes another person unveil his true nature unintentionally in a state of intoxication. And thirdly the element of completeness is important; it belongs to truth to be uttered completely. Thus, the meaning of *alethes* and *aletheia* combined with a *verbum dicendi* is to tell everything that you see, know or think, without exaggeration or invention. These three aspects have some impact on how οἶνος καὶ ἀλάθεα must be properly understood. It seems that this formula expresses the compulsion on the *sympotes* to expose his thoughts frankly and completely. Thus both fragments of Alcaeus would not be identical but complementary in regard to their content: οἶνος γὰρ ἀνθρώπω δίοπτρον refers to the other person, οἶνος καὶ ἀλάθεα is a maxim for one's own behaviour.

The following two quotations show that this is in fact the case. The first passage I have already mentioned. It is the beginning of Theocritus's *Carmen* 29. After quoting Alcaeus, the *erastes* goes on:

> κἄμμε χρὴ μεθύοντας ἀλάθεας ἔμμεναι.
> κἄγω μὲν τὰ φρένων ἐρέω κέατ' ἐν μύχῳ.   (Theocritus, *Carmen* 29.2-3)

Before I translate these verses I would like to add that as early as Homer's *Iliad* (xii. 433), *alethes* is applied not only to that which is said, but also to human beings. Corresponding to the meaning of the neuter just discussed, it denotes also a person who knows everything and forgets nothing about the subject under discussion.[6] It is this meaning Theocritus is using here: 'Now that we are drunk[7] we are not allowed to leave out anything. In my case, I will utter what is in my innermost heart'. The second passage is from Alcibiades's speech about Socrates in Plato's *Symposium*. Alcibiades tells how, when he was still a *pais*, he tried to make Socrates his *erastes*. 'Up to this moment', he says (217E), 'it is possible to tell this matter to everybody. But you would not hear from me what happened next', εἰ μὴ [...] τὸ λεγόμενον οἶνος [...] ἦν ἀληθής, 'if it were not that, according to the proverb, wine leaves out nothing'. In both cases the situation of the *symposion* is said to be responsible for the fact that everything has to be revealed: even our innermost feelings (Theocritus), and a very delicate incident (Alcibiades in Plato's

---

[5]Snell (1978); Heitsch (1979); Cole (1983).
[6]According to Snell (1978), 94: '*in einem bestimmten Wissens-Kontinuum nichts der* Lethe *anheimfallen zu lassen*'.
[7]Gow (1952) *ad locum*: '*μεθύοντας*: suggesting that a symposium is the occasion of the poem'.

Symposium). There is something of a compulsion (the *erastes* in Theocritus's poem says *chre*) to leave nothing out. Furthermore we can see that this feature of the *symposion* is taken for granted in both texts. This becomes clear from the fact that a short reference to the proverb is enough: Theocritus quotes it, Plato refers to it in a slightly altered form.

* * *

At this point we should stop for a moment and clarify how this evidence contributes to our understanding of the Greek *symposion*. A *symposion* was separated from everyday life. An external feature is that there had to be an especially equipped and furnished room. But the detachment was not only external. Washing one's hands and wearing a wreath are ritual acts, which indicate that a *symposion* was regarded as initiation, as transition to a different state of existence;[8] and consequently, it is from this conception that the *sympotai* were required to give up their mental disposition of everyday life, including dissembling, tactical considerations and inaccuracies. The *symposion* was the place of truth, and the means to this end was through drinking wine. A certain kind of dialectics was conceived: on the one hand, wine is λαθικάδης (Alcaeus fr. 346.3 V.); it makes man forget his troubles.[9] On the other hand, this illusion of a better reality leads to a higher state of consciousness which is characterized by just the opposite of forgetting, that is full understanding and unrestrained communication. In the *symposion* 'one speaks freely about everything' — it is exactly this term, *parrhesia* (which is composed of *pas* and *rhesis*), which is used in Greek to characterize the frankness released by drinking wine (Pl. *Leg.* i. 849B; Philochorus, below).

     With some hesitation I would like to draw a parallel with the encounter groups of present-day psychotherapy: these groups help the patient to reveal himself without inhibitions, and also to evaluate those aspects of his personality which he himself views negatively, and therefore tries to suppress in ordinary life. Group therapy aims to overcome this self-assessment. It aims at enabling the patient to feel: if I reveal myself completely, including all those aspects of my personality which I myself imagine as being problematical, not only will I not be rejected, but rather I will get thereby much closer to other people. Is this not the core of the logic of οἶνος καὶ ἀλάθεα, at least to a considerable extent? In the *Corpus Theognideum* (that is in sympotic poetry) this problem is clearly indicated:

> ἀλλ'εἴη τοιοῦτος ἐμοὶ φίλος, ὅς τὸν ἑταῖρον
>   γινώσκων ὀργὴν καὶ βαρὺν ὄντα φέρει
> ἀντὶ κασιγνήτου.

[8]Von der Mühll (1975), 489.
[9]This thought is extended by Pindar (fr. 124ab.5ff. Sn.-M.):
ἀνίκ᾽ἀνθρώπων καματώδεες οἴχονται μέριμναι
στηθέων ἔξω· πελάγει δ᾽ ἐν πολυχρύσοιο πλούτου
πάντες ἴσα νέομεν ψευδῆ πρὸς ἀκτάν.
ὃς μὲν ἀχρήμων, ἀφνεὸς τότε, τοὶ δ᾽ αὖ πλουτέοντες

    * * *

<> ἀέξονται φρένας ἀμπελίνοις τόξοις δαμέντες.
Cf. also Pl. *Leg.* i. 849A: πιόντα τὸν ἄνθρωπον αὐτὸν αὑτοῦ ποιεῖ (sc ὁ οἶνος) πρῶτον ἵλεων εὐθὺς μᾶλλον ἢ πρότερον.

Such a man should be my friend, who, when recognizing his comrade, can accept him even if he has a difficult personality, just as if he were his brother.

(*Corpus Theognideum* 97-9)

Obviously the *symposion* was the right place to encourage mutual acceptance. It seems significant that what could be fulfilled by a social institution in ancient Greece, nowadays is the responsibility of a psychotherapist. But it needs to be added that *aletheia* in the Greek *symposion* was not limited to the expression of personal problems; a *symposion* was more than the session of an encounter group. At this point Philochorus, an early Hellenistic historian, may be quoted (*FGrH* 328 F 170): οἱ πίνοντες οὐ μόνον ἑαυτοὺς ἐμφανίζουσιν οἵτινές εἰσιν, ἀλλὰ καὶ τῶν ἄλλων ἕκαστον ἀνακαλύπτουσι παρρησίαν ἄγοντες. ('People who are drinking wine do reveal not only their own inner being but also everything else, observing no restriction of speech'.) Philochorus obviously wants to express the idea that within the *symposion* truth and frankness in the most comprehensive sense of the words are required: the *sympotes* tells the truth about himself and about everything else.[10] This was the ideal of the Greek *symposion*, against which reality was measured, however far it might fall short. Alcaeus's outrage at the treachery of Pittacus, for example, can only be understood if one recalls the many sympotic occasions when the *hetairoi* had celebrated with Pittacus. The 'crafty fox', as Alcaeus characterized him (fr. 69.6 f. V.), had concealed his true intentions from his comrades. It was this behaviour, and not only his breaking of the oath, which was regarded as a grave offence.

* * *

On this basis we can now take into account two components of the Greek *symposion* which are connected to the relationship of wine and truth: the *symposion* as a place of education and as a place of poetry.

The *symposion* was a place of education since adolescents (*paides*) were present and used to attend the *sympotai*, and, listening to their conversation, they learnt the system of aristocratic norms and values, of which they were the inheritors.[11] This can be seen very clearly in the *Corpus Theognideum*. Theognis announces to Cyrnus that he is going to teach him what he himself as an adolescent learned from 'the good men', *hoi agathoi* (27-8). It is people like that whom Cyrnus should join for drinking and eating (33): καὶ μετὰ τοῖσιν πῖνε καὶ ἔσθιε. These words indicate that the *symposion*, along with the preceding meal, was an important place for instruction. The subsequent request (33-4) belongs also to sympotic practice: καὶ μετὰ τοῖσιν ἵζε ('take your seat among them'). We know that during the *symposion* the *paides* used to sit, not to recline.[12] Later in the *Corpus Theognideum* it becomes clear that the poet had this in mind as the basic idea of the collection as a whole: an adult (the poet) teaches an adolescent (Cyrnus) in the *symposion*. This can be inferred from the famous elegy σοὶ μὲν ἐγὼ πτέρ' ἔδωκα

---

[10]This meant to the other *sympotai* absolute discretion: μισέω μνάμονα συμπόταν (*PMG* 1002 P.).

[11]Bremmer (1990).

[12]Bremmer (1990), 139-40.

(237ff.) which has the character of an epilogue. The poet's witty remark at the end of the elegy ('I have made you immortal but you keep putting me off with poor excuses') calls up the fact that the paedagogic relationship between *pais* and *aner* merged with the homoerotic relationship between *eromenos* and *erastes*.[13] From this viewpoint it is significant that our proverb is directed to a *pais* on its first occurrence:

οἶνος, ὦ φίλε παῖ, καὶ ἀλάθεα.

Obviously instruction and truth are closely connected: one cannot teach lies. This is especially the case for the concept of ἀληθές and ἀλήθεια: communicating completely and honestly everything one knows and thinks. We can presume that for a Greek 'to tell the truth' and 'to instruct' were almost identical. Again, a glance at Theognis is illuminating: he shows a concern for completeness, so that his teaching may add up to a comprehensive canon of aristocratic virtues.[14] At the same time in Theognis the quest for trustworthiness (*pistis*) and the identity of thought and speech is a recurrent motive.

As the *Corpus Theognideum* shows, there is no clear borderline between the *symposion* as a place of instruction and the *symposion* as a place of poetry. Of course not all of the sympotic poetry was as explicitly instructive as that of Theognis. But, to start with a truism, all sympotic poems were utterances in the *symposion*: the maxim οἶνος καὶ ἀλάθεα basically held true for them as well. How does this affect sympotic poetry? I shall conclude with this question.

There was a natural tendency for sympotic conversation to proceed from immediate experiences to more general questions. 'To tell everything' implied to speak about gods and men, life and death. Thus, the *symposion* was not least of all the place of wisdom. It is significant that the Seven Sages were imagined to have met in the *symposion*[15] and that the philosophic *symposion* became a literary genre.[16] This is reflected in a remark by Horace (*c.* iii. 21.14ff.), who sees one of the effects of wine in its revealing the thoughts of wise men (*sapientium curas*). But wisdom belonged to the *symposion* already in the archaic period, and it is sympotic poetry which shows this. In sympotic poetry the element of reflection is characteristic. We do not find it only in texts addressed to a *pais* which have a decidedly didactic intention, like the elegies of Theognis. Let us have a look at the whole of Alcaeus's fragments. They abound in sententious expressions — like οἶνος καὶ ἀλάθεα and οἶνος ἀνθρώπω δίοπτρον. These expressions are a means of legitimation; they make what is said appear based on the order of the world. There are also many poems which bring present events into relation with the activities of the gods. This can be done by addressing the gods directly, with a hymn or prayer, as well as indirectly (like in fr. 70.11ff. V.). Again, myth and allegory need to be considered. The representation of reality on a different level is the result of reflection on the part of the author, as well as an appeal for reflection to the audience. Finally there is the type of the quasi-philosophic poem, which deals with an existential problem. An example is fr. 38a V., in which Alcaeus denies the hope of his friend Melanippus to return to a new life

[13]Patzer (1982); Bremmer (1990), 142ff.
[14]Patzer (1981).
[15]Snell (1971), 62ff.
[16]Martin (1931).

after death.[17] That is what conversations in the *symposion* were like! Taking all this together we find that sympotic poetry fully complies with the principle οἶνος καὶ ἀλάθεα. In order to characterize the poet's role I would like to adopt a term which Marcel Detienne created for a different context and with a different intention:[18] the poet in the *symposion* was '*maître de vérité*'.

He was '*maître de vérité*' in two respects. To explain this I shall return to the definition of *alethes* and *aletheia* I started with: to tell everything that you see, know or think, without exaggeration or invention. This definition implies that *alethes* and *aletheia* are opposed to both *lethe* (oblivion) and *pseudos* (untruth, lie). Thus there are, as we have seen, two responsibilities combined in sympotic *aletheia*. On the one hand, the *sympotes* was obliged to unreserved candour, he was not allowed to withhold anything for reasons of opportunism and considerateness. On the other hand, he was answerable for what he said; lies and exaggerations were severe offences against the rules of the *symposion*. This was, in a nutshell, the meaning of the proverb οἶνος καὶ ἀλάθεα. But what was the particular responsibility of the poet? What made him a '*maître de vérité*'? The answer follows from the early Greek conception of poetry. The essence of this conception is the poet's particular relation to truth, which results from his special relationship to the Muses, the daughters of Mnemosyne.[19] Here, too, both aspects of *aletheia* are implied: the poet's task is to preserve the tradition both faithfully and completely. This concept was not restricted to narrative poetry, but universal: the lyric poet Pindar makes the truth of poetry a central issue. It is especially this last aspect, based on an opposition to the *pseudos*, which played an important role in the poetological discussions of the Greeks. We repeatedly hear of the accusation that poets do not tell the truth, as in Xenophanes's famous criticism of Homer and Hesiod. Criticism of this kind shows that the demand for the poet to speak the truth was taken seriously. Aristotle was the first to free poetry from this restriction. It is Xenophanes again, who clearly shows that both concepts of *aletheia*, the poetic and the sympotic, are united in the *symposion*. In his elegy on the proper procedure of a *symposion* he prescribes:

οὔ τι μάχας διέπειν Τιτήνων οὐδὲ Γιγάντων
οὐδὲ < > Κενταύρων, πλάσμα<τα> τῶν προτέρων

not to dwell on the battles of the Titans, Giants, and Centaurs, which are inventions of the past.
(Xenophanes fr. 1 D.-K.= W.= G.-P., 21-2)

These are the words of a '*maître de vérité*' in the *symposion*, who was at the same time *sympotes* and poet.[20]

---

[17] Rösler (1980a), 264ff.
[18] Detienne (1979).
[19] Rösler (1980b); Puelma (1989).
[20] I am grateful to Antje Märtin (Konstanz) for her translation.

REFERENCES

Bremmer, J.N. (1990) Adolescents, symposion, and pederasty, in O. Murray (ed.), *Sympotica: a Symposium on the* Symposion: 135-48. Oxford.

Cole, Th. (1983) Archaic Truth. *QUCC* ns 13: 7-28.

Detienne, M. (1979) *Les maîtres de vérité dans la Grèce archaïque*, third edition. Paris.

Gow, A.S.F. (1952) *Theocritus*, second edition. Cambridge.

Heitsch, E. (1979) Der Ort der Wahrheit. Aus der Frühgeschichte des Wahrheitsbegriffs, in E. Heitsch, *Parmenides und die Anfänge der Erkenntniskritik und Logik*: 33-69. Donauwörth.

Lissarrague, F. (1987) *Un flot d'images: une esthétique du banquet grec*. Paris.

Lissarrague, F. (1990) *The Aesthetics of the Greek Banquet: Images of Wine and Ritual* (English translation of Lissarrague 1987). Princeton.

Martin, J. (1931) *Symposion*. Paderborn.

Page, D. (1955) *Sappho and Alcaeus*. Oxford.

Patzer, H. (1981) Der archaische Areté-Kanon im Corpus Theognideum, in G. Kurz, D. Müller and W. Nicolai (eds), *Gnomosyne. Festschrift für Walter Marg zum 70. Geburtstag*: 197-226. Munich.

Patzer, H. (1982) *Die Griechische Knabenliebe*. Wiesbaden.

Puelma, M. (1989) Der Dichter und die Wahrheit in der griechischen Poetik von Homer bis Aristoteles. *MH* 46: 65-100.

Rösler, W. (1980a) *Dichter und Gruppe*. Munich.

Rösler, W. (1980b) Die Entdeckung der Fiktionalität in der Antike. *Poetica* 12: 283-319.

Snell, B. (1961) *Poetry and Society*. Bloomington.

Snell, B. (1971) *Leben und Meinungen der Sieben Weisen*, fourth edition. Munich.

Snell, B. (1978) Die Entwicklung des Wahrheitsbegriffs bei den Griechen, in B. Snell, *Der Weg zum Denken und zur Wahrheit*: 91-104. Göttingen.

Tecuşan, M. (1990) *Logos Sympotikos*: patterns of the irrational in philosophical drinking: Plato outside the *symposium*, in O. Murray (ed.), *Sympotica: a Symposium on the* Symposion: 238-60. Oxford.

Trumpf, J. (1973) Über das Trinken in der Poesie des Alkaios. *ZPE* 12: 139-60.

Voigt, E.-M. (1971) *Sappho et Alcaeus*. Amsterdam.

Von der Mühll, P. (1975) Das griechische Symposion, in P. Von der Mühll, *Ausgewählte Kleine Schriften*: 483-505. Basel.

8

Wine in Old Comedy

E.L. BOWIE

The poets of Attic Old Comedy present wine as a central constituent of the good life and an important catalyst of well-being, provided that it is correctly used. This is hardly surprising in a form of entertainment which, from the early and mid fifth century respectively, had played a large and formal part in the Great Dionysia and the Lenaia, two of the Athenians' major festivals in honour of Dionysus. These festivals were themselves characterized by both ceremonial and casual consumption of wine. This is made clear by other evidence,[1] even if we do not wholly accept the report of Philochorus[2] that in the old days Athenian audiences had already consumed food and drink by the time they reached the theatre and continued to do so profusely throughout performances. However some features of the presentation of wine are, if not surprising, at least remarkable, and cohere with many other elements of Old Comedy which show that, like tragedy, it had detached itself almost wholly from its religious context. It is striking, for example, how small a part is played by scenes in which wine is consumed on stage in a way that can be seen as ritual. This in turn will no doubt have made scenes in which wine was in any way ritually consumed all the more effective theatrically and, if I may so express it, theorically, that is, in relation to the overall themes of the festival. But that is a by-product and not a reason for the paucity of such scenes, which is perhaps partly to be sought in the dramatists' wish to present scenes that must be perceived as drama and that could not be mistaken for ritual and real life.

Of course the poet's ability to portray drinking by characters played by actors was constricted by the genre's limitation on their number (whether that limitation was formal or practical).[3] A *symposion* of typical size could not be played out on the stage by speaking characters. Accordingly *symposia* in Old Comedy involving only characters

---

[1]Cf. A.W. Pickard-Cambridge, *Dramatic Festivals of Athens*, revised by J. Gould and D.M. Lewis (Oxford, 1968), 30-4, on the possibility that *stamnoi* with maenadic scenes and then (*c.* 440 BC) scenes with stately ladies consecrating wine may be linked with the Lenaia. For an instance of drunken behaviour during the πομπή Dem. 19 (*In Midian*) § 180.

[2]*FGrH* 328 F 171 (= Ath. xi. 464E-F): λέγει δὲ περὶ τούτων ὁ Φιλόχορος οὑτωσί, Ἀθηναῖοι τοῖς Διονυσιακοῖς ἀγῶσι τὸ μὲν πρῶτον ἠριστηκότες καὶ πεπωκότες ἐβάδιζον ἐπὶ τὴν θέαν καὶ ἐστεφανωμένοι ἐθεώρουν, παρὰ δὲ τὸν ἀγῶνα πάντα οἶνος αὐτοῖς ᾠνοχοεῖτο καὶ τραγήματα παρεφέρετο, καὶ τοῖς χοροῖς εἰσιοῦσιν ἐνέχεον πίνειν, καὶ διηγωνισμένοις ὅτ' ἐξεπορεύοντο ἐνέχεον πάλιν· Cf. Ar. fr. 513K.-A. (= 496Kock, from *Tagenistae*).

[3]Cf. Pickard-Cambridge, *Dramatic Festivals of Athens* (above, n. 1), 136, 149-53.

played by actors must either be narrated, whether in prospect or in retrospect, or take an unusual form.

The narrated *symposion* is best exemplified by *Wasps* (*Vespae*). First Bdelycleon's re-education of Philocleon sets out the normal sympotic pattern; then Philocleon's obtuse perversions anticipate what is later going to happen — off-stage.[4] Finally the disastrous events that actually took place at the party are reported by a slave and corroborated by Philocleon's reappearance on stage, blind-drunk, with a torch in one hand and a naked *auletris* in the other. The audience does not actually see Philocleon drinking here or in any other part of the play.

A distorted form of the *symposion* may plausibly be seen in the concluding scenes of some other plays of Aristophanes, where the central character, for whom Whitman's term 'comic hero' is not always appropriate, is launched upon climactic self-indulgence in wine, food and sex. This is a type of scene where the half-imaginary world of the play does overlap with the half-real world of the festival. No doubt many Athenian males in the audience recalled or hoped for some approximation to this ideal in the course of their own private celebrations during the festival.[5] But this sort of drinking is private rather than public and nearer to the secular than to the religious. That is so even if it can be overlaid with elements drawn from religious ritual, as it is in *Acharnians* where Dicaeopolis's competition with Lamachus draws on the ritual not of the Lenaia or Dionysia but of the Anthesteria. Precisely because it involves one single character who drinks, this scene is not sympotic in the normal sense. Its combination of delights, however, can readily be associated with those of the *symposion*, since in the real world that will have been for many male Athenians one of the most likely contexts in which they might drink and engage in casual sex with *auletrides*. And Aristophanes does ask his audience to see it as a sort of *symposion* when he has Dicaeopolis refer to competition with his *sympotai* (1135) and commend his situation with the words συμποτικὰ τὰ πράγματα (1142). For Aristophanes, of course, it was both necessary and expedient that this should be a one-man *symposion* — necessary because he could not use other actors in sufficient number to create a *symposion*, expedient because it emphasized the unique triumph of his central character.

There were indeed other, non-sympotic forms of drinking which actors might without difficulty portray. But here too the instances — usually representations of drinking in a bad light, as some I later consider show — are fewer than we might expect. The number of drunkards in our texts is remarkably small given that *methuontas* are clearly seen as an important feature of Old Comedy by the writer of the *de comoedia* (who credits Crates with their introduction).[6]

---

[4]Ar. *Vesp.* 1122-264, on which see M. Vetta, 'Un capitolo di storia di poesia simposiale (Per l'esegesi di Aristofane, "Vespe" 1222-1248)', in M. Vetta (ed.), *Poesia e simposio nella Grecia antica* (Rome/Bari, 1983). Narrative of sympotic scenes is also found in Ar. fr. 482K.-A. (= 466Kock) from the *Proagon* of 422, and fr. 444K.-A. (= 430Kock) from the *Pelargoi* (*c.* 400).

[5]Note the interest in conducting an adulterous affair foisted by the chorus on members of the audience of *Birds* (*Av.* 793-6).

[6]Anon. *de comoedia* (*Prolegomena de comoedia* iii) p. 8 = *PCG* IV Crates, *testimonium* 2a: πρῶτος μεθύοντας ἐν κωμῳδίᾳ προήγαγεν. The presence in Old Comedy of drunks may perhaps be corroborated by the vase cited in n. 12 below, unless, of course, the conjecture made there about the identity of the φιλοπότης is correct.

The few cases of religious ritual drinking that might have involved actors seem also to have been kept off-stage. The celebration of the rural Dionysia by Dicaeopolis at *Acharnians* 241-79 will in due course involve ritual drinking, but does not do so in the part of the ritual represented to the audience. We have fragments of Aristophanes's *Telmessians* relating to a ritual banquet, but that banquet was narrated, not played out on stage.[7] The one ritual use of wine that is not uncommon in stage action is for libation — for example at *Peace* 424-38. But there is no indication that this or other libations were followed by drinking, far less finishing the cup without taking breath (*amustin*) as urged in a fragment of Cratinus.[8]

There was more scope for ritual drinking by a chorus, whether in a *symposion* or in a more specifically religious ritual. Twenty-four would have been an unusually large number of participants for an Attic *symposion*, but not perhaps impossible, and certainly within the known limits for some sorts of ritual banqueting.[9] A poet determined to represent a characteristic Attic *symposion* might have done so by dividing his *choreutai* into two groups of twelve, as was often done for other dramatic ends. But as far as I know no such scene was demonstrably created in Old Comedy. We have no title *Sympotai* or *Symposiastai*. It may be that the accident of survival or the lack of such scenes' dramatic possibilities should be considered as explanations. We do, however, know of two plays entitled *Comastai*, by Ameipsias and Phrynichus. These may have involved choral drinking, but no fragment establishes this. The same is true of Pherecrates's *Deserters* (*Automoloi*), but in the case of *Deserters* any drinking there may have been is unlikely to have been ritual (see further below, note 14).

One comedy whose title suggests that it might have involved ritual drinking of a more religious sort is Aristophanes's first play, *Fellow banqueters* (*Daitales*). The chorus seems to have consisted in *thiasotai* of a cult of Heracles: but on our limited evidence they seem only to have come into the orchestra as a chorus after they had (supposedly) had their ritual *deipnon* in the precinct of Heracles.[10] A rather different sort of ritual drinking might also have taken place in one or more of the several plays entitled *Satyrs* (*Satyroi*) — by Ecphantides, Cratinus, Phrynichus and perhaps Callias — but it is no more than a presumption that satyrs will have engaged in one of their two favourite activities (the other is of course sex).[11] When we turn, however, to comic representations of women engaged in cult, the picture is unambiguous: audiences of comedy were amused by the presentation of womens' cults as an excuse for heavy drinking — so, for example, Aristophanes in *Women at the Thesmophoria* (*Thesmophoriazusae*) (especially 630-2),

---

[7] Ar. fr. 545-6K.-A.

[8] Cratinus 322K.-A. (= 291Kock), cf. 132K.-A. (= 124Kock), from his *Nomoi*, a reference to libations from a golden cup to snakes. By contrast Strepsiades denies that he will engage in libations at *Nub.* 426.

[9] Cf. B. Bergquist, 'Sympotic space: a functional aspect of Greek dining-rooms', in O. Murray (ed.), *Sympotica: a Symposium on the Symposion* (Oxford, 1990), 38-65.

[10] See A.C. Cassio, *Aristofane. I Banchettanti* (Pisa, 1977), 21-3 and his *testimonium* h = K.-A. test. iii (*ad finem*).

[11] For a *Satyrs* in 437 BC, probably by Callias, see *PCG* IV p. 38 *test* 4; by Cratinus in 424 BC (when it was second to *Knights*) *Hypothesis to Knights* A5; by Ecphantides, see *PCG* V Ecphantides frs 1 and 2; and by Phrynichus *PCG* VII Phrynichus *test.* 1 = *Suda* Φ 763.

in the oath scene of *Lysistrata* (194ff.), and in his lost *Women at the festival of Adonis* (*Adoniazousai*) and *Women in festival huts* (*Skenas katalambanousai*). The same is likely for the *Bacchants* of Diocles and Lysippus.

This offers a convenient transition to a different approach. I return later to sympotic aspects of drinking, but now I wish to explore how the comic perception of wine and of drinking differs according to the sex, age and class of the drinker. It will emerge that drinking by zeugite males in company is usually perceived as good; that drinking by males of a higher or lower class, or by a zeugite solo (*en Suisse*) can often be seen as bad; that drinking by females is invariably regarded as bad; and the older the women are the worse it is regarded.

Part of the rationale of these perceptions is that sympotic drinking is kept orderly by the rules of the *symposion* (when these are contravened, as by Philocleon in *Wasps*, even sympotic drinking is no longer laudable), whereas the other types of drinking are not moderated by that or by any other principle of order. But this is only a partial explanation. Upper-class Athenians, *chrestoi*, are branded with a penchant for drinking in the opening dialogue between the slaves in *Wasps* 77-80 — they are *philopotai* — though the categorization of this as a disease (*nosos*) should not be pressed, since it is required by the poet's intention of presenting Philocleon's addiction to jury-service as a disease. It may be doubted whether there was indeed a greater fondness for drink among the upper classes, but no doubt their *symposia* were more lavish, and the zeugites who constituted the majority of the spectators in the theatre could interpret more generous provision of wine as reflecting a stronger attachment to its consumption. Moreover the term *philopotes* seems not to involve very serious criticism. A character in Eupolis's *Cities* used it of Cimon — καλὸς μὲν οὐκ ἦν, φιλοπότης δὲ κἀμελής (fr. 221K.-A. = 208Kock) — suggesting an indulgent tut-tutting rather than identification of a grave moral weakness. The same mixture of the positive and negative may be there in its use on an Apulian vase of *c.* 380-360 BC to label an old man in a comedy who is tottering home from a party carrying a torch and wine vessel.[12] There is criticism, not untinged with envy, of the *symposia* at which the depraved young man in *Fellow banqueters* drank special wine (from Chios) out of imported Laconian vessels and sang rude songs.[13] But this behaviour cannot have been seen as wholly alien, since singing was a part of most *symposia*, and, as we shall see, the audience was reckoned to be familiar with the features of Chian and other imported wines. More alien, perhaps, were the bibulous habits with which *Deserters* (*Automoloi*) as a class are charged[14] — or at least they could be perceived as the behaviour of 'the other' by those zeugites who dutifully performed their hoplite service.

---

[12]See A. Greifenhagen, 'Philopotes', *Gymnasium* 82 (1975), 26-32. Like scholars hitherto Greifenhagen took the figure to be a Phlyax, but as O. Taplin argues in *Comic Angels* (Oxford, 1993), the comic scenes on South Italian vases of the fourth century — before the composition of Phlyax plays is attested — more probably refer to Attic Old Comedy. We should therefore consider whether the old man on this vase is actually 'Cratinus' in his *Pytine* (see below, text at nn. 40-2).

[13]Ar. fr. 225K.-A. (= 216Kock):

ἀλλ' οὐ γὰρ ἔμαθε ταῦτ' ἐμοῦ πέμποντος, ἀλλὰ μᾶλλον
πίνειν, ἔπειτ' ᾁδειν κακῶς, Συρακοσίων τράπεζαν,
Συβαρίτιδάς τ' εὐωχίας καὶ Χῖον ἐκ Λακαινᾶν.

On Chian, see below, n. 34.

[14]Pherecrates 34K.-A. = 29Kock, see below, n. 28.

Chrestoi and *automoloi* are the only groups of male citizens lambasted as *philopotai*. It is easier to find individual Athenians who are represented as too fond of drink, sometimes with the hint that their drinking was solitary. Alongside Cimon, mentioned above, they include a potter Chaerestratos, suggested by Phrynichus in his *Comasts* (fr. 15K.-A. = 15Kock) as capable (were he able to pot all day at home) of knocking back 100 *kantharoi* of wine daily. Among Aristophanes's dramatic characters Philocleon in his great defence of his lifestyle in the *agon* claims that if his son does not pour him wine he drinks direct from his *onos* (616-7), hinting at solitary and excessive drinking, and preparing the audience for his excesses later in the play.

By contrast citizen women are repeatedly presented as inveterate tipplers and, when given the chance, as consuming wine in excessive quantities or in an unacceptably strong mixture. This perception is of course part of a wider web of fear and suspicion that was interwoven with other emotions in Athenian citizens' attitudes to their womenfolk.[15] It is clearest in *Women at the Thesmophoria*, where one of the charges that the women level against Euripides is that he has portrayed women as bibulous, a charge to which they object not because it is false but because it is true (*Thesm.* 689ff.). This is not just a joke devised to help along the plot, but a comic stereotype well-documented elsewhere in Aristophanes and other poets of Old Comedy. In Aristophanes we find it in *Lysistrata* (200ff.), produced, like *Women at the Thesmophoria*, in 411 BC. Again in *Women in festival huts*, in which women appear to have contested with men the occupation of *skenai* provided for a festival, a woman complains about the loss or breakage of her *lekuthos*, its capacity comically exaggerated to seven *kotylai*.[16] Finally at the end of Aristophanes's career, in his *Cocalos*, produced at the Dionysia of 388/7 BC, there was a sung description of an orgy in which 'other and somewhat more elderly old women poured out a vessel full of red Thasian wine into their bodies without ceremony, serving themselves with large *kotylai*, compelled by lust for the unmixed red wine'.[17]

Other comic poets present the same caricature. It was already there in a play in which Cratinus seems to have parodied the *Stheneboea* of Euripides: the heroine drank wine either undiluted or mixed with an equal proportion of water, calling on Bellerophon

---

[15]The classic treatment remains that of J. Gould, 'Law, custom and myth: aspects of the social position of women in classical Athens', *JHS* 100 (1980), 43-59. For a good recent discussion with the last decade's bibliography see J.J. Winkler, *The Constraints of Desire* (London-New York, 1990).

[16]Ar. fr. 487K.-A. (= 472Kock): a κοτύλη contained six of the usual measure, κύαθοι.

[17]Fr. 364K.-A. (= 350Kock): the text of Ath. xi. 478D is differently restored by different editors, and the following is Hermann's:

$$...\check{\alpha}λλαι <δ'>$$

ὑποπρεσβύτεραι γρᾶες ἀκράτου
Θασίου μέλανος μεστὸν κέραμον
ταμιευόμεναι κοτύλαις μεγάλαις
ἐνέχεον, < ὑπ'> ἔρωτι βιαζόμεναι
  σφέτερον δέμας οὐδένα κόσμον.

In fr. 365K.-A. from the same play (= 351Kock) a character narrates how vomiting had been precipitated by the consumption of unmixed wine, but it is not certain that the speaker is one of these old dames. For the charge that women exploited ritual occasions to get drunk cf. *Lys.* 194ff., *Thesm. passim*, *Eccl.* 132ff.

as she played *kottabos*.[18] In his *Tyranny*, exploiting the theme of a state run by women, Pherecrates had a male speaker (probably the *koruphaios*) complain that for men the women had had made flat drinking vessels that held nothing, for themselves deep cups, like wine-ships, so that they could drink as much wine as they could unmonitored. 'Then when we accuse them of drinking up the wine they turn nasty and swear they have only drunk one cup — but that one outdoes a thousand of our vessels'.[19]

Sometimes the charge is directed more specifically against old women. An early use of drunken old women on the comic stage is credited to Phrynichus by Aristophanes in the passage of the revised *Clouds* where he accuses Eupolis of having plagiarized his *Knights* in *Maricas*.[20] But once introduced the caricature was assured of a long stage existence.[21] Thus in Pherecrates's *Corianno* the eponymous heroine's old nurse Glyce comes thirsty from her bath, responds eagerly to the offer of a drink, but vehemently prohibits use of a small *kotyliske*: it has made her ill, the bigger one must be used. In another fragment that seems to follow closely on, Glyce is upset by the mixture:

'Has he poured you too watery a mixture?'
'No, it's nothing but water'
[to the wine pourer] 'What have you done? What proportions did you pour, you villain?'
'Two of water, gran'
'And of wine?'

Two of water to three of wine was the accepted strength, so when the pourer replies 'four of wine' we know that he had indeed meant to give Glyce a stronger mixture. But she is outraged, and would have liked something much stronger:

'Go to hell. You ought to be a butler to frogs'.[22]

[18]Cratinus 299K.-A. (= 273Kock):
πιεῖν δὲ θάνατος οἶνον ἢν ὕδωρ ἐπῇ.
ἀλλ' ἴσον ἴσῳ μάλιστ' ἀκράτου δύο χοᾶς
πίνουσ'ἀπ' ἀγκύλης ἐπονομάζουσα< >
ἵησι λάταγας τῷ Κορινθίῳ πέει.
[19]Pherecrates fr. 152K.-A. (= 143Kock). Cf. fr. 207 (= 192Kock) where Pherecrates is said to have slandered women in connection with taking a Chian cup down from its peg.
[20]Ar. *Nub.* 553-6:
Εὔπολις μὲν τὸν Μαρικᾶν πρώτιστος παρείλκυσεν
ἐκτρέψας τοὺς ἡμετέρους Ἱππέας κακὸς κακῶς
προσθεὶς αὐτῷ γραῦν μεθύσην τοῦ κόρδακος οὕνεχ', ἣν
Φρύνιχος πάλαι πεπόηχ', ἣν τὸ κῆτος ἤσθιεν.
Cf. Phrynichus 77K.-A. (= 71Kock), and for an illustration of an old and ugly woman dancing vigorously and (one would guess) drunkenly, A.D. Trendall and T.B.L. Webster, *Monuments Illustrating Greek Drama* (London, 1971), 129 no. iv 12.
[21]The charge is not made in early iambic poetry. Neoboule is accused of many things, but not drink, even when old, unless 42W relates to her. Hipponax's Arete drinks copiously, but no more than her sexual partner, cf. frs 13-14W; Semonides's long list of charges against women in fr. 7W omits tippling.
[22]Pherecrates frs 75K.-A. (= 69Kock) and 76K.-A. (= 70Kock):
...(A.) ἄποτος, ὦ Γλύκη.
(Γλ.) ὑδαρῆ 'νέχεέν σοι; (A.) παντάπασι μὲν οὖν ὕδωρ.
(Γλ.) τί ἠργάσω; πῶς ὦ κατάρατε <δ'> ἐνέχεας;
(B.) δύ' ὕδατος, ὦ μάμμη. (Γλ.) τί δ' οἴνου; (B.) τέτταρας.
(Γλ.) ἔρρ' ἐς κόρακας. βατράχοισιν οἰνοχοεῖν σ' ἔδει...
It may also have been in his *Corianno* that Pherecrates had a woman described as 'a he-goatess, drunkard and witch', ἀνδροκάπραινα καὶ μεθύση καὶ φαρμακίς, fr. 186K.-A. (= 17 Dem.). For women's predilection for neat wine cf. Ar. *Eccl.* 153-5, 1123-4; *Lys.* 197, 200-1.

The *Corianno* scene was clearly made all the funnier by Glyce's age. Likewise in Philyllius's *Auge* the drinking (unqualified) of men and boys is contrasted with the pleasure of old women in large flagons of wine.[23]

Another improper use of wine is illustrated by the behaviour of slaves. The line that divides good and bad drinking can be seen in Aristophanes's *Knights*. To escape from their predicament Nicias suggests death by drinking bull's blood, but Demosthenes proposes drinking unmixed wine, as in honour of the *agathos daimon*, and praises wine's capacity to nurture human fantasy — a case not of *in vino vera* but of *in vino vana*. In broad daylight he reclines and gets Nicias to steal wine from the house of Demos, where the reviled Paphlagonian, standing for Cleon, is snoring on his back already drunk. Demosthenes has Nicias pour him a large libation, and despite Nicias's urging him to pour it as a libation to the *agathos daimon* he gulps it down himself: then a plan does indeed strike him, that of stealing the Paphlagonian's oracles.[24]

Although there are some elements in this scene that touch on real or comic images of the politicians, such as Nicias's piety and inclination to sobriety, the charge of proclivity to drink is not elsewhere brought against Demosthenes. The similar scene in *Wasps* (9ff.) where one of the two slaves may have been drinking suggests that in *Knights* this penchant for unmixed wine relates to masters' perceptions of their house-slaves. However in the case of Cleon/the Paphlagonian the charge is repeated later and associated with gluttony: the Paphlagonian ridicules the sausage-seller for water-drinking, and he in return asks what the Paphlagonian has done for the city by drinking — the Paphlagonian replies that he will gulp down hot tunny, drink a *chous* of unmixed wine and then abuse the generals at Pylos.[25] The link with gluttony is important: Cleon's consumption of unmixed wine is an aspect of his excessive consumption in general, and he is not being picked on simply as *philopotes*. But his declaration that he will drink unmixed wine classes his use of wine with that of Demosthenes (in his dramatic role as a slave) and apart from that of respectable citizens.

How then do respectable citizens take their wine? The formal answer 'at the right time and in due quantity' can be given fairly precise content. Drinking during the day is reprehensible. It should happen after a *deipnon*, which in turn belongs at the end of the day, when men's shadows are seven or ten feet long.[26] Indeed the midday self-indulgence that brings on sleep can be dismissed as a shortcut to the underworld.[27] Even

[23]Philyllius fr. 5K.-A. (= 5Kock):
πάντα γὰρ ἦν
μέστ᾿ ἀνδρῶν <καὶ> μειρακίων
πινόντων· ὁμοῦ † δ᾿ ἄλλων
γραιδίων μεγάλαισιν οἴ-
    νου χαίροντα λεπασταῖς.
[24]Ar. *Eq.* 80-125.
[25]Ar. *Eq.* 349-58, esp. 353-5:
ἐμοὶ γὰρ ἀντέθηκας ἀνθρώπων τίν'; ὅστις εὐθὺς
θύννεια θερμὰ καταφαγών, κᾷτ᾿ ἐπιπιὼν ἀκράτου
οἴνου χοᾶ καταλβάσω τοὺς ἐν Πύλῳ στρατηγούς.
For a drunken (female) slave cf. *Pax* 535.
[26]Ar. *Eccl.* 651, fr. 695K.-A. (= 675Kock).
[27]Pherecrates 85K.-A. (= 80Kock) from Κραπάταλοι with the interpretation of Kock (cited by Kassel and Austin in *PCG*).

worse is the behaviour described in Pherecrates's *Deserters* — presumably but not certainly referring to the deserters — drinking and getting drunk before the agora is full. Its discreditable image is confirmed by Eupolis, who has Alcibiades claim drinking early in the day as his invention, along with the practice of calling for a chamber-pot in mid drinking-bout.[28]

For drinkers at the *symposion* after a *deipnon* the sympotic order will allow drinking (*pinein*) that does not lead to getting drunk (*methuein*). Wine will be consumed along with τραγήματα which will reduce its intoxicating effect and enhance the pleasure of drinking.[29] It will be served by waiters who have been trained, as in Pherecrates's *Trainer of slaves* (*Doulodidaskalos*), to pour wine through a strainer into a clean *kylix*,[30] who add water in the proportions prescribed by the symposiarch, and who may include *oinopotai* whose specific task is to monitor these proportions.[31] Among the games played at *symposia* is one involving wine itself, *kottabos*, which can almost be used as a metaphor for drinking.[32] Drinking can also lead to telling riddles, *muthoi* and singing, a tradition given less prominence in comic drama than in archaic song, and mocked in *Banqueters* (*Daitales*) and by Pheidippides in *Clouds*.[33]

Drink can also lead on to sex. I shall later look more closely at the link set up between wine and sex in *Acharnians*, where it is integral to the purpose of the play. But the link is clear elsewhere too. A fragment of Aristophanes calls wine 'the milk of Aphrodite', and in the second *Women at the Thesmophoria* a character said that (she?) would not allow (?her man) to drink Pramnian or Chian or Thasian or Peparethian wine, 'or any other that will rouse the battering-ram'.[34]

This passage shows that just as the Attic theatre audience could be relied upon to distinguish appropriate and inappropriate proportions, so too it was expected to have some, albeit modest level of connoisseurship. The prized wines were all imported.[35]

---

[28]Pherecrates 34K.-A. (= 29Kock), Eupolis 385K.-A. (= 351Kock).

[29]Cf. Ar. *Eccl.* 306, and the mini-*symposion* set up in Pherecrates's *Corianno*, fr. 73K.-A. (= 67Kock), though here the elegant imitation is deflated by the refusal of beans as bad for the breath. For the distinction between the potentially good activity πίνειν and the bad μεθύειν cf. Ar. frs 225K.-A. (= 216Kock) from *Banqueters* (Δαιταλῆς) where πίνειν accompanied by song is part of traditional education, and 135K.-A. from *Old Age* (Γῆρας), where a man μεθύων vomits by the ἀρχηγέται; *Eq.* 1400, where the Paphlagonian μεθύων ταῖς πόρναισι λοιδορήσεται. But πίνειν can be used of excessive drinking, as by Philocleon in his parodic *schetliasmos* at *Vesp.* 1253-5.

[30]Pherecrates fr. 45K.-A. (= 41Kock).

[31]Cf. Eupolis fr. 219 (= 205Kock) from *Cities* (Πόλεις). On the proportions themselves cf. Eupolis 6K.-A. (= 8Kock), Ameipsias 4K, Hermippus 24K.-A. (= 25Kock) (all five of water and two of wine); Diocles 7K.-A. (= 6Kock) (four and two); Ar. *Eq.* 1187-8 (with van Leeuwen's note) and Cratinus 195K.-A. (= 183Kock) (three and two) and 196K.-A. (= 184Kock) (equal proportions).

[32]Ar. fr. 960K.-A. (= *adespota* 586Kock). Cf. Cratinus fr. 124K.-A. (= 116Kock) from his *Nemesis*, τὸν δὲ κόττοβον προθέντας συμποτικοῖσι νόμοις, and fr. 299K.-A. (= 273Kock) of Stheneboea's drinking (cf. above, n. 18); Hermippus fr. 48K.-A. (= 47Kock).

[33]Ar. Δαιταλῆς, fr. 225K.-A. (= 216Kock); *Nub.* 1354-72.

[34]Ar. fr. 613K.-A. (= 596Kock):
ἡδύς γε πίνειν οἶνος, 'Αφροδίτης γάλα;
334K.-A. (= 317Kock):
οἶνον δὲ πίνειν οὐκ ἐάσω Πράμνιον,
οὐ Χῖον, οὐχὶ Θάσιον, οὐ Πεπαρήθιον,
οὐδ' ἄλλον ὅστις ἐπεγείρει τὸν ἔμβολον.

[35]Ar. fr. 435K.-A. (= 423Kock) from *Merchant vessels* ('Ολκάδες).

One of Philyllius's characters promised wines that were not to cause hangovers —
Lesbian, Chian, Thasian, Biblian (from Thrace) and Mendaean.[36] Phrynichus in his
Grass-cutters (Poastriai) compared Sophocles to wine that was 'not bland or diluted, but
Pramnian'.[37] Athenaeus quotes Aristophanes (meaning a character in Aristophanes) as
saying that 'the Athenian people didn't like poets who were tough and unyielding nor
Pramnian wines which contracted your eyebrows and stomach, but flowery wine and
mature nectar-drop'.[38] Only Dionysus, so far as we know, may perhaps have demanded
wine from that island linked to him in the Ariadne myth, Naxos.[39]

This last comparison may serve to introduce my two final themes, both of which
concern the symbolic use of wine, and both of which corroborate the importance of
wine as an element in the good life.

First I consider the close relation portrayed as linking the drinking of wine and the
production of comic poetry. Archilochus (fr. 120W) had already proclaimed a link
between the consumption of wine and the composition of another form of poetry
specially connected with Dionysus, the dithyramb. But it was left to Cratinus, in a
magnificent fantasy of self-caricature, to create a dramatic character, *Methe*,
(Drunkenness) and have her contest control of the poet himself with another
personification, *Komodia* (Comedy). No wonder that the play, *Wine-flask (Pytine)*, won first
prize in the Dionysia of 424/3. Cratinus's relationship with Comedy is presented as prior
to that with Drunkenness — she had been his wife, abandoned by him when he took up
with Drunkenness. But the allegory is complex. Cratinus's attraction to drink is
particularized in his weakness for individual wines, represented, since *oinos* is masculine, as
young boys: 'But now, if he sees a little Mendaean wine, just coming to maturity, he follows
it and trails after it, and says "My god! How soft and white he is! Will he take three?"'.[40]

A similar double entendre on the technical terminology of proportions is exploited
in 'and another who goes half and half: meanwhile I waste away'.[41]

It will have been such scenes as this that gave a cue to ancient biography for its
representation of Cratinus as φιλοπότης καὶ παιδικῶν ἡττημένος.[42] Even more

---

[36]Philyllius fr. 23K.-A. (= 24Kock). For Chian cf. Ar. fr. 546K.-A. (= 531Kock), for Mendaean
Cratinus fr. 195K.-A. (= 183Kock); for Thasian Ar. *Lys.* 196; *Plut.* 1021, fr. 364K.-A. (= 350Kock) from
Cocalos (cf. above, n. 14). Mendaean, Magnesian, Thasian and Chian are all praised at Hermippus
77K.-A. (= 82Kock), while Peparethian is dismissed as fit for enemies.

[37]Phrynichus fr. 68K.-A. (= 65Kock): οὐ γλύξις οὐδ' ὑπόχυτος, ἀλλὰ Πράμνιος. Cf. Ar. fr.
334K.-A. (= 317Kock, cf. above, n. 34).

[38]Ar. fr. 688K.-A. (= 579Kock): τὸν Ἀθηναίων δῆμον οὔτε ποιηταῖς ἥδεσθαι σκληροῖς καὶ
ἀστεμφέσιν οὔτε Πραμνίοις οἴνοις συνάγουσι τὰς ὀφρῦς καὶ τὴν κοιλίαν, ἀλλ' <ἀνθ> οσμίᾳ καὶ
πέπονι νεκταροσταγεῖ. Note also the term καπνίας in Cratinus fr. 462K.-A. (= 334Kock).

[39]Eupolis 271K.-A. (= 253Kock) from *Taxiarchs* (the speaker is uncertain):
δίδου μασᾶσθαι Ναξίας ἀμυγδάλας
οἶνόν τε πίνειν Ναξίων ἀπ' ἀμπέλων.

[40]Cratinus fr. 95K.-A. (= 183Kock):
νῦν δ' ἢν ἴδη Μενδαῖον ἡβῶντ' ἀρτίως
οἰνίσκον, ἔπεται κἀκολουθεῖ καὶ λέγει
'οἴμ' ὡς ἀπαλὸς καὶ λευκός· ἆρ οἴσει τρία';
For the proportions cf. above, n. 31.

[41]Cratinus fr. 196K.-A. (= 195Kock): τὸν δ' ἴσον ἴσῳ φέροντ'. ἐγὼ δ' ἐκτήκομαι.

[42]*Suda* K 2344, and for the possibility that this image was also picked up by a vase-painter, see
above, n. 12. Cf. Ath. x. 428F = Ar. T 55K.-A., asserting that Aristophanes used to compose drunk.

influential, and taken up half-seriously by later poets, was one of Cratinus's defences: 'If you drink water you could never produce a work of art'.[43]

Clever and theatrically effective though the idea of the Pytine was, it should not be interpreted as making a serious statement about the relationship between wine and the composition of poetry. It is a *jeu d'esprit* in which a typical ploy of Old Comedy, the personification of common phenomena in the audience's life, is ingeniously applied to subject-matter that was already firmly at home in the genre; and it is one in which Cratinus would hardly have indulged if he had expected his audience to view fondness for wine as wholly disreputable.

There is a more serious purpose in the second symbolic use of wine with which I conclude, the occasions where it appears in visions of peace and plenty. Ideal worlds are regularly imagined as providing an amplitude of wine. Admittedly wine plays a smaller role in these than food, and some descriptions of plenty have no reference to wine at all, at least in the form in which they survive.[44] In attempting to explain this I am not sure how much weight should be given to the fact that man can live by food and water, but not by wine alone; how much to the incomparably wider range of foods that an Attic poet can exploit in building up that favourite comic device, a list; and how much to the fact that in Attica of the fifth century and later food shortages could easily occur whereas domestic production of wine could if necessary meet the demands of the home market. Nevertheless, wine remains important. In a picture of the golden age in Pherecrates's *Persians* a chorus imagines how Zeus will rain smokey wine.[45] His *Miners* (*Metalles*) had a long description of the foods on offer in the underworld (33 lines are quoted by Athenaeus) which include four lines on fragrant wine, sloshed out into full cups to all who want it by nubile girls scantily enough clad to show off their elegantly styled pubic hair.[46] In his *Friers* (*Tagenistai*) Aristophanes too envisaged drinking starting as soon as we reach the underworld.[47]

More realistically the peaceful life of the Attic countryside involves harvesting grapes and drinking wine.[48] In Aristophanes's *Islands* it included the bleating of sheep and the sound of 'wine lees being thrust into a bowl (*lekane*)', and 'one man harvesting

---

[43]Cratinus fr. 203 (= 199K; from Nicaenetus *Anthologia Palatina* xiii. 29 = *HE* Nicaenetus 5, cf. Horace, *Epist.* i. 19.1-2): ὕδωρ δὲ πίνων οὐδὲν ἂν τέκοις σοφόν.

[44]Philyllius 12K.-A. (= 13Kock), 18K.-A. (= 19Kock), 26K.-A. (= 27Kock); Pherecrates 50K.-A. (= 45Kock); Hermippus 63K.-A. (23 lines listing imports mostly of food, none of wine).

[45]Pherecrates fr. 137.6-8K.-A.) (= 130Kock) (the fragment is ten lines in all):
ὁ Ζεὺς δ' ὕων οἴνῳ καπνίᾳ κατὰ τοῦ κεράμου βαλανεύσει,
ἀπὸ τῶν δὲ τεγῶν ὀχετοὶ βοτρύων μετὰ ναστίσκων πολυτύρων
ὀχετεύσονται θερμῷ σὺν ἔτνει καὶ λειριοπολφανεμώναις.

[46]Pherecrates fr. 113.28-31K.-A. (= 108Kock):
κόραι δ' ἐν ἀμπεχόναις τριχάπτοις, ἀρτίως
ἡβυλλιῶσαι καὶ τὰ ῥόδα κεκαρμέναι,
πλήρεις κύλικας οἴνου μέλανος ἀνθοσμίου
ἤντλουν διὰ χώνης τοῖσι βουλομένοις πιεῖν.

[47]Ar. fr. 504K.-A. (= 488Kock): for the idea in serious speculation about the afterlife see *PCG ad locum.*

[48]For the link in Attic comedy between ideas of a golden age and the peace and plenty of the countryside see A.C. Cassio, *Commedia e participazione. La Pace di Aristofane* (Naples, 1985), 27-33.

vines, another gathering olives'.[49] But the fullest and most complex elaboration of the intimate relation between wine and the ideal life is offered in *Acharnians*. Here wine appears time and again as a symbol of the peace that Dicaeopolis seeks, pointed up by occasional illustrations of the abuse of wine which act as foils to the images of its correct use.[50]

The theme is introduced in a low key: in his catalogue of city woes Dicaeopolis complains (35) that *oxos* (vin ordinaire/*Tafelwein*),[51] along with charcoal and olive oil, is something he has never before had to buy. By contrast we shortly hear that the Athenian envoys to Persia had been drinking unmixed sweet wines (ἄκρατον οἶνον ἡδύν from crystal and gold cups (73-4). By then there has already been the first mention (at 52 by Amphitheus) of a treaty with Sparta. The term he uses, *spondai*, is ambiguous, connoting both the contract and the libations of wine that will seal it. At 178-83 we learn that the Acharnians have caught a whiff of the *spondai* carried by Amphitheus and have protested at his act — a protest based on the violence that has been done to their own vines (τῶν ἀμπέλων τετμημένων). Again at 232 the enemy's trampling of their vines is chosen as the symbol of his aggression.[52]

The analogy between *spondai* and wine is entertainingly elaborated at 187-203. *Spondai* come in three flavours, of five, ten and 30 years. The 30-year *spondai* have a bouquet of ambrosia and nectar,[53] and of no need to keep three days of provisions in stock. In Dicaeopolis's mouth they speak to him of freedom of movement. Dicaeopolis's response opens with the ecstatic 'O Dionysia', and announces that he will use his freedom of movement to celebrate the rural Dionysia.

When part of that celebration is enacted, Dicaeopolis's hymn to Phales (263-79) does not give first place to drink. The earlier lines of the song focus on casual sex — with boys, with other men's wives and with the Thracian slave-girl of Strymodorus. But he concludes with a parodic vow — 'if you drink with us you will slurp up a cup of peace the morning after' (277-8).[54]

It might be fanciful to see the theme of wine given a further subtle twist in the fact that at 420 the first ragged character whom Euripides offers to Dicaeopolis is Oeneus, or in Dicaeopolis's order to his *thumos* at 484 'Drink up Euripides and get moving' (οὐκ εἶ καταπιὼν Εὐριπίδην). But it certainly returns at 499 when Dicaeopolis calls the

[49]Ar. frs 402K.-A. (= 387Kock) and 406K.-A. (= *adespota* 437Kock). Cf. *Pax* 535, τρυγοίπου, προβατίων βληχωμένων, and 578, and the praise of Attica that emphasizes mid-winter grapes, fr. 581K.-A. (= 569Kock) from the *Seasons* (Ὧραι).

[50]See the basic discussions of H.-J. Newiger, *Metaphor und Allegorie* (Munich, 1957), 52-3, 104-6 and 'War and peace in the comedies of Aristophanes', *YClS* 26 (1980), 220-4. In other comedians cf. Hermippus fr. 48 for a link between *kottabos* and peace; his fr. 55 takes a wine-cup's relegation to its peg as a mark of war.

[51]Only to be drunk when wine of quality is not available, cf. Eupolis fr. 355K.-A. (= 326Kock).

[52]Cf. Dicaeopolis's point at 512 that his vines have been damaged too.

[53]Cf. Ar. fr. 688K.-A. (= 579Kock, cited above at n. 34). The 30-year σπονδαί reappear in *Knights* as beautiful 30-year old women offered by the sausage-seller to Demos, but there, despite earlier mentions of σπονδαί noted by H.-J. Newiger, *Metapher und Allegorie* (Munich, 1957), 106, they are much less integral to the play and its imagery.

[54]ἐὰν μέθ' ἡμῶν ξυμπίῃς, ἐκ κραιπάλης ἕωθεν εἰρήνης ῥοφήσεις τρύβλιον.

play a *trugoidia*, a term picked up by the *koruphaios*'s words χοροῖσιν...τρυγικοῖς at 628 and by his own τρυγωδικοῖς χοροῖς at 886.

The theme of wine is then suspended for several hundred lines. It may be distantly alluded to in the reference to Pericles's laws written like *skolia* (532), songs invariably associated with the *symposion*, and in the reference to wine-skins and jars (*askoi* and *kadoi*) among the military provisions of 549. But it is not mentioned in the scene with the Megarian, which moves along the axis of the more fundamental necessities of life, food and sex, nor that with the Boeotian, where music leads into food. Perhaps this is partly because wine is too important to the representation of Dicaeopolis's peace to be simply bartered and thus diluted (just as Dicaeopolis refuses to share the *spondai* with the farmer and the best man (παράνυμφος) at 1018ff. and 1048ff). When it next appears, at 936, it is again allusively and in a negative context: the *sukophantes* who is to be carried off is described as a 'mixing-bowl of evils' (κρατὴρ κακῶν) and as a cup for stirring up trouble (κύλιξ τὰ πράγματ᾽ ἐγκυκᾶσθαι). Then at 961 we first hear of the competition of the Cups (*Choes*) — not from Dicaeopolis's perspective, but from that of Lamachus, who wants to buy some thrushes and eel for his celebration of this festival.

This sequence of chiefly negative images of wine is gathered together in the choral song at 979-87. The chorus declares that it will never welcome Polemos into its house, nor will it be he who reclines beside them and sings the Harmodius song, because he has been a man who abused wine (*paroinos*), setting off in a *komos* against people who had every good and wreaking every evil ... Despite many appeals 'drink, lie down, take this cup of friendship' (cf. *Lys.* 203) he all the more set fire to the vine-poles and violently spilled the wine from their vines.[55]

It is as a contrast to this abuse of wine that the audience approaches the glorious competitive sequence between Dicaeopolis and Lamachus. At 1000 the herald proclaims the traditional competition of the *Choes* — the first man to drain his cup will get the wine-skin of Ctesiphon. In response Dicaeopolis urges preparation of his banquet, and at 1067 asks for his wine-ladle so that he can pour into it wine for the *Choes*. Shortly, at 1085, Dicaeopolis is invited by the Priest of Dionysos to a *deipnon* which certainly involves the consumption of wine, even if it is not mentioned at 1090-3, whereas Lamachus has been ordered to remain sober and prepare to resist a Boeotian incursion. The contrasts continue: at 1132-5 Lamachus asks his slave to bring out his breastplate, Dicaeopolis his to bring out his cup as a breastplate with which he will tank himself up in competition with his *sympotai*.[56] For him, as we earlier noted συμποτικὰ τὰ πράγματα (1142). The chorus cue the audience (1143) on the contrast between

---

[55] Οὐδέποτ᾽ ἐγὼ Πόλεμον οἴκαδ᾽ ὑποδέξομαι,
οὐδὲ παρ᾽ ἐμοί ποτε τὸν Ἁρμόδιον ᾄσεται
ξυγκατακλινείς, ὅτι πάροινος ἀνὴρ ἔφυ,
ὅστις ἐπὶ πάντ᾽ ἀγάθ᾽ ἔχοντας ἐπικωμάσας
ἠργάσατο πάντα κακά, κἀνέτρεπε κἀξέχει
κἀμάχετο καὶ προσέτι πολλὰ προκαλουμένου·
'Πῖνε, κατάκεισο, λαβὲ τήνδε φιλοτησίαν',
τὰς χάρακας ᾗπτε πολὺ μᾶλλον ἔτι τῷ πυρί,
ἐξέχει θ᾽ ἡμῶν βίᾳ τὸν οἶνον ἐκ τῶν ἀμπελων.
[56] Cf. above on how this scene involves a mini-*symposion* for Dicaeopolis.

Lamachus's and Dicaeapolis's lot — Dicaeopolis's is to drink garlanded, and to lie down with a lovely girl and have his thingy rubbed.

When at 1198 Dicaeopolis returns he is supported by two firm-breasted *hetairai* from whom he requests kisses 'for I was first to drain my cup'. Expertise with wine has been one of the chief symbols of Dicaepolis's wine-based σπονδαί, and has secured him another important symbol of peace, sexual gratification. Now it will also secure him still more wine. For (1225), just as Lamachus asks to be taken to the doctor Pittalos, so Dicaeopolis asks to be taken to the judges of the *Choes*: 'Where is the *basileus*? Give me the wineskin'. He brandishes the cup that he has drained in one (1229) and the chorus tells him to carry off the wine-skin: it will follow celebrating the victory of Dicaeopolis and his wine-skin (1230-4).

Together the *Pytine* and *Acharnians* show how an individual's indulgence in wine can be heroized. In a non-festive context that of Cratinus may be laughed at, but there is no hint or likelihood that the poet held it up for censure; in a festive context the unadulterated tippling of Dicaeopolis can be presented as an unadulterated good. It is, overall, as an important constituent of the good things of life, though not of its necessities, that wine is presented by Old Comedy. It is a good which in real life or in contexts approximating to it a citizen can be expected to enjoy in moderation and preferably in the company of other citizens, but which slaves and women are likely to abuse.

9

Un Rituel du Vin: la Libation

FRANÇOIS LISSARRAGUE

L'imagerie attique du *symposion* et du *komos* est — on le sait — d'une grande richesse. Les pratiques sociales autour du vin mélangé, partagé entre les convives, font l'objet d'une abondante iconographie dont le développement sur les vases à boire ne saurait surprendre. Je ne reviendrai pas ici sur ces aspects qui ont été étudiés à satiété,[1] sinon pour relever une absence quasi totale dans l'imagerie des vases: celles des libations au *symposion*. Ce rituel — au sens strict — du vin ne semble pas avoir retenu l'attention des peintres, qui ont choisi de représenter d'autres aspects du *symposion* et ont réservé à la libation proprement dite une place à part dans le répertoire.

On examinera donc ici ce qu'il en est de la libation en images, à partir des objets manipulés, des gestes et des rôles qu'un tel acte suppose, des moments et des espaces mis en scène par l'image.[2]

Les textes et les allusions littéraires à la libation ne nous donnent pas exactement sur cet acte rituel les mêmes informations que les images, non que ces deux séries de données soient contradictoires, mais elles procèdent d'une logique et de moyens d'expressions distincts et proposent donc des points de vue différents sur une même pratique rituelle. Un premier écart concerne ce qui est dit de la nature des liquides versés en libation. Le plus souvent il s'agit de vin, mais on sait que de manière exceptionnelle d'autres liquides sont employés, dans certains rituels spécifiques qui se distinguent par là et s'opposent à la libation ordinaire, comme l'a bien montré F. Graf.[3] Ce peut être du lait, du miel ou tout simplement de l'eau. Ainsi nous savons que des libations d'eau, les *choai*, sont réservées aux morts.[4] En règle générale les images ne peuvent spécifier la nature du liquide versé, sauf par le truchement des vases à contenir. On peut parfois identifier les *choai* sur certaines images, rares il est vrai, où non

---

[1]Voir B. Fehr, *Orientalische und Griechische Gelage* (Bonn, 1971); J.-M. Dentzer, *Le motif du banquet couché dans le proche-orient et le monde grec du VIIe au IVe siècle avant J.-C.* (Rome-Paris, 1982); O. Murray (ed.), *Sympotica: a Symposium on the* Symposion (Oxford, 1990); F. Lissarrague, *Un flot d'images: une esthétique du banquet grec* (Paris, 1987).

[2]Sur la libation en général, voir W. Burkert, *Greek Religion* (Oxford, 1985), 70-3; J. Rudhardt, *Notions fondamentales de la pensée religieuse et actes constitutifs du culte dans la Grèce classique*, seconde édition (Paris, 1992), 240-8; P. Stengel, *Opferbrauche der Griechen* (Leipzig, 1910), 178-86. Je reprends ici en partie certaines remarques faites dans mon article: 'La libation: essai de mise au point', *Image et rituel en Grèce ancienne. Recherches et documents du centre Thomas More* 48 (déc. 1985), 3-16.

[3]F. Graf, 'Milch, Honig und Wein', dans *Perennitas. Studi in onore di A. Brelich* (Rome, 1980), 209-21.

[4]*Cf.* Rudhart, *Notions fondamentales de la pensée religieuse* (ci-dessus, n. 2), 246-8.

FIG. 1. Lécythe de Carlsruhe. Deux femmes se tiennent devant une stèle ornée de bandelettes (Carlsruhe 234) *(D'après photo du Musée)*

seulement le contexte funéraire permet de supposer un tel type de libation, mais où la
présence du vase à eau par excellence, l'hydrie,[5] rend le fait explicite. Ainsi sur un
lécythe de Carlsruhe (Fig. 1) deux femmes se tiennent devant une stèle ornée de
bandelettes; l'une à droite tient la *phiale* de la libation tandis que l'autre à gauche,
penchée sur la tombe, verse l'eau que contient son hydrie.[6]

De même, et c'est là un autre écart entre textes et images, plusieurs textes spécifient
le destinataire des libations au *symposion*; certains font allusion au rituel des 'trois
cratères', ces libations offertes successivement, chaque fois que l'on mélange un nouveau
cratère, à Zeus et aux Olympiens, puis aux Héros, enfin à Zeus Teleios, ou bien en
premier lieu à l'Agathos Daimon et en conclusion à Hermès; toutes ces formules,
susceptibles de variantes et d'ajouts au gré des buveurs, nous indiquent que boire et
faire libation sont deux actes étroitement associés.[7]

[5]Sur l'hydrie dans le rituel funéraire voir D.C. Kurtz et J. Boardman, *Greek Burial Customs* (Londres,
1971), 161 et 209; E. Diehl, *Die Hydria* (Mayence, 1964), 65-168, en particulier p. 137.
[6]Carlsruhe 234; *ARV*[2] 1372.17 (Woman painter). *Cf.* aussi New York 34.32.2; *ARV*[2] 1168.131
(Peintre de Munich 2335).
[7]Voir Burkert, *Greek Religion* (ci-dessus, n. 2), 70-1; K. Kircher, *Die Sakrale Bedeutung des Weins im Alter-
tum* (Giessen, 1910); M. Nilsson, 'Die Götter des symposions', *Opuscula Selecta* I (Lund, 1951), 428-42; D.
Tolles, *The Banquet Libations of the Greeks* (Dissertation, Bryn Mawr, 1943). (Je remercie H.A. Shapiro qui
m'a rendu ce dernier ouvrage accessible.)

Rien en image ne correspond à ces invocations, sinon, peut-être, une coupe fragmentaire qui provient de l'Acropole d'Athènes (Fig. 2).[8] Il s'agit, dans la production céramique, d'un objet prestigieux puisque l'intérieur est à fond blanc.[9] On y voit la déesse Athéna, debout, armée d'une lance, tendant une *phiale*, dans l'attitude typique des dieux faisant libation. L'extérieur est très fragmentaire; sur la face A un homme barbu, couronné, tourné vers la gauche, tend de la main droite une *phiale*; sur son épaule gauche est appuyée une lance qui passe entre ses doigts. Devant sa bouche ouverte, on

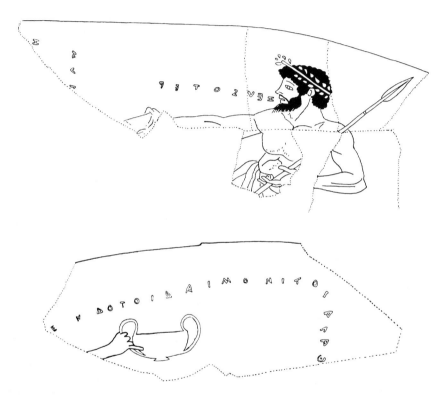

FIG. 2. Coupe fragmentaire de l'Acropole d'Athènes. (A) Un homme, tenant de la main droite une *phiale*, avec les mots ZEU SOTER, rétrogrades; (B) Une main droite, tenant un canthare, avec l'inscription ΣΠ]ΕΝΔΟ ΤΟΙ ΔΑΙΜΟΝΙ ΤΟΙ ΑΓΑΘ[ΟΙ (Athènes Acr. 434) *(D'après O. Benndorf, Griechische und Sikilische Vasenbilder II (Berlin, 1870), Pl. 29 (A et B) , et G.C. Richards, 'Selected vase fragments from the Acropolis of Athens III', JHS 14 (1894), 383, figg. 2 et 3 (A))*

[8]Athènes, Acr. 434; *ARV*[2] 330.5 (Manière d'Onésimos); attribué au Peintre d'Antiphon par D.J.R. Williams.

[9]Sur la valeur votive des vases à fond blanc voir les remarques de D.J.R. Williams, 'An oinochoe in the British Museum and the Brygos painter's work on white ground', *JBerlM* 24 (1982), en particulier 27-9.

lit les mots ZEU SOTER, rétrogrades.[10] La trajectoire de l'écriture suit le mouvement du bras, créant un effet dynamique dans l'image, qui anticipe sur la trajectoire du vin versé. La prière à Zeus Sauveur est proche des formules que l'on vient d'évoquer. L'attitude du personnage est difficile à préciser: il pourrait être allongé sur un lit de banquet, mais on s'attendrait à voir un coussin sous son coude gauche, or ce n'est pas le cas. Peut-être est-il assis. De plus, il tient une lance, ce qui est inhabituel dans les images attiques de banquet à cette date;[11] aussi ne peut-on assurer qu'il s'agisse effectivement d'un banquet. Benndorf, qui le premier publia ces fragments, a songé à un sacrifice public,[12] mais il est difficile d'en dire plus. L'état fragmentaire du revers B réduit l'image à son expression minimale: une main droite tend un canthare. L'inscription, incomplète, qui traverse le tesson lui donne toute sa valeur; on peut lire ΣΠ]ΕΝΔΟ ΤΟΙ ΔΑΙΜΟΝΙ ΤΟΙ ΑΓΑΘ[ΟΙ, 'je verse pour le Bon Génie'. Ici encore la trajectoire de l'inscription produit un effet dynamique; elle part probablement de la bouche du locuteur, comme au revers, mais s'incurve à mi-parcours comme pour s'orienter vers le point d'arrivée de la libation, dont l'inscription décrit métaphoriquement le parcours.[13]

L'emploi du verbe *spendo*[14] correspond bien à la catégorie des libations faites au banquet, les *spondai*; ces mêmes libations peuvent marquer la fin d'une guerre, et désigner un traité de paix. Ici, à défaut d'une image complète, qui nous permettrait d'identifier les acteurs de la libation, symposiastes ou guerriers, seuls les mots nous restent qui décrivent l'action de manière quasi redondante, comme le font souvent les inscriptions parlées. Elles n'ajoutent pas d'éléments nouveaux à l'image, mais en précisent le champ sémantique. Ici, entre guerre et banquet, le contexte de la libation reste indécidable.

Un *stamnos* du Louvre,[15] des années 490 av. J.-C., associe deux scènes de distribution du vin qui se déroulent au plan divin et au plan humain. Au droit, c'est un satyre muni d'une *oinochoe* qui s'apprête à remplir le canthare que lui tend Dionysos. De la main gauche il salue le dieu, maître de la vigne et du vin: un large rameau, tenu par Dionysos, se déploie dans le champ, faisant apparaître de lourdes grappes au dessus du

---

[10]Le fragment qui porte l'épithète Soter, publié par O. Benndorf, *Griechische und Sikilische Vasenbilder* II (Berlin, 1870), Pl. 29, Ib, a aujourd'hui disparu; mon dessin combine celui de G.C. Richards, 'Selected vase fragments from the Acropolis of Athens - III', JHS 14 (1894), 383, figg. 2 et 3 et celui de Benndorf. Sur ces fragments, *cf.* Tolles, *The Banquet Libations of the Greeks* (ci-dessus, n. 7), 61-2. Sur une *pelike* de Naples RC 117; *ARV* [2] 1209.57 (Peintre de Shuwalow; *cf.* A. Lezzi, *Der Shuwalow Maler* (Mayence, 1976), 87) on lit l'inscription, complète, EUSOTER, sans rapport avec une libation. E. Greco, que je remercie, m'a fait observer que la formule 'Zeus Soter' sert de mot de passe aux Grecs lors de la bataille de Cunaxa (Xen. *An.* i. 8).

[11]On voit rarement des armes à coté des buveurs sur les images de cette période; *cf.* toutefois les fragments de coupe Paris, BN, Cabinet des Médailles 546; *ARV* [2] 372.26 (Peintre de Brygos). La panoplie est en revanche souvent représentée sur les images archaïques en particulier corinthiennes; sur ce point voir P. Schmitt-Pantel, *La cité au banquet. Histoire des repas publics dans les cités grecques* (Paris-Rome, 1992), 17-31.

[12]Benndorf, *Griechische und Sikilische Vasenbilder* (ci-dessus, n. 10), 49.

[13]Sur ce type d'effet voir F. Lissarrague, 'Paroles d'images: remarques sur le fonctionnement de l'écriture dans l'imagerie attique', dans A.M. Christin (ed.), *Ecritures II* (Paris, 1985), 71-93.

[14]Voir J. Casabona, *Recherches sur le vocabulaire des sacrifices en Grec* (Aix-en-Provence, 1966), 231-68.

[15]Paris, Louvre G 54 bis; *ARV* [2] 246.8 (Peintre de l'Amphore de Munich).

FIG. 3. *Stamnos* du Louvre. Une femme verse le contenu de son *oinochoe* dans la *phiale* d'un guerrier; avec deux inscriptions (Louvre G54 *bis*) *(D'après l'original)*

canthare. Au revers (Fig. 3), une femme, elle aussi saluant de la main gauche, verse le contenu de son *oinochoe* dans la *phiale* d'un guerrier. Deux inscriptions se lisent, entre ces personnages; l'une, horizontale, à hauteur des visages, donne le nom du guerrier Menandros (rétrograde). L'autre, verticale, se lit ΚΑΛΟΣ ΧΕΟ, 'je verse bien'. Les lettres suivent, de haut en bas, la trajectoire du vin versé par la femme de l'*oinochoe* dans la *phiale*, et par le guerrier de la *phiale* au sol. Le peintre a en effet indiqué en rehaut violet le trajet que fait le vin d'un vase à l'autre, puis vers le sol, d'une seule traite. Ce n'est pas la succession des gestes, la décomposition des actes dont est constituée la libation que le peintre a voulu montrer, mais au contraire, en une image synthétique qui ne se soucie pas de réalisme technique, la circulation d'un bout à l'autre de sa trajectoire du vin parmi les hommes et vers les dieux. Si l'on regarde les deux faces du vase on y découvre le vin du dieu qui, selon le mot de Tirésias,[16] s'offre lui-même en libation, puis le vin des hommes qui fait retour aux dieux sous forme de libation. Le parcours graphique du rehaut crée, entre les hommes et les dieux, un lien symbolique matérialisé par la ligne violette qui court d'un vase à l'autre et vers le sol. L'inscription renforce cet effet visuel en redoublant ce tracé.

L'emploi du verbe *cheo* est remarquable; le verbe *leibo*, qui indique que l'on verse goutte à goutte,[17] s'appliquerait mal au flot que l'on voit ici; *spendo* serait plus approprié au geste du guerrier et *cheo* à celui de la femme. Ce dernier verbe est en effet le moins technique qui soit, indiquant simplement l'action de verser, sans impliquer nécessairement une connotation rituelle.[18] On le retrouve dans les composés qui désignent soit l'échanson lui-même, au *symposion*, *oinochoos*, soit le vase à verser par excellence, *oinochoe*. On remarquera qu'ici, pas plus qu'ailleurs, le verbe *cheo* n'implique le type spécifique de libation que désigne le nom dérivé de ce verbe, *choé*, et qui est exclusivement réservé aux morts.[19] Rien n'indique en effet dans l'image un contexte funéraire; on n'y voit ni stèle ni offrande. La femme verse du vin au guerrier et le guerrier fait une libation; c'est avant tout la qualité des deux gestes combinés qui est mise en évidence par l'inscription καλῶς χέω.

Un tel geste est peu fréquent dans l'iconographie du banquet. Peut-être apparaît-il sur une intéressante coupe de Berlin à décor en zone (Fig. 4).[20] Au médaillon central un jeune homme debout devant un autel tend de la main droite une *phiale* pour faire libation; dans la zone qui entoure ce médaillon, encadrée par deux frises de méandres, se déploie un cercle ininterrompu de cinq symposiastes dont l'un joue de l'*aulos*. Ils ne tiennent aucun vase à boire, mais l'espace du *symposion* est ici clairement indiqué par les coussins sur lesquels ils s'accoudent et la circularité conviviale qui caractérise souvent ce type d'images.[21] On peut en fait lire de deux manières cette double image emboîtée: soit en continuité, comme une libation au banquet précédant ou concluant une beuverie;

---

[16]Eur. *Bacch.* 284.

[17]Casabona, *Recherches sur le vocabulaire des sacrifices en Grec* (ci-dessus, n. 14), 271; Rudhardt, *Notions fondamentales de la pensée religieuse* (ci-dessus, n. 2), 240.

[18]*Ibid.* pp. 264-7.

[19]Sur ce dernier type de libation, voir ci-dessus, nn. 4-5.

[20]Berlin F 2299, non attribuée. Voir G. von Lucken, *Griechische Vasenbilder* (Berlin, 1921), Pl. 93. Sur ce type de coupes à zone *cf.* D. Buitron, *Douris* (Dissertation, Ann Arbor University Microfilm, 1976), 214.

[21]Sur type d'espace voir Lissarrague, *Un flot d'images* (ci-dessus, n. 1), 23-30; comparer en particulier avec une coupe de New York 16.174.41; *ARV*[2] 355.35 (Peintre de Colmar).

FIG. 4. Coupe de Berlin. Entouré de cinq symposiastes, au médaillon un jeune homme tend de la main droite une *phiale* (Berlin F2299) *(D'après von Lücken, Griechische Vasenbilder, Pl. 93)*

soit comme deux manières de faire circuler le vin, entre hommes, au *symposion*, ou bien des hommes aux dieux, devant l'autel. En juxtaposant ainsi ces deux images, le peintre n'a pas ajouté d'indice contraignant qui permettrait de choisir l'une ou l'autre de ces deux lectures et de fait il ne paraît pas nécessaire de trancher ni de réduire la polysémie d'une telle juxtaposition. La libation à l'intérieur d'une scène de banquet, si c'en est une, reste en tout cas une exception. Les *phiales* sont rares aux mains des convives et le plus souvent indiquent la nature divine ou héroïque de ceux qui les manipulent.[22] De même le lien explicitement indiqué par Xénophane entre l'autel et le cratère,[23] entre le partage des viandes sacrifiées et la distribution du vin mélangé, est très rarement montré en image.[24] On le rencontre plutôt dans des scènes dionysiaques, rituelles ou

[22]*Cf.* par exemple la coupe attribuée au peintre de Codros, Londres E 82, *ARV*[2] 1269.3 ici étudiée par T. Carpenter. *Cf.* aussi Louvre G 152 et Tarquinia RC 6846; *ARV*[2] 369.1,4 (Peintre de Brygos).

[23]Xénophane fr. B1 West, *apud* Ath. xi. 462C-F.

[24]On trouve ensemble: sacrifice et *symposion*, sur une pyxide béotienne de Berlin F 1757, *CVA* Berlin 4, pl. 196; sur une pyxide corinthienne de Paris, BN, Cabinet des Médailles 94, *CVA* BN 1, pl. 17; découpe des viandes et vin mélangé, sur un cratère corinthien du Louvre, E 635, *CVP* 147,1; *symposion* et sacrifice, sur une coupe attique de Tarente IG 4346, *ABV* 54,70 (Peintre C); *comos* et sacrifice, sur une coupe attique de Florence 5B2, *ARV*[2] 146.3 (Peintre d'Epeleios).

mythiques,[25] ou dans des scènes qui montrent le dérèglement de la *xenia*, le mépris des lois de l'hospitalité et des dieux qui les régissent, par exemple lorsqu'aux noces de Pirithoos les Centaures veulent violer la mariée.[26] Il arrive que l'on voie alors un cratère renversé, signe d'une violence extrême, et un autel qui rappelle à quel point les dieux sont bafoués.[27] En fait la valeur religieuse et rituelle du vin est davantage mise en évidence dans d'autres séries iconographiques qui ne sont pas liées à ce type de consommation du vin, soit lors de libations à l'autel, soit dans des scènes de départ de guerriers. En image la libation apparaît alors comme un geste par lequel se définit un lieu d'échange entre les partenaires de cette libation, un espace symbolique distinct de celui du banquet. Il s'agit d'un acte rituel isolé, ou du moins isolable par l'image, et dont on voudrait ici définir les modalités.

La libation est caractérisée à la fois par un geste, celui de verser, et par des instruments: la cruche, *oinochoe*, et un récipient, coupe ou *phiale*. La *phiale* est l'objet technique par excellence; à l'époque classique[28] ce terme désigne une coupe sans pied ni anses, pourvue d'un bossage en son centre (*omphalos*). Cet objet qui permet de faire l'offrande du vin est lui-même souvent offert aux dieux, le contenant se substituant au contenu. Il fait alors partie de ces *agalmata* de type quasi monétaire que l'on empile et thésaurise dans les sanctuaires.[29] On en voit, dans cette fonction paramonétaire, par exemple dans certaines scènes du rachat d'Hector, parmi d'autres vases métalliques, hydries ou bassins, et de riches armes[30] ou bien, dans la célèbre scène du tribut perse, sur le cratère apulien attribué au peintre de Darius, parmi les objets remis au souverain.[31] La *phiale* est donc à la fois un objet précieux et un objet technique.

[25]Scène rituelle: coupe attribuée à Macron, Berlin F 2290, *ARV*[2] 462.48 (pour l'ensemble de cette série voir F. Frontisi-Ducroux, *Le dieu-masque* (Paris-Rome, 1991)). Scène mythique (thiase de Dionysos): Athènes MN 1262, *ARV*[2] 587.62 (Maniériste Indéterminé).

[26]Voir F. Lissarrague, 'Le banquet impossible', dans M. Aurell, O. Dumoulin et F. Thelamon (edd.), *La sociabilité à table: commensalité et convivialité à travers les âges* (Rouen, 1992), 54-64.

[27]Ainsi sur le cratère de Vienne 1026; *ARV*[2] 1087.2 (Peintre de la Nékyia). *Cf.* aussi les images représentant Héraclès chez Ops, identifiées par D.J.R. Williams, 'Herakles and Peisistratos', dans F. Lissarrague et F. Thelamon (edd.), *Image et céramique grecque* (*Colloque Rouen 25-26 nov. 1982*) (Rouen, 1983), 138: Paris, Louvre G 50, *ARV*[2] 188.70 (Peintre de Cléophradès); New York 12.231.2, *ARV*[2] 319.6 (Onésimos).

[28]Voir en général H. Luschey, *Die Phiale* (Bleicherode, 1939), et *RE Suppl.* VII, coll. 1026-1030. Le terme *phiale* peut avoir un sens différent dans les poèmes homériques; *cf.* N. Valenza Mele, 'Da Micene a Omero: dalla *phiale* al *lebete*', *AION(archeol)* 4 (1982), 97-133.

[29]Un bel exemple publié par D. von Bothmer, 'A gold libation bowl', *The Metropolitan Museum of Art Bulletin* (déc. 1982), 154-66. *Cf.* également D. von Bothmer, 'A Greek and Roman Treasury', *The Metropolitan Museum of Art Bulletin* (summer 1984), n° 1, 2, 12, 16-19, 25-32, 79, 86, 89, 90, 100. *Cf.* surtout la *phiale* offerte par les Cypsélides à Olympie (Boston, 21.1843; L. Jeffery, *The Local Scripts of Archaic Greece* (Oxford, 1961), 131, n° 13 et pl. 19). Sur les *agalmata* voir L. Gernet, 'La notion mythique de la valeur', dans L. Gernet, *Anthropologie de la Grèce ancienne* (Paris, 1968), en particulier p. 132.

[30]Amphore de Toledo 72.54.0; *LIMC* Achilleus 656 (Peintre de Rycroft) — Coupe de Munich 2618; *ARV*[2] 61.74 (Oltos) — Skyphos de Vienne 3710; *ARV*[2] 380.171 (Peintre de Brygos); *LIMC* Achilleus 659 — Coupe de la Collection White/Levy; *ARV*[2] 399.1650, *Paralipomena* 369 (Peintre du quatorzième Brygos); *LIMC* Achilleus 661; *Glories of the Past* (exposition New York sept. 1990), n° 118.

[31]Naples H 3253; voir M.-C. Villanueva-Puig, 'Le vase des Perses', *REA* 91 (1-2) (1989), 1-2, 277-98, en particulier pp. 292-3.

Ce n'est pourtant pas l'instrument exclusif de la libation. Tout vase à boire peut être utilisé à cet effet, une simple coupe[32] ou plus rarement un canthare, comme sur une amphore à figures noires de la Villa Giulia.[33] Dans ce cas, c'est souvent Dionysos lui-même qui verse le contenu de son canthare sur un autel.[34] Il arrive même que l'on utilise directement l'*oinochoe* pour verser la libation, comme sur une coupe du Musée d'Athènes (Fig. 5)[35] où un jeune homme en *himation*, qui pourtant tient une coupe de la main gauche, tend son *oinochoe* vers l'autel, faisant le geste de verser avec la cruche.

La libation apparaît donc, du point de vue instrumental, comme un geste rituel susceptible de variantes. Il en va de même de l'espace et du contexte dans lequel elle peut ou non s'insérer, soit qu'elle reste un acte isolé, soit qu'elle s'agrège à un ensemble plus ou moins complexe d'actes rituels. Ni le contexte de la libation, ni l'espace dans lequel elle a lieu ne sont déterminés de manière univoque et contraignante. Les peintres ont en général retenu deux mises en scène: soit, comme on vient de le voir, à l'autel, soit, en un lieu non spécifié architecturalement, entre plusieurs personnages, le plus souvent dans un départ de guerrier.

[32]Par exemple sur:

Chiusi C 1837; *CVA* 2, pl. 16,3; non attribué;

Leningrad 1898.42; *ARV*[2] 311.2 (Painter of the Leningrad Herm-mug);

Tarquinia RC 1918; *ARV*[2] 366.88 (Peintre de Triptolème);

Kassel T 436; *ARV*[2] 626.105 (Peintre de la Villa Giulia; à noter que le personnage ne fait pas le geste de verser; Beazley le décrit comme un 'comaste à l'autel'. Voir sur ce point Ch. Bron, 'Le lieu du comos', dans J. Christiansen et T. Melander (edd.), *Third Symposium on Ancient Greek and Related Pottery* (Copenhague, 1987), 71-9).

Dans des scènes sacrificielles: J.L. Durand, *Sacrifice et labour en Grèce ancienne* (Paris-Rome, 1986), figg. 56, 65, 66.

[33]Rome Villa Giulia 20842; *ABV* 381, sub. 297 (non attribué). *Cf.* également Brooklyn 59.34; *ARV*[2] 604.57 (Peintre des Niobides). On trouve aussi un canthare utilisé pour des libations à l'intérieur d'une scène sacrificielle: Wurzburg L 474; *ARV*[2] 173.10 (Peintre d'Ambrosios); Palerme V 661a; *ARV*[2] 472.210 (Macron); Darmstadt 478; *ARV*[2] 1146.48 (Peintre de Cléophon); Ferrare T 343 B; Durand, *Sacrifice et labour en Grèce ancienne* (ci-dessus, n. 32), fig. 64; A. Lezzi-Hafter, *Der Shuwalow-Maler* (Mayence, 1976), Pl. 118.

[34]Ainsi sur:

Boston 00.334; *ARV*[2] 126.27 (Peintre de Nicosthénès);

Londres E 350; *ARV*[2] 256.2 (Peintre de Copenhague);

Londres E 257; *ARV*[2] 604.50 (Peintre des Niobides);

Ferrare 2683; *ARV*[2] 606.77 (Peintre des Niobides);

Wurzburg L 503; *ARV*[2] 611.32 (manière du Peintre des Niobides); la présence de l'autel garantit la lecture rituelle et distingue cette image de celles où il s'agit simplement de servir le dieu.

Je n'entrerai pas ici dans la discussion des libations executées entre dieux, puisque mon exposé se limite au vin des hommes. Sur cette question voir E. Simon, *Opfernde Götter* (Berlin, 1953), qui interprète ces scènes comme la représentation d'un rituel d'auto-célébration divine. Ce point de vue a été discuté et contesté dans un important article d'A.-F. Laurens, 'La libation: intégration des dieux dans le rituel humain?', *Images et rituel en Grèce ancienne. Recherches et documents du centre Thomas More* 48 (1985), 35-59. Voir aussi l'analyse encore plus radicale de P. Veyne 'Divinités à la patère', *Métis* 5 (1990), 17-30.

[35]Athènes MN 1666; *ARV*[2] 1567.13 (non attribuée).

FIG. 5. Coupe du Musée d'Athènes. Un jeune homme, qui pourtant tient une coupe de la main gauche, tend son *oinochoe* vers l'autel (Athènes MN 1666) *(D'après J.E. Harrison, 'Two cylices relating to the exploits of Theseus', JHS 10 (1879), pl. 1)*

La libation à l'autel est fréquente au médaillon des coupes et présente souvent en pareil cas une figure isolée.[36] On peut la considérer comme un segment d'une scène plus complexe, et il arrive que certains éléments présents dans l'image renvoient à d'autres activités, soit la guerre, soit le *symposion*, soit, et c'est le cas le plus fréquent, le sacrifice. Ainsi sur la coupe du Louvre G 629 un jeune homme est assis, faisant libation avec une

[36]Ainsi par exemple:
Bonn 1227; *ARV* [2] 324.63 (Onésimos);
Tarquinia RC 1918; *ARV* [2] 366.88 (Peintre de Triptolème);
Athènes Agora P 42; *ARV* [2] 415.1 (Peintre d'Agora P 42);
Athènes MN 1666 (ci-dessus, n. 35);
Londres E 53; *ARV* [2] 435.87 (Douris);
Louvre G 149; *ARV* [2] 473.212 (Macron);
Toledo 72.55; *CVA* 1, pl. 53 (Macron);
Kassel T 436; *ARV* [2] 626.105 (Peintre de la Villa Giulia);
Harvard Fogg 1927.155; *ARV* [2] 803.58 (successeur de Douris);
Florence PD 272; *ARV* [2] 834.4 (Peintre de Londres E 100);
Chiusi C 1837; *CVA* 2, pl. 16,3; non attribuée;
Vérone 51 Ce; *ARV* [2] 1023.148 (Peintre de la Phiale).

phiale sur un autel; au dessus de lui, dans le champ, est suspendu un bouclier qui évoque une scène d'armement.[37] Sur une coupe publiée par O. Jahn (Fig. 6)[38] une femme debout près d'une *trapeza* tient une *phiale* et une *oinochoe*; cette table peut évoquer aussi bien le contexte du *symposion* que celui du sacrifice;[39] en l'absence de lit ou d'autel pour confirmer l'une ou l'autre lecture cette image reste 'ouverte', comme au croisement de deux espaces rituels proches mais le plus souvent distincts en image. Le médaillon d'une

FIG. 6. Coupe. Une femme tient une *phiale* et une *oinochoe* (Coll. privée) *(D'après O. Jahn, 'Herakles und Syleus', AZ 18 (1861), Pl. 149)*

[37]Louvre G 629; *ARV*[2] 962.78 (Peintre de Londres D12); il me semble que l'objet semi-circulaire suspendu dans le champ est à lire comme un bouclier; E. Pottier (*Vases antiques du Louvre*, III (Paris, 1922, 296) considère qu'il s'agit d'un panier, le contexte serait alors le *symposion*. Sur les libations dans les scènes d'armement, voir ci-après.

[38]Le vase a disparu; *ARV*[2] 429.25 (Douris); mon dessin reprend, malgré ses déformations probables, la gravure parue dans O. Jahn, 'Herakles und Syleus', *AZ* 18 (1861), Pl. 149.

[39]Pour une table dans un contexte sacrificiel, *cf.* Durand, *Sacrifice et labour en Grèce ancienne* (ci-dessus, n. 32), figg. 36 et 53. *Cf.* également, en rapport avec un autel et une libation, effectuée par Zeus, les tables qui figurent sur la *pyxis* de Berlin, inv. 3308; *ARV*[2] 977.1 (Peintre d'Agathon).

coupe de Macron est en revanche tout à fait explicite (Fig. 7):[40] une femme se tient devant un autel où le feu sacrificiel est allumé; elle verse le contenu de son *oinochoe* sur la flamme tandis que sur le bras gauche elle porte un panier sacrificiel, *kanoun*; derrière elle un *thymiaterion* est posé sur une base, autre forme d'offrande sacrificielle. Ici l'ensemble des éléments renvoie clairement au sacrifice, et les exemples ne sont pas rares, où une femme, porteuse de *kanoun*, fait une libation à l'autel.[41] Il faut cependant relever une distinction nette entre ce type d'image, que l'on pourrait décrire comme une libation évoquant le sacrifice et d'autres images plus complexes où la libation se combine effectivement, dans une scène sacrificielle, à d'autres actes rituels comme le rôtissage des

FIG. 7. Coupe de Macron. Une femme verse le contenu de son *oinochoe* sur le feu sacrificiel tandis que sur le bras gauche elle porte un panier sacrificiel (*kanoun*) (Toledo 72.55) *(D'après CVA Toledo 1, pl. 53)*

[40]Toledo 72.55; *CVA* 1, pl. 53 (Macron).
[41]Ainsi:
Kassel T 551; *CVA* Kassel 1, pl. 41, 5-7;
Agrigente Giudice 55; *ARV*[2] 652.31 (Peintre de Nicon);
Perdu; A. Greifenhagen, *Alte Zeichnungen nach Unbekannten Griechischen Vasen* (München, 1976), n. 11, Fig. 30 (Peintre de Dresde, D. von Bothmer);
Akrai, Etolie; P. Zaphiropoulou, in *Magna Grecia* 14, n° 5-6 (mai-juin 1979), 9 (Peintre de Bowdoin);
Cyrenia (Chypre) 111; K. Nicolaou, 'Archaeology in Cyprus, 1969-76', *AR* (1975-6), 53, fig. 39;
Vérone 51 Ce; *ARV*[2] 1023.148 (Peintre de la Phiale).

viandes par exemple.[42] C'est alors le problème de la mise en séquence de l'ensemble du sacrifice par l'image qui se pose.[43]

Dans la série qui nous retient, au médaillon des coupes ou sur certain *lecythoi*,[44] la libation à l'autel apparaît donc soit comme le fragment d'un ensemble, soit comme un geste isolé et autonome, qui parfois est visiblement accompagnée d'une prière. Il arrive en effet qu'une inscription vienne préciser le destinataire de l'offrande, comme sur une coupe de Bonn (Fig. 8), où l'on lit ἄναξ Ἑρμῆ;[45] plus souvent qu'une inscription, c'est le geste de la main levé, paume ouverte qui visualise la prière, comme sur une coupe de Tarquinia (Fig. 9).[46] La libation apparaît ainsi comme un geste rituel minimal, qui a son autonomie et que les peintres ont isolé sur de petites surfaces, cercle du médaillon des

A N A + ϟ
E] Ρ Μ E

FIG. 8. Coupe de Bonn. Une inscription précise le destinataire de l'offrande: ἄναξ Ἑρμῆ (Bonn 1227) *(D'après CVA Bonn 1, pl. 7)*

[42]Par exemple sur:
Berlin inv. 3232; *ARV*² 117.2 (Peintre d'Epidromos);
Palerme V 661a; *ARV*² 472.210 (Macron);
Gotha Ahv 51; *ARV*² 1028.10 (Polygnotos);
Londres E 456; *ARV*² 1051.17 (Groupe de Polygnotos, indéterminé);
Darmstadt 478; *ARV*² 1146.48 (Peintre de Cléophon);
Paris Louvre G 402; *ARV*² 1214.2 (Peintre de Craipale).

[43]Sur ce point voir J.L. Durand, 'Du rituel comme instrumental', dans J.P. Vernant et M. Detienne, *La cuisine du sacrifice en pays grec* (Paris, 1979), 167-81; l'analyse de la libation dans le cadre du sacrifice sanglant a fait l'objet du séminaire de J.L. Durand, *AEHE(V^e sect.)* 93 (1984-5), 325.

[44]Les exemples sont fort nombreux en particulier au chapitre 39 des *ARV*² (Painter of slight Lekythoi and Nolans): *e.g. ARV*² 686.204 à 206; 688.230; 690.9; 691.28; 698.35-6; 703.39-42,46; 706.5; 711.50-1; 719.3,11; 723.6.

[45]Bonn 1227; *ARV*² 324.63 (Onésimos); sur la Fig. 8 l'inscription (invisible sur la photo du *CVA*) n'est pas à sa place, elle a été transcrite à l'extérieur du médaillon.

[46]Tarquinia RC 1918; *ARV*² 366.88 (Peintre de Triptolème); pour le geste, voir G. Neumann, *Gesten und Gebarden in der Griechischen Kunst* (Berlin, 1965), 78-82.

FIG. 9. Coupe de Tarquinia. Le geste de la main levée qui visualise la prière (Tarquinia RC 1918) *(D'après La cité des images (Lausanne, 1984), fig. 33)*

coupes ou cylindre des lécythes. Dans une présentation de ce type où figure un seul acteur devant un autel, c'est avant tout le rapport avec les dieux qui est mis en évidence, et la verticalité du lien qui unit les hommes aux dieux.

Dans les images où figurent, autour de la libation, plusieurs personnages, l'accent est plutôt mis sur la circulation collective du vin entre les partenaires du rite. On sait par les textes que la libation comporte deux temps au moins; d'abord on offre une part de liquide aux dieux, puis on boit tour à tour dans une *phiale* qui circule ou chacun dans sa *phiale*. Ainsi sont marqués les deux axes de la circulation du vin, d'une part des hommes aux dieux par l'offrande versée, d'autre part entre hommes que l'acte rituel rend solidaires et qui consomment ensemble le même breuvage. La libation implique en effet un double lien, entre hommes et des hommes aux dieux.

En image ceci correspond aux deux scénographies que l'on remarque, à l'autel, ou en groupe.[47] Mais, tout comme dans l'iconographie du *symposion*, la consommation du

[47]Il existe bien sûr des interférences entre ces deux schémas; on peut être plusieurs à l'autel, par exemple dans certains départs de guerriers:
Paris, Louvre G 431; *ARV*[2] 604.48 (Peintre des Niobides);
Rhodes inv. 13205; *ARV*[2] 610.24 (Manière du Peintre des Niobides);
Syracuse 30747; *ARV*[2] 1153.17 (Peintre du Dinos).

vin est rarement montrée, et les exemples de buveur à la *phiale* sont rares.[48] Le caractère collectif de la libation est parfois marqué par la présence de plusieurs *phiales* que l'on voit présentées en piles, non plus en tant qu'objet thésaurisé mais comme un objet qui se démultiplie à proportion des participants, prenant ainsi une valeur non pas cumulative mais distributive.[49]

La majorité des scènes collectives représente des guerriers, hoplites ou éphèbes; la libation y est toujours servie par une femme[50] qui joue un rôle médiateur essentiel. En dehors des scènes d'armement, il est difficile de savoir si la libation marque un départ ou un retour; le temps en image n'est pas toujours vectorisé de manière explicite. Mais il est clair que la libation accompagne ce moment de séparation ou de retrouvailles, et sert à marquer symboliquement les liens qui unissent entre eux les acteurs de ce rituel. Le passage ainsi célébré peut être purement temporel — départ ou retour — ou bien correspondre à un changement de statut, un passage d'éphèbe à hoplite, comme semblent l'indiquer les images où, comme sur un cratère de Tübingen, un jeune homme en chlamyde et pétase reçoit des armes hoplitiques (Fig. 10).[51] Certaines représentations de départ soulignent par le geste de la *dexiosis*, des mains serrées, ce rapport étroit entre

---

[48]Buveur dans une *phiale*:

Oxford 270; *ARV*^{2} 820.52 (Peintre de Télèphe);

Athènes Acr 396; *ARV*^{2} 628.1 (apparenté au Peintre de Penthésilée; le renvoi à la p. 932 dans l'index des *ARV*^{2} est inexact);

Naples 146741; *ARV*^{2} 1275.3 (entre le Peintre de Codros et Aison).

Sur l'amphore de Bale, Ka 424, *ARV*^{2} 183.8 (Peintre de Cléophradès), un guerrier boit dans une coupe.

[49]Plusieurs *phiales* empilées:

Leningrad b 1584 (St. 1528); *ARV*^{2} 207.134 (Peintre de Berlin) — Niké;

Tarente; *ARV*^{2} 553.35 (Peintre de Pan) — Niké;

Ferrare 3169; *ARV*^{2} 590.9 (Peintre des Niobides) — *phiales* posées sur une table;

Boston 97.371; *ARV*^{2} 1023.146 (Peintre de la *phiale*);

Florence 15 B 24, etc.; *ARV*^{2} 1269.7 (Peintre de Codros); Greifenhagen, *Alte Zeichnungen* (ci-dessus, n. 41), 11, n° 3, Fig. 6.

Femme (ou Niké) tenant plusieurs *phiales*:

Athènes, coll. priv.; *ARV*^{2} 310.3 (Peintre de Palerme 4) — Niké;

Bruxelles A 1579; *ARV*^{2} 486.41 (Hermonax) — Niké;

Londres E 723; *ARV*^{2} 664 (comparer avec Mys);

Palerme; *ARV*^{2} 678.13 (Peintre de Bowdoin) — Niké;

Athènes MN 1827; *ARV*^{2} 685.181 (Peintre de Bowdoin) — Niké;

Perdu, ex Cattaneo; *ARV*^{2} 691.22 (manière du Peintre de Bowdoin) — Niké;

Athènes MN 1749; *ARV*^{2} 697.27 (Peintre d'Icare);

Paris, commerce; *ARV*^{2} 717.220 (Peintre d'Aischines);

Athènes MN 1625; *ARV*^{2} 719.3 (manière du Peintre d'Aischines);

Hannovre 1968,50; *ARV*^{2} 1681/1065.4 bis (Peintre de Mannheim);

Paris, Louvre Cp 10808; *ARV*^{2} 1067.13 (Peintre de Barclay);

Rome, Vatican 17903; *ARV*^{2} 1214.2 (Peintre de Leipzig T 64).

Sur un cratère de Leningrad 634 [(St. 1713); *ARV*^{2} 234.15 (Peintre de Gottingen)] une femme nue effectue un curieux exercice d'équilibre avec trois *phiales*.

[50]La femme apparaît ainsi à la fois comme une servante et un acteur indispensable. Sur cette série voir F. Lissarrague, *L'autre guerrier* (Paris, 1990), 35-53.

[51]Tübingen E 104; *ARV*^{2} 603.35 (Peintre des Niobides).

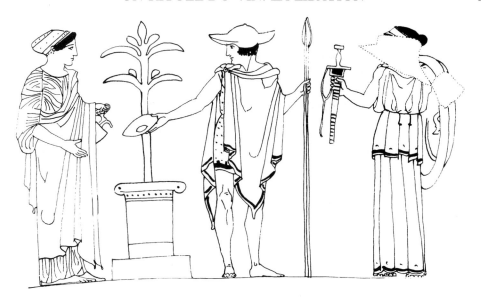

FIG. 10. Cratère de Tübingen. Un jeune homme en chlamyde et pétase reçoit des armes hoplitiques (Tübingen E 104) *(D'après C. Watzinger, Griechische Vasen in Tübingen (Tübingen, 1924), 47)*

les acteurs de la scène; ainsi sur un *stamnos* de Londres (Fig. 11),[52] au centre de l'image, un hoplite tout armé serre la main d'un vieillard à gauche tandis qu'à droite se trouve une femme avec *oinochoe* et *phiale*. La main tenue et la libation sont en quelque sorte deux signes symétriques, deux marques symboliques équivalentes, dans l'ordre du geste et dans l'ordre du rite, pour montrer les liens qui unissent ce groupe.[53]

Le rapport au divin est souvent renforcé dans ces scènes de départ de guerrier par la présence d'une Niké, qui donne ses armes à l'hoplite ou qui présente les instruments de la libation. La figure divine fonctionne alors visuellement comme un embrayeur entre le monde des dieux et le monde des hommes. Un cratère aujourd'hui disparu[54] propose deux scènes parallèles: d'un côté un hoplite et une femme, de part et d'autre d'un autel, offrent une libation aux dieux; de l'autre figure aussi une scène de libation entre femme et guerrier, sans autel, mais en présence d'une Niké qui porte le bouclier de l'hoplite. Autel et Niké fonctionnent dans ces deux scènes comme des signes homologues du rapport au divin, soit sous la forme construite d'un lieu rituel, soit sous la forme d'une présence divine que l'image rend visible.

[52]Londres E 448; *ARV*² 992.65 (Peintre d'Achille); on notera qu'au revers figure également une scène de libation avec un jeune hoplite que sert une femme.

[53]Voir, pour sur cette équivalence *spondai/dexiosis*, Laurens, 'La libation' (ci-dessus, n. 34), 58 n. 29, qui renvoie à *Il.* ii. 339-41 et Eschine iii. 224. Sur le geste dans l'imagerie, Neumann, *Gesten und Gebarden in der Griechischen Kunst* (ci-dessus, n. 46), 49-58 et M. Meyer, *Die Griechischen Urkundenreliefs* (*MDAI(A)* Beiheft 13) (Berlin, 1989), 140-5.

[54]*Cf.* le dessin que publie A. Greifenhagen, 'Zeichnungen nach attisch rotfigurigen Vasen im DAI Rom', *AA* 78 (1977), 211, Fig. 15.

FIG. 11. *Stamnos* de Londres. Un hoplite tout armé serre la main d'un vieillard à gauche tandis qu'à droite se trouve une femme avec *oinochoe* et *phiale* (Londres E 448) *(D'après J.D. Beazley, 'The master of the Achilles amphora in the Vatican', JHS 34 (1914), pl. 15)*

On comprend mieux ainsi la multiplicité des représentations de Niké isolées, en particulier sur des lécythes,[55] où on les voit tenant une *phiale* et assurant la circulation du vin entre hommes et dieux. Ces images sont susceptibles de s'intégrer à l'ensemble des schémas que l'on vient d'évoquer. Niké peut verser une libation dans une scène sacrificielle complexe,[56] ou bien participer à une scène d'armement, de départ, de retour. Dans la mesure où elle marque, plus que la victoire au sens militaire du terme, la réussite, le bon accomplissement, elle peut être présente pour chaque acte humain, que ce soit le travail de l'artisan qu'elle couronne ou la mariée qu'elle salue.[57] Niké est souvent l'officiante d'une libation totalement ouverte, sans destinataire ni acteur spécifié par l'image. L'acte rituel est isolable, autonome, on l'a vu; mais les imagiers accentuent ce caractère en transformant la scène rituelle en un pur signe de ritualité. De même qu'on peut offrir, au lieu de la libation, une *phiale*, on a représenté cette figure divine

[55]Même remarque qu'à la note 44; *e.g. ARV* [2] 678.13-29; 685.181-4; 686.188-95; 687.227,229; 690.1-4; 691.22-3; 699.66; 701.1; 702.10,18,19; 703.39-42,46; 707.2; 721.2.

[56]Ainsi sur:
Londres E 455; *ARV* [2] 1028.9 (Polygnotos);
Gotha Ahv 51; *ARV* [2] 1028.10 (Polygnotos).

[57]Niké couronnant un potier: Milan, Torno; *ARV* [2] 571.73 (Peintre de Leningrad). Les exemples de Niké dans des scènes de mariage ne sont pas rares, en particulier sous les anses des *lebetes gamikoi*; sur ce point *cf.* F. Lissarrague, 'Les femmes au figuré' in P. Schmitt Pantel (ed.), *Histoire des femmes* (Paris, 1991), 159-251, en particulier pp. 174-7.

comme signe du rituel; à l'usager du vase, au spectateur d'intégrer ou non ce signe dans l'acte rituel spécifique qui lui convient.

La figure d'Eros joue parfois en image un rôle équivalent. Ainsi sur une amphore du Louvre (Fig. 12)[58] le jeune dieu vole au dessus d'un autel et tient une *phiale* dans chaque main. Nous retrouvons ici les divers aspects notés jusqu'à présent: le caractère collectif de la libation avec les deux *phiales*, le rapport vertical avec les dieux qu'implique l'autel, enfin la présence effective d'une puissance divine, la plus séduisante, celle qui accompagne Aphrodite et dont les chants des buveurs célèbrent sans cesse les charmes: Eros en personne.

FIG. 12. Amphore du Louvre. Eros vole au dessus d'un autel et tient une *phiale* dans chaque main (Paris, Louvre G 337) *(Musée du Louvre, Chuzeville)*

[58]Paris, Louvre G 337; *ARV* ² 654.11 (Peintre de Charmidès).

Une telle image, et la série qui s'y rattache,[59] réintroduit dans le rituel de la libation un double aspect: d'une part celui de la charis et des valeurs de séduction associées à Eros, d'autre part le plaisir du vin qui rapproche Aphrodite et Dionysos.[60] La libation n'est pas en elle même un acte de séduction, mais on n'est pas surpris de voir Eros voler au devant de Ménélas qui poursuit Hélène et lui offrir une libation qui doit rétablir entre eux des rapports sans violence.[61] De même voit-on Himéros verser une libation au dessus de la tête d'Ariane lorsque Dionysos s'en approche.[62]

En image, la libation prend ainsi des formes variées, selon les espaces où elle se déroule. Bien que ce soit un acte essentiel du *symposion*, auquel elle donne sa dimension religieuse, elle n'est pratiquement pas représentée dans les scènes de *symposion*. En revanche, à travers les vases à boire sur lesquels elle est souvent représentée, elle est intégrée au répertoire visuel du *symposion*. Les nombreuses scènes de libation au départ des guerriers sont vues par les convives qui sont eux mêmes des soldats citoyens.

Ainsi l'image rituelle du vin, dans la libation, construite et codifiée par les peintres de vases, prend place dans l'espace rituel — au sens large — de la consommation du vin.

---

[59]Sur Eros faisant libation ou tenant une *phiale*, voir *LIMC* s.v. 'Eros', nn° 457-9, ainsi que 116 et 661. *Cf.* également A. Greifenhagen, *Griechische Eroten* (Berlin, 1957), 23, Fig. 18 (Munich 2686, non attribué). On remarquera la conjonction Eros/Niké avec *phiales* sur l'*askos* de Londres E 723; *ARV*[2] 664 (comparer avec Mys).

[60]*Cf.* le proverbe: 'Aphrodite et Dionysos vont ensemble', Apostolius iv. 58, E.L. Leutsch et F.G. Schneidewin, *Corpus Paroemiographorum Graecorum* ii (Hildesheim-Olms, 1958-61), 320 et commentaire *ad locum*.

[61]Pyxis de Brauron; *ARV*[2] 631.42 (Peintre de Chicago).

[62]Cratère de Tübingen 5439; *ARV*[2] 1057.97 (Groupe de Polygnotos); le nom d'Himéros est précisé par une inscription.

10

A *Symposion* of Gods?

T.H. CARPENTER

On both the inside and outside of an Attic red-figure cup in London[1] five gods, named, recline on *klinai*, while their wives, also named, sit, or (in one case) stand, by their feet. The painter of the cup, who worked in the 430s, is called the Codrus Painter after a figure on one of his vases in Bologna. He is careful and imaginative in his choice and use of scenes, and his figure-style seems to show the influence of sculpture from the Parthenon. All of the nearly 50 vases attributed to him are drinking vessels.[2]

On the inside of the London cup a bearded Hades (inscribed Plouton) cradles a large empty horn against his shoulder with his left hand and holds up a *phiale* with his right (Fig. 1). Persephone (inscribed Pherrephatta, a variant name for her) sits on the *kline* by his feet; her feet do not reach the ground. She raises up her hands from her lap as if to take the *phiale*.

On the outside of the cup there are four more *klinai*, two on each side. On one side a Doric column must indicate an interior setting (Fig. 2). Poseidon holds a *phiale* in his left hand, a trident in his right, and Amphitrite dips a long pin into an *alabastron*[3] presumably full of perfume. On the other *kline*, Zeus, resting his sceptre against his left shoulder, holds a *phiale* with his left hand and reaches out toward Hera's veil with his right. She wears a diadem and veil and also holds a sceptre. Ganymede stands at the head of the *kline* holding a wine strainer.

On the other side Ares rests his spear against his left shoulder and reaches out toward Aphrodite who stands at his feet holding a *pyxis* (Fig. 3). His *phiale* sits on a table beside the *kline*; the tables beside the other gods are all empty. Dionysus, on the next *kline*, rests his *thursos* against his left shoulder and holds up a *phiale* with his right hand. Ariadne, who sits by his feet, raises her hands in a gesture similar to Persephone's, as if to take the *phiale*. A balding satyr named Komos stands by the head of the *kline*. The feet of all of the women on the outside touch the ground-line.

This is a family gathering of the three brothers who, between them, rule the heavens, the seas and the underworld, together with two sons of Zeus, one legitimate and one not, all with their wives. The disposition of the scenes on the cup — a single

---

[1]London 1847.9-9.6 (E82); *ARV*² 1269.3; *AJA* 82 (1978), 365-6.

[2]*ARV*² 1268-72, 1689; *Paralipomena* 472. In *Attische Vasenmaler des Rotfigurigen Stils* (Tübingen, 1925), 425 Beazley writes, '*sehr feine Schalen mit Anklängen an Parthenonisches*'. Named after Bologna PU 273, *ARV*² 1268.1.

[3]For the gesture, see B. Ridgway, 'The banquet relief from Thasos', *AJA* 71 (1967), 307-8.

FIG. 1. Attic red-figure cup (BM 1847.9-9.6) of the Codrus Painter. View of inside, showing Hades and Persephone *(Courtesy of the Trustees of the British Museum)*

kline in the *tondo* and two on either side of the exterior — is a common one for fifth-century depictions of mortal *symposia*.[4] On the London cup, however, in place of cups or *skyphoi*, the gods hold *phialai*, which are normally used to make offerings. Yet none is pouring or about to pour a libation — Ares has put his on the table beside him while he deals with Aphrodite. Perhaps this is a sign of the painter's wit — having gods in a *symposion* drinking directly from *phialai*.[5] The infibulated penis of the satyr also has its comic side — though it is an old joke since similar satyrs appear as early as 490. Such tying of the foreskin is often shown in depictions of athletes, and it surely interfered with erotic pursuits.[6]

At first glance the scene seems unexceptional — except that the mortal symposiasts we expect to see have been given attributes that turn them into gods. It is something of a surprise, then, to realize that the subject is unique. In fact, of the five male deities, only Dionysus is shown reclining on a *kline* on any other Attic vases before the end of the fifth century.[7]

---

[4]E.g. Villa Giulia 63691, *ARV*[2] 792.52; 8342, *ARV*[2] 792.56. Cf. Gotha 49, *ARV*[2] 467.19, *CVA* 1 pl. 45.

[5]For gods pouring libations, see E. Simon, *Opferende Götter* (Berlin, 1953).

[6]London E 768, *ARV*[2] 446.262, *CVA* 6 pl. 105. For infibulation, see recently D. Sansone, *Greek Athletics and the Genesis of Sport* (Berkeley, 1988), 119-20; and F. Lissarrague, 'Sexual life of Satyrs', in D. Halperin, J. Winkler and F. Zeitlin (eds), *Before Sexuality* (Princeton, 1990), 59-60. Cf. Aesch. *Theoroi* fr. 78a Radt.

[7]Cf. Florence 73127, *ARV*[2] 173.4, *CVA* 3 pl. 75 where Poseidon and Apollo recline on the ground.

FIG. 2. Attic red-figure cup (BM 1847.9-9.6) of the Codrus Painter. View of the outside, showing Poseidon and Zeus reclining on *klinai*, accompanied by Amphitrite, Hera and Ganymede *(Courtesy of the Trustees of the British Museum)*

John Boardman noted in his paper at the first of these *symposia*, in 1984, that the *symposion* form was 'deemed inappropriate for Olympians' and that 'it was only exceptional demi-gods who had much to do with mortals and mortal ways, like Dionysus, Hermes and Herakles who might be shown reclining'.[8] He is, of course, right; gods together either stand or sit — except on this cup. I propose, then, to consider why the Codrus Painter chose to put the gods in a *symposion* when no one before had painted, and no one after him would paint, a similar scene. The Codrus Painter is a painter of considerable subtlety, and I think it can be assumed safely that his choice of images was careful and considered, and that the implications of his choice are worth exploring.

Dionysus is the key to the puzzle. He is pre-eminently the god who reclines. He is shown reclining on Attic vases from the 520s down to the end of red-figure in the fourth century, and, of course, this is the pose Phidias chose for him for the east pediment of the Parthenon — as later did the sculptor of the Lysicrates monument. Outside Attica he is shown reclining in terracotta figurines from Taranto[9] from the beginning of the fifth century on into the fourth, and on coins of Mende[10] from as early as 460 down to 423. However, the faulty syllogism — Dionysus is the god of wine; the *symposion* is about wine; therefore, it is natural for Dionysus to be shown in the *symposion* — is, as we will

[8]J. Boardman, 'Symposium furniture', in O. Murray (ed.), *Sympotica: a Symposium on the* Symposion (Oxford, 1990), 124.

[9]R. Higgins, *Greek Terracottas* (London, 1967), 91.

[10]C. Kraay, *Archaic and Classical Greek Coins* (London, 1976), 136-7.

Fig. 3. Attic red-figure cup (BM 1847.9-9.6) of the Codrus Painter. View of the outside, showing Ares and Dionysus reclining on *klinai*, accompanied by Aphrodite, Ariadne and Komos *(Courtesy of the Trustees of the British Museum)*

see, of little help. The source and significance of the reclining Dionysus must be sought elsewhere. On several fifth-century vases Dionysus is shown picnicking on the ground beneath a vine or a tree, but the intent and imagery of these scenes is only loosely connected with scenes where he reclines on a *kline*.

* * *

Dionysus first appears in Greek art on an Attic black-figure *dinos c.* 580, and by the middle of the fifth century canons for depicting him, at least on Attic vases, are well established.[11] On early Attic black-figure vases he is above all the god of wine. The earliest depictions of him reclining, however, do not appear before the 520s and then he is not a participant in a convivial *symposion*, but is shown on a solitary *kline*, reclining by himself or with a woman.

Symposion scenes were first popular on Corinthian vases and then, by the beginning of the sixth century, on Attic vases.[12] The Heidelberg Painter, who was instrumental in establishing the canon of Dionysian imagery, often painted *symposia* on his cups, but he never included Dionysus in those scenes, nor did he ever show the god reclining.[13] In

[11]See T.H. Carpenter, *Dionysian Imagery in Archaic Greek Art* (Oxford, 1986), 30-54.
[12]For the *symposion* in Greek art see J.-M. Dentzer, *Le motif du banquet couché dans le proche-orient et le monde grec du VII͏ᵉ au IV͏ᵉ siècle avant J.-C.* (Rome-Paris, 1982).
[13]Carpenter, *Dionysian Imagery* (above, n. 11), 31-43.

short, before the 520s vase-painters did not see the reclining pose as appropriate for Dionysus.

Prior to the 520s Achilles and Herakles were the only recognizable figures from myth to be shown reclining on Attic vases. From before the middle of the sixth century Achilles is shown reclining on a solitary *kline*, feasting, while the body of Hektor lies beneath it.[14] From not much later, Herakles is shown reclining on a solitary *kline* in the presence of Athena and Iolaos.[15] Both of these subjects are also depicted by early red-figure painters. In the 520s, when Dionysus adopts a similar pose on a solitary *kline*, it is unlikely to be an entirely independent development. In fact, one of the earliest, on a bilingual amphora by Psiax, is part of a group of three related vases, one of which shows the reclining Herakles (Fig. 4).[16]

Surely the term *symposion* is inappropriate for these scenes which show Achilles or Herakles as reclining banqueters. They are not abbreviations of larger scenes and there is nothing convivial about them. Rather, a much closer parallel is provided by the seventh-century relief from the palace of Ashurbanipal at Nimrud.[17] Thematic and

FIG. 4. Amphora by Psiax (Munich, Antikensammlungen 2301). Herakles reclines on a *kline (Courtesy of the Münchner Stadtmuseum)*

[14]Oxford B 131.30, *CVA* 2 pl. 2.18.

[15]Basel, Cahn 919, H.A.G. Brijder (ed.), *Ancient Greek and Related Pottery. Proceedings of the International Symposium in Amsterdam, 12-15 April 1984* (Amsterdam, 1984), 244, fig. 1.

[16]Munich 2302, *ARV*[2] 6.1, *CVA* 4 pls 153-4; Munich 2301, *ARV*[2] 4.9, *CVA* 4 pls 155-9; Reggio, *ARV*[2] 3.6, B. Cohen, *Attic Bilingual Vases* (New York, 1978), pl. 33.1-4.

[17]London 124920, R. Barnett, *Sculptures from the North Palace of Ashurbanipal at Nimrud* (London, 1976), 56-7, pls 63-5 = Reade pl. 23.

iconographic parallels between that relief and Attic depictions of Achilles in the Ransom of Hektor are striking. On the Assyrian relief the king feasts in the presence of the decapitated head of his foe, the Elamite king Teumman, while servants and submissive captives bring him gifts and food.[18] So, on Attic vases, a reclining Achilles feasts in the presence of the body of his foe while, on most examples, Priam leads a procession of servants with gifts. On the Nineveh relief a table stands by the head of the *kline* with the sword, bow and quiver on it. On one of the earliest examples of Achilles in the Ransom, Hektor's body lies underneath a table to the right of the *kline* on which are a helmet and cuirass.[19]

On shield bands roughly contemporary with the earliest depictions of Achilles reclining in the Ransom of Hektor, Achilles, Hermes and Priam stand over the supine body of Hector.[20] On fragments of an Attic Siana cup contemporary with the shield bands,[21] Achilles and Priam also stood over the body of Hektor, but this form does not appear on later vases. Present evidence allows the conclusion, then, that in about 560 the form of Achilles reclining as he receives Priam replaced an older version where he stood.

The actual link between the Assyrian relief and the Attic depictions has not yet been discovered and may never be, but it seems unlikely that the parallels are accidental.[22] Inded, Åkerstrom is surely right in his conclusion that the oriental royal type, as in the Ashurbanipal relief, 'was adopted in Greece for special purposes'.[23] It was used to show the heroes Achilles and Herakles, and later it was used in so-called *Totenmahl* reliefs to show deceased heroes.[24] That it was also used for Dionysus is, to say the least, puzzling, and it introduces a new and complex dimension to the iconography of the god.

On the amphora by Psiax,[25] Dionysus reclines on a *kline*, naked to the waist and holding a *kantharos* with his left hand. Ivy grows beside him. A woman with *krotala* (Eumelpes) dances by his feet, a satyr (Hiachos) dances at his head. The table is underneath the *kline* with part of the god's *himation* hanging in front of it, and there is no

---

[18]Barnett, *ibid.* p. 56, writes that 'the dead Te-umman's hand, still holding his wand or sceptre, is fixed in a tree above a table bearing what is presumably his bow, his quiver full of arrows and his sword'. H. Frankfort, *The Art and Architecture of the Ancient Orient*, fourth edition (Harmondsworth, 1970), 390 n. 52, notes: 'a hand holding a long stick appears to emerge from the palm tree to the right. Andrae sees in it the act of the numen embodied in the tree'. P. Albenda, 'Landscape bas-reliefs in the *Bit Hilani* of Ashurbanipal', *BASO* 224 (1976), 65-7 shows that the hand belongs to an attendant and holds a 'bird chaser rod'. She notes that 'the original drawing shows the tip of one foot (of the attendant), but this corner of the slab is now broken away'.

[19]Swiss Private, *Paralipomena* 32.1bis, *BJ* 161 (1961), pl. 47.

[20]E.g. Berlin 8099, *LIMC* I, pl. 121, Achilleus 642. See E. Kunze, *Archaische Schildbänder* (Berlin, 1950), 145-8.

[21]Once Curtius, *ABV* 66.50. Drawings of the fragments are in the Beazley Archive, Oxford. For a description of them see F. Johansen, *The Iliad in Early Greek Art* (Copenhagen, 1967), 137.

[22]Dentzer, *Banquet* (above, n. 12), 151 suggests tapestry as a possible medium. For recent comments on the iconography of classical tapestries, see E. Barber, *Prehistoric Textiles* (Princeton, 1991), ch. 16.

[23]A. Åkerstrom, 'Etruscan tomb painting - an art of many faces', *ORom* 13 (1981), 19.

[24]R. Thönges-Stringaris, 'Das griechische Totenmahl', *MDAI(A)* 80 (1965), 1-98; Dentzer, *Banquet* (above, n. 12), ch. 7. See also O. Murray, 'Death and the Symposion', *AION(archeol)* 10 (1988), 239-55.

[25]Munich 2302; see above, n. 16.

footstool. A large piece is missing from the centre of the scene, but two curious semicircles remain at the bottom, just above the ground-line. No similar objects appear beneath a *kline* on other black- or red-figure paintings. One scholar's reconstruction of the missing fragment as part of huge fillets is clearly wrong — if only because there is no place from which they can properly hang. Langlotz, in the *Corpus Vasorum Antiquorum*, also calls them parts of fillets, though he does not suggest a parallel.[26]

Rather, I suggest that these semicircles are the lower parts of two coils of a large snake (Fig. 5). A snake with Dionysus in a gigantomachy by the Syleus Painter *c.* 480 on a *stamnos* in the Louvre[27] best illustrates the way the snake appeared in Psiax's scene. Similar snakes often appear in other Dionysian scenes as well.[28]

A snake does appear beneath the *kline* of the reclining figure on many of the *Totenmahl* reliefs, but not until the fourth century — more than a century after this vase was painted — so the connection is at best tenuous. At the least, however, the snake beneath Dionysus's *kline* and perhaps in some other Dionysian scenes, hints at chthonic connections.[29]

FIG. 5. Reconstruction of the decoration of the Psiax amphora (Munich, Antiken-sammlungen 2302) showing Dionysus reclining on a *kline* (*Photograph courtesy of the Münchner Stadtmuseum; reconstruction drawn by L.C. Lancaster*)

[26] H.R.W. Smith, *New Aspects of the Memnon Painter* (Berkeley, 1929), 47; *CVA* 4 p. 7.

[27] Louvre C11073, *ARV*^{2} 251.37, *RA* 28 (1947), 6-7.

[28] E.g. Tarquinia RC 6848, *ARV*^{2} 60.66, P.E. Arias, M. Hirmer and B.B. Shefton, *A History of Greek Vase-Painting* (London, 1963) pl. 100.

[29] For connections between snakes and the dead see J. Bremmer, *The Early Greek Concept of the Soul* (Princeton, 1983), 80-7, and nn. 22-4 for bibliography.

Another group of scenes showing Dionysus on a solitary *kline* becomes popular with black-figure painters during the last two decades of the sixth century. In these he is shown reclining with a woman, and it is this group of scenes that will lead us back to the Codrus Painter's cup. The earliest is on an amphora in Cambridge[30] *c.* 520. A man and a woman, both naked to the waist and both wearing ivy wreaths, recline on a *kline*. The man holds a *phiale*, the woman touches her wreath with her right hand, perhaps crowning herself. A table stands next to the *kline* with another *phiale* and with food and ivy sprigs on it. By it stands a small naked youth with an *oinochoe* in his right hand, a flower (?) in his left; below it is a dog chewing on a bone. At either end a satyr holds up a maenad; one plays pipes, the other *krotala*.

The dog beneath the *kline* suggests that the painter was drawing on traditional Corinthian and Attic imagery from the convivial *symposion*,[31] but the ivy wreaths and the presence of the satyrs and maenads urge the identification of the man as Dionysus. On the assumption that this is a correct identification, the woman has usually been identified as Ariadne. Before accepting this, however, we need to consider the source of the imagery and the problems raised by such an identification. Not least of the problems is the idea of depicting the wife of a god in such an immodest pose.

* * *

Naked women reclining with men on *klinai* appear as early as 590 on Corinthian vases where couples are shown on adjacent *klinai*.[32] In each instance the man and the woman gaze at each other. Beside each *kline* is a table with food and a stool, and lyres hang from the walls above them. It is generally accepted that the women in these scenes are *hetairai*.[33]

Not much later than the Corinthian vases are some Attic examples. On an amphora in Omaha[34] *c.* 580 animated couples recline on three *klinai*, each with food-laden tables beside it and a dog beneath one. A lyre and a pipes case hang beside them. On a contemporary amphora in the Vatican[35] a man and woman recline on each of two *klinai*. There, however, the women have more modestly pulled their *himatia* up over their left shoulders. Both of these scenes are quite clearly related to Corinthian models and there is little reason to see the women as other than *hetairai*; so too the half-naked women on both sides of a slightly later amphora in the Louvre, one playing pipes.[36] This vase is of particular interest because on one side men and women recline on two *klinai*, while on the other there is only one. Surely the setting is the same on both sides and the single *kline* is to be understood as an abbreviation of a larger scene.

On an Attic black-figure amphora by Lydos from before the middle of the sixth century (Fig. 6), a single *kline* is shown on which a man and a woman recline.[37] The man

---

[30]Cambridge GR27.1864, *ABV* 259.17, *LIMC* III pl. 388, Dionysos 757.

[31]E.g. Louvre 635, Arias, Hirmer and Shefton pl. 32; Louvre E 876, *ABV* 90.1, *CVA* 2 pl. 21.

[32]E.g. D. Amyx, *Corinthian Vase Painters of the Archaic Period* (Berkeley, 1988), pl. 120.

[33]*Ibid.* p. 647.

[34]Omaha, Joslyn Art Museum 1963.480, *Paralipomena* 34, *CVA* 1, pls 10-11.

[35]Vatican 39515, *ABV* 84.3.

[36]Louvre F2, *CVA* 3, pl. 147.1,4.

[37]Florence 70995, *ABV* 110.32, *LIMC* III pl. 388, Dionysos 756. Cf. New York 59.64, *Paralipomena* 31, *CVA* 4 pls 1-2.

Fig. 6. Attic black-figure amphora (Florence, Museo Archeologico 70995) by Lydos, showing a man and woman reclining on a single *kline (Courtesy of the Soprintendenza Archeologica per la Toscana — Firenze)*

and woman, both with *himatia* pulled over their left shoulders, gaze at each other. Their hands are empty. The table has been pushed underneath the *kline*, so there is no food visible, and a large dog lies beneath it; a drinking horn hangs above. At either end of the *kline* komasts (women and naked men) dance. At first glance, this scene also appears to be an abbreviation of larger *symposion* scenes. The komasts, however, give pause, though komasts (usually male) are not infrequently included in Attic *symposion* scenes.[38] Also, the absence of both food and drinking vessels in the couple's hands or on the table is noteworthy.

This scene is often described as Dionysus and Ariadne, but the identifications are surely wrong. Quite simply, we know the genealogy of the scene and no new attributes have been added for the reclining figures. The only possible basis for the identifications is the occurrence of scenes where Dionysus and Ariadne probably do recline together on vases from nearly half a century later — such as the Cambridge *hydria*. The most one can say with any confidence is that the painters of the early scenes might have excerpted a detail from a conventional *symposion* scene to show a specific event rather than a specific couple.

[38]E.g. Taranto 4339, *ABV* 52.28, H. Brijder, *Siana Cups I and Komast Cups* (Amsterdam, 1983), pl. 16c; Helgoland, Kropatscheck, Brijder pl. 43c. See also B. Fehr, 'Entertainers at the Symposion', in Murray, *Sympotica* (above, n. 8), 185-95.

Before returning to the Cambridge vase, a word should be said about the connection between Dionysus and Ariadne. During the course of the sixth century Dionysus often stands or sits with women. Many of these women are simply nymphs or, later, his nurses, but some of them are clearly intended to be specific women. They are rarely named, but when they are named on black-figure vases, they are never Ariadne — which of course does not necessarily mean that the woman never is Ariadne. However, in depictions of the wedding of Peleus and Thetis by both Sophilos and Kleitias, where Zeus, Poseidon and Ares are shown with their wives, Dionysus walks alone. On a later black-figure depiction of gods with the chariot of Peleus and Thetis, Ares and Aphrodite appear together, but Dionysus is accompanied by his mother. Dionysus's mother Semele is named with him on at least three black-figure vases and Aphrodite on two,[39] and most of the women with him in scenes from before about 520 can be explained in terms of one of these two. The first named Ariadne with Dionysus is on a red-figure vase from about 470.

Just what a sixth-century Athenian understood to be the connection between Dionysus and Ariadne is not altogether clear. According to Homer (*Od.* xi. 321-5) Dionysus had Ariadne killed by Artemis on the island of Dia when she had abandoned him for Theseus. Hesiod (*Theog.* 947-9) gives a different version where Dionysus made her his wife and Zeus made her immortal; however, West, among others, has argued that this part of the *Theogony* is a later addition to the poem, probably dating to the sixth century.[40]

By about 470 Attic vase-painters showed a version of the Ariadne story in which Theseus abandons Ariadne at Athena's bidding and Dionysus rescues her. This version is clearest on a *hydria* in Berlin. During the last decades of the sixth century new Theseus stories begin to appear in some quantity as he was rejuvenated or reinvented to become the hero of the new democracy. A late sixth-century date has been posited for a *Theseid* mentioned by Aristotle (*Poet.* 1451ª), to provide the literary versions for the painted scenes.[41] Perhaps that too was the source for the imagery on these vases with Theseus abandoning (and Dionysus saving) Ariadne.[42] Other versions where Ariadne was killed continued to be known, as Polygnotos's mid-fifth-century painting in Delphi shows (Pausanias x. 29.3), where he put her in the underworld with her sister Phaedra. The Attic vases with Dionysus taking Ariadne from Naxos give us a *terminus ante quem* of 470 for her union with the god, though the story need not have become current before the late 500s.

To return to the identity of the half-naked woman reclining with Dionysus on the Cambridge amphora, it seems clear that she is neither Semele nor Aphrodite — nor does it seem likely she is a nymph/*hetaira* Dionysus happened to fancy one night. Of the gods, Dionysus is singularly lacking in lovers.[43] His one amorous adventure involves Ariadne and by a process of elimination she seems to be the only woman who could be shown reclining with him here.

[39]See Carpenter, *Dionysian Imagery* (above, n. 11), 23-4.
[40]*Theogony*, ed. M.L. West (Oxford, 1966), 398.
[41]See, most recently, H.A. Shapiro, *Art and Cult under the Tyrants* (Mainz, 1989), 144.
[42]See T.B.L. Webster, 'The myth of Ariadne from Homer to Catullus', *G&R* 13 (1966), 22-31.
[43]S. Kaempf-Dimitriadou, *Die Liebe der Götter in der Attischen Kunst des 5. Jahrhunderts v. Chr.* (Bern, 1979), 30-2.

The immodesty of the scene must be intentional and must have specific meaning. We know where the imagery comes from, and its intent was obviously erotic. The most likely explanation is that the scene represents the marriage bed and that the painter has borrowed an old form for a new story. A related scene on a contemporary vase, an amphora in Boston,[44] supports this conclusion. There Dionysus stands beside a woman between amorous satyrs and maenads — they are the *komos*. The couple faces, to the right, the end of a *kline*, which is surely intended for them. The atmosphere of the scene is highly erotic, and this can only be Dionysus and Ariadne approaching their marriage bed.

That it was not inappropriate under some circumstances to show explicitly the foreplay of Dionysus and Ariadne on their wedding night is made very clear by the pantomime at the end of Xenophon's *symposion* (9.2-7) where actors depict the couple in their wedding chamber. It is perhaps significant that as the couple headed for the bridal couch, those guests 'who were unwedded swore that they would take themselves wives and those who were already married mounted horse and rode off to their wives that they might enjoy them'. The eroticism led to thoughts of marriage!

A comparison between the Cambridge scene and a contemporary scene with mortals is useful here. On one side of an amphora in the White/Levy collection, recently displayed in New York,[45] a bearded man and a woman who is naked to the waist recline on a *kline* (Fig. 7). The man rests his right hand on the woman's shoulder. Beside the *kline* is a table with food on it, and at either end is a naked man. The man at the foot of the *kline* holds out a wreath toward the couple; the man at the head dances. There are no drinking vessels. The scene is an heir to the imagery on the amphora in Florence. This is not an extract from a *symposion*, it is a celebration — most likely a marriage scene — and perhaps it makes clearer the meaning of the earlier scenes.

The connection between this vase and the Cambridge vase is made even clearer by the scenes on the obverse of each. Here a woman playing pipes leads a procession of three naked men, two carrying wine-skins and one carrying a large volute *krater* (Fig. 8). Under each handle a naked man vomits. On the other side of the Cambridge amphora is a procession of satyrs — one plays pipes, one carries a column *krater* and an *oinochoe* and one carries a wine-skin. Both vases tell the same story — one on a level of myth, the other on the level of mortal life. The latter has been borrowed to tell the former. The new Dionysiac scene with Dionysus and Ariadne reclining together on a *kline* is quite popular with black-figure vase-painters during the last decades of the sixth century and the first decades of the fifth, particularly on cheap black-figure *lekuthoi*, though in most Ariadne is fully clothed.

Red-figure painters, after about 470, put the union between Dionysus and Ariadne into a narrative context. On a fragment of a red-figure *krater* in Tübingen[46] from after the middle of the fifth century Dionysus with a *thursos* approaches a woman named 'Ariadne', in a *chiton*, who reclines on a mattress that seems to rest on a pile of rocks —

[44]Boston 76.40, *Paralipomena* 144.1, *CVA* 1 pl. 39.

[45]New York, White/Levy: D. von Bothmer (ed.), *Glories of the Past* (New York, 1990), 140-1. See also Amherst College 1950.59, *ABV* 321, D. Buitron, *Attic Vase Painting in New England Collections* (Harvard, 1972), 50-1, no. 20.

[46]Tübingen 5439, *ARV*² 1057, *CVA* 4 pl. 18.

FIG. 7. Amphora (New York, Shelby White and Leon Levy collection), showing a bearded man and a woman reclining on a *kline (Courtesy of the Shelby White and Leon Levy Collection. Photograph by Sheldon Collins)*

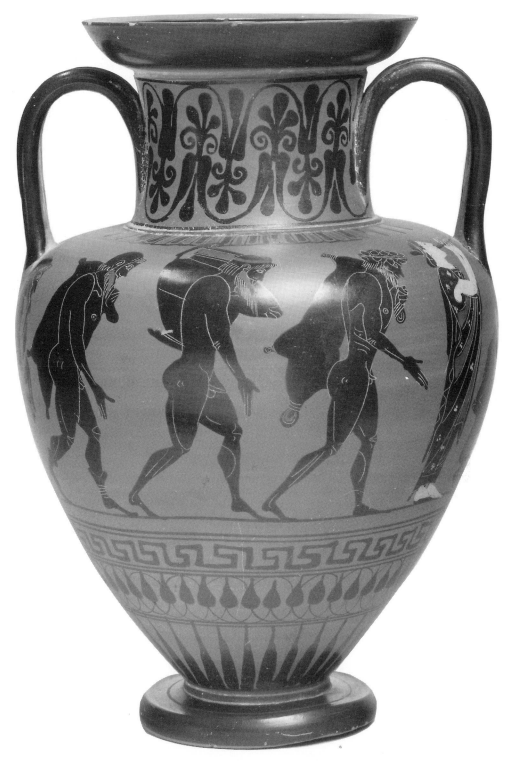

FIG. 8. Amphora (New York, Shelby White and Leon Levy collection), showing a woman playing pipes leading a procession of three naked men *(Courtesy of the Shelby White and Leon Levy Collection. Photograph by Sheldon Collins)*

presumably on Naxos. 'Himeros' holds a *phiale* above her and a naked figure, probably a satyr, follows Dionysus with a *kantharos* and *oinochoe* (*chous*). Of this scene Erika Simon has written that 'the picture shows an etiological myth closely connected with the sacred wedding of the Anthesteria'.[47] Walter Burkert agrees that in such scenes Ariadne and the *basilinna* are interchangeable.[48] Simon and Burkert are, of course, referring to the ritual performed each year during the festival of the Anthesteria in Athens, where the *basilinna*, the wife of the *archon basileus*, was married to Dionysus in the Boukolion in or near the Agora. Though no ancient source tells of the nature of this union, there has been much speculation, and several red-figure vases have been said to show elements of that sacred marriage.[49]

Presumably this principle of interchangeability between the unions of Dionysus and Ariadne and Dionysus and the *basilinna* would have to apply to the earlier scenes as well. This is, in some ways, an attractive solution to the problem of the meaning of the procession on the back of the White/Levy amphora. This is no normal sympotic *komos*, if only because drinking vessels are completely absent. On the other hand, the wineskins might allude to the prize for the drinking contest on the second day of the Anthesteria festival, and the vomiting men could well allude to a common result of that same contest. The satyrs, then, on the Cambridge amphora raise the scene to the level of myth. However, given the ambiguity of Ariadne's relationship with Dionysus before the end of the sixth century, and given the antiquity of the Anthesteria, it seems unlikely that the union of Dionysus should be considered an *aition* for the union with the *basilinna*; perhaps, rather, the reverse.

Around 520 another scene appears with Dionysus reclining in the presence of a woman and the format here is close to that on the Codrus Painter's cup. The earliest of these scenes is on an amphora in Boston (Fig. 9).[50] Dionysus, wearing an ivy wreath and holding a cup, reclines on a *kline*. A woman wearing a *himation* over a *chiton* sits on the edge of the *kline* by his knees and offers him a flower. A table with food on it stands beside them and she rests her feet on a stool. A grapevine, in which a satyr climbs, grows up to the right of the *kline* and spreads across the top of the scene. At the foot of the *kline* are two satyrs, one playing pipes, and a nymph with *krotala*. Several other similar scenes appear on vases from the end of the sixth century.[51]

It seems likely that this is simply a more modest variation on the other scene and that the woman is again Ariadne. The similarities between these scenes and the form of the Dionysus group on the Codrus Painter's cup in London, where Ariadne is named, support this, though the gap of as much as seven decades between the black-figure scenes and the later one might make us pause. However, a named Ariadne in a similar

[47]E. Simon, *Festivals of Attica* (Madison, 1983), 97; also, 'Ein Anthesterien Skyphos des Polygnotos', *AK* 6 (1963), 12.

[48]W. Burkert, *Homo Necans* (Berkeley, 1983), 233.

[49]Simon, 'Ein anthesterien Skyphos des Polygnotos' (above, n. 47), 6-22.

[50]Boston 01.8052, *ABV* 242.35, *CVA* 1 pl. 24.

[51]E.g. Bologna G.M.5, *CVA* 1 pl. 7. See also Rothschild, Pregny, *ABV* 268.30, J. Burow, *Der Antimenesmaler* (Mainz, 1989), pl. 60. Cf. Berlin F 1890, *ABV* 269.34; Burrow pl. 61; Louvre C 11288; *CVA* 12 pl. 188; once D.M. Robinson, 'Unpublished Greek vases in the Robinson Collection', *AJA* 60 (1956), pl. 6.28.

FIG. 9. Amphora (Boston, Museum of Fine Arts 01.8052) showing Dionysus reclining on a *kline*, accompanied by a woman and a satyr, with a
table of food at the side of the *kline (Courtesy of the Boston Museum of Fine
Arts)*

pose on a *psykter/krater c.* 470 recently purchased by the Metropolitan Museum in New York[52] helps to establish the link (Figs 10-11).

I suggest, then, that the woman who reclines with Dionysus and the woman who sits at his feet as he reclines on black-figure vases are both Ariadne. Furthermore, I suggest that these are the first depictions of Ariadne with Dionysus on Attic vases and that the imagery here is specifically connected with her marriage to the god. The underlying tone is erotic, and in fact Ariadne appears in no other context with Dionysus on Attic vases of any period. With her comes romance.

FIG. 10. *Psykter/krater* of *c.* 470 (New York, Metropolitan Museum of Art 1986. 11.12), showing Dionysus and Ariadne reclining on a *kline (Courtesy of the Metropolitan Museum of Art, New York, Classical Purchase Fund, 1986)*

[52]New York 1986.11.12, Christies sale catalogue 16 July 1986, no. 141. I am grateful to Carlos Picón for providing me with pictures of this vase and granting me permission to publish them.

FIG. 11. *Psykter/krater* of *c.* 470 (New York, Metropolitan Museum of Art 1986. 11.12), showing Dionysus and Ariadne reclining on a *kline (Courtesy of the Metropolitan Museum of Art, New York, Classical Purchase Fund, 1986)*

Turning back to the London cup, it seems clear that the imagery used to depict Dionysus and Ariadne here is wedding imagery, which was originally borrowed from the convivial *symposion* and which ironically and perhaps inappropriately is here returned to that context. Significantly, nothing about Dionysus in this scene connects him with his function as wine god — even his *kantharos* is missing.

Some of the imagery used to depict other couples on the London cup also seems inappropriate for a convivial *symposion*. Appearing on the same side of the cup with Dionysus and Ariadne, Aphrodite stands by Ares holding up a *pyxis*, which in Attic vase-paintings and in the paintings on Attic *pyxides* is almost always associated with women, and often in a wedding context.[53] Assuming that it holds Aphrodite's perfumes or potions, this, surely, is an odd vessel to appear in a *symposion*.

Erika Simon has argued convincingly that the *hieros gamos* lies behind the imagery of the depiction of Zeus and Hera on the other side of the cup,[54] and she points to parallels in the east frieze of the Parthenon, where Hera, seated in front of Zeus, unveils

[53]See S. Roberts, *The Attic Pyxis* (Chicago, 1978), 4, 178. E.g. London E744, *ARV* [2] 1250.32.
[54]Simon, *Opfernde Götter* (above, n. 5), 60; cf. K. Arafat, *Classical Zeus* (Oxford, 1990), 7, 98-9.

herself as she turns to look at him, and a metope from Temple E at Selinus, where she stands in front of Zeus unveiling herself as Zeus, seated on a rock, reaches up to grasp her wrist. It was this *hieros gamos* that was celebrated at the Theogamia in Athens, the festival that gave its name to the month of its celebration, Gamelion.

Amphitrite, seated by Poseidon, dips a long pin into an *alabastron*, which is presumably full of scented oil, before perfuming her hair. The *alabastron*, like the *pyxis*, is almost exclusively a woman's vase, and it too is associated with wedding scenes. Both the gesture and the vessel, like Aphrodite's, seem inappropriate for a *symposion*.

In short, the imagery used to depict each of the four groups allows each to be understood as a couple on its nuptial couch. Iconographic parallels support such an interpretation for Zeus and Dionysus, vessels usually associated with marriage support a similar interpretation for Aphrodite and Amphitrite.

Plouton with Persephone in the *tondo* remains to be explained. It was, and is, the easiest scene on the cup to look at closely, and, set by itself in the centre of the cup, it makes a stronger impression than those on the outside. Where the column on the outside suggests that the setting is indoors, presumably on Olympos, there is no setting here and the figures are isolated from the others. The scene recalls the passage in the Homeric *Hymn to Demeter* (343), where Hermes seeks out Hades in his house and finds him on a couch with Persephone beside him. On this cup, her feet dangling in the air may refer to her helplessness as she sits there, yearning to be with her mother, away from him. The connotations are ambiguous. On the one hand this is Plouton with his *cornucopia*, symbolizing the wealth of the earth — though here, ironically, the *cornucopia* is empty. On the other hand, he is Hades, ruler of the underworld, with his captive bride. The *kline*, it is worth remembering, is a proper place to dine and drink and to make love, but it is also a proper place to be laid out when dead.

The scenes on the Codrus Painter's cup have mainly to do with marriage, and depictions of the marriage bed of Dionysus and Ariadne provide the formula for depictions of the other deities. From the earliest depictions of the gods on Attic pottery, Zeus and Hera, Poseidon and Amphitrite, and Ares and Aphrodite are paired as paradigms of the divine family. Hera and Aphrodite are thematically necessary as well. As Walter Burkert has written, '... the archetype of consummated marriage ... Hera is everywhere the goddess of weddings and marriage — while seduction and carnal pleasure remain the responsibility of Aphrodite'.[55] So Hera is shown with Zeus in a pose that reflects other depictions of the 'sacred marriage' and Aphrodite, alone of the women, stands. She is in control, albeit beside her legal spouse, with her *pyxis* of perfume or potions.

There at the centre of the cup, the most important place, is Persephone, the unwilling bride, sitting helplessly on the *kline* with her feet hanging in the air, an image many would have recognized from the Homeric *Hymn to Demeter*. The painter has given us all types and sorts of marriages, but the greatest emphasis seems to be on Persephone whose lot, it should be remembered, is not altogether negative. Rather, the focus is on the ambiguity of her plight and this ambiguity is further highlighted by the nature of the

---

[55]W. Burkert, *Greek Religion* (Oxford, 1985), 132.

wedding imagery and its connection with funerary imagery. So, for example, the *alabastron* and *pyxis*, appropriate at a wedding, also have distinct funerary connotations.[56]

It is unlikely that the painter was unaware of the growing popularity of carved reliefs that showed a man reclining on a *kline* with a woman seated by his feet — the so-called *Totenmahl*-reliefs. On the earliest surviving example, *c.* 520 from Tegea,[57] the woman seated on a chair at the foot of the *kline* holds back her veil with her left hand in a gesture similar to Hera's on the Parthenon and Selinus reliefs. On another early example, *c.* 460 from Thasos,[58] the woman seated on a chair at the head of the *kline* holds an *alabastron* with her left hand and a pin with her right, just as Amphitrite does on the London cup. So too the banquet couch in these reliefs may be seen as the marriage bed, yet at the same time it is, of course, the *kline* of a deceased hero.

* * *

We can probably assume that a fifth-century Athenian would have been as surprised as we are to see the gods in a *symposion* — and it should be repeated that the form and disposition of the scenes on this cup are explicitly used by many painters to depict convivial *symposia*. The Codrus Painter clearly wanted the viewer to be surprised. The presence of Ganymede with a wine-strainer by the *kline* of Zeus can only be explained as another direct allusion to the *symposion*. Yet the scene is clearly not a *symposion* in the strict sense of the word — each of the couples is self-contained — none interacts with other couples — nor is there drinking or eating or singing or music of any sort — only the satyr Komos by the *kline* of Dionysus hints at such activity — a subtle reminder of the komos before the wedding night.

Rather, we have here the *kline* as nuptial couch. The erotic elements of the *symposion*, where men cavort with *hetairai*, have been taken over for divine couples. So, while the scene is eminently respectable, the underlying tone is erotic. Yet at the same time there is a reminder of the *kline* as funerary couch — through the presence of Hades, the use of funerary/wedding imagery and the parallels with the *Totenmahl*-reliefs. Above all, the many layers of interconnecting allusion, on a cup which was surely intended for the drinking of wine, show the breadth and variety of meanings which the imagery from the *symposion* could have for classical painters and sculptors.

[56]Roberts, *Pyxis* (above, n. 53), 4; see Athens, NM, 1963, *ARV*[2] 995.122, *CVA* 1 pl. 3,4; Athens, NM, 12784, *ARV*[2] 998.162, *CVA* 1 pl. 5.2.

[57]Athens, NM, 55, *AM* 80 (1965), pl. 6.1.

[58]Istanbul 1947, *AM* 80 (1965), pls 3-4.

WINE AND SOCIETY IN ETRURIA AND ITALY

11

Il Banchetto in Italia Centrale: Quale Stile di Vita?

ANNETTE RATHJE

The ways people eat, dress, or lodge, at the different levels of that society, are never a matter of indifference.

F. Braudel, *Civilization and Capitalism, 15-18th Century I. The Structures of Everyday Life* (London, 1981): 29

La nozione secondo cui il posto che un individuo occupa a banchetto corrisponde a quello che gli è assegnato nella società è oramai acquisita, come ha ricordato J.M. Dentzer in occasione di una discussione svoltasi a Roma alcuni anni fa.[1] Si tratta ora di evitare il pericolo delle generalizzazioni astratte e schematiche: il nostro compito attuale è quello di studiare a fondo i vari contesti storici in cui troviamo il banchetto, per comprenderne ancor meglio le diverse problematiche ed il vero significato, anche quando non siamo in grado di ricostruire l'atteggiamento mentale che sta dietro tutti i contesti esaminati. Nel caso dell'Etruria, in particolare, non possiamo collegare le rappresentazioni figurative del banchetto con testi letterari e poetici, come si è fatto per la Grecia e per le varie culture del vicino Oriente.

Nel mio caso, lo studio del banchetto ha costituito un elemento unificante rispetto a due ambiti di ricerca nei quali ho lavorato: da una parte mi sono trovata ad occuparmene in relazione al materiale restituito dagli scavi di Ficana, dall'altra il mio interesse per il commercio a lunga distanza (inteso come veicolo per lo scambio di informazione oltrechè di merci) mi ha indotto a prendere in considerazione la situazione globale dell'area mediterranea. Il risultato per me è stato che il banchetto ha assunto un ruolo centrale nel mio modello di studio sui processi di acculturazione,[2] dal momento che nell'epoca in questione — il periodo orientalizzante — si verifica un vero cambiamento nella cultura materiale, corrispondente ad un mutamento nelle

---

[1] In occasione della tavola rotonda '*Aspects du banquet dans le monde grec et l'Italie antique*', svoltasi il 9 maggio 1984 presso l'École française de Rome.

[2] A. Rathje, 'Banquet and ideology. Some new considerations about banqueting at Poggio Civitate (Murlo)', in R. de Puma e J.P. Small (edd.), *Murlo and the Etruscans. Essays in Memory of Kyle Meridith Phillips Jr* (Wisconsin, 1994), 95-9.

abitudini alimentari di cui si è già tanto parlato e su cui non ritornerò in questa sede.[3]

L'orientalizzante in Etruria è un fenomeno complesso da studiare, anche perchè si afferma in un periodo di transizione tra età del ferro ed età arcaica, vale a dire in un ambito cronologico a cavallo tra gli studi di preistoria e quelli di archeologia storica (per usare una distinzione convenzionale). Siamo ancora ben lontani da una piena comprensione dell'orientalizzante in tutte le sue sfumature, siamo, anzi, appena agli inizi, ed anche la semplice raccolta di tutti i dati necessari per una sintesi seria è compito assai impegnativo.

Cio che mi propongo di fare in questo contributo è di usare il banchetto come ottica per comprender meglio questo fenomeno, nella consapevolezza che esso fornisce un punto di vista divenuto oramai assolutamente centrale. Il che non può che colpire, quando si pensi — come ci ha ricordato Oswyn Murray — alla posizione occupata dagli studi sul banchetto ed il simposio agli inizi degli anni '80.[4] I dati che ho potuto utilizzare per questo tipo di indagine sono esclusivamente archeologici, come del resto nel caso di un mio precedente contributo alla raccolta di *Sympotica*, che considero solo un primo passo di un lungo itinerario ancora da percorrere.[5]

Dalla discussione di quel mio primo contributo con Oswyn Murray emerse una certa ambiguità delle mie conclusioni: non avevo a quel punto le idee chiare su ciò che andava attribuito ad influenza greca e quello che mi pareva fosse invece da considerare come 'orientale'; nel caso, in particolare, delle posizione — seduta o reclinata — adottata dai commensali il quadro appariva assai confuso.

Dal momento che secondo il modello generalmente accettato gli Etruschi avrebbero adottato il banchetto dai Greci, o meglio che i Greci avrebbero importato in Etruria l'idea stessa del banchetto (idea questa frutto di una concezione degli Etruschi come rappresentanti di una *Randkultur* ai margini del mondo civile[6]) mi è parso opportuno mettere a confronto l'impatto greco con quello 'orientale' per verificare se tale modello fosse valido o se non fosse invece una conseguenza della ben nota posizione egemone della Grecia nell'ambito degli studi sul Mediterraneo antico.[7] La mia impressione è che nel dimostrare l'inattendibilità del racconto erodoteo di una migrazione etrusca dall'oriente, si sia finito col negare l'influsso orientale sulla civiltà etrusca. Da diversi anni sono venuta ribadendo la necessità di non sottovalutare l'impato che il contatto con la rete commerciale fenicia ha avuto con la società etrusca,

[3]M. Gras, 'Vin et société à Rome et dans le Latium à l'époque archaïque', in *Modes de contacts et processus de transformation dans les sociétés anciennes. Actes du colloque de Cortone 1981* (Pisa-Roma, 1983), 1074; cfr. anche J. Goody, *Cooking, Cuisine and Class. A Study in Comparative Sociology* (Londra, 1982), *passim*, e da ultimo M. Botto, 'Sul commercio fenicio nel Tirreno nell'VIII e nel VII sec. a.C.', *AION(archeol)* 12 (1990), 213.

[4]'Sympotic history', in O. Murray (ed.), *Sympotica: a Symposium on the* Symposion (Oxford, 1990), 7.

[5]A. Rathje, 'The adoption of the Homeric banquet in central Italy in the Orientalizing Period', in Murray, *Sympotica* (sopra, n. 4), 279-88.

[6]J. Boardman, *The Greek Overseas*, terza edizione (Londra, 1980), 199; G. Camporeale, 'La cultura dei principi', in M. Cristofani (ed.), *Civiltà degli Etruschi* (Milano, 1985), 79-80.

[7]Sulla tendenza 'greco-centrica' degli studi sul Mediterraneo antico, problema storiografico di grande importanza, vedi ora M. Bernal, *Black Athena. The Fabrication of Ancient Greece 1785-1985* (Londra, 1987); cfr. anche D.W.J. Gill, 'Pots and trade: spacefillers or *objects d'art?*', *JHS* 111 (1991), 41.

e mi rallegro che studiosi illustri, partendo da approcci ben diversi, siano giunti ad una conclusione simile.[8] Alcuni anni orsono Moorey già notava la popolarità dei servizi da bere nel commercio tra l'Italia e l'Oriente,[9] ed io cercavo a mia volta di dimostrare come la maggior parte degli oggetti di lusso in questo commercio appartenesse a servizi da banchetto,[10] compreso un *rhyton* con testa leonina uguale a quelli conosciuti dai rilievi dei palazzi neo-assiri.[11] Alla fine sono arrivata a domandarmi se non fosse l'idea stessa del banchetto ad essere stata trasmessa dall'Oriente, come del resto altre idee risultanti nell'adozione di usi orientali nella società etrusca.[12] Nel prendere l'impegno di ripubblicare il fregio architettonico da Murlo, avevo trovato ispirazione nelle parole di Bruno D'Agostino: 'Si avverte invece ora l'esigenza di rielaborare le iconografie adattandole ai contenuti locali ed inserendo temi e scene estranei alla tradizione greca'.[13]

Il sito di Poggio Civitate, Murlo, occupa una posizione chiave nello studio dei cambiamenti di costume. Si tratta di un centro remoto, miracolosamente preservato per il fatto che non fu mai più riedificato dopo la sua distruzione nel sesto secolo a.C. Come ben capito dal Prof. Phillips più di vent'anni orsono, i ritrovamenti da questo sito sono di importanza cruciale: possiamo qui studiare vari aspetti della società che altrove devono essere ricostruiti, come in un *puzzle* di cui non possediamo tutte le tessere.[14] Ed uno degli aspetti che Poggio Civitate ci permette di studiare è proprio la funzione ed il significato del banchetto. Ricordo brevemente il contesto: su una collina toscana, ben difesa, si trovano i resti di due ampi edifici sovrapposti, *lower* e *upper building*.[15] Gli scavatori pur affermando di non essere 'in grado di stabilire con assoluta certezza la funzione dei complessi orientalizzante ed arcaico' credono però che essa fosse 'la stessa per entrambi i gruppi di edifici'.[16] Si tratta di una affermazione molto importante perchè a tutt'oggi solo loro conoscono il materiale nella sua totalità. Per E. Nielsen l'emergere di un complesso monumentale su questa scala va visto come una manifestazione della ricchezza acquisita nella zona delle colline metallifere.[17] Il primo edificio appartiene al mondo orientalizzante ben noto dalla *facies* delle tombe principesche:[18] a Murlo si sono trovati infatti avorio lavorato, calderoni di bronzo e

---

[8]M. Martelli, 'I Fenici e la questione orientalizzante in Italia', in *Atti del II congresso internazionale di studi Fenici e Punici* III (Roma, 1991), 1049-72.

[9]P.R.S. Moorey, 'Metal wine sets in the ancient Near East', *IA* 15 (1980), 181-97.

[10]A. Rathje, 'I Keimelia orientali', *Opus* 3 (1984), 341-54.

[11]A. Rathje, 'Oriental imports in Etruria in the eighth and seventh centuries BC: their origins and implications', in D. Ridgway e F.R. Ridgway, *Italy before the Romans* (Londra, 1979), 145-83, e fig. 1. Ma ora penso che il *rhyton* sia stato prodotto a Sam'al e spero di tornare sull'argomento.

[12]A. Rathje, 'Manners and customs in central Italy', *Acta Hyperborea* 1 (1988), 81-90.

[13]B. D'Agostino, 'L'immagine, la pittura e la tomba nell'Etruria arcaica', *Prospettiva* 32 (1983), 2-12.

[14]K.M. Phillips Jr., 'Bryn Mawr College excavations in Tuscany, 1966', *AJA* 71 (1967), 139.

[15]Per la bibliografia generale del sito rimando al lavoro di I.E. Berry in K.M. Phillips Jr., *In the Hills of Tuscany. Recent Excavations at the Etruscan Site of Poggio Civitate (Murlo, Siena)* (Philadelphia, 1993), 107-40.

[16]E.O. Nielsen e K.M. Phillips Jr., in S. Stopponi (ed.), *Case e palazzi d'Etruria* (Milano, 1985), 64.

[17]'Some observations on early Etruria', in T. Hackens, N.D. Holloway e R.R. Holloway (edd.), *Crossroads of the Mediterranean* (Louvain-Providence, 1984), 255-9; cfr. ora E. Mangani, 'L'orientalizzante recente nella valle dell'Ombrone', *AION(archeol)* 12 (1990), 11.

[18]Il fenomeno merita uno studio approfondito, che possa avvalersi della pubblicazione in forma scientifica del materiale. Ci auguriamo di avere presto la ripubblicazione di vecchi scavi, sul modello, ad esempio, di F. Canciani e F.W. von Hase, *La tomba Bernardini di Palestrina* (Roma, 1979).

soprattutto molto vasellame di ceramica fine che formava servizi da banchetto.[19]
L'edificio fu decorato con terraccotte architettoniche che secondo la collega svedese Eva
Rystedt esprimono la volontà di autocelebrazione di una élite aristocratica.[20] Quando
questo edificio fu distrutto da un incendio (fortuito), venne costruito il cosidetto *upper
building* che testimonia ancor meglio la pratica del banchetto. Da qui proviene infatti,
oltre al cospicuo servizio da banchetto trovato insieme a numerosi resti ossei di animali,
la decorazione dell'edificio, con la più antica rappresentazione ritrovata in Italia di una
scena di banchetto con persone sdraiate, anche se alla rovescia.[21] Non è questa la sede
per discutere della decorazione figurata nel suo complesso, ne' di commentare le altre
scene del fregio, del resto ben note: la corsa a cavallo, l'assemblea e la processione. Sto
lavorando alla pubblicazione del fregio nel suo insieme e la mia ipotesi di lavoro è che i
quattro motivi formino un programma ideologico e che il fregio rappresenti una serie di
momenti reali nella vita di Murlo. La stessa ricchezza di dettagli fornisce un argomento
a sostegno di questa ipotesi. Quanto alla vecchia discussione sulla possibilità che le
immagini vadano intese come rappresentazioni di divinità, possiamo piuttosto pensare
ad esseri umani che hanno scelto di farsi raffigurare come divini.[22] Ciò che è certo è che
nel caso delle scene di banchetto la corrispondenza del tema figurativo con la vita reale
di questa comunità trova ampia conferma nei reperti archeologici.

Murlo ha assunto senza dubbio un significato particolarmente rilevante nella storia
degli studi, poichè si tratta di uno dei pochi contesti non funerari ad essere conservati; in
questo senso la sua funzione è paragonabile a quella svolta dall'Ara Pacis per la nostra
conoscenza dell'arte propagandistica augustea. Due aspetti fondamentali emergono
dallo studio del fregio; la cospicua presenza femminile[23] e l'ostentazione di lusso ed
opulenza come indicatori di status. Questo secondo aspetto si spiega ancora bene
nell'ambito dello stesso fenomeno rappresentato dall'esibizionismo delle grandi tombe
del settimo secolo a.C. La connessione, già proposta ormai da diversi anni,[24] mi fa
pensare alle rappresentazioni del fregio come ancora appartenenti alla sfera
dell'orientalizzante, o meglio me le fa vedere come pertinenti ad uno stile di vita
proprio del secolo precedente, come, in altre parole, un anacronismo. È per questo che
non guardo alla rappresentazione del banchetto di Murlo come alla prima di una serie
ampiamente documentata nelle decorazioni di terracotta,[25] nelle pitture tombali, sui

---

[19]Stopponi, *Case e palazzi* (sopra, n. 16), 80-8, 138-48.

[20]E. Rystedt, 'Architectural terracotta as aristocratic display: the case of seventh century Poggio
Civitate (Murlo)', *Opus* 3 (1984), 367-76.

[21]J.P. Small, 'The banquet frieze from Poggio Civitate (Murlo)', *SE* 39 (1971), 25-61; *eadem*, 'Directions in Etruscan art', *ORom* 15 (7) (1987), 125-35; *eadem*, 'Eat, drink and be merry: some thoughts on
Etruscan banquets', in de Puma e Small, *Murlo and the Etruscans* (sopra, n. 2) 85-94.

[22]Per l'argomentazione di questa ipotesi mi sia consentito rimandare al mio studio d'insieme sul
fregio (in preparazione).

[23]Fatto che ho analizzato nel mio contributo 'Alcune considerazioni sulle lastre da Poggio Civitate
con figure femminili', in A. Rallo (ed.), *Le donne in Etruria* (Roma, 1989), 75-84.

[24]M. Torelli, *Storia degli Etruschi* (Bari, 1981), 83-98; l'idea è ripresa da M. Menichetti, *Archeologia del
potere* (Milano, 1994), 35-8.

[25]Come ha fatto Small (vedi sopra, n. 21).

cippi chiusini, le ciste d'avorio etc.:[26] perchè penso che le immagini offerte da tutti questi altri monumenti riflettano una realtà diversa, più nettamente ellenizata, in cui, ad esempio, si riconosce chiaramente la rappresentazione di esseri divini. Il fregio con banchetto di Murlo si colloca invece alla fine di una serie di raffigurazioni del banchetto tipiche dell'orientalizzante, anche se in Etruria i partecipanti sono presentati in una posizione diversa, cioè seduti anzichè sdraiati. Il che non costituisce alcun problema, come ha ben dimostrato Dentzer,[27] e come emerge dalle varie rappresentazioni del Vicino Oriente.

Cerchiamo ora di comprendere meglio queste immagini, partendo dal punto di vista che esse sono state scelte con cura per riflettere una determinata ideologia. Come ricordavo sopra tutto il fregio è ricco di dettagli eseguiti con una minuzia non facile a riprodursi in terracotta.[28] Balza anzitutto agli occhi la posizione centrale del calderone con il suo sostegno chiaramente metallico che, da una parte, divide la scena in due sezioni o gruppi, e dall'altra enfatizza la funzione dell'oggetto stesso, un contenitore per miscelare vino ed acqua; il quale dunque unisce al tempo stesso i due gruppi, dal momento che i commensali hanno già cominciato a bere il vino miscelato (Fig. 1). Risalta immediatamente, anche ad uno sguardo superficiale, l'organizzazione della scena in due gruppi antitetici, costituiti ciascuno da una coppia sdraiata su un letto, davanti ad una tavola sulla quale sono collocati dei cibi. È quest'ultimo elemento a farmi parlare in questo caso di banchetto: l'esibizione di beni di consumo che caratterizza questa rappresentazione la distingue nettamente dal contesto greco del simposio, dove si beve soltanto. I due gruppi sono accuditi ciascuno da un inserviente con brocca e coppa, ma si nota subito l'assenza di ripetizione tra le due sezioni, tranne che nel caso di elementi secondari: i tavoli, gli animali sottostanti, ed i letti, che sono dello stesso tipo del magnifico esemplare d'avorio trovato nel Kerameikos ed appartenente alla tomba di un *aristos* d'Asia Minore,[29] e che possiamo ben immaginare anche qui come d'avorio. Grande cura è stata posta nel differenziare i due gruppi, sia nel caso dei personaggi sdraiati che di quelli stanti, e l'elemento che fa da raccordo nella composizione è proprio il vasellame per bere. Si distinguono due tipi di coppa: la coppa emisferica semplice e la coppa a due anse orizzontali. La prima corrisponde al tipo classico noto dal Vicino Oriente: esemplari di questo tipo venivano importati in Etruria (ricordo lo splendido esemplare, in vetro, dalla Tomba Bernardini) e furono imitati in bronzo e metalli preziosi.[30] Di questo tipo sono le coppe in mano ai due banchettanti che considero sicuramente maschili ed all'inserviente che accudisce uno di loro. L'altro

[26]Una sintesi è proposta da M. Cristofani, 'Il banchetto in Etruria', nel volume *L'alimentazione nel mondo antico. Gli Etruschi* (Roma, 1987), 123-32; l'esegesi più approfondita rimane quella di S. Stopponi, *La tomba della Scrofa Nera* (Roma, 1983), 42-64; vedi anche B. D'Agostino, 'Image and society in archaic Etruria', *JRS* 79 (1989), 1-10, e M.-F. Briquet, *Le sarcophage des époux de Cerveteri du Musée du Louvre* (Firenze, 1989), 105-47.

[27]J.-M. Dentzer, *Le motif du banquet couché dans le proche-orient et le monde Grec du VIIe au IVe siècle avant J.C.* (Roma-Paris, 1982), 54.

[28]J. MacIntosh, 'Representations of furniture on the frieze plaques from Poggio Civitate', *MDAI(R)* 81 (1974), 36.

[29]U. Knigge, *Kerameikos* 9 (Atene, 1976), 60-83; cfr. A. Mastrocinque, 'Avori intarsiati in ambra da Quinto Fiorentino', *Bollettino di archeologia* 10 (1991), 1-10.

[30]Canciani e von Hase, *La tomba Bernardini* (sopra, n. 18), 77 no. 148; cfr. anche Rathje, 'I Keimelia orientali' (sopra, n. 10), 345.

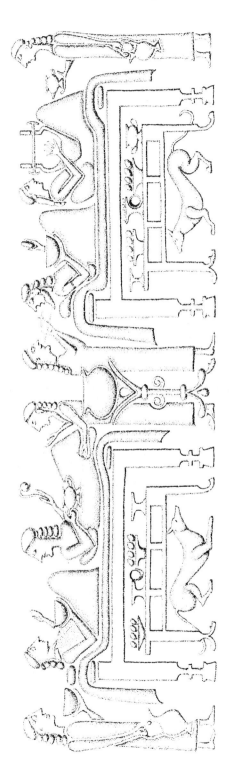

Fɪɢ. 1. Fregio con una rappresentazione del banchetto da Poggio Civitate (Murlo) *(Disegnato da Thora Fisker)*

tipo di coppa, identificata con la cosiddetta coppa ionica,[31] compare tre volte: in mano al personaggio che io sostengo essere una donna, sul tavolo davanti al citarista (da notare l'espressionismo di questo dettaglio) ed infine in mano all'inserviente che chiude la scena. Anche le brocche in mano agli inservienti sono uguali ed appaiono di aspetto decisamente metallico. Dal momento che non si sono trovate sul sito coppe emisferiche, presumo che queste fossero di metallo, mentre si sono trovati vari esemplari in ceramica di coppe ioniche. Dal punto di vista della antitesi riproposta recentemente da Michael Vickers ed altri,[32] si può concludere che il servizio era misto e 'gerarchizzato' — conclusione simile a quella cui ero arrivata indipendentemente anche nel caso del materiale di Ficana.[33] Anche in questo caso, dunque, è molto importante distinguere tra vari tipi di vasellame.

Quanto ai piatti, con o senza alto piede, anch'essi sono ben rappresentati nella ceramica trovata a Murlo. Più difficile è stabilire cosa contenessero: alcuni degli oggetti ovali rappresentano forse frutti. Anche nell'oggetto in mano all'uomo barbato, ritenuto comunemente un uovo, preferisco riconoscere un frutto, come nel caso di un frammento d'avorio da Nimrud (Fort Shalmaneser[34]). Va pure notata, a conclusione di questa breve descrizione, la presenza di musicisti, giustamente sottolineata da Cristiano Grottanelli: uno sta in piedi e fa da *pendant* all'inserviente dietro la donna, il quale è l'unico personaggio a non tenere niente in mano, mentre sul letto si trova un citarista.

La rappresentazione del banchetto che compare nel fregio di Murlo viene solitamente paragonata a quelle che appaiono sui crateri corinzi trovati, per la maggior parte, in Italia.[35] Dal momento però che l'arte corinzia mostra notevoli influssi di origine orientale, soprattutto neo-assira, il confronto che vorrei proporre — con un salto paragonabile a quello delle sette mila tese di Kierkegaard — è con le immagini della famosa, e spesso menzionata, festa di Assurbanipal e della regina Ashurshurat.[36] Va ricordato, innanzitutto, che quest'ultima rapresenta una sezione soltanto di una composizione più grande, in cui occupa una posizione preminente al centro del pannello superiore. La coppia assira è circondata da inservienti che distribuiscono vino e cibo, con accompagnamento di musica; anche qui spicca la presenza di un calderone con relativo sostegno. La solennità celebrativa, certamente comune ad entrambe le rappresentazioni, non è tuttavia identica: il rilievo neo-assiro mostra un personaggio nello splendore della sua opulenza e potere, mentre il fregio di Murlo celebra non un singolo individuo ma un gruppo, il quale però, quando si consideri il fregio nel suo

[31]Sull'esportazione ionica vedi R. Cook, 'East Greek influences on Etruscan vase-painting', *PP* 44 (1989), 161-73, specialmente 170-3.

[32]D.W.J. Gill e M. Vickers, 'Reflected glory. Pottery and precious metal in classical Greece', *JDAI* 105 (1990), 1-30.

[33]A. Rathje, 'A banquet service from the Latin city of Ficana', *ARID* 12 (1983), 15.

[34]M. Mallowan, *Nimrud and its Remains* (Londra, 1966), 504, fig. 405.

[35]J. De la Genière, 'Les acheteurs des cratères corinthiens', *BCH* 112 (1988), 83-90; cfr. A. Rathje, 'Il fregio di Murlo: status sulle considerazioni', in E. Rystedt, Ch. Wikander e Ö. Wikander (edd.), *Deliciae fictiles. Proceedings of the First Conference on Central Italic Architectural Terracotta* (Stoccolma, 1993), 135-8, n. 26. Ho ripreso lo studio del banchetto corinzio che merita un approfondimento dopo il lavoro di Dentzer, *Le motif du banquet couché* (sopra, n. 27).

[36]P. Albenda, 'Landscape bas-reliefs in the Bit Hilani of Ashurbanipal', *BASO* 224 (1976), 49-72, e 225 (1977), 29-48; K. Deller, 'Assurbanipal in der Gartenlaube', *BaM* 18 (1987), 229-38.

insieme, emerge chiaramente come ben distinto: un gruppo assistito da numerosi inservienti in vesti orientali, fortemente caratterizzato da segni di lusso e *status* che ho rintracciato in dettagli di rappresentazioni dal Vicino Oriente che mi accingo a pubblicare.

Sebbene nel fregio di Murlo manchi qualsiasi allusione ad un ambito spaziale nel quale collocare la scena di banchetto, si può tuttavia ipotizzare che funzioni di questo tipo si avessero luogo nell'ampio cortile. Con il che si torna al problema del contesto architettonico, anche se non è questa la sede per dilungarsi sull'argomento. Tanto più che, in attesa della pubblicazione finale dei risultati dello scavo, qualsiasi affermazione a questo riguardo va presa con cautela. È certo però che l'*upper building* con una pianta a tre o quattro ali raggruppate intorno ad un cortile, 3.600 mq in tutto, rappresenta un caso piuttosto singolare tra gli edifici conosciuti in Etruria. Recentemente, una delle studiose impegnate negli scavi di Aquarossa ha ribadito che il paragone tra 'palazzi' di quel tipo e gli esempi di Roma e Satricum non è pertinente.[37] A mio giudizio, tuttavia, non si può condurre un discussione a questo riguardo solo sulla base di piante (tanto più quando si ha a che fare con ricostruzioni congetturali) senza tenere conto delle funzioni di ciascuno dei vari edifici. È pur vero, d'altra parte, che le funzioni si possono comprendere solo studiando ogni singolo contesto nel suo insieme, e che per far questo i dati a disposizione sono purtroppo ancora insufficienti. Aggiungo, tra parentesi, che per quanto riguarda il caso specifico di Murlo, il materiale complicatissimo di Larisa non è, a mio parere, utilizzabile per confronti.[38] Le terracotte sono prive di contesto ed il cosiddetto 'palazzo', stando agli studi di Lauter, sembrerebbe essere un *megaron*.[39]

Nel caso di Murlo, come altrove, la situazione risulta ancora assai confusa. Vorrei sottolineare, in particolare, che tipologie e funzioni edilizie appaiono miste, come nel caso ben noto di Roma, e ricordare a questo riguardo le conclusioni di Filippo Coarelli, secondo cui l'edificio chiamato *regia* doveva far parte di un complesso più grande.[40] Quanto alla figure che compaiono nelle scene da Murlo, si tratta senz'altro di personaggi di alto rango i quali uniscono in sè sfere diverse (religiosa, politica, giuridica, forse militare). Essi compaiono in una serie di situazioni rappresentative in generale del loro *status*, ma che non permettono il riconoscimento di funzioni distinte. Non sarà un caso che questa narrazione si trovi a decorare il fregio di un grande edificio la cui planimetria viene sempre ritenuta di ispirazione orientale. Le immagini di Murlo suggeriscono infatti il paragone con ciò che avviene nell'arte propagandistica per eccellenza, quella dei grandi rilievi dei palazzi reali neo-assiri. Il messaggio di potere e prestigio che in entrambi i casi si vuole affermare appare così immediatamente simile, che penso si possa ricondurre ad una comune ideologia, la quale può trovare espressione, di volta in volta, in terracotta, pietra, o marmo.[41] Di questa ideologia il banchetto costituisce un aspetto ben definito. Nel caso di Murlo, in particolare, non credo si debba vedere, come in certi esempi più tardi, la monotona ripetizione di una

[37]C. Scheffer, '"Domus Regiae" - a Greek tradition?', *OAth* 18 (13) (1990), 185-91.

[38]Cristofani, 'Il banchetto in Etruria' (sopra, n. 26), 126.

[39]H. Lauter, 'Die beiden ältere Tyrannen Paläste in Larisa am Hermos', *BJ* 175 (1975), 33-57.

[40]F. Coarelli, *Il foro romano. Periodo arcaico* (Roma, 1983), 58-70.

[41]Per una analoga conclusione cfr. anche J. Christiansen, 'Comments on the iconography of some early Etruscan revetment plaques', *ARID* 17-18 (1989), 43-51.

formula consueta, ma piuttosto un riferimento ad una occasione particolare, un grande banchetto collettivo a cui forse allude anche un'altra sezione del fregio, se si accetta che nella scena di processione i personaggi che conducono il carro portano in un caso una mannaia da carne e nell'altro uno strumento nel quale si potrebbe riconoscere uno spiedo.[42] Ciò che è certo è che questo banchetto etrusco trova confronti nei banchetti orientali associati al mondo delle corti principesche, come si vede descritto e rappresentato sia nei testi che nei monumenti (ad esempio nelle coppe fenicie[43]).

Anch'io avrei voluto partecipare alle discussione avviata da Oswyn Murray sulla storia dei piaceri ed i piaceri nella storia, ma le mie fonti, purtroppo, non me lo permettono. Per far questo, infatti, è necessario potere entrare nei meccanismi psicologici che informano di volta in volta le varie attività umane ed in particolare poter comprendere i meccanismi che regolano la dialettica tra lusso da una parte, e *status* dall'altra, ed i piaceri connessi a ciascuno di questi due poli.

La conclusione di carattere generale che penso invece si possa trarre è che in questo tipo di studi, soprattutto per il periodo in discussione, non ci si può limitare ad uno stretto ambito etnico. In questo senso il progetto *In Vino Veritas* assume un valore fondamentale. Uno degli aspetti che tanto ha unito ed unisce le diverse culture del Mediterraneo è proprio la produzione ed il consumo di vino, ed in questo senso questo convegno ha ribadito la necessità della collaborazione tra studiosi di civiltà diverse.

[42]Come da me suggerito ('Alcune considerazioni sulle lastre da Poggio Civitate' (sopra, n. 23)).

[43]A. Rathje, 'Il banchetto presso i Fenici', in *Atti del II congresso internazionale di studi Fenici e Punici* III (sopra, n. 8), 1165-8.

12

Simposio e Élites Sociali nel Mondo Etrusco e Italico

ANGELA PONTRANDOLFO

Nel volume *Sympotica* Oswyn Murray ha presentato recentemente un bilancio critico di numerosi e importanti lavori che, con svariate prospettive di indagine e con ricerche orientate su evidenze e problematiche diverse, hanno contribuito a fissare l'attenzione sul valore delle pratiche di commensalità come aspetti e segni non secondari dell'organizzazione sociale del mondo greco.

In questo quadro lo studioso si chiede se è possibile illuminare lo sviluppo della *polis* in Grecia attraverso l'interpretazione funzionale dei corredi funerari rinvenuti in Etruria e nel Lazio e letti dagli archeologi come la recezione di un costume greco da parte di comunità non greche all'interno di un complesso processo di urbanizzazione segnato dalla nascita di una aristocrazia.[1]

Non credo che a questa domanda si possa rispondere in maniera categorica sia in senso affermativo che in senso negativo, ma si avverte piuttosto l'esigenza di una riflessione di metodo che investa il problema del rapporto tra analisi di contesti archeologici e uso di modelli interpretativi desunti da altri tipi di evidenze: penso in particolare alle fonti letterarie che spesso assurgono a paradigmi onnicomprensivi. Infatti, nella letteratura archeologica talvolta la specificità dei modelli desunti dai contesti tirrenici, in particolare etruschi e laziali dell'orientalizzante, è stata successivamente usata in maniera generalizzata, in altri ambiti temporali e spaziali, senza tentare di distinguere di volta in volta l'opzione interpretativa a cui si faceva riferimento. Ha in sostanza dominato e prevalso fino ad oggi il tentativo di mettere in evidenza la necessità di interpretare una serie di determinati oggetti — vasi di bronzo, alcune forme ceramiche, alari e spiedi in ferro — non come singoli elementi inseriti in una tomba, ma come sistema rapportabile ad una pratica. Senza dubbio questo tipo di approccio è servito a prendere coscienza della possibilità di un contributo archeologico al problema che, tuttavia, diventa fuorviante se risolto con giustapposizioni combinatorie e non radicato in una ben dichiarata lettura grammaticale dei contesti, ancorati, a loro volta, a tutti gli elementi che nell'interpretazione possano concorrere a delineare in primo luogo i molteplici aspetti di una microstoria territoriale.

Pertanto, in questa sede e nel quadro della più ampia problematica relativa alla commensalità, usando i mezzi che da archeologo ho per approfondire il problema,

---

[1]O. Murray, *Sympotica: a Symposium on the* Symposion (Oxford, 1990), 10.

essenzialmente quelli dell'analisi socio-economica condotta su vasti complessi omogenei, presenterò alcuni esempi. Da essi cercherò di far scaturire spunti di riflessione che possano arricchire i termini della questione in relazione al valore che le pratiche di commensalità assumono quando, nella loro trasmissione/ricezione in ambiti diversi, si inseriscono in dinamiche di 'acculturazione' intese non nei termini di un modello diffusivo, che presuppone una centralità precostituita, ma in quelli di un tipo dinamico-conflittuale che di volta in volta induce a ridefinire i limiti e gli scambi tra centro e periferia.[2]

Un esempio è offerto dai rinvenimenti della Lucania centro-meridionale localizzati in un'area compresa tra le medie vallate del Sinni e dell'Agri dove a partire dalla fine del settimo secolo a.C. e per tutto il secolo successivo fiorirono una serie di insediamenti testimoniati essenzialmente da numerose e ricche necropoli.

L'analisi condotta su un gruppo di sepolture prese come campione — 80 da Chiaromonte e 125 da Alianello — ha portato a registrare i segni di una stabilizzata stratificazione sociale, espressa attraverso una codificata gerarchia di valori.[3]

In entrambi questi siti tra le tombe maschili, caratterizzate normalmente dalla lancia e dal coltello, se ne distingue un numero limitato — cinque nel primo e sei nel secondo — che aggiunge alle armi più ricorrenti la spada e altri oggetti in ferro: uno strumento arcuato, simile ad un falcetto e da alcuni interpretato come *drepanon*, ma soprattutto scuri, alari, spiedi, e ancora, bacili di bronzo ad orlo perlinato a cui, in un numero ancora più limitato di sepolture, si accompagna un 'servizio da vino' in bronzo composto da una *oinochoe* trilobata di tipo rodio, da una *kotyle* e da due coppe a calotta emisferica.

Questi strumenti e utensili sono associati a una notevole quantità di vasi ceramici che sono presenti, spesso reiterati, anche in tutte le altre sepolture di queste necropoli. Tali oggetti ceramici, sia destinati a contenere offerte solide, sia adatti a versare e consumare liquidi, sono in buona parte di produzione locale e greca coloniale: generalmente coppe di tipo ionico e *oinochoai* di tradizione sia corinzia che greco-orientale, mentre più rari sono i vasi importati dalla Grecia e i buccheri etruschi.

A buon diritto i corredi che esibiscono utensili in ferro e un servizio composto da vasi di lusso di bronzo sono stati letti come espressione delle *élites* di queste comunità che sembrano voler rimarcare l'acquisizione di pratiche alimentari riservate a personaggi di rango quali il consumo aristocratico delle carni arrostite e del vino.

Tale interpretazione si rifà ad un modello di comportamento che sottende la presenza di oggetti di prestigio e che è stato generalmente definito 'tirrenico'.

---

[2]Per la definizione del paradigma funzionale del sistema di azione cfr. T. Parson e N.J. Smelfer, *Economy and Society* (Londra, 1966). Per i problemi di acculturazione in Italia meridionale cfr. A. Pontrandolfo, 'Greci e indigeni', in *Un secolo di ricerche in Magna Grecia. Atti del XXVIII convegno di studi sulla Magna Grecia (Taranto 1988)* (Napoli, 1989), 329-50.

[3]M. Tagliente, 'Elementi del banchetto in un centro arcaico della Basilicata (Chiaromonte)', *MEFRA* 97,1 (1985), 159-91. Cfr. inoltre in un quadro di sintesi più generale: A. Bottini, 'I popoli indigeni fino al V secolo', in C. Ampolo, A. Bottini e P. Guzzo, *Popoli e civiltà dell'Italia antica* 8 (Roma, 1986), 176-94; M. Tagliente, 'Mondo etrusco-campano e mondo indigeno dell'Italia meridionale', in G. Pugliese Carratelli (ed.), *Magna Grecia. Lo sviluppo politico, sociale ed economico* 2 (Milano, 1987), 135-40; B. D'Agostino, 'Il processo di strutturazione del politico nel mondo oscolucano. La protostoria', *AION(archeol)* 9 (1987), 36; *idem*, 'Il rituale funerario nel mondo indigeno', in G. Pugliese Carratelli (ed.), *Magna Grecia. Vita religiosa e cultura letteraria, filosofica e scientifica* 3 (Milano, 1988), 195-9.

È sul questo modello che vorrei porre una serie di interrogativi. Mi chiedo se è corretto considerare il vasellame prezioso di indubbia provenienza etrusca, vale a dire bacili a orlo perlinato, *oinochoai* di tipo cosidetto rodio, vasi di bucchero, e oggetti quali gli spiedi, particolarmente connotati nel loro uso funzionale, come semplice trasmissione fossilizzata di un modello culturale affermatosi molto tempo prima per influsso degli *hippobotai* cumani nell'area centrale tirrenica tra Vetulonia e Pontecagnano. Se spostiamo, infatti, la nostra attenzione dai segni distintivi che apparentemente sembrano omologare le aristocrazie italiche verifichiamo che, a partire dal momento di passaggio dall'orientalizzante recente all'alto arcaismo, oggetti indicatori di prestigio, simili e talvolta identici, sono inseriti in contesti molto più differenziati di quanto non avvenisse in precedenza. Essi suggeriscono la messa in campo di un ampio ventaglio di referenti ideologici che acquistano maggiore spessore quando allarghiamo il nostro campo di indagine all'esame dei sistemi in cui gli oggetti 'preziosi' sono inseriti e all'intero contesto di cui fanno parte.

Mi sembra sufficiente citare come punto di confronto la tomba ceretana 170 della Buforaleccia,[4] pressappoco coeva a quelle aristocratiche delle valli del Sinni e dell'Agri, ma con un corredo totalmente differente benchè comprensivo di alcuni oggetti in metallo simili a quelli presenti nelle ricche sepolture di area enotria.

Nella tomba a camera ceretana oltre a due *olpai* e a una *oinochoe* di bronzo di tipo rodio è presente prezioso materiale di diversa origine: un'*amphora* e un cratere laconici, un'altra *amphora* attica del 'pittore della Gorgone', *kylikes* di tipo ionico, *kantharoi* di bucchero, un *diphros* e numerosi gioielli che fanno presumere si tratti di una deposizione femminile quella pertinente alla banchina di destra.

I segni distintivi espressi dalle tombe 'aristocratiche' di Chiaromonte e Alianello sono, invece, contrassegnati dal costante accoppiamento delle armi, tra cui significativa è la presenza della spada, degli oggetti in bronzo, quali i bacili destinati a contenere offerte, sempre affiancati da numerosi vasi ceramici adatti a versare e a consumare liquidi, e che trovano la reiterazione più ridondante nella *kotyle* e nella *oinochoe* di bronzo.

La stessa suppellettile è presente senza alcuna variazione sostanziale nelle tombe elitarie di Armento e Rivello,[5] siti che gravitano nello stesso ambito territoriale mediano tra la costa tirrenica e quella ionica, collegato da un lato con Pontecagnano e dall'altro con il mondo greco coloniale acheo che vede agli inizi del sesto secolo la indiscussa supremazia sibarita (Figg. 1-4).

Forte è la suggestione di leggere in questa esibizione di ricchezza riconosciuta, nei segni di valore legati alla guerra e nella ostentazione di supremazia, tutti così profondamente correlati, la riplasmazione di un modello di comportamento di quella aristocrazia militare sibarita a cui, agli inizi del sesto secolo a.C., era propria la logica della *habrosune-truphé* come simbolo di *status*, la stessa logica delle opulente aristocrazie dell'Asia Minore, adottata anche dagli Etruschi e adattata alla loro organizzazione

---

[4]Cfr. M.A. Rizzo, in M. Cristofani (ed.), *Civiltà degli Etruschi* (Milano, 1985), 195-9.

[5]Cfr. D. Adameşteanu, 'Una tomba arcaica di Armento', in *Atti e memorie della società Magna Grecia* 11-12 (1970-1), 83ss.; P. Bottini, 'Il Lagonegrese in età arcaica', in *Siris-Polieion (Atti del convegno)* (Galatina, 1986), 49ss.

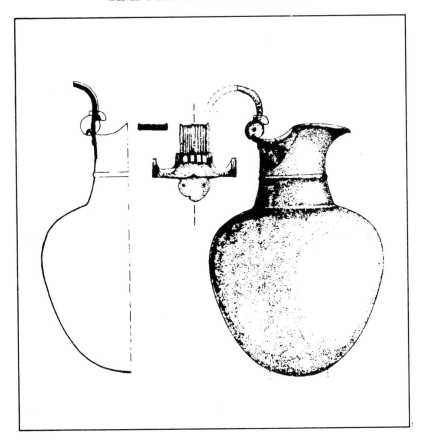

FIG. 1. Vaso in bronzo dalla Tomba A di Armento *(Tratto da Adameşteanu, 'Una tomba arcaica di Armento'; permesso dato dalla Soprintendenza archeologica della Basilicata)*

sociale, e che verrà tratteggiata con accenti di riprovazione da fonti letterarie greche ideologicamente rispondenti a *poleis* ispirate ad altri modelli di comportamento.[6]

Del resto, atteggiamenti del tutto simili a quelli sibariti dominavano, prima dell'arrivo di Pitagora, a Crotone, dove *populus* e *multitudo* erano in preda ad una *luxuria* fatta di vesti preziose, sacrifici dispendiosi, sepolture e funerali costosi con lamentazioni, libagioni, sacrifici senza risparmio.[7]

Se questa mia interpretazione è valida ne deriva che i vertici delle comunità indigene della Lucania centro meridionale esibiscono segni di tipo aristocratico recepiti in maniera non sclerotizzata attraverso una serie di mediazioni diluite nel tempo, ma in seguito a rapporti di reciprocità con la *polis* che, dopo la vittoria su Siris, non solo

---

[6]Erodoto vi. 126.1; Timaeus fr. 97 Jacobi; Diod. viii. 18.2; 19.2. Per un inquadramento critico di queste problematiche cfr. A. Mele, 'Crotone e la sua storia', in *Crotone. Atti del XXIII convegno di studi sulla Magna Grecia (Taranto 1983)* (Napoli, 1984), 26-9.

[7]Just. xx. 4.1-2; 11.8; Iambl. *Vita Pythagorica* 56, 54, 122.

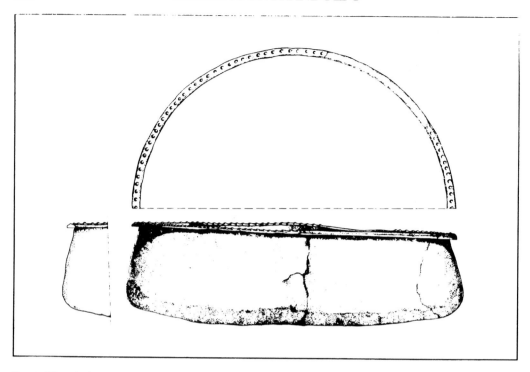

FIG. 2. Vaso in bronzo dalla Tomba A di Armento *(Tratto da Adameșteanu, 'Una tomba arcaica di Armento';*
permesso dato dalla Soprintendenza archeologica della Basilicata))

godette dell'*arché* su quattro *ethne* e 25 città, ma, intorno a sè, si sforzò di costruire una
sua autonoma centralità politica, economica, ideologica.[8]

Vi è inoltre un altro aspetto relativo ai rituali funerari di queste comunità indigene
enotrie su cui vorrei soffermarmi perchè permette di entrare più nel merito dei problemi
che in questa sede sono al centro dell'attenzione.

Riesaminando la letteratura archeologica e analizzando in dettaglio i dati
filologicamente editi ne deriva che nella disposizione degli oggetti nelle sepolture
'emergenti' la spada è disposta aldisopra del petto dell'inumato, mentre lungo il fianco
destro vi sono le lance e gli utensili in ferro. Nella sepoltura gerarchicamente più

[8]Mentre gli atti di questo convegno erano in stampa a Metaponto, la più recente colonia achea
della costa jonica, sono state portate alla luce un gruppo di tombe del primo quarto del sesto secolo a.C.
che si distaccano dal resto delle necropoli note per ubicazione, per struttura e per corredo. Esse, infatti,
pur appartenendo alle necropoli urbane, sono raggruppate tra loro ma fisicamente isolate dalle altre
sepolture; sono costituite da monumenti di notevole impegno architettonico; sono contraddistinte da
ricchi corredi che esibiscono tra gli altri oggetti *oinochoai* di bronzo di tipo rodio, coppe di bronzo e in un
caso la patera d'argento, spade, scuri e un numero elevatissimo di spiedi. Queste sepolture metapontine,
le prime di tal genere rinvenute in una delle colonie achee della costa jonica, mostrano la volontà di
accentuare con il rituale funerario il carattere timocratico della comunità politica e potrebbero concorrere ad avvalorare l'ipotesi da me avanzata che un atteggiamento non dissimile dovesse contraddistin-
guere le sepolture aristocratiche alto arcaiche di Sibari e Crotone. Ringrazio l'amico A. De Siena per
aver voluto mettermi immediatamente a conoscenza di questa straordinaria scoperta.

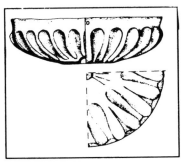

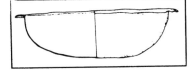

FIG. 3. Vaso in bronzo dalla Tomba A di Armento *(Tratto da Adameşteanu, 'Una tomba arcaica di Armento'; permesso dato dalla Soprintendenza archeologica della Basilicata)*

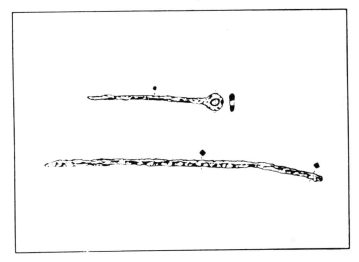

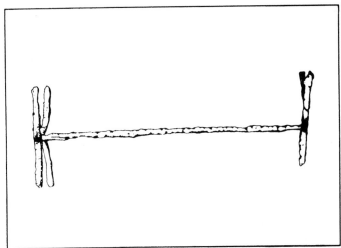

FIG. 4. Utensili in bronzo dalla Tomba A di Armento *(Tratto da Adameşteanu, 'Una tomba arcaica di Armento'; permesso dato dalla Soprintendenza archeologica della Basilicata)*

prestigiosa rispetto alle altre simili, quella 26 di Chiaromonte sotto la Croce,[9] lungo il fianco destro del defunto furono rinvenuti anche i vasi di bronzo destinati a mescere e a bere, cioè la *kotyle* e l'*oinochoe* trilobata; ai piedi dell'inumato erano ammassati tutti gli altri vasi che ripetono forme adatte a bere e a versare, affiancati, come ho già detto, da oggetti in bronzo e in ceramica, funzionali a contenere offerte di cibo.

Nelle rimanenti sepolture di questa comunità, pur con varianti tipologicamente dettate da fattori di gusto, sono costantemente presenti vasi per offerte, soprattutto coppe su alto piede con vasca a profilo carenato, *thymiateria*, *kylikes*, *oinochoai* e il *deinos* fittile che chiaramente ripete prototipi metallici. Tali oggetti appaiono come l'elemento che ideologicamente unifica il rituale di questi gruppi sociali, enfatizzato dal valore intrinseco e dalla qualità del vasellame di bronzo, insieme all'aggiunta di altri segni, nelle sepolture aristocratiche che peraltro sono fisicamente distinte dalle altre e spesso raggruppate tra loro.

Pur con tutte le cautele necessarie quando si cerca di trovare lo specchio di situazioni archeologiche in altri tipi di evidenze, e in particolare nelle fonti letterarie, mi chiedo se in queste forme rituali di 'banchetto funerario' non possiamo anche vedere riflesse quelle strutture enotrie concepite come *syssitia* da Aristotele nella *Politica*[10] che, come ha più volte sottolineato Ettore Lepore, probabilmente riferisce notizie provenienti da Antioco di Siracusa, anche quando fa riferimento alla loro sedentarietà organizzata κατὰ γένη.[11]

Tirando le fila delle osservazioni sin qui presentate, sottopongo all'attenzione il quesito se questo rituale possa essere interpretato come il segno di una pratica comunitaria, il *syssition*, che nel caso specifico della realtà enotria assume sfumature differenti da quelli spartani definibili, sulla base delle notizie tramandate, come pratica quotidiana di articolazioni fisse del corpo civico,[12] e sembrerebbe piuttosto sancire l'identità dell'intero gruppo sociale anche attraverso la connotazione aristocratica dei vertici che le fonti scritte, d'altro canto, individuano come *dynastai* proprio per il tipo di rapporto stabilito con i Greci, basato sul potere personale arbitrario.[13]

Sulla costa tirrenica, immediatamente a nord dell'area occupata da genti enotrie e controllata da Poseidonia, la relativamente recente colonia sibarita, a partire dagli inizi del sesto secolo a.C. riscontriamo, invece, l'attestazione di altri modelli di comportamento.

Ad esempio, la necropoli di Pontecagnano, come chiaramente si evince dalle ricerche in corso e parzialmente edite,[14] conosce un significativo processo di ristrutturazione reso tangibile dalla formazione di nuovi appezzamenti funebri che si

---

[9]G. Tocco Sciarelli, 'Aspetti culturali della Val d'Agri dal VII al VI secolo a.C.', in *Attività archeologica in Basilicata 1964-1977. Studi in onore di Dinu Adameşteanu* (Matera, 1983), 439ss.

[10]vii. 10.2-3 (1329b).

[11]Cfr. *Atti del convegno di studio su le genti della Lucania antica e le loro relazioni con i Greci dell'Italia (Potenza-Matera 1971)* (Roma, 1972), 48-50.

[12]Cfr. M. Lombardo, 'Pratiche di commensalità e forme di organizzazione sociale nel mondo greco: symposia e syssitia', *ASNP* 18,2 (1988), 263-86.

[13]Cfr. A. Mele, 'Il Pitagorismo e le popolazioni anelleniche d'Italia', *AION(archeol)* 3 (1981), 61-96.

[14]L. Cerchiai, 'Modelli di organizzazione in età arcaica attraverso la lettura delle necropoli: il caso di Pontecagnano', in *La presenza etrusca in Campania meridionale. Atti del colloquio internazionale svoltosi a Pontecagnano e Salerno nel 1990* (in corso di stampa).

impiantano in zone precedentemente non sfruttate e con una evidente discontinuità rispetto al tessuto sepolcrale del periodo orientalizzante, nonchè al rituale funerario allora espresso e ai cui vertici si pongono le tombe 'principesche' con i defunti incinerati o scarnificati deposti in grandi lebeti di bronzo.

Si formano ora settori funerari ben distinti e circoscritti in cui l'organizzazione planimetrica sembra voler mettere in evidenza in maniera più marcata i legami di parentela degli occupanti. Alcuni gruppi sociali privilegiati esibiscono ceramiche di tipo etrusco-corinzio prodotte localmente in officine da loro controllate in cui operavano artigiani specializzati trapiantati, e, insieme, ceramica corinzia in proporzione ignota al resto della necropoli, e, soprattutto, con esemplari di qualità eccezionale quali crateri e *oinochoai*.

Nelle stesse tombe, inoltre sono presenti numerose anfore vinarie di tipo etrusco, talvolta anche in più esemplari per tomba.

Si ha percezione di gruppi che saremmo tentati di definire di stampo gentilizio e che sembrano voler mettere in evidenza gerarchie indicate in relazione al diverso grado di integrazione sociale, goduto in base all'appartenenza ad una linea privilegiata di parentela.

Questo modello di comportamento subisce nello stesso sito una ulteriore trasformazione nel corso della prima metà del sesto secolo quando le tombe sembrano strutturarsi in nuclei distinti in base alle classi di età e danno l'impressione di appartenere ad un gruppo ricomposto su basi solidali, mentre, poco lontano, un altro nucleo ancora usa nello stesso periodo cronologico altri segni distintivi che nella gerarchia di valori si presentano come più connotanti. Si tratta di ceramica attica figurata, vasi di bucchero con iscrizioni di appartenenza; queste ultime permettono di riconoscere nei personaggi sepolti, sia maschili sia femminili, individui di origine campana o comunque italica non solo perfettamente integrati nella originaria compagine etrusca, ma anche inseriti a livelli piuttosto alti nell'organizzazione complessiva di questa comunità di tipo urbano.

È all'interno di questo secondo gruppo che si manifesta in maniera netta nelle deposizioni di particolare rilievo l'uso differenziato della *kylix* nelle tombe maschili e dello *skyphos* nelle tombe femminili, oggetti entrambi funzionali al bere, ma che lasciano trasparire l'esistenza di una partecipazione sessualmente diversificata in un rituale che presumiamo potesse prevedere il consumo del vino anche se non possiamo escludere altri liquidi. Tali oggetti — *kylix/oinochoe* — diventano più frequenti e più evidenti, sempre nella loro opposizione/complementarietà funzionale, a partire dalla fine del sesto secolo a.C. e nella prima metà di quello successivo.

In sintesi, è ben evidente che mentre nel mondo enotrio i processi avviati agli inizi del secolo si esauriscono in seguito alla rottura degli equilibri causati dalla sconfitta di Sibari e dal conseguente crollo del suo 'impero', sulla costa tirrenica, a Pontecagnano, ma anche nei numerosi centri interessati da quella che è stata definita 'colonizzazione etrusca', si consolidano fenomeni di trasformazione urbana incentrati sulla inter-relazione tra Etruschi, Greci e Italici, e che danno vita a nuove realtà con una complessa stratificazione ideologica, frutto dell'intreccio e dell'osmosi di molteplici referenti sociali e istituzionali.

L'insediamento di Fratte ne offre la testimonianza più completa sulla base della documentazione nota.[15] Anche qui, come a Pontecagnano, a Nola, a Capua, lo spazio sepolcrale si articola per nuclei fisicamente ben distinti tra loro e gerarchicamente differenziati per tipi di corredo non solo al loro interno, ma anche gli uni dagli altri.

Su una base comune, che nel rituale privilegia essenzialmente le coppe, le *oinochoai* e le *kylikes*, un primo livello di distinzione è rappresentato dai grandi vasi contenitori: olle biansate, anfore da trasporto, crateri di bucchero acromi o a vernice nera, deposti sia singolarmente, sia accostati come a costituire un insieme. Tali vasi furono rinvenuti sia all'interno, sia all'esterno delle tombe, e, pertanto, ambiguamente assumono da un lato la valenza di oggetti che accompagnano il morto, dall'altro di offerte.

Tutti connessi al vino in quanto contenitori, essi mettono in campo una gamma articolata di variabili e suggeriscono diverse implicazioni ideologiche che travalicano l'importanza del contenuto creando una complessa scala di valori a cui non so trovare adeguate risposte interpretative, nemmeno in via ipotetica.

Un altro livello, gerarchicamente più forte e riservato ad un numero ancora più ristretto di sepolture, è segnato dal sistema costituito dal cratere, prevalentemente attico figurato e di notevole qualità, deposto ai piedi del morto e in stretta connessione con i vasi per bere e per versare, anch'essi molto spesso attici anche se appartenenti ad una produzione più corrente, talvolta collocati all'interno dello stesso cratere.

Cratere, anfora, *kylix*, *skyphos*, *oinochoe* o *olpe* compongono in queste sepolture il servizio tipo usato che, senza alcuna forzatura, possiamo dire ripete e adotta i vasi peculiari del simposio così come è rappresentato nel repertorio figurativo della ceramica attica, e con una mediazione logica riscontriamo tramite gli oggetti la pratica di un comportamento che ideologicamente sembra ricalcare quella del simposio greco.

Ma, il *set* vascolare sopra elencato, nella staticità paradigmatica di servizio che accompagna il morto 'eccellente' e comunque 'diverso' e distinto dagli altri del gruppo di appartenenza e dall'intera comunità, rimanda, più che agli oggetti che nel gioco delle immagini circolano nella scena tra le mani o accanto ai simposiasti, a quelli spesso rappresentati in *silhouette* nera su fondo rosso nelle fasce risparmiate che corrono aldisotto delle scene conviviali, contrapponendosi anche con un gioco cromatico e nello stesso tempo rinviando ad esse.[16]

Le *oinochoai*, le *olpai*, gli *skyphoi* e le *kylikes* paratatticamente affiancati non sono più i vasi manipolati durante il simposio, e, al pari di quelli disposti nelle tombe, quasi si dematerializzano diventando dei segni indicatori di tutte le virtuali potenzialità del bere che travalicano il primario piacere dello stesso atto conviviale.

Inoltre, il cratere, in quanto oggetto privilegiato e prestigioso, accresce il valore simbolico nell'insieme di vasi a lui collegati, e, deposto quasi sempre ai piedi del morto, metaforicamente sembra quasi voler strutturare e definire anche nel sepolcro uno spazio che oserei chiamare 'sacro'.

Diversi piani concettuali si intrecciano in maniera complessa quando vediamo trasparire l'allusione ad un simposio che trasferisce l'esperienza forte e positiva

---

[15]G. Greco e A. Pontrandolfo (edd.), *Fratte. Un insediamento etrusco-campano* (Modena, 1990), 168-278, in particolare pp. 276-9; A. Pontrandolfo, 'Modelli di organizzazione in età arcaica attraverso la lettura delle necropoli: il caso di Fratte', in *La presenza etrusca* (sopra, n. 14).

[16]Cfr. F. Lissarrague, *Un flot d'images. Une esthétique du banquet grec* (Parigi, 1987).

dell'espressione di socialità per eccellenza nel mondo greco in contesti sepolcrali dove si ingigantisce il suo valore di esperienza per simulazione.

Non so superare la soglia della registrazione di *semeia* intesi, facendo ricorso alla definizione aristotelica, come segni che non danno certezza e che, pertanto, possono risultare ingannevoli proprio per la loro intrinseca ambiguità.[17]

Indubbio è il dato che siffatti corredi sono prerogativa solo di alcune tombe a Fratte, come a Padula, a Palinuro e in numerosi altri centri di comunità non greche ma decisamente ellenizzate, e che queste sepolture si pongono sempre al livello più alto della scala di valori espressa da ciascun contesto di appartenenza.

Inevitabile è, infine, il parallelo tra valenza ideologica dei corredi che esibiscono esclusivamente un completo servizio da vino e il programma decorativo della famosissima *Tomba del Tuffatore*,[18] macroscopica anomalia tra le sepolture posidoniati di quinto secolo a.C.

Le sue scene fissano in uno stretto rapporto di complementarietà l'immagine del tuffo, inteso come rappresentazione simbolica del passaggio dalla vita all'oceano della morte, e quella del simposio, e, quindi, nell'insieme si pongono come metafora dell'immersione in una dimensione della conoscenza 'altra' da quella normale e accessibile ad una entità umana.

Molto si è discusso su questo documento così complesso;[19] a me interessa riprendere in questa sede quanto già messo in evidenza da Oswyn Murray, vale a dire che essa non rispecchia l'atteggiamento mentale diffuso nelle comunità politiche greche dove il mondo della morte e quello del simposio si collocano come entità polari.[20]

Tra tutte le tombe della Poseidonia greca, dove non è stato rinvenuto nemmeno un corredo costituito da un servizio simposiale, nè mai un cratere è stato deposto accanto al morto all'interno della sepoltura,[21] quella del *Tuffatore* rappresenta, a mio giudizio, una manifestazione di devianza da una norma, che è anche segno di integrazione politica, e privilegia piuttosto una risposta individuale alla morte che, proprio attraverso la scena del simposio, sembra esaltare altre forme di integrazione. Non a caso questa tomba non fa corpo con quelle delle necropoli urbane, ma faceva parte di un piccolo nucleo di sepolture articolate nel tempo e situate alcuni chilometri più a sud della città.[22] La *Tomba del Tuffatore* si colloca a parte dalle altre coeve anche fisicamente e rimane un monumento isolato proprio in un momento cronologico che vede l'esplosione di una nuova necropoli urbana, quella di S. Venera, impiantata e rigorosamente programmata

---

[17]Per una discussione sulla semiotica nell'antichità cfr. G. Manetti, *Le teorie del segno nell'antichità classica* (Milano, 1987).

[18]M. Napoli, *La Tomba del Tuffatore* (Bari, 1970).

[19]B. D'Agostino, 'Le sirene, il tuffatore e le porte dell'Ade', *AION(archeol)* 4 (1982), 43-50; L. Cerchiai, 'Sulle tombe del Tuffatore e della Caccia e della Pesca: proposta di lettura iconologica', *DArch* 5 (1987), 113-23; A. Pontrandolfo, 'L'escatologia popolare e i riti funerari greci', in Pugliese Carratelli (ed.), *Magna Grecia* 3 (sopra, n. 3), 183ss.; A. Bottini, *Archeologia della salvezza. L'escatologia greca nelle testimonianze archeologiche* (Milano, 1992), 85ss.

[20]O. Murray, 'Death and the Symposion', *AION(archeol)* 10 (1988), 241ss.

[21]Cfr. A. Pontrandolfo, 'Le necropoli dalla città greca alla colonia latina', in *Poseidonia-Paestum. Atti del XXVII convegno di studi sulla Magna Grecia (Taranto 1987)* (Napoli, 1992), 225-44.

[22]E. Greco, 'Non morire in città: annotazioni sulla necropoli del Tuffatore di Poseidonia', *AION(archeol)* 4 (1982), 51-6.

in un'area vergine con le tombe allineate su file regolari secondo assi perfettamente orientati.[23]

Riflettendo su questi dati ne deriva la sensazione che rispetto ad un corpo civico che si manifesta organizzato in senso 'democratico', o che comunque in relazione alla morte tende ad annullare le differenze, la *Tomba del Tuffatore* voglia mettere in evidenza l'unità ideale dell'individuo sepolto, connotato come un μουσικὸς ἀνήρ dalla *lyra* deposta accanto a lui, con i partecipanti al simposio raffigurati sulle pareti, quasi a sancire e suggellare l'identità e l'appartenenza ad un gruppo. I codici e le formule usate sono perfettamente rispondenti a quelli che governano il simposio nella città greca, ma in questo caso, in maniera anomala, il piacere del vino è inequivocabilmente proiettato oltre la vita.

Gli esempi addotti mostrano come l'adattamento della pratica simposiale al costume funerario ha terreno fertile, a partire dalla fine del sesto secolo, soprattutto in area tirrenica gravitante intorno a Cuma e a Poseidonia. Quest'ultima con la *Tomba del Tuffatore* offre il documento più esplicito dell'ideologia che sottende un modello di comportamento prodotto dall'osmosi tra grecità coloniale e i vertici delle molteplici e articolate comunità circostanti.

Da un lato, dunque, sembra abbastanza chiaro che il cratere e i vasi per bere e versare diventano in ambito indigeno un elemento centrale del corredo delle tombe pertinenti ad individui di elevato rango sociale, mentre nelle necropoli delle città greche dell'Italia meridionale questo vaso veniva deposto all'esterno della sepoltura, probabilmente come *sema* o come elemento funzionale a rituali periodici, secondo una prassi ben nota e diffusa in tutto il mondo greco. D'altro canto, tuttavia, vi sono alcuni contesti, almeno in base ai dati noti, divergenti da questo panorama tendenzialmente uniforme e che, pertanto, è indispensabile richiamare all'attenzione benchè siano filologicamente editi e patrimonio della letteratura archeologica da molto tempo.

Tra le tombe tarantine ritenute pertinenti ad alcuni degli atleti tramandati nelle liste di vincitori nelle più importanti competizioni panelleniche degna di particolare interesse è quella rinvenuta nel 1917 in via Crispi, solo in parte esplorata e poi scavata interamente nel 1921.[24] È una grande tomba a camera costruita con blocchi parallellepipedi di carparo disposti a secco in robusta opera isodoma; anche il piano di calpestio era completamente pavimentato da blocchi di carparo perfettamente squadrati, e si presuppone che in lastroni dello stesso materiale dovesse essere costituito il tetto già completamente asportato al momento del rinvenimento.

Il monumento, di notevole impegno architettonico, ha la camera sepolcrale a pianta quadrata con all'interno due colonne, a fusto liscio e capitello dorico, disposte sull'asse centrale alla cui estremità si trova l'ingresso (Figg. 5-6). Questo risulta spostato a sud rispetto all'asse della tomba e, all'interno sette sarcofagi sono perfettamente

---

[23]M. Cipriani, 'Morire a Poseidonia nel V secolo. Qualche riflessione a proposito della necropoli meridionale', *DArch* 7 (1989), 71-91.

[24]F.G. Lo Porto, 'Tombe di atleti tarentini', in *Atti e memorie della società Magna Grecia* 8-9 (1967-8), 31-98; E. Lippolis, 'Taranto, tomba a camera: crateri attici a figure nere', in *Vecchi scavi. Nuovi restauri (Catalogo della mostra - Taranto 1991)* (Taranto, 1991), 37-9; N. Valenza Mele, 'Solo "tombe di atleti" a Taranto?', *Prospettiva* 63 (1991), 4-16.

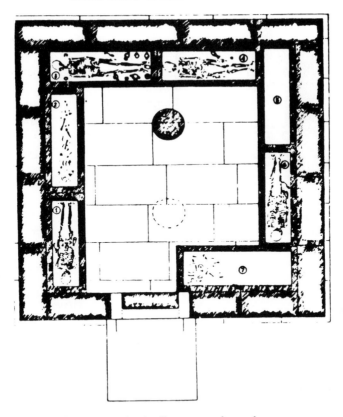

Fig. 5. Camera sepolcrale di una grande tomba a camera a
Taranto: pianta *(Tratto da Lo Porto, 'Tombe di atleti tarentini';
permesso dalla Soprintendenza archeologica della Puglia (Museo
archeologico di Taranto)*

allineati lungo le quattro pareti tranne, naturalmente, nel tratto riservato all'accesso.
L'impianto è esattamente quello di un *andreion* dove i sarcofagi prendono il posto delle
klinai e gli inumati sembrano consegnati ad un eterno convivio. Inoltre, subito dopo la
porta di accesso, nello spazio compreso tra due sarcofagi, furono trovati ben quattro
crateri a volute attici a figure nere (Fig. 7), una *kelebe* a figure rosse, un'anfora
panatenaica, numerose *oinochoai* e numerose *kylikes* sia figurate sia semplicemente
verniciate di nero.

Nonostante alcune incertezze sull'esatta collocazione dei materiali perché la tomba
era stata depredata in antico, la ricostruzione filologica del rinvenimento fatta
dall'editore del complesso rende certa la distinzione tra gli oggetti deposti nello spazio
libero della camera, e quindi comune a tutti gli inumati, e quelli rinvenuti all'interno di
ciascun sarcofago. Dei sette, uno risultò non essere stato mai occupato, mentre negli
altri il defunto era accompagnato dallo strigile e dall'*alabastron*, collocati presso le mani.
Faceva eccezione il terzo a sinistra dell'ingresso che aveva, oltre allo strigile, due *kylikes*,
un *cup-skyphos*, due *lekythoi*, un boccaletto, disposti lungo gli arti inferiori, e una corona
d'oro che gli cingeva il capo.

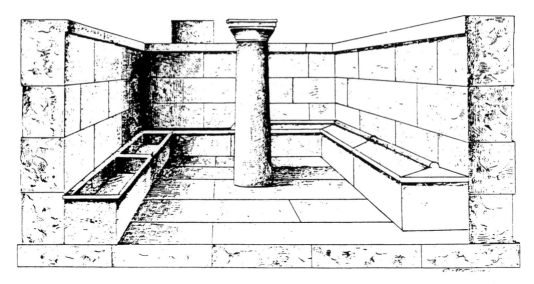

FIG. 6. Ricostruzione del camera sepolcrale di una grande tomba a camera a Taranto *(Tratto da Vecchi scavi. Nuovi restauri; permesso dalla Soprintendenza archeologica della Puglia (Museo archeologico di Taranto)*

È probabile che molte delle *kylikes* e delle *oinochoai* recuperate in frammenti nell'intero vano e sui pezzi di coperture rotte violentemente dai depredatori completassero, come in questo sarcofago, il corredo personale degli inumati dove si sono conservati *in situ* solo gli strigili e gli *alabastra*. Tuttavia va osservato che la volontà di distinguere dagli altri, sia pure all'interno di uno stesso modello ideologico, il defunto del terzo sarcofago, è manifestata dal fatto che è l'unico ad avere la copertura piana e le pareti interne intoncate di rosso. Purtroppo la situazione di giacitura primaria alterata da manomissioni e la impossibilità di una verifica osteologica non consentono di accertare se le leggere distinzioni fra corredi personali corrispondano ad una differenza per classi di età. È invece indubbio che gli individui per cui era stata predisposta questa magnifica tomba fossero tutti di sesso maschile, connotati in senso atletico da un sodalizio che supera i legami familiari e sancisce una unità ed identità di gruppo imperitura anche dopo la morte.

L'ideale che informa questo gruppo sociale è quello aristocratico che trova nel mondo greco di età arcaica una delle espressioni più compiute nel simposio. La tomba tarantina riproduce esattamente la 'stanza in cui gli uomini si riuniscono e a cui è legato il simposio' sia nella pianta con l'ingresso decentrato, sia nella disposizione dei sarcofagi che prendono il posto delle *klinai* tanto che, sulla scia di Plutarco,[25] avremmo quasi la tentazione di individuare il 'padrone di casa', o comunque il personaggio più importante, nell'individuo sepolto nel primo sarcofago entrando sulla destra, e ancora, sia per i crateri e per i vasi indispensabili a questo tipo di riunione deposti nello spazio centrale, poco oltre l'ingresso, come se almeno cinque dei defunti sepolti nella tomba a camera fossero stati accompagnati dall'intero servizio personale.

[25] *Quaest. conv.* 619C.

Fig. 7. Cratere a volute attico a figure nere dalla camera sepolcrale di una grande tomba a camera a Taranto *(Tratto da Vecchi scavi. Nuovi restauri; permesso dalla Soprintendenza archeologica della Puglia (Museo archeologico di Taranto)*

I materiali rinvenuti nella sepoltura ne collocano l'impianto e l'uso in un arco di tempo che va dalla fine del sesto fino ai primi decenni del quinto secolo a.C., vale a dire alla vigilia della sconfitta di quei *gnorimoi* tarantini decimati dagli indigeni e che provocò nella città l'avvento di un ordinamento di tipo democratico.

L'ipogeo di via Crispi e alcune altre tombe a camera ad esso simili possono essere considerate espressione di 'eterie' aristocratiche tarantine che trasferiscono in ambito funerario una pratica sociale, in maniera del tutto eccezionale rispetto alla norma che sembra governare il mondo greco. Esse spingono ad una più approfondita riflessione, già avviata da altre angolazioni, sulla specificità della grecità occidentale, o forse meglio delle grecità che, spesso, per mancanza di dati finiamo per appiattire su un modello ideale, piuttosto statico, creato dall'immaginario dei moderni.

Una ulteriore testimonianza sulle possibili connessioni esistenti nel rituale funerario tra il vino e il defunto è offerta dalla ben nota iscrizione tardo arcaica di Cuma in cui si ricorda che sotto una *kline* è deposto un *lenos*, termine che in questo contesto, a mio avviso, gioca ambiguamente sul significato di tino, di oggetto legato alla pressa del vino e quello di contenitore del morto.[26]

L'iscrizione occupava due blocchi di una grande tomba a camera, rinvenuta nell'800 nel fondo Correale, di cui, purtroppo, sappiamo solo che aveva quattro sarcofagi disposti lungo le pareti e che 'la poca ceramica e le quattro monetine raccolte sul fondo non possono essere a nessun costo contemporanee dell'iscrizione' che correva su una delle pareti interne, verosimilmente in corrispondenza della *kline* a cui fa riferimento.[27]

La tomba rientra tra quelle monumentali con deposizioni plurime, attestate a Cuma già nel sesto secolo a.C., in particolare nell'area dove operò il conte di Siracusa, a ridosso del ben più famoso fondo Artiaco.

In attesa della edizione delle necropoli cumane a cui si sta lavorando cercando di ricomporre i corredi sulla base dei taccuini Stevens, ai fini del discorso che interessa in questa sede, e in forma del tutto problematica per un arricchiamento della discussione, vorrei annotare che dai dati pubblicati dal Gabrici si ricava la testimonianza di alcune tombe a camera, definite di tipo a schiena e collocabili tra il sesto e la prima metà del quinto secolo, oltre che nel fondo Correale, in quelli Maiorano e d'Isanto. Tutte di notevole impegno architettonico, avevano sarcofagi disposti lungo le pareti e deposizioni plurime sia ad inumazione che ad incinerazione. Una proposta interpretativa in chiave sociologica sull'uso nelle necropoli cumane del rituale differenziato è stata avanzata da N. Valenza che considera le tombe a schiena con deposizioni multiple come l'evidente espressione di un nucleo familiare o unito da altro tipo di affinità.[28] A me interessa sottolineare alcune similitudini con le tombe tarantine prima menzionate, pur con la sostanziale differenza che a Cuma nelle casse-sarcofago trovano posto sia gli inumati che gli incinerati, individui chiaramente distinti per classi di età secondo un costume di tradizione euboica-pithecusana. E partendo da questa suggestione credo non si possa del tutto escludere un uso funzionale del cratere attico a figure rosse rinvenuto sul pavimento della tomba a camera LXXII di fondo

---

[26]Cfr. E. Gabrici, 'Cuma', *MonAL* 22 (1913), col. 573, dove il termine *lenos* viene letto, aderendo all'ipotesi del Sogliano e dell'Hoffman, come un nome proprio, al contrario del Kaibel, che lo interpretava nel senso di loculo. M. Guarducci, *Epigrafia greca* 3 (Roma, 1975), 145, dà alla parola il significato 'sarcofago', facendo riferimento ad una iscrizione da Tessalonica e specificando che nell'iscrizione cumana il termine compare 'in significato non sicuro'.

[27]Cfr. E. Gabrici, 'Cuma', *NSA* (1884), 348ss.

[28]N. Valenza Mele, 'La necropoli cumana di VI e V a.C. o la crisi di una aristocrazia', in *Nouvelle contribution à l'étude de la société et de la colonisation eubéennes (Cahiers du Centre Jean Bérard 6)* (Napoli, 1981), 97ss.

Maiorano,[29] purtroppo l'unica un pò meglio documentata, che aveva tre sarcofagi 'con l'orlo al livello del pavimento', addossati uno, di dimensioni maggiori e con all'interno un inumato, lungo la parete di fondo, e gli altri due, più piccoli, e con ossa cremate, lungo quelli laterali.

In sostanza, una serie di elementi sembrano concorrere sottilmente a caratterizzare anche qui le sepolture monumentali collettive come proiezione di un momento emblematico della vita di gruppi aristocratici, e, inevitabilmente, le collocano ad un livello gerarchicamente più alto rispetto a tutte le altre sepolture coeve.

Se questo assunto è condivisibile, ne consegue un ulteriore dato di distinzione e articolazione del complesso e stratificato rituale funerario cumano tra sesto e quinto a.C., già correttamente letto come rispecchiamento del modificarsi e complicarsi dell'originario assetto sociale, ed è pertanto necessario introdurre concettualmente una separazione tra i crateri rinvenuti nelle tombe a schiena e che non risulta contenessero resti inumati, e quelli, anche molto rari, usati come cinerari nelle sepolture monosome sia a ricettacolo che a cassa monolitica. Mi chiedo se siano omologabili e se possano essere indifferentemente intesi come il risultato di una lineare evoluzione del ceto aristocratico che manifesta la propria appartenenza a forme di socialità conviviale.

Ancora una volta non si può trascurare la specificità di alcuni ambiti magno-greci in queste forme di espressione nel rituale funerario, e, soprattutto nel caso cumano il fenomeno non può essere considerato senza tener conto di quanto avviene nel corso del sesto secolo in Etruria, proprio nell'ottica di quelle dinamiche di acculturazione non diffusive a cui si faceva riferimento nelle prime pagine di questo intervento. Le tombe a schiena cumane per la loro monumentalità, per l'uso di *klinai* come contenitori degli individui qui sepolti, siano essi incinerati che inumati, per la presenza al centro della stanza di un vaso quale il cratere, mettono in campo valenze ideologiche espresse in maniera più decisa dal programma decorativo della *Tomba delle Leonesse*[30] che, unica tra quelle tarquiniesi degli ultimi decenni del sesto secolo a.C., nel proporre una delle più antiche scene di simposio rappresenta sulle pareti laterali due coppie di uomini sdraiati su *klinai* e, al centro di quella di fondo, un grande cratere a volute intorno al quale sembra svolgersi un rituale che prevede danza e musica.

Se l'insieme cratere + vasi per bere e per versare richiama modelli simposiali le cui valenze in ambito funerario andranno meglio definite, altri tipi di associazioni arricchiscono la sfera delle nostre conoscenze ampliandone gli interrogativi e le problematiche.

A Fratte, per citare un esempio meglio noto, accanto al sistema di oggetti illustrato ve ne è un altro, parallelo ad esso e riservato ad un numero ancora più ristretto di individui, incentrato, invece, sull'*hydria-kalpis*, sovente attica figurata e di ottima qualità, accompagnata da un servizio di oggetti di bronzo, di probabile fattura vulcente, composto da situle, colini, attingitoi, brocchette e bacili, oltre che dagli spiedi, gli alari e il coltello di ferro.[31]

---

[29]Cfr. Gabrici, 'Cuma' (sopra, n. 26), coll. 450-1; Valenza Mele, 'La necropoli cumana' (sopra, n. 28), 111-2, n. 65, dove si ritiene probabile che il cratere potesse essere stato usato come cinerario.

[30]S. Steingraber, *Catalogo ragionato della pittura etrusca* (Milano, 1985), 322, n. 77, tavv. 97-104. Per il significato di queste scene: B. D'Agostino, 'L'immagine, la pittura e la tomba nell'Etruria arcaica', *Prospettiva* 32 (1983), 2-12.

[31]Cfr. n. 15 e in particolare Greco e Pontrandolfo (edd.), *Fratte* (sopra, n. 15), 242-4.

Questo tipo di corredo, a differenza del primo, gioca su due livelli proiettando riferimenti anche alla sfera della cucina e del sacrificio.

È non secondario, e forse chiarificatore, a mio avviso, il particolare che questi corredi appartengono a sepolture che si affiancano e comunque insistono nello stesso spazio occupato da quelle a cui è riservato un servizio di vasi che richiama il simposio.

A livello elitario, dunque, ritroviamo, bene inteso in rapporto a questa microstoria, i segni di una partecipazione differenziata nell'ambito di un rituale che presuppone con segni diversi il consumo di vino: in un caso espresso mediante un codice di riferimento 'greco', nell'altro connotandolo piuttosto come 'banchetto'. Non so trovare per quest'ultimo un termine diverso che riesca a definire un modello di comportamento che mette in campo una pratica regolamentata in cui il bere vino sembra accompagnarsi alla manipolazione e alla spartizione di carne. Tuttavia, nel complesso, si avverte una netta sensazione che con questa articolazione si tenda a sottolineare la complementa-rietà tra un ruolo di consumo, probabilmente maschile, ed uno femminile connesso piuttosto ad una funzione di distribuzione/manipolazione, quest'ultimo più aderente a moduli già registrati, anche attraverso altre serie di dati, in parecchi ambiti del mondo etrusco-tirrenico a partire dall'età arcaica.

La lettura grammaticale dei contesti esemplificativi presi come campione permette di ricavare che in una realtà composita caratterizzata da una forte mobilità sociale i gruppi che la compongono si articolano in maniera stratificata e proiettano nel rituale funerario questa articolazione e stratificazione attraverso una molteplicità di segni che, pur rinviando tutti a pratiche collettive del consumo del vino, mettono in campo una vasta gamma di comportamenti e quindi di modelli di riferimento.

'In vino veritas', dunque, o 'in vino veritates'?

Non so trovare risposte soddisfacenti e preferisco fermarmi allo stadio della registrazione.

Tuttavia un ultimo quesito desidero sottoporre all'attenzione: quale tipo di mediazione rispetto alle realtà che hanno prodotto tali comportamenti nel rituale funerario è possibile operare interpretando i sistemi di oggetti sopra elencati quali segni di recezione di un costume proprio dell'organizzazione sociale del mondo greco senza ignorarne, però, le numerose variabili e tenendo ben presente che spesso il panorama si complica quando alcuni di questi stessi oggetti giocano in altri contesti in modo ancora differente e assumono ulteriori valenze ideologicamente più complesse che lasciano percepire anche forme di religiosità individuale.

Mi sembra opportuno, infatti, richiamare alla memoria l'esistenza di un numero significativo, benchè limitato all'interno di alcune necropoli note, di vasi attici a figure nere e rosse di dimensioni notevoli, pregevoli per qualità e destinati a contenere vino — *deinoi*, crateri, anfore — usati come cinerari. Nella stessa necropoli di Fratte, a partire dalla fine del sesto e per tutto il quinto secolo a.C., questo rituale è riservato ad un gruppo di individui sepolti in una stessa area come a comporre un gruppo ben distinto dagli altri distribuiti nello spazio della necropoli, anche da quelli deposti con il rito dell'inumazione e accompagnati dai corredi non usuali, spesso con crateri e oggetti per bere e versare, sopra menzionati.

L'interpretazione più immediata che ho già proposto[32] induce a vedere i grandi vasi attici figurati, generalmente destinati per contenere vino e usati per deporre le ceneri, come prerogativa dei membri più elevati del ceto dominante a cui viene riservato un rituale di tipo 'eroico'. Senza dubbio tale lettura è insoddisfacente e una risposta più articolata non potrà prescindere da una più globale impostazione del problema che pone l'uso del cratere come cinerario.[33]

Esemplari sono noti già dal secondo quarto del sesto secolo a.C. a Cuma e Capua dove un cratere corinzio viene utilizzato per cremazioni secondarie.[34] Nella seconda metà dello stesso secolo sono attestati come cinerari un cratere a volute di bucchero pesante e uno di bronzo a Capua,[35] un cratere laconico a Reggio,[36] ma soprattutto nelle necropoli della Sicilia orientale e meridionale: Naxos,[37] Gela[38] e Selinunte.[39] Dalla fine del secolo e per tutto il quinto, la funzione di ossuario viene assunta dai crateri attici figurati, sostituiti in alcuni siti, intorno alla fine del secolo, da quelli italioti usati prevalentemente fino alla metà del quarto. I crateri-cinerario rimangono però nell'ambito di ciascuna necropoli sempre prerogativa di un numero molto limitato d' individui; tali vasi sono stati rinvenuti a Cuma e Fratte, come si è detto, ma anche a Pithecusa[40] e, soprattutto, in Sicilia a Siracusa,[41] Megara Hyblaea,[42] Camarina,[43] Gela,[44] Selinunte[45] e Lipari.[46]

---

[32]Cfr. n. 15.

[33]Alcuni problemi sono affrontati da J. De La Génière, 'Des usages du cratère', in *Grecs et Ibères. Commerce et iconographie* (Parigi, 1989), 271-7.

[34]Cfr. per Cuma: Gabrici, 'Cuma' (sopra, n. 29), coll. 462-3, tomba CVI da fondo Scala; per Capua: W. Johannowsky, *Materiali di età arcaica dalla Campania* (Napoli, 1983), 187-8, tomba 168.

[35]Cfr. Johannowsky, *Materiali di età arcaica* (sopra, n. 34), 66-7, tomba 994; *idem*, 'Un corredo tombale con vasi di bronzo laconici da Capua', *RAAN* 49 (1974), 3-20, tomba 1426.

[36]N. Putori, 'Reggio di Calabria. Nuove scoperte in città e dintorni', *NSA* (1924), 88-90.

[37]A. Rastrelli, 'La necropoli del Poker Hotel, scavi 1973', *NSA* (1984-5), 337-8, tomba 24.

[38]P. Orsi, 'Gela. Scavi del 1900-1905', *MonAL* 17 (1906), col. 325, tomba 6 dal 'Gruppo sepolcrale al Cimitero'; P. Orlandini, 'Gela. Scoperta di tombe greche in via Francesco Crispi', *NSA* (1960), 140-1, tomba 3.

[39]V. Tusa, *Odeon* (Palermo, 1971), 26, tomba senza numero. Il vaso è conservato presso la fondazione Mormino, n. inv. 286, e reca sul corpo l'iscrizione: *Sino Mennaros (Figlio) di Kalikratos*.

[40]G. Buchner, 'Articolazione sociale, differenze di rituale e composizione dei corredi nella necropoli di Pithecusa', in G. Gnoli e J.-P. Vernant (edd.), *La mort, les morts dans les sociétés anciennes* (Cambridge, 1982), 275-87, tombe 93 e 94.

[41]P. Orsi: *NSA* (1891), 410-1, tomba XIV; *NSA* (1893), 462, tomba LV; *NSA* (1897), 471-504, tomba DXIX; *NSA* (1901), 337, tomba 8; *NSA* (1903), 528-31, tomba 552; *NSA* (1907), 741-7, tombe 563 e 574; *NSA* (1915), 181-5; G. Cultera: *NSA* (1938), 262-4; *NSA* (1943), 69-71, tomba XLI; B. Pace: *MonAL* 28 (1922), coll. 596-8, tombe 616, 639, 640, 651.

[42]P. Orsi, *MonAL* (1892), coll. 830-1, tomba LXX; G.V. Gentili, *NSA* (1954), 104, tomba M.

[43]P. Orsi, *MonAL* (1904), coll. 787-888, tombe 119, 127, 148, 280, 289, 379, 385, 413, 476, 503, 524; M.T. Lanza (ed.), 'P. Orsi, la necropoli di Passo Marinaro a Camarina. Campagne di scavo 1904-1909', *MonAL* 54 (1990), tombe 534, 573, 578, 615, 764, 768, 856, 891, 903, 974, 1029, 1096, 1145, 1157, 1252, 1307, 1316.

[44]P. Orsi, 'Gela. Scavi del 1900-1905', *MonAL* 17 (1906), coll. 399-513, tombe 13 e 28 dal Predio Leopardi, e quelle senza numero dal Predio Jozza; P. Orlandini, 'Via Cicerone - Via Palazzi, Predio Minardi già Leopardi - Rinvenimento di sepolture greche del VI e V sec. a.C.', *NSA* (1956), 380-1, tomba 2; *idem*, 'Gela. Scoperta di tombe greche in via Francesco Crispi', *NSA* (1960), 138-9.

[45]Cfr. Tusa, *Odeon* (sopra, n. 39), 199-226, tombe 20, 2, 26, 6, 8, 9, 13, 15, 1 dalla contrada Gaggera, tombe 36, 11, 4 dalla contrada Manicalunga.

[46]L. Bernabò Brea e M. Cavalier, *Meligunìs-Lipàra* II (Palermo, 1965), 14, tomba 24; 65-6, tomba 198; 68, tomba 207 *bis*; 78-9, tomba 229 *bis*; 131, tomba 367; 142-3, tomba 402; 162, tomba 446; L. Bernabò Brea e M. Cavalier, *Meligunìs-Lipàra* V (Roma, 1991), 107, tomba 1553; 122, tomba 1596; 123-4, tomba 1600; 132-3, tomba 1617; 161-4, tomba 2184.

A Cuma grazie all'ausilio delle fonti il cratere-cinerario chiuso in un ricettacolo è stato letto come il segno dell'adozione di una nuova istituzione sociale, il simposio, che sostituisce la più vecchia ideologia del banchetto, pur rimanendo sempre espressione della classe aristocratica.[47]

Da questa angolazione bisognerebbe comprendere meglio nel caso cumano le differenze tra i crateri-cinerari in ricettacolo, quelli deposti nella terra con protezione di tegole e quelli in cassa monolitica e, più in generale, la distinzione tra il cratere-ricettacolo e quello altrettanto raro usato come elemento del corredo nelle tombe a schiena.

Non va inoltre trascurata la presenza frequente, ma non diffusa, di incinerazioni in altri vasi sempre di produzione attica e di notevole qualità e dimensioni come ad esempio le *pelikai* cumana e neapolitana, quella rinvenuta a Pontecagnano,[48] nonchè le *pelikai* note di Siracusa, Gela, Camarina[49] e quelle italiote di Eraclea di Lucania e Acrae,[50] forma vascolare frequentemente usata come cinerario anche nelle necropoli attiche.[51]

Nè va ignorato che il rituale dell'incinerazione nel corso del quinto secolo non sembra essere destinato esclusivamente agli uomini: ad Agrigento, nella necropoli di contrada Mosè, ad una donna si pensa possa appartenere la sepoltura costituita da un pozzetto che racchiudeva un enorme cratere-cinerario di bronzo a volute con attachi a testa di cigno, circondato da oggetti di corredo e da toilette.[52]

Dall'insieme di questi elementi scaturisce l'interrogativo se sia possibile ipotizzare una mutazione ideologica che nell'unione incinerato-cratere assomma all'identificazione simbolica del piacere del vino e della vita simposiale quella derivata dal privilegio di una conoscenza mistica riservata agli iniziati, un processo che vede gli esiti più espliciti, ma non semplificati, alla fine del quarto secolo a.C. nel cratere bronzeo con scene dionisiache dalla tomba B di Derveni il cui incinerato era sepolto con gli stessi segni di quello, accompagnato da un testo orfico, della tomba A poco distante.[53]

---

[47]Cfr. n. 28.

[48]Cfr. per Cuma: Gabrici, *Cuma* (sopra, n. 26), col. 461; per Napoli: W. Johannowsky, in *Napoli antica (Catalogo della mostra)* (Napoli, 1985), 203-31; per Pontecagnano: Cerchiai, 'Modelli di organizzazione' (sopra, n. 14).

[49]Cfr. per Siracusa: P. Orsi, *NSA* (1901), 337, tomba 8 - dove la *pelike* era deposta nella stessa fossa del cratere usato anch'esso come cinerario; per Gela: Orsi, 'Gela' (sopra, n. 44), coll. 367-71, tomba 11 dal Predio N. Salerno; coll. 504-8, la *pelike*-cinerario senza numero di tomba dal predio Jozza; per Camarina: Lanza, 'P. Orsi, la necropoli di Passo Marinaro' (sopra, n. 43), 65, tomba 903.

[50]Cfr. per Eraclea: G. Pianu, *La necropoli meridionale di Eraclea* I (Roma, 1990), 31-2, tomba 2; 23-4, tomba 53; per Acrae: P. Orsi, *NSA* (1915), 210-1.

[51]S. Karouzou, 'Un cimetière de l'époque classique à Athènes', *BCH* 71-2 (1947-8), 385-91; *eadem*, 'L'usage funéraire de la péliké', *BCH* 95 (1971), 138-45.

[52]*Veder Greco. Le necropoli di Agrigento (Catalogo della mostra)* (Roma, 1988), 245. Una lettura antropologica delle necropoli di Agrigento è stata proposta da M. Torelli nella relazione svolta al convegno *I vasi attici ed altre ceramiche coeve in Sicilia*, organizzato dall'Università di Catania nel 1990 (atti in corso di stampa).

[53]H. Macaronas, 'Taphoi para to Derbeni Thessalonikes', *ArchDelt* 18 (1963 (1964)), 193ss.; S.G. Kapsomenos, 'O Orphikos panyros tes Thessalonikes', *ArchDelt* 19 (1964 (1965)), 17-25; e in particolare l'inquadramento problematico del cratere e del contesto di rinvenimento di R. Bianchi Bandinelli, 'Il cratere di Derveni', *DArch* 8 (1974-5), 179-200; A. Bottini, *Archeologia della salvezza* (Milano, 1992), 134-48.

Credo che un filone di ricerca impostato in questa prospettiva debba mettere in gioco non solo una revisione sistematica di tutti i crateri-cinerario fino ad oggi rinvenuti in rapporto ai contesti di appartenenza, ma debba anche tener conto delle scene che li decorano. Infatti, un lavoro avviato di recente[54] permette di registrare che alle scene dionisiache e di *komos* prevalenti si affiancano nel corso del quinto secolo, soprattutto ad Agrigento e Selinunte, quelle mitologiche che rappresentano il rapimento di un mortale, uomo o donna, da parte di una divinità anch'essa maschile o femminile: Zeus ed Egina, Eos e Kephalos, Nike o Iris e un giovinetto, così come su di un cinerario di Agrigento è raffigurato il volo magico di Trittolemo sul carro alato insieme a Demetra. Dal vino come elemento di aggregazione sociale all'allusione simbolica di forme di coesione fondate su scelte individuali? La ricerca futura potrà aiutarci a dare spessore a tale ipotesi e a verificare i modi di questo processo che dilata gli innumerevoli aspetti della 'verità'.

---

[54]La ricerca è in atto presso l'Università di Salerno e un primo contributo sta per essere edito da D. Panza, *Vasi attici e italioti figurati come cinerari in Magna Grecia e Sicilia.*

13

Vino e Ideologia nella Roma Arcaica

FILIPPO COARELLI

La produzione e il consumo del vino nel mondo arcaico, particolarmente in Italia, erano inseriti nell'ambito di un complesso tessuto di rapporti ideologici — oltre che, naturalmente, economici — il cui esame non può essere in alcun modo trascurato, se vogliamo accedere alla comprensione di fenomeni che fanno parte, in primo luogo, della sfera magico-religiosa. Fra i numerosi temi che si potrebbero prendere in considerazione a questo proposito ne ho trascelti un paio, tenendo conto soprattutto in questa scelta della possibilità intrinseca che essi presentano di consentire analisi complesse, tramite una pluralità di approcci disciplinari (storico-letterario, storico-religioso, archeologico in senso ampio), e quindi di permettere verifiche incrociate.

Anche a rischio di sovrappormi in parte al contributo che segue — rischio inevitabile, ma al tempo stesso, almeno spero, non inutile per il confronto di varie opinioni su temi analoghi — non posso non iniziare il mio intervento con un esame, anche se sommario, dei dati conosciuti sulle tre grandi feste del vino, inserite già nel feriale arcaico di Roma: i Vinalia Priora del 23 aprile, i Vinalia Rustica del 19 agosto e i Meditrinalia dell'11 ottobre: tutte studiate infinite volte, ma che solo di recente, per merito di Mario Torelli, hanno conosciuto un'esposizione d'insieme sistematica e coerente.[1]

Si tratta di cerimonie dedicate, rispettivamente, alla prima degustazione del vino nuovo (Plin. *HN* xviii. 287: *Vinalia priora quae ante hos dies sunt, VIII kalendas Maias, degustandis vinis instituta, nihil ad fructus attinent*), alla vendemmia e a libazioni di mosto subito dopo la pressatura dell'uva, a fini magico-medicamentosi.

Non è qui il caso di affrontare in pieno tutti i complicatissimi problemi tecnici e storici che un tale compatto plesso festivo propone: sarà, penso, il compito di Olivier De Cazanove (sotto, capitolo 14). Vorrei soltanto accennare ad alcuni aspetti fondamentali, che sono alla base di tutto quanto dirò in seguito, e non possono quindi venir tralasciati.

In primo luogo, voglio sottolineare ancora una volta, dopo molti altri, la pertinenza originaria di queste feste — in particolare dei Vinalia Priora — al culto di Iuppiter, prevalente rispetto a quello di Venere;[2] quest'ultimo si aggiunse, a quanto

---

[1] M. Torelli, *Lavinio e Roma* (Roma, 1984). Cfr. anche M. Gras, 'Vin et société à Rome et dans le Latium à l'époque archaïque', in *Forme di contatto e processi di trasformazione nelle società antiche* (Pisa-Roma, 1983), 1069ss.; *idem, Trafics tyrrhéniens archaïques* (Roma, 1985), 367ss.; E. Montanari, 'Funzioni della sovranità e feste del vino nella Roma repubblicana', *SMSR* 49 (1983), 150ss.; A. Mastrocinque, *Lucio Giunio Bruto* (Trento, 1988), 245ss.

[2] Varrone, *Ling.* vi. 16; Macrob. *Sat.* i. 4.6; Ov. *Fast.* iv. 863ss.; Fest., p. 322 L.; Paul.-Fest., p. 57 L., p. 517 L.

sembra, solo in un secondo tempo, almeno nella forma specifica che ci è nota;[3] in ogni caso, anche questa seconda presenza divina non può essere trascurata, dal momento che essa è certamente funzionale ad aspetti essenziali del culto, che vanno spiegati. Basterà qui ricordare che Venere è presente tanto al momento dei Vinalia Priora del 23 aprile (con il culto di *Venus Erucina extra portam Collinam*),[4] quanto al momento dei Vinalia Rustica del 19 agosto (con il più antico culto attestato della divinità, quello di *Venus Obsequens* fondato da Q. Fabius Gurges presso il circo Massimo nel 295 a.C.;[5] ma anche con il culto di Libitina, più tardi anch'essa identificata con Venere: culto certamente arcaico, che dimostra la presenza di elementi 'afrodisiaci' già nella festa originaria).[6]

Un secondo punto che mi premeva mettere in luce è il rapporto astronomico che lega i primi con i secondi Vinalia: sappiamo infatti da Columella[7] che il 23 aprile (cioè il giorno dei Vinalia Priora) coincideva con il sorgere della costellazione della Lira (*Fidicula*), mentre Varrone fissava al 19 agosto (giorno dei Vinalia Rustica) il tramonto della stessa costellazione.[8] Ambedue i momenti sarebbero stati caratterizzati da *tempestates*, contro le quali bisognava tutelare le viti con tutti i mezzi, anche magici (ad esempio, collocando nelle vigne un grappolo di uva finta, dipinto).[9]

È difficile pensare che questa coincidenza astronomica non sia da porre alla radice delle feste del vino, che risultano attraverso di essa strettamente collegate tra loro.

Questa osservazione può servirci per abbozzare un'altra serie di considerazioni: l'uva dipinta collocata nelle vigne il giorno dei Vinalia Rustica, subito prima della vendemmia (forse per attirare magicamente su di sé le intemperie, risparmiando l'uva vera?) evoca irresistibilmente la cerimonia dell'*auspicatio vindemiae*, che veniva compiuta lo stesso giorno dal *flamen dialis*:[10] ancora una volta, dal sacerdote di Iuppiter. Si trattava probabilmente di scegliere un grappolo particolare — *vinum legere* — probabilmente il più grande di tutti quelli presenti in una vigna sacralmente designata. Questa *auspicatio vindemiae* è probabilmente da identificare, o comunque è collegata, con l'*auguratio* dei vineta ricordata da Cicerone,[11] anche se in quest'ultimo caso sono gli auguri a intervenire, non più il *flamen dialis*: possiamo però pensare a una collaborazione dei due sacerdozi, resa indispensabile dalle competenze tecniche dei primi. Il particolare segno 'augurale' che concerne le vigne si ricava anche dal linguaggio utilizzato da Plinio, che sottolinea la divisione di esse tramite *cardines* e *decumani*, tecnica ovviamente legata all'arte degli auguri.[12]

---

[3]Il culto di Venere non è noto a Roma prima del 295 a.C., quando fu dedicato il tempio di *Venus Obsequens in circo*. Naturalmente, le funzioni di 'Afrodite' si ritrovano nel Lazio fin da età arcaica, sotto nomi diversi (Fortuna, Libitina, ecc.). Con prospettiva diversa, R. Schilling, *La religion romaine de Vénus* (BEFAR 178) (Parigi, 1954).

[4]Schilling, *La religion romaine de Vénus* (sopra, n. 3), 248ss.

[5]*Ibid.* pp. 147-8.

[6]F. Coarelli, *Il Foro Boario* (Roma, 1988), 283-4.

[7]*Rust.* xi. 2.36.

[8]Varrone, in Plin. *HN* xviii. 289 e 284.

[9]Plin. *HN* xviii. 289.

[10]Varrone, *Ling.* vi. 16. Forse nella *vinia publica* (sull'*arx*?) restaurata da Vespasiano nel 75, menzionata in un'iscrizione (*CIL* VI, 933).

[11]Cic. *Leg.* ii. 20-1.

[12]Plin. *HN* xvii. 169.

È probabile di conseguenza che il noto passo di Cicerone relativo ad Atto Navio,[13] che ricorda la prima operazione compiuta in gioventù dal celebre augure proprio su una vigna, e proprio per scoprire il grappolo più grande (analogo a quello che verrà *lectus* nell'*auspicatio vindemiae*), debba essere considerato niente altro che l'*aition* mitico di questa particolare operazione augurale. È da sottolineare, a questo proposito, che Cicerone era augure.

Aggiungerei solo una breve considerazione sui Meditrinalia dell'11 ottobre.[14] In primo luogo, è importante notare che Varrone, il nostro informatore principale, cita come sua fonte un Flaccus, *flamen Martialis*:[15] considerato l'aspetto tecnico di questo testo, ciò dovrebbe significare che quest'ultimo, e non il *flamen dialis*, era il sacerdote incaricato della cerimonia. Si tratta di un dato particolarmente interessante, se lo consideriamo in rapporto alla posizione calendariale dei Meditrinalia, l'11 ottobre, e cioè subito prima dei Fontinalia (13 ottobre) e soprattutto dell'*equus October* (15 ottobre).[16] In quest'ultima, arcaicissima festa, che si svolge lo stesso giorno dei *ludi Capitolini*, mi è sembrato di dover identificare il trionfo arcaico, svolgentesi a data fissa (come risulta anche dal trionfo di Romolo, che avverrebbe proprio il 15 ottobre).[17] Trattandosi di Idi, siamo certamente in ambito di *feriae Iovis*.

Il possibile collegamento dei Meditrinalia con Marte e con cerimonie di vittoria non dovrebbe sorprendere: già più volte è stato sottolineato, per gli altri da Dumézil,[18] lo stretto rapporto esistente tra il vino e la vittoria, per esempio nel mito di Mesenzio (ma anche assai più tardi: impressionante, a questo proposito, il caso di L. Papirio Cursore che, nel 293 a.C., nello scontro con i Sanniti ad Aquilonia *voverat Iovi Victori, si legiones hostium fudisset, pocillum mulsi priusquam temetum biberet sese facturum*).[19]

Il rito principale dei Meditrinalia, e comunque l'unico che conosciamo, consisteva essenzialmente in una libazione di mosto, cioè in un'offerta di primizie, a scopo magico-medicamentoso (come indica del resto il nome stesso della festa, derivato da *medeor*, 'guarire'), utilizzando una formula trasmessaci, con minime differenze, da Varrone e da Festo: *novum vetus vinum bibo, novo veteri morbo medeor*.[20] È interessante, a questo proposito, il confronto con l'iscrizione del cosiddetto 'vaso di Duenos', ove troviamo una formula del tutto analoga, sia nell'uso di ottonari trocaici che in certi giochi linguistici (*duenos-malos* rispetto a *novus-vetus*).[21] Tra l'altro, nel vaso è da riconoscere un recipiente destinato all'offerta di primizie, come risulta dalla caratteristica forma di *kernos* e dal luogo di ritrovamento, la stipe votiva di un santuario del Quirinale.[22] La datazione di esso nel corso della prima metà del sesto secolo a.C. costituisce un indizio anche per la cronologia della formula utilizzata nel corso dei Meditrinalia, festa a sua volta inserita

---

[13]Cic. *Div.* i. 17; cfr. *Nat.D.* ii. 3.9; Dionigi di Alicarnasso iii. 70.

[14]Varrone, *Ling.* vi. 21; Paul.-Fest., p. 110 L.

[15]Varrone, *loc. cit.*

[16]A. Degrassi, *Inscriptiones Italiae* XIII 2 (1963), 519, 521-2.

[17]Coarelli, *Foro Boario* (sopra, n. 6), 432-4.

[18]G. Dumézil, *Fêtes romaines d'été et d'automne* (Parigi, 1975), 98-107; Schilling, *La religion romaine de Vénus* (sopra, n. 3), 131ss.

[19]Livio x. 42.7.

[20]Cfr. n. 14: Festo rovescia l'ordine delle parole: *vetus novum vinum bibo / veteri novo morbo medeor*.

[21]Sul 'vaso di Duenos' da ultimo, Coarelli, *Foro Boario* (sopra, n. 6), 285-93.

[22]*Ibid.* p. 290.

nel feriale arcaico romano, e quindi certamente non posteriore alla metà del sesto secolo a.C.[23]

* * *

Il vino a Roma non appartiene a Dioniso (Liber), ma a Iuppiter.[24] Questo dipenderebbe, secondo Dumézil,[25] non da eventuali 'funzioni agrarie' di Giove, ma dalla sua natura essenziale di dio sovrano. Ora, il rapporto tra vino e sovranità a Roma sembra accertato, e dovremo tornarci tra poco a proposito del trionfo arcaico. Tuttavia sembra difficile escludere del tutto caratteristiche 'ctonie' in un particolare culto di Giove a Roma. Come ha notato già Heurgon (seguito da De Cazanove)[26] conosciamo nell'Italia tirrenica arcaica un 'dionisismo senza Dioniso': in Etruria e nel Lazio tutto l'apparato figurativo del *thiasos* è presente in modo quasi ossessivo, ma manca proprio la divinità che in Grecia è centrale, Dioniso. Tutto ciò va spiegato, mi sembra, proprio in relazione con la preminenza del culto di Giove nella sfera del vino, ma di un Giove che doveva necessariamente possedere almeno alcune delle caratteristiche di Dioniso: quindi, una divinità sovrana, certo, ma non solo celeste, in cui dovevano essere presenti notevoli caratteristiche ctonie.[27]

Conosciamo a Roma divinità altrettanto ambigue, che vanno collocate nella stessa sfera: basti qui ricordare Veiove e soprattutto il trasparente Iuppiter Liber dell'Aventino.[28] Del resto anche in Grecia non mancano figure divine analoghe, come Zeus Meilichios, il cui culto non a caso ebbe tanta fortuna in Italia.[29]

Mi sembra che il nucleo mitistorico che si concentra intorno alla figura di Mesenzio possa notevolmente contribuire al chiarimento di questo problema.

Si deve anzitutto ricordare che una scoperta recente ha permesso di verificare la storicità del nome, presente a Cerveteri fin dal settimo secolo a.C.[30] Tutto fa pensare che la leggenda si sia formata a partire da un nucleo reale, il rapporto storico tra un tiranno di Cerveteri e un re latino di Lavinio (non a caso, la tomba identificata più tardi come *heroon* di Enea appartiene anch'essa al settimo secolo).[31]

Il mito è noto a tutti: un tiranno di Cerveteri, cacciato dalla sua città, si allea con i Rutuli contro i Latini, alleati dei Troiani, e finirà ucciso da Enea.[32]

---

[23]Sulla cronologia del feriale arcaico romano, cfr. F. Coarelli, *Foro Romano. Periodo arcaico* (Roma, 1983), 185-6.

[24]Cfr. sopra, n. 2.

[25]Dumézil, *Fêtes romaines* (sopra, n. 18), 87-97.

[26]J. Heurgon, 'Le satyre et la ménade étrusques', *MEFRA* 46 (1929), 102; O. De Cazanove, 'Le thiase et son double', in *L'association dionysiaque dans les sociétés anciennes* (Roma, 1986), 179; Coarelli, *Foro Boario* (sopra, n. 6), 421-3.

[27]Coarelli, *Foro Boario* (sopra, n. 6), 421-6.

[28]Su questo, A. Bruhl, *Liber Pater* (BEFAR 175) (Parigi, 1953), 19ss.

[29]Su Zeus Meilichios, cfr. da ultimo D. Russo, *Il tempio di Giove Meilichio a Pompei* (Napoli, 1991), 119ss.

[30]D. Briquel, 'A propos d'une inscription redécouverte au Louvre: remarques sur la tradition relative à Mézence', *REL* 67 (1989), 78ss.

[31]Torelli, *Lavinio e Roma* (sopra, n. 1), 189ss.

[32]La spiegazione qui accettata è quella di H.S. Versnel, *Triumphus* (Leiden, 1970), 285-6. Cfr. A. La Penna, 'Mesenzio', in *Enciclopedia Virgiliana* III (Roma, 1987), 510-15. Inoltre, Schilling, *La religion romaine de Vénus* (sopra, n. 3), 137-41; M. Sordi, *I rapporti romano-ceriti e l'origine della* civitas *sine suffragio* (Roma, 1960), 10-16.

In realtà, la tradizione conosce molte varianti: secondo altri, Ascanio e non Enea ucciderà il tiranno etrusco.[33] È del resto evidente che la figura di Mesenzio è modellata sostanzialmente su quella di Tarquinio il Superbo: si tratta di un'osservazione più volte ripetuta,[34] ed evidente, ma di una certa importanza per quanto diremo più avanti.

A parte le varianti della tradizione, la figura di Mesenzio appare centrale per il rapporto, nel Lazio arcaico, tra vino e sovranità. Nella festa dei Vinalia Priora (che, come si è visto, è la festa dell'apertura dei *dolia* contenenti il vino nuovo, analoga agli Anthesteria di Atene), la storia di Mesenzio funziona come un *aition*, un mito di fondazione. Qual è dunque il significato di questo rapporto?

Il motivo che connette Mesenzio con il vino nella vulgata dipende dalla richiesta (avanzata dal tiranno ai Latini, ma in precedenza già ai Rutuli) di consegnargli tutto il vino di un anno.[35] In realtà la richiesta è più precisa: si tratta di tutte le libazioni di vino destinate teoricamente agli dei, e a Giove in particolare.[36] Il nucleo centrale del mito si coglie, a mio avviso, in un passo delle *Origines* di Catone citato da Macrobio,[37] in cui viene spiegata la caratteristica di Mesenzio, ripetuta da tutte le fonti: l'empietà. Perché Mesenzio è *contemptor deorum*? Non perchè *sine respectu deorum in homines impius fuit*, ma perchè aveva chiesto ai Rutuli prima, ai Latini poi *quas diis primitias offerebant*, le primizie del vino destinate agli dei. Quindi la colpa di Mesenzio si identifica col fatto *quod divinos honores sibi exegerat*, di essersi sostituito agli dei nel richiedere per sé le primizie. Di qui l'iniziativa dei Latini di dedicare tutta la libazione di vino a Giove, che darà loro la vittoria.[38] Appare qui evidente, tra l'altro, quello che chiamerei il 'modello di Tarquinio': la critica cioè a un comportamento religioso che mirava a identificare, in un certo modo, il tiranno con la divinità, in contrapposizione al 'modello di Enea', alternativo al primo, quello cioè del sovrano pio, rispettoso delle prerogative della divinità.[39]

Questo mito 'fonda' il rito dei Vinalia Rustica, nel corso dei quali in effetti, come ricorda Plutarco, si versavano a terra, davanti ai templi, tutte le primizie del vino.[40]

Ma la possibilità che un uomo possa sostituire il dio (cioè Giove) in certe occasioni non è sconosciuta a Roma in età storica. Il trionfo, nelle forme che ci sono tramandate, rappresenta proprio questo: la momentanea identificazione del trionfatore con Giove, di cui il primo riveste le insegne (le vesti, la corona). Il problema è stato esaminato minutamente da Versnel,[41] con risultati che io stesso ho potuto utilizzare proficuamente nel mio libro sul Foro Boario.[42] Il dato più interessante in questa sede è che il trionfo rivestiva caratteristiche evidentemente dionisiache: a parte il fallo che veniva legato

---

[33]Catone, *Orig.* fr. 10-11 Schr.

[34]La Penna, 'Mesenzio' (sopra, n. 32), 513-14.

[35]*Fasti Consulares Praenestini*, 23 aprile (Degrassi, *Inscriptiones Italiae* (sopra, n. 16), 446); Ov. *Fast.* iv. 877ss.; Dionigi di Alicarnasso i. 65.1ss.; Plin. *HN* xiv. 88; Plut. *Quaest. Rom.* 45.

[36]Macrob. *Sat.* iii. 5.10.

[37]Macrob. *Sat.* iii. 5.9-11.

[38]Cfr. sopra, n. 35. Inoltre, Fest., p. 322 L.

[39]Schilling, *La religion romaine de Vénus* (sopra, n. 3), 144ss.

[40]Plut. *Quaest. Rom.* 45.

[41]Versnel, *Triumphus* (sopra, n. 32).

[42]Coarelli, *Foro Boario* (sopra, n. 6), 414-37.

sotto il carro, il corteo di Sileni e Satiri che formava una parte della *pompa*,[43] il canto di versetti di carattere osceno da parte dei soldati, ecc. è qui determinante il nome stesso della cerimonia: come sapevano perfettamente gli scrittori antichi, *triumphus* deriva (probabilmente via Etruria) da *thriambos*.[44] Né si può pensare, con Jeanmaire, a un tardo adeguamento romano a modelli ellenistici[45] (scappatoia abituale dell'ipercritica ottocentesca), dal momento che gli elementi dionisiaci riguardano proprio il trionfo arcaico: la parola appare del resto già nel *carmen fratrum arvalium*, la cui antichità non può essere messa in dubbio.[46]

La proposta di Versnel, basata su confronti con complessi mitico-rituali del Vicino Oriente e dell'Egitto, è più o meno la seguente:[47] il trionfo si spiega come cerimonia di introduzione al potere del nuovo sovrano, ripetuta periodicamente (a Roma ogni anno) e legata ai riti di capodanno. Essa è sistematicamente in rapporto con una ierogamia, preceduta dalla 'morte rituale' del dio (Tammuz-Adone, Melqart, Osiride ecc.), che viene sostituito provvisoriamente dal futuro sovrano, il quale proprio attraverso questa identificazione con il dio, e la conseguente *mixis* con la dea, acquista le prerogative che autorizzano il suo potere. Un numero notevole di miti greci legati alla successione dinastica e alla fondazione di città, regni o *ethne*, da Edipo a Telefo a Teseo, possono essere letti e spiegati attraverso questo schema strutturale.[48]

La conoscenza in ambiente tirrenico di un analogo contesto, fornitoci dal santuario di Pyrgi, permette di dimostrare l'esistenza di analoghi cerimoniali (riti e probabilmente miti) in territorio etrusco fin da età arcaica:[49] qui il culto di Uni-Astarte, venerata nel tempio B a partire dal 500 a.C. circa, fa coppia con un Tin ctonio, venerato in un'adiacente area sacra *sub dio*, che è collegata da un canale con il sottosuolo. Che il dio etrusco vada qui interpretato come *paredros* di Astarte, e sia quindi da identificare con Melqart, si ricava anche dalle celebri lamine d'oro iscritte, in cui è questione di una cerimonia (probabilmente di una ierogamia) che si deve svolgere 'il giorno del seppellimento della divinità', evidentemente lo stesso Tinia-Melqart, che anche qui è dunque un dio morente.[50] Le caratteristiche del santuario sono completate dalla presenza della *hierodulia* di carattere orientale, testimoniata sia dai resti delle celle destinate alle *pornai*,[51] rivelati dagli scavi, sia dalla notizia luciliana relativa a *scorta pyrgensia*,[52] evidentemente passati in proverbio.

Ora, tutto questo sistema di origine orientale, costituito da una divinità femminile dell'*eros* e della riproduzione (ma anche della guerra), legata ad un dio morente, quindi di carattere ctonio, anche a Pyrgi sembra avere la stessa funzione che nel Vicino Oriente: le lamine iscritte ci rivelano infatti che il culto, e una particolare cerimonia

---

[43]Da ultimo, De Cazanove, *L'association dionysiaque* (sopra, n. 26).

[44]Versnel, *Triumphus* (sopra, n. 32), 11-55; Coarelli, *Foro Boario* (sopra, n. 6), 418.

[45]H. Jeanmaire, *Dionysos. Histoire du culte de Bacchus* (Parigi, 1951), 234.

[46]Cfr. Versnel, *Triumphus* (sopra, n. 32), 11-55.

[47]*Ibid.* pp. 201-35.

[48]Cfr. W. Burkert, *Mito e rituale in Grecia* (Roma-Bari, 1987), 14-15.

[49]Coarelli, *Foro Boario* (sopra, n. 6), 328-63.

[50]*Ibid.* pp. 357-8.

[51]G. Colonna, 'Il santuario di Leucotea e Ilizia a Pyrgi', in *Santuari d'Etruria (Catalogo della mostra di Siena)* (Milano, 1985), 128-9.

[52]Lucil. fr. 1271 M (da Serv. *Comm. in Verg. Aen.* x. 184).

traducibile in una *hierogamia* collegata alla morte del dio maschio, servono sostanzialmente a giustificare e garantire il potere di un tiranno di Cerveteri, Thefarie Velianas.

Perfettamente simmetrico a quello di Pyrgi è a Roma il culto serviano di Fortuna e Mater Matuta:[53] *hierogamia* e intronizzazione del sovrano vi sono illustrate, miticamente, dal rapporto erotico tra Servio e la Fortuna; ritualmente, il santuario assolve alla funzione di luogo di inizio del trionfo, che si conclude all'altro capo davanti al tempio di Giove Capitolino, divinità con la quale il trionfatore stesso si identifica nel corso della cerimonia.

Il mito di Mesenzio, *contemptor deorum*, sembra dunque da leggere come il rovesciamento di un rito originario di intronizzazione, come sempre legato al motivo della vittoria e del trionfo, pertinente ai 'tiranni' dell'età dei Tarquinii, non più capito, o meglio rifunzionalizzato negativamente, a confronto con un modello 'positivo', che è la regalità latina originaria, preetrusca: quella di Latino e di Enea. Sembra che una tale destrutturazione non si possa spiegare, ideologicamente, se non in rapporto alla cacciata dei Tarquinii e all'inizio della repubblica; essa è del tutto analoga alla contemporanea eliminazione del trionfo di tipo 'etrusco', con la quadriga di cavalli bianchi, che assimilava il trionfatore a Giove.[54]

Non mancano nella stessa Roma altri indizi che permettono di ricostruire una fase arcaica in cui il vino è legato — tramite una figura di Giove ctonio con forti elementi dionisiaci — alla sovranità e al potere. Principale tra questi è la decorazione architettonica della Regia, pertinente al secondo quarto del sesto secolo a.C., e quindi attribuibile all'epoca tradizionale di Servio Tullio.[55] Le lastre decorative presentano un'alternanza di pantere e altri felini con trampolieri e con la rappresentazione del Minotauro. Che si tratti di quest'ultimo e non di una generica figura di uomo a testa di toro (del resto improponibile in un contesto ormai ellenizzante come questo) risulta anche dalla associazione non banale con i trampolieri, nei quali è agevole identificare delle gru, e cioè gli uccelli che avrebbero dato il nome alla danza rituale di Teseo che celebrava la vittoria cretese, la *geranos*.[56] Una gru appare anche in un'altro fregio arcaico di terracotta con rappresentazione di *komos*.[57]

Ora, la struttura del mito di Teseo, letta come trasposizione di un rituale, non differisce da uno stereotipo diffusissimo in Grecia, e al quale abbiamo già accennato in precedenza; si tratta sostanzialmente di un problema di trasmissione del potere, legato a riti di passaggio, i cui elementi salienti sono sempre gli stessi:

(1) l'oracolo annuncia a un sovrano che il figlio nato da sua figlia lo ucciderà;

(2) di conseguenza, il re provvede a isolare la figlia, e a consacrarla a un culto che preveda la verginità;

(3) un dio o un eroe viola la fanciulla; il figlio che nascerà sarà esposto (oppure l'ordine di ucciderlo non verrà eseguito);

---

[53]Coarelli, *Foro Boario* (sopra, n. 6), 358-63.

[54]*Ibid.* pp. 431-4.

[55]Coarelli, *Foro Romano* (sopra, n. 23), 63-4.

[56]M. Verzar, 'Pyrgi e l'Afrodite di Cipro', *MEFRA* 92 (1980), 35-84.

[57]G. Pellegrini, 'Fregi arcaici etruschi in terracotta a piccole figure', in L.A. Milani, *Studi e materiali di archeologia e numismatica* 1 (Firenze, 1899-1901), 87-118; G. Mancini, in *NSA* (1915), 68-88.

(4) cresciuto ignaro della sua origine, il giovane compie una serie di imprese (uccisione di briganti, di mostri ecc.);

(5) tornato in patria, il giovane uccide inavvertitamente il padre (e talvolta sposa la madre), assumendo il potere o fondando una città.

Nella struttura che dobbiamo immaginare come originaria, il padre si identifica con lo stesso dio morente, e la madre con la dea.[58] Tracce evidenti di questo schema si riscontrano quasi sempre, e in particolare nel mito di Teseo, dove appaiono del resto quasi tutti gli stereotipi elencati in precedenza. Fermiamoci piuttosto sugli elementi di chiara origine rituale, che costituiscono nel loro insieme, al di là della ricontestualizzazione post-arcaica, una struttura perfettamente leggibile.

Teseo uccide il Minotauro (nel quale è stato agevole riconoscere Dioniso, il dio-toro, forse di ascendenza minoica),[59] si unisce con Arianna (altra divinità originaria, attestata nelle tavolette micenee, ed assimilabile ad Afrodite)[60] e accede così al potere (tramite la morte del padre, da lui provocata, sia pure involontariamente): sarebbe difficile non riconoscere qui tutti gli elementi della struttura rituale che abbiamo vista presente e operante nell'Italia arcaica.

Del resto, gli elementi superstiti dei rituali ateniesi delle Anthesteria[61] e delle Oschophoriai[62] ci forniscono il contesto cultuale più evidente nel senso indicato: le prime sono una festa primaverile, che iniziava il primo giorno con l'apertura dei dolii del vino nuovo, associata (il secondo giorno) con una processione che rappresentava l'ingresso trionfale in città di Dioniso sul carro navale. Seguiva la celebrazione dello *hieros gamos* tra Dioniso e la *basilinna*, la moglie dell'arconte *basileus* (quest'ultimo si sostituiva nella realtà al dio). Il rapporto con i Vinalia Priora (e il connesso mito di Mesenzio) da un lato, con il trionfo arcaico ricostruito in precedenza dall'altro non potrebbe essere più chiaro: con il vantaggio, nel caso ateniese, del collegamento tra festa del vino e trionfo, ricostruibile a Roma solo ipoteticamente.

Il collegamento tra Teseo e Dioniso si ricava da un'altra festa attica, le Oschophoriai, appunto: queste comprendevano la rappresentazione dello sbarco di Dioniso al Falero, che illustrava l'introduzione in Attica della vite da parte del dio. Nella stessa occasione veniva rappresentato anche il ritorno di Teseo da Creta con i quattordici giovani salvati dal Minotauro:[63] particolare notevole, tra di questi erano due ragazzi vestiti da donne, travestimento rituale che si spiega chiaramente come rito di passaggio d'età, e la cui presenza in Roma nell'ambito del culto di Fortuna-Venere (e cioè sempre in collegamento con feste del vino) è stata già segnalata in precedenza.

La rappresentazione del Minotauro e delle gru, in un contesto chiaramente dionisiaco (espresso dalle pantere) nella Regia dell'età di Servio Tullio non può essere dissociata, di conseguenza, da rituali greci (non solo attici, ma diffusi anche in Ionia,

[58]Versnel, *Triumphus* (sopra, n. 32), 235ss. V.J. Propp, *Edipo alla luce del folclore* (trad. ital.) (Torino, 1975).

[59]*Ibid.* p. 246 n. 7. Non a caso lo *hieros gamos* (unico conosciuto ad Atene) ha luogo nel *Boucoleion*.

[60]Jeanmaire, *Dionysos* (sopra, n. 45), 22; M. Delcourt, *Hermaphrodite* (Parigi, 1958), 13-14.

[61]Anthesteria: L. Deubner, *Attische Feste* (Berlino, 1952), 93ss., 148ss.; H.M. Parke, *Festivals of the Athenians* (Londra, 1977), 107-20.

[62]Oschophoriai: Deubner, *Attische Feste* (sopra, n. 61), 46-8; Parke, *Festivals of the Athenians* (sopra, n. 61), 77-80.

[63][Plut.] *De mus.* capp. 22-3 Lasserre.

come quello del carro navale)[64] collegati con il mito di Teseo; riti di passaggio strettamente funzionali alla trasmissione del potere e alla vittoria del re. Trovarli rappresentati nel palazzo di colui che era considerato il vero fondatore della città, la cui nascita era avvolta in un'aura leggendaria per tanti versi analoga a quella dell'eroe greco, difficilmente potrà esser considerato un fatto casuale.

* * *

Dopo aver preso in considerazione il livello rituale e quello mitico, ci resta da esaminare l'uso reale del vino in contesti precisi. Altri hanno esaminato, nel corso del convegno, i dati che si possono ricavare dall'archeologia per la ricostruzione dei fatti economici (produzione e commercio/distribuzione) e di particolari fatti ideologici (ad esempio, l'aspetto funerario del vino, il banchetto ricostruito attraverso la scoperta di servizi di vasi, e così via).[65] Per quanto mi riguarda, intenderei qui occuparmi di un aspetto ideologico particolare del banchetto, quello relativo ai *carmina convivalia*.

Si tratta, come è noto, di un terreno minato, su cui, a partire dall'interpretazione romantico-popolare del Niebuhr,[66] si sono esercitati praticamente tutti gli storici della letteratura romana arcaica (meno frequentemente gli storici *tout-court*): le conclusioni più recenti degli specialisti sono improntate in genere al più profondo scetticismo, in perfetta sintonia con le conclusioni cui era giunta la storiografia del tardo ottocento.[67]

Solo da poco, in parallelo a una tendenza di prudente rivalutazione della tradizione romana arcaica, il problema è stato riconsiderato in tutta la sua complessità (che mal si concilia con gli approcci tradizionali, improntati in genere al più miope e gretto specialismo), con il risultato di una complessiva rivalutazione del quadro tradizionale. Intendo riferirmi soprattutto agli studi recenti di Momigliano e di Zorzetti.[68]

Il tema non è infatti risolvibile all'interno della tradizionale ricostruzione filologico-letteraria: le limitatissime indicazioni delle fonti, in sé considerate, non permettono di esprimersi né in senso negativo né in senso positivo. Solo un'analisi assai ampia di carattere comparativo (anche in senso etno-antropologico) e la considerazione dei dati archeologici possono ricollocare questa tematica su un terreno più solido.

La perdita quasi totale della più antica antiquaria romana (e in particolare delle *Origines* di Catone e del *De vita populi Romani* di Varrone) ci lascia singolarmente disarmati per tutto quanto concerne gli usi quotidiani di Roma arcaica, sui quali essa ci appare, a giudicare dai frammenti conservati, piuttosto bene informata. Basterà qui ricordare le notizie sull'apparizione delle statue di culto nel periodo di Tarquinio Prisco,[69]

---

[64]Smirne: *Hymn. Hom. Bacch.* 7; Deubner, *Attische Feste* (sopra, n. 61), 162-3.

[65]Si vedano le communicazioni di A. Rathje e A. Pontrandolfo.

[66]Su questo cfr. A. Momigliano, 'Perizonius, Niebuhr and the character of early Roman tradition', in A. Momigliano, *Secondo contributo alla storia degli studi classici* (Roma, 1960), 69-86.

[67]Caratteristico ad esempio H. Dahlmann, 'Zur Überlieferung über die "altrömischen Tafellieder"', *AAWM* 17 (1950), 1191-202, seguito da J.H. Waszink, 'Tradition and personal achievement in early Latin literature', *Mnemosyne* ser. 4, 13 (1960), 17.

[68]Momigliano, 'Perizonius, Niebuhr' (sopra, n. 66); V. Zorzetti, 'The *carmina convivalia*', in O. Murray (ed.), *Sympotica: a Symposium on the* Symposion (Oxford, 1990), 289-307.

[69]Varrone, *Antiquitates Rerum Divinarum* fr. 18 Cardauns.

confermate in pieno dalla ricerca archeologica o, per un tema più vicino al nostro, l'informazione varroniana sull'uso di mangiare seduti, che precedette a Roma l'uso di mangiare sdraiati;[70] indicazione che si potrebbe anche far risalire all'analogo sviluppo riconoscibile in Grecia, a partire da Omero, se non ci fosse l'ulteriore precisazione, secondo la quale le donne continuarono a restare sedute anche in seguito; ciò che corrisponde in effetti a un uso attestato da rappresentazioni figurate.[71] In questo caso, le informazioni di Varrone sono dunque perfettamente attendibili, perchè confermate dalla documentazione archeologica.

Possiamo così procedere, con accresciuta fiducia, ad esaminare i pochi frammenti che ci hanno trasmesso il ricordo dei *carmina convivalia*.

(1) Cicerone, *Tusculanae Disputationes* i. 3: *sero igitur a nostris poetae vel recogniti vel recepti. Quamquam est in Originibus solitos esse in epulis canere convivas ad tibicinem de clarorum virorum virtutibus.*

(2) Cicerone, *Tusculanae Disputationes* iv. 3: *gravissimus auctor in Originibus* (fr. 118 Peter) *dicit Cato morem apud maiores hunc epularum fuisse, ut deinceps qui accubarent canerent ad tibiam clarorum virorum laudes atque virtutes. Ex quo perspicuum est et cantus tum fuisse discriptos vocum sonis et carmina ...*

(3) Cicerone, *Epistulae ad Brutum* 75: *Atque utinam extarent illa carmina, quae multis saeculis ante suam aetatem in epulis esse cantitata a singulis convivis de clarorum virorum laudibus in originibus scriptum reliquit Cato.*

(4) Varrone, *de Vita Populi Romani*, in Nonnus p. 83 L.: *In conviviis pueri modesti ut cantarent carmina antiqua in quibus laudes erant maiorum et assa voce et cum tibicine.*

(5) Orazio, *Carmina*, iv. 15.25-32:

Nosque et profestis lucibus et sacris
inter iocosi munera liberi
        cum prole matronisque nostris
                rite deos prius adprecati

virtute functos more patrum duces
Lydis remixto carmine tibiis
        Troiamque et Anchisen et almae
                progeniem Veneris canemus.

(6) Dionigi di Alicarnasso i. 79.10: οἱ δὲ ἀνδρωθέντες γίνονται κατά τε ἀξίωσιν μορφῆς καὶ φρονήματος ὄγκον οὐ συοφορβοῖς καὶ βουκόλοις ἐοικότες, ἀλλ᾽ οἵους ἄν τις ἀξιώσειε τοὺς ἐκ βασιλείου τε φύντας γένους καὶ ἀπὸ δαιμόνων σπορᾶς γενέσθαι νομιζομένους, ὡς ἐν τοῖς πατρίοις ὕμνοις ὑπὸ Ῥωμαίων ἔτι καὶ νῦν ᾄδεται.

(7) Dionigi di Alicarnasso viii. 62.3: ἐτῶν δὲ μετὰ τὸ πάθος ὁμοῦ τι πεντακοσίων ἤδη διαγεγονότων εἰς τόνδε τὸν χρόνον οὐ γέγονεν ἐξίτηλος ἡ τοῦ ἀνδρὸς μνήμη, ἀλλ᾽ ᾄδεται καὶ ὑμνεῖται καὶ πρὸς πάντων ὡς εὐσεβὴς καὶ δίκαιος ἀνήρ.

(8) Quintilianus, *Institutio oratoria* i. 10.19-20: *Unde etiam ille mos, ut in conviviis post cenam circumferretur lyra, cuius cum se imperitum Themistocles confessus esset, ut verbis Ciceronis utar, 'est habitus indoctior' (Tusc. i. 2.4). Sed veterum quoque Romanorum epulis fides ac tibias adhibere moris fuit; versus quoque Saliorum habent carmen. Quae cum omnia sint a Numa rege instituta, faciunt manifestum ne illis quidem, qui rudes ac bellicosi videntur, curam musices, quantam illa recipiebat aetas, defuisse.*

---

[70]Varrone, *de Vita Populi Romani* fr. 30 a Riposati, da Isid. *Etym* xx. 11.9.
[71]L'uso sembra diffondersi in periodo post-arcaico (nel sesto secolo le donne appaiono anch'esse sdraiate): cfr. S. De Marinis, *La tipologia del banchetto nell'arte etrusca arcaica* (Roma, 1961).

Se stiamo alle indicazioni di Catone, trasmesse da Cicerone, nella Roma arcaica sarebbe esistito l'uso nei banchetti di cantare le lodi dei *clari viri* (certamente degli antenati, come precisa Varrone): sarebbero stati gli stessi convitati a cantare, accompagnati dalle tibie. L'epoca dei *carmina* (che non si conservavano più al tempo di Cicerone)[72] sarebbe stata comunque di molto anteriore allo stesso Catone: *saecula* a mio avviso, tenuto conto del contesto, va interpretato non con 'generazioni', come ritiene Momigliano,[73] ma proprio con 'secoli', durata massima della vita di un uomo. Si vuole quindi alludere a una grande antichità rispetto al secondo secolo a.C., ciò che ci riporta comunque ad età arcaica: non può in alcun caso trattarsi del quarto secolo, cioè di un'età di pochi decenni anteriore all'inizio della poesia letteraria.

Un indizio cronologico interessante potrebbe forse riconoscersi nella precisazione che i convitati mangiavano già sdraiati (*qui accubarent*): ma potrebbe trattarsi anche di una inavvertita modernizzazione di Cicerone (o dello stesso Catone, se il suo testo qui è riferito alla lettera).

Si è molto insistito, anche di recente, sulle discrepanze tra Catone e Varrone:[74] quest'ultimo infatti attribuisce la *performance* non già ai convitati, ma a *pueri modesti*[75] che avrebbero cantato o senza accompagnamento oppure accompagnati dalle tibie. Ora, questo dettaglio potrebbe esser utilizzato, semmai, per dimostrare che Varrone non dipende da Catone (ciò che mi sembra del tutto evidente). I critici più recenti della tradizione antica, mentre da un lato ritengono che il primo derivi le sue notizie dal secondo, dall'altro ritengono che le abbia a sua volta modificate.[76] Quanto al testo di Catone, esso viene interpretato come una voluta attribuzione ai Romani di usi greci arcaici, senza alcun riscontro nella realtà.[77]

Mi sembra che la critica di Momigliano colga perfettamente nel segno: i due stili di *performance* conviviale ricordati da Catone e da Varrone esistevano ambedue in Grecia, e nulla impedisce che fossero importati a Roma (con adattamenti locali, beninteso) fin da età arcaica: più o meno contemporaneamente all'introduzione del banchetto sdraiato, anch'esso giunto in Etruria e a Roma fin dalla fine del settimo secolo, probabilmente dalla Ionia.[78]

---

[72]Ciò sembrerebbe contrastare con l'affermazione di Dionigi di Alicarnasso, secondo il quale i *carmina convivalia* erano ancora eseguiti al suo tempo: più che a una invenzione di Dionigi si potrebbe pensare a un *revival* augusteo, di cui è traccia forse in Orazio, *Carm.* iv. 15.25-32. Se, come pensa S. Timpanaro, 'Note a Livio Andronico, Ennio, Varrone, Virgilio', *ASNP* 18-19 (1949), 194-200, il *carmen Priami*, almeno nella forma che ci è giunta nei frammenti, è una ricostruzione erudita tardo — repubblicana, avremmo un conferma di tale interpretazione.

[73]Momigliano, 'Perizonius, Niebuhr', (sopra, n. 67), 82.

[74]Dahlmann, 'Überlieferung' (sopra, n. 67).

[75]La correzione che in genere si vuole introdurre di *modesti* (ad esempio, *domestici* in Dahlmann) deriva, al solito, dalla incomprensione del contesto. Qui Varrone vuole distinguere gli usi del banchetto arcaico romano da quelli, impudici, dei Greci: significa *non petulantes*.

[76]Dahlmann, 'Überlieferung' (sopra, n. 67).

[77]*Ibid.*

[78]J.-M. Dentzer, *Le motif du banquet couché dans le proche-orient et le monde grec du VIIe au IVe siècle avant J.C.* (Roma-Paris, 1982), 51ss.

Tutto dipende in realtà dall'idea obsoleta che ci si fa di Roma arcaica, che porta ad attribuire al periodo tardo-repubblicano ogni traccia di influsso greco che si riscontri nella cultura romana.[79] In realtà, usi greci (a cominciare dalla scrittura) furono introdotti in Roma già del pieno settimo secolo, se non prima: l'enorme congerie di dati archeologici accumulati soprattutto negli ultimi decenni — e sistematicamente ignorata dai filologi — non permette ormai alcuna conclusione diversa.

Ancora una volta, problemi di questo tipo possono essere affrontati correttamente solo in un contesto più ampio, che non può venir ricostruito se non a partire da una base interdisciplinare molto più estesa e articolata della semplice escussione di quattro o cinque frammenti letterari, esaminati per di più alla luce di una banale ipercritica, completamente digiuna di conoscenze e di stimoli non strettamente pertinenti alla disciplina professata.

Partendo da un modello, che non potrà non identificarsi nel banchetto (ed eventualmente nel simposio) greco arcaico,[80] dovremo prendere in esame i dati disponibili sull'Italia tirrenica, utilizzando tutti i materiali possibili, ed in particolare quelli epigrafici e archeologici, oggi disponibili in quantità e qualità molto superiori a quanto non fosse anche solo pochi decenni orsono. Si tratta, in altri termini, di adeguare, in un contesto unitario, i livelli di conoscenza disponibili sul piano archeologico (ancora insufficientemente elaborati e non utilizzati in genere per problemi del tipo che qui ci interessa) a quelli di origine letteraria, su cui si è invece esercitata una critica più che secolare.

Gli elementi del simposio greco, quale lo conosciamo a partire dall'età arcaica, possono essere sommariamente schematizzati come segue:

(1) la presenza di eterie;
(2) il bere separato dal mangiare (polarità banchetto-simposio);
(3) l'esistenza di canti simposiali (politici, erotici, encomiastici);
(4) l'uso di banchettare sdraiati;
(5) il *komos*.

Dobbiamo subito precisare che il punto (2), almeno a giudicare dalla nostra informazione iconografica, non appare mai realizzato appieno in Etruria e a Roma:[81] sembra, in altri termini, che qui ci troviamo di fronte ad uno di quei tipici limiti dell'acculturazione, che dipendono da elementi costitutivi 'forti' della società che riceve, e che determinano varianti anche di rilievo nella determinazione delle strutture locali 'acculturate'.

---

[79] Tipica, a riguardo, la posizione di Dahlmann, 'Überlieferung' (sopra, n. 67).

[80] Su questo, oltre alle comunicazioni del convegno, cfr. Dentzer, *Motif du banquet couché* (sopra, n. 78) (per le rappresentazioni figurate) e i contributi comodamente raccolti da M. Vetta, con un'esauriente introduzione, in *Poesia e simposio nella Grecia antica. Guida storica e critica* (Roma-Bari, 1983).

[81] Ringrazio Oswyn Murray, che nella discussione mi ha chiarito questo punto: sembra che il banchetto in Italia non abbia mai assunto completamente le forme greche, in particolare per quanto riguarda la netta separazione tra banchetto e simposio. Piuttosto che di 'incomprensione', però, si dovrà parlare di adattamento a situazioni locali diverse.

L'uso del simposio si scontrava, evidentemente, con componenti della società tirrenica non omologabili ad esso, che ci sembra di poter identificare soprattutto nel ruolo diverso della donna. Varrone,[82] come si ricorderà, afferma la presenza delle donne nei banchetti, ai quali esse tuttavia partecipavano sedute: ci è sembrato di identificare in questo dettaglio tutt'altro che irrilevante la prova dell'attendibilità di Varrone, che qui non può dipendere da fonti greche.

Ora, la partecipazione della donna libera al banchetto, inconcepibile in Grecia (di qui lo scandalo di Aristotele e di altri per la 'scostumatezza' delle donne etrusche),[83] era tale da impedire lo sviluppo completo degli usi greci in Italia, almeno nelle forme più 'pure', il cui culmine è appunto costituito dal simposio.

Sembra dunque che in Etruria e a Roma il banchetto conservi più a lungo, per queste ragioni strutturali, le sue forme più antiche, anteriori all'introduzione del simposio, che in Grecia sono conosciute per il periodo eroico.[84]

Una volta riconosciuta questa fondamentale divergenza, frutto ineliminabile delle costanti sociali italiche, e della pressione da queste esercitata sugli apporti culturali greci, resta comunque il fatto, innegabile, che gli usi del banchetto in Italia sono sostanzialmente il risultato dell'acculturazione, che si verifica in età molto antica, e comunque non dopo la fine del settimo secolo a.C.

Se infatti esaminiamo le altre caratteristiche del banchetto e del simposio greco enumerate in precedenza, ci accorgiamo rapidamente che altre due di esse, i canti simposiaci (almeno quelli di carattere politico-encomiastico: quelli di carattere erotico sono probabilmente esclusi dalla particolare struttura sociale tirrenica, ricordata in precedenza, che anche per questo aspetto rimane più arcaica, più vicina alla Grecia dell'età eroica) e il banchetto sdraiato sono attestati come esistenti *ab antiquo* dalle fonti romane: per il secondo poi, come marginalmente anche per il *komos*, possediamo un'abbondantissima documentazione iconografica contemporanea, che ci toglie ogni dubbio sull'attendibilità dei dati trasmessi dall'antiquaria romana.[85]

Tutto ciò naturalmente costituisce anche un indizio favorevole all'esistenza dei *carmina convivalia*: per una società strutturata, come quella romana arcaica, su rigide basi gentilizie, tutto compreso analoghe a quelle che in Grecia andarono coagulandosi con circa un secolo di anticipo, è difficile negare l'esistenza di un'epica di tipo eroico, funzionale alla coesione del gruppo agnatizio, e quindi al culto degli antenati. Tracce di una tale cultura arcaica sono evidenti ancora nella tradizione funeraria di età medio-repubblicana. Un'epica 'gentilizia' del genere è del resto diffusa in tutte le epoche e in tutte le società pervenute a un certo grado di sviluppo delle forze produttive.[86]

---

[82]Sopra, n. 70.

[83]M. Torelli, *Storia degli Etruschi*, seconda edizione (Roma-Bari, 1990), 81-3.

[84]Ad esempio, Omero, *Il.* ix. 185ss.

[85]De Marinis, *Tipologia del banchetto* (sopra, n. 71).

[86]Il tema è quello, notissimo, di M. Parry. Per la bibliografia, immensa, basterà rimandare a B. Gentili, *Poesia e pubblico nella Grecia antica* (Roma-Bari, 1984), 327ss.

Ma anche se si accantonano queste considerazioni di carattere generale (che a mio avviso restano comunque determinanti), non mancano precisi indizi coevi, suscettibili di confermare la storicità dei *carmina convivalia*.

In primo luogo, vanno qui ricordate le testimonianze epigrafiche più antiche a noi pervenute, che attestano l'esistenza di *carmina* metrici, probabilmente di carattere lirico, almeno in un caso inquadrabili entro un contesto del tutto analogo a quello del simposio greco.[87] Il carattere metrico di tutte le iscrizioni arcaiche di una certa lunghezza conservate risulterebbe chiaramente, ritengo, da un esame sistematico esteso anche a quelle di più recente scoperta.[88] Non mi sembra che sia stato notato, ad esempio, che ambedue le lamine bronzee iscritte di Lavinio sono metriche.[89] La più antica di esse, ancora del sesto secolo a.C., sembra da interpretare come un tetrametro trocaico, analogo a quelli riconoscibili nel 'vaso di Duenos' e nella formula dei Meditrinalia:[90]

Castorei Podlouqueique qurois

(*CIL* I², 2933);

Iovesat deivos qoi med mitat

(*CIL* I², 4);

novum vetus vinum bibo

(Varrone, *Ling.* vi. 21).

Del resto, anche per monumenti da tempo conosciuti, come il cippo del Foro,[91] è possibile, in base alla ricostruzione praticamente certa della formula standardizzata iniziale, identificare un perfetto saturnio:

quoi hon[k stloqom violasid/ manibos] sakros esed.

Ciò significa che il saturnio 'canonico' doveva essere ormai formato fin dalla prima metà del sesto secolo a.C., come aveva giustamente proposto Giorgio Pasquali.[92]

In precedenza, si possono rintracciare singoli *cola* di saturnio, analoghi a quelli che possiamo trovare in Grecia, utilizzati come metri lirici, accompagnati dalla musica.[93] L'analisi di *carmina* antichissimi, come quello dei *fratres arvales*,[94] dimostra l'esistenza di tali *cola* lirici, destinati quindi al canto ed eventualmente alla danza, con accompagnamento della lira o delle tibie.[95] Da questo punto di vista quindi la possibilità, almeno teorica, dell'esistenza di *carmina convivalia*, lirici nella forma, epici nei contenuti può considerarsi acquisita.

---

[87]Si tratta, come vedremo in seguito, dell'iscrizione arcaica scoperta a Satricum: C.M. Stibbe, G. Colonna, C. De Simone e H.S. Versnel, *Lapis Satricanus* (Roma, 1980).

[88]Per le quali si veda la lista in Colonna, *Santuari d'Etruria* (sopra, n. 51), 53ss.

[89]*CIL* I², 2833, 2847.

[90]Sui quali cfr. sopra, nn. 21 (Duenos) e 14 (Meditrinalia).

[91]Da ultimo, R.E.A. Palmer, *The King and the* Comitium (*Historia, Einzelschriften* 11) (1969), e Coarelli, *Foro Romano* (sopra, n. 23), 178ss.

[92]G. Pasquali, *Preistoria della poesia romana*, seconda edizione (Firenze, 1981) (con importante saggio introduttivo di S. Timpanaro), 139ss.

[93]*Ibid.* pp. 143ss.

[94]*Ibid.* p. 73.

[95]*Ibid.* pp. 114ss.

Un passo avanti decisivo è consentito da un'iscrizione rinvenuta di recente, il *lapis Satricanus*, su cui moltissimo si è scritto, senza tuttavia esaurirne il potenziale documentario.[96]

È stato già osservato[97] che l'iscrizione sembra di carattere metrico, senza tuttavia portare fino in fondo l'analisi su questo terreno. Ora, non c'è dubbio che la parte sicuramente comprensibile del testo, letta di seguito, costituisca un saturnio perfetto:

Popliosio Valesiosio / suodales Mamartei

(*Lapis Satricanus*).

Addirittura, anzi, un verso identico al 'modello teorico' del saturnio, che ricorre solo raramente:

malum dabunt Metelli / Naevio poetae.[98]

(Caesinus Bassino, *Fragmentum de metris*, in H. Keil,
Grammatici Latini VI (Leipzig, 1874), 265-6)

A mio avviso, il collegamento in un unico verso impone anche un'interpretazione diversa da quella che ha finito per imporsi, e che separa *suodales* da *Mamartei*, identificando l'epigrafe con una dedica a Marte. Mi sembra invece inevitabile leggere *suodales Mamartei* come *suodales Martiales*, analogamente a quanto troviamo a Capua ancora nel secondo secolo a.C.: *magistrei Spei, Fidei, Fortunae; magistrei Iovei Optumo Maxumo; magistrei Castori et Polluci; ministri Laribus*,[99] ecc. In conclusione, si dovrà tradurre: 'i *sodales Martiales*'.

Ciò che significa anche che il dedicatario va cercato, come di regola, all'inizio del testo,[100] e va riconosciuto nell'enigmatico [...]*ieisteterai*, che proporrei di integrare con qualcosa come [*Man*]*ieis Teterai* = *diis chtoniis*, con un raddoppiamento enfatico *tetera* per *tera=terra*, del tutto analogo al seguente *Mamartei*.[101] Il testo completo suonerebbe come 'I *sodales Martiales* (di Publio Valerio) (dedicano) agli dei Mani di Publio Valerio'. Potrebbe, in altri termini, trattarsi di un epitaffio, il che non contraddice al luogo di ritrovamento nella struttura del tempio di *Satricum*, dal momento che si tratta di un reimpiego. Si noterà che, se l'integrazione proposta è accettabile (ma anche integrazioni diverse non darebbero risultati diversi, dal momento che all'inizio dell'iscrizione mancano pochissime lettere, e quindi in ogni caso una sola sillaba), ne risulta ancora una volta un itifallico, cioè un secondo *colon* del saturnio, del tutto analogo a *suodales Mamartei*: ciò che conferma la lettura metrica del resto ed entro certi limiti l'integrazione proposta, ma anche l'uso di *cola* del saturnio isolati, che sembra da spiegare come metro lirico.

Ora, in questo possibile epitaffio (genere poetico strettamente connesso con i *carmina convivialia*, come si è detto in precedenza) vediamo convergere quasi tutti gli elementi che si sono enumerati come tipici del simposio: oltre all'aspetto metrico, che rimanda al canto accompagnato dalla musica, il contenuto ideologico (la stessa

---

[96]Cfr. sopra, n. 87.

[97]Colonna, *Santuari d'Etruria* (sopra, n. 51), 41ss.

[98]Sul saturnio si veda da ultimo, oltre a Timpanaro, 'Note a Livio Andronico' (sopra, n. 72), B. Luiselli, *Il verso saturnio* (Roma, 1967).

[99]*ILLRP* 707, 708, 712, 715, 718.

[100]F. Coarelli, *Roma sepolta* (Roma, 1984), 60ss.

[101]*Ibid.* p. 62

eccezionalità di un'epigrafe, forse funeraria, in onore di un privato nel sesto secolo a.C. si spiega solo con la personalità assolutamente fuori del comune del personaggio, appartenente alla *gens patricia* dei *Valerii*, l'unica per cui ci viene ricordata l'esistenza di un sepolcro gentilizio già all'inizio della repubblica:[102] l'aspetto encomiastico insomma è implicito nella struttura stessa della dedica); ma soprattutto, i dedicanti sono *sodales* di Publio Valerio: una sodalità nata in relazione al culto di Marte. Tutto ciò rimanda a una eteria di carattere militare, tipicamente arcaica, che sembra connessa all'*ara Martis* del Campo Marzio, fondata, secondo una tradizione, all'inizio della Repubblica, e forse proprio da P. Valerio Poplicola,[103] in cui, giustamente a mio avviso, si è voluto riconoscere il dedicatario del *lapis Satricanus*.

Quest'ultimo ci fornisce, di conseguenza, la prova innegabile dell'esistenza di *sodalitates* arcaiche a Roma, la cui natura e la cui funzione sono assimilabili a quelle delle eterie greche. È particolarmente importante che questa testimonianza sia emersa dallo stesso documento da cui ricaviamo l'attestazione di *carmina* metrici, lirici nella forma e sostanzialmente encomiastici nel contenuto.

In altri termini, le condizioni che ci sono sembrate necessarie per confermare l'esistenza dei *carmina convivalia* si trovano tutte riunite in un documento databile agli ultimi decenni del sesto secolo a.C.

Non mancano nella letteratura latina (soprattutto annalistica) gli accenni all'esistenza di *sodalitates* arcaiche, affini per caratteristiche e funzioni alle eterie greche (pur con quelle differenze strutturali che abbiamo segnalato in precedenza).[104] Un chiaro indizio ne ritroviamo nella tradizione relativa a Mastarna — Servio Tullio, nell'interpretazione claudiana: Servio vi appare come *sodalis fidelissimus* di Celio Vibenna, e tutta la complessa vicenda della conquista del potere a Roma, anche in base alle pitture della Tomba François, ci si rivela come opera di una eteria di tipo politico, quali quelle che ci sono ben note nella Grecia arcaica.[105] Lo stesso circolo tirannico dei Tarquini è più volte caratterizzato nelle fonti come una tipica eteria,[106] e così pure i circoli aristocratici che furono artefici della repubblica:[107] ciò che rende ancor più affascinante il documento di Satrico, che probabilmente ci restituisce una testimonianza contemporanea di queste *sodalitates* gentilizie filorepubblicane.

* * *

Per finire, occorrerà prendere in esame le testimonianze archeologiche, che presentano il vantaggio, come quelle epigrafiche, di offrirci documenti coevi e scevri di rielaborazioni ideologiche successive, diversamente dalle fonti letterarie. Interessano

---

[102]Coarelli, *Foro Romano* (sopra, n. 23), 79-83.

[103]J. Gagé, *La chute des Tarquins et les débuts de la république romaine* (Parigi, 1976), 78-105.

[104]Cfr. H.S. Versnel, 'Historical implications', in Stibbe *et al.*, *Lapis Satricanus* (sopra, n. 87), 95ss.

[105]Gaius, *Digesta* 47, 22, 4. *Tabula Claudiana*: *CIL* XIII, 1668 = *ILS*, 212, 1, 17ss. Per le eterie in Grecia, C. Talamo, 'Per l'origine delle eterie arcaiche', *PP* 16 (1961), 297-303.

[106]Livio i. 57.5: *regii quidem iuvenes interdum otium conviviis comisationibusque inter se terebant*; Livio ii. 3.2; 4.5.

[107]Livio i. 59.5, 12.

qui soprattutto le abitazioni regie o gentilizie, sedi privilegiate del banchetto arcaico,[108] e le rappresentazioni iconografiche che, nel nostro caso, vanno scelte in primo luogo tra quelle destinate a decorare questi stessi edifici[109] (sulle rappresentazioni funerarie potrebbe infatti gravare il sospetto di una connotazione determinata esclusivamente dal contesto).

Se torniamo per un momento alla lastra della *regia* con rappresentazione del Minotauro, già considerata in precedenza, potremmo essere tentati di stabilire un rapporto tra questa immagine e una funzione non esclusivamente simbolica di essa: in altri termini, l'uso del mito, e di questo mito particolare, le cui valenze ideologiche ci sono sembrate evidenti nel contesto di un palazzo regale di Roma forse appartenente a Servio Tullio, non potrebbe aver costituito il contenuto di canti epici, di *performances* avvenute nella stessa sede, eventualmente nella forma di *carmina convivalia*? È importante sottolineare, a questo proposito, che i due *carmina* ritenuti arcaici di cui ci è rimasta notizia, il *carmen Nelei* e il *carmen Priami*,[110] trattano di argomenti mitistorici, certamente in connessione con genealogie locali, tra le quali bisogna identificare i committenti. Per quanto riguarda Priamo, il fatto appare evidente, ma anche Neleo e i Nelidi (soprattutto Nestore) erano considerati fondatori di città e probabilmente anche antenati mitici di famiglie aristocratiche in Italia.[111] Il mito di Teseo può aver conosciuto un'analoga fortuna nell'ambito di una dinastia regia romana.

I dati più importanti, perché la loro integrità ci permette di ricostruire il sistema complessivo di cui essi fanno parte, sono però quelli che provengono dallo scavo di alcuni 'palazzi' etruschi, in particolare quelli di Murlo e di Acquarossa.[112] L'interpretazione complessiva che ne ha dato Mario Torelli, a mio avviso impeccabile, costituirà il presupposto di queste mie considerazioni.[113]

Il palazzo di Murlo, nella sua seconda fase, databile al secondo quarto del sesto secolo a.C., costituisce un esempio impressionante di organismo accentrato, risalente a prototipi orientali. Il cuore ne è costituito da un grande cortile quadrato (lato di 40 m) intorno al quale si dispongono ordinatamente i quartieri di abitazione, i magazzini, le sale cerimoniali. La principale tra queste è collocata sul lato nordovest: qui forse avevano luogo i banchetti ufficiali; particolare notevole, un sacello, sede del culto domestico, si dispone in asse con questa sala. Lungo il crinale del tetto erano collocate grandi statue sedute di terracotta, certamente rappresentazioni degli antenati.[114] La decorazione architettonica comprendeva anche una serie di lastre fittili a rilievo con la raffigurazione di banchetti, corse di cavalli, una processione nuziale, un'assemblea di divinità.

---

[108]Cfr. da ultimo M. Torelli, introduzione a S. Stopponi (ed.), *Case e palazzi d'Etruria* (Milano, 1985), 21-32.

[109]*Ibid. passim.*

[110]Timpanaro, 'Note a Livio Andronico' (sopra, n. 72).

[111]Si veda il caso della Tomba François, F. Coarelli, 'Le pitture della tomba François a Vulci: una proposta di lettura', *DArch* 3ª ser. 1,2 (1983), 43ss.

[112]Stopponi (ed.), *Case e palazzi* (sopra, n. 108), 41ss., 64ss.

[113]*Ibid.* pp. 21ss.

[114]Si veda già R. Bianchi Bandinelli, 'Qualche osservazione sulle statue acroteriali di Poggio Civitate (Murlo)', *DArch* 6 (1972), 236ss.; M. Torelli, 'Polis e "palazzo". Architettura, ideologia e artigianato greco in Etruria tra VII e VI sec. a.C.', in *Architecture et société* (Parigi-Roma, 1983), 471ss.

Nel più tardo (terzo quarto del sesto secolo a.C.) palazzo di Acquarossa tra i fregi figurati vediamo apparire quello con la rappresentazione delle fatiche di Ercole:[115] gli antenati non sono più gli dei, ma gli eroi. Coerentemente, il culto non è più interno alla struttura gentilizia, come dimostra il fatto che il sacello, analogo a quello di Murlo, sorge al di fuori del 'palazzo'.

Anche in questo caso appaiono scene conviviali e di *komos*, attestazione della posizione ormai centrale del banchetto, in rapporto con una probabile eteria.

Il fatto che le scene di banchetto appaiano solo in edifici 'privati' (tali debbono essere considerati anche gli esemplari di fregi fittili con analoghe rappresentazioni, provenienti dal Palatino, da Velletri, da Cisterna)[116] e mai in veri e propri edifici templari dimostra che ci troviamo in presenza di rappresentazioni non generiche, ma strettamente funzionali alle strutture palaziali in cui erano inserite: in altri termini, si tratta di un imagerie che riproduce la sostanza delle attività reali che avevano luogo negli edifici stessi.

L'esame di queste rappresentazioni è dunque essenziale per i nostri scopi. In esse appaiono, coerentemente con l'uso etrusco, uomini e donne distesi su *klinai*, ai quali si accostano inservienti per versare il vino, attinto dai vicini crateri. Quello che più conta per noi è la presenza di musici con lire e tibie. Nel caso di Murlo è anzi uno dei banchettanti a suonare la lira, secondo un costume tipicamente greco.[117] Nello stesso rilievo un tibicine si accosta a un convitato che si volge verso di lui e apre la bocca per cantare.

L'atto non permette equivoci, e costituisce l'illustrazione perfetta del passo di Catone già ricordato in precedenza: *solitos esse in epulis canere convivae ad tibicinem.*[118]

Certo, ci piacerebbe restituire la voce a questo personaggio; ma anche in mancanza di ciò il contesto è parlante: la scena si svolge in una sala del palazzo, affacciata su di un sacello destinato al culto dinastico, sul cui tetto si dispone la teoria delle statue degli antenati. Il canto, possiamo esserne certi, esponeva *clarorum virorum laudes atque virtutes.*

---

[115]Torelli, introduzione a Stopponi (ed.), *Case e palazzi* (sopra, n. 108), 31-2.

[116]*Ibid.* pp. 31-2.

[117]R.L. Lacy, in Stopponi (ed.), *Case e palazzi* (sopra, n. 108), 125.

[118]Catone, *Orig.* fr. 118 Peter.

14

Rituels Romains dans les Vignobles

OLIVIER DE CAZANOVE

La fête romaine qu'on célébrait le 19 août, les Vinalia Rustica, a toujours suscité une certaine perplexité de la part des modernes. Th. Mommsen écrivait voilà un siècle: 'la signification originelle des deuxièmes Vinalia' [*sc.* les Vinalia Rustica] est aussi incertaine qu'est certaine celle des premiers'[1] [*sc.* les Vinalia de printemps]. Et, voilà une quinzaine d'années, Dumézil, dans le livre qu'il consacrait aux *Fêtes romaines d'été et d'automne*, confessait la même ignorance: 'des Vinalia Rustica, on ne connaît que l'intention'.[2]

Incertitude donc, sur les rites et le sens même de cette journée. S'il existe à Rome deux fêtes du même nom,[3] célébrées à quatre mois d'intervalle, le 23 avril et le 19 août, s'il existe un petit dossier de textes qui se rapportent à ces Vinalia,[4] les quelques renseignements précis dont on dispose intéressent la cérémonie printanière.[5] Les Vinalia

---

[1] *CIL* I², 325ss.

[2] G. Dumézil, *Fêtes romaines d'été et d'automne* (Paris, 1975), 87.

[3] Sur l'appellation usuelle de chacune des deux fêtes dont le nom officiel est identique, voir ci-dessous, n. 52.

[4] On le trouvera commodément réuni par R. Schilling, *La religion romaine de Vénus* (Paris, 1954), 98-107. Des cadres généraux d'interprétation des Vinalia sont fournis par Fr. Bömer, 'Juppiter und die römischen Weinfeste', *RhM* 90 (1941), 30-58; par Schilling, *op. cit.*, 107-8; par G. Dumézil à plusieurs reprises, et surtout *Fêtes romaines* (ci-dessus, n. 2), 87-8; *idem*, 'Virgile, Mézence et les Vinalia', dans *L'Italie préromaine et la Rome républicaine. Mélanges offerts à Jacques Heurgon* (Collection de l'École française de Rome 27) i (Paris, 1976), 253-63 (= *Mariages indo-européens* (Paris, 1979), 198-209). Le travail plus récent de E. Montanari, 'Funzione della sovranità e feste del vino nella Roma repubblicana', *SMSR* 49 (1983), 243-62, s'attache, non pas 'à reconstruire l'exacte répartition des rites à Jupiter dans chacune des fêtes du vin' (p. 247), mais à explorer le rapport 'Jupiter-vin-victoire'.

[5] Les informations de type rituel qu'on possède sur les Vinalia du 23 avril sont: (a) la prohibition d'importer du vin en ville (à Rome et dans le Latium) avant l'indiction de la fête (*antequam Vinalia kalentur*: Varron, *Ling.* vi. 16, voir ci-dessous, à la n. 8) ou le jour même de celle-ci (*quo die primum in Urbem vinum deferebant*: Paul.-Fest., p. 323 L.), avec une confusion évidente entre les Vinalia d'automne et ceux de printemps): (b) effusion d'une grande quantité de vin (πολὺν οἶνον) hors du temple de Vénus (Erycine, dont le 23 avril est le *dies natalis*), geste qui répète celui, mythique, d'Enée répandant le produit de la vendange [latine] en acquittement du voeu souscrit [envers Jupiter] (Plut. *Quaest. Rom.* ch. 45; et *cf.* les sources relatives au mythe d'origine des Vinalia: *CIL* I², 236 (*Fasti Praenestini*); Cato *apud* Macrob. *Sat.* iii. 5.10; Varron *apud* Pline, *HN* xiv. 88; Fest., p. 322 L.; Ov. *Fast.* iv. 877-900); (c) une libation à Jupiter de vin nouveau qui porte, pour l'occasion, un nom special: *calpar* (Paul.-Fest., p. 57 L.: *calpar vinum novum quod ex dolio demitur sacrificii causa, antequam gustetur. Iovi enim prius sua vina libabant, quae appellabant festa Vinalia; cf. idem*, p. 517 L.); cette libation étant effectuée *ex dolio*, avant toute consommation profane, on en déduira que le *calpar* était — en principe — prélevé sur chaque jarre qu'on ouvrait ce jour-là; (d) une dégustation

214

Rustica, eux, restent un cadre vide. Ce cadre, une partie de la critique récente[6] a pensé le remplir en rattachant à la fête du 19 août un rituel qu'évoque Varron dans un développement consacré — justement — aux Vinalia: celui de l'ouverture solennelle des vendanges par le flamine de Jupiter. Pour ma part, je crois que ces deux événements sont distincts et non superposables. Pour le montrer, je vais m'intéresser un peu longuement à la cérémonie qui marque le début de la vendange, avant de revenir aux Vinalia Rustica et à leur contenu.

L'OUVERTURE RITUELLE DES VENDANGES

Il faut citer tout au long le développement bien connu que Varron consacre aux Vinalia, dans la liste des fêtes romaines qu'il dresse au sixième livre du *De Lingua Latina*:

'Les Vinalia dérivent du mot vin. Ce jour appartient à Jupiter, non à Vénus. Les soins dont on entourait ce produit[7] n'étaient pas peu de chose dans le Latium. Car, dans un certain nombre d'endroits, les vendanges étaient faites en premier lieu par les prêtres, au nom de l'Etat. A Rome, il en est encore ainsi maintenant: car c'est le flamine de Jupiter qui prend les auspices de la vendange et, lorsqu'il a donné l'ordre de cueillir le raisin, il sacrifie une agnelle; dans l'intervalle de temps entre le découpage des entrailles et leur présentation, c'est le flamine qui, le premier, cueille le raisin. Sur les portes de Tusculum se trouve l'inscription: défense de transporter le vin nouveau en ville, avant la proclamation des Vinalia.'[8]

De quels indices dispose-t-on pour identifier les Vinalia Rustica et le cérémonial d'ouverture des vendanges? D'un argument et d'un seul. Que la description varronienne de ce rituel est comprise dans un développement consacré aux Vinalia. Mais l'argument est sans valeur, du moment que Varron parle, dans ce passage, de la fête d'avril (il cite les Vinalia après les Megalesia du 10 avril, les Fordicidia du 15, les Palilia et les Cerialia du 21 et du 19; et avant les Robigalia du 25). Dans la même notice,

---

(publique, un peu comparable à la premiere partie des Antesthéries grecques: Pithoigia, jour de l'ouverture des jarres, *Choès*, jour du concours des buveurs, comme le voulait déjà L. Deubner, *Attische Feste* (Berlin, 1932), 94): Pline, *HN* xviii. 287: *Vinalia priora, quae ante hos dies* (sc. Robigalia et Floralia = 25 et 28 avril) *sunt Vlll kal. Mai. degustandis vinis instituta, nihil ad fructus attinent; cf.* Paul.-Fest., p. 57 L.

[6]Entre autres W. Warde Fowler, *The Roman Festivals of the Period of the Republic* (Londres, 1899), 104; J. Carcopino, *s.v.* 'Vinalia', dans Dar.-Sag. 5 (1919), 893-6; Bömer, 'Juppiter und die römische Weinfeste' (ci-dessus, n. 4). Et, plus recemment, H.H. Scullard, *Festivals and Ceremonies of the Roman Republic* (Londres, 1981), 177; M. Torelli, *Lavinio e Roma* (Rome, 1984), 164-5. *Contra* (se prononcent donc pour l'autonomie de la cérémonie d'ouverture des vendanges par rapport au Vinalia Rustica), entre autres: Th. Mommsen, *CIL* I[2], 326; G. Wissowa, *Religion und Kultus der Romer*, seconde édition (Munich, 1912), 115; Dumézil, *Fêtes romaines* (ci-dessus, n. 2), 94, n. 3; P. Catalano, *Contributi allo studio del diritto augurale* (Turin, 1960), 359.

[7]*Huius rei*, c'est-à-dire le vin, comme le comprenait correctement Wissowa, *Religion und Kultus* (ci-dessus, n. 6), 115, n. 5.

[8]Varron, *Ling.* vi. 16: *Vinalia a vino; hic dies Iovis, non Veneris; huius rei cura non levis in Latio; nam aliquot locis vindemiae primum ab sacerdotibus publice fiebant ut Romae etiam nunc; nam flamen Dialis auspicatur vindemiam et, ut iussit vinum legere, agna Iovi facit, inter exta caesa et porrecta* (porrecta *corr.*; proiecta *codd.*), *flamen primus* (corr. Müller; porus, poorus *codd.*) *vinum legit. In Tusculanis portis* (corr. Bergk, sortis, ortis *codd.*) *est scriptum: vinum novum ne vehatur in urbem antequam Vinalia kalentur.*

l'inscription de Tusculum se réfère évidemment aux Vinalia de printemps. En fait, le raisonnement de Varron est le suivant: il cherche quelle est la preuve la plus éclatante de l'importance religieuse du vin dans le Latium (qui explique que la fête du vin soit consacrée au plus grand des dieux, de préférence à tout autre), et il trouve celle-ci: les vendanges étaient ouvertes *publice*, au nom de l'Etat.

Il est donc clair qu'il faut dissocier la fête célébrée à date fixe, le 19 août, et l'ouverture rituelle des vendanges qui, elle, est mobile. En effet, les vendanges latines étaient effectuées, comme il est normal, à date variable.[9] Pline, comme les autres agronomes, multiplie les conseils aux paysans sur le moment le plus favorable pour les commencer,[10] d'après le stade de maturation du raisin et, inversement, énumère les circonstances qui peuvent faire différer l'entreprise: si le raisin est chaud, s'il est couvert de rosée etc.[11] Aussi bien, on assigne aux vendanges une période assez longue, à l'interieur de laquelle l'opération peut être menée à bien à tout moment: Varron, approuvé par Pline, dit: à partir de l'équinoxe d'automne et pendant 44 (ou 48) jours, jusqu'au coucher des Pléiades (11 novembre).[12] Le code théodosien, quant à lui, place les Vindemiales Feriae plus tôt: du 23 août aux Ides d'octobre.[13] Mais cette tendance à avancer l'époque des vendanges est relativement tardive,[14] Pline en est garant.

Dans les calendriers latins, le 19 août est marqué par différents sigles, comme s'il y avait incertitude sur le statut réel de cette journée: *F* ('faste') selon les Fasti Antiatini et Allifani; *NP* ('néfaste'?) pour les Fasti Vallenses; *FP* (de sens incertain) selon les Fasti Antiatini Veteres, les Amiterni et les Maffeiani.[15] En fait, le seul sigle du calendrier qui ne soit pas associé à cette journée, le sigle *EN*, est justement celui qu'on devrait trouver, si le rituel de l'ouverture des vendanges tombait le 19 août. Les jours *EN* (*dies endotercisi*, forme archaïque pour *dies intercisi*) étaient, comme leur nom l'indique, des 'jours coupés par le milieu', 'entrecoupés', c'est-à-dire néfastes, frappés d'interdit religieux le matin et le soir, tandis que le milieu de la journée était faste, concédé aux affaires humaines et, en particulier, aux actions en justice. Cette parenthèse faste s'insère dans un jour néfaste au moyen d'un sacrifice sanglant; elle s'ouvre au moment de la mise à mort; elle se clôt lorsque, après un laps de temps plus ou moins long, les entrailles de la victime sont

---

[9]Sur l'*indictio* des vendanges, *Dig.* ii. 12.24.

[10]Pline, *HN* xviii. 316 (on notera la formule récurrente *vindemiare incipito*).

[11]*Ibid.* 315. Il s'agit de préceptes (*leges*).

[12]Varron, *Rust.* i. 34.2: *uvas autem legere et vindemiam facere inter aequinoctium et Vergiliarum occasu*; Pline, *HN* xviii. 319: *iustum vindemiae tempus ab aequinoctio ad Vergiliarum occasu dies XLIIII*. Mais il s'agit en fait de 48 jours, puisque l'équinoxe tombe le 24 septembre (*ibid.* 311).

[13]*Cod. Theod.* ii. 8.19.

[14]R. Billiard, *La vigne dans l'antiquité* (Lyon, 1913), 429-30.

[15]Sur le sens — controversé — de ces différents sigles, voir *e.g.* G. Dumézil, 'Matralia, N ou NP', dans G. Dumézil, *Mythe et épopée*, iii (Paris, 1973), 331-7. Mommsen, *CIL* I² (au-dessus, n. 6) faisait observer que les lettres *FP* ne caractérisent que trois fêtes: les Feralia du 21 février, et les deux Vinalia du 23 avril et du 19 août. Il interprétait *FP* comme *F(astus) P(rincipio)*. Cette théorie revient à faire des jours *FP* une catégorie de ces *dies fissi* dont parle Serv. *Comm. in Verg. Aen.* vi. 37, dont la *prima pars*, ou la *media*, ou la *postrema* est seule faste. Mais tandis qu'on connaît bien les deux dernières catégories (*media pars* de la journée faste: *intercisi dies*, voir au-dessous; *postrema pars* de la journée faste: 24 mars et 24 mai, jours *Q(uando) R(ex) C(omitiauit) F(as)*; et 15 juin, jour *Q(uando) S(tercus) D(elatum) F(as)*), on ne sait rien de la première, si bien que l'interprétation proposée par Mommsen (reprise récemment par Torelli, *Lavinio e Roma* (au-dessus, n. 6), 167-8) reste purement hypothétique.

'expédiées'[16] à la divinité au moyen du feu allumé sur l'autel qui les consume entièrement. C'est pourquoi on parle, en termes techniques, d'intervalle *inter hostiam caesam et exta porrecta*.[17] Or, c'est précisément à un intervalle de ce genre qu'on a affaire dans le cas du rite d'ouverture des vendanges: car le flamine de Jupiter cueille bien, le premier, le raisin *inter exta caesa et porrecta* d'une agnelle. Le jour (mobile) où la vendange est 'auspiciée' est donc, de toute evidence, un *dies intercisus*.[18]

Pourquoi commencer à récolter le raisin *inter exta caesa et porrecta*? Dumézil avançait, voilà 30 ans, une réponse ingénieuse:[19] parce que le *flamen Dialis* procède à la cueillette des premières grappes de manière à pouvoir les offrir, comme prémices, à Jupiter. Pour ce faire, il lui faut incorporer ces offrandes à la part qui revient de droit aux dieux dans le sacrifice: les *exta* justement, ces organes internes auxquels on ajoute, avant de les 'expédier' sur l'autel à la divinité, quelques autres morceaux qui portent le nom significatif d'*augmenta* et de *magmenta*.[20]

L'explication proposée par Dumézil garde certainement sa valeur. L'enjeu de la cérémonie est bien, en effet, une offrande de prémices.[21] Mais il convient aussi de

[16]L'expression est de G. Dumézil, *La religion romaine archaïque*, seconde édition (Paris, 1974), 550. Celui-ci avait déjà remarqué que les Vinalia Rustica ne sont pas jour *EN*: p. 97, n. 1.

[17]Varron, *Ling.* vi. 31: *intercisi dies sunt per quos mane et vesperi est nefas, medio tempore inter hostiam caesam et exta porrecta fas; a quo, quod fas tum intercedit aut eo intercisum nefas, intercisi*; Ov. *Fast.* i. 45-6; Macrob. *Sat.* i. 16.2-3: *diesque omnes aut festos, aut profestos, aut intercisos. Festi dies dicati sunt; profesti hominibus ob administrandam rem privatam publicamque concessi; intercisi deorum hominumque communes sunt ... intercisi in se, non in alia dividuntur. Illorum enim dierum quibusdam horis fas est, quibusdam fas non est ius dicere. Nam, cum hostia caeditur, fari nefas est; inter caesa et porrecta fari licet; rursus, cum adoletur, non licet. Cf. CIL I[2] 1, 231 (Fasti Consulares Praenestini)*; Cic. *Att.* v. 18; Serv. *Comm. in Verg. Aen.* vi. 37 (ci-dessus, n. 15).

[18]Un autre indice possible dans ce sens: l'*agna* sacrifiée avant la vendange rentrait peut-être dans la catégorie des *hostiae praecidaneae* (à côté de la *porca praecidanea*, que Cato *Agr.* 134 prescrit d'offrir avant la moisson, il existait une *agna praecidanea*: Paul.-Fest., p. 250 L.; *cf.* H. Le Bonniec, *Le culte de Cérés à Rome* (Paris, 1958), 155ss.) qu'on immolait également les veilles de sacrifices solennels (Gell. *NA* iv. 6.7). Or les jours *EN* se répartissent bien, en effet, tout au long de l'année, la veille des fêtes publiques: le 10 et le 14 janvier, veilles des doubles Carmentalia; le 16 février, veille des Quirinalia; le 26 février et le 13 mars, veilles des doubles Ecurria; le 14 octobre, veille de l'Equus October; le 12 décembre, veille des Ides. Le 22 août, jour *EN*, constitue une exception à cette règle. Mais on observera qu'il s'agit justement de la veille de l'ouverture théorique des vendanges selon le code théodosien (ci-dessus, n. 13) — donc, dans ce système, de la première date possible pour le rituel mobile d'*auspicari vindemiam*.

[19]G. Dumézil, 'Quaestiunculae indo-italicae. 16. Inter exta caesa et porrecta', *REL* 39 (1961), 270-4 (= *Fêtes romaines d'été et d'automne* (Paris, 1975), 93-7).

[20]Varron, *Ling.* v. 112.

[21]S'il y a offrande de prémices, c'est que le représentant du dieu sur terre, le flamine, prélève la part divine, en commençant à vendanger avant les autres, le premier: *flamen primus vinum legit*. Il est vrai que *primus* est une correction (de Müller) pour *porus* ou *poorus* que portent les manuscrits (les *recentiores*, puisque nous ne possédons la leçon du manuscrit principal, le Florentinus, qu'à partir du ch. 61 pour le livre vi du *De Lingua Latina*). On a donc parfois proposé d'autres corrections d'un texte de toute façon altéré: récemment Torelli, *Lavinio e Roma* (ci-dessus, n. 6), 167-8, a avancé *porris*. Il est inutile de s'attarder sur ces hypothèses, du moment que *primus* est une restitution pratiquement certaine: (a) du point de vue de la structure même du texte: Varron parle d'abord d'une situation generale; dans le Latium, en certains lieux (*aliquot locis*), les vendanges étaient faites d'abord (*primum*) par les prêtres. Varron passe ensuite à un cas particulier: à Rome (*Romae*), les vendanges étaient faites d'abord (*primus*) par le flamine; (b) d'un point de vue paléographique: la faute s'explique facilement si le modèle direct (ou plutôt le modèle du modèle direct) du manuscrit F était en onciales et qu'on y trouvait la forme abrégée '*pmus*'. Un 'm' oncial ressemble à deux 'o', ou à 'or'; la faute se serait produite lors du passage de l'onciale à la bénéventine (écriture de F). Je remercie vivement L. Holtz, directeur de l'Institut de Recherche et d'Histoire des Textes (CNRS — Paris) et 'réviseur' du livre vi du *De Lingua Latina* pour la CUF, d'avoir bien voulu me livrer l'état de ses reflexions sur ce passage très corrompu.

déterminer très précisement le statut du rite au regard du droit pontifical. Et donc, pourquoi l'ouverture de la vendange requiert-elle une parenthèse faste, et pourquoi doit-on, en conséquence, y procéder *inter exta caesa et porrecta*? La réponse, aussi simple qu'évidente, est fournie par Columelle. Les *feriae* sont, en principe, des 'temps où l'homme renonce à ses activités profanes',[22] en d'autres termes des jours chômés. Columelle, donc, énumère scrupuleusement ce que les paysans peuvent, et ne peuvent pas faire, durant les *feriae*.[23] Le *ritus maiorum* leur donnait la permission de piler le blé, de confectionner des torches et des chandelles, de cultiver une vigne affermée etc. Mais il leur refusait celle de labourer la terre, d'élaguer les arbres ... Parmi beaucoup d'autres interdictions figurait en bonne place celle-ci: *ne vindemiam quidem cogi per religiones pontificum feriis licet*, 'selon les prescriptions religieuses des pontifes, il n'etait pas permis de faire la vendange les jours de fête'.[24] Il y avait donc nécessité absolue d'entreprendre la vendange dans un laps de temps faste. Celui-ci était, dans tous les cas, garanti par la procédure *inter exta caesa et porrecta* même si, pour des raisons contingentes, il avait fallu commencer la cueillette durant l'une de ces journées de fête que comptait la période des vendanges.[25]

Parvenus à ce point, nous pouvons affirmer que les Vinalia Rustica et le rituel mobile d'*auspicari vindemiam* sont distincts. Il convient donc d'envisager séparément ce dernier, qui s'intègre d'ailleurs parfaitement dans la séquence des fêtes latines du vin. Il répond symétriquement, d'une part aux Meditrinalia (ouverture et clôture des opérations de vendange),[26] d'autre part aux Vinalia d'avril (offrande des prémices du raisin arrivé à maturité en automne; du vin arrivé à maturité au printemps).[27] Et, comme les autres fêtes du vin, il est placé sous le signe de Jupiter.

La présence de Jupiter est en effet triplement requise dans le rite que nous examinons. D'abord l'officiant. Le *flamen Dialis* est davantage encore que le prêtre de Jupiter: il est une 'statue vivante' du dieu.[28] Ensuite le sacrifice. Les *exta*, la grappe de vin sont présentés à un destinataire qui ne peut être que Jupiter. Mais le dieu souverain prend aussi une part active et directe au déroulement des operations, en manifestant son accord (et éventuellement son désaccord) par l'envoi de signes, *auspicia*.

---

[22]Dumézil, *La religion romaine archaïque* (ci-dessus, n. 16), 552.

[23]Columelle, *Rust.* ii. 21.1: *nos quoque monendos esse agricolas existimamus, quae feriis facere quaeque non facere debeant.*

[24]*Ibid.* 3-4.

[25]La période varronienne-plinienne des vendanges (ci-dessus, nn. 12-13) comporte cinq jours de *feriae* du plus ancien férial (1 octobre, *N*, Tigillum Sororium; 11 octobre, *NP*, Meditrinalia; 13 octobre, *NP*, Fontinalia; 15 octobre, *NP*, Equus October; 19 octobre, *NP*, Armilustrium; à quoi il faut ajouter un jour *EN*, le 14: ci-dessus, n. 18). La période théodosienne des vendanges (ci-dessus, n. 13) en compte éga-lement cinq (23 août, *NP*, Volcanalia; 25 août, *NP*, Opiconsiua; 27 août, *NP*, Volturnalia; 13 Septembre, *NP*, Epulum Iouis; 1 Octobre, *N*, Tigillum Sororium). On ajoutera encore à cette liste celle des *dies religiosi* et, en particulier, dans la période qui nous occupe, les trois jours où *mundus patet*: 24 août, 5 octobre, 8 novembre. Un *dies fissus* (*EN* entre autres) est en effet, par définition, non *totus religiosus* (Serv. *Comm. in Verg. Aen.* vi. 37).

[26]Sur les Meditrinalia, voir ci-dessous, n. 51.

[27]Conformément à la formule générale donnée par Pline, *HN* xviii. 8: *ne degustabant quidem novas fruges aut vina antequam sacerdotes primitias libassent.*

[28]Expression de Plut. *Quaest. Rom.* 290C (question 111), mise en valeur et commentée par J. Scheid, *Religion et piété a Rome* (Paris, 1985), 39-40; *idem*, 'Le flamine de Jupiter, les Vestales et le général triom-phant', *Le temps de la reflexion* 7 (1986), 213-14.

Que veut dire au juste la formule varronienne *flamen Dialis auspicatur vindemiam*? Le verbe *auspicari* signifie-t-il ici simplement 'commencer', 'ouvrir', sans connotation rituelle particulière?[29] Non. A l'époque de Varron et dans ce contexte technique, *auspicari* ne peut que revêtir son sens propre,[30] ce qui d'ailleurs pose un épineux problème de droit public. Un flamine jouit-il du pouvoir de prendre les auspices? Oui, selon Catalano qui postule l'existence d'*auspicia* sacerdotaux à côté des *auspicia publica* et des *auspicia privata*.[31] Non, si l'on s'en tient à la stricte doctrine mommsénienne d'équivalence entre *auspicium* et *imperium*.[32] La vérité doit se situer entre ces deux extrêmes, sans qu'il faille reléguer ces auspices parmi les *privata* puisque le flamine agit en l'occurrence, selon Varron, *publice*. De manière on ne peut plus conforme à la doctrine augurale, le représentant de l'Etat est ici chargé de constater l'assentiment[33] des dieux au choix d'un jour précis (le jour même de la consultation)[34] pour le commencement d'une tâche qui intéresse la communauté tout entière: la vendange. Au fond, cette prise d'auspices et le sacrifice qui la suit, avec sa conclusion différée (*inter victimam caesam et exta porrecta*), poursuivent le même but, même s'ils mettent en oeuvre des techniques différentes: il s'agit, à chacune des étapes du rituel, d'éliminer toute possibilité que le jour retenu pour l'ouverture de la vendange soit néfaste.

LA VOCATION D'ATTUS NAVIUS

Où le *flamen Dialis* prenait-il les auspices? De l'un des *auguracula* de Rome? C'est possible.[35] Ou bien sur le lieu même où devait être accomplie l'opération subséquente, d'après un principe général posé par Mommsen?[36] Dans ce dernier cas, il faudrait que le vignoble dans lequel le *flamen Dialis* ouvre solennellement la vendange ait été constitué en *templum*, en *templum terrestre* selon une distinction fameuse qu'on doit à Varron.[37] Or, nous possédons justement un épisode qui montre comment on transforme une vigne en *templum* pour y prendre les auspices. C'est à I.M.J. Valeton[38] que revient le mérite

[29]Ainsi le pensait Bömer, 'Juppiter und die römischen Weinfeste' (ci-dessus, n. 4), 41.

[30]Voir Catalano, *Contributi allo studio del diritto augurale* (ci-dessus, n. 6), 358-9, qui fait remarquer que 'i primi prosatori in cui auspicium, auspicor assumono senso di exordium, initium facere *sono dell'età dei Claudi*' (*cf. ibid.* p. 74), et signale un tour analogue chez Liv. xxvi. 2.2: *sollemne auspicandorum comitiorum*.

[31]*Ibid.* pp. 357-84.

[32]Th. Mommsen, *Droit public romain* (trad. française, Paris, 1887), 86-7.

[33]Sur la signification que les Romains donnaient à cet assentiment, voir les remarques récentes de J. Scheid, 'La parole des dieux. L'originalité du dialogue des Romains avec leurs dieux', *Opus* 6-8 (1987-9), 125-36.

[34]Sur l'efficacité limitée dans le temps (à un jour) de la prise d'auspices, voir particulièrement Catalano, *Contributi allo studio del diritto augurale* (ci-dessus, n. 6), 42-3, 124-5.

[35]L'*auguraculum* de l'*arx* est l'unique lieu d'où les augures exerçaient leur activité, selon I.M.J. Valeton, 'De inaugurationibus Romanis caerimoniarum et sacerdotum', *Mnemosyne* 19 (1891), 407-8. Mais voir, sur les autres *auguracula* de Rome, F. Coarelli, 'La doppia tradizione sulla morte di Romolo e gli auguracula dell'arx e del Quirinale', dans *Gli Etruschi e Roma (Atti dell'incontro di studio in onore di Massimo Pallottino)* (Rome, 1981), 173-88.

[36]Mommsen, *Droit public romain* (ci-dessus, n. 32) I, 116-17.

[37]Varron, *Ling.* vii. 6 et 8: *templum tribus modis dicitur ab natura, ab auspicando, ab similitudine. Natura in caelo; ab auspiciis in terra; ab similitudine sub terra ... In terris dictum templum locus augurii aut auspicii causa quibusdam conceptis uerbis finitus*; *cf.* I.M.J. Valeton, 'De templis romanis', *Mnemosyne* 21 (1893), 84.

[38]I.M.J. Valeton, 'De modis auspicandi Romanorum', *Mnemosyne* 17 (1889), 448ss.

d'avoir, il y a un siècle, établi un rapprochement suggestif entre le rite et un mythe: le récit de la vocation d'Attus Navius, archétype légendaire de l'augure. L'épisode est bien connu:[39] tout jeune, Attus Navius garde les porcs de son père, un pauvre paysan. L'un des porcs s'égare et Navius fait le voeu, s'il le retrouve, d'offrir à la divinité la plus grosse grappe de la vigne.[40] Il est exaucé: il retrouve la bête. Denys d'Halicarnasse, plus prolixe, ajoute que l'enfant se trouve alors plongé dans une profonde perplexité: car comment découvrir à coup sûr la plus grosse grappe de raisin? Et c'est alors qu'une inspiration divine le saisit. Cicéron, plus sobre, se contente de décrire la séquence des opérations qu'accomplit Attus Navius pour découvrir la grappe requise. Il se place, face au midi, au milieu du vignoble, et le divise en quatre parties. Dans trois de ces régions, les oiseaux ne donnent pas de signes favorables. Dans la quatrième, Navius trouve une grappe d'une incroyable grosseur.

Quelle est la divinité bénéficiaire de l'offrande d'Attus Navius? Denys d'Halicarnasse dit que l'augure fait son voeu et porte son offrande 'à la chapelle des héros' (*kalia ton heroon*), c'est-à-dire celle des *Lares Compitales*. Mais Denys est certainement influencé par le développement, à son époque, des Compitalia (peut-être même, précisément, par la restauration augustéenne du culte).[41] Cicéron, plus fiable, dit *deo* au singulier. Et comme les signes auguraux sont toujours donnés par Jupiter (les augures sont appeles *interpretes Iovis O. M.*),[42] on voit mal le dieu souverain indiquer une offrande destinée à d'autres qu'à lui.

Prise d'auspices, avec construction d'un temple augural. Puis cueillette de la grappe agréée par Jupiter. Les analogies, qui avaient frappé Valeton, entre l'histoire d'Attus Navius et la prise d'auspices préliminaire à la vendange, ne peuvent toutefois être poussées dans le détail. Car si, on l'a vu, le but de la consultation 'réelle' est de déterminer l'idonéité d'un *jour* préalablement choisi, celui de la consultation 'mythique' est d'élire un *lieu* (le lieu d'un objet), qui n'était pas connu à l'avance, mais que l'opération de découpe augurale permet précisément de découvrir. Ce dernier type de demande ('*en quel lieu* doivent être accomplies les [actions pour lesquelles on prend les] augures')[43] reste, pour autant qu'on puisse juger, très marginal dans la discipline d'interprétation des signes telle que la mettaient en pratique les Romains.[44] On lui donne — en se fondant sur des notices assez peu claires de Servius — le nom d'*augurium*

---

[39] ... essentiellement par les récits de Cic. *Div.* i. 30-1, et, de manière plus étendue, de Denys d'Halicarnasse iii. 70.2-4. Pour les autres références, on se reportera à A.S. Pease, éd. du *Div.* (Darmstadt, 1973), 143, n. 1.

[40] Cic. *Div.* i. 30-1: *uvam se deo daturum quae maxima esset in vinea.* Denys d'Halicarnasse iii. 70.2-4: θύσειν αὐτοῖς ὑπέσχετο τὸν μέγιστον τῶν ἐκ τοῦ χωρίου βοτρύων.

[41] Denys d'Halicarnasse iv. 14.3-4. Denys écrit la préface de son oeuvre en 7 avant J.-C. (i. 3.4). La restauration du culte des *Lares* et des *Vicomagistri* est datée de 12, 9 ou 7 av. J.-C. (Mommsen, *Droit public romain* (au-dessus, n. 32), IV, 213, n. 2).

[42] Cic. *Leg.* ii. 20.

[43] Serv. *Comm. in Verg. Aen.* iii. 84: *quo in loco auguria peragi debeant.* C'est la définition de l'*augurii genus quod stativum dicitur.*

[44] Aussi bien Catalano, *Contributi allo studio del diritto augurale* (au-dessus, n. 6), 308-9, pense qu'il s'agit d'un aspect de l'art augural étranger à la *disciplina* romaine; au contraire 'l'augurio stativo, nella precisa formulazione di cui è esempio in Cicerone e Dionisio per l'episodio dell'uva, è da riportarsi all'arte divinatoria etrusca'. Mais on sait bien qu'on est tenté de donner une origine étrusque à tout ce qui résiste à l'analyse ...

stativum.[45] Aussi ne faut-il pas voir entre le mythe et le rite de correspondance stricte, ni penser que l'un forme le pendant étiologique de l'autre. Si rapport il y a, il est d'ordre plus général et peut être résumé dans cette formule: Jupiter est chez lui dans le vignoble. Il en reçoit les produits, il y envoie des signes. On comprend mieux pourquoi, alors, l'épisode du porc perdu d'Attus Navius constitue l'un des récits fondateurs de l'art augural à Rome.[46] Non pas, comme on l'a quelquefois pensé, parce que les vignes auraient été des lieux inaugurés.[47] Mais parce que le dieu souverain est, à la fois, dans le ciel, le maître des auspices et, sur la terre, le propriétaire de la vendange latine. Et cela, depuis qu'en des temps primordiaux Enée la lui a vouée tout entière, dans un mythe qui, de son côté, constitue l'un des récits fondateurs du sacrifice à Rome.[48] On voit l'importance, dans cette société, de la vigne et du vin puisqu'autour d'eux s'articulent une série de mythes d'origine qui touchent aux principaux points de la pratique religieuse.

VINALIA RUSTICA

La prise d'auspices du flamine de Jupiter ouvre donc la période des vendanges et, plus largement, tout le cycle de la vinification qui ne prendra fin qu'environ sept mois plus tard, lorsque la fermentation du vin nouveau sera achevée, au moment de la libation (et de la dégustation) des Vinalia du 23 avril.[49]

---

[45] Serv. *Comm. in Verg. Aen.* iii. 84; x. 423. Valeton, 'De modis auspicandi Romanorum' (ci-dessus, n. 38), 451-2, voit précisément dans la prise d'auspices du *flamen Dialis* un *augurium stativum* qui répondrait, sur le plan du rite, à l'*exemplum* mythique d'Attus Navius. Mais rien, dans la cérémonie d'ouverture des vendanges décrite par Varron, ne permet d'étayer cette interprétation. Rien ne suggère que la consultation augurale n'ait pas comme objet, comme il est habituel, la vérification de l'assentiment des dieux à la réalisation tel jour de telle tâche, mais plutôt l'identification de telle ou telle grappe comme prémices.

[46] ... avec, bien sûr, ces autres épisodes fameux que sont ceux des vautours de Romulus ou de l'inauguration de Numa sur l'*arx*. Ce qui est exposé, en effet, ce n'est rien moins que la vocation du plus célèbre des augures (après Romulus), de leur archétype (*cf.* W. Kroll, *s.v.* 'Navius', *RE* XVI 2 (1935), coll. 1933-6): le bâton augural de Navius, son *lituus*, restait le plus fameux dans la tradition avec celui de Romulus; la *descriptio regionum* à laquelle il avait procédé pour trouver la plus grosse grappe était toujours citée en exemple (Cic. *Div.* i. 31: *quid, multis annis post Romulum regnante Tarquinio, quis veterum scriptorum non loquitur, quae sit ab Atto Navio per lituum regionum fata discriptio?* Cic. *Nat. D.* ii. 3: *an Atti Nauii lituus ille, quo ad investigandum suem regiones uineae terminavit, contemnendus est? Crederem, nisi eius augurio rex Hostilius maxima bella gessisset.*).

[47] Cette théorie se fonde essentiellement sur Cic. *Leg.* ii. 20-1: *interpretes autem Iovis Optumi Maxumi, publici augures, signis et auspiciis postea vidento, disciplinam tenento sacerdotesque docento, vineta virgetaque et salutem populi auguranto*; *cf.* également le passage de Pline, *HN* xvii. 169, selon lequel les *vineae* auraient été tracées selon un *decumanus* et un *cardo*; et, sur tout cela, voir A. Bouché-Leclercq, *Histoire de la divination dans l'antiquité* IV (Paris, 1882), 191-4. Mais G. Wissowa, *s.v.* 'augures', *RE* II (1896), col. 2329, reconnaissait à bon droit dans l'expression *vineta virgetaque* un fragment d'une formule allitérante qu'on retrouve dans la prière du paysan catonien à Mars (Cato, *Agr.* 141): *utique tu fruges frumenta vineta virgultaque grandire beneque evenire siris.* L'identification que fait ensuite Wissowa de l'office augural mentionné par Cicéron avec l'*augurium canarium* reste bien sûr hypothétique. Ce qu'il y a de certain, c'est qu'on ne peut détacher arbitrairement les vignobles du *De Legibus* de leur contexte — en premier lieu des *virgeta* cités en même temps: fourrés, broussailles, oseraies? — et donc parler d'une inauguration spécifique des vignes.

[48] Ainsi que l'a mis en évidence J. Scheid, *AEHE(V^e sect.)* 88 (1979-80), 327-33.

[49] Ci-dessus, n. 5.

A l'intérieur de ce cycle long peuvent être identifiés des cycles courts (par exemple celui du pressurage, dont Jupiter est absent, alors qu'il s'agit du temps propre d'intervention de Liber),[50] repérés des équilibres et des parallélismes secondaires (par exemple, le rituel appelé *sacrima* fait pendant, à la fois aux Meditrinalia et à la libation de *calpar* des Vinalia d'avril).[51]

Mais alors, quelle place occupent les Vinalia d'août qui précèdent la vinification et restent en dehors du système rituel qui s'y superpose? Une brève note de Varron jette quelque lueur sur les rites qu'on pouvait célébrer à cette occasion.

Au livre xviii de son *Naturalis Historia*, Pline rapporte l'opinion de Varron selon lequel les Vinalia (d'août)[52] ont été institués pour mettre fin au mauvais temps (ou l'apaiser — les leçons des manuscrits diffèrent: *tempestatibus finiendis* ou *leniendis institutum*). Il ajoute qu'ils prennent place au coucher de la Lyre (*Fidicula incipiente occidere*), lequel coïncide, toujours selon Varron, avec le début de l'automne.[53] Quelques paragraphes plus loin, après avoir parlé des périls qui menacent les cultures, Pline ajoute: 'Varron nous est garant que, si au coucher de la Lyre (*Fidiculae occasu*), c'est-à-dire au début de l'automne, on consacre une grappe peinte (*uva picta*) au milieu des vignes, le mauvais temps fera moins de mal'.[54]

Coucher de la Lyre, début de l'automne, protection contre les *tempestates*. Nous sommes exactement à la date indiquée précédemment par Varron pour les Vinalia Rustica, et dans l'énoncé des motifs de la fête. Bien entendu, la 'recette' indiquée par

---

[50]Liber patronne les opérations de pressurage parce que le produit obtenu n'est, à ce stade, que du moût, boisson 'immonde' (*spurcum vinum*) impropre au sacrifice et dont, pour cette raison, Jupiter se désintéresse: *cf.* O. De Cazanove, 'Jupiter, Liber et le vin latin', *RHR* 205 (1988), 245-65.

[51]*Sacrima* est un nom rituel du moût qu'on offre à Liber dans un rituel qui transpose, sur le plan religieux, la plus simple des techniques de frelatage du vin. Il s'agit donc d'une offrande de prémices qui vaut pour toute cette partie du moût qui, immédiatement après le pressurage, va être dénaturée, sans poursuivre sa fermentation: De Cazanove, 'Jupiter, Liber et le vin latin' (ci-dessus, n. 50), 260-1. Symétriquement, les Meditrinalia du 11 octobre, fête jovienne, constituent en quelque sorte une réaffirmation des droits que possède le dieu souverain sur le 'vin nouveau', au moment précisément où est introduit, dans sa structure encore instable, du 'vin vieux' comme fixateur, pour lui permettre de poursuivre sa fermentation: *ibid.* pp. 253-4; le véritable enjeu du rituel a été mis en lumière par Dumézil, *Fêtes romaines* (ci-dessus, n. 2), 98-107. Quant au *calpar*, il représente les prémices, non plus du vin frelaté, mais de celui qui est arrivé 'naturellement' à maturité.

[52]Pline appelle cette fête Vinalia Altera (*NH* xviii. 289; voir la note suivante). C'est la seule fois qu'on rencontre cette dénomination. Il est clair qu'elle n'est pas officielle et qu'elle n'a de sens que dans le passage du naturaliste, où elle s'oppose au Vinalia Priora cités quelques paragraphes plus haut (ch. 287). Cette appellation de Vinalia Priora n'est d'ailleurs pas plus officielle que l'autre puisqu'on ne la rencontre, elle aussi, que dans ce contexte. On n'est donc autorisé a parler que de Vinalia Rustica pour la fête d'automne (l'adjectif ne se rencontre pas dans les calendriers, mais il était couramment accolé par les antiquaires au *dies festus* du 19 août: Varron, *Ling.* vi. 20; *Rust.* i. 1.6; Fest. et Paul.-Fest., pp. 322-3 L.), et de Vinalia tout court pour la fête de printemps (ceux-ci auraient cependant quelque titre à être appelés Vinalia Urbana, par opposition à la cérémonie rustique, et parce que c'est à cette occasion que le vin nouveau rentre en ville, *in urbem*: *cf.* ci-dessus, n. 45).

[53]289: *Extra has causas sunt Vinalia altera, quae aguntur a. d. Xllll kal. Sept. Varro ea, Fidicula incipiente occidere, mane determinat, quod uult initium autumni esse et hunc diem festum tempestatibus leniendis institutum*; *cf.* 284: *Tria namque tempora fructibus metuebant, propter quod instituerunt ferias diesque festos, Robigalia, Floralia, Vinalia.*

[54]Varron *apud* Pline xviii. 294: *Varro auctor est, si Fidiculae occasu, quod est initium autumni, uua picta consecretur inter uites, minus nocere tempestates* (trad. H. Le Bonniec, Les Belles Lettres (Paris, 1972)).

l'agronome aux paysans ne saurait, en aucun cas, être assimilée à un acte du culte public. Elle donne toutefois une indication sur la manière dont pouvait être conçue une réponse rituelle aux périls de l'heure. Or, cette réponse est ambiguë. Il y a bien consécration, mais seulement d'un simulacre d'offrande, puisqu'il s'agit d'une fausse grappe, d'une grappe peinte. Pourquoi? Après l'analyse qui vient d'être faite de la cérémonie d'ouverture solennelle des vendanges, la solution est évidente. Parce qu'on ne peut pas, bien sûr, prélever une vraie grappe de la vigne avant que le flamine ait offert officiellement les prémices du raisin à Jupiter. Aux Vinalia Rustica, à défaut de prémices, sont offerts par les paysans, dans le culte privé, des simulacres de prémices.

On pourrait, dans ces conditions, se demander pourquoi le cycle des fêtes du vin latin débute avant la vendange et non au moment de celle-ci, lorsqu'il devient possible d'offrir à la divinité une parcelle de la récolte. La réponse doit être cherchée, encore une fois, dans le mythe étiologique des Vinalia. Toutes les versions insistent sur le fait que Mézence réclame pour lui, et qu'Enée voue à Jupiter, la *prochaine* vendange du Latium — c'est-à-dire, au moment où le voeu est prononcé, du raisin encore sur pied.[55] Dès lors, pour l'accomplissement correct de celui-ci, il importe que la vigne arrive sans incident à maturité complète, alors que les périls (atmosphériques en particulier) s'accumulent dans la période qui précède immédiatement la récolte. D'où l'intérêt de Jupiter pour une vendange qui n'est encore, à ce moment, que potentielle. D'où la présence, dans les calendriers, de deux fêtes identiquement appelées Vinalia qui se répondent, à huit mois d'intervalle, comme, dans le mythe, le voeu acquitté répond au voeu souscrit.[56]

---

[55]Le texte le plus clair est, de ce point de vue, celui d'Ov. *Fast.* iv. 887-8. (Mézence s'adresse à Turnus): *Qui petis auxilium, non grandia divide mecum / praemia, de lacubus proxima musta tuis.* En contrepartie, Enée fait son propre voeu à Jupiter au futur (893): *Iuppiter, e Latio palmite musta feres.* Vient ensuite l'automne, le pressurage et la vendange, enfin l'acquittement du voeu (897-898): *Venerat Autumnus calcatis sordidus uuis / redduntur merito debita vina Iovi.* Par ailleurs, une note des *Fasti Consulares Praenestini* (*CIL* I², 236) précise même qu'a été voué *Io(vi) ... si subsidio venisset* (sic) *omnium annorum vini fructum.* Pour Cato *apud* Macrob. *Sat.* iii. 5.10, les Latins s'engagent (par avance, évidemment) à lui offrir les *primitiae* plutôt qu'à Mézence. L'expression de Varron *apud* Pline, *HN* xiv. 88 (Mézence secourt les Rutules contre les Latins *vini mercede quod tum in Latino agro fuisset*) implique, à mon avis, que ce *vinum* dont on spécifie l'extension géographique a ici pour sens — comme il est courant — 'vigne', 'vignoble'. Enfin, Plut. *Quaest. Rom.* ch. 45 se sert d'une expression de sens plus general: ἐπέτειος οἶνος, 'le vin de l'année'.

[56]Cf. Schilling, *La religion romaine de Vénus* (ci-dessus, n. 4), 141-2: '[la] fête ... développe le même compas temporel que le *vovit - dedicavit*'. A ceci près que pour cet auteur, les Vinalia Rustica ont pour objet l'ouverture de la vendange, il faut souscrire à sa reconstruction du 'système orienté' (p. 125) des Vinalia, et à son analyse du rôle qu'y joue Vénus (pp. 146ss.) qui 's'explique à la fois par le rite et par le mythe'. J'aurais, pour ma part, tendance à mettre davantage encore l'accent sur le récit étiologique. Le prestige de ce mythe fondateur fait qu'il devient le principal point d'ancrage de la legende troyenne dans le férial et donc, par voie de conséquence, le biais par lequel Vénus troyenne, mère d'Enée, pouvait rentrer dans le calendrier et acquérir un ou des *dies festi*. C'est le mythe, doublement présent aux Vinalia d'avril et d'août, qui explique en dernière analyse qu'autour de ces deux dates se 'coagulent' des dédicaces de temples à Vénus.

15

In vino stuprum

M. BETTINI

Il divieto di bere vino, notoriamente imposto alla donna romana, non sembra avere particolare bisogno di essere 'giustificato': le nostre fonti[1] lo spiegano e lo giustificano già a sufficienza. Dionigi di Alicarnasso (ii. 25.6) narra che Romolo stabilì questo divieto in quanto 'l'adulterio è origine di follia (apónoia), e l'ubriachezza è origine di adulterio'; mentre Valerio Massimo (ii. 1.5; cfr. vi. 3.9) spiega che alle antiche donne romane era stato imposto il divieto di bere vino *ne scilicet in aliquod dedecus prolaberentur, quia proximus a Libero patre intemperantiae gradus ad inconcessam Venerem esse consuevit*. E tutti ricordano certamente il moralistico pezzo di bravura in cui Plinio (*HN* xiv. 140) dichiara che l'ubriachezza insegna di per se stessa la libidine (*tamquam per se parum doceat libidinem temulentia!*): e descrive l'onesta matrona valutata e soppesata, come in una vendita all'asta, da occhi vogliosi.[2]

La cultura romana aveva insomma una sua idea riguardo al divieto del bere vino imposto alle donne: non possiamo ignorare che, coloro i quali ci descrivono questo divieto dall'interno della cultura romana, lo mettono stabilmente in relazione con l'adulterio e la trasgressione sessuale. Così secondo Dionigi (ii. 25.6) Romolo permise che esattamente queste due colpe femminili, l'adulterio e il bere vino, fossero punite con la morte: mentre ancora queste due trasgressioni appaiono nominate, e punite, insieme in un frammento del *De dote* di Catone (fr. 221 Malc.[2]). D'altra parte, è noto che il costume dello *ius osculi*, ossia il 'bacio' sulla bocca che le donne ricevevano dai loro parenti maschi sino al grado di *sobrinus*,[3] si muoveva proprio nella doppia sfera della sanzione della castità femminile e del controllo sull'uso del vino. Da un lato, infatti, le nostre fonti ci dicono stabilmente che l'*osculum* parentale veniva dato alle donne per controllare se 'odorassero di vino'; dall'altro, sappiamo che questo bacio veniva rifiutato

---

[1]Plin. *HN* xiv. 89ss.; Plut. *Quaest. Rom.* cap. 6; Dionigi di Alicarnasso ii. 25.6; Gell. x. 23; Valerio Massimo ii. 1.5; Serv. *Comm. in Verg. Aen.* i. 737; Non. 68, 26, ecc. Per la possibile origine varroniana di queste testimonianze cfr. la discussione di B. Riposati, *Marci Terenti Varronis de vita populi romani* (Milano, 1939), 53ss., 143ss., 290ss. (raccolta delle testimonianze).

[2]Cfr. anche Sen. *Controv.* i. 2.10: con la descrizione della *puella* che aspira al sacerdozio ed invece *inter ebriorum convivarum iocos iactatur*.

[3]Cfr. Polyb. vi. 11a.4 (in Ath. 10, 440E); Plut. *Quaest Rom.* cap. 6 (265C); Gell. x. 23; Plin. *HN* xiv. 90, ecc. Cfr. M. Bettini, 'Il divieto fino al "sesto grado" incluso nel matrimonio romano', *Athenaeum* 66 (1988), 69-96 (con bibliografia). È possibile che le notizie relative allo *ius osculi* abbiano ascendenza varroniana: cfr. Riposati, *Marci Terenti Varronis* (sopra, n. 1), 53ss., 144ss., 290ss. (raccolta delle tesimonianze).

alla donna che godesse di cattiva fama.[4] Anche dal punto di vista di questo costume, insomma, l'associazione fra 'divieto del vino' e 'castità femminile' appare espressa molto chiaramente.

Questa stabile correlazione fra vino e adulterio può anzi spiegare perché, sia quando si tratta di giudicare un adulterio femminile, sia quando occorre esercitare il controllo sulla *temulentia* della donna, si verifica un identico intervento del gruppo parentale di cui la donna fa parte. Erano infatti i *sungeneis* che, assieme al marito, avevano competenza in materia di adulterio e di 'colpa del vino';[5] così come era ugualmente il gruppo dei parenti al completo che, tramite la citata pratica dello *ius osculi*, esercitava il controllo sul rispetto del divieto del vino. Nella consapevolezza diffusa, insomma, una donna che 'beve vino' compie una trasgressione che va a colpire tutto il gruppo parentale di cui fa parte: proprio come nel caso dell'adulterio. A Roma, una donna che beve vino commette una colpa che sembra essere concepita come contigua alla trasgressione sessuale, un atto che, proprio come l'adulterio, altera la purezza e l'integrità del corpo femminile:[6] e di conseguenza, sparge vergogna sull'intero gruppo parentale cui la donna appartiene.

Naturalmente, queste considerazioni non escludono che, all'interno dei modelli culturali che regolavano il buon uso del vino nella cultura romana, e la sua esclusione dalla sfera femminile, giocasse un ruolo importante anche il significato sacrificale posseduto da questa bevanda. Da tempo M. Gras, in un contributo di grande chiarezza, ha infatti richiamato la nostra attenzione sul fatto che il *temetum* da cui le donne sono escluse era anche il *vinum merum* usato per il sacrificio.[7] A nostro avviso, questa osservazione aggiunge qualcosa di importante a quanto già sappiamo dalle nostre fonti, ma non le sostituisce. Dopo il contributo di Gras, si può certo affermare che la logica simbolica in cui agiva il divieto contemplava anche la sfera del sacrificio: ma con questo non ci sentiamo di cancellare il carattere sessuale e adulterino che le nostre fonti sottolineano così concordemente a proposito di questo divieto. Non è probabile che quanto esse ci dicono costituisca una semplice 'riscrittura moralistica' di ciò che sarebbe stato solamente un tabù religioso. Tanto più che la tendenza ad istituire una qualche forma di opposizione fra 'donna' e 'vino' sembra costituire un modello molto generale, una sorta di ricorrente tentazione, comune ad altre culture e ad altri momenti storici. Ad esempio, nelle *Baccanti* di Euripide il re Penteo dichiara esplicitamente (260ss.) che 'quando in un banchetto scintilla il vino per le donne, allora io affermo che in questi

---

[4]Cic. *Rep.* iv. 6.6 (in Non. 476,1 L.): *si qua erat famosa, ei cognati osculum non ferebant.*

[5]Cfr. Dionigi di Alicarnasso ii. 25.6.

[6]Non credo perciò che le note interpretazioni del divieto fornite da P. Noailles ('Les tabous de mariage dans le droit primitif des Romains', in P. Noailles, *Fas et jus* (Parigi, 1948), 1-27) e M. Durry ('Les femmes et le vin', *REL* 33 (1955), 108-13) siano così lontane dal vero come a taluni è sembrato. Noailles insisteva infatti sull'*élement extérieur* che il vino avrebbe introdotto nel sangue della donna e della famiglia; Durry, sul vino come bevanda che produce aborto. Anche se si può non condividere in tutto queste spiegazioni, esse hanno comunque il merito di restare attaccate al valore di trasgressione familiare, parentale, contenuta nella colpa del vino, e di mantenere viva la relazione fra corpo femminile e gruppo parentale.

[7]M. Gras, 'Vin et société à Rome et dans le Latium à l'époque archaïque', in *Forme di contatto e processi di trasformazione nelle società antiche* (Pisa-Roma, 1983), 1067-75. Questa interpretazione era già stata in qualche modo anticipata da G. Piccaluga, 'Bona dea. Due contributi all'interpretazione del suo culto', *SMSR* 35 (1964), 195-237 (p. 207).

culti non c'è nulla di sano'. Mentre ancora ai tempi di Monica, la madre di Agostino, si trovava del tutto sconveniente che una fanciulla bevesse vino (Agostino, *Confessiones* ix. 8.17): *modo aquam bibitis, quia in potestate vinum non habetis*.

La tendenza al *Besserwissen*, ovvero la convinzione secondo cui noi ne sappiamo sempre 'di più' degli autori antichi rispetto alle cose di cui essi ci parlano, finirebbe per portarci solo fuori strada. Il divieto del vino femminile non ha bisogno di una interpretazione, tantomeno della scoperta di qualcosa che ci è rimasto (o ci è stato tenuto) segreto: questo costume sembra piuttosto aver bisogno di ritrovare un suo contesto etnografico. In altre parole, si sente la necessità di inserire questo divieto in un reticolo culturale che, secondo un procedere più orizzontale che verticale, sia in grado di fornirci maggiori informazioni sui rapporti di incompatibilità che nella cultura romana esplicitamente intercorrono fra il 'vino' da un lato e la 'donna' dall'altro. Cominceremo con alcune precisazioni.

I 'VINI' PERMESSI ALLA DONNA

Nello stesso capitolo in cui ci informa sull'antico costume femminile di astenersi dal vino (*temetum*), Aulo Gellio (x. 23) ci dà anche interessanti informazioni sulle bevande che le donne usavano invece bere: *bibere autem solitas ferunt loream, passum, murrinam et quae id genus sapiant potu dulcia*. Da notare subito la definizione riassuntiva che viene data di queste bevande: *quae ... sapiant potu dulcia*. Nonio (551 L.)[8] ripete informazioni analoghe, ed enumera anzi i vari tipi di 'vino' permessi alle donne, con l'aggiunta di qualche spiegazione relativa al modo in cui li si preparava.

Queste notizie tramandateci da Gellio e da Nonio potrebbero sembrare contraddittorie: da un lato si dice che la donna non poteva bere vino, dall'altro si afferma che esistevano però dei vini a lei permessi, pur se erano di sapore dolce. In realtà, non c'è alcuna contraddizione. Perché si vede bene che a Roma i *vina* da un lato, e i *dulcia* dall'altro, erano concepiti come due tipi di bevande assolutamente diverse. Non solo perchè i *dulcia* venivano preparati secondo un procedimento del tutto differente rispetto a quello che veniva usato per produrre il vino,[9] ma perchè, esplicitamente, i *dulcia* non erano considerati vini. Questo dato emerge chiaramente da Plinio (*HN* xiv. 93), un passo in cui, dopo aver discusso della *murrina* (non a caso uno dei vini permessi alla donna), l'autore conclude: *quibus apparet non inter vina modo murrinam, sed inter dulcia quoque nominatum*. Dunque un conto sono i *vina*, un conto sono i *dulcia*. Ma importante si presenta anche quest'altro passo di Plinio (*HN* xiv. 83): *medium inter dulcia vinumque est quod Graeci 'aigleucos' vocant, hoc est semper mustum*. Insomma i *dulcia* (o *quae ... sapiant potu dulcia*, come dice Gellio) erano concepiti come bevande di tipo diverso dal

---

[8]Sui difficili problemi testuali, e di interpretazione, posti da questo importante lemma, cfr. la discussione di Riposati, *Marci Terenti Varronis* (sopra, n. 1), 145ss., 292ss.

[9]La caratteristica comune di queste bevande elencate da Gellio e Nonio sembra infatti essere l'assenza di vera e propria 'fermentazione': si tratta di mosto cotto, o di uva più acqua, o di mosto semplicemente, ecc. Cfr. la ricostruzione di Riposati, *Marci Terenti Varronis* (sopra, n. 1), 145ss. (svolta a partire dalle indicazioni di Non. 551 L.).

vino: la *lorea*, il *passum*, ecc., non erano dei vini, ma altro. Quindi non c'era alcuna contraddizione nel fatto che la donna potesse berne.

In effetti il *vinum* non è affatto *dulce*. Ancora Plinio (*HN* xiv. 124ss.) lo descrive come qualcosa che deve avere *saporis quaedam acumina*, ovvero come un prodotto che possiede *virus* (*ibid.*), cioè 'sapore forte': un *virus* che occorre o moderare quando è eccessivo o addere quando manca (a tale scopo, si usava aggiungere *pix crapulana* o *crapula* al mosto che bolle). Questo termine *virus* è molto interessante, e merita di essere brevemente analizzato.

Nella sua accezione fondamentale, *virus* sembra infati designare il *sucus* caratteristico di una certa pianta, o di un altro elemento naturale,[10] percepito come qualcosa che esprime la forte 'essenza' di ciò che lo contiene. Ad esempio, secondo Plinio (*HN* xix. 89) la *pastinaca* era caratterizzata dal fatto di mantenere un *virus intractabile* anche se preparata in *patina*; mentre in xxx. 44 egli ci descrive il *virus cochlearum*, il forte umore dei frutti di mare, che produce alito cattivo. Questo carattere 'forte' espresso dalla parola *virus* spiega perché Lucrezio (ii. 475) usi l'espressione *taetri primordia viri* per designare i caratteri specifici dell'acqua di mare opposta a quella dolce: ciò che Manilio (v. 683) designerà come *virus ponti*. *Virus* sembra insomma designare ciò che ha sapore od odore 'forte', a volte addirittura sgradevole,[11] come nel caso dell'acqua marina: e designarlo sotto la forma di un *sucus*, di una sorta di essenza che riassume i poteri più 'forti' della sostanza che lo contiene o lo esprime. A questo valore di *virus* si riconnette il noto significato di 'veleno' posseduto da questa parola: il veleno visto come essenza o succo potente, iniettato da un serpente o distillato dalla malvagità umana. Questo carattere di 'distillazione', quasi di quintessenza, espresso da *virus*, emerge anzi con particolare chiarezza dal modo in cui Virgilio (*G.* iii. 281) descrive l'*hippomanes*: un *virus* che *lentum destillat ab inguine* [*equarum*], un succo 'viscido' (così Servio *ad locum*) che *destillat*, scende 'goccia a goccia' in modo vischioso. La caratteristica di essenza, o succo, 'forte' espressa da *virus*, spiega infine un altro aspetto molto rilevante del campo semantico che questa parola ricopre: essa infatti si usa anche per indicare il *semen* maschile (Plin. *HN* ix. 157 e xxviii. 155). Ma di questo dovremo riparlare anche più sotto.

Dunque il *vinum* ha sapore acuto (*saporis quaedam acumina*), possiede *virus*, ossia sapore ed odore forte. Questo tratto del forte odore del vino lo troviamo spesso ribadito: e sempre in opposizione ai *dulcia*, che invece ne sono privi. Ancora Plinio ci informa del fatto che *vinum omne dulce minus odoratum, quo tenuius eo odoratius* (*HN* xiv. 80).[12] Lo stesso in xv. 110: *Nam et vinum tale* [*scil dulce*] *sine odore, tenue odoratius multoque celerius talia ad usum veniunt quam pinguia.*[13] Dunque ciò che è *dulce* ha meno odore: e anzi, fra i vini ha più

[10]Cfr. A. Ernout e A. Meillet, *Dictionnaire étymologique de la langue latine* 3ᵉ ed. (Paris, 1951) *s.v.* '*virus*': '*suc des plantes; humeur (sperme) ou venin des animaux*'.

[11]Cfr. per esempio Lucr. ii. 852; Marziale i. 88; Plin. *HN* xi. 277, ecc. (odore); Orazio, *Epist.* ii. 2.158 (sapore).

[12]Questa caratteristica, dell'avere profumo debole, è tratto caratteristico non solo dei vini ma di tutti gli alimenti dolci. Cfr. ancora Plin. *HN* xv. 110: *sua et in odore miracula: malis acutum, persicis dilutum, dulcibus nullus*.

[13]Con l'espressione *celerius in usum venire* Plinio vuol dire, naturalmente, che questi vini danno più rapidamente alla testa (come si ricava dal confronto con *HN* xxiii. 40): non che 'se ne consuma di più', come qualche volta il passo viene tradotto.

odore quello che è *tenue*, cioè il vino 'spogliato', filtrato, il contrario cioè di un vino *pingue*.[14] Vale la pena di notare, a questo punto, che tale caratteristica dei *dulcia*, cioè di avere minor odore, concorda perfettamente con quanto sappiamo a proposito dello *ius osculi*, e della forma di controllo che i parenti maschi esercitavano, tramite il bacio parentale, sulla sobrietà della donna. Gellio (x. 23) spiega che il bacio veniva dato *deprehendendi causa, ut odor indicium faceret, si bibissent*; così come Plinio (*HN* xiv. 90) ci dice che i parenti baciavano la donna *ut scirent an temetum olerent*. Dunque è l''odore' del vino ciò che costituisce la prova dell'avvenuta trasgressione. Ma visto che i *dulcia* non avevano odore, non era certo a loro che si rivolgeva il controllo dell'*osculum*.[15]

Un'ultima osservazione. Il fatto che i vini permessi alla donna siano caratterizzati dal tratto della 'dolcezza', avvicina queste bevande alla sfera del 'latte' e del 'miele'.[16] Una sfera che, come vedremo sotto, si presenta da un lato opposta a quella del vino: dall'altro, strettamente contigua allo spazio culturale della donna.

AI SACRA DELLA *BONA DEA*

Com'è noto, il culto della *bona dea* costituisce un complesso religioso di grande rilevanza per ciò che riguarda la definizione dello statuto culturale della donna a Roma. Si tratta di una cerimonia rigidamente femminile, da cui sono esclusi non soltanto gli uomini (vedi lo scandalo di Clodio), ma anche ogni animale di sesso maschile, e persino qualsiasi 'pittura' rappresentante uomini o esseri comunque di sesso maschile.[17] Ora, nell'insieme di riti e di 'racconti' di fondazione che costituisce la sostanza di questo culto così gelosamente femminile, il divieto del bere vino gioca un ruolo molto esplicito. Cercheremo dunque di approfondire brevemente questo aspetto del rito, con l'intenzione di muovere un secondo passo verso l'ampliamento del contesto culturale in cui inserire il divieto del vino femminile. D'altro lato, bisogna anche notare che il rituale della *bona dea* viene registrato dalle fonti romane come qualcosa di particolarmente antico, e risalente all'epoca dei re (Cic. *Har. Resp.* 37: *vetustum ... a regibus aequale huius urbis accepimus*): dunque, sul piano della simbolica culturale questo culto è concepito come *aequaevus* alle prescrizioni romulee e regali sul divieto del vino di cui ci stiamo occupando.

Procederemo esaminando, una dopo l'altra, le principali fonti che trattano del ruolo giocato dalla 'colpa del vino' nel mito di fondazione relativo all'origine del culto.

---

[14]Questo è infatti il senso da dare all'espressione *vinum tenue*, e non, come a volte accade, quello di 'vino leggero'. Cfr. Plin. *HN* xxiii. 40, dove del *vinum tenue* è detto *tanto magis capita temptat*; xxiii. 45, in cui l'azione del *vinum tenue* è posta in relazione col il filtraggio di esso tramite un *saccus*; cfr. soprattutto Verg. *G.* ii. 93, e il commento di Serv. *ad locum*.

[15]Per l'odore del vino bevuto confronta anche Plin. *HN* xiv. 142, e l'*halitus cadi* che caratterizza il fiato del 'giorno dopo'.

[16]Palladio xi. 19.2 nota esplicitamente che il *passum ... conditum vasculo mellis more servatur*. Quanto al rapporto di questi *dulcia* con il latte, si ricordi che una mistura di *lac* e *sapa* si beveva in occasione dei Parilia: Ov. *Fast.* iv. 779ss.

[17]Cfr. Juv. vi. 340 e scolio *ad locum*; Sen. *Ep.* 97.2; Fest. 348 L.; Ov. *Ars Am.* iii. 243ss., ecc. Su *bona dea* e le sue caratteristiche cfr. Piccaluga, 'Bona dea' (sopra, n. 7); H.H.J. Brower, *Bona dea* (Leiden, 1989); L. Beltrami, *L'impudicizia di Tarpeia* (Tesi di dottorato, Pisa, 1989), 79ss.

PLUTARCO, *QUAESTIONES ROMANAE* xx

La domanda specifica posta nella *quaestio* è la seguente: 'perchè al culto di Bona dea non si portano fronde di mirto, benchè le donne gareggino fra loro nell'offrire alla dea ogni genere di piante e di fiori ?' (268D).

Secondo Plutarco, il mito di fondazione relativo all'istituzione del culto sarebbe il seguente: la moglie di Fauno beveva segretamente, e per punirla il marito la uccise colpendola con rami di mirto. Per questo il mirto è escluso dal rito. Plutarco suggerisce una seconda spiegazione possibile per questa esclusione rituale del mirto dalla cerimonia: dato che le donne, celebrando questa festa, debbono restare pure, e dato che il mirto è sacro a Venere, il mirto è escluso dal rituale. A riprova del fatto che il mirto è sacro a Venere, Plutarco porta il fatto che, quella che ora viene chiamata *Venus Murcia*, portava un tempo il nome di *Venus myrtea*. La notizia trova riscontro in Varrone, *De Lingua Latina* v. 154, che parla di un *sacellum ... Murteae Veneris*, e in Plinio, *Naturalis Historia* xv. 121: *Veneri Myrteae, quam nunc Murciam vocant*.

Vediamo schematicamente i principali elementi messi in gioco dal resoconto plutarcheo:

(1) parentela. La relazione operante è quella moglie/marito, con una 'moglie' che trasgredisce il divieto del vino. La situazione è identica a quella, assai nota, della moglie di Egnatius Matennus, analogamente punita dal marito perchè aveva trasgredito il divieto del vino.[18]

(2) vino: la moglie beve volontariamente.

(3) mirto: usato come strumento di punizione.

(4) castità delle donne coinvolte nel rituale: e mirto escluso dal rito in quanto sacro a Venus.

Il consumo femminile di 'vino' viene dunque punito tramite 'mirto'. La significazione amorosa del 'mirto', ed il suo legame con Venus, è ben nota.[19] Basta ricordare Plinio, *Naturalis Historia* xv. 121 ss.: *et in ea quoque arbore genus suffimenti habetur, ideo tum electa, quoniam coniunctioni et huic arbori Venus praeest*; ancora, si parla di una *myrtus* esplicitamente definita *coniugula* (Catone, *Agr.* 8 e 33; Plin. *HN* xv. 122). Per questi motivi, si può realmente pensare che la pianta *myrtus* venga esclusa dal culto della *bona dea* perchè rappresenta quella *libido* che, come sappiamo, il 'vino' è in grado di suscitare: sembra probabile che questa pianta venga utilizzata come specifica punizione per la donna che beve proprio a significare che si punisce l'ubriachezza tramite una pianta capace di simboleggiare le conseguenze della *temulentia*. La punizione della colpa 'vinaria' è realizzata in termini 'amorosi': ed avviene in un contesto di rigorosa *castitas*.

MACROBIO, *SATURNALIA* i. 12.24ss.

Il racconto relativo al mito di fondazione del culto si presenta più lungo, e leggermente diverso, rispetto a quello che sta in Plutarco. Stavolta Fauno non è più un 'marito' ma un 'padre', il quale voleva commettere incesto con la propria figlia. La ragazza appare

---

[18]Cfr. Plin. *HN* xiv. 90; Valerio Massimo vi. 3.9; Serv. *Comm. in Verg. Aen.* i. 737.

[19]Cfr. J.G. Frazer, *Publius Ovidius Naso. Fastorum libri sex* III (Londra, 1929), 164, 191, 399, ecc. Piccaluga, 'Bona dea' (sopra, n. 7), 219ss.

caratterizzata da una straordinaria pudicizia, tanto che, si diceva, non era mai uscita dal gineceo, e nessun uomo l'aveva mai vista. Per ottenere il suo scopo, Fauno fa 'ubriacare' la ragazza ma lei gli resiste ugualmente, tanto che deve farle violenza colpendola con una *virga myrtea*. Tra gli *indicia* rituali che secondo Macrobio sarebbero relativi a questo racconto di fondazione, i seguenti presentano per noi particolare interesse: nel tempio non si introducono verghe di mirto; il vino che si introduce nel tempio porta il nome di *lac*, mentre il vaso in cui è contenuto ha quello di *mellarium*, 'vaso da miele'.

Vediamo anche qui, schematicamente, i principali elementi messi in gioco nel mito di fondazione e nel rituale:

(1) parentela. In questo caso si tratta non di un rapporto moglie/marito, ma di un rapporto padre/figlia. L'importanza del legame parentale appare accresciuta dall'estrema 'pudicizia' della figlia.

(2) vino. Esso non è bevuto volontariamente dalla donna, ma le è imposto per costringerla ad una gravissima trasgressione sessuale, l'incesto.

(3) mirto. Stavolta la pianta è esplicitamente usata come strumento per giungere alla *libido*.

(4) Eufemismi rituali, riguardanti entrambi il vino: questa bevanda viene infatti chiamata 'latte', mentre il 'vaso da vino' viene introdotto sotto il nome di 'vaso da miele'.

Dunque il mirto non è utilizzato qui come punizione per la 'colpa del vino', ma come strumento per costringere ad un rapporto sessuale che, da solo, il vino somministrato alla donna non è stato capace di produrre. Resta però la valenza erotica di questa pianta. Una interessante novità appare poi portata dai due eufemismi con cui si designano il 'vino' rituale ed il suo contenitore: essi mettono in gioco infatti due sostanze di grande interesse all'interno dell'orizzonte culturale femminile, il 'latte' ed il 'miele'. Più sotto le analizzeremo in modo dettagliato.

LATTANZIO, *DIVINAE INSTITUTIONES* xxii. 9, E ARNOBIO, *ADVERSUS NATIONES* v. 18

Il mito di fondazione è più o meno identico a quello che conosciamo da Plutarco, con una moglie che beve di nascosto dal marito. Quanto al vaso che contiene il vino per il rituale, esso non è presentato sotto particolari eufemismi, ma è detto semplicemente *obvoluta vini amphora* (Lattanzio) o *vini amphora ... obtecta* (Arnobio).

Mettendo insieme le informazioni che ci vengono da queste varianti, si ha la possibilità di chiarire alcuni punti fondamentali del contesto culturale presupposto dal mito e dal rituale della *bona dea*.

In primo luogo, si vede chiaramente che il vino femminile gioca *negativamente* nei confronti della parentela: da un lato si ha infatti una moglie che 'trasgredisce' la legge ed è uccisa dal marito; dall'altro, un padre che vuol commettere incesto con la figlia e cerca di ubriacarla. Tale costante presenza di un rapporto parentale nelle diverse varianti del mito di fondazione, che prevede la presenza di una moglie/figlia 'ubriaca', ci riporta naturalmente allo *ius osculi*: che costituisce appunto una forma parentale di controllo sulla 'colpa del vino' che la donna potrebbe commettere. Tutto ciò mostra che le nostre fonti, quando mettono lo *ius osculi*, ovvero il bacio parentale, in stabile connessione con il controllo sul vino femminile, non ci danno una informazione arbitraria o infondata, ma rispecchiano un modello culturale reale. Anche nella rappresentazione religiosa, la 'colpa del vino' compare stabilmente associata ad una relazione di parentela.

In secondo luogo, emerge chiaramente che il carattere negativo del vino femminile (che come abbiamo visto ha una valenza parentale) si esplica proprio nel campo della *libido* e della trasgressione sessuale: è quanto ci dice sia l'esplicito uso sessuale del vino fatto da Fauno/padre per sedurre la figlia; sia la costante presenza del mirto nel mito di fondazione, e l'esclusione di questa pianta dal rito effettivo. Il contesto mitico e rituale conferma dunque l'impostazione degli autori che ci informano sul divieto del vino: i quali, costantemente, riconnettono questo divieto alla sfera dell'adulterio e della trasgressione di tipo sessuale.

Ma l'informazione più nuova e più interessante che ci viene dal culto della *bona dea*, è certo costituita dagli eufemismi linguistici e culturali che camuffano la presenza del 'vino' in questo contesto rituale. Come abbiamo visto, si ha a che fare con un'anfora vinaria 'velata' o 'coperta', ovvero con un 'vino' chiamato 'latte' e con un 'vaso da vino' che va sotto il nome di 'vaso da miele'. Naturalmente, questo carattere 'coperto' del vaso da vino usato per il rito, e più ancora la sua simulazione in termini di 'vaso da miele' contenente 'latte', corrispondono a quello che, sul piano del codice di comportamento, è espresso dal divieto del vino femminile. Vietato alla donna nella vita quotidiana, nel rito il vino può entrare solo in modo camuffato, negato:[20] come sappiamo, la donna non può aver niente a che fare con il *temetum* sacrificale.[21] Così come il mirto, connesso alla trasgressione sessuale, è escluso dal rito, il vino vi è ammesso solo se camuffato da 'latte' e da 'miele'.

Ma dato che si tratta di simulazioni rituali, sembra a questo punto opportuno vedere quale possa essere il significato espresso da queste metafore: esaminando brevemente il valore simbolico di 'latte' e 'miele' in relazione al vino da un lato, ed al mondo femminile dall'altro.

LATTE E MIELE

Inutile sottolineare la stabile connessione culturale, e quasi il carattere di polarità, che lega fra loro 'latte' e 'miele' nelle tradizione.[22] Ma vediamo intanto il miele. Questo alimento, che pure intrattiene con il vino numerosi rapporti di utilizzazione, si oppone però ad esso in alcune tradizioni culturali. Plutarco (*Quaest. conv.* iv. 6.672) dice esplicitamente che la $\phi\acute{\upsilon}\sigma\iota\varsigma$ del miele è contraria a quella del vino.[23] Mentre Nonno

---

[20]È possibile che anche ai riti della *bona dea* si riferisse il noto passo di Serv. *Comm. in Verg. Aen.* i. 737: *feminae non utebatur vino, nisi sacrorum causa certis diebus.*

[21]Cfr. Gras, 'Vin et société' (sopra, n. 7).

[22]Cfr. H. Usener, 'Milch und Honig', *RhM* 57 (1902), 177-95.

[23]A proposito della festa ebraica del Sabato confrontata con i culti di Dioniso: 'Non offrono mai miele nelle loro oblazioni perché sembra che questa sostanza guasti il vino quando vi viene mescolata. Era con questa sostanza che si facevano libazioni, e che veniva bevuta, prima che la vigna fosse conosciuta. Ancora oggi, quei barbari che non conoscono l'uso del vino preparano una bevanda a base di miele e di cui alterano la dolcezza con delle radici dal gusto aspro e vinoso. I Greci praticano delle offerte analoghe che chiamano Nefalia o Melisponda, e le praticano perché il miele possiede una natura contraria a quella del vino'.

(*Dion.* xiii. 258ss.; xix. 228ss.) narra della gara fra Dioniso, dio del vino, ed Aristeo, signore del miele e delle api, che fu vinta da Dioniso. In effetti, sembra proprio che sul piano della rappresentazione religiosa il 'miele' potesse essere concepito come un alimento in qualche modo anteriore al 'vino', e con esso posto in rapporto di esclusione.[24] Se poi dal miele passiamo agli animali che lo producono, le api, anche qui troviamo segni consistenti di incompatibilità con il vino. Delle api sappiamo infatti che sono animali sobri per eccellenza (Porph. *De Antr. Nymph.* 19), le quali non solo rifuggono dal vino ma addirittura si allontanano da coloro che, semplicemente, hanno addosso questo odore (Ael. *NA* i. 58; v. 11; *Geoponica* xv. 2.19; Palladio iv. 15.4).

Per quanto poi riguarda il rapporto fra il miele ed il mondo della donna, dato il contesto in cui ci troviamo (un rituale di rigida castità femminile) si potrà ricordare che le api, oltre che animali sobri, si configurano come creature 'caste' per eccellenza. Basti citare qui il celebre passo virgiliano: *neque concubitu indulgent, nec corpora segnes / in Venerem solvunt.*[25]

È noto, inoltre, che le api rifuggono da coloro che provengono da un convegno amoroso, ed odiano ogni forma di mollezza.[26]

Sembra dunque comprensibile che 'miele' e 'vino', nel contesto del rituale per la *bona dea*, possano essere concepiti in rapporto di opposizione: una opposizione che ben si intreccia con quella fra 'ape' e 'vino', fra 'ape' e 'trasgressione sessuale'. Si può dunque dire che la trasformazione del 'vino' in 'miele' al rituale di *bona dea*, tramite la definizione di *mellarium* data al *vas* in cui è contenuto il vino, corrisponde alla isotopia generale della donna che celebra il rito: una persona che deve essere 'opposta' al vino e, contemporaneamente, caratterizzata da estrema castità. Il miele evocato dal *mellarium* si presenta come una sostanza che la casta e sobria matrona romana può maneggiare molto più propriamente che non il vino.

Vediamo ora il latte. Come già si diceva, si tratta di una sostanza molto vicina al miele, unita ad essa da un'antica polarità. Proprio il latte, ad esempio, è in grado di riconciliare gli sciami separati (Plin. *HN* xi. 58). Sembra anzi interessante notare che, ancora secondo Plinio (*HN* xi. 58), questo medesimo scopo si potesse ottenere tramite l'uso di *aqua mulsa*: quasi che il latte fosse concepito come equivalente ad una mistura di acqua e miele. D'altro lato, si vede bene che 'vino' e 'latte' si oppongono direttamente nella cultura romana. Da questo punto di vista, è esplicita una testimonianza di Paolo-Festo p. 382 L.: *sobrium vicum Romae dictum putatur ... quod in eo Mercurio lacte, non vino supplicabatur* (pare inoltre che in questo *vicus* non ci fossero *tabernae*).[27] La *sobrietas* si configura come utilizzazione del 'latte' in luogo del 'vino'. Questa opposizione latte/vino funziona anche sull'asse diacronico. La cultura romana sembra infatti presentarsi come una cultura che ha accettato il vino solo nel corso del tempo: ma che aveva il

---

[24]A.B. Cook, 'The bee in Greek mythology', *JRS* 25 (1895), 1-24: la tradizione orfica raccontava di Kronos ubriacato 'di miele' da Zeus perché il vino ancora non esisteva (Porph. *De Antr. Nymph.* 16); cfr. anche Epiph. *Adv. Haeres.* ii. 485: 'alcuni chiamano "miele" l'aceto'.

[25]Verg. *G.* iv. 196ss. Cfr. M. Bettini, *Antropologia e cultura romana* (Roma, 1986), 208ss. (= *Anthropology and Roman Culture* (Baltimore, 1991)).

[26]*Ibid.*

[27]I sacrifici a base di latte, e non di vino, sono ovviamente frequenti: cfr. per esempio il caso delle Camenae, cui (secondo Serv. *ad Verg. ecl.* vii. 21) *'non vino sed aqua et lacte sacrificari solet'*. Cfr. G. Wissowa, *Religion und Kultus der Römer*, seconda edizione (Monaco, 1912), 411 n. 7.

'latte' in luogo del 'vino' al suo mitico inizio. È noto infatti che Romolo non sacrificava con 'vino' ma con 'latte' (Plin. *HN* xiv. 87ss.); e che in antico *inter dona* si trovavano *sextarii* di latte e non di vino (*ibid.*, 91). Da un passo di Gellio si ricava inoltre che Romolo, il fondatore, era caratterizzato da grande 'sobrietà' (xi. 14). E Plinio sosteneva che proprio questa straordinaria sobrietà degli inizi di Roma potesse giustificare il semplice *pocillum vini* promesso come *votum* da L. Papirius a Giove qualora avesse riportato la vittoria contro i Sanniti.[28]

Per quanto poi riguarda il rapporto fra il latte ed il mondo femminile, si può notare che, alla festa dei Veneralia, si offrivano miele e latte misti a papavero (Ov. *Fast.* iv. 151ss.). Nel mito di fondazione relativo alla cerimonia, così come è raccontato da Ovidio, si dice che Venus, dopo questa assunzione rituale, potè considerarsi realmente nupta. La mistura di latte e miele avrebbe dunque designato, per una sposa, la sanzione definitiva del suo carattere di donna sposata.[29]

Del resto, anche dal punto di vista biologico, dei liquidi 'interni' alla donna, il latte costituisce una marca caratteristica dell'essere femminile. Nella donna, l'umore vitale per eccellenza, il *sanguis*, ha infatti la capacità di trasformarsi in *lac*: e questo la distingue radicalmente dal maschio. È noto infatti che il 'sangue' della donna, dopo il concepimento, si fa 'latte' nelle parti superiori (*superna*: Macrob. *Sat.* v. 11.16), ovvero che il suo latte è concepito come un *sanguis che exalbuit* (Favorino fr. 38 Barigazzi = Gell. *NA* xii. 1.12). Che il 'latte' sia considerato umore femminile equivalente al sangue, emerge anche da singolari espressioni linguistiche del tipo *assa nutrix*, 'balia asciutta'. L'aggettivo *assus* si usa propriamente per indicare la carne quando è arrostita,[30] ossia quando è stata liberata del suo *cruor*: quel 'sangue' o meglio 'succo carneo'[31] che la vivanda, ancora cruda, secerne. Dunque una *assa nutrix*, una 'balia che non ha latte', sarebbe propriamente una balia privata dal suo *cruor* specifico, del suo sangue e *sucus* vitale. Il latte femminile sembra proprio essere stato concepito come 'sangue trasformato', non solo nelle teorie di tipo scientifico ma anche a livello di cultura diffusa.

La donna, dunque, è un essere biologicamente contiguo al latte: la sua stessa natura la rende prossima a questo elemento. Ma allora bisognerà ricordare che, anche sul piano dei liquidi interni al corpo femminile, il 'latte' si oppone molto rigidamente al vino. La *temulentia* infatti è assolutamente vietata per la *nutrix*, o per la donna che allatta (Favorino fr. 38 Barigazzi = Gell. *NA* i. 12.17; Soranus *Gynaecia* ii. 19).[32]

Se ci è anzi concesso, alla fine di questo paragrafo, aprire una breve parentesi sul mondo vegetale, possiamo notare che questo rapporto privilegiato fra 'latte' da un lato e 'natura femminile' dall'altro, trova interessanti proiezioni nelle credenze relative ad alcune erbe. Quella che porta il nome di *lactuca*, e che come tale si designa linguisticamente quale pianta legata alla sfera del *lac*, è contemporaneamente giudicata

---

[28]*Loc. cit.*; cfr. Livio x. 42.7.

[29]Secondo Frazer, *Publius Ovidius Naso* (sopra, n. 19), 194, è possibile che questo racconto ovidiano rispecchi l'uso (peraltro non testimoniato) di offrire questa bevanda alle spose romane. L'autore riporta usi analoghi nella cultura popolare di Calabria e Grecia.

[30]Cfr. M. Bettini e G. Pucci, 'Del fritto e d'altro', *Opus* 5 (1986), 153-65.

[31]F. Mencacci, 'Sanguis/cruor. Designazioni linguistiche e classificazione antropologica del sangue nella cultura romana', *MD* 17 (1986), 25-62.

[32]Cfr. K.R. Bradley, 'Wet-nursing at Rome: a study in social relation', in B. Rawson (ed.), *The Family in Ancient Rome* (Ithaca, 1986), 201-29.

pianta anafrodisiaca per gli uomini (*Geoponica* xii. 13.2), ed è considerata fredda (Plin. *HN* xix. 154).[33] Quest'erba stabilisce una polarità, non solo suffissale e linguistica, ma anche di funzione culturale, con quella che porta il nome di *eruca*: la quale, al contrario, è considerata eccitante per gli uomini (Plin. *HN* x. 182), ed è specificamente dotata di *fervor*, oltre ad essere *frigoris contemptrix* (*HN* xix. 154). Si mescola perciò alla *lactuca* per bilanciare il 'freddo' di quest'erba col suo 'calore' (*ibid.*). Questa sezione del codice vegetale, se così possiamo chiamarlo, relativo al rapporto *lactuca/eruca*, ripropone dunque un'opposizione più vasta e generale: quella fra maschile e femminile. È noto infatti che la donna è tradizionalmente considerata 'fredda', rispetto all'uomo concepito come 'caldo'.[34] L'erba *lactuca*, lattea, fredda e anafrodisiaca per gli uomini (i quali trovano invece eccitamento nel calore e nel sapore acuto della *eruca*) ripropone dunque nel mondo vegetale quel rapporto fra 'latte' e caratteristiche di tipo 'femminile' che ci era già noto per altra via.

NELLA PROVINCIA DI LIBER

In alcuni passi del settimo libro del *De Civitate Dei*, Agostino, sulla scorta di Varrone, ci fornisce preziose notizie sulle funzioni del dio Liber nell'antica religione romana. In vii. 21 ci dice che [*Liberum*] *liquidis seminibus ac per hoc non solum liquoribus fructuum, quorum quodam modo primatum vinum tenet, verum etiam seminibus animalium praefecerunt.* Dunque Liber sarebbe stato il dio specificamente preposto ai 'semi liquidi': come tale, egli aveva giurisdizione sia sui 'succhi' dei frutti (fra cui spicca il *liquor* del vino) sia sui semi prodotti dagli animali. L'informazione contenuta in questo passo diventa ancora più interessante se la si confronta con quanto viene detto in vii. 16: *Liberum et Cererem praeponunt seminibus, vel illum masculinis, illam femininis.* Dunque Liber, come 'dio dei semi', fa coppia con Ceres: e trova precisata la sua funzione come divinità non solo dei semi 'liquidi' (animali o vegetali), ma anche dei semi 'maschili'. Da queste due notizie si può dunque concludere che Liber, secondo la codificazione religiosa arcaica, presiedeva una provincia seminale caratterizzata dai seguenti tratti: 'liquido' e 'maschile'. Tale provincia si biforcava, se così si può dire, in due rami, rispettivamente 'vegetale' 'animale':

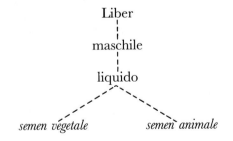

[33]Cfr. le note pagine di M. Detienne, *I giardini di Adone* (trad. italiana, Torino, 1975), 88-93 (= *Les jardins d'Adonis* (Parigi, 1972)).
[34]Cfr. per esempio Arist. *Gen. An.* 738ª; Censorinus *D.N.* vi. 4ss.

Già questo abbozzo di classificazione risulta per noi interessante: esso pone infatti il vino (che, come dice Agostino, detiene il *primatus* fra i *fructuum liquores*) in una luce molto nuova. In primo luogo perchè ci accorgiamo che, nel codice simbolico connesso all'organizzazione religiosa, il *vinum* era considerato una sostanza affine alla sfera dei *semina*, e come tale raggruppabile assieme con i *semina* prodotti dagli animali; in secondo luogo, perchè scopriamo che il vino possedeva una caratterizzazione dichiaratamente 'maschile'.

Continuiamo con Liber. La pertinenza specificamente 'maschile' attribuita a questa divinità, non che alla sua provincia seminale, viene confermata in vii. 2, dove Liber è definito *qui marem effuso semine liberat*: una identica funzione, per la donna, è invece attribuita a Libera (*quae hoc idem beneficium conferat feminae ut etiam ipsa emisso semine liberetur*). Il quadro continua ad ampliarsi, ma resta coerente. In quanto dio dei semi 'liquidi'/'maschili'/'animali', Liber funge anche da divinità che presiede specificamente alla effusione del seme nel maschio.

Il modello religioso e antropologico che emerge da queste notizie agostiniane, come dicevamo, si presenta di grande rilevanza. Tramite il comune referente religioso, il 'seme maschile' da un lato, ed il 'vino' dall'altro, vengono posti in stretto rapporto di contiguità: uno stesso dio presiede alla sfera del vino e, addirittura, a quella della effusione del seme nel maschio. Potremmo anzi richiamare, a questo punto, quanto dicevamo sopra a proposito del termine *virus*, usato sia per designare il seme maschile sia per evocare le caratteristiche salienti del vino. Il seme maschile (in quanto *liquidum semen*, o *liquor* assimilabile a quello dei frutti) può ben essere definito *virus*, cioè 'succo' dalle caratteristiche 'forti' ed inconfondibili; inversamente, si può ben dire che il vino (in quanto *liquor* di carattere seminale) possiede in sè un determinato *virus*.

Proviamo dunque a riferire questo quadro antropologico e religioso al problema costituito dal divieto del vino femminile. Come dicevamo all'inizio, le nostre fonti lo pongono regolarmente e concordemente in relazione con l'adulterio e la trasgressione sessuale: ce lo dicono gli autori che spiegano perché esso fu istituito al tempo dei re; ce lo comunica il costume dello *ius osculi*, che pone in relazione il vino femminile con la castità della donna; ce lo comunica anche il mito di fondazione di *bona dea*, in cui la castità femminile è stabilmente posta in conflitto con il bere vino. Dunque, sappiamo già che secondo i modelli del comportamento sociale e secondo quelli dei rituali femminili, l'assunzione di vino da parte di una donna equivale ad una esplicita spinta verso la trasgressione sessuale. Adesso, dopo aver brevemente esaminato quanto Varrone ed Agostino ci dicono del dio Liber, possiamo aggiungere che secondo i modelli della codificazione religiosa arcaica questa medesima assunzione di vino da parte di una donna avrebbe significato metterla in rapporto con una divinità che presiede anche al seme maschile ed alla sua emissione. Secondo il codice simbolico che organizza la tassonomia dei *semina* dal punto di vista religioso, il 'vino' si colloca in una provincia che è assolutamente maschile, come il seme di cui il maschio si libera. È ovvio che la donna non possa assolutamente berne. Nella sua logica astratta, la codificazione religiosa fornisce un contesto antropologico molto utile per comprendere le regole applicate nel comportamento sociale: e molto coerente con esse.

WINE AND SOCIETY IN REPUBLICAN AND IMPERIAL ROME

16

The Decoration of Roman *Triclinia*

ROGER LING

The object of my paper is to examine the subject-matter of decorations in Roman *triclinia* and in particular to determine to what extent they incorporated references to wine and to the god of wine, Dionysus.[1] I hope to show that, in one group of decorations at least, these references were less common than tends to be assumed.

My starting-point is a passage in Karl Schefold's classic study of the ideology of Pompeian painting *Pompejanische Malerei. Sinn und Ideengeschichte*:

> *Schon immer hatte man ... im Männersaal beim Gelage dem Weingott geopfert. Auf seine Herrschaft spielen in reicheren Häusern seit klassischer Zeit Mosaiken des Fussbodens an, Weihgeschenke an Dionysos, mit Bildern seines Gefolges, der Tiere und Geräte, die ihm heilig sind, und der Helden, die am Symposion besungen werden. In der Römerzeit werden diese Themen als Wandschmuck von Speisezimmern reicher ausgestaltet.*
>
> (Schefold 1952: 34-5; cf. Schefold 1972: 53)

Schefold is writing about the Greek roots of certain conceptions that in his view underlie Roman wall-painting. It is my contention, however, that, as the Greek *symposion* gave way to the Roman *convivium*, so Dionysiac themes lost a little of their force and relevance. They therefore play a relatively small part in the decoration of the room which was the Roman counterpart of the *andron*. The last sentence of the quotation, in fact, gives a false impression both of the extent to which Roman decorations depended on Greek ones and of the actual nature of the themes employed in *triclinia*. It is true that many dining-rooms in Roman houses were decorated with Dionysiac subjects or with allusions to the world over which Dionysus presided: thus there are representations of satyrs and maenads, Cupids, wild animals, fruit and flowers, and wine-vessels. But many more decorations show simply generic references to dining — that is representations of food-stuffs — or subjects which are not related to Dionysus at all: for example, myths of Aphrodite (Venus) or Artemis (Diana); sacro-idyllic or villa landscapes; still life assemblages of athletics vases or attributes of deities other than Dionysus; even Nilotic scenes with pygmies hunting crocodiles and the like.

To determine the extent to which Dionysiac themes appeared in the decorations of Roman dining-rooms I decided to carry out a statistical check. The problems of any

---

[1] I am grateful to various delegates at the conference for their comments on this paper when it was delivered, and to Andrew Wallace-Hadrill for reading the text afterwards; he has made a number of valuable criticisms and suggested possible directions for further research. That I have not acted upon all these suggestions is due primarily to the need to preserve, as far as possible, the general form of the paper given in Rome.

such operation are obvious. It is not always easy to judge whether a room functioned as a dining-room; one must beware of identifying function on the basis of decoration, lest we get involved in circular argument. Ideally, we need to use external criteria — especially evidence for the presence of the three couches of a *triclinium*. The chief indications of these are the demarcation of the position of the couches in the pattern of a decorated pavement, or the presence of a recess for the foot of a couch in the far end of the left wall (provided that the room is of appropriate size — at least 3.5 m wide and 4.5 m deep). Another criterion is the division of space by means of an architectural or decorative caesura into inner and outer parts, the former roughly twice as deep as the latter; the inner part would have contained the couches of the diners, the outer part the area for service (and possibly for entertainments such as dancers and musicians). More generally, it can be assumed that a room which stands out in a house by reason of its size, position and fine decoration is likely to have been used for banquets.

To get a good sample I have chosen to tackle Schefold 'on home ground' by concentrating on Pompeii.[2] For lack of time I have not been able to do much by way of checking the functions of rooms myself but have relied upon Schefold's own identifications (Schefold 1957), along with those of the photographic index *Pitture e pavimenti di Pompei* (Bragantini *et al.* 1981; 1983; 1986); I have accordingly analysed the decorations of the rooms termed by them '*triclinium*'.[3] Within these rooms I have not listed every single decorative motif, many of which are clearly stock fillers used by painters to save time, but have concentrated on the most important subjects, that is the mythological pictures or other subjects in the central position of a wall-, ceiling-, or pavement-decoration, the figures or motifs in the side-fields of the main zone of a wall-decoration, and the principal motifs in the subsidiary areas (dado and upper zone of a wall-decoration; outer parts of a ceiling or pavement). Only those decorations which contain figure-subjects (whether human or animal), landscapes or still-lifes are included; and I have also eliminated those *triclinia* in which the surviving decorations are so incomplete that only subsidiary motifs can be identified. Generally speaking, the criterion for inclusion is the survival of the central subject on at least one wall — a situation which is too incomplete for comfort, but which nonetheless gives a guide to the overall content.

The result (Fig. 1) is a total of 137 *triclinia*, of which seven have decorations which are predominantly Dionysiac and 39 have decorations which contain some Dionysiac elements. This leaves 86 decorations which can be described as non-Dionysiac (plus five where there are some doubts over the interpretation of the subjects). Admittedly these are very crude statistics. Several of the decorations classed as non-Dionysiac may have contained Dionysiac elements on walls or parts of walls which no longer survive. On the

---

[2]I had hoped to cover a wider range of material, including figured mosaics from the Roman provinces, but was frustrated by lack of time. Concentrating on Pompeii, however, has the advantage of providing a sample closely circumscribed in place and time: all the decorations considered belong to the period from the late Second Style to the Fourth — i.e. *c.* 40 BC - AD 79. The sample excludes residences outside the walls of the city, such as the Villa Imperiale and the Villa dei Misteri, which are not in Bragantini *et al.* (1981; 1983; 1986).

[3]This involves discounting those large, more square-shaped rooms, usually called *oeci*, which may equally have been used for dining and drinking. The data that I have collected for such rooms suggest a range and statistical pattern of subjects very similar to those found in *triclinia*.

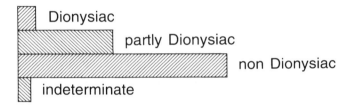

FIG. 1. Decorations of Pompeian *triclinia*: general content *(Drawn by Roger Ling)*

other hand, some of the decorations classed as 'predominantly Dionysiac' are so described on the basis of incomplete information; the missing walls or parts of walls might, for all we know, have been decorated with non-Dionysiac subjects. The important point to emerge is that Dionysiac themes do not prevail in the decorations under review.

At this point I shall look at one or two of the decorations in the different categories to see what sort of material we are dealing with. First of all, let us consider a decoration which is predominantly Dionysiac: that of the *triclinium* (room 16) to the right of the *tablinum* in the House of M. Lucretius (IX 3, 5). This is almost the archetypal Dionysiac decoration, and as such is considered in some detail by Schefold (1952: 132-4; 1972: 193-7; cf. 1962: 76) and by Mary Lee Thompson in her study on programmatic painting in antiquity (Thompson 1960-1: 66-7).[4] The central pictures are all related to Bacchus and the effects of wine. On the back wall (Fig. 2) Herakles, crowned with a vine-wreath, holding a *thyrsus* in his left hand, supported by Silenus, an *amorino* playing the pipes in one ear, a maenad clashing cymbals in the background, reels drunkenly while Omphale, wearing Herakles's lion-scalp helmet and holding his club, looks on with regal self-satisfaction. The picture illustrates the power of wine, and its companion-pieces on the side-walls pick up the same idea in the form of the conquests of the wine-god himself. On the left wall Dionysus erects a trophy to commemorate his Indian victory. On the right wall he is shown as an infant in a triumphal cortège. The Bacchic theme is continued in many of the subsidiary motifs. In the side-fields are little panels with Cupids (beings who are often members of the entourage of Bacchus) engaged alternately in banqueting and in rehearsing dramatic or musical performances.

In this case the imagery is carefully selected to project a common theme of the power of wine and the all-conquering nature of the wine-god Dionysus. These messages are specifically stated in the central pictures, while the activities over which Dionysus presides (banqueting, drama and choral performances) are extolled in the side-panels. But this kind of decoration is an exception to the rule. To illustrate a heterogeneous repertory we may take the decoration of the *triclinium* (room 9) in the Casa del Fabbro (I 10, 7). Whatever its final function (at the time of the eruption it contained only a single couch, by which two skeletons were found), this room was certainly designed as a *triclinium*: this is suggested by its size and position (it being the largest room in the house

---

[4]The programmatic nature of the decoration was first pointed out by Trendelenburg (1873: 48).

FIG. 2. East wall of the *triclinium* (room 16) to the right of the *tablinum*, House of M. Lucretius (Pompeii IX 3, 5) *(After Zahn 1828-59: vol.3, pl. 84)*

and opening through a wide southern doorway to a view of the garden), and confirmed by the recess at the north end of the west wall, designed for the foot of a couch, and by the pattern of the pavement, which clearly marks the position of couches against the north, west and east walls. Here the central pictures of the Third Style wall-decoration are decidedly heterogeneous in subject-matter. The west wall shows the fall of Icarus; the north wall (Fig. 3) shows a scene with grazing cattle and a little rural shrine thought to represent Paris and Hermes on Mount Ida; and the east wall (Fig. 4), pierced by a *lararium* niche, shows further grazing cattle, this time perhaps in association with a scene of Marsyas and Athena (Schefold 1957: 46-7). The main things which these pictures have in common are their bucolic setting and their similar colour-scheme, and it is my belief that this kind of formal balance was as a rule more important to artists and their clients than any attempt to achieve thematic links.[5] The subsidiary motifs reinforce the disparate character of the subject-matter. Most important is a series of still lifes in the *predella*, consisting respectively of fruits, athletics objects, and birds and plants — all favourite motifs of Pompeian wall-painting, and probably in the present context having no symbolic value. A female figure in the centre of the upper zone on the east wall may possibly have been a maenad but is too incomplete for identification. The only motifs which can more specifically be linked with Bacchus and his beverage are *rhyta* attached to the plant-festooned poles which separate the panels of the main zone, hanging *cistae* in the dado, and wine-cups standing on entablatures in the pseudo-architectural structures of the upper zone.

A couple of further examples may be cited. A Third Style decoration from a winter *triclinium* in the House of Orpheus (VI 14, 20), recorded in a coloured lithograph by P. D'Amelio (Fig. 5),[6] is focused upon a landscape painting of a rustic sanctuary which may

[5]Cf. Ling (1991: 135-41). Some good observations on this point are made by Trendelenburg (1876: 1-8).
   [6]The decoration is now largely destroyed: see Bragantini *et al.* (1983: 279).

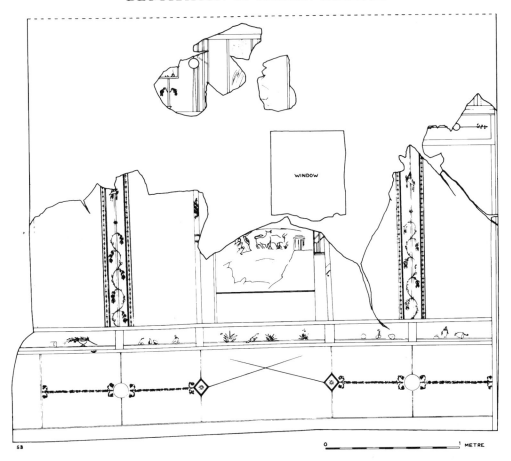

FIG. 3. North wall of the *triclinium* (room 9), Casa del Fabbro (Pompeii I 10, 7) *(Courtesy of the Pompeii Research Committee; drawn by S. Bird and S. Gregory)*

or may not be Dionysiac (the statue is a kind of herm growing from a vegetal calyx and holding a *pedum*). The herons, plants and swimming ducks in the dado could make a general reference to the world of nature over which Dionysus holds sway, while the vignettes containing theatrical masks in the frieze may refer to his patronage of drama; but the assemblages of athletics prizes also in the frieze take us further from the world of Dionysus, and the sphinxes in the side-fields and Egyptianizing statues of the upper zone belong to a totally different world. Other motifs, such as the swans and pegasi which serve as *acroteria*, even the wine-jugs standing on cornices, are little more than stock fillers.

A Fourth Style decoration from room r in the House of Queen Margherita (V 2, 1), again best studied in a nineteenth-century lithograph (Fig. 6),[7] has marginal elements

[7]Cf. Schefold (1962: pl. 108). The paintings survive but in a damaged state: see Bragantini *et al.* (1983: 56-7).

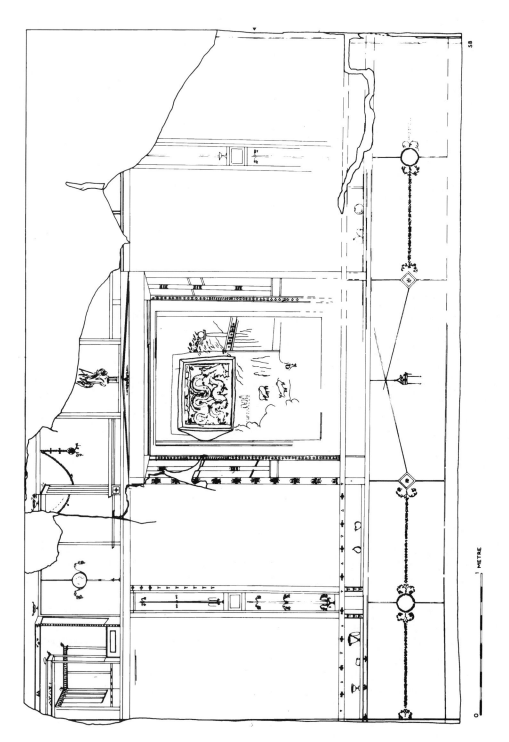

Fig. 4. East wall of the *triclinium* (room 9), Casa del Fabbro (Pompeii I 10, 7) *(Courtesy of the Pompeii Research Committee; drawn by S. Bird and S. Gregory)*

FIG. 5. North wall of a winter *triclinium* (room l), House of Orpheus (Pompeii VI 14, 20) *(After a coloured lithograph by P. D'Amelio)*

which could be regarded as Dionysiac — a dancing maenad (?) in the centre of the upper zone, lion-griffins in the dado, and *amorini* with plates of fruit in the side-fields. But the central panel, representing Narcissus among nymphs and Cupids, belongs to a different repertory, while the subsidiary motifs are as miscellaneous as ever — peacocks, antelopes, goats and birds.

In this last decoration, however, the central panels on the remaining walls of the room were more closely connected with the mythology of the wine-god. One showed the abandonment of Ariadne by Theseus, the prelude to her discovery by Dionysus; the other the madness of Lycurgus, punished for attacking the infant god and his nurses.

Examples like this suggest that decorators and their patrons were aware of the appropriateness of Dionysiac myths and motifs in the decoration of dining-rooms but did not feel the need to make them the exclusive, or even the dominant, theme. What then were the principles which dictated choices of subject-matter? To answer this question we may go back to the 137 *triclinia* in our Pompeian sample; and, to simplify

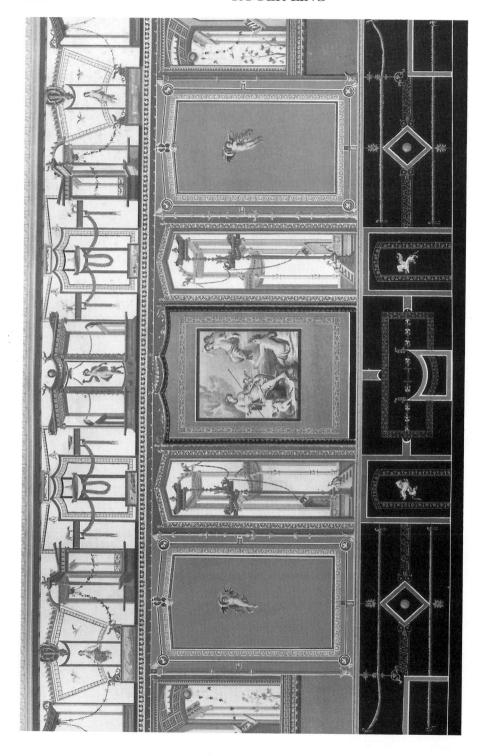

FIG. 6. East wall of a *triclinium* (room r?), in the House of Queen Margherita (Pompeii V 2, 1) *(After a coloured lithograph by P. D'Amelio)*

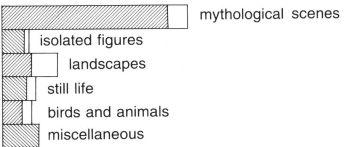

Fɪɢ. 7. Decorations of Pompeian *triclinia*: central subjects. The unhatched tips of the columns represent decorations in which the relevant subject is combined with another or others. *(Drawn by Roger Ling)*

the terms of reference, we may concentrate on the central panels and vignettes, which can reasonably be regarded as the likely focus of any decorative programme.

The range of subjects is illustrated diagrammatically in Fig. 7. Of the 137 *triclinia* 69 have mythological panel-pictures and a further eight combine such pictures with other kinds of picture (landscape or genre). Nine contain isolated figures or vignettes, generally where identifiable of mythological or allegorical subjects, such as maenads and satyrs, Cupids and Psyches, Victories, and Seasons. Two combine such figures with other subjects. Twelve contain only landscapes, and a further eleven combine landscapes with other subjects (mythological scenes, isolated figures, still lifes, animals). Ten contain only still lifes, and a further four combine still lifes with other subjects (landscapes, animals and isolated figures). Eight contain only animals and birds, with a further four showing animals and birds in combination with other subjects. This leaves fifteen rooms with miscellaneous subjects, of which the most important are genre scenes (including banquets and religious ceremonies, some of which feature Cupids or Dionysiac figures) and painted gardens.

The preponderance of mythological pictures is not surprising. The dining-room, the place of entertainment *par excellence*, inevitably receives one of the finest decorations in the house, and the mythological picture, often adapted from a Greek 'old master', is the most costly and prestigious form of representational painting. The less prestigious subjects, such as isolated figures, still lifes, and especially animals and birds, derive from the dining-rooms of more modest houses, whose owners could not afford the luxury of a mythological picture.

More interesting is the choice of subjects within the mythological series. Here we may digress for a moment. In only five rooms do the pictures appear to form clearly linked pendants or cycles. Apart from the Dionysiac cycle already described in the House of M. Lucretius, there are decorations on the theme of Daedalus and Pasiphae (V 2, 10 room n), Paris (VI 9, 2 room 27), Thetis and the armour of Achilles (VII 2, 25 room n), and possibly episodes from the career of Achilles (VII 3, 29 room 1).[8] Otherwise, unless one looks for moral themes such as Schefold's favourite antithesis of

---

[8]To these can be added the Cretan cycle in Triclinium A of the Villa Imperiale: see Von Blanckenhagen (1968: 116); Pappalardo (1985: 9).

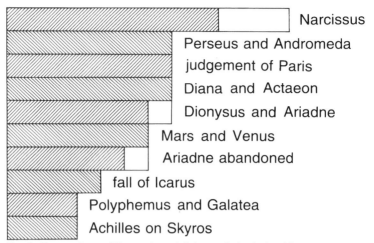

FIG. 8. Decorations of Pompeian *triclinia*: mythological subjects most commonly depicted. The unhatched tips of the columns represent pictures where the interpretation is uncertain. *(Drawn by Roger Ling)*

'*Held und Frevler*', the mythological subjects seem to have been put together in a random way. A table of the most popular subjects (Fig. 8) places Narcissus at the top (nine certain and three possible occurrences), Perseus and Andromeda, the judgement of Paris, and Diana and Actaeon joint second (seven occurrences), Dionysus and Ariadne fifth (six + one?), Mars and Venus sixth (six), Ariadne abandoned by Theseus seventh (five + one?), the fall of Icarus eighth (four), Polyphemus and Galatea and Achilles on Skyros joint ninth (three). These subjects are joined in almost every conceivable combination. Only on three occasions (all, curiously, involving pictures of Diana and Actaeon) do two of them recur together. In no case do three subjects recur in combination.

A similar pattern of usage would certainly emerge if we extended the enquiry to cover other sorts of rooms. Among the hundreds of Pompeian wall-decorations still extant or known from drawings and descriptions there are only one or two instances, to my knowledge, of different rooms combining precisely the same groups of pictures. At the same time, I suspect that the range of subjects in other kinds of rooms is very similar to that found in dining-rooms. A glance at the indexes in Schefold's *Die Wände Pompejis* (1957) shows that the five most popular mythological scenes overall are all in our top ten for dining-rooms: Narcissus (38 + two?), Mars and Venus (35 + one?), Ariadne abandoned (30), Perseus and Andromeda (26 + one?), Polyphemus and Galatea (twenty + one?). The inevitable inferences are: (1) that there were no consistent patterns of selection in Pompeian wall-decorations; (2) that there were no significant differences in subject-matter between dining-rooms and other sorts of room.[9]

[9]A different line of argument which could be used against Schefold is to collect statistics of houses where Dionysiac subjects decorate areas other than the *triclinium*. In the Casa della Venere in Bikini, for example, there is a painting of Dionysus and a maenad in the *tablinum* and non-Dionysiac pictures in the *triclinium*. I suspect that such examples can be multiplied.

To return to the main point of this enquiry: the decorations of Pompeian dining-rooms are not predominantly Dionysiac. They do not often show the myths of Dionysus, or 'representations of his retinue, of the animals and instruments which are sacred to him'. Nor, incidentally, do many of them give prominence to the theme of dining. *Xenia*, still life paintings of food, occur in only seven of our 137 rooms (and in some of these alongside other forms of still life); scenes of non-mythological banquets are found in only one, or possibly two.

Schefold may be nearer to the mark, however, when he refers to 'representations ... of the heroes who are celebrated in the course of the *symposion*' (Schefold 1952: 34; cf. p. 239 above). The mythological and other subjects could relate to stories told, or poems recited, in dining-rooms. More generally, they could be designed simply to appeal to the literary taste of educated diners. A clear instance from a later period is the mosaic pavement in the *triclinium* of the Roman villa at Lullingstone in Britain, where a representation of Europa and the bull, orientated towards the couches (or better *stibadium*) of the diners (Toynbee 1962: no. 192, pl. 229; 1964: 263-4; Meates 1979: 76-8), is accompanied by an elegiac couplet which would make no sense to any one who did not know the first book of Virgil's *Aeneid*:

invida si ta[uri] vidisset Iuno natatus
iustius Aeolias isset adusque domos

if jealous Juno had seen the swimming of the bull, more justly would she have gone to the halls of Aeolus.

At Pompeii, one painting at least seems to refer explicitly to the *Aeneid*. The picture of the wounded Aeneas from a *triclinium* in the Casa di Sirico (VII 1, 25) closely follows *Aeneid* xii. 383-416: Aeneas stands leaning on a tall spear, his son weeping at his side, himself in pain but tearless; the doctor Iapyx is grasping the bolt with his forceps; Venus is arriving with a sprig of healing dittany (Naples 9009: illustrated by Rizzo (1929: pl. 195 right), Borda (1958: 239), and De Franciscis (nd: pl. 21)). Other paintings have a literary 'feel' without referring to specific passages. Sacro-idyllic landscape paintings, for instance, may have been designed to conjure up the world depicted in the bucolic poetry of Theocritus and Virgil. In a more general way the predominance in our top ten mythological subjects of the love-stories which feature in the poems of Ovid and other Augustan or Julio-Claudian poets could be a token of the success of those poets in popularizing the tales in question.[10]

But the primary inspiration for the painted pictures in dining-rooms, as in other rooms, is not literary but artistic. Many of the paintings of Pompeii clearly go back, in however debased a form, to famous prototypes — the old masters which were brought to Rome for display in temples or collected and reproduced in the villas and houses of the wealthy. The wall-pictures at Pompeii and Herculaneum represent the aspirations of the municipal bourgeoisie to ape the *luxuria* of the contemporary nobility. Their choice of subjects was to a large extent conditioned, like that of upper-class collectors, not by a desire to create moral and intellectual programmes, but by the pressures of the market-

---

[10]The bibliography on the relationship between poetry and painting in the ancient world is very large. It is clear, however, that with few exceptions the influence of literature upon art was of a very general kind. For some sensible observations on the subject see Wallace-Hadrill (1983).

place — namely by the range of pictures that the firms of painters could offer. The painters certainly had pattern books of some form (cf. Ling 1991: 217-20), and the patron was no doubt invited to select items from them. In making his selection he may have been influenced by various motives — by the snob value of having what purported to be a copy of a Zeuxis or an Apelles, for example (one thinks of the picture gallery visited by Encolpius in the *Satyricon*: Petronius 83), or simply by his liking for a certain story or for a certain composition. His taste may have been shaped by literary culture or, more vaguely, by romantic notions of heroic deeds and remote places. Above all he was anxious to display his culture. The dining-room was not just a place where hospitality was dispensed, it was also a place where a host advertized his wealth and taste.

I conclude, therefore, by taking an 'agnostic' line on the decorations of Roman *triclinia*. There is no special tendency towards a relationship between the function of wining and dining and the range of subjects employed in decorations; the choice of subject-matter in our sample seems to be eclectic and, with a few exceptions, not unified in coherent programmes. This does not mean to say that ancient viewers did not look for programmatic links; Encolpius's response to three of the pictures in the gallery just mentioned (he lumps them together as examples of the love-affairs of gods, more fortunate than his own) suggests that they sometimes did. But they may have done so as a kind of intellectual after-dinner exercise; in other words, like Schefold and Mary Lee Thompson (and like Karl Lehmann (1941) in his analysis of the *Imagines* of the Elder Philostratus), they may have tried to identify hidden meanings and subtle interrelationships that the patron and artist (and ekphrasist) had never intended.[11]

REFERENCES

Bartman, E. (1991) Sculptural collecting and display in the private realm, in E.K. Gazda (ed.), *Roman Art in the Private Sphere*: 71-88. Ann Arbor.

Borda, M. (1958) *La pittura romana*. Milan.

Bragantini, I., De Vos, M. and Parise Badoni, F. (1981) *Pitture e pavimenti di Pompei* I (*Repertorio delle fotografie del Gabinetto Fotografico Nazionale*). Rome.

Bragantini, I., De Vos, M. and Parise Badoni, F. (1983) *Pitture e pavimenti di Pompei* II (*Repertorio delle fotografie del Gabinetto Fotografico Nazionale*). Rome.

Bragantini, I., De Vos, M., Parise Badoni, F. and Sampaolo, V. (1986) *Pitture e pavimenti di Pompei* III (*Repertorio delle fotografie del Gabinetto Fotografico Nazionale*). Rome.

Curtius, L. (1929) *Die Wandmalerei Pompejis*. Leipzig.

[11]Among the questions raised by the audience in response to this paper was one on the programmatic nature of Roman sculpture-displays. My view on such displays is very similar to my view on assemblages of pictures (cf. Ling (1986: 727-31)). To most collectors formal balance was more important than thematic links, and, when links did occur, they were often of a banal kind. This view is reinforced by a recent article by S. De Caro (1987), which attempts, not very successfully, to formulate programmes in the garden statuary of the villa of the Poppaei at Oplontis. That there was a similar lack of coherent and consistent programmes among sculptural collections in public bath-buildings is demonstrated by Manderscheid (1981: 38-45). For an excellent discussion of the principles of sculptural collecting and display in the private sphere see Bartman (1991).

De Caro, S. (1987) The sculptures of the Villa of Poppaea at Oplontis: a preliminary report, in E.B. MacDougall (ed.), *Ancient Roman Villa Gardens* (*Dumbarton Oaks Colloquium on the History of Landscape Architecture* X): 77-133. Washington D.C.

De Franciscis, A. (nd) *La pittura pompeiana* (*Forma e colore* 5). Florence.

Lehmann, K. (1941) The *Imagines* of the elder Philostratus. *ArtB* 23: 11-44.

Ling, R. (1986) The arts of living, in J. Boardman, J. Griffin and O. Murray (eds), *The Oxford History of the Classical World*: 718-47. Oxford.

Ling, R. (1991) *Roman Painting*. Cambridge.

Manderscheid, H. (1981) *Die Skulpturenausstattung der Kaiserzeitlichen Thermenanlagen* (*Monumenta artis Romanae* XV). Berlin.

Meates, G.W. (1979) *The Roman Villa at Lullingstone, Kent* I. *The Site* (*Monograph Series of the Kent Archaeological Society* I). Chichester.

Pappalardo, U. (1985) Die 'Villa Imperiale' in Pompeji. *AW* 16 (4): 3-15.

Rizzo, G.E. (1929) *La pittura ellenistico-romana*. Milan.

Schefold, K. (1952) *Pompejanische Malerei. Sinn und Ideengeschichte*. Basel.

Schefold, K. (1957) *Die Wände Pompejis*. Berlin.

Schefold, K. (1962) *Vergessenes Pompeji*. Bern-Munich.

Schefold, K. (1972) *La peinture pompéienne. Essai sur l'évolution de sa signification*. Brussels. (Revised ed. of Schefold 1952)

Thompson, M.L. (1960-61) The monumental and literary evidence for programmatic painting in antiquity. *Marsyas* 9:36-77.

Toynbee, J.M.C. (1962) *Art in Roman Britain*. London.

Toynbee, J.M.C. (1964) *Art in Britain under the Romans*. Oxford.

Trendelenburg, A. (1873) Erotenfries aus Pompeji. *AZ* 31: 44-8.

Trendelenburg, A. (1876) Gegenstücke in der campanischen Wandmalerei. *AZ* 34: 1-8, 79-93.

Von Blanckenhagen, P.H. (1968) Daedalus and Icarus on Pompeian walls. *MDAI(R)* 75: 106-43.

Wallace-Hadrill, A. (1983) Ut pictura poesis? *JRS* 73: 180-3.

Zahn, W. (1828-59) *Die Schönsten Ornamente und Merkwürdigsten Gemälde aus Pompeji, Herculanum und Stabiae* III. Berlin.

17

Scenes from the Roman *Convivium*: *Frigida non derit, non derit calda petenti* (Martial xiv. 105)

KATHERINE M. D. DUNBABIN

Around the turn of the fourth to fifth century AD, the owner of a wealthy house at Complutum, modern Alcalà de Henares in Spain, decorated it with a series of mosaic pavements.[1] As is often the case, the most impressive of these were reserved for the main dining-room, and the corridor by which it was approached. Guests invited to dinner were greeted in the corridor by the images of six servants, nearly lifesize, with napkins over their arms, and holding out cups in three different shapes and sizes (Fig. 1).[2] The mosaic is a clear indication of the hospitality which awaits the guests; set as they are before the entrance, it is tempting to see the drink that the servants offer as meant for *mulsum*, which Roman sources tell us was served as an aperitif, before the main meal began.[3] The *triclinium* itself has its pavement marked out in the traditional way for three couches, although by this date the single semicircular couch known as the *stibadium* was much more common.[4] In the centre is a figured panel showing Dionysus, leaning drunkenly on a satyr and flanked by Silenus and maenad, while below five vintagers tread the grapes. In a panel at either side, confronted pairs of leopards drink from a *crater*. The iconography, like the layout of the room, is traditional — amazingly so for this date; and everything is designed to stress the pleasures of wine as the central element of the owner's hospitality. Beyond the figured panel is a semicircular space, evidently intended for service, and especially doubtless to hold the apparatus needed for the wine. We get no indication here, however, of how the wine is prepared or dispensed; for that we have to turn to other illustrations.

---

[1] This paper has been left essentially in the form in which it was delivered at the conference. A longer version dealing with the Roman use of *craters* and hot-water heaters has been published as 'Wine and water at the Roman *Convivium*', *JRA* 6 (1993), 116-41.

[2] D. Fernandez-Galiano, *Complutum, I: Excavaciones* (Madrid, 1984), 129-36; *II: Mosaicos*, 135-47, pls lxxi-ix.

[3] Cf. A. Hug, *RE* XVI (1935), 513-4, *s.v.* '*mulsum*'; J. Marquardt, *Das Privatleben der Römer*, second edition (revised by A. Mau) (Leipzig, 1886), 323; J. André, *L'alimentation et la cuisine à Rome* (Paris, 1981), 166.

[4] Fernandez-Galiano, *Complutum* (above, n. 2) II, 148-86, pls lxxxi-ci. For the *stibadium*, see K. Dunbabin, 'Triclinium and Stibadium', in W. Slater (ed.), *Dining in a Classical Context* (Ann Arbor, 1991), 121-48.

FIG. 1. Mosaic from the corridor of a house at Complutum (Spain), showing servants offering drink
(Courtesy of D. Fernández-Galiano)

My second example is nearly 100 years earlier, and comes from the opposite side of the Empire: another mosaic, from Ephesus, probably early fourth century (Fig. 2).[5] It decorated an apsidal space, inserted into one side of an older peristyle, which was presumably used as a *stibadium*-dining room, with the couch around the outer space. In the centre is a scene of the banquet. Four revellers, apparently two male and two female, recline on the cushions, the two men drinking from beakers, the women passing a cup from one to the other. Three separate tables stand in front of them; this is, to my knowledge, unique for *stibadium* scenes, where the diners usually share a common table. Indistinct traces of food may be seen on the tables, and the animals gnawing crumbs on the ground imply that a meal has taken place. In front, the wine is prepared and served. A large, wide-mouthed *crater* stands on the ground; beside it a nude boy holds a wine-jug, and an object with a handle which might be either the *cyathus* to ladle the wine, or the *colum*, the strainer.[6] Equally prominent beside the *crater* is a cylindrical metal container with a high pointed lid; I shall return to this later.

My two examples give some notion of the difficulty of handling the artistic evidence when we wish to assess the role, actual and symbolic, of wine at the Roman *convivium*. The artistic vocabulary combines elements which may be more than half a millennium old, like the drunken Dionysus at Complutum, with others which are more recent, and which appear to bear more reference to contemporary reality: but these too can be deceptive, and include conventional elements. The geographic and chronological range is immense; we can certainly not assume that customs in Spain were identical with those in Asia Minor, nor that they remained unchanged from the first century BC to the fourth century AD. Only in a few special cases, some of which I consider later, is there a homogeneous group of monuments which form a coherent series, limited chronologically and geographically. My aim in this paper is therefore to raise questions rather than to answer them, and especially to suggest a few ways in which the evidence of texts and of images may be mutually enlightening. With all their shortcomings, what the visual representations can do, I believe, is to indicate what seemed important to Romans

[5]W. Jobst, 'Das "öffentliche Freudenhaus" in Ephesos', *JÖAI* 51 (1976-7), 73-84, figs 21-3.

[6]For these implements, see W. Hilgers, *Lateinische Gefässnamen* (Düsseldorf, 1969), 56-7, 166 no. 132, 150 no. 108. These objects need further study.

FIG. 2. Banquet scene on a mosaic from Ephesus *(After Jobst 1976-7, fig. 22; courtesy of W. Jobst and Österreichisches Archäologisches Institut)*

of different origins, what they themselves chose to stress about their use of wine. And, at the risk of tilting at antiquated windmills, I want particularly to question the assertion of most of the classic handbooks that the Roman practice was simply that of the Greeks, in somewhat degenerate form.[7]

Let us therefore examine more closely the relationship between the *crater* and the object beside it on the Ephesus mosaic. The importance of the *crater* in images of the Greek *symposion* has been repeatedly stressed in recent studies, especially by François

---

[7]E.g. A. Mau, *RE* IV.1 (1901), 610-19, *s.v. 'comissatio'*; H. Blümner, *Die Römischen Privataltertümer* (*Handbuch der Klassischen Altertums-Wissenschaft* IV.2(2)), third edition (Munich, 1911), 400-10.

Lissarrague and his collaborators.[8] The adoption of the *crater* in Rome, and the mixing of wine and water which it is taken to imply, is seen as a sign of the Hellenization of Roman drinking customs.[9] But it is necessary to ask whether the practice was indeed the same, whether the Romans invariably used *craters* in the same way as the Greeks.

First, let us look at some examples where *craters* appear in what would seem to be their traditional role. They figure prominently in some early imperial representations of the banquet, and of its apparatus. For example, the Tomb of Vestorius Priscus at Pompeii contains an illustration of a display of table silver, the status symbols of a wealthy, and doubtless fashionable, local magistrate.[10] Among them are three *craters*, accompanying drinking cups of various shapes, wine-jugs, *cyathi* to ladle the wine, and other implements. Their importance here is echoed in at least one collection of real table silver, the Augustan Hildesheim treasure, which included two large and elegant *craters*, one standing 0.36 m high, the other 0.524 m.[11] That these are centrepieces of the collection, and therefore presumably of the whole process of serving the wine, can hardly be doubted.

Crater-shaped vessels can also be used with an emblematic value, as indicators of the place where wine is drunk. The pavements of two small structures, apparently taverns, propped against the façade of the Caserma dei Vigili at Ostia (ii v.1) are decorated simply with large *craters*.[12] The *crater* can also be a sign for the drink it contains: the Dionysiac leopards drinking from the *crater* on the Complutum mosaic[13] belong with a host of other creatures and, especially, birds, who drink from the *crater*, until the theme passes into Christian iconography.

Such conventional images tell us little about the actual role of the *crater* at Roman banquets. However they also play a dominant part in some illustrations of banquets and drinking, not only in the early empire but throughout antiquity. Several such scenes appear among the mosaics of Antioch, though with very varying contexts. If a scene of the Drinking Contest of Dionysus and Herakles, of the third century AD, places the silver *crater* prominently in the foreground, between Herakles's club and Dionysus's drinking-horn, this may be due to the traditional nature of the mythological scene (Fig. 3).[14] However on the fourth-century mosaic from the Tomb of Mnemosyne, where two women recline on the *stibadium*-couch and a third sits, the figures wear contemporary dress (Fig. 4); it is rightly seen by Levi as representing a memorial banquet for the

[8]E.g. J.-L. Durand, F. Frontisi-Ducroux and F. Lissarrague, 'L'entre-deux-vins', in C. Bérard *et al.* (eds), *La cité des images: religion et société en Grèce antique* (Lausanne, 1984), 124: '*Le cratère définit à lui seul le mélange et le partage du vin. Sa seule présence permet d'indiquer toutes les valeurs symboliquement associés aux banquets et aux beuveries*'.

[9]Cf. P. Villard, 'Le mélange et ses problèmes', *REA* 90 (1988), 19-33, esp. 19, n. 2: '*Il va de soi que cette pratique grecque est également romaine, même si il y a sans doute plus de déviances chez les romains*'.

[10]G. Spano, 'La tomba dell'edile C. Vestorio Prisco in Pompei', *Atti della Reale Accademia d'Italia, Memorie della classe di scienze morali e storiche* ser. 7a, vol. 3, fasc. 6 (1943), 266-7, fig. 8; Hilgers, *Lateinische Gefässnamen* (above, n. 6), 53, pl. 5.

[11]U. Gehrig, *Hildesheimer Silberfund in der Antikenabteilung Berlin* (Berlin, 1967), 20, figs 2-6; E. Pernice and F. Winter, *Der Hildesheimer Silberfund* (Berlin, 1901), 61-5, pls xxxii-v.

[12]G. Becatti, *Scavi di Ostia 4, Mosaici e pavimenti marmorei* (Rome, 1961), 62-3, nos. 77-9, pls cxcii-iii.

[13]Cf. above, n. 4.

[14]D. Levi, *Antioch Mosaic Pavements* (Princeton, 1947), 156-9, pl. xxx.

Fig. 3. Mosaic from the House of the Drinking Contest, Antioch, showing a drinking context of Herakles and Dionysus *(Courtesy of the Department of Art and Archaeology, Princeton University)*

dead.[15] A tall, high-necked metal *crater* stands beside the table, an amphora in its stand is in the corner, and a girl-servant stands between the two with jug and bowl; presumably she draws wine from the *crater*.

Also at Antioch is the well-known mosaic of the House of the Buffet Supper.[16] It shows the entire course of the banquet, with a wide variety of food, spread out on the mosaic inside the curve where the *stibadium*-couch would have been set. Wine does not figure very prominently among the food, though there is a drinking cup beside the ham. But in the rectangular panel behind stands a large *crater*, liquid overflowing its rim, and surrounded by birds, peacocks and Erotes, all tokens of luxury. As close as possible to it within the horseshoe section are two shallow silver vases of the type known as saucepans or casseroles, with wreaths above them. The function of this type of vessel has been much disputed, and Levi interpreted them here as holding gravy and sauces for the meat; but their proximity to the *crater* leaves little doubt that here they are to serve the wine.[17]

[15]*Ibid.* pp. 295-304, pl. lxvi.

[16]*Ibid.* pp. 129-36, pls xxiii-iv.

[17]Cf. S. Tassinari, 'Il vasellame di bronzo', in F. Zevi (ed.), *Pompei 79* (Naples, 1979), 235; A. Carandini, 'Alcune forme bronzee conservate a Pompei e nel Museo Nazionale di Napoli', in *L'instrumentum domesticum di Ercolano e Pompei nella prima età imperiale* (*Quaderni di cultura materiale* 1) (Rome, 1977), 163-8.

FIG. 4. Mosaic from the Tomb of Mnemosyne, Antioch, showing a banquet *(Courtesy of the Department of Art and Archaeology, Princeton University)*

In these examples (which are noticeably all from the Greek East, presumably conservative in these matters), it looks as though the *crater* maintains its traditional role, as the one big vessel for serving the wine, in which we therefore assume it to have been mixed. But at Ephesus — also a city of the Greek East — it shares its prominence with another vessel.[18] This may be identified by analogy with a famous vessel of just this form from Pompeii, where a door in the side allows charcoal to be introduced, while above is a container for liquid; it is a hot-water heater (Fig. 5).[19] Another vessel from Pompeii designed for this function has an inner channel for the charcoal, the outer basin for the liquid (Fig. 6); simpler types also occur, that is, cauldrons or jars with containers for the fuel.[20]

The first type, as at Ephesus, occurs on another mosaic, from Spain again, in the midst of a display of provisions and apparatus for the banquet. This is the black-and-white frieze which ran around the edge of one side of the peristyle in a villa at Marbella, probably dating to the later part of the second century AD (Fig. 7).[21] The villa was only

[18]Above, n. 5.

[19]E. Pernice, *Gefässe und Geräte aus Bronze (Die Hellenistische Kunst in Pompeji* 4) (Berlin-Leipzig, 1925), 30-7, pl. vii.

[20]*Ibid.* p. 9, pl. ii; J. Overbeck and A. Mau, *Pompeji in seinen Gebäuden, Alterthümern und Kunstwerken,* fourth edition (Leipzig, 1884), 441-3.

[21]A. Garcia y Bellido, 'El mosaico de tema culinario de Marbella', *Hommages à Marcel Renard* 3 (Brussels, 1969), 241-6; J.M. Blazquez, *Mosaicos romanos de Córdoba, Jaén y Málaga (Corpus de Mosaicos de España* 3) (Madrid, 1981), 81-3, no. 55, figs 22-3, pls 62-6; A. Balil, 'Un bodegon en mosaico hallado en Marbella (Malaga)', *Baetica. Estudios de arte, geografía e historia* 6 (1983), 159-70.

FIG. 5. Hot-water heater from Pompeii *(After Pernice, Gefässe und Geräte aus Bronze (Berlin-Leipzig, 1925), pl. vii)*

partially excavated, and the location of the *triclinium* is not known; most parallels would suggest that it lay on the main axis opposite the entrance. The frieze would then lead from entrance to dining-room. It starts with items of bathing equipment — for example, strigils and oil-flasks; a bath was the regular prelude to a meal. At the angle, a wide-mouthed *crater*, with a ladle or strainer resting on it, introduces the display of food: set out on trays, hanging from racks, lying on plates. Various cooking equipment, some of it not easy to recognize, is interspersed with the food; so is the drinking apparatus: an amphora, *oinochoe*, another *crater* with a *cyathus*, a table with wine jug and beakers, and, towards the end of the preserved section, the hot-water heater. Sparks or embers are shown issuing from its side, leaving no doubt here of its function.

The presence of the hot-water heaters indicates a fundamental difference in the Roman way of handling wine from that of the Greeks. Texts from the late Republic onwards speak frequently of the mixing of *calda*, and, rather less often, of *frigida*, with the

FIG. 6. Hot-water heater from Pompeii *(After Pernice, Gefässe und Geräte aus Bronze (Berlin-Leipzig, 1925), pl. ii)*

wine.[22] The use of *calda* was already recognized in antiquity as a specifically Roman custom; Athenaeus (iii. 123) raises the question, whether the ancients (that is the Greeks) drank hot water at their banquets. The Greek sources that he quotes in answer refer only to drinking or using warm water by itself; none shows unequivocally that it was mixed with wine. The other typical Roman luxury, on the other hand, the use of very cold water or snow as a mix, was known to the Greeks, though the Romans undoubtedly introduced refinements. What seems to me important, however, is not so much the use of *calda* itself, as that the Roman texts repeatedly make it clear that the mixing was normally done at the guest's request and to his taste, in his own cup. I quote a few examples out of many.

[22]Cf. Dar.-Sag. 1.2 (1887), 820-1, *s.v.* 'calda'; Mau, *RE* III (1899), 1346, *s.v.* 'calda'.

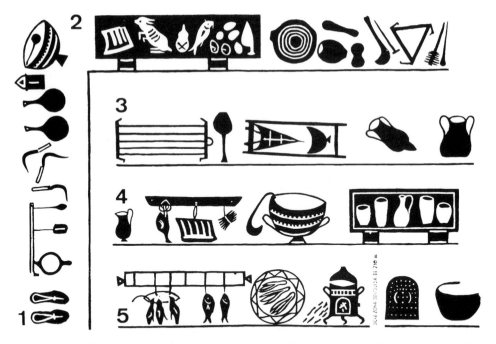

FIG. 7. Frieze of household and cooking utensils from a villa at Marbella *(After A. Garcia y Bellido, Hommages à Marcel Renard 3 (Brussels, 1969), pl. xcvi)*

Varro (*Rust.* iii. 5.15-16) describes the dining facilities in his aviary. The guests are served by a rotating table in the middle of the little lake, which conveys their food and drink to them; among its features are taps, *epitonia*, of hot and cold water, which the guests evidently operate themselves. The special circumstances here might justify unusual behaviour; but other authors imply mixing to individual taste as a normal practice. Juvenal, for instance, speaks of the poor guest ignored by the elegant page, who does not know how to mix for poor men, and will not answer his call for hot water or cold: *quando rogatus adest calidae gelidaeque minister?* (v. 63). Seneca (*Ep.* lxxviii. 23), comments that the sick man cannot mix his wine with snow, nor chip ice into the drink, which he has mixed in a capacious *scyphus, quam capaci scypho miscuit.* Or Petronius 65, where Habinnas, immediately after lying down, calls for *vinum et caldam.* There is in fact only one mention of preliminary mixing in the whole *Cena Trimalchionis*, and it is notable that it is not for the guests: in chapter 64, Trimalchio orders a *camellam grandem* (which seems to be a cheap wooden bowl) to be mixed up for the slaves. If anyone doesn't drink it, he adds, it should be poured over his head. This is not Falernian; cheap wine perhaps, or even *mulsum.*

Other indications point the same way. The notorious practice, attacked by the satirists, of the great man and his friends drinking superior wine while serving inferior to the more lowly guests, clearly implies that the wine has not been previously mixed for common consumption.[23] So probably do the proposals, of Trimalchio and of

---

[23]Juv. v. 24-37; Martial iii. 82.22-5, 9.2; Pliny, *Ep.* ii. 6.

Nasidienus to Maecenas in Horace's *Satire* ii. 8, to send the wine back and replace it with something else.[24] It may be questioned, in fact, whether the mystique of quality wine — the '*grand cru*', the named variety and vintage — does not discourage preliminary mixing.

The whole Roman practice seems in marked contrast to Greek ideals of *koinonia* and the symbolic role of the *crater*. The handbooks solve the dilemma by proposing a distinction between mixing in the cup, *during* the meal, and the *comissatio* after the meal, where, they say, the mixing is performed in the *crater* following traditional Greek custom.[25] But they do not clearly substantiate the distinction, and there seems in fact to be remarkably little Roman evidence for the latter practice. We hear nothing in Roman sources of the proportions of mixing in a *crater*, so important to the Greeks that Athenaeus devotes much of a book (x. 426-31) to discussing it. Plautus once quotes the traditional, though enigmatic, Greek saying, ἢ πέντ' ἢ τρία πῖν' ἢ μὴ τέτταρα, presumably from a Greek original, only deliberately to misunderstand it as referring to the quantity to be drunk, not the mixture (*Stich.* 708). The Roman rules for the *comissatio*, as we find them reflected in Horace, Martial, and other sources, seem to have governed the quantity of wine drunk, specifically the number of *cyathi* measured into the cup; the proportions of a mixture do not seem to have been of significance.[26]

Another difference of emphasis should also be noted. The Greeks apparently drank little during the actual meal: serious drinking begins only afterwards. With the Romans, food becomes much more important: the variety of food offered at the banquet and the elegance and complexity of its preparation are major signs of luxury in themselves. The separation between eating and drinking is correspondingly less clear; and a large proportion of the Roman references to wine refer to its use during the banquet, as an accompaniment to food. The *comissatio*, by contrast, as an independent entity, attracts very much less attention.

With all this in mind, I want to go back to Roman representations of dining and drinking, and particularly to two groups which are sufficiently numerous, and sufficiently homogeneous, to constitute a series. The first decorate the lids of a number of sarcophagi from the city of Rome, between the second and early fourth centuries AD. The banquet, always at a *stibadium* cushion on the ground, occurs here in various contexts: mythological, as the meal after the hunt of the Calydonian boar; as a hunters' picnic on hunt sarcophagi; and as a genre scene of daily life (Fig. 8).[27] In all these contexts, the preparation of the wine plays an important part, and frequently includes a scene of the heating of a cauldron on a fire. This should not be confused with the preparation of the boar's carcase, as seen on some of the Meleager sarcophagi; a cauldron may also be used for this, but both appear together at least once. Wine is

---

[24]Petron. *Sat.* 48; Hor. *Sat.* ii. 8.14-17.

[25]E.g. Marquardt-Mau, *Das Privatleben der Römer* (above, n. 3), 402; Blümner, *Die Römischen Privatalter-tümer* (above, n. 7), 333; Dar.-Sag. 1.2 (1887), 1373, *s.v.* '*comissatio*'; Mau, *RE* IV.1 (1901), 612, *s.v.* '*comissa-tio*'.

[26]Cf. above, n. 25.

[27]G. Koch, *Die Mythologischen Sarkophage* 6, *Meleager* (*Die Antiken Sarkophagreliefs* 12.6) (Berlin, 1975), 48-50, 125-9; B. Andreae, *Die Sarkophage mit Darstellungen aus dem Menschenleben* 2, *Die Römischen Jagdsarkoph-age* (*Die Antiken Sarkophagreliefs* 1.2) (Berlin, 1980), 102-3; F. Gerke, *Die Christlichen Sarkophage der Vorkonstanti-nischen Zeit* (Berlin, 1940), 110-20; N. Himmelmann, *Typologische Untersuchungen an Römischen Sarkophagreliefs des 3. und 4. Jahrhunderts n.Chr.* (Mainz am Rhein, 1973), 24-6, 57-66.

FIG. 8. Fragment of a sarcophagus lid with a picnic scene (Vatican, Museo Chiaramonti 214; Arch. Fot. XXXI.20.49) *(Courtesy of the Vatican Museums and Dr E. Cicerchia)*

sometimes shown poured from an amphora into another bowl on the ground, sometimes apparently directly from the amphora into the cauldron on the fire. This is the only indication that I know that the wine itself may have been heated, not just the water. There seems to be no sign of the traditional *crater*, unless the bowl on the ground takes its place.

The hunters' banquet might seem to be a special case; its picnic character justifies the omission of the regular *crater*. It is more surprising to find the heating of the cauldron as part of the banquet on Dionysiac sarcophagi.[28] *Craters* of traditional shape are of course present here (though we do not see the wine poured into them): as part of classic Dionysiac apparatus they could hardly be omitted. But even in this traditional context, the heating of *calda* has come to be regarded as an integral part of the sympotic scene.

My second group consists of paintings from the Roman catacombs showing the Christian meal.[29] Argument has raged over the nature of the meal represented: funerary or memorial, communal meal of the living or banquet in paradise; it seems accepted now at least that they do not represent the Eucharist. The context would nevertheless

[28]F. Matz, *Die Dionysischen Sarkophage 3* (*Die Antiken Sarkophagreliefs 4.3*) (Berlin, 1969), 328-39, esp. nos 184, pl. 205.3; 191, Beilage 87.4; 193, Beilage 86.6; and 4.2 (1968), nos 108, pl. 134.2; 152, pl. 168.2; 4.4 (1975), no. 265, pl. 284.2.

[29]Cf. E. Jastrzebowska, 'Les scènes de banquet dans les peintures et sculptures chrétiennes des IIIᵉ et IVᵉ siècles', *Recherches Augustiniennes* 14 (1979), 3-90, esp. 62-9, with references; for their significance, J. Engemann, 'Der Ehrenplatz beim antiken Sigmamahl', in *Jenseitsvorstellungen in Antike und Christentum. Gedenkschrift für Alfred Stuiber* (*JbAC* Ergänzungsband 9 (1982)), 248-50.

seem to require a greater decorum than the normal secular banquet; and indeed many either omit wine altogether or place little emphasis on it. But one series of at least eight paintings from the catacomb of Santi Pietro e Marcellino forms a group apart (Fig. 9).[30] These paintings show the guests reclining, again at the *stibadium* cushion, eating fish or, once, chicken. The serving of drink plays a prominent part: the servants bring goblets and jugs, whilst bottles or an amphora stand ready. The hot-water heater appears twice, once in a panel of its own. Inscriptions address the servants: *Irene da calda, Agape misce mi, Sabina misce.* Mixing is again clearly an individual act, even in this context where the communal sense is so important; and the greatest stress is laid upon the *calda.*

FIG. 9. Arcosolium painting from the catacomb of Santi Pietro e Marcellino, showing a *stibadium* scene with *authepsa* *(Courtesy of the Pontificia Commissione di Archeologia Sacra, Lau L45)*

The comparatively simple meals represented in the catacomb paintings or on the sarcophagi give little indication of another aspect which was crucial in more elaborate banquets: the ceremonial which surrounded the serving of wine. I can only touch on this subject, but here too, I think the illustrations can supplement the written sources, and point the way to more fruitful lines of research. I select two examples from opposite ends, chronologically, of the Roman Empire. Firstly, there is a painting from Pompeii showing an open-air banquet of Erotes; the central place is occupied by an Eros, who

[30]J. Deckers, H.R. Seeliger and G. Mietke, *Die Katakombe 'Santi Marcellino e Pietro'. Repertorium der Malereien (Roma sotteranea cristiana 6)* (Vatican City-Münster, 1987), nos 39, pp. 255-7; 45, pp. 266-70; 47, pp. 271-3; 50, pp. 278-81; 75, pp. 336-8; 76, pp. 338-40; 78, pp. 343-8. Heaters in no. 75, pls 55a, 56a, col. pl. 55; no. 76, col. pl. 76. Cf. also P.-A. Février, 'À propos du repas funéraire: culte et sociabilité', *CArch* 26 (1977), 29-45.

dances to the music of the lyre with an amphora against his shoulder (Fig. 10).[31] That
the production of food and drink could form a spectacle in its own right is clear from
many sources: the carver Carpus at Trimalchio's feast (Petron. *Sat.* 36), or the singing
cooks in Athenaeus (ix. 381F). Illustrations such as these suggest a more moderate form
of fanciful production: the presentation of the amphora before the assembled company
is accompanied by music and dance. Secondly, let us consider a miniature from a late
antique manuscript, the *Vergilius Romanus*, showing the banquet of Dido (Fig. 11).[32] Here
we do not see any of the larger vessels for wine or water, but two elegant long-haired
pages are serving the diners. One, on the left, holds a jug and a goblet, and may safely
be taken to be serving the wine. The other also holds a jug; since this must contain
something different from the first, presumably it is water, hot or cold. The two recall the
elaborate series of titles for attendants at the banquet recorded in some inscriptions: *a
cyatho, a potione, a lagona*;[33] their bearers were evidently valued for the skill and elegance
with which they manipulated the apparatus of drinking.

FIG. 10. Painting of a banquet of Erotes (Pompeii IX 3, 5) *(Photo S.
Jashemski, courtesy of W. Jashemski, from W. Jashemski, The Gardens of
Pompeii, Herculaneum, and the Villas Destroyed by Vesuvius (New Rochelle,
Caratzas Bros., 1979), fig. 153)*

[31]W. Helbig, *Wandgemälde der vom Vesuv Verschütteten Städte Campaniens* (Leipzig, 1868), 149, no. 759;
W. Jashemski, *The Gardens of Pompeii* (New Rochelle, 1979), 97, fig. 153.
[32]E. Rosenthal, *The Illuminations of the Vergilius Romanus* (Zürich, 1972), 54-8, pl. ix: fol. 100v.
[33]E.g. *CIL* VI, 1884; 8815-17; 8866; cf. Blümner, *Die Römischen Privataltertümer* (above, n. 7), 396;
Hilgers, *Lateinische Gefässnamen* (above, n. 6), 166 no. 132.

FIG. 11. Miniature of the banquet of Dido, from the *Vergilius Romanus*
(Cod. Vat. Lat. 3867, fol. 100v) *(Courtesy of the Biblioteca Apostolica Vaticana)*

My collection of material so far has been disparate, but I think it allows certain
tentative conclusions. On most of the Roman monuments drinking is presented as an
accompaniment to the meal, and usually the food is as prominent as the wine. The
service of the wine is accompanied, at grander feasts, by considerable ceremonial, from
the moment of its first production. *Crater* and hot-water heater may appear together or
separately; in the later examples, the hot-water heater is more frequent. A very few
monuments may imply preliminary mixing, but much more emphasis is placed on
pouring and mixing in the cup. It is this act and, above all, the use of *calda*, which seem
to have become the essential constituents of Roman conviviality.

18

Il Vino di Orazio: nel *modus* e contro il *modus*

ANTONIO LA PENNA

VINO E CONVITO

Orazio associa generalmente il vino al convito, cioè alla cena, più raramente ad atti rituali (libagioni, sacrifici). Dai riferimenti ad atti rituali non mi sembra si possa ricavare una fedeltà rilevante ad antiche tradizioni romane; segnalo, tuttavia, qualche accenno che si può prendere in considerazione. Il vino entra nel sacrificio al *Genius*, che Elio Lamia celebrerà in campagna, in un giorno di tempesta, quindi non adatto ai lavori della villa:

> *cras Genium mero*
> *curabis et porco bimenstri*
> *cum famulis operum solutis.*

(Orazio, *Carm.* iii. 17.13-15)

Il *Genius* era divinità romana di antichità veneranda, che si identificava, in origine, con la fecondità dell'uomo (come dimostra l'espressione *lectus genialis*), in contrapposizione con *Iuno*, la divinità corrispondente della donna; ma abbastanza presto indicò, più genericamente, la forza vitale dell'uomo, la sua capacità di godere dei piaceri elementari.[1] Il *Genius* veniva onorato con vino e fiori specialmente nel *dies natalis*, ma anche in altre occasioni, non necessariamente festive; nel caso di Lamia si tratta solo di un giorno di riposo forzato, che Orazio esorta a considerare come una buona occasione per un convito accanto al focolare. Il maialino non rientrava nel rito per il *Genius*, ma rientrava in quello per i Lari, e il *Genius* nel culto veniva talvolta associato a queste divinità della famiglia. Il culto del *Genius* è per Orazio una manifestazione tipica della sana Roma arcaica nelle sue giornate di riposo: in un quadro di quella Roma troviamo, appunto, gli agricoltori che dopo il raccolto fanno festa e onorano *Tellus* col sacrificio di un porco, Silvano col latte, il *Genius* con fiori e vino (*Epist.* ii. 1.143-4; cfr. anche *Ars P.* 209-10). Al culto dei Lari fu associato, dopo la vittoria in oriente, per una decisione del senato, anche quello del *Genius* dell'imperatore. Il salvatore, che aveva dato pace e sicurezza all'Italia e al mondo, poteva essere invocato in qualunque parte della giornata, specialmente la mattina e la sera; una preghiera particolarmente solenne, che lo associa

---

[1]Per il *Genius* rimando a K. Latte, *Römische Religionsgeschichte* (Monaco, 1960), 103-4; sul *Genius* in Orazio cfr. il commento di O. Brink al secondo libro delle *Epistulae* (Cambridge, 1982), nota a ii. 1.144.

ai Lari, gli viene rivolta durante abbondanti libagioni che si collocano nelle *secundae mensae* della cena (*Carm.* iv. 5.33-40). Seguiva la recitazione di *carmina convivalia*, che celebravano le origini troiane e le gesta di eroi romani (*Carm.* iv. 15.24-32). Specialmente questa parte del rito inquadra il tutto in un risveglio arcaizzante di antichi costumi, caratteristica ben nota dell'età augustea; l'accostamento alle invocazioni dei Dioscuri e di Ercole in Grecia (*Carm.* iv. 5.35-6) serve a legittimare il particolare culto dell'imperatore, non indica un'origine greca del rito, che ha radici salde nella più antica tradizione indigena.[2] Si tratta, però, di casi rari nella selva dei riferimenti al vino nell'opera di Orazio, riferimenti che portano generalmente al convito privo di significato religioso.

Proprio perché l'associazione del vino al convito è, in Orazio, così frequente, si acuisce l'attenzione per i casi in cui l'associazione non sussiste o suscita dei dubbi: dubbi dai quali talvolta è difficile, o impossibile, liberarsi. Qui debbo limitarmi ad alcuni casi. Alla fine dell'epodo 9 (33ss.) il poeta invita lo schiavo a portare grandi coppe di vino di Chio o di Lesbo o a versare con più misura il Cècubo, *quod fluentem nauseam coerceat*: il vino dovrebbe dissolvere le preoccupazioni e i timori, che ancora sussistono circa l'esito della battaglia di Azio. Chi colloca la situazione dell'epodo nella battaglia stessa, pensa alle coppe bevute sulla nave, come in un frammento di Archiloco (5 A D = 7 Tarditi); ma, se, come anch'io credo, Orazio è a Roma, la nausea è quella provocata dal cibo: la situazione, dunque, è quella del convito. Ma non è il caso di riprendere in quest'occasione un problema che si dibatte senza fine. Nell'epodo 13 il convito non è richiamato esplicitamente; l'unguento, la musica fanno pensare ad un convito, anzi ad una cena non parca, se l'unguento richiama il lusso degli Achemenidi; tuttavia già in un caso come questo ci si può chiedere se l'invito implichi necessariamente il banchetto. Quando Leuconoe è invitata a 'filtrare il vino' (*Carm.* i. 11.6: *vina liques*), l'invito si riferisce alla preparazione di una cena (in casa dell'etèra, o anche in casa dello stesso Orazio), o il vino servirà solo ad allietare l'incontro, la conversazione, l'amore? La sicurezza del banchetto non c'è neppure nel caso di Taliarco (*Carm.* i. 9): il vino, nella rigida giornata invernale, sarà bevuto con larghezza davanti al focolare acceso, ma non c'è il chiaro preannunzio di un convito. D'estate il vino si beve all'aperto, in luoghi ben riparati dal sole, all'ombra di alberi. L'incontro con Tindari avverrà *in reducta valle*, all'ombra, e sarà allietato dal vino di Lesbo, innocuo perché non molto forte, e dal canto e dalla musica dell'etèra, esperta di tali arti (*Carm.* ii. 17.17ss.). Nell'ode a Dellio lo sfondo è quello della natura, forse chiusa nel giardino di una ricca villa romana: un prato lontano dai rumori della gente (*in remoto gramine*); probabilmente rientrano nel paesaggio anche il pino dall'ampia ombra, il pioppo dalle foglie argentate, il rapido ruscello evocati poco dopo, elementi soliti del *locus amoenus* antico: qui si portino vino, unguenti, rose (*Carm.* ii. 3.6-16). Analogo il paesaggio nell'ode a Quinzio Irpino (solo un altro platano sostituisce il pioppo), analogo l'invito (rose, profumo, Falerno; *Carm.* ii. 11.13-20). Naturalmente anch'io sono propenso a credere che in tutti questi casi ci si appresta ad un convito; ma non mi pare futile lasciare un margine di dubbio: il termine 'simposio' lo userei con fiducia, il termine 'banchetto' esiterei ad usarlo.[3] Comunque

---

[2]Altre menzioni del vino nel contesto di cerimonie religiose in *Carm.* i. 19.15; iii. 18.5ss.

[3]Credo che una ricerca approfondita sulle affinità e differenze tra συμπόσιον, δεῖπνον, *convivium*, *cena* non sarebbe inutile. Il problema si pone anche per le rappresentazioni figurative del simposio.

due considerazioni emergono da questi casi che abbiamo affrontati per primi: la mancanza di attenzione per il cibo nel simposio, su cui tornerò tra poco; l'associazione del simposio col paesaggio, sia esso la tempesta, l'inverno, da cui il vino difende, sia il *locus amoenus* che difende dalla calura estiva.[4] E qui ci torna alla mente l'importanza che nella poesia di Orazio hanno le stagioni, in quanto scandiscono il fluire inesorabile del tempo.

LA FUNZIONE DEL CONVITO E LA FUNZIONE DEL VINO NEL CONVITO

Il convito di Orazio è la *cena* romana: ciò si vede bene dalle *Satire*: sono nella tradizione romana l'ora e la divisione del convito (*gustatio, primae mensae, secundae mensae*). Orazio conosce bene la mensa romana dei ceti più ricchi, quale si presenta ai suoi tempi, dopo quasi due secoli di progresso del lusso: una mensa molto ricca, molto varia nelle vivande, poiché può profittare, oltre che dei prodotti indigeni, di prodotti rari provenienti dalle provincie, talvolta anche lontane; una mensa che dà non poco spazio a cibi complicati. Ben poco erano servite come freno al lusso le *leges sumptuariae* del secondo e del primo secolo a.C., rivolte specialmente contro il lusso della tavola. Personalmente il poeta preferisce, com'è ben noto, la mensa parca, che non coincide, però, con la mensa misera: egli rifiuta la scelta cinica non meno della scelta voluttuaria; oltre a sentirsi poco attratto dalla mensa lussuosa, dai cibi rari, dalla crapula, egli è disgustato dalla dottrina gastronomica, che i padroni di casa ricchi e intenditori esibiscono ai loro ospiti: lo sappiamo dalla nota caricatura di Nasidieno. Tuttavia la posizione di Orazio verso il lusso della mensa non è così semplice. La satira più impegnativa sull'argomento, ii. 4, non è una caricatura né della mensa lussuosa né dell'arte gastronomica: in uno svolgimento del tema improntato ad una giocosa eleganza, ma privo di aggressività satirica, Orazio si preoccupa, sì, di evitare eccessi di raffinatezza, ma soprattutto fa molti passi avanti nella legittimazione del lusso della tavola, accogliendo un'esigenza di fondo dei ceti ricchi e decorosi del suo tempo.[5] È ovvio che ciò vale anche per i vini, tra cui quelli greci sono comunemente presenti, ma prevalgono, tuttavia, quelli italiani, specialmente del Lazio e della Campania, e tra questi alcuni, soprattutto il Cècubo, sono pregiati. Non manca qualche raro accenno all'uso di vini romani, come il Falerno, o di vini greci, come quello di Chio e quello di Cos, nella preparazione delle vivande (*Sat.* ii. 4.19, 29; 8.9, 47ss.).

Tuttavia questa tradizione romana con i suoi problemi serve solo in parte a capire il senso e il rilievo che il convito assume nella lirica e nelle epistole di Orazio. Nel costume la cena aveva assunto una funzione non priva di ambiguità: momento necessario nel

---

[4]Sulla funzione poetica, specialmente simbolica, del vino in Orazio, segnalo S. Commager, 'The function of wine in Horace's Odes', *TAPhA* 88 (1957), 68-80; per altri aspetti cfr. P.A. McKinlay, 'The wine element in Horace', *CJ* 42 (1946-7), 161-7, 229-35; R.L. Frieman, 'Wine and politics in Horace', *EMC* 16 (1972), 84-91; H. Wuilloud, 'À propos de deux bi-millénaires. La vigne et le vin dans Virgile et Horace', in *Forschungen auf dem Gebiete der Wirtschaftswissenschaft des Landbaues, Festgabe für E. Laur* (Brugg, 1937), 167-85.

[5]Su questo problema rimando al mio studio 'La legittimazione del lusso privato da Ennio a Vitruvio. Momenti, problemi, personaggi', *Maia* NS 41 (1989), 3-10 (= autori vari, Contractus e pactum. *Tipicità e libertà negoziale nell'esperienza tardo-repubblicana* (Napoli, 1990), 252-9).

ritmo della giornata, in quanto rilassamento e preparazione di nuove energie per i nuovi *negotia* (così come l'*otium* nella cultura scipionica; comunque niente di simile agli odierni detestabili costumi del *fast food* o delle colazioni di lavoro), ma nello stesso tempo rottura dei *negotia* e loro rimozione, almeno per un tempo limitato, dalla coscienza. Il secondo aspetto si era accentuato, naturalmente, col progresso del lusso; ma Orazio, che pure rifiuta decisamente la gozzoviglia, accentua ulteriormente la funzione di rottura: il convito, attraverso la pausa dei *negotia*, ha il compito di interrompere e cancellare le *curae*, sia come tensione dell'animo negli affari sia come angoscia (nel senso del greco *mérimnai*; anzi Orazio gli assegna per lo più la funzione di superare la fondamentale angoscia lucreziana dell'esistenza, acuita da una sensibilità particolare per il tempo come corsa ineluttabile e logoramento o distruzione: perciò è il vino come causa di oblio, come droga, che assume nel convito la funzione centrale. Nelle satire del secondo libro Orazio si è dilettato a dissertare di gastronomia in versi; nelle odi conviviali i cibi non vengono descritti: il convito è evocato col profumo delle rose, degli unguenti, ma soprattutto col vino. Naturalmente si deve tener conto della differenza dei generi letterari: la lirica filtra in modo diverso la realtà quotidiana: anche ad un livello non sublime, quale vuol essere per lo più quello di Orazio lirico, una descrizione delle portate, quale ricorre più volte in epigrammi di Marziale, sarebbe riuscita sconveniente; ma una ragione più sostanziale è che il vino, molto più del cibo, dà al convito la sua funzione liberatoria. Nel definire questa funzione Orazio si ispira decisamente alla lirica greca arcaica (Archiloco, Alceo, Anacreonte), e nello stesso tempo all'epicureismo: dunque le radici del senso poetico che assume la cena romana di Orazio, vanno cercate quasi tutte nella cultura greca; ma nuova, e felice, è la sintesi di motivi della lirica greca arcaica, o, talvolta, della poesia ellenistica, con la meditazione epicurea: una sintesi la cui importanza, per millenni, nella poesia europea è facile valutare.

Richiamare a questo proposito i passi opportuni mi pare superfluo, perché sono nella memoria di tutti quelli che hanno letto Orazio, magari costretti dalla scuola; tuttavia ne ricorderò alcuni fra quelli che meglio dimostrano la funzione liberatoria del convito e del vino in quanto meglio fanno sentire il senso di precarietà, l'angoscia per la mancanza di dominio sulla realtà che acuiscono il bisogno di liberazione. Incomincerò dal grande messaggio epicureo a Mecenate (*Carm.* iii. 29). Certo, è epicureo l'invito a *componere quod adest*, mettere ordine nel presente, nel breve spazio che noi possiamo controllare; ma il saggio epicureo arriva a questa conclusione fondandosi sulla piena conoscenza della natura: egli sa come la natura funziona, da dove veniamo e dove andiamo, cioè come saremo dissolti. Non di questo si occupa Orazio: oltre il breve spazio controllabile c'è la notte caliginosa in cui la divinità ci avvolge, irridendo le nostre ambizioni di eternità:

> *Prudens futuri temporis exitum*
> *caliginosa nocte premit deus*
> *ridetque, si mortalis ultra*
> *fas trepidat.*

(Orazio, *Carm.* iii. 29.29-32)

Al di là di quell'angusto cerchio tutto scorre come un fiume, che ora scende placido al mar Tirreno, ora travolge, selvaggiamente tempestoso, alberi, animali, case, con un fragore che si spande per monti e le selve (pensa alle inondazioni del Tevere). Questa tempesta, quasi alla fine della prima raccolta delle odi, ci riporta ad uno degli epodi ritenuti più antichi, al 13, che si apre con la tempesta che soffoca il cielo e la musica grandiosa e terribile del vento di Tracia sul mare e nelle selve. Il dio che ci avvolge nell'oscurità e ride *si mortalis ultra / fas trepidat*, ci fa capire meglio lo *scire nefas* con cui veniva ammonita Leuconoe; il mare dell'ode a Leuconoe è anch'esso un mare in tempesta, il Tirreno che l'inverno scaglia e infrange contro le rocce. Se teniamo conto di questi passi, risulta, forse, meno banale l'opposizione tempesta/convito con cui viene formulata l'esortazione a Munazio Planco:

> *Albus ut obscuro deterget nubila caelo*
> *saepe Notus neque parturit imbris*
> *perpetuo, sic tu sapiens finire memento*
> *tristitiam vitaeque labores*
> *molli, Plance, mero...*

(Orazio, *Carm.* i. 7.15ss.).

Dietro la metafora della tempesta emergono, forse, le turbinose vicende di Munazio Planco attraverso le guerre civili; l'accenno esplicito, comunque, va alle sue fatiche di capo militare, fra lo splendore delle insegne; i *labores* non mancheranno neppure nell'ombra fitta di Tivoli: probabilmente Orazio allude alle mansioni politiche che attendono il grande personaggio. I personaggi a cui il poeta rivolge i suoi inviti, sono angustiati dai loro *negotia*, politici o economici: sembra che nessuno svolga le sue occupazioni con serenità, letizia, entusiasmo. Mecenate è, sotto questo aspetto, un caso tipico: negli inviti a cena Orazio non giustifica l'esortazione ad afferrare i doni dell'ora presente con la morbosa inquietudine del suo carattere. Il convito e il vino sono rimedio alle *civiles curae*, che il grande personaggio sente pesare su di sé, anche quando per l'impero le preoccupazioni causate dai nemici esterni non sono affatto gravi (*Carm.* iii. 8); non l'orgoglio del potere, non la sicurezza dell'efficienza caratterizzano l'uomo di stato, ma il timore quasi affannoso (*Carm.* iii. 29.26: *Urbi sollicitus times*). I destinatari, se non sono stressati dalla politica, sono stressati dalle loro attività lucrose, come Manlio Torquato, l'importante oratore forense di *Epist.* i. 5, o l'ignoto Virgilio di *Carm.* iv. 12. Insomma l'invito al simposio e al vino raramente si stacca da un contrasto acuto con una vita affannosa (*Carm.* ii. 11.17-18: *dissipat Euhius / curas edacis*), e in questo modo s'inserisce in una meditazione lirica di carattere generale, dove si carica di una ricca funzione simbolica.

Il rilievo del vino nel simposio è sottolineato talvolta da una finezza stilistica, che era gradita a Orazio ed ai poeti augustei: la collocazione artistica del vocativo, che mira ad associare il nome del destinatario ad un motivo chiave del componimento. Un caso l'abbiamo già incontrato: Planco non è nominato all'inizio dell'ode, ma dopo diciotto versi e associato strettamente al vino: *molli, Plance, mero*. Poco diverso è il caso di Taliarco: il vocativo ricorre alla fine della seconda strofa, associato strettamente con l'anfora di vino sabino: *benignius / deprome quadrimum Sabina, / o Thaliarche, merum diota*; analogamente, ma con più luminosa grazia, il vocativo di Mecenate, all'inizio del messaggio epicureo, è circondato dalle rose del banchetto: *cum flore, Maecenas, rosarum*; il vino, però, viene subito prima: *tibi / non ante verso lene merum cado*.[6]

[6]Su questo procedimento stilistico cfr. il mio studio '... *cum flore, Maecenas, rosarum* ... Su una collocazione artistica del vocativo in poesia latina', in autori vari, *Mnemosynum. Studi in onore di Alfredo Ghiselli* (Bologna, 1989), 335-53.

IL FASCINO AMBIGUO DELL'IRRAZIONALE

A rigore, la funzione del vino in quanto cancellazione temporanea della realtà, in quanto droga, non potrebbe trovare posto in una meditazione epicurea: questa filosofia voleva dare la felicità, l'atarassia, eliminando le paure che possiedono l'uomo; ma le paure si eliminano rendendo l'uomo più lucido, dandogli la conoscenza giusta della natura e dell'animo, non procurandogli l'oblio irrazionale. Problemi di ortodossia come questo non angustiavano né Orazio né altri poeti augustei (e il non voler riconoscerlo ha portato talvolta a forzature o a discussioni tanto sottili quanto futili); il poeta, che aveva familiarità con i lirici greci e i poeti ellenistici (lirici ed epigrammisti), non si preoccupava certo di far collimare l'invito al vino come donatore di gioia e di oblio con l'etica del giardino. Ma sia l'esaltazione della vitalità sia l'oblio e il torpore, che Orazio vedeva come gli effetti fondamentali del vino (effetti ovviamente contrastanti fra loro), ponevano problemi che egli non si nascondeva. Invece che alla gioia si arrivava alla rissa. Fra le odi si distingue per vivacità quella (*Carm.* i. 27) che si apre con una scena di banchetto in cui i convitati combattono scagliandosi coppe:

> *Natis in usum laetitiae scyphis*
> *pugnare Thracum est ...*

(Orazio, *Carm.* i. 27.1-2).

I Traci sostituiscono degnamente gli Sciti nell'ode di Anacreonte (43 Diehl) che, probabilmente, suggerì a Orazio l'ammonimento iniziale: anche altrove nelle odi (i. 36.14; ii. 7.26-7) essi sono l'esempio classico dei bevitori sfrenati. Il poeta romano accentua la diversità fra la letizia del convito e la degradazione nella barbarie; ma la seconda incombe sulla prima come un pericolo non lontano (*Carm.* i. 18.9-10):

> *[...] fas atque nefas exiguo fine libidinum*
> *discernunt avidi.*

(Orazio, *Carm.* i. 18.9-10)

Dal mito e dalla poesia venivano ammonimenti a non oltrepassare la misura: l'esempio più noto era la rissa dei Centauri e dei Lapiti, che lo stesso Orazio ricorda a questo proposito nell'ode famosa che sto citando (7ss.).[7] Non è escluso che l'ammonimento venisse dall'ode di Alceo a cui Orazio rimanda col 'motto' iniziale. Le risse sono evocate come episodi soliti nei banchetti di città, in contrasto col calmo e dolce simposio che Orazio prospetta a Tindari in campagna (*Carm.* i. 17.22ss.). L'altro pericolo, quello a cui si arriva per la via dell'oblio, un pericolo a cui Orazio si sente più esposto, è evocato con la musica adatta allo scopo, all'inizio di un epodo probabilmente influenzato dall'elegia: al torpore dato dal vino è assimilata la *mollis inertia* causata dall'amore:

> *Mollis inertia cur tantam diffuderit imis*
> *oblivionem sensibus,*
> *pocula Lethaeos ut si ducentia somnos*
> *arente fauce traxerim,*
> *candide Maecenas, occidis saepe rogando [...]*

(Orazio, *Epod.* 14.1-5).

---

[7]Su *Carm.* i. 18 cfr. G. Pasquali, *Orazio lirico* (Firenze, 1920 (nuova edizione, 1964)), 1ss.; una fine analisi (ma con qualche eccesso di sottigliezza) dei motivi e dell'architettura in V. Pöschl, 'Horazens Ode an den Weingott (c. 1, 18) *Nullam Vare sacra*', *WS* NF 20 (99) (1986), 193-203; attendibile, anche se meno nuova, l'analisi di E. Römisch, 'Horaz, *Nullam, Vare, sacra ...* (c. I 18)', *AU* 20.4 (1977), 14-28.

Non per caso in questo epodo è richiamato esplicitamente Anacreonte, che soleva unire le gioie del vino e le gioie dell'*eros*.

Contro questi pericoli Orazio si difende con la sua morale della misura: l'atteggiamento è così chiaro, e così noto, che sarebbe del tutto inutile insistervi. Alla barbarie delle risse sanguinose si contrappone il *verecundus Bacchus* (*Carm.* i. 27.3-4); nell'ode a Varo l'ammonimento mira a che, nell'accogliere i doni di Bacco, non si saltino i limiti del *modicus Liber* (*Carm.* i. 18.7). Ma l'atteggiamento di Orazio verso il dio del vino e dell'estasi è complicato e ambiguo. Si ricorderà che nell'ode a Varo l'ammonimento ad evitare i pericoli in cui fa precipitare l'uso eccessivo del vino, egoismo cieco, vana superbia, violazione della *fides*, fa tutt'uno con un senso di paura di fronte ai riti misterici con cui il dio viene adorato e che sono evocati con l'agitazione del tirso, la musica dei corni e dei timpani; Pasquali, limitando la presenza di Alceo, mise decisamente l'accento su questo motivo dell'ode e presuppone, non senza ragione, l'esperienza di riti dionisiaci praticati a Roma. La paura non porta, nell'ode a Varo, a un divieto rigoroso, ma Orazio insiste sulla cautela, che è quasi un'astensione. Altrove, però, l'esperienza dell'estasi dionisiaca lo affascina; certo, nei casi che si possono segnalare, il dio misterioso è quello della poesia, non quello del vino, ma i due aspetti si connettono nell'esperienza dell'ebbrezza, sentita esplicitamente come esperienza dell'irrazionale. L'estasi dionisiaca di Orazio si caratterizza come mescolanza di entusiasmo e di paura:

> *Euhoe! recenti mens trepidat metu*
> *plenoque Bacchi pectore turbidum*
> *laetatur. Euhoe! parce, Liber,*
> *parce gravi metuende thyrso*

> (Orazio, *Carm.* ii. 19.5-8).

Non voglio insistere su questa visione di Bacco *in remotis ... rupibus*, perché la sua evocazione e i sentimenti di gioia e di paura sono alleggeriti, mi sembra, da un tono elegantemente giocoso.[8] Ma non direi lo stesso della bellissima ode sull'altro invasamento bacchico, preludio alla nuova poesia in onore di Augusto (*Carm.* iii. 25). L'entusiasmo per la nuova esperienza poetica è accostato allo stupore della Baccante davanti al paesaggio della Tracia candida di neve, toccata solo da piede barbaro; ma l'entusiasmo è nello stesso tempo trepidazione, paura: *Dulce periculum est* [...] *sequi deum* (*Carm.* iii. 25.17-18).[9] Uno stato d'animo simile, anche se l'ambiguità e il contrasto sono attenuati, prende il poeta al rivelarsi della Musa all'inizio della quarta ode romana: *amabilis insania* (*Carm.* iii. 4.5-6). Lo stato d'animo e l'atteggiamento di Orazio davanti all'estasi dionisiaca non sono certo isolati nella cultura latina del tempo, anzi ci sono chiare affinità con un atteggiamento diffuso, alla fine della repubblica e nell'età

---

[8] L'interpretazione del tono, però, è discussa; un'interpretazione del tono come serio e sublime è sostenuta decisamente, dopo molti altri, da V. Pöschl, 'Die Dionysosode des Horaz (c. 2, 19)', *Hermes* 101 (1973), 208-30, utile anche per una dossografia sulla questione. La finezza critica del Pöschl è stata da me più volte riconosciuta; ma egli soffre di una certa tendenza dei professori tedeschi a prendere tutto sul serio (insigne il caso di H. Fränkel come interprete di Ovidio). Wilamowitz notò il tono ironico; si è detto talvolta che il grande filologo fosse '*geschmacklos*' (in effetti egli era talvolta freddo e pedante di fronte all'alta poesia); ma da questo caso si vede che aveva più gusto dei latinisti tedeschi venuti dopo.

[9] Su quest'ode rimando al mio studio 'Estasi dionisiaca e poetica callimachea', in autori vari, *Studi in onore di Vittorio De Falco* (Napoli, 1971), 229ss.

augustea, verso culti orgiastici: il fascino è irresistibile, ma se ne ha paura, anche da parte di scrittori più aperti di Orazio all'esperienza religiosa. Senza dubbio l'*Attis* di Catullo è dominato dal fascino di un'esperienza tormentosa di furore e languore, la musica esotica dei timpani e dei cimbali è evocata in un metro che ai lettori romani doveva apparire un'audace novità; ma come finisce il carme? Con un'invocazione alla Grande Madre perché altri, non il poeta romano, siano posseduti da quel furore:

[...] *procul a mea tuos sit furor omnis, era, domo;*
alios age incitatos, alios age rabidos.

(Catullo, *Attis* 92-3)

Non c'è bisogno di ricordare, dal poemetto di Arianna, il pezzo sulla danza selvaggia e la musica del coro al seguito di Bacco, musica che è un turbine di suoni cupi ed acuti, timpani e cimbali, corni e flauti (64, 254-64). Sono evidenti, comunque si debbano spiegare, e ben note le affinità di questo pezzo con l'evocazione del culto di Cibele da parte di Lucrezio (ii. 600-43): la musica è press'a poco la stessa; più spaventoso è il corteo, qui identificato con i Cureti, un coro di danzanti in armi, inondati e inebriati dal sangue. L'attrattiva dello spettacolo è innegabile, e non è certo per caso che Lucrezio vi insiste così a lungo; ma nell'evocazione domina insieme un senso di repellenza e di orrore; atterrite sono le folle delle città attraverso cui passa questo corteo frenetico, intorno alla statua severa e muta della dea. In confronto è molto meno truce, benché stimolato da Aletto, il coro bacchico guidato da Amata nel settimo libro dell'*Eneide* (385-405): chiome al vento in danze frenetiche, tremuli ululati, tirsi agitati; in mezzo la regina, dagli occhi macchiati di sangue, che innalza una grande torcia di pino come torcia nuziale. Qui il senso di paura che incute di per sé il coro dionisiaco con il suo furore, con i suoi ululati, è accentuato dalla particolare circostanza, che fa di quell'orgia la parvenza di un'ispirazione infernale. Da Catullo a Virgilio, in misura diversa, ebbrezza e paura si mescolano in una persistente ambiguità.[10]

DULCE MIHI FURERE

Un filo essenziale che si può rintracciare nella meditazione di Orazio, è la tendenza a relativizzare la propria morale, cioè a non considerare mai la propria scelta, e, quindi, i valori su cui si fonda, come l'unica giusta, a rifiutarsi di imporla agli altri; si sa quanto sia vivo nelle *Epistole* il bisogno di una *virtus* certa e stabile; ma *insani sapiens nomen ferat, aequos iniqui, / ultra quam satis est virtutem si petat ipsam* (*Epist.* i. 6.15-16). La norma del *modus* è quella a cui Orazio, negli ondeggiamenti tra una filosofia e l'altra, resta più fedele; ma proprio Dioniso è il dio che più lo tenta a rompere la norma sovrana: proprio nel convito e nel piacere del vino, che, come abbiamo visto, meglio assume su di sé la funzione del convito, vi sono occasioni in cui si può, o addirittura si deve, andare oltre il *modus*.

[10]Naturalmente a questo proposito va richiamata la ben nota teoria del 'numinoso', elaborata da Rudolph Otto, in cui terrore per il *mysterium tremendum* e attrazione del *mysterium fascinans* sono compresenti. L'ambiguità è, per Otto, di ogni autentica esperienza religiosa; ma nella religione più propriamente romana, prima di questi culti da me segnalati, non si avverte: non è un caso che Otto non si riferisca a religione romana.

L'invito a bere è impetuoso, come uno scoppio di gioia, quando arriva la notizia della morte di Cleopatra e della definitiva vittoria in oriente. Alceo offriva uno spunto incomparabile per l'espressione adatta a quella situazione; ma Orazio, con felicità perfetta, trovò il modo di essere fedele, nel 'motto' iniziale, ad Alceo e di richiamare nello stesso tempo l'inizio dell'epodo in cui aveva cantato l'attesa del banchetto per la vittoria, da festeggiare nel palazzo di Mecenate: alla domanda 'Quando potrò bere il Cècubo riposto per festeggiare la vittoria di Cesare?' si risponde ora: 'Ora è il momento di bere'. La situazione dell'ode per la morte di Cleopatra è, probabilmente, una festa privata in concomitanza con cerimonie pubbliche. È difficile immaginare una situazione di tripudio più eccezionale. La danza sarà più sfrenata del solito (*pede libero*); le vivande saranno sontuose, degne dei banchetti dei Salii; il vino sarà il Cècubo, cioè il vino romano più pregiato, e sarà di antichità rispettabile; ma proprio riguardo al vino un'esortazione esplicita a rompere la misura non c'è, e si nota come l'invito a bere sia più temperato rispetto alle espressioni forti di Alceo (*methysthen*, *pros bian*). Appaiono, invece, in quest'ode, gli effetti funesti del vino: il *furor* di Cleopatra è quello di una mente sconvolta dal vino mareotico; dietro la regina ebbra il lettore vedeva emergere l'uomo dell'orgia, della crapula, della vergognosa ubriachezza, il non nominato Antonio; l'allusione alla propaganda di Ottaviano contro Antonio negli anni fra la rottura dei rapporti e la fine della guerra d'oriente, propaganda in cui il nuovo Dioniso veniva accusato e deriso come un ubriacone, è probabile. Su di essa non m'intratterrò perché è ben nota, ma in una trattazione sul vino in età augustea va segnalata; può darsi che un'eco si debba avvertire anche nell'ode a Varo (fra le conseguenze dell'ubriachezza appare la *tollens vacuum plus nimio gloria verticem*), ma è meglio essere prudenti nella caccia ai sottintesi.

L'esortazione che non compare esplicita nell'ode per la vittoria d'oriente, è chiara, comunque, in altre occasioni festive. Non per caso due di queste feste sono celebrate per il ritorno di amici da terre lontane, dopo vicende più o meno pericolose (sia il carattere del rito sia il genere di componimento sono stati illustrati adeguatamente dai commentatori). Quando Numida, l'amico fraterno di Elio Lamia, torna dalla Spagna (probabilmente è stato al seguito di Augusto nella campagna del 27-25 a.C.), un vitello viene sacrificato per ringraziare gli dèi e al sacrificio segue il banchetto (*Carm.* i. 36). La prima raccomandazione è di bere senza misura: *neu promptae modus amphorae*; in questo caso anche la dismisura barbarica dei Traci è permessa. Anche qui la danza sfrenata *morem in Salium*. I desideri dell'*eros*, i cui piaceri raramente mancano nel convito greco e romano (io non ne ho trattato perché l'associazione è ben nota), trovano qui nella cortigiana Damalis uno stimolo ardente e implacabile: qualche cosa di diverso dalla *decens Venus* di altri conviti. Molto diversa nello svolgimento l'ode per il ritorno di Pompeo Varo, il compagno d'armi della giovinezza (*Carm.* ii. 7), ma vi ritorna con chiarezza il salto oltre il limite del *modus*. La parte maggiore dell'ode è la rievocazione del passato lontano: le lunghe cene, ma soprattutto la lunga tempesta delle guerre civili. Ora il vino non dona solo l'oblio dei *negotia*: dona l'oblio di tutta una vita e il dono è da accogliere senza risparmio:

> oblivioso levia Massico
> ciboria exple, funde capacibus
> unguenta de conchis.

                                                                      (Orazio, *Carm.* ii. 7. 21-3)

I suoni sono scelti in funzione della musica suadente dell'oblio. Le porte del *furor* barbarico vengono aperte e l'irrazionale dionisiaco irrompe con la sua violenza fascinosa:

Non ego sanius
bacchabor Edonis: recepto
dulce mihi furere est amico.

(Orazio, *Carm.* ii. 7.26-8)

Una traccia, tuttavia, dell'ambiguità dell'esperienza dionisiaca, di cui ho parlato poco fa, persiste nell'espressione quasi ossimorica *dulce furere*, che richiama il *dulce periculum* di *Carm.* iii. 25.18 e a cui si può accostare il *lene tormentum* di *Carm.* iii. 21.13. Più tardi la violazione della misura viene giustificata anche in occasioni meno straordinarie. Nella lettera con cui viene invitato a cena Manlio Torquato, pazzo viene considerato non chi gode dei piaceri del convito e del vino, ma chi risparmia per l'erede; preferibile, semmai, uscire dai limiti della saggezza solita nell'abbandonarsi ai piaceri della mensa:

potare et spargere flores
incipiam, patiarque vel inconsultus haberi.

(Orazio, *Epist.* i. 5.14-15)

Sia pure in tono minore rispetto ad altre odi, l'esortazione a non costringersi entro i limiti della saggezza chiude l'invito a cena rivolto, verso l'inizio della primavera, all'ignoto Virgilio:

misce stultitiam consiliis brevem:
dulce est desipere in loco.

(Orazio, *Carm.* iv. 12.27-8)

L'avvertimento *in loco* non è superfluo: aprire le porte all'irrazionale si può, o si deve, solo in determinate e limitate occasioni: la *stultitia brevis* non deve diventare lunga; l'invasione del furore barbarico si addice solo ad occasioni straordinarie, come il ritorno di un amico che riemerge dalle tempeste del passato. Comunque c'era nel lucano e romano Orazio un fondo di vitalità più vicino alla gioia dei lirici greci che alla morigerata e tristemente serena saggezza di Epicuro, e in quella persistente forza vitale si nascondeva una tentazione contro la saggezza e la misura.

GLI ELOGI DEL VINO

La funzione liberatoria del vino è confermata dai due elogi che al vino Orazio ha dedicati nelle *Odi* (iii. 21) e nelle *Epistole* (i. 5.16-20); ma in questi elogi compaiono anche altri motivi, e su questi vorrei fermarmi un momento prima di finire, tralasciando molti problemi, del resto in gran parte ben risolti, relativi alla composizione, cioè alla parentela con la poesia religiosa, ed ai rapporti con gli svolgimenti anteriori nella lirica e nell'epigramma greco, da Alceo, Pindaro, Bacchilide, a Posidippo ed altri epigrammisti.[11] Nei due elogi non manca la funzione di liberare dagli affanni (cfr. specialmente

[11]Su *Carm.* iii. 21 le classiche trattazioni di Norden e Pasquali sono ben note; mi limito a segnalare studi recenti: J.N. Grant, 'The wine jar as lover in Horace, *C.* 3.21', *CJ* 73 (1977), 22-6, dove l'interpretazione dell'ode come parodia della poesia erotica è alquanto forzata; E. Dont, 'Horaz *C.* iii 21 und die Gattung des Dinggedichts', in P. Händel e W. Meid (edd.), *Festschrift für R. Muth zum 65. Geburtstag am 1. Januar 1981 Dargebracht von Freuden und Kollegen* (Innsbruck, 1983), 89-93; lo studio di I. Borzsáck, '*O nata mecum consule Mantw* ... (Zu Horaz *C.* iii 21)', *ACD* 12 (1976), 47-52, riguarda la fortuna dell'ode.

Epist. i. 5.18: *sollicitis animis onus eximit*); in ambedue è lodata la funzione di rendere l'uomo trasparente, di scoprirne affanni e segreti, di *operta recludere* (*Carm.* iii. 21.14-16; *Epist.* i. 5.16); il concetto appariva già nell'ode a Varo, ma come un pericolo: la rivelazione dei segreti può essere un tradimento della *fides* (*Carm.* i. 18.16). Altro motivo di elogio, svolto specialmente nell'epistola, è che il vino non solo cancella con l'oblio una realtà, specialmente la miseria, ma ne crea, nella speranza o nell'illusione, un'altra più bella; tuttavia Orazio non insiste molto su questo motivo, svolto splendidamente da Pindaro e Bacchilide e ripetuto da epigrammisti di età ellenistica e romana;[12] opportunamente è stato ricordato che il motivo fu svolto nel *Symposium* di Mecenate e che in questo dialogo questa ragione di elogio del vino veniva argomentata da Messalla, il destinatario dell'inno oraziano all'anfora: dunque si tratta di un tema d'attualità nei circoli letterari del tempo. Altra ragione di lode celebrata da Orazio, in particolare nell'ode, è che il vino corregge in modo positivo il carattere ispido, duro, severo del filosofo; dice di Messalla:

Non ille, quamquam Socraticis madet
sermonibus, te negleget horridus:
narratur et prisci Catonis
saepe mero caluisse virtus.

Tu lene tormentum ingenio admoves
plerumque duro...

(Orazio, *Carm.* iii. 21.9-14).

Dell'uso, dell'utilità, dei pericoli del vino non avevano mancato di occuparsi i filosofi; più degli altri, a quanto pare, gli stoici, e con orientamenti un po' diversi tra loro; le dispute stoiche offrirono l'appiglio anche ad esercizi retorici, che si svolsero, forse, anche ai tempi di Orazio o in tempi non lontani.[13] Una legittimazione di un uso non

[12]Orazio svolge brevemente l'elogio del vino anche in *Epist.* i. 15.18-21 (il vino scaccia gli affanni, dà speranza e facondia, ringiovanisce e dà vigore per l'*eros*). Nella sua brillante introduzione al convegno e questo libro il collega Murray ha citato l'elogio del vino come la cosa più forte di tutte che ricorre in uno dei testi apocrifi dell'Antico Testamento, il terzo libro di Ezra (3.17-24). Questo libro ci è conservato solo in greco, ma il testo greco è, con tutta probabilità, traduzione di un testo aramaico o ebraico; la traduzione greca si colloca probabilmente nella seconda metà del secondo secolo a.C. L'elogio del vino ricorre al primo posto in una specie di gara fra tre giovani paggi di Dario (il secondo elogia la forza del re, il terzo la forza della donna e, in un secondo momento, quella insuperabile della verità). La gara di sapienza, motivo non raro in racconti orientali, pare un'aggiunta posteriore al complesso del racconto; ed è probabile che l'elogio della verità sia un'innovazione rispetto allo schema originario della gara che l'autore trovava in tradizioni orientali. Per i difficili problemi che pone il terzo libro di Ezra rimando all'approfondita introduzione che Paolo Sacchi ha premessa alla traduzione, nella raccolta di *Apocrifi dell'Antico Testamento* (Torino, 1981) da lui curata. Nell'elogio del vino l'affinità con i passi di Pindaro e Bacchilide è evidente: il vino sconvolge la mente; dà illusione di ricchezza e di potenza; fa dimenticare dolori e colpe; ma porta anche alla rissa e al delitto. Se non i lirici direttamente, l'autore avrà tenuto presente una rielaborazione ellenistica del *topos*; risalire ad una fonte orientale più antica di Pindaro e di Bacchilide non è assurdo, ma, tuttavia, rischioso. Nella lunghissima storia del motivo nelle letterature moderne il posto d'onore spetta a Baudelaire; echi diretti, e molto filtrati, di Orazio si possono supporre almeno in due delle sue poesie sul vino, *Le vin du chiffonnier* e *Le vin du solitaire*, che è un'allocuzione alla *bouteille profonde*.

[13]Sulla teoria storica relativa all'ubriachezza, cfr. M. Pohlenz, *La Stoa. Storia di un movimento spirituale* I (trad. dal tedesco) (Firenze, 1967), 259 n. 10. Temo che non esista una trattazione adeguata sull'argomento.

strettamente parco del vino, specialmente del vino puro (*akratos*), che, come si sa, i Greci bevevano solo eccezionalmente, non si poteva trovare negli stoici più antichi. Zenone non ammetteva che il saggio potesse ubriacarsi (*SVF* i. 229); Crisippo distingueva nettamente il bere vino (*oinousthai*), concesso anche allo *spoudaios aner*, dall'ubriacarsi (*methysthai*), che porta all'umor nero o alla stoltezza nell'azione e nella parola (*SVF* iii. 643, 644); Cleante riteneva che l'ubriachezza non potesse influire sulle salde conoscenze del saggio (*SVF* i. 229). Ma di Zenone, il quale pure sentiva schifo per l'ubriachezza di Antigono (*SVF* i. 289), si raccontava che non sempre fosse moderato nel bere; essendogli stato chiesto perché non si frenasse abbastanza, avrebbe risposto: 'Anche i lupini, che sono amari, bagnati si addolciscono' (Diogene Laerzio vii. 1.5 = *SVF* i. 1; cfr. le altre testimonianze date dal von Arnim insieme con questo passo). Crisippo qualche volta, dopo aver bevuto, non si reggeva bene sulle gambe, ma la sua schiava diceva: 'Di Crisippo sono ubriache solo le gambe' (*SVF* ii. 7 da Diogene Laerzio). Perseo, che frequentava le corti, usava più indulgenza verso il *kalos kagathos* che si ubriacava (*SVF* i. 451). In tempi più vicini ad Orazio si contrapponevano, probabilmente anche in ambienti stoici, la tesi di chi non ammetteva affatto l'ebbrezza (*methe*) per il saggio, e la tesi di chi ammetteva che ci fosse una *methe* non più nociva dell'*oinousthai*, che si collocava al di qua della stoltezza. Del dibattito possiamo farci un'idea grazie a due opere di Filone di Alessandria, probabilmente già nato prima che Orazio morisse: l'opera *Sull'ubriachezza* (περὶ μέθης) e specialmente quella *Sul lavoro di Noè come piantatore*.[14] Uno degli argomenti usati per dimostrare che la μέθη non è indecente per lo *spoudaios aner* è che essa addolcisce l'aspetto truce e austero del saggio. Cito qualche punto di questa argomentazione: 'Il saggio, quando ha bevuto, diviene più piacevole di se stesso quando era sobrio ... Inoltre bisogna aggiungere che l'aspetto della saggezza non è triste e severo, ma, al contrario, lieto e sereno, pieno di gioia e di allegria; e da questi sentimenti si fu indotti spesso a giocare e celiare non senza grazia: tale gioco si armonizza pienamente con la gravità e la serietà come in una lira ben accordata suoni contrari si fondono in una sola melodia' (*Sul lavoro di Noè come piantatore*, 167-8). Un esempio eccellente di tale armonia è, per il dotto ebreo, Mosé. Dunque è evidente che il saggio si ubriacherà (*methysthesetai*), giacché l'ubriachezza forma il carattere e gli dà rilassamento e semplicità. E viene spiegato che il vino puro tende e rafforza le qualità insite nell'individuo, siano esse buone o cattive: quindi anche la virtù dell'uomo giusto (170-1).[15] In base ad una teoria come questa si può capire meglio come la *virtus* di Catone si scaldasse col vino puro. Dell'amore di Catone per il vino non abbiamo indizi consistenti, ma la tradizione doveva esistere al tempo di Orazio (*narratur*), e anch'io credo che si tratti di Catone il Censore, non dell'Uticense (ma non sarebbe fruttuoso riprendere qui il problema): per Orazio, come per Cicerone, l'antico grande personaggio romano non era autorità morale inferiore a quella di Zenone o di Crisippo.

---

[14]Sulle fonti dei due opuscoli di Filone rimando alla bibliografia segnalata nella nota citata del Pohlenz e nell'edizione di Filone della collezione Loeb, iii (Londra, 1930), trad. di F.H. Colson e G.H. Whitaker, p. 209 nota *a*. Sul problema occorrerebbe un'indagine a parte, che non mi sono proposta.

[15]Alla fine dell'opuscolo *Il lavoro di Noè come piantatore* è perduta la replica alla difesa del vino, cioè l'attacco contro l'uso del vino, a cui poteva fornire molti argomenti lo stoicismo più antico; di questi argomenti possiamo farci un'idea da Sen. *Ep.* 83.8-27; cfr. anche lo stesso Filone, *Sull'ubriachezza*, spec. 138-53.

A questa funzione del vino rivendicata da alcuni filosofi Orazio è restato fedele, come abbiamo visto, anche nella prima raccolta delle epistole; ma non ha rivendicato la funzione del vino come ispiratore di poesia. Tuttavia la caricatura dei poeti che, forti dell'autorità di Cratino e di Ennio, puzzano di vino fin dal mattino (*Epist.* i. 19.1ss.), va collocata nel suo contesto, che è la polemica contro il gregge degli imitatori servili: non basta ubriacarsi per diventare poeti: ciò non significa bandire Dioniso dal regno della poesia. D'altra parte per Orazio l'esperienza positiva dell'entusiasmo dionisiaco era connessa con la sublimità della poesia civile; dopo la prima raccolta di liriche egli è convinto che non è quella la via giusta per la sua vocazione. Della raccomandazione data nell'*Ars Poetica* (412ss.) ai giovani di faticare e sudare e astenersi *venere et vino* non si deve sopravvalutare l'importanza, perché si riferisce, appunto, al periodo di formazione; d'altra parte, però, è noto che nella poetica Orazio si preoccupa molto più dell'*ars* che dell'*ingenium*. La maturità lo ha portato ad una più chiara coscienza della propria vocazione; non è escluso che, come non raramente accade, una decisa scelta abbia comportato anche la mortificazione di una parte vitale di sé. Comunque, per molte ragioni, forse anche perché infastidito dall'inclinazione di certi giovani per la poesia sublime, pindarica o epica, egli ha cercato di bandire il *furor* dal regno delle Muse: *furere* è bello e giusto in certe occasioni; ma la poesia, per Orazio, richiede freno dei sentimenti e lucidità di visione e di elaborazione. Nell'ultima lirica di Orazio ci sono momenti alti, come, per esempio, in *Diffugere nives*; ma è lirica che nasce da una coscienza più lucida dei limiti che all'uomo pone la necessità della natura, non da nuove speranze o illusioni o invasamenti.

LA SCOPERTA POETICA DEI VINI ITALIANI

Richiamo ancora una volta la diversità di raffigurazione del convito fra le satire e le odi: nella lirica l'attenzione ai cibi scompare. La differenza di genere letterario non spiega tutto: nelle epistole il convito appare molto meno: quando appare, il posto dominante è dato ancora al vino: sono menzionati i fiori, la *munda supellex*, non i cibi: una prova eloquente è nell'invito a Manlio Torquato (*Epist.* i. 5). Nella lirica il vino, che, ripeto, quasi assume su di sé tutta la funzione liberatoria del convito, compare con le sue varietà locali. Non direi che l'indicazione delle etichette (*Caecubum, Falernum, Massicum, Chium, Lesbium,* ecc.) vada assimilata all'uso degli epiteti nella poesia elevata; penso, piuttosto, che essa rientri in quella patina di quotidianità con cui Orazio nelle odi limita il sublime; e mi pare che ciò sia confermato dalle indicazioni dell'annata nel caso di vini più o meno vecchi.

Nella *Satira* i. 10 Orazio mette in ridicolo l'uso gratuito e affettato di grecismi nella lingua; obietta l'immaginario interlocutore:

At sermo lingua concinnus utraque
suavior, ut Chio nota si commixta Falerni est.

(Orazio, Sat. i. 10.23-4)

Verso la fine della repubblica vini greci erano usati comunemente, dai ceti ricchi, insieme con quelli romani. Una trattazione tecnica sui vini di Orazio non rientra affatto nei miei propositi; del resto niente saprei aggiungere a quanto è noto dai manuali;[16] ma alcune riflessioni sui vini da lui menzionati sono utili, io credo, per capire un fine che egli si è proposto riguardo ai vini romani.

Si osserva, innanzitutto, l'emarginazione dei vini greci. Il più menzionato e il più pregiato fra questi è il vino di Chio;[17] si tratta di sei menzioni in tutto; un paio di volte è menzionato quello di Coo, un paio di volte il vino lesbio:[18] tutto qui. È interessante anche constatare come queste menzioni sono distribuite nelle opere: il vino di Chio ricorre quattro volte nelle *Satire*, una volta sola nelle *Odi* (iii. 19.5); nelle *Satire* ricorrono le menzioni del vino di Coo (ii. 4.29; ii. 8.9); il vino di Lesbo è nominato in un *Epodo* (ix. 34) e in un'*Ode* (i. 17.21). I vini italiani o, più precisamente, i vini del Lazio e della Campania (fuori di queste regioni credo che si collochi solo il vino di Taranto in *Carm.* ii. 6.18-20), prevalgono chiaramente. Il re dei vini pare il Cècubo; non per caso le menzioni, eccetto una, cadono negli epodi e nelle odi;[19] ma il buon vino più comunemente usato è il Falerno, e il poeta gli rende alti onori;[20] altro vino da lui onorato è il Massico;[21] a distanza si pongono altri vini menzionati qua e là, provenienti sempre da Lazio e Campania (Tivoli, Alba, Sabina, Cales, Formia, Sorrento).[22] Sulla scelta delle annate è prudente non azzardare congetture. Si nota una convergenza delle date verso l'anno di nascita o gli anni dell'infanzia del poeta: 66 a.C. (consolato di Volcacio Tullo, benché non si possa escludere con sicurezza il console del 33 a.C.: *Carm.* iii. 8.12), 65 a.C. (consolato di Manlio Torquato: *Epist.* xiii. 6; *Carm.* iii. 21.1); 59 a.C. (consolato di Bibulo, forse scelto per il nome: *Carm.* iii. 19.5); 26 a.C. (consolato di Statilio Tauro: *Epist.* i. 4.4). C'è una giocosa solennità nel proclamare l'etichetta, ma soprattutto un accostamento all'uso quotidiano del convito. In un caso, comunque, la ragione della scelta è chiara: il 65 è l'anno della nascita del poeta (*O nata mecum consule Manlio*), e il vino diventa qualche cosa di simile al *Genius* della sua vita. Ma non è per queste considerazioni frivole che ho voluto soffermarmi su questo aspetto della presenza del vino in Orazio: ciò che vorrei sottolineare è piuttosto la funzione che queste indicazioni hanno nell'accentuare il colore romano in una poesia conviviale le cui radici greche erano evidenti. Probabilmente c'è di più: quasi una rivendicazione 'nazionale' del prestigio dei vini laziali e campani. Ennio negli *Hedyphagetica*, scostandosi dal suo *auctor* Archestrato di Gela, dava un posto d'onore, nella cucina, ai pesci della Magna Grecia; ora siamo ben al di là di quei timidi passi: Orazio vuol dare ai vini romani, nel

---

[16]Rimando al alcune trattazioni sui vini antichi: R. Billiard, *La vigne dans l'antiquité* (Lione, 1913); F. von Bassermann-Jordan, *Geschichte des Weinbaus* (Francoforte, 1923); C. Seltman, *Wine in the Ancient World* (Londra, 1957); per il mondo romano a P. Remark, *Der Weinbau im Römerreich* (Monaco, 1927), e a J. André, *L'alimentation et la cuisine à Rome* (Parigi, 1981), 162-71. Da Orazio si ricava anche qualche indicazione utile sull'importanza della vigna e dei vini nella ricchezza: *Epod.* iv. 13; *Carm.* i. 31.9ss.; ii. 14.25-6; iii. 1.29.

[17]*Epod.* ix. 34; *Sat.* i. 10.24; ii. 3.115; ii. 8.15, 48; *Carm.* iii. 19.5.

[18]Dall'isola di Lesbo, precisamente da Metimna, proviene anche un'uva pregiata (*Sat.* ii. 8.50).

[19]*Epod.* ix. 1.9, 36; *Carm.* i. 20.9; 37.5; ii. 14.25ss.; iii. 28.3.

[20]*Sat.* i. 10.24; ii. 2.15; 4.19; 4.24; 4.55; 8.16; *Carm.* i. 20.10; 27.10; ii. 3.8; 6.19-20; 11.19; iii. 1.43; *Epist.* i. 14.34.

[21]*Sat.* ii. 4.51; *Carm.* i. 1.19; ii. 7.21; iii. 21.5.

[22]Per Tivoli, cfr. *Carm.* i. 18.1-2; per Alba, *Sat.* ii. 8.16; *Carm.* iv. 11.1-2 (l'uva in *Sat.* ii. 4.72); per la Sabina, *Carm.* i. 9.7-8; 20.1; per Cales, *Carm.* i. 20.9; 31.9; iv. 12.14; per Formia, *Carm.* i. 20.11; per Sorrento, *Sat.* ii. 4.55; si aggiunga la zona fra Minturno, alla foce del Liri, e l'odierna Mondragone (Petrinum), indicata in *Epist.* i. 5.4-5.

regno delle Muse, un posto non meno prestigioso di quello che i poeti greci avevano dato ai loro vini: si tratta, insomma, di una consacrazione poetica. La fama del Cècubo o del Falerno per due millenni dimostra con evidenza che il poeta romano conseguì pienamente il suo scopo.

* * *

'Intervento' by Michael C.J. Putnam: Thoughts on Horatian modus

I would like to pursue for a few minutes the notion Professor La Penna so nicely outlines of the *convivium* as a segment of *otium* demarcated between the demands of *negotia*, of 'security' between oppressions of *curae*. This centrality works in many ways, both literal and figurative. The *convivium* is usually at night and indoors, a circumscribed event in a private setting apart from the public responsibilities which the day brings. Horace also regularly offers wine to his addressees during daylight hours, and outdoors. In this case, as we snatch an instant of rest *solido de die* (in the phrase of the initial ode), shade is essential to protect the symposiasts from the sun's glare. But just as the brilliance of the heavens offers analogy for the trials of daily reality, so the day is metonymic for life itself and the *convivium* becomes a moment that not only prepares us for sleep and for on-going existence but also sequesters us briefly from that final care, death. In good Epicurean fashion it emphasizes presentness in contrast both to what has happened and to what might be in store.

This notion in Horace of wine-drinking as a time apart brings with it a series of creative contradictions. The *convivium* offers us an occasion of forgetting, of putting aside remembrance of past trials or future problems, but it also provides opportunity for freedom in which the mind becomes more supple in its thinking and in which the secrets of the wise are unlocked and open discourse is fostered. Yet a paradox lies here, for Horace's *convivium* has aspects of a cult refuge or even a prison where matters are locked as well as unlocked. It is the place where the initiates keep their mysteries intact and where fidelity is a paramount virtue and trust essential.

Horace, though he often puts the matter lightly, takes this idea of ritual celebration very seriously. The *deductio* of the wine jug in procession, subject of *Carm.* iii. 21, is one instance. *Carm.* iii. 8 — *Martiis caelebs* — offers another example. Here the bachelor poet invites his patron to celebrate the Matronalia whose major festivity took place in the temple of Juno Lucina on Maecenas's Esquiline. But Maecenas, though he is *docte sermones utriusque linguae* (5), learned in the λόγοι of both Greek and Latin, able to converse wisely in two tongues, does not understand. Horace alone can initiate him into the special symbolism involved.

The poet was once saved from death on 1 March, and therefore in a sense is reborn on the feast of Juno the Light-Giver. But this will also be an occasion from which the *profani*, uninitiates such as Uproar and Rage, will be prohibited — *procul omnis esto / clamor et ira.* No shouting or anger at the end. No severity either, which Maecenas has left behind. In the middle we have the poet's private ritual, the reasons for which Maecenas must needs have explained to him, and a celebration of Horace as priest-seer-sage, receiving his friend and ritually excluding those unworthy of participating in his private wine-drinking ceremony of survival.

Though my point has validity for all the symposiastic odes, let me pursue it briefly in two odes of the first book. My exposition springs from lines in *Epistles* i. 5 which follow on the aretology of *ebrietas* to which Professor La Penna alluded. This is what Horace promises that Torquatus will find in his dinner's setting: that the coverlet and napkin be clean and bright,

> et cantharus et lanx
> ostendat tibi te, ne fidos inter amicos
> sit qui dicta foras eliminet, ut coeat par
> iungaturque pari: ...

... and that tankard and plate show you to yourself, that there be none to carry beyond the house's threshold what is said among faithful friends, that like may meet and conjoin with like ...
(Hor. *Epist.* i. 5.23-6).

To take Horace's pledges in reverse order, all distinctions, social or otherwise, are at least here obliterated through the symposium's equalizing power. There is to be complete trust that whatever is said will be held inviolate, and the plate, which is to say also the wine, the conversation and, on a deeper level, the poetry that tells of each, will serve as a mirror. Its reflection will reveal the truth of self to self, as well as the truths of others, in a context where the resultant clarity will never be betrayed.

Two brief examples, which Professor La Penna looked at from other points of view, must here suffice to illustrate how this intellectual setting is figured, and refigured, in the *Odes*. I choose adjacent poems, the seventeenth and eighteenth of Book 1, which as so often in this great poet serve to elucidate each other. The first is a day-time invitation to Tyndaris, Helen *rediviva*, to join the speaker in the enclosure of his magic *paesaggio*, a setting where nothing, neither the sun's heat nor Mars's wolves, menaces his flock and where the smooth rocks re-echo the flute's sweetness. Two threats are here named only to be kept at bay. One is the person of glassy Circe (*vitream Circen*), symbol of treachery especially by contrast to faithful Penelope, whose epic doings are now reduced to being sung on Anacreon's lyre. The speaker will offer his guest no transforming, bestializing drink, only 'goblets of innocent Lesbian wine' (*innocentis pocula Lesbii*). His lyric's harmless seduction will not serve as occasion when the drinkers will overindulge and 'pour together' Mars and Bacchus.

The other averted threat is the presence of Cyrus who will not (25-6) 'thrust uncontrolled hands on someone ill-suited for such treatment' (... *male dispari / incontinentis iniciat manus* ...). Equal will meet with equal in an isolated setting whence poetic wizardry has excluded both infidelity and disequilibrium's brutality.

My second example is the end of the subsequent poem, *Carm.* i. 18, where the speaker comments on the aftermath of violence breaking out, and of mysteries being made public, at a *convivium*. What results is the ungentle tympanum's roar (no sweet flute resounding off smooth rocks now, no Teian lyre)

> . . . quae subsequitur caecus amor sui
> et tollens vacuum plus nimio gloria verticem
> arcanique fides prodiga, perlucidior vitro.

. . . which blind Self-Love follows, and Vainglory lifting its empty head too far aloft, and Faith that betrays its trust, more transparent than glass.

(Hor. *Carm.* i. 18.14-16)

Without wine, says our poet elsewhere, we cannot unravel the concerns of the wise and their secret counsels, we cannot apply force to the bastions of wisdom. Here we learn that under the influence of too much wine we, on the contrary, become either addicts of self-importance, which means that we become unseeing of ourselves, or practitioners of infidelity and betrayal. We become more treacherous than glassy Circe because, to those whom overindulgence has rendered incapable of honest vision, transparency betokens non-existence.

Just as the setting of the true Horatian *convivium* is based on *mediocritas*, so too the intake of wine on the part of the participants must be measured. Only thus can wine decipher the abstruse and clarify the arcane. Moderate drinking holds mysteries sacred and keeps intimate truths private. It equalizes the disparate and, above all, in the hands of a master entertainer, it shows self to self in the conversation of friends and in the mirror of a poet's brilliant words.

19

Regalis inter mensas laticemque Lyaeum: Wine in Virgil and Others

JASPER GRIFFIN

Heroic characters in epic poems are subject to very strict conventions. It was pointed out in antiquity that their eating is in principle limited to roast beef. Ancient commentators tended to see in this a matter of moral and stylistic elevation;[1] some modern scholars have seen rather a memory of the time when the ancestors of the Greeks lived on the great plains and were ignorant of the sea.[2] The ancient explanation seems to me much the more plausible. Something not dissimilar is true of wine. Like the god Dionysus, who in myth is regularly represented as an outsider, a disruptive new arrival, wine itself is depicted in a number of myths as a new and revolutionary invention, suddenly revealed to mankind through the medium of a man like Icarius or Oeneus or another.[3] Yet the god Dionysus was already known in the twelfth century BC, when his name appears on the Pylos tablets,[4] and wine is utterly familiar to the characters in Homer. They are, indeed, seldom shown drinking water. Yet the gods, we are told, do not drink wine.[5]

Iliadic men are wine drinkers; but the poet shows great care and tact in handling the subject. There is no drunkenness. There are in the *Iliad* no violent quarrels at table, like those where Oedipus cursed his sons for using the wrong cups, where the three goddesses quarrelled over the prize for beauty, or where the centaur in his violent inebriation tried to lay hands on the Lapith women;[6] the great quarrel between Achilles and Agamemnon is set in a very different atmosphere, and while Achilles does, uniquely, go so far in rudeness as to call the king of men a drunkard as well as a coward — οἰνοβαρές, κυνὸς ὄμματ' ἔχων, κραδίην δ' ἐλάφοιο[7] — the motif is not pursued. In the ethos of the *Iliad* it cannot be. The writer on agriculture in the

---

[1] Ath. 9Aff.

[2] Thus A. Lesky, *Thalatta* (Vienna, 1947).

[3] Icarius: [Apollod.] iii. 14.7. Several other such stories are alluded to by the ancient sources, cf. W. Burkert, *Homo Necans* (English trans. by Peter Bing) (California, 1983), 222 n. 34.

[4] Tablets PYXa 102; PYXb 1419. Cf. G. Aurelio Privitera, *Dioniso in Omero* (Rome, 1970), 9.

[5] *Il.* v. 341; but observe the word οἰνοχοεῖν used of nectar, i. 598; iv. 4; xx. 234.

[6] *Thebais*, fr. 2 Davies (but cf. also fr. 3); *Cypria, Enarratio* 7-10; *Od.* xxi. 295ff. Cf. also the evidently proverbial fear of violence at drinking parties μή πως οἰνωθέντες ἔριν στήσαντες ἐν ὑμῖν... *Od.* xvi. 492 = xix. 11.

[7] *Il.* i. 225.

Archaeologia Homerica[8] observes that intoxication is mentioned '*auffallenderweise fast nur in der Odyssee*'. That is, more than he seems to realize, related to the whole stylistic level of the two poems.

In the *Iliad*, revealingly, the word μεθύω can be used only in a metaphor, of an ox-skin soaked in grease, βοείην-μεθύουσαν ἀλοιφῇ, while in the *Odyssey* the beggar Irus, knocked out by Odysseus, ἧσται νευστάζων κεφαλῇ, μεθύοντι ἐοικώς.[9] In the *Iliad* we find two delicate and distant approaches to the theme of drunken behaviour at a party. In *Iliad* Book Eight, when Hector is driving the Achaeans back to the ships, Agamemnon shouts, 'For shame! Where have the boastings gone which you uttered vaingloriously on Lemnos, eating in plenty the flesh of straight-horned cattle, drinking the cups crowned with wine, saying that each of you would face one hundred or two hundred Trojans?' Twelve books later, as the Trojans retreat before Achilles, Apollo says to Aeneas, 'Where are the threats, the promises which you made to the Trojan chiefs as you drank your wine, saying that you would fight Achilles face to face?'[10] These reproaches refer to the past[11] and keep the motif of intoxication to a delicate and evanescent hint: contrast the bluntness with which in the *Odyssey* the hero himself can say εὐξάμενός τι ἔπος ἐρέω· οἶνος γὰρ ἀνώγει[12] — 'I shall speak out boldly, for the wine gives me the order'. More importantly, in the *Odyssey* we find several times repeated the motif of drunken and disastrous celebrations. Odysseus captures a city of the Cicones, loots it, and urges a quick getaway; but his men insist on staying. 'Then much wine was drunk, and many sheep and oxen they slaughtered on the sea-shore' — and an avenging party of Cicones, as numerous as the leaves in spring, inflict heavy losses on his troops. Even more damaging were the consequences of the Achaean celebration of the taking of Troy. A disorderly ἀγορή was held, μάψ, ἀτὰρ οὐ κατὰ κόσμον, until the setting of the sun, 'and they arrived heavy with wine, the sons of the Achaeans'.[13] The result was disaster for many of them. So too in the Cyclic epics, the *Ilias Parva* and the *Iliou Persis*, we read that the Achaean capture of Troy was made easier because on the last night the Trojans 'revelled to celebrate defeating the Greeks'.[14] From there it is a short step to the motif of the bloodstained celebration, of slaughter in the midst of festivity, with blood staining the table and being shed among the wine; the scene which we hear described movingly by the ghost of Agamemnon, and enacted triumphantly when Odysseus gets his hands on the bow and shoots Antinous as he drinks his wine at his ease.[15]

---

[8] W. Richter in *Archaeologia Homerica* II H (Göttingen, 1968), *Die Landwirtschaft im Homerischen Zeitalter*, 127.

[9] *Il.* xvii. 390; *Od.* xviii. 240. The word μέθυ occurs fifteen times in the *Odyssey*, but only twice in the *Iliad*. The *Odyssey* also uses the un-Iliadic words ἐκπίνω, οἰνοβαρείω, οἰνοποτάζω, οἰνοποτήρ, οἰνωθείς, and the revealing phrase οἶνος πανδαμάτωρ (viii. 228-33; xx. 82-4).

[10] *Il.* viii. 228-33; xx. 82-4.

[11] Cf. the boaster Othryoneus, *Il.* xiii. 363-82 (no mention of drinking).

[12] *Od.* xiv. 463. He is accused of being drunk by Melantho, *Od.* xviii. 331; by Eurymachus, xviii. 31; and by Antinous, xxi. 23.

[13] *Od.* ix. 39-61; iii. 137ff.

[14] Proc. 30: εὐωχετοῦνται ὡς νενικηκότες τοὺς Ἕλληνας. It is only in the *Cycle*, not in the great epics, that we find an explicit praise of wine as the remedy for cares: *Cypria* fr. 15D.

[15] *Od.* xi. 405-34 and cf. iv. 534-5; xxii. 8-21. The cannibal feast of the Cyclops in *Od.* ix is of course akin.

That development made little appeal, on the whole, to the tragic poets. For the Attic tragedians Agamemnon was not killed at the table but in the bath,[16] and Euripides, who several times in the extant plays evokes with pathos and power the last night of Troy, is careful to exclude from those touching passages any hint of intoxication. In the *Troades* the chorus sings only of the music of that night, and we observe the exactness of the poet's reticence in the *Hecuba* when the chorus says that the horrors began ἦμος ἐκ δείπνων ὕπνος ἡδὺς ἐπ᾽ ὄσσοις/σκίδναται, 'when after supper sweet sleep was spread over our eyes'.[17] In tragedy, in fact, reference of any kind to wine is surprisingly infrequent. The word πίνω, 'drink', occurs seven times in the extant plays of Aeschylus, and of those seven occurrences five refer to the drinking of human blood (twice by Erinyes, thrice of the earth). That verb is used in the extant plays of Sophocles three times, every one of them referring to blood; with the exception of the *Cyclops* and *Alcestis*, Euripides uses πίνω only once, when the shade of Achilles is summoned to 'drink the dark unmixed blood' of Polyxena.[18] It can indeed seem that in the world of tragedy blood is the most frequent drink.

By contrast, the word οἶνος appears only twice in Aeschylus, and once in Sophocles:[19] in the unjovial context of the first revelation to Oedipus that he was not in reality the son of his supposed parents.[20] In Euripides it appears, outside the special cases of the *Cyclops*, *Bacchae* and *Alcestis*, only once, in the *Ion*: revealingly, in a deadly context, that of the poisoned wine with which Creusa attempted to kill her unrecognized son.[21] It is a neglected mark of the non-Euripidean authorship of the *Rhesus* that its chorus is more explicitly attracted to the theme of wine and its accompanying pleasures.[22] The motif of the bloodstained meal, which is familiar to tragedy, is characteristically different from that of the epic. In the *Odyssey* we find the slaughter of an enemy, his blood flowing amid the wine and food[23] — 'That was the most pathetic sight you could ever have seen, the way we lay in the hall among the wine bowl and the tables loaded with food, while the whole floor ran with blood', and 'He fell backwards, and the wine-cup fell from his hand as he was hit, and instantaneously a thick gout of his blood streamed from his nostrils; he kicked over the table and sent the food on to the floor'.[24] Spilt wine and spilt blood are readily imagined together. In tragedy the corrupted feast is rather a cannibal banquet, the nightmare feeding of a Thyestes or a

---

[16] So in Aesch. *Ag.* 1108ff., 1382ff.

[17] Eur. *Tro.* 542ff.; *Hec.* 915-16; cf. also *Andr.* 1037ff., *Hel.* 1107ff.

[18] Aesch. *Sept.* 736, 821; *Ag.* 1188; *Cho.* 578; *Eum.* 980; and *Supp.* 953, fr. 124; Soph. *OT* 1400; *Trach.* 1056; *OC* 622; Eur. *Hec.* 538, cf. fr. 687.2, ἐμπλήσθητί μου / πίνων κελαινὸν αἷμα.

[19] And μέθυ once in Aeschylus and once in Sophocles.

[20] Soph. *OT* 780-1 (the sole occurrence both of οἶνος and μέθη).

[21] Eur. *Ion* 1184.

[22] προπότας...θιάσους ἐρώτων/ψαλμοῖσι καὶ κυλίκων οἰνοπλανήτοις + ... + ἁμίλλαις, *Rhes.* 360ff. That recalls the manner of the *sympotica* of Pindar and Bacchylides; genuine Euripides, as far as we can see, never sounds like that.

[23] From a more modern writer compare A. Conan Doyle, 'The Gloria Scott', in *The Memoirs of Sherlock Holmes*: 'When (the smoke) cleared away again the place was a shambles. Wilson and eight others were wriggling on the top of each other on the floor, and the blood and brown sherry on that table turn me sick now when I think of it'.

[24] *Od.* xi. 428-30.

Tereus upon the flesh of his own children.[25] Those horrors are alien to the Homeric manner, and in the great epics cannibalism is restricted to the non-human figure of the Cyclops.

We turn, with a broad leap, to Virgil and the *Aeneid*. It must be said at once that not only Virgil but also his Latin successors were anxious on the topic of wine. Ovid, who enjoys wine in the *Amores*, is very sparing in the use of wine to motivate action in his epic poem. It is not until the Tenth Book of the *Metamorphoses* that we find it playing any role of that sort. Myrrha's nurse gets Cinyras's consent to make love with an unknown girl, in reality his incestuous daughter, by taking advantage of his tipsy state: *nacta gravem vino Cinyram male sedula nutrix ... exponit amores.*[26] Up to that point it has been assumed that the passionate loves and sexual assaults which make up so much of the poem have been sufficiently motivated simply by one partner catching sight of the other; in so erotic a world no other stimulant is necessary. Even with Cinyras, all that is really motivated by the drink is not his sexual drive but his lack of scruples in admitting to his bed a young woman whom he has not even seen. It is only the non-human Centaurs of Book Twelve in whom desire is actually said to be kindled by drink; of Eurytion we read, *ardet, et ebrietas geminata libidine regnat.*[27] *Vina dabant animos*; they fight, using the *krater* and the rest of the sympotic furniture as weapons.

That was a special case, as even Homer had said that it was wine which drove the Centaur on to misbehave in the house of Pirithous.[28] At the great battle in Book Five, when Andromeda's old suitor Phineus tries to reclaim her by force, the setting is a feast; but there is no mention of wine, and no such episodes as the use of a great wine-bowl to brain an adversary.[29] The only element of what might be called sympotic furniture is the musician Lampetides, who, as he falls, strikes his lyre with his hand, 'and by chance it was a pitiable strain';[30] and we hear, not of dying men defiling the festive table and the spilt wine with their blood, but in the most general terms that 'Bellona drenched the polluted house with much gore'.[31]

On the whole, except for the rather grotesque episode of the Centauromachy, Ovid avoids the subject of wine in the *Metamorphoses*. It becomes clear why he does so, when we observe its use in the *Fasti*. In Book One Ovid tells at length the comic story of Priapus and his midnight assault on the nymph Lotis. The whole company had plenty to drink (*vina dabat Liber*[32]); they went off in a drunken sleep:

> *nox erat, et vino somnum faciente iacebant*
> *corpora diversis victa sopore locis*

(Ov. *Fast.* i. 421-2).

[25] Aeschylus, *Agamemnon*; Sophocles, *Tereus*; Seneca, *Thyestes* (the play which accounts for four of the five occurrences of the word *vinum* in Seneca's tragedies — only in connection with a cannibal feast will the poet mention something so commonplace, and normally so genial, as wine). The other occurs in his *Agamemnon*, a play in which the hero is murdered at table while feasting, so that *sanguinem extremae dapes domini videbunt et cruor Baccho incidet* (885-6). On the last feature mentioned, see the note of R.J. Tarrant in his *Commentary* (Cambridge, 1976) *ad locum*: he calls it, rather unsympathetically, a 'picturesque detail'.

[26] Ov. *Met.* x. 348.

[27] Ov. *Met.* xii. 295-6.

[28] *Od.* xxi. 295-6.

[29] Ov. *Met.* xii. 235-40.

[30] *casque fuit miserabile carmen*: Ov. *Met.* v. 118.

[31] Ov. *Met.* v. 115-16.

[32] Ov. *Fast.* i. 403.

Priapus tried his assault and cut a ludicrous figure when a donkey brayed and aroused all the company. That is why Priapus welcomes the sacrifice of donkeys. The aetiology is, says Ovid, *pudenda*:[33] no matter for serious treatment. In the very next Book Ovid tells another, rather similar: the lustful Pan once tried to assault Omphale, when all her party were 'unstrung by wine and sleep', but found Hercules in her clothes,[34] with disastrous results. That story is *antiqui fabula plena ioci*, a tale full of old-time mirth. In Book Six there is a second story of Priapus,[35] exactly like that in Book One, except that this time it is told of the goddess Vesta: that, too, is a story of drunkenness (*in multo nox est pervigilata mero*), and a low but droll little tale:

> *praeteream referamne tuum, rubicunde Priape,*
> *   dedecus? est multi fabula parva ioci*

(Ov. Fast. vi. 319-20).

No doubt the poet, had he completed his poem, would have done something to reduce the repetitiveness of these narratives. We see, however, that in Ovid's view the combination of love and wine, appropriate enough to the *Amores* and even to the *Fasti*, was not suitable to the dignity of epic.

He will indeed go so far, in the *Fasti*, as to include a tale, tragic in its outcome, which starts with a scene of men drinking and becoming indiscreet: the Tarquin and his guests, and the rape and suicide of Lucretia. That began when Tarquinius entertained his friends *dapibus meroque*. Each man praises his own wife: *et fervet multo linguaque corque mero*.[36] The result will be terrible — and momentous for Rome, as the kings take their flight from the city for ever. Yet the story retains a kinship more with the tales of Priapus and Pan than with the amours of the *Metamorphoses*. Only at a stylistic level of that kind can such a motive be acknowledged, and even then the wine and the lust of Tarquinius are not brought into direct contact. That might have recalled the ethos of the *Amores* in too disruptive a way.

From another side, we can form an idea of the hesitancy with which Latin poets of the high style approached vinous questions by considering a few statistics about word usage. The word *calix*, quite at home in elegy and lyric, was not dignified enough for epic: like the *Aeneid*, the *Metamorphoses* admit only *pocula* (*calices* comes twice in the *Fasti*), as Statius confined *calix* to the *Silvae* (three appearances), drink being served exclusively in *pocula* in the *Thebais*. More startlingly, Lucan and Silius agree in banning all parts of the word *vinum* itself from their epics, although Statius and Valerius Flaccus both admit it, or rather its plural, *vina*, a fact which shows how difficult and personal such decisions were. The word they use is *merum*, precisely because outside epic it was not what you drank. On the other hand Valerius, who uses the word *vinum* nine times, strictly avoids the verb *bibo*, which was good enough for Virgil, and which is used by Silius. Lucan even eschews the word *crater*, for which most epic poets show a positive liking, its Greek origin as a word, and its massive presence as a thing, conferring on it the status which ladles

---

[33] Ov. *Fast.* i. 392.

[34] Ov. *Fast.* ii. 333, 335-56, 304.

[35] Ov. *Fast.* vi. 32-3, 319-20.

[36] Ov. *Fast.* ii. 725, 732. So too Livy: the quarrel arose over the wine (*incaluerant vino*), but the act of list is sober: i. 57-8.

and lesser pieces of equipment seem to lack. Yet it is Silius, fastidious enough to exclude the word *vinum*, who alone among the Latin epic poets likes to refer, in a connoisseur-like way, to different growths of wine; a taste which he shares only with Horace.[37]

Virgil is not immune to such anxieties. It is noticeable that he does not choose to show his gods drinking, even nectar. When the gods of the *Iliad* gazed down on Troy, at the beginning of *Iliad* Book Four, 'Hebe poured out nectar like wine' (νέκταρ ἐῳνοχόει), 'and they pledged each other in golden goblets as they gazed at the city of the Trojans'.[38] The scene that follows, with Zeus deliberately teasing and stirring up the goddesses Hera and Athena, has among other things the feeling of a real party, with drinking and playful malice. Very different is the atmosphere in the only full-scale divine assembly of the *Aeneid*, at the opening of Book Ten. Jupiter speaks in tones from which all teasing is conspicuously absent, gives a crushing decision, and sweeps out, respectfully accompanied to the door by the other gods.[39] They can hardly, one feels, have expected to be offered a drink in that austere atmosphere; and they are not. Dido, too, when it is time for her to pledge the health of her guests, has an antique and precious vessel filled, but herself barely touches it with her lips before handing it to a doughty local drinker, who takes a gargantuan draught.[40] Servius observes, doubtless correctly, that the poet 'demonstrates the queen's self-restraint and the Roman custom', for in the good old days women drank wine only for religious reasons and on holidays, *sacrorum causa*. Homer does not show his ladies drinking wine, but he avoids the slightly obtrusive, if charming, note struck by the explicit contrast between heroine and hero.

Virgil goes well beyond his Homeric model in describing the night expedition of Nisus and Euryalus. In the Tenth Book of the *Iliad*, the marauding heroes Odysseus and Diomedes enter the enemy camp by night. The Trojans are on watch; Hector has summoned a council, and the sentries are duly keeping each other awake. Only the allies, the ἐπίκουροι, are asleep, allowing themselves the luxury of leaving this unpleasant duty to their hosts,[41] and their slackness allows the Achaean pair to get unobserved into the Thracian encampment and kill a dozen men as they sleep. Their sleep is perfectly respectable: 'they were asleep, exhausted by their toil, and their armour lay on the ground beside each man, in good order'.[42] Very different is the scene in the Rutulian camp in the *Aeneid*. The whole army, we read, 'indulge in wine and upturn the brazen bowls', *indulgent vino et vertunt crateras aenos*. Nisus is justified in saying to Euryalus that the self-confident enemy are 'sunk in wine and sleep'. Arrived in the

---

[37] All these poets avoid *vinum* and use only *vina* in the nominative and accusative; cf. Austin's note on *Aen.* iv. 455. Silius refers to wines from Spain (i. 237), Entella (xiv. 204), Tarraco (iii. 370), Setia (viii. 736); and tells us that Falernian (he tells the story of Falernus the Icarius-figure) exceeds in quality the wines of Tmolus, Ariusia, and Methymna (vii. 209-11). We recall that he was a millionaire; and doubtless a gourmet.

[38] *Il.* iv. 1-4.

[39] Verg. *Aen.* x. 116-17.

[40] Verg. *Aen.* i. 728-39.

[41] Trojan council, *Il.* x. 299-300, 413-14; Trojan sentries, *Il.* x. 418-19; allies are relaxed, *Il.* x. 420-2.

[42] οἱ δ' εὗδον καμάτῳ ἀδηκότες, ἔντεα δέ σφιν / καλὰ παρ' αὐτοῖσι χθονὶ κέκλιτο εὖ κατὰ κόσμον: *Il.* x. 471-2.

enemy camp, they see 'on all sides bodies stretched on the grass in sleep and wine', and wine as well as weapons surrounding the unconscious bodies of their owners.[43] Rhamnes is snoring heavily (*toto proflabat pectore somnum*); Serranus is 'overcome by the god in force';[44] Rhoetus, who is awake, hides behind a large *krater*, and when he is stabbed spews up his crimson life and wine mixed with blood.[45]

That last detail finds a partial Homeric precedent in the disgusting Cyclops of the *Odyssey*, who after his anthropophagous meal and the wine which Odysseus gives him reclines in drunken sleep, 'and from his gullet there issued wine and gobbets of man's flesh'.[46] It also, however, is different: the Cyclops vomits not his own blood but that of others, and the mixture of blood and wine takes its place in the long list of passages, Near Eastern as well as classical, in which the idea of wine as the blood of the grape, and of wine and blood as essentially akin, finds expression. We shall return to it in connection with Dido's eerie sacrifice in Book Four. The whole conception of the Rutulian camp as helplessly in the grip of wine, quite alien to the *Doloneia*, is presumably a Virgilian transposition of the motif familiar (though not in the *Iliad* or *Odyssey*) of the fall of Troy. He has already shown its attraction for him by making Troy itself lie 'overwhelmed with sleep and wine'.[47] But the other Virgilian innovation in this episode is of course the homosexual love of Nisus and Euryalus, something which Homer does not admit to his world at all. Nor is that alone here. We find also the good-looking Serranus, *insignis facie*:[48] if only he had gone on all night with his game, then Nisus, the lover of beautiful youth, would not have killed him. Love and wine go together, and, bringing both of them to bear, in the Ninth Book of the *Aeneid*, the poet has reduced rather than doubled the arbitrariness of his transformation of the Iliadic ethos. From a world of straightforward fighting and killing he leads us into an atmosphere clouded and made less transparent by passion and loss of control. Nisus and Euryalus went on their expedition to carry vitally important news to Aeneas; in the darkness of night, love, and revenge they lose sight of it and think only of a *Liebestod*. In the darkness of night and wine the Rutulians are massacred; in that same darkness the lover kills a pretty young man.

Homer is aware of the god Dionysus, and also of the Maenads who worship him. The story of Lycurgus, who chased the nurses of the god of madness and was justly punished for it,[49] stands with two passages in which the anxious Andromache is compared to a maenad.[50] Aurelio Privitera is probably right to infer the existence, behind the *Iliad*, of a body of poetry concerned with the childhood and persecutions of

---

[43] Verg. *Aen.* ix. 165, 189, 316.

[44] Verg. *Aen.* ix. 326 (Rhamnes), 336 (Serranus): *multoque iacebat / membra deo victus*. Commentators ancient and modern have been unsure of the identity of the *deus* here (*vel vino vel somno*, Servius); the parallel of Stat. *Theb.* ii. 76-7 seems to prove that it is wine.

[45] *purpuream vomit ille animam et cum sanguine mixta / vina refert moriens*: *Aen.* ix. 349.

[46] *Od.* ix. 373. Heyne was disgusted by the Virgilian passage: *sensum igitur foedae et ingratae rei poeta habuit nullum, qui ista memorare non dubitavit.*

[47] *Aen.* ii. 265. The motif occurs of course also in historians: e.g. the fall of Syracuse, Livy xxv. 24 (*aut sopiti vino erant, aut semigraves potabant ... gravatis omnibus vino somnoque ...*).

[48] Verg. *Aen.* ix. 336.

[49] *Il.* vi. 132ff.: ὅς ποτε μαινομένοιο Διωνύσοιο τιθήνας / σεῦε κατ' ἠγάθεον Νυσήιον....

[50] *Il.* vi. 389 μαινομένῃ ἐικυῖα; xxii. 460 μαινάδι ἴση.

the god.[51] But in the Homeric text such allusions are kept to an absolute minimum, and the ecstasy characteristic of Dionysus's cult is on the whole excluded from the Homeric world. Virgil follows up the Homeric hints and carries them much farther.

At the rumour that Aeneas intends to leave Carthage and abandon her, Dido goes crazy:

> *saevit inops animi totamque incensa per urbem*
> *bacchatur, qualis commotis excita sacris*
> *Thyias, ubi audito stimulant trieterica Baccho*
> *orgia nocturnusque vocat clamore Cithaeron*

(Verg. Aen. iv. 300-3).

Like a maenad she rushes madly (*bacchatur*) through the city, like a votary of the god at one of his Boeotian festivals. The comparison with a specific cult of mainland Greece has an oddity which resembles anachronism without necessarily being one: the comparison is in our minds, not in that of Dido, but such a simile is unusual in kind. Its fullness of detail and specific application takes it far from the two-word comparisons which are applied in the *Iliad* to Andromache. But not only Dido; Fama behaves in the same way: *concussam bacchatur Fama per urbem*.[52] When Allecto stirs up Lavinia's mother, Amata, to oppose her daughter's marriage to Aeneas, the queen goes off like a maenad:

> *quin etiam in silvas simulato numine Bacchi*
> *maius adorta nefas maioremque orsa furorem*
> *evolat et natam frondosis montibus abdit...*
> *euhoe Bacche fremens...*

(Verg. Aen. vii. 385-8).

It appears from this passage that Virgil means the Dionysiac possession of Amata to be seen as a piece of pretence; but a few lines later we read:

> *tale inter silvas, inter deserta ferarum*
> *reginam Allecto stimulis agit undique Bacchi.*

(Verg. Aen. vii. 404-5)

Is her Bacchic possession real or pretended? Richard Heinze[53] observed that 'It is not easy to say how Virgil wants the description of this *baccheia* interpreted', and concluded that Amata was really possessed, but by Allecto; and claimed that it was by Bacchus.

It is perhaps worth remarking that a similarity of sound enters in. Virgil shows a strongly formulaic vocabulary in these repeated scenes in which female persons or personifications behave like maenads. Of Dido we read that she *incensa per urbem / bacchatur*; of Fama, *concussam bacchatur Fama per urbem*; of Amata, *immensam sine more furit lymphata per urbem*, and *per medias urbes agitur populosque ferocis*. Fama appears again on other occasions: at the death of Euryalus, *pavidam volitans pennata per urbem / nuntia Fama ruit*, through the Trojan camp; as the fall of Latinus's town seems imminent, *hinc totam infelix vulgatur Fama per urbem*; elsewhere, *Allecto medias Italum bacchata per urbes*.[54] The phrase *per urbem/s* is evidently regular. Another word family which is at home in this context is that

---

[51] Aurelio Privitera, *Dioniso in Omero* (above, n. 4), 53ff.
[52] Verg. *Aen.* iv. 666.
[53] *Virgils Epische Technik*, fourth edition (Stuttgart, 1957), 184.
[54] *Aen.* iv. 300; iv. 666; vii. 377, 384; ix. 473; xii. 608.

of *stimulus* and *stimulo*. Dido, we saw, is compared to a maenad, *ubi audito stimulant trieteria Baccho / orgia*; Allecto drives Amata — *reginam stimulis agit undique Bacchi*.[55] This word family is far from common in the *Aeneid*, verb and noun having a total of only eight appearances; of those eight a third is also closely akin, when Virgil says of the Sibyl, in the grip of prophetic frenzy, first that she *bacchatur*, then that the god spurs her: *stimulos sub pectore vertit Apollo*.[56]

The sound of those words is strikingly recalled when we hear, of Amata, that she *in silvas simulato numine Bacchi ... evolat*, and again of Helen, on the fatal night of the sack of Troy, that *illa chorum simulans euhantis orgia circum / ducebat Phrygias*.[57] I think it likely that the curious ambiguity about Amata was in part produced by a slide from one similar sounding word, familiar to the poet in this context, to another: *stimulo — simulo*. And, of course, whether her possession was genuinely Bacchic or not is a detail which makes very little difference. Like all Virgilian females, from Andromache and Creusa to the collective matrons of Troy, like Dido and Euryalus's mother[58] and Allecto and Fama, she is at home in madness and raving, and any provocation suffices to precipitate her into it.

The third and last vinous phenomenon which we can discuss in the *Aeneid* is the horrid and ill-omened scene when Dido makes her vain offerings to the gods, praying as she does so for death. 'She saw, frightful to tell, as she placed her offerings on the altars where incense burned, that the consecrated liquid turned black and the wine she poured out changed into loathsome blood':

> *vidit, turicremis cum dona imponeret aris,*
> *horrendum dictu, latices nigrescere sacros*
> *fusaque in obscenum se vertere vina cruorem*

(Verg. *Aen*. iv. 455-7).

Knauer in his great book *Die Aeneis und Homer* cites no Homeric model for this portent, and the ancients observed: *de augurali disciplina translatum est* — the long Italian tradition of statues sweating, androgynous infants coming into the world, and natural waters turning into blood.[59] We can, however, point to the sinister episode of the 'second sight' in the Twentieth Book of the *Odyssey*, when in the vision of the seer Theoclymenus the wicked Suitors 'laughed with mouths not their own, and ate food dabbled with blood'; the seer adds that the walls are running with blood.[60] That this episode was in Virgil's mind is perhaps supported by the fact that in the Virgilian passage, as in that in the

---

[55] Verg. *Aen*. iv. 302; vii. 405; x. 41.

[56] Verg. *Aen*. vi. 78, 101.

[57] Verg. *Aen*. vii. 385; vi. 517.

[58] Andromache: *arma* amens *vidit, magnis exterrita monstris / deriguit visu in medio ... lacrimasque effudit et omnem / implevit clamore locum. / vix pauca furenti / subicio*: *Aen*. iii. 306-7, 312-14. Creusa: *talia* vociferans gemitu *tectum omne replebat, Aen*. ii. 679. Trojan matrons: *attonitae monstris actaeque* furore / *conclamant, rapiuntque focis penetralibus ignem;* / pars spoliant aras, 659-61. Euryalus's mother: *evolat infelix et femineo ululatu / scissa comam muros* amens *atque agmina cursu / prima petit*, ix. 477-9.

[59] Virgil asserts that wells 'did not cease' to run with blood at the time of Caesar's assassination: *G*. i. 485.

[60] *Od*. xx. 347-54.

Odyssey, it is left delicately unclear how much of the vision is vouched for by the poet and how much is only in the eye of one specific onlooker.[61]

Confusions and substitutions between water, wine, and blood present a rather complex picture, which has not interested Virgil's commentators as much as might have been expected. Water turns into blood repeatedly, both in the Old Testament — it is one of the plagues of Egypt[62] — and among the Greeks and Romans, where A.S. Pease can observe, comfortably, that 'Rivers, springs, pools, or lakes flowing with blood are one of the commonest of portents'.[63] It is a favourite spine-chiller of the author of the Revelation,[64] and another anti-Roman writer in the Sibylline oracles uses the image in his fantasies of vengeance on Rome.[65]

Akin to it is the picture, very attractive to many Roman poets, of blood staining water. A few illustrations will suffice. The Sibyl foresees the Tiber foaming with much blood; Horace asks pathetically 'What sea-shore is free from our Roman blood?' and, in lighter mood (but not to the taste of all his readers), speaks of the blood of a sacrificial kid staining the cool spring Bandusia.[66] Statius took up the theme with some gusto, writing of the spring Dirce streaming with gore,[67] but it was to Lucan that it made most appeal: we find a lengthy and energetic development of the idea of the Tiber running with blood:

> *tandem Tyrrhenas vix eluctatus in undas*
> *sanguine caeruleum torrenti dividit aequor*

a stream of blood parting the waters of the Tyrrhenian sea

(Luc. ii. 219-20);[68]

the sea (or the sea-god Nereus) blushing red with the blood of civil war; blood foaming in the sea at Massilia and the waves setting hard with gore; the River Enipeus turbid

---

[61] Servius on *Aen.* iv. 455 argues that Virgil asserts only that the change seemed to Dido to take place, not that it really happened, *quod contra naturam est.*

[62] Exodus 4.9; 7.17.

[63] A.S. Pease, *Commentary on Cicero, de Divinatione i.98* (Illinois, 1920 (repr. 1963), with many references.

[64] This writer is literally as well as metaphorically blood-thirsty. Revelation 8.8, 'the third part of the sea became blood'; 16.3, '(the sea) became as the blood of a dead man'; 16.4-6, 'the rivers and fountains of waters ... became blood ... For they have shed the blood of saints and prophets, and thou hast given them blood to drink'.

[65] πρῶτα δὲ Ῥωμαίων ἀπαραίτητος χόλος ἔσται, / αἱμοπότης καιρὸς καὶ δύστηνος βίος ἥξει. / αἲ αἲ σοί, ἰταμὴ χώρη, μέγα βάρβαρον ἔθνος, *Oracula Sibyllina* viii. 94-6.

[66] *Thybrim multo spumantem sanguine cerno*, Verg. *Aen.* vi. 87; *quae caret ora cruore nostro?* Hor. *Carm.* ii. 1.36; *gelidos inficiet tibi / rubro sanguine rivos / lascivi suboles gregis*, Hor. *Carm.* iii. 13.6-8. R.G.M. Nisbet quotes with approval the comment of A.Y. Campbell: 'Who wants a drink out of the fountain of Bandusia after that?' ('Romanae fidicen lyrae: the Odes of Horace', in J.P. Sullivan (ed.), *Critical Essays on Roman Literature: Elegy and Lyric* (London, 1962), 198). That response perhaps shows a certain refusal to allow the poet his harder, more dandyish, side.

[67] *sanguine Dircen / irriguam*, Stat. *Theb.* iv. 374; cf. also v. 4ff., *sanguineis mixtum ceu fontibus ignem / hausissent belli magnasque in proelia mentes* (a typical exaggeration).

[68] The whole passage extends from 209 to 220. Prose authors dwell on Sulla making the Tiber run with blood: Val. Max. ix. 2.1.

with blood of Romans, and so on.[69] The motif goes back ultimately to the *Iliad*: Achilles's battle with the River in Book Twenty-One is mostly concerned with the blocking of the stream with corpses and its inability to flow, but at line 21 we do find 'and the water was reddened with blood'.[70] Aeschylus makes little use of it in the *Persae*, but Timotheus fancies it more, dwelling on the way 'the emerald-haired sea reddened in its furrows with rain of ship-blood'.[71] Timotheus's friend Euripides also liked it.[72] When dwelt upon by a poet, as by Virgil it is not, it always I think conveys a certain aestheticism. Virgil prefers, but again does not linger on, a motif in some ways adjacent to this one: that of pouring wine into the sea,[73] an offering to the marine deities.

Blood in the water is horrid but also picturesque: one thinks, in Shakespeare, of Macbeth imagining the blood from his hands staining the whole ocean:

> This my hand would rather
> The multitudinous seas incarnadine,
> Making the green one red.

(Shakespeare, Macbeth ii. 2.62-4)

Less picturesque is that of the earth stained with blood — ἐρυθαίνετο δ᾽ αἵματι γαῖα, in Homeric phrase.[74] This lends itself to development in a different direction: that of the earth thirsting for human blood, growing rich on it, receiving it like rain. Deadly weapons, too, can be said to thirst for blood. Closely akin is the pervasive idea of the thirst of the dead, to be slaked by bloody draughts, and of the gods of the dead. Time forbids anything like the full unpacking of the evidence for these widespread, deep-seated, and haunting notions, which go all the way from the spears lusting to taste flesh, λιλαιόμενα χροὸς ᾆσαι, of the *Iliad*, and the ghosts who must drink blood in order to speak, of the *Odyssey*, to Virgil's lament that the gods did not mind that the fields of Thessaly should twice grow fat on Roman gore, and the blood-drinking Furies of Aeschylus's *Eumenides*, and their overstrained and lurid descendants in Petronius's epic poem, complaining that they are parched for human blood.[75]

Wine and blood were both used in sacrificial ritual: the blood must flow, and the ashes of the fire were quenched with wine.[76] Blood was appropriate as a libation to the dead, to whom also wine was poured out.[77] Indeed, wine and blood were poured out

---

[69] Luc. ii. 713; ili. 572-7; cf. also iv. 566-8, 785; vii. 292, 700, 789-90. The Nile, *infando pollutus sanguine*, vi. 307; *sanguine Romano quam turbidus ibit Enipeus* vii. 116.

[70] ἐρυθαίνετο δ᾽ αἵματι ὕδωρ (κῦμα coni. Bentley), *Il.* xxi. 21.

[71] Timoth. *Pers.* 31-3: I borrow the translation from J. Herington, *Poetry into Drama* (California, 1985), 155.

[72] ὥσθ᾽ αἱματηρὸν πέλαγος ᾽ἐξανθεῖν ἁλός, Eur. *IT* 300; αἵματος δ᾽ἀπορροαὶ / ἐς οἶδμ᾽ ἐσηκόντιζον οὔριοι ξένῳ, *Hel.* 1587-8.

[73] *Aen.* iii. 525ff.; v. 238, 776.

[74] *Il.* x. 484. This idea is developed with electrifying energy by Aeschylus's Clytemnestra: *Ag.* 1389ff.

[75] *nec fuit indignum superis bis sanguine nostro / Emathiam et latos Haemi pinguescere campos*, Verg. *G.* i. 491-2; *iam pridem nullo perfundimus ora cruore / nec mea Tisiphone sitientes perluit artus ...*, Petron. 120.96-7, cf. 116ff. Silius has the bad taste to make Juno thirsty for Roman blood, viii. 204.

[76] W. Burkert, *Greek Religion* (Oxford, 1985), 70-1.

[77] From *Il.* xxiii. 218, ὁ δὲ πάννυχος ὠκὺς ᾽Αχιλλεὺς / χρυσέου ἐκ κρητῆρος, ἑλὼν δέπας ἀμφικύπελλον, / οἶνον ἀφυσσάμενος χαμάδις χέε, δεῦε δὲ γαῖαν, / ψυχὴν κικλήσκων Πατροκλῆος δειλοῖο.

together as an offering to the dead.[78] Wine was typically red wine, οἶνος ἐρυθρός; its colour resembles that of blood; and taboos and fears were attached to its drinking, reflected in the myths of its introduction which cost the lives of Icarius and other Bacchic εὑρεταί.[79] The expression 'the blood of the grape' for wine is very ancient,[80] and the Bible is full of language which conflates the two liquids: 'they shall be drunken with their own blood, as with sweet wine'; 'the sword shall devour, and it shall be satiate and made drunk with their blood'; 'And I saw the woman drunken with the blood of the saints, and with the blood of the martyrs of Jesus'.[81] Even the Elder Pliny, a rather prosaic writer, says of M. Antonius's notorious book *On my Drunkenness* that he was 'already drunk on the blood of Roman citizens' when he 'vomited it forth'.[82] There were creatures which drank blood: the *striges* of Latin superstition, the Erinyes of Attic drama.

Humans might drink blood; in Herodotus, queen Tomyris plunged the severed head of Cyrus into a bucket of blood, to satisfy his limitless thirst for it: he had caused her son to be full of wine and killed him in his helplessness.[83] The conqueror is glutted with blood, as his victim was with wine. In the motif of the evil feast, where the scene typical of ease and well-being is transmuted into its loathsome opposite, wine and blood might flow together, or even be mixed, as in the bowl offered to Thyestes, on which Seneca, above all, dilated with such gusto.[84] It is only to be expected that Seneca also finds the same ghastly relish in speaking of Achilles's ghost drinking the blood of Polyxena, even to the horridly exaggerated point of saying that the girl's blood did not stay on the surface but was immediately swallowed down.[85]

Virgil's invention for Dido of wine turning into blood was, it seems, without complete precedent, but it fitted well into the patterns of ancient thought, religion, and poetry. It lingered in the mind of Seneca, who based on it several horrid and portentous happenings in his tragedies. Tiresias's daughter, in Seneca's *Oedipus*, is shocked to see the wine of her libation turn to blood, as happens also in his *Thyestes*.[86] Statius, in the grimmest of Latin epics, finds a variant, describing the horrors on Lemnos, when the women massacred the men. One could see, he says, 'mixing-bowls upset and banquets floating in gore, and mingled wine and blood streaming back like a torrent to the goblets from gaping throats'.[87] As so often, Virgil goes well beyond Homer in the direction of the lurid, and his successor in turn surpasses him. The horror of these passages rests on

---

[78] *Aen.* v. 77-9, Aeneas's offering of his father's grave: *hic duo rite mero libans carchesia Baccho / fundit humi, duo lacte novo, duo sanguine sacro.* In the *Odyssey* Odysseus must pour out a libation of wine to the ghosts and offer them blood to drink: x. 516ff.; xi. 25ff.

[79] Burkert, *Homo Necans* (above, n. 3), 220ff.

[80] In Ugaritic: *Baal* ii. 4.37, *ANET³* 133; *Genesis* 49.11

[81] Isaiah 49.26; Jeremiah 46.10; Revelation 17.6.

[82] Pliny, *HN* xiv. 148. Cf. Sid. Apoll. *Carm.* v. 32 *cuspis ... ebria caede virum.*

[83] Hdt. i. 211-14. Michael Putnam reminds me of the warning given to Alexander the Great by the philosopher Androcydes: *Vinum poturus, rex, memento bibere te sanguinem terrae; cicuta homini venenum est, cicutae vinum* (Pliny, *HN* xiv. 58) — wine is 'the blood of the earth'.

[84] Sen. *Thyests* 65 *mixtus in Bacchum cruor / spectante te potetur ...*; 917 *mixtum suorum sanguinem genitor bibat,* etc., especially the actual drinking of the mixture, 983ff.

[85] *non stetit fusus cruor / humove summa fluxit; obduxit statim / saevusque totum sanguinem tumulus bibit,* Sen. *Troades* 1162-4.

[86] *genitor, horresco intuens: / libata Bacchi dona permutat cruor ...,* Sen. *Oedipus* 324-5; cf. *Thyestes* 700-1.

[87] Stat. *Theb.* v. 255-7 (Loeb translation by J.H. Mozley).

two facts: wine and blood resemble each other, both in colour and also in being both extraordinary, dangerous, and not entirely canny fluids; but they also are at the opposite extreme points, as the embodiment of good cheer and of horror. Their resemblance gives point and force to their opposition. In a wine drinking society, which performed and watched animal sacrifice constantly, the resemblance and the opposition were both more urgently present to the mind than they can be in a society which pours its wine from glass bottles and buys its meat at the supermarket wrapped in plastic. Dido saw a sight which spoke to her nearest feelings: all that was good and sweet, wine like love, had turned into something which resembled it yet was its repulsive opposite — blood and hatred.

> Sweet love, I see, changing his property,
> Turns to the sourest and most deadly hate.

(Shakespeare, Richard II iii. 2.135-6)

Love and hate are akin, as well as being opposites: the unhappy queen's gruesome vision makes that perceptible. With his usual skill, Virgil took a hint from Homer in leaving open the question of the objective reality of Dido's vision. On the public level, that of events, it means her death; on the private level, that of feelings, it means her love turned to hatred. The power of the image comes from the seamless interweaving of the two. And we are reminded that the history of Pleasure will be also a history of pain, of anxiety, of death: *surgit amari aliquid quod in ipsis floribus angit.*

* * *

'Intervento' by Michael C.J. Putnam: Dido and wine

I would like for a moment to help bridge the gap between the Dido who merely touches the *patera* to her lips and the Dido whose magic turns wine to blood in a rite which, as Jasper Griffin so tellingly puts it, serves to exemplify the metamorphosis of sweet love to hatred in her life.

Dido's fastidiousness is only superficial. Within a few lines of her initial gesture Virgil offers a far different picture of the enraptured queen:

nec non et vario noctem sermone trahebat
infelix Dido longumque bibebat amorem.

And unfortunate Dido, too, with varied conversation prolonged the night and drank deep draughts of love.

(Verg. Aen. i. 748-9)

As restraint turns to gratification in Dido's life, the poet changes literal to figurative, giving particular emphasis to her metaphorical act of drinking because this is the only occasion in the *Aeneid* where the verb *bibo* is allotted to a human being.

Setting, too, is important, as this recklessness continues apace. Her original act of wine-sipping took place where 'in the midst of the palace they prepare a banquet' (*mediis ... parant convivia tectis*, 638). It is no accident, to continue in a statistical mode, that

Virgil's only other use in the *Aeneid* of the noun *convivium* occurs in Book Four where the infatuated queen asks for a renewal of the same feast:

> *nunc eadem labente die convivia quaerit,*
> *Iliacosque iterum demens audire labores*
> *exposcit.*

> Now, as day wanes, she seeks the same banquet, and again, in her madness, demands to hear the sorrows of Troy.

> (Verg. *Aen.* iv. 77-9)

In her lovesickness, she has already drunk deep of Aeneas's words and now, as her regal individuality yields to someone else's rhetorical iteration, she requests a new performance. The tale that she had heard, and yearns to hear again, concerns a city whose invaders find it 'buried in sleep and wine' (*somno vinoque sepultam*, ii. 265). Overindulgence in love's liquor will not allow her to perceive that, as Aeneas repeats the tale of Troy's drunken demise, her own urban dreams have come to a halt. Virgil tightens the parallel at the moment of her suicide by comparing the re-echo of the city's lamentation in simile to the collapse of Carthage or Tyre, become prey to an enemy's flames.

The 'releasing god' of wine in Jasper Griffin's title, Lyaeus, whose presence Venus anticipates at Dido's ceremony of reception, reappears in the *Aeneid* only at the opening of Book Four where *pater Lyaeus* (58) is among the divinities to whom the wavering Dido, once more with *patera* in hand, offers libation. Release here will be from the *pudor* that only momentarily keeps her recklessness in control. The ultimate freeing come only with death.

Finally let me offer a word on wine become blood as the nearly last stop on this journey from love and celebration to suicide. The word Virgil adopts for the transformed liquid is not *sanguis* but *cruor*. The choice anticipates the final metamorphosis Dido effects on herself, from life to death. Both at the moment when she kills herself and as her sister staunches her wounds, Virgil makes use again of *cruor*. The first instance is particularly noteworthy, dwelling as it does on 'her sword frothing with blood' (*ensem ... cruore / spumantem*, 664-5). Virgil has carefully kept the image of frothing before our attention earlier in Book Four when he describes the frothing reins of Dido's steeds, prior to the hunt, or the frothing boar Ascanius imagines as his quarry. This continuum aids in recalling the still earlier moment of the feast in Dido's palace when the queen merely tastes the wine while Bitias, at her challenge:

> *... ille impiger hausit*
> *spumantem pateram et pleno se proluit auro*

> Briskly drained the foaming cup, and drank deep from the gold's fullness

> (Verg. *Aen.* i. 738-9).

On the literal level her moderation here is counterbalanced by the deep, foaming draughts in which Bitias and his fellow courtiers find pleasure. As restraint in her life yields to self-indulgence and then to suicide, the poet with consummate irony reverses his usage, appropriately giving the metaphor to dying Dido as frothing and then release, attribute and trait of wine in other circumstances, help articulate her final moments.

20

Le Vin et l'Honneur

ANDRÉ TCHERNIA

Mort il y a peu d'années, le baron Philippe de Rothschild, propriétaire à Pauillac du célèbre château Mouton-Rothschild, était aussi un fin lettré, savant traducteur de poèmes élisabéthains. Pendant quinze ans de sa vie, il a bataillé pour que le Mouton-Rothschild, classé second cru par le syndicat des courtiers de commerce près la Bourse de Bordeaux en 1855, acquît le rang de premier cru, et il a fini par obtenir gain de cause en 1973. La devise du Mouton-Rothschild, qui avait été jusque-là 'Premier ne puis, second ne daigne, Mouton suis', devint 'Second fus, premier suis, Mouton reste'.

Trois siècles plus tôt, le 10 avril 1663, Samuel Pepys notait dans son journal qu'il était passé à la taverne du Chêne Royal dans Lombard Street à Londres, où il avait rencontré le poète Alexander Brome: '*a merry and witty man, I believe, if he be not a little conceited. And here drank a sort of French wine called Ho Bryan that hath a good and most perticular taste that I never met with*'. C'est la plus ancienne mention littéraire d'un cru identifié par le nom de la propriété, et limité à elle: en l'occurrence, le Château Haut-Brion. Quelques années plus tard, son propriétaire Arnaud de Pontac, qui était aussi le brillant premier président du Parlement de Bordeaux, eut l'idée remarquable d'envoyer son fils François-Auguste fonder en 1666 à Londres un établissement à l'enseigne de 'Chez Pontac' qui tenait à la fois de l'épicerie fine, de la taverne de luxe et du restaurant gastronomique. Bientôt fréquentée par l'aristocratie et l'intelligentsia de Londres, cette maison contribua à étendre et à assurer la réputation du Château Haut-Brion. Vingt ans après Samuel Pepys, John Evelyn, son ami et rival en journal, familier de la Cour, juge digne de consigner le 13 juillet 1683 non seulement la qualité des vins, mais l'intérêt d'avoir eu une conversation avec François-Auguste: '*I had much discourse with Monsieur de Pontaq; this gentleman, who is the famous and wise President of Bordeaux' son, is the owner of the delightful vineyards of Pontac and O' Brien, whence come our finest and best Bordeaux wines*'.[1]

Personne, je pense, même parmi les plus fervents partisans de l'implication de l'élite romaine dans le commerce, n'imaginerait qu'on pût avoir à Rome ou à Alexandrie une taverne au nom d'un chevalier ou même d'un juge de la quatrième décurie. Je passe là-dessus, qui n'est pas de notre sujet. Si j'ai cité ces deux exemples, c'est pour montrer que la qualité du Château Haut-Brion a manifestement fait honneur au dix-septième siècle à une famille de noblesse de robe, récente mais déjà célèbre, comme celle des Pontac, et que de notre temps Philippe de Rothschild trouvait

---

[1]Sur les Pontac, voir R. Pijassou, *Un grand vignoble de qualité: le Médoc* (Paris, 1980), 330-40.

conforme à sa dignité de faire tous ses efforts pour que son vin reçût officiellement le rang qu'il estimait lui revenir. Il est beaucoup plus connu comme propriétaire du Château Mouton-Rothschild que comme traducteur de poèmes élisabéthains.

Aucun texte latin ne va dans ce sens-là; aucun ne nous donne le nom du propriétaire d'un vignoble de qualité exceptionnelle. Personne ne s'est jamais flatté, dans les textes qui nous sont parvenus, de produire un meilleur vin que les autres. Plusieurs personnages, en revanche, se sont fait un nom grâce au rendement de leurs plants: les viticulteurs du monde romain ont mis leur point d'honneur dans la quantité.

Marcius Libo, *praefectus fabrum* de Varron au moment de la guerre des pirates, a laissé son nom dans l'histoire parce que sa propriété de Faventia rapportait 300 amphores par jugère, c'est-à-dire un rendement difficilement croyable de 316 hectolitres/hectare (Varron, *Rust.* i. 2.7). Columelle est heureux de pouvoir au moins avancer, pour quelques-unes de ses vignes, 100 amphores au jugère (*Rust.* iii. 3.3). Mais l'histoire la plus significative est celle d'Acilius Stenhelus, un affranchi qui s'était fait une spécialité d'augmenter la valeur des terres en les plantant de vignes à haut rendement: voilà, selon Pline (*HN* xiv. 48-51), l'exemple du parfait vigneron. Après avoir réussi à vendre 400.000 sesterces 60 jugères de vignes qu'il possédait près de Nomentum, il travailla sur un vignoble voisin appartenant au célèbre grammairien Remmius Palémon: au bout de huit ans, la récolte d'un domaine acheté 600.000 sesterces fut adjugée sur pied pour 400.000. 'Tout le monde courut voir les monceaux de raisins dans ces vignes'. La réputation et la séduction de ces hauts rendements furent tels que Sénèque — *minime utique miratore inanium, vir excellentis ingenii atque doctrinae*, précisent Pline et Columelle (*Rust.* iii. 3.3) à propos de cette affaire — acheta deux ans plus tard le domaine de Remmius Palémon quatre fois ce qu'il avait coûté à celui-ci. Il put ainsi se faire honneur d'un vignoble produisant 160 amphores par jugère, soit 170 hectolitres/hectare d'un vin qui ne pouvait, avec ce rendement-là, qu'être des plus communs. Il confirmait ainsi la formule d'une de ses lettres à Lucilius (41. 7): *Vitem laudamus, si fructu palmites onerat, si ipsa pondere ad terram eorum quae tulit adminicula deducit: num quis illam proferret vitem cui aureae uvae, aurea folia dependent? Propria virtus est in vite fertilitas.*

Comme on est loin de ce que dirait le marquis de Lur-Saluces, propriétaire du Château d'Yquem, qui se flatte de ne pas faire produire plus d'un verre à chacun de ses ceps porteurs de raisins d'or!

Comment expliquer que la hiérarchie si ostensible des vins romains n'ait joué que pour la consommation, sans entraîner une rivalité des producteurs vers la qualité? On alléguera la lenteur avec laquelle la notion de cru individuel s'est dégagée de celle de cru régional — il a fallu, nous venons de le voir, attendre le dix-septième siècle. On notera que les agronomes latins n'ont pas clairement aperçu la relation inverse qu'entretiennent quantité et qualité. Pline se contredit là-dessus à quelques pages d'intervalle puisque, après avoir raconté l'histoire de Remmius Palémon et de Sénèque, il ajoute : 'De tels efforts mériteraient de profiter aux terroirs du Cécube et de Setia'; mais un peu plus loin il regrette que les vignerons du Falerne s'attachent de son temps plus à la quantité qu'à la qualité (*HN* xiv. 52 et 62). Derrière tout cela, je crois que l'idée de base est que l'honneur d'un propriétaire terrien était avant tout de s'enrichir en cultivant son domaine, le moyen le plus honorable qui soit de gagner de l'argent. L'agriculture, et particulièrement la viticulture, ne sont pas une forme d'art qui pourrait, au moins quelquefois, trouver sa fin en lui-même; elles se jugent aux profits qu'elles rapportent. Même Graecinus, qui a le mieux perçu le choix radical que doit faire le viticulteur entre la qualité et la quantité, ne plaide pas pour un effort systématique dans le sens de la qualité; c'est le profit qui compte: *Ubi multa invitabunt regionis commoda ut nobilem vitem conseramus generosam requiremus; ubi nihil erit aut non multum quod proritet, feracitatem potius sequamur, quae non eadem portione vincitur pretio quam vincit abundantia* (Columelle, *Rust.* iii. 2.31). Et la *sententia* brillante revient à Pline: *Bene colere necessarium est, optime damnosum* (*HN* xviii. 37). Aussi est-il particulièrement intéressant — je le dis entre parenthèses — de noter que Remmius Palémon vend sa récolte sur pied: même pour cet athlète de la productivité agricole, le profit s'arrête là; il ne cherche pas à l'étendre par une opération proprement commerciale.

Bien entendu, ces remarques ne doivent pas faire oublier que la possession de vignes du Falerne, du Cécube ou d'autres crus très célèbres fait partie, dans de nombreux poèmes en particulier, des signes qui manifestent une richesse hors de l'ordinaire. Les vins venant de ces régions se vendaient cher, facilement et rapportaient beaucoup, et c'est peut-être justement parce que cela suffisait que ne s'est pas exercée entre les propriétaires de ces crus une rivalité de qualité qui aurait fait dégager la notion de clos ou de château. Le succès des appellations régionales a peut-être empêché la naissance des vins de propriété: si on en voit poindre l'idée, c'est dans le plus ancien de nos textes, quand Caton recommande de vendanger tardivement *ne vinum nomen perdat* (*Agr.* 25).

***

S'il semble indifférent à un grand personnage de produire sur ses terres du bon ou du mauvais vin, il lui est tout à fait nécessaire d'en boire du bon. La règle générale est claire: à un rang social différent correspond une catégorie de vin différente. Pour me mettre en conformité avec le titre de ce colloque, je dirai que la vérité de l'homme est dans ce qu'il boit.

La création d'une hiérarchie codifiée des grands crus accompagne la phase ultime de l'enrichissement de l'élite romaine. On trouve en 102 avant notre ère la plus ancienne mention du Falerne sur une amphore du Castro Pretorio (*CIL* XV, 4554). D'autres noms s'y sont ajoutés dans la première moitié du premier siècle et, pour nous, la première liste structurable s'établit d'après Horace. Le livre xiv de Pline (*HN*) présente un système complet avec quatre catégories hiérarchisées de 'grands crus classés' (comportant quatorze noms), et 28 crus non classés ayant une réputation reconnue. La liste sera tenue à jour ultérieurement. J'attribuerais assez volontiers maintenant le point de départ de cette liste à Asclépiade de Pruse, le médecin de Crassus, qui a été surnommé *oinodotes* parce qu'il avait écrit un traité sur l'administration du vin aux malades.

De fait, il faut, pour que naissent des grands crus, une société fortement différenciée; inversement, il fallait à la société romaine une échelle bien différenciée des vins pour coller à l'échelle bien différenciée des fortunes, sauf à laisser, de façon humiliante pour la Romanité, les vins grecs jouer seuls le rôle de signes distinctifs. Il fallait enfin à Horace une liste de vins bien hiérarchisée pour créer une poésie du symposium romain puisque, au contraire de la poésie grecque, elle insiste, comme l'a bien souligné Oswyn Murray, sur l'inégalité.[2] Le Falerne et le Cécube vont devenir des termes du vocabulaire poétique quelque temps après que les grands vins seront entrés dans la série des signes de raffinement obligés, et inversement les mauvais dans celle des signes de grossièreté.

Quand Cicéron veut discréditer Pison, prouver qu'il ne vaut même pas le *praeco* de Milan qui lui a servi d'aïeul, il dit que 'sa table est chargée non de coquillages ou de poissons, mais d'énormes pièces de viande un peu rance: des esclaves salement vêtus font le service; plusieurs même déjà vieux; le même lui sert de cuisiner et de portier; chez lui ni panetier, ni sommelier: le pain se prend chez le boulanger et le vin au litre' (*Pis.* 67). J'ai emprunté cette traduction à l'édition Pancoucke de 1840, qui a joué avec bonheur sur l'anachronique litre pour traduire *de cupa*; le sens exact est que Pison se fournit dans un débit de boissons qui conserve en cuve un vin évidemment commun et le débite aux acheteurs dans les récipients qu'ils apportent eux-mêmes.

A l'inverse, le mauvais buveur déshonore le vin, comme le mauvais vin déshonore le buveur. Il faut avoir, comme Trimalcion, le génie de la grossièreté et de la sottise dans l'étalage de ses richesses pour donner du Falerne aux masseurs de ses thermes (Pétrone, *Sat.* xxviii. 3). Martial, en connaisseur polémiste, s'acharne sur deux vins qui lui paraissent sans doute surfaits: le vin de Marseille et le vin des Marses. Le premier fera l'affaire si l'on doit distribuer des sportules par centaines (xiii. 123); le second, mieux vaut le donner à un de ses affranchis que le boire soi-même (xiii. 121).

* * *

C'est par Horace que nous apercevons le mieux la complexité de la répartition qui joue sur une fourchette: le vin des jours de fête et le vin quotidien. Même Mécène semble réserver le meilleur de tous à l'époque, le Cécube, pour les jours de fête (*Epod.* ix. 1-4). Horace, ces jour-là, s'élève jusqu'à l'Albanum, au Massique, ou au vin de Calès. Mais il boit plus souvent du vin de Sabine, vieux de quatre ans dans l'*Ode* i. 9, et qu'il a mis lui-même en amphores, dans la célèbre *Ode* i. 20: *Vile potabis* .... Si Antonius Musa l'envoie pour sa santé à Vélia ou à Salerne, il se préoccupe de faire venir un vin qui lui convienne, *nam vina nihil moror illius orae*. Bien loin de lui, tout en bas de l'échelle, le marinier qui conduit la barque halée sur le canal des Marais Pontins s'enivre de *vappa*, un vin tourné après une fermentation secondaire (*Sat.* i. 5.16), et l'image de l'avarice extrême est donnée par qui boit de la *vappa* tous les jours et l'affreux rosé de Véies les jours de fête (*Sat.* ii. 3.142-4).

Les extrêmes ne se rencontrent jamais, non seulement parce que les grands vins sont bien évidemment inaccessibles aux plus pauvres, mais aussi parce qu'il serait inconvenant pour un grand personnage de boire leur vin. L'exemple le plus flagrant et le plus tragique à la fois en est donné par l'histoire de l'orateur M. Antonius que raconte Plutarque dans sa *Vie de Marius*. Nous sommes en 87, au moment des proscriptions de Marius. Antoine a trouvé refuge chez un ami sûr, mais pauvre et plébéien (πένης καὶ δημοτικός). En tant que tel, il boit d'ordinaire un vin qui est lui aussi plébéien et, pire encore, nouveau (νέον καὶ δημοτικόν). Impressionné par l'arrivée

---

[2]O. Murray, 'Symposium and genre in the poetry of Horace', *JRS* 75 (1985), 39-50.

d'Antoine, ancien consul, ancien censeur, il envoie un esclave en acheter du meilleur, de l'excellent, du cher, chez son boutiquier habituel. Celui-ci s'étonne, interroge l'esclave qui dit naïvement la vérité, sans se douter que le boutiquier est un scélérat et un impie qui va aller aussitôt dénoncer Antoine à Marius. Sans attendre d'avoir fini de dîner, celui-ci donne ordre de faire massacrer Antoine et de lui apporter sa tête, ce qui fut fait.

Que ce récit soit vrai ou faux, Plutarque y ajoutait foi et le souci du pauvre plébéien prend tout son relief quand on replace la scène dans le contexte de ces journées de massacre, où les cadavres jonchaient les rues et où les partisans et les esclaves de Marius traquaient leurs victimes dans toute la ville: il a fallu quand même offrir à Antoine un vin moins indigne de lui, et éviter de lui faire boire un vin de l'année. C'est en effet le pire des défauts, et il est vrai que, pour être encore buvable après un an, le vin, tant qu'on n'avait pas pris l'habitude de le traiter au soufre, devait témoigner d'une bonne qualité naturelle.

Avant d'avoir passé un an, le vin est donc nouveau, et les gens bien nés n'en boivent pas. Voyons dans Elien (*Lettre* viii. 30) l'amusante colère de la courtisane Opora à qui son amant a cru spirituel d'envoyer à l'automne des cadeaux inspirés par son nom: 'Beaux cadeaux que les tiens, des fruits de deux sous et du vin dont la jeunesse fait un affront' (ὑβριστὴς διὰ νεότητα).

Il n'y a sans doute qu'une chose plus outrageante que d'offrir du vin nouveau: faire boire son hôte dans de la terre-cuite. Car une hiérarchie de la vaisselle accompagne celle des vins et doit s'harmoniser avec eux. Martial se fâche d'autant plus du vin nouveau qu'on le lui fait boire dans de l'argenterie d'antiquaire (viii. 6.16), qui conviendrait à un vieux Falerne, ou qu'on lui propose de l'accompagner d'une coupe d'or: *Quisquam plumbea vina vult in auro?* (xi. 49.5). L'idée de mettre un grand vin dans de la terre-cuite serait bouffonne. Q. Aelius Tubéron a fait preuve de grossièreté stoïcienne selon Cicéron (*Mur.* 75), d'une sorte d'héroïsme immortel selon Sénèque (*Ep.* xcv. 72-3) quand il a fait, à la fin du deuxième siècle avant notre ère, placer des *fictilia* devant les convives d'un repas funèbre dressé en souvenir de Scipion l'Africain. L'absence de vaisselle d'argent suffit comme référence à Suétone pour montrer l'*inopia* et l'*infamia* dans lesquelles Domitien a passé son adolescence (*Dom.* 2). Mais l'anecdote la plus étonnante, racontée à la fois par Tacite (*Hist.* i. 48.6), Suétone (*Claude* 32) et Plutarque (*Galba* 12. 4), porte sur une mésaventure de Titus Vinius, le futur conseiller de Galba: Claude le soupçonnait d'avoir volé une coupe d'or à sa table; pour toute et suffisante punition, il le réinvita le lendemain et le fit servir dans de la terre-cuite. Toutefois, dans ce cas, je crois qu'il s'agit avant tout d'un jeu pédant de l'érudit Claude, qui s'est sans doute souvenu d'un passage où Ctésias dit que 'chez les Perses, celui à qui le roi veut marquer son mépris use de coupes en terre-cuite' (παρὰ Πέρσαις, φησίν, ὅν ἂν βασιλεὺς ἀτιμάσῃ, κεραμέοις ποτηρίοις χρῆται (in Ath. xi. 464A).

* * *

A l'intangibilité de la hiérarchie que j'essaie de démontrer, on objectera sans doute le *Vile potabis modicis Sabinum cantharis* d'Horace à Mécène (*Carm.* i. 20) et la série des poèmes d'invitation où le poète s'excuse de ne pouvoir offrir à son hôte le grand vin auquel il est habitué. Il est amusant que le modèle en soit, dans l'*Anthologie grecque* (xi. 44), un poème adressé par Philodème à Pison que nous venons de voir décrit par Cicéron comme un grossier personnage. La différence avec le poème d'Horace — et là encore je cite Oswyn Murray — est que Philodème indique clairement à Pison que, s'il en reçoit plus d'argent, il le fera mieux dîner. Mais l'un et l'autre manifestent la dignité de leur hôte en soulignant la différence entre les possibilités médiocres de leur modeste statut et l'excellence des vins qui font partie de son ordinaire et devraient normalement lui convenir: le Chio pour Pison, le Cécube, le Calès, le Falerne pour Mécène. Les poèmes d'invitation constituent l'exception qui confirme la règle. Horace, du reste, est loin de faire boire n'importe quoi à Mécène et à Torquatus, et surtout pas du vin nouveau: les vins qu'il servira ont vieilli entre six et huit ans; par leur millésime pour Mécène, par leur terroir pour Torquatus, ils forment aussi une allusion flatteuse à l'histoire de ces grands hommes.

Voyons maintenant un phénomène inverse qui semble s'être développé dans le courant du premier siècle de notre ère. César dans sa munificence sert apparemment à tous du Falerne et du Chio dans les banquets qu'il dresse pour ses triomphes (Pline, *HN* xiv. 97). A l'époque de Martial et de Juvénal, quand un personnage important offre un banquet à de nombreux convives, il ne leur sert pas à tous le même vin et veille à ce que la qualité des crus réponde à celle des dîneurs. Les plaintes de Martial là-dessus (iii. 49; vi. 11.2-3; x. 49) et la *Satire* v de Juvénal sont bien connues. La *Lettre* ii. 6 de Pline le Jeune est particulièrement intéressante: d'une part elle montre une hiérarchie à trois niveaux: *sibi et nobis, minoribus amicis, suis nostrisque libertis*; d'autre part elle indique cette pratique comme nouvelle: *istam luxuriae et sordium nova societas*.[3] La première mention que j'en connaisse est effectivement dans Pline l'Ancien, où elle apparaît comme moins générale (*HN* xiv. 91). S'il s'agit alors vraiment d'une nouveauté, on serait tenté de mettre en relation ce mélange de luxe et d'économie (*luxuria specie frugalitatis*, dit Pline le Jeune) avec la disparition progressive de la prodigalité de la table que Tacite (*Ann.* iii. 55) remarque en particulier après Vespasien. Il est intéressant que nos sources donnent deux interprétations de l'usage: celle de Juvénal (v. 156-74), pour qui il s'agit d'une façon qu'a l'hôte de marquer son pouvoir sur son client, et celle strictement économique que suggère le dialogue cité (ou imaginé) par Pline, que nous examinons: à son interlocuteur qui lui demande s'il approuve les trois catégories de leur hôte, il répond que non:

-Eadem omnibus pono.
-Etiamne libertos?
-Etiam.
-Magno tibi constat!
-Minime.
-Quid fieri potest?
-Potest quia scilicet liberti mei non idem quod ego bibunt, sed idem ego quod et liberti.

(Pline, *Ep.* ii. 6)

Depuis Caton, qui disait boire en temps de guerre le même vin que ses rameurs, Pline est la première personne à se vanter de partager le vin d'inférieurs. Savoir

---

[3]Sur ce passage, et sur la hiérarchie inégalitaire du banquet romain en général, voir J. D'Arms, 'The Roman *Convivium* and the idea of equality', dans O. Murray (ed.), *Sympotica: a Symposium on the Sym-posion* (Oxford, 1990), 308-20.

quelle est dans cette lettre la part de pose philosophique éloignée de la pratique réelle, ou celle de l'envahissement des exercices de tempérance liés à la culture de soi chère à Michel Foucault, est un point difficile à trancher; c'est sans doute par malveillance que je pencherais pour la première solution. Pline, en tout cas, n'a pas fait école puisque 50 ans plus tard, dans les *Saturnales* de Lucien (17-22), les pauvres se plaignent à Kronos dans les mêmes termes que se plaignaient Martial et Juvénal, et Kronos lui-même se sent obligé de dire un mot aux riches de ἐκεῖνο τὸ μὴ τοῦ αὐτοῦ οἴνου συμπίνειν, Ἡράκλεις, ὡς ἀνελεύθερον. A quoi les riches répondront que les pauvres boivent trop, qu'une fois ivres ils se conduisent fort mal et qu'après avoir vomi dans toute la salle à manger, ils la quittent en insultant leur hôte et en les accusant à tort de les laisser affamés et assoiffés.

Tous ces exemples se rangent sans peine parmi les signes multiples de différenciation sociale d'une société où chacun existait d'abord comme membre d'un ordre déterminé et occupant un rang bien précis. L'admiration du pauvre pour les biens dont use le riche commande l'admiration que celui-ci a pour lui-même, et son plaisir d'être riche serait bien moins grand si les pauvres n'étaient pas là pour l'admirer. Avant Veblen et Veyne, le Kronos des *Saturnales* de Lucien (29-35) l'avait parfaitement expliqué.

S'agissant du vin, il y a peut-être quelque chose à ajouter. Dans son livre xxiii, où il parle des propriétés médicales des fruits, Pline l'Ancien ouvre son chapitre sur la santé et le vin par cette phrase: *Saluberrimum liberaliter genitis Campaniae quodcumque tenuissimum, vulgo vero quod quemque juverit validum.* Je cite la traduction de Jacques André (Les Belles Lettres (Paris, 1971)): 'Tous les vins les plus légers de Campanie sont les plus sains pour les gens comme il faut, pour les gens du peuple de complexion robuste, celui qui plaît à chacun'. La traduction de *liberaliter geniti* est reprise de Littré. Les traducteurs de l'édition Einaudi disent *gente di origine aristocratica*.

L'intérêt de la phrase de Pline est qu'il n'y est plus question de rang social, mais de nature. L'organisme des *liberaliter geniti* a besoin d'un vin fluide, venant d'une région de bons crus; l'organisme des autres peut s'accommoder de n'importe quoi qui leur plaise: ils ont une nature plus résistante. On pense au sens de 'délicat, fragile' qu'*ingenuus* reçoit dans les textes poétiques. Avec cette phrase, nous touchons au problème de la part de l'*adscription* et de celle de l'*achievement* dans la société romaine, de la confluence de la naissance, de la richesse et de la carrière dans la définition du statut personnel. C'est un autre et vaste sujet; contentons-nous de verser cette phrase au dossier de la naissance et, en ce qui concerne le vin, au dossier de la complexité de cette boisson qui, plus que toute autre nourriture, est à la fois aliment, remède, plaisir et symbole.

21

Heavy Drinking and Drunkenness in the Roman World:
Four Questions for Historians

JOHN H. D'ARMS

DRUNKENNESS AND *DECORUM*

In the second book of his *Paedagogus* (*The Instructor*), Clement of Alexandria urges his readers 'to drink without contortions of the face, not greedily grasping the cup, nor before drinking making the eyes roll with unseemly motion; nor from intemperance draining the cup at one draught; nor besprinkling the chin, nor splashing one's garments while gulping down all the wine at once — the face all but filling the bowl, and drowned in it'.[1]

In strikingly visual language, Clement here succeeds in bringing the ancient drinker before our very eyes; and the passage performs another function, too, in underscoring the way in which the upper classes connect proper control of physical gesture with proper behaviour (εὐσχημοσύνη) which the Romans, for their part, knew as *decorum*. Two centuries before, Cicero, in the *de Officiis*, discoursed at length upon *decorum* (τὸ πρέπον) and its place within the Roman aristocratic system of values; in practical terms, he argued, *quod decet honestum est, et quod honestum est, decet*; and although he admits that the difference between *honestum* and *decorum* is 'more easily felt than explained', firm control of the appetite for food and drink — indeed, resisting overindulgence of any sensual sort — is integral, he makes clear, to the observance of *decorum*.[2]

Clement's emphasis was on the manner of drinking: more commonly the focus is upon the quantities of wine consumed. When the *vir bonus* drinks, *salubris moderatio* is always observed; Seneca's *sapiens* will always stop short of *ebrietas*; men of *dignitas* will

---

[1] Clem. Al. *Paedagogus* ii. 2.31 (mens' drinking: for unseemly drinking by women cf. ii. 2.34; below, n. 66; Ath. x. 440F, an important passage). See now N. Purcell, 'Women and wine in ancient Rome', in M. McDonald (ed.), *Gender, Drink and Drugs* (Oxford, 1994), 191ff. For the Stoic elements in Clement, see P.A. Brunt, 'Stoicism and the Principate', *PBSR* 43 (1975), 35.

[2] Cic. *Off.* i. 93-106. The logical relationship between *decorum* and the four moral virtues is not made very clear from Cicero's discussion; but Brunt's description ('Stoicism and the Principate', above, n. 1) of Panaetius's conception of the links between virtues and *decorum* is pertinent: '... the virtues are inter-twined; "decorum" is a sort of bloom on them all, though most conspicuous in the control of the passions' (p. 34).

observe strict limits at their *convivia*: limits to ostentatious display, to the time spent at table, and to drinking.[3] Excess in high political circles might have especially damaging consequences for social order, and so required extraordinary measures: among the reasons for Augustus's exile of Julia were her revelling and drinking bouts and Suetonius notes that she was forbidden wine during her banishment.[4] This emphasis on moderation is unremarkable in general terms; parallels may be found in other private spheres.[5] But wine and wine-drinking hold special fascination for moralists, philosophers, and other members of the educated élite, owing in part to their inherent potential for danger — for wine causes inebriation, a consequent loss of control over other appetites, and hence constitutes a special threat to the breaching of propriety (*decorum*).

All the more interesting, therefore, are the many passages that seem to condone inebriation. *Dulce est desipere in loco*: La Penna notices some Horatian instances of such 'places' elsewhere in these pages; for instance, victory at Actium, or the safe return of an absent friend.[6] Seneca admits that the *sapiens* can be so taken up with the social virtue of *hilaritas in convivio*, that he can move rather far along the path to drunkenness; and he actually recommends, in the *de Tranquillitate Animi*, that 'occasionally we should reach the point of drunkenness' (*usque ad ebrietatem veniendum*).[7] Indeed, *liberalior potio* was so often and obviously considered acceptable by the Roman governing classes, and phrases such as *bene poti*, and *supermodum poti* are so routinely encountered,[8] that we might be prompted to ask: what are the types of case (for Roman mentalities) which sociologists of drink would term 'permissible insobriety'; under what circumstances might a Roman notable be drunk without impropriety, without a breach of *decorum*?

Prima facie, given the firm Roman distinction between *negotium* and *otium*, between behaviour appropriate for the hours of work and that appropriate for periods of leisure, we might expect to find the clearest and most conspicuous cases of *impermissible* drunkenness outside the *triclinium*, where a man's intemperance can be seen as interfering with his proper conduct of the public business. In this connection, let us consider, as a case-study, some of the prodigious Roman drinkers who appear in the well-known discussions of drunkenness in Seneca and Pliny the Elder. Novellius Torquatus, who could empty three *congii* at a single go, L. Piso, who held the dubious distinction of participating in the longest Roman drinking bout on record, and Cossus,

---

[3] Sen. *Tranq.* 17.9 (*salubris moderatio*); *Ep.* lxxxiii. 17 (*sapiens*); Pliny, *Ep.* iii. 12 (limits); cf. also Cic. *Off.* i. 106, on the need to keep the promptings of *voluptas* under strict control. Many of the Horatian allusions to moderation in drinking were assembled long ago by A.P. McKinlay, 'The wine element in Horace', *CJ* 42 (1946-7), 165-6. Cf. also C.R. Haines, *The Correspondence of M. Cornelius Fronto* I (London, 1919), 276 (a large proportion of water is mixed with wine ἐν τοῖς σώφροσιν συμποσίοις).

[4] Suet. *Aug.* 65.3.

[5] For emphasis upon *moderatio* (along with *frugalitas* and *parsimonia*) in eating habits, see now M. Corbier, 'The ambiguous status of meat in Ancient Rome', *Food and Foodways* 3 (1989), 246ff.; on individuals' control of personal consumption in the face of luxurious excesses of the state, see E. Gowers, *The Loaded Table* (Oxford, 1993), 13-14.

[6] Hor. *Carm.* iv. 12.28; ii. 7.27ff.; cf. also i. 36 — discussed by La Penna in this volume; i. 37. Cf. also McKinlay, 'The wine element in Horace' (above, n. 3), 161-5.

[7] Sen. *Ep.* lxxxiii. 17; *Tranq.* 17.9.

[8] See e.g. Cic. *Fam.* 7.22 (*etsi domum bene potus seroque redieram*); cf. Apul. *Met.* iii. 5 (*potulentus alioquin*, another late and tipsy return home); Macrob. *Sat.* vii. 3 (*vino vel infusum vel aspersum*); Suet. *Otho* ii. 1. Cf. the *seribibi universi*, electoral supporters in Pompeii (*CIL* IV, 581 — surely ironic).

described as *mersus et vino madens*, were notorious. Piso, we are informed, routinely slept off his intoxication throughout the mornings, and Cossus, once unable to be roused from drunken slumber at a meeting of the senate, had to be physically removed and carried home.[9] And yet, both Pliny and Seneca are at pains to emphasize that these topers had distinguished careers and earned plaudits as highly effective public figures.

To be sure, these persons need to be seen in a larger context; they have their place within a group of Roman politicians and public officials known to combine, to an extraordinary degree, *industria* and ability on the one hand, *luxuria* and other defects of character on the other. M. Caelius Rufus, Maecenas, Petronius, Otho, Mucianus are examples, men termed *personalità paradossali* by La Penna, who has well analyzed these and other cases, and clarified the historiographical tradition to which they belong.[10] But we still might ask: does not the emphasis upon the distinguished public achievements of men singled out for drunkenness help to create the impression that upper-class ranks close rather protectively around the conduct of fellow notables? Are we not left wondering how far, in the eyes of senatorial peers, stigma actually attached even in such conspicuous cases of drunken conduct as these?

'How many the evils which he inflicted upon the world through this vice of drunkenness'.[11] About M. Antonius, last on Pliny's list of notorious drunkards, it was easy to be unambiguous; Antonius was publicly discredited, having chosen the wrong side at the battle of Actium, and earlier having put to death the father of Latin letters; by Pliny's day, Antonius was universally judged to be an enemy of the state.[12] Cicero had much earlier formulated the case against his drinking in hyperbolic language. Antonius had consumed vast quantities of wine at Hippias's wedding: that was no disgrace. What caused unspeakable offence occurred next morning when, carrying out public business as *magister equitum*, Antonius 'vomited and filled his own lap and the whole tribunal with bits of food reeking with wine'.[13] To be sure, this is the M. Antonius of Cicero's second *Philippic*, where the veracity of any particular allegation is hugely suspect. And hence we have all the more reason to regret that the contents of the *de Ebrietate Sua*, Antonius's defence of his own conduct,[14] have not come down to us: they might have done much to clarify (among other things) the ways in which one Roman notable articulated the relationship between drunkenness and *decorum*.

[9] Sen. *Ep.* lxxxiii. 14-15; Pliny, *HN* xiv. 144. The same tale about L. Calpurnius Piso Frugi (cos. 15 BCE) is reported by Suet. *Tib.* 42.3.

[10] A. La Penna, 'Il ritratto "paradossale" da Silla a Petronio', in A. La Penna, *Aspetti del pensiero storico latino* (Turin, 1978), 193ff.; and, more recently, 'Ancora sul ritratto "paradossale"', *SIFC* 52 (1980), 244-50. For good remarks on the magnetism of such *exempla*, see J. Griffin, 'Propertius and Antony', *JRS* 67 (1977), 21-2 (= *Latin Poets and Roman Life* (North Carolina, 1985), 39-40).

[11] Pliny, *HN* xiv. 148.

[12] For public perceptions and artistic representations of M. Antonius prior and subsequent to Actium, see now P. Zanker, *Augustus und die Macht der Bilder* (Munich, 1987), 65-73 (= *The Power of Images in the Age of Augustus* (Michigan, 1988), 57-65).

[13] Cic. *Phil.* ii. 63 (where however Hippia (bride) may be the correct reading); the later episode occurred in the *porticus Minucia* (cf. ii. 84). Cf. Quint. viii. 6.68 on the hyperbole.

[14] Pliny, *HN* xiv. 148 ... *volumine de sua ebrietate, quo patrocinari sibi ausus* ... Pliny dates the work just before the battle of Actium. On Antonius's drunkenness see also Sen. *Ep.* lxxxiii. 25 (without reference, however, to the *de Ebrietate Sua*). Zanker, *The Power of Images* (above, n. 12), 60, plausibly notes that 'the work was directed at people who not only could read, but understood such aspects of Hellenistic culture as lavish banquets and Dionysiac symposia'.

Thus, even in the cases examined here, in which *intemperantia bibendi* plays itself out in the public sphere, one wonders how far anybody seriously believed aristocratic reputations could be irreparably damaged as a result simply of heavy drinking. When we move to the more private world of *otium* — to the *convivium*, where *hilaritas* reigned, and the *comissatio* — we want first to know how far these were routine experiences for aristocrats, and how far, rather, the revelry and heavy drinking so often associated with those social institutions were exceptional, reserved for weddings, augural banquets, *cenae adventiciae*, and other culturally 'marked' occasions. Numbers, frequency, and quantities matter, for without a surer sense of these, we cannot really begin to establish the level of the upper-class Roman tolerance for wine.

But this much at least seems clear: *epulae*, *convivia*, and *comissationes* functioned in part as culturally protective devices to legitimize upper-class drinking. Drinking contests with their elaborate rules; toasts, to be drunk in as many measures as the honoured person had letters to his name; prizes given to promote *ebrietas* — all these offerred considerable scope for 'permissible insobriety'.[15] And when a drinker exceeded what might be thought to be the bounds of propriety, it is interesting to notice the kinds of excuses which members of the upper classes sometimes offered up to justify their conduct. Seneca condones the behaviour of his *sapiens*, who, as we have seen, is occasionally permitted to come perilously close to drunkenness, by ascribing it not to the *sapiens*'s own desires, but to the wish to please a friend.[16] The younger Cato's late and deep drinking was notorious; but, says Plutarch, Cato's friends took pains to explain this away by citing his passion for literary and philosophical conversation, which, owing to Cato's active public career, he had time to pursue only over the cups (again we may note the justificatory role of friends).[17] According to Pliny the Younger, when Cato staggered home drunk at dawn, he remained so awe-inspiring (*venerabilis*) that it was the passers-by who blushed with embarrassment, not Cato (*erubuisse*; would these unnamed 'passers-by' have actually reacted, one wonders, as Pliny maintains that they did?) and even Caesar (Pliny claimed) had found as much to praise as to blame in Cato's conduct.[18]

What conclusions might we draw from the texts inspected above? Firstly, *decorum* — which I take to mean the implied code of behaviour which was prevalent among Roman notables of senatorial (and sometimes sub-senatorial) rank, and which was adopted by those who wished to gain standing as members of that group — was a concept which embraced conduct both public and private. Secondly, *decorum* patently included directives for appropriate convivial conduct: if a father's chastizing of his son for causing public embarrassment by misbehaviour at a banquet can appear among the

[15] Pliny, *HN* xiv. 146: *haec ars (sc bibendi) suis legibus constat*; Novellius Torquatus is here described as an 'acute observer of the regulations intended to prevent all shirking on the part of drinkers'. For toasts, see e.g. Martial i. 71; xi. 36 (Gaius Julius Proculus, whose health was drunk with five, six and eight *cyathi* (more than four-fifths of a litre); cf. also i. 11; i. 26; x. 47, Lucian, *de Mercede Conductis* 16. The *arbiter* (or *magister*) *bibendi*, or *rex mensae* established the procedures for drinking: Cic. *Sen.* 46 (*magisteria ... a maioribus instituta*); Hor. *Carm.* ii. 7.25; Macrob. *Sat.* ii. 1 (*rex mensae*); Macrob. *Sat.* ii. 8.4 (*arbitris et magistris conviviorum*). For drinking contests, see e.g. Pliny, *HN* xiv. 140 (*certamina in bibendo*).

[16] Sen. *Ep.* lxxxiii. 15 (*aliena causa*).

[17] Plut. *Cat.* 6.2-3.

[18] Pliny, *Ep.* iii. 12.

subjects treated in a Latin school exercise book from fourth-century Gaul, we can safely conclude that notions of correct convivial deportment had long since been culturally engrained. These notions (as I have argued elsewhere) were normative to an extent, or at least coherent enough to be set down in something very like manuals of conduct: Varro discoursed on the ideal dinner party in one of his *Menippean Satires*, and a contemporary of Martial's devoted an entire work to the *optimum convivium* (appropriate drinking behaviour will certainly have been part of the contents).[19] Thirdly, excessive drinking was indeed objected to as a breach of *decorum*, especially by those skilled in invective or diatribe: what more disgraceful, Cicero once rhetorically asks, than Piso emerging, his breath reeking with drink, from a foul tavern (*taeterrima popina*) in mid-morning?[20]

But on the other hand, if Cicero had not had potent political reasons for attacking Piso, would we have known of this breach of *decorum* at all? And when we find Cicero on the defensive rather than on the attack — as in the *pro Caelio*, for example — his client's crapulous excesses are airily waved away, regarded as a merely trivial failing, to which all human beings are susceptible.[21] Indeed, and as we have seen above, all manner of excuses might be offered up by a man's friends to justify excessive drinking. I conclude that the concept of *decorum* was sufficiently elastic to ensure that some, perhaps most, aristocratic drinkers were never in serious danger of breaching it. Is it not in the interests of any educated élite to promote precisely this view, and to close their ranks in protective solidarity around the heavy drinking of fellow notables?

Finally, any discussion of *decorum* needs to take account of changes over time. Especially, the arrival of the emperor on the social scene gave the concept a new embodiment, and provided a new point of reference for the moral discourse about what constitutes excess. A particular emperor's convivial practices are likely to be reflected in the discourse of the educated élite: *decorum*, in short, like other ideologies, is a dynamic, not a static, concept.

DRINKING AND CHILDHOOD

Drunkenness, the anthropologists rightly emphasize, is learned behaviour. Rather than viewing all drunken conduct as a relaxation of cultural constraints before the levelling effects of nature, we need to recognize that drunkenness is itself culturally expressive, for it takes the form of highly patterned, learned conduct, which varies considerably from one culture to another.[22] Here is one reason why the distinctively Roman rules, contests,

---

[19] School excercise from Gaul: A.C. Dionisotti, 'From Ausonius' schooldays: a schoolbook and its relatives', *JRS* 72 (1982), 103, lines 66-7. See also P. Brown's discussion in *The Body and Society: Men, Women and Sexual Renunciation in Early Christianity* (New York, 1988), 22-4. Gell. xiii. 11.1ff. (... *in quo disserit* [sc. M. Varro] *de apto convivarum numero deque ipsius convivii habitu cultuque*); Martial ix. 77 (manuals of conduct); cf. J.H. D'Arms, 'The Romam *convivium* and the idea of equality', in O. Murray (ed.), *Sympotica: a Symposium on the* Symposion (Oxford, 1990), 317.

[20] Cic. *Pis.* 13.

[21] Cic. *Cael.* 39-47, esp. 44: ... *vitium ventris et gurgitis non modo non minuit aetas hominibus, sed etiam auget.*

[22] See M. Douglas (ed.), *Constructive Drinking: Perspectives on Drink from Anthropology* (Cambridge, 1987),

and formal codes surrounding drinking hold a special interest: they may be keys to unlocking some of the distinctive features of Roman culture. But emphasis upon learned behaviour prompts a prior question: how did young Romans of the upper classes learn what they later came to 'know' about wine and its effects? What was the relative importance of parents, the extended *familia*, and peers in the process of enculturation?

So far as I can tell, this is largely *terra incognita* within Roman cultural history; the standard works on Roman education — not surprisingly — offer no guidance; neither do the various authors in the recent volume edited by Paul Veyne, intended to advance the modern study of Roman private life to a new and higher standard;[23] and Wiedemann is similarly silent in his recent book on Roman children.[24] (Although in fairness it needs to be conceded that anthropologists themselves are only now beginning to address such matters.)[25] There may be, therefore, no definitive answers, but only a series of further questions: these may at least help to point us on the way.

First, a personal anecdote. Late in the evening of my own wedding reception, family lore has it that my father-in-law spied his youngest son, then nine years old, slumped in a chair with a glassy smile on his face and a champagne bottle — nearly empty — at his side. My father-in-law interrogated him sternly: 'When, my boy, did you last draw a sober breath?' My brother-in-law pondered briefly and then replied: 'the day before yesterday, Papa'. This banal tale may be a helpful reminder of just how wide is the gulf between learning to drink and learning to be drunk; and that we should be prepared for the appearance of these at different phases in the life cycle. Fronto once remarks that all remedies for children's sore throats are to be found in milk.[26] When did they first taste wine? Doctors prescribed it, as is clear from Celsus's observation that for *pueri*, wine needs to be diluted.[27] Other notices — for instance, that in cases of cardiac disease it is better to administer wine to a *iuvenis* than to a *puer* or that, during fever, children ought not to be given wine — may be taken to imply that wine was medicinally recommended.[28] Wine's powers to comfort the sick child have been discovered by many ages: I think it not at all fanciful to suppose that among the reasons for the emperor Augustus's known predilection for Setinum was his familiarity with it from his boyhood years in Velitrae. Galen, however, strongly opposes administering wine to children.[29]

It is just possible that family slaves played some role in introducing children to the joys of mild intoxication — at such special occasions as the *Saturnalia*, since we hear that the children of great houses sometimes waited on slaves at meals during the festivals

[23] P. Veyne (ed.), *A History of Private Life. Vol. 1. From Pagan Rome to Byzantium*, trans. A. Goldhammer (Cambridge MA, 1987).

[24] T. Wiedemann, *Adults and Children in the Roman Empire* (London, 1989). Similarly silent is M. Kleijwegt, *Ancient Youth: the Ambiguity of Youth and the Absence of Adolescence in Greco-Roman Antiquity* (Amsterdam, 1991).

[25] See e.g. D. Heath, 'A decade of development in the anthropological study of alcohol use 1970-80', in Douglas, *Constructive Drinking* (above, n. 22), 47: 'Despite the continuing importance that is placed on drinking and drunkenness as learned behaviors, there have been few attempts to study in detail the ways in which young people learn what they do "know" about alcohol and its effects'.

[26] C.R. Haines, *The Correspondence of M. Cornelius Fronto* 2 (London, 1920), 42 (162 CE).

[27] Celsus i. 32.

[28] Pliny, *HN* xxiii. 51 (cardiac disease); Celsus iii. 7.1 c (fevers).

[29] Augustus: Pliny, *HN* xiv. 61; for Augustus's tastes in wine cf. also 72. Galen: Kühn iv, 809ff.; vi, 54-5.

(and so were presumably alone with them).[30] It is possible, too, that weddings, or other family feasts — the *Caristia*, for instance, where *hilaritas* was a stated objective of the occasion[31] — helped to habituate the young to wine. In one of the imperial donations, well-known from inscriptions, by a local magistrate of pastry and sweetened wine (*crustulum* and *mulsum*) to a town's citizens, *pueri* are explicitly mentioned among the recipients.[32] On the other hand, the *pueri* in this inscription were the sons of local senators, and the text is exceptional also in other ways: it would be imprudent to infer general practice from it. All the more so, since drinking children are not to be seen, as far as I have been able to discover, in any of the representations of diners at *convivia* known from paintings and mosaics (the presence of two Christian children in the dining scene from the catacomb of San Pietro in Marcellino, which Dunbabin discusses elsewhere in this volume, belongs to a different iconographical context).[33]

Furthermore, children's access to wine-drinking as routine experience was severely impeded by another factor: they did not normally attend *convivia*. One of Plutarch's *Quaestiones Romanae* — why did Roman fathers of early times always take their young children with them to dinners — makes no sense unless *praetextati* had, as a general rule, long since been excluded from *convivia* — as Alan Booth has rightly seen.[34] Children at the imperial court sometimes attended *convivia*, but there the ambiguous status of imperial princes was reinforced by separating them physically from the company which reclined, either by seating them at the foot of the emperor's couch (rarely, in the case of Caius and Lucius Caesar in boyhood; routinely, in the case of Claudius's children) or else by providing them and their contemporaries with a table in sight of their elders but at a distance from them (as with Britannicus, when he met his death by poison in his thirteenth year).[35]

No, we should look outside family households — and past the moment when the *toga virilis* was assumed — for the settings in which young men 'learned' their heavy drinking. Two well-known critics of conditions in the Roman family under the principate implicitly suggest as much: Juvenal and Tacitus hold the moral failings of

---

[30] Lucian, *Chronos* 18.

[31] Val. Max. ii. 1.8.

[32] *CIL* X, 5853 (= *ILS*, 6271).

[33] See K. Dunbabin in this volume, pp. 262-3. For children at a banquet (seated at the ends of couches), see Veyne, *A History of Private Life* (above, n. 23), 188 (relief from the Museum of Plovdiv). Representations of drunkenness in Pompeian painting are normally restricted to the expected figures of mythology: Bacchus, Silenus, Hercules, and (from the *triclinium* from the House of the Citharist) the well-known drunken Maenad (Mus. Naz. Nap. inv. 11283). The only drunken human in painting known to me is the man supported by a slave (part of the sequence purportedly displaying the three phases of a banquet): Mus. Naz. Nap. inv. 120029; see *Pompei, Pitture e mosaici* III (Rome, 1991), 815, no. 41 (from an unnamed house, *regio* V 2, 4). But the Church fathers devote considerable attention to drinking by the young, and heavy drinking seems widespread in Roman Gaul between the third and seventh centuries: see M.B. Lancon, '*Vinolentia*: l'ivrognerie en Gaule à la fin de l'antiquité d'après les sources littéraires', *Archéologie de la vigne et du vin* (= Université de Tours, *Caesarodunum* 24) (Paris, 1990), 155-61.

[34] Plut. *Quaest. Rom.* 33 (272C); on which see A. Booth, 'The age for reclining and its attendant perils', in W.J. Slater (ed.), *Dining in a Classical Context* (Michigan, 1991), 109.

[35] Suet. *Aug.* 64.3 (Gaius and Lucius); *Claud.* 32 (his children seated at the ends of couches *cum pueris puellisque nobilibus*); Tac. *Ann.* xiii. 16.1; cf. Suet. *Ner.* 33.2; and Booth, 'The age for reclining and its attendant perils' (above, n. 34), 110: 'So, in proper imperial practice, before assumption of the *toga virilis*, princes did not recline but sat, and they did not participate fully in the *convivium*'.

parents or slave tutors directly responsible for the corruption of children, and from their lists of vices (including gluttony) passed from one generation to the next, drunkenness is conspicuous by its absence.[36] That the young first indulged in heavy drinking at a safe remove from parental influence is inherently more plausible, is strongly implied by the author of '*The Education of Children*', and is strikingly corroborated by the case of Cicero's son Marcus, whom Pliny the Elder includes among emblematic Roman drinkers. Dispatched by his father at the age of twenty to study in Athens, Marcus there came under the spell of Gorgias the rhetorician, who steered him εἰς ἡδονὰς καὶ πότους, prompting the orator to command his son to get rid of Gorgias at once.[37]

The assumption of the *toga virilis* is often viewed as the critical point in a young Roman's assertion of his individual identity, and in the serious social drinking that so often accompanied this. The experience is variously described as enabling — so Perseus would have us believe his was, under the influence of his friend and learned mentor Cornutus — or destructive: when Apuleius's stepson came under the sway of his uncle, the young man straightaway received the *toga virilis*, abandoned school and study and serious friends, and, along with other dissolute youths, took to whoring and drinking (*cum adulescentulis postremissumis inter scorta et pocula*).[38] We should look to circles of *iuvenes* and their peers, rather than across generations, for the settings which forwarded the taste for strong drink: the contemporaries of Scipio Aemilianus (then seventeen) who, says Polybius, had abandoned themselves (unlike the blameless Scipio) to musical entertainment and drinking parties, and the extravagance which these involved;[39] young officers on military assignment in the provinces, quaffing in the general's tent; *sodales*, familiar from Horace's *Odes*, who cemented youthful friendships through long hours of drinking; Catiline's sleek and luxury-loving cronies, expending their energies together at bibulous banquets which lasted till dawn (these last more than faintly reminiscent of the world of Roman elegy).[40]

'In his younger days he was too much addicted to wine'.[41] The person in question happens to be Tiberius, but it would have been easy to say the same about countless others — of the youthful Otho, or the eighteen-year old Nero and his companions, rampaging drunk through the streets, the brothels, and the wine shops of the capital; or of M. Caelius Rufus, who, in giving free reign to his *adulescentiae cupiditates* (including drinking parties) was doing no more, Cicero insists, than what nature dictated and all of mankind indulgently condoned.[42] I conclude that most Roman upper-class males will

[36] Juv. 14; Tac. *Dial.* 29.
[37] In Plut. *Mor.* 13F (*Education of Children*), a father is advised not to be critical when a son returns home with breath reeking from yesterday's debauch — that young man's drinking clearly occurred outside the household. Plut. *Cic.* 24; Cic. *Fam.* 16.21.6; on Marcus's drinking cf. Pliny, *HN* xiv. 147.
[38] Pers. v, esp. 41-4; Apul. *Apol.* 98; both texts are cited also by Booth, 'The age for reclining and its attendant perils' (above, n. 34), 108-9.
[39] Polyb. xxxi. 25.4.
[40] Gell. xv. 12 (officers); Hor. *Carm.* ii. 7 (*sodales*); Cic. *Cat.* ii. 22 (Catiline's cronies). For reflections of such entertainments in Latin literature, see J. Griffin, 'Augustan poetry and the life of luxury', *JRS* 66 (1976), 87-105 (= *Latin Poets*, above n. 10, 1-31); T.P. Wiseman, *Catullus and his World: A Reappraisal* (Cambridge, 1985), 44-7.
[41] Pliny, *HN* xiv. 145 (*ad merum pronior*).
[42] Suet. *Otho* 2; Tac. *Ann.* xiii. 26; Cic. *Cael.* 28.

have first 'learned' to be drunk at this stage in the life cycle, in the company of their youthful peers.

THE SOCIO-ECONOMIC LOCATION OF HEAVY DRINKING AND DRUNKENNESS

In '*Le vin de l'Italie romaine*', Tchernia was right to insist upon the close connection between grand wine and high status.[43] In this regard, I find satisfyingly appropriate the recent news (from the Masada texts), that a prestige wine from Italy previously unknown — Philonianum — reached the cellars of king Herod the Great and his highly sophisticated court.[44] Purcell has also contributed significantly to the question of the relationship between wine and status; in the course of making a strong case for an early imperial boom in Italian viticulture, he argues for 'a great downward diffusion of wine drinking in social terms'.[45] From various interesting questions suggested by this thesis, I single out two: first, what evidence have we for the penetration of high quality wine into lower social strata; second, is it possible to detect signs of increased heavy drinking and drunkenness in circles outside those of the élite?

Clearly, we ought not to expect to find anything like Caecuban in lower-class settings — Horace knew it of course, but seems never to have actually served it, and (if Tchernia is right) even Maecenas appears to have reserved it for feast days.[46] But Horace did drink Falernian in his more expansive moods — and Falernian could also be bought for four *asses* at the bar of Hedonius in Pompeii, where it was the highest priced of the three wines sold.[47] (I think it quite likely that some wines of superior quality were available also at the large and increasingly well-appointed wine counters which turn up in Ostia from the Flavian period.)[48] In an early second-century epitaph from Ostia, the deceased also claims close familiarity with Falernian: this man was certainly sub-equestrian in status, probably with a background in slavery.[49] We do not know the names of the wine which a slave member of the funeral college at Lanuvium was obliged to offer to *socii* to celebrate the day on which he had received his freedom — but the rules prescribed that it be *vinum bonum*.[50] An epitaph in hexameters

---

[43] A. Tchernia, *Le vin de l'Italie romaine* (BEFAR 261) (Rome, 1986), 28ff.

[44] H.M. Cotton and J. Geiger, *Masada II: The Latin and Greek Documents* (Jerusalem, 1989), 145ff. According to the editors, the type of amphora cannot be specified (p. 140), but the shipment appears to date to 19 BCE (p. 144). And as the editors rightly observe (p. 148), 'the importing of high quality wine from Italy to serve at [Herod's] table is in harmony with Josephus' testimony that he kept a special wine steward (οἰνοχόος, *AJ* xv. 223)'.

[45] N. Purcell, 'Wine and wealth in Ancient Italy', *JRS* 75 (1985), 1-19; cf. esp. p. 5.

[46] Tchernia, *Le vin de l'Italie romaine* (above, n. 43), 28-34, citing Hor. *Epod.* ix. 1-4, and astutely noting that Horace's wines were far removed from those of the *plebs sordida* on the one hand, and from the wines of Maecenas on the other. See also Griffin, *Latin Poets* (above, n. 10), 65-87.

[47] Hor. *Epist.* i. 14.34; *CIL* IV, 1679.

[48] G. Hermansen, *Ostia, Aspects of Roman City Life* (Edmonton, 1981), 125ff., discusses 38 Ostian taverns; cf. also T. Kleberg, *Hôtels, restaurants et cabarets dans l'antiquité romaine* (Uppsala, 1957); on which however see Purcell's criticisms ('Wine and wealth in Ancient Italy', above, n. 45), 14.

[49] *CIL* XIV, 914 (C. Domitius Priscus).

[50] *CIL* XIV, 2112 (= *ILS*, 7212), Lanuvium, 136 CE.

adorned the tomb of a municipal *popinaria* 'owing to whom Tibur's fame was spread wide abroad':[51] her respectability suggests something equally respectable about her clientele, for it cannot have been only Roman aristocrats (like Juvenal's Lateranus, who enjoyed drinking with social riff-raff in an Ostian *popina*)[52] who were the sole consumers of decent wines in establishments like these. Finally, we should keep in mind that the socially heterogeneous character of Roman *convivia* must have introduced many a non-notable to prestige wines: to be sure, *amici minores* at grand dinners complained about ill treatment on this score, but we also know of cases where someone new to the household (and to the quality of its cellar) misjudged the power of such unaccustomed tipple and ended up drunk.[53]

As for drunkenness in lower-class housing, a passage of the *Satyricon* presents what is perhaps the most explicit evidence, a vivid scene of lodgers drinking together *in eodem synoecio*, and the *diversitor* accusing Eumolpus and the others of fleeing the *insula* rather than pay for their night's lodging: a crowd of drunken lodgers (*hospitum ebriorum frequentia*) and building attendants (*insularii*) all participate in the ensuing rumpus.[54] Widespread and heavy drinking in the *insulae* must have been as much a part of the urban atmosphere as the drunks one regularly encountered on Roman streets at night. And, while some of the latter, no doubt, were tipsy Roman notables, making their late way home after *convivia*, it will surely have been inebriates of non-illustrious status whom (if Suetonius is to be believed) the youthful Otho enjoyed catching unawares on the streets at night and tossing about in blankets.[55]

Drunken donkey-drivers and others in intoxicated condition — some rich, but most of marginal status — turn up too in Roman Egypt, where in a number of papyri complaints are lodged against violent and illegal attacks.[56] The penalty for personal injuries perpetrated when drunk (like those committed at night-time, in temples, or in the market-place) was twice that normally prescribed:[57] the explicit penalties prove the place of drunken violence in social reality. Roman jurists, on the other hand, show

---

[51] *CIL* XIV, 3709 (= *ILS*, 7477): *... quam propter multi Tibur celebrare solebant.*

[52] Juv. viii. 171-8.

[53] Lucian, *de Mercede Conductis* 18 (newcomer to a grand household unaccustomed to powerful wine); Pliny, *Ep.* ii. 6; Juv. v. 125-7, etc. (complaints of ill treatment); Pliny, *Ep.* ix. 24 (*vir municipalis*, on his first day in Rome, attends a grand dinner); cf. also, on the heterogeneous character of *convivia*, D'Arms, 'The Roman *convivium*' (above, n. 19), 318-19.

[54] Petron. *Sat.* 93-5; for *insularii*, see B.W. Frier, 'The rental market in early imperial Rome', *JRS* 67 (1977), 28, n. 8. For the staff of Petronius's lodging house and its social composition, cf. B.W. Frier, *Landlords and Tenants in Imperial Rome* (Princeton, 1980), 28.

[55] Cic. *Fam.* vii. 22; Apul. *Met.* iii. 5; Pliny, *Ep.* iii. 12; Juv. iii. 278 (deep-drinking notables on the streets late at night); Suet. *Otho* ii. 1 (Otho's escapades). For references to heavy drinking among the graffiti of Pompeii, see e.g. *CIL* IV, 1819, 1831, 8492.

[56] H.C. Youtie, 'Drunken rowdies', *ZPE* 31 (1978), 167-9 (translating P. Mich. inv. 4195): '... at a late hour ... both of them donkey-drivers ... becoming drunk made an assault on my house and inflicted no little violence ...'. Other drunks: P. Isid. 75 (rich men); H. Hauben, 'On the Melitians in P.London VI (P.Jewws) 1914: the problem of Papas Hebraiscus' *Proc. XVI Congr. Papyr.* (New York, 1980) (= *American Studies in Papyrology* 23 (Chico CA., 1981)), 447-56 (drunken soldiers); cf. also *PLondon* vii, 2009, 3a (245-244 BCE), *POxy.* xxxvi, 2758 (110-112 CE).

[57] *P.Hal.* 1, 193-5 (= A.S. Hunt and C.C. Edgar, *Select Papyri* vol. ii (London, 1932-4), no. 202, pp. 193ff.): 'Injuries done in drunkenness or by night or in a temple or in the market-place shall forfeit twice the amount of prescribed penalty'.

almost no interest in drunkenness; I confess to finding this baffling, since they have much to say about wine in general (texts on the wine trade number some 200), and one might have anticipated arguments based on the premise that the drunkard could not be held as responsible for his acts as someone fully in his senses. Still, drunken slaves do appear in the legal texts (drunkenness being one of the specified defects of slaves sold in the market-place), and in a text from Nero's day a group of nocturnal disturbers of the peace in a lower-class apartment block were quite naturally assumed to be 'drunkards or runaway slaves, or both'.[58]

In second-century Lanuvium, strict regulations were aimed at discouraging the lowly members of a *collegium* from drunken rowdiness; in first-century Alexandria, Philo claimed to know of 'organizations in whose fellowship you could find no sound elements but only liquor, tippling, drunkenness and the outrageous conduct they lead to'.[59] In short, it seems that we can with some confidence locate heavy drinking and drunkenness outside upper-class circles as well as within them, and long before the end of the fourth century, when Ammianus Marcellinus painted his famous picture of 'bibulous Rome'.[60]

DOCTORS AND WINE

Fourth and finally, the subject of doctors and wine deserves discussion. Many aspects of the general topic seem to me to hold quite exceptional interest: for instance, doctors mixed and often prescribed spiced wine; since Galen's Roman offices, as Filippo Coarelli reminds me, were near the Horrea Piperataria, what is the full nexus of association involving spices, doctors, and wine?[61] What social meaning lies behind the complex medical classifications of wines, and what was the role of the medical profession not just in assessing wine's therapeutic properties, but in helping to shape aristocratic tastes? Did doctors, by promoting certain wines at the expense of others, or by introducing novel drinking habits, succeed simultaneously in influencing the market

[58] Ulpian (1 Ed. Aed. Cur.), *Digest* xxi. 1.4.2.; xxi. 1.14.4; Ulpian (1 Ed. Aed. Cur.), *Digest* xxi. 1.25.6. In the single occurrence of *ebrietas* in the *Digest* (xlviii. 19.11.2, Marcian) which distinguishes among offences committed by design, impulse, or accident, drunkenness is placed in the second category (*impetus*). Nero's day: Petron. *Sat.* 95; cf. also Philo, *In Flacc.* 4 (heavy drinking in Egyptian σύνοδοι).

[59] *CIL* XIV, 2112 (= *ILS*, 7212), cited also above, n. 50 (Lanuvium); Philo, *In Flacc.* 136-7 (Alexandria); this and other texts cited also by R. MacMullen, *Roman Social Relations, 50 BC to AD 284* (New Haven, 1974), 77-8.

[60] Amm. Marc. xiv. 6.25; xxviii. 4.29 (tavern life) cited also by Purcell, 'Wine and wealth in Ancient Italy' (above, n. 45), 15, who appositely notices also the wine-drinking in the imperial *collegia* of the urban poor, and the 'development of a vigorous drinking-place culture among the urban communities of Roman cities' (p. 14).

[61] Galen and Rome: *PIR²* G, 24; G.W. Bowersock, *Greek Sophists in the Roman Empire* (Oxford, 1969); spiced wines: Pliny, *HN* xiv. 92; Macrob. *Sat.* vii. 7; Ath. xi. 464C-D; doctors: Tchernia, *Le vin de l'Italie romaine* (above, n. 43), 203ff. For '*ypocras*', a highly spiced mulled wine served for medicinal purposes at the end of feasts in the Middle Ages, cf. L.J. Sass, 'Religion, medicine, politics and spices', *Appetite* (1981), 10.

(they certainly seem to have incurred the hostility of both emperors and members of the educated élite)?[62]

But in the present context my question needs to be focused far more narrowly. The American Medical Association designated alcoholism a 'disease' or 'illness' in 1956, and later (1980), a 'handicap' or 'disability'.[63] Meanwhile, medical journals have been publishing their share of papers on ancient Roman drinking; in one of these, *The British Journal of Addiction*, the author asserts that 'descriptions of acute alcoholic psychosis go back to ... Galen'.[64] Assertions like this are freighted with assumptions which require unpacking; we need first to ask, of which of the prodigious drinkers in Seneca's or Pliny's lists might 'alcoholic' seem a reasonable description? Do modern notions of 'alcoholism' conform even approximately to Roman conceptions of their own drinking behaviours, to what they understood by *vinolentia*?

To begin with, a note of caution. We will do well to guard against privileging modern western presumptions about disease, and so crowding out the traditions and values that shaped attitudes and behaviour in ancient Rome.[65] A more circumspect approach is required: if one were to seek evidence for 'alcoholism' in Roman society, which did not think in these categories, what signs might be thought to be particularly suggestive? Indications of a deeply ingrained propensity to drink, perhaps — *consuetudo*? Old Leaena, the doorkeeper in Plautus's *Curculio*, is a type who might be thought to qualify: she is described as *multibiba atque merobiba ... vinosissuma* (77-9). While still a girl (*puella*) the mother of Saint Augustine came perilously close to *vinolentia* — as her son says he learned much later from Monica's domestic servant. Assigned by her parents the household chore of fetching wine from the cellar, Monica would take a sip from the cup before pouring it into the wine-jar; 'and so adding to that daily small quantity every day a little more ... she developed such a *consuetudo* that she soon was greedily drinking down cups of wine almost brimful'. But God, says

---

[62] Observe *CIL* X, 388 (L. Manneius, the 'winegiving' doctor of Tralles and later of Atinum). For medical classifications of wine and their implications, see the suggestive remarks of N. Purcell, *JRS* 78 (1988), 195. Doctors influence aristocratic taste: Pliny, *HN* xiv. 73 (*auctoritas* of Erasistratus), 96 (Chian wine first prescribed), 144 (drinking habits the result of doctors' policy of perpetually advertizing themselves by some novelty); xiv. 64 (Tiberius's complaints about doctors' exaggerated claims for Sorrentine wine); xxiii. 32 (*discordes medicorum sententiae*). But Pliny is far too harsh on doctors: see V. Nutton, 'The perils of patriotism: Pliny and Roman medicine', in R. French and F. Greenway (eds), *Science in the Early Roman Empire: Pliny the Elder, his Sources and Influence* (Kent, 1986), 30-58. For Galen's strictures against self-indulgent doctors, drinking at the tables of the rich, see e.g. Kühn i, 59; xvii B, 151.

[63] D.B. Heath, 'A decade of development in the anthropological study of alcohol use: 1970-1980', in Douglas (ed.), *Constructive Drinking* (above, n. 22), 48; for the contributions of Alcoholics Anonymous to the development of the 'disease model' (beginning in 1937), see P. Antze, 'Symbolic action in Alcoholics Anonymous', in Douglas (ed.), *Constructive Drinking* (above, n. 22), 154-8.

[64] J.O. Leibowitz, 'Studies in the history of alcoholism II: acute alcoholism in ancient Greek and Roman medicine', *British Journal of Addiction* 62 (1967), 83-6 (quotation from p. 83).

[65] The use of the term 'alcoholic' is far too free in the secondary literature: see for example E.M. Jellinek, 'Drinkers and alcoholics in ancient Rome', *Journal of Studies on Alcohol* 37 (1976), 1718-41, where 'alcoholic' is never defined, and where such statements as the following are routinely encountered: '... it is evident that in Rome of the first century not only excessive drinkers but true alcoholics as well were frequent among the wealthy freedmen, the upper-middle and upper classes' (p. 1737). Somewhat better are the sections on 'inebriety prevalence' by G.A. Austin *et al.*, *Alcohol in Western Society from Antiquity to 1800: a Chronological History* (Santa Barbara, 1985), 38-50.

Augustine, was watching over Monica; she was put suddenly back on the right path by the same servant: she taunted Monica with being a wine bibber (*meribibula*) and so returned her instantly to sanity.[66]

This passage is indeed suggestive, the more so since Augustine characterizes the insult as helping to 'cure' a 'secret disease' (*latentem morbum*), and since Brent Shaw has now invoked what he takes to be 'the pervasive problem of excessive drinking' to explain the later unprovoked outbursts of anger (*ira*) to which Augustine's father seems to have been frequently subject.[67] But on the other hand, Augustine's reference to a 'disease' is clearly metaphorical; Shaw's hypothesis, as he himself recognizes,[68] is unable to be properly tested; and in any event the handmaiden's insult seems the only intervention Monica ever required: she is presented in later life as the soul of sobriety, piously conveying bread and wine to the oratories of the saints in North Africa and Milan, and — on the conclusion of her duties — never taking more than a small cup of heavily watered wine as refreshment — her palate sober, her spirit wholly free of *vinolentia* and *amor vini*.[69] The case for Monica's 'alcoholism', to my mind, has not been made.

I do not hereby mean to imply that 'alcoholism', in its presently accepted sense, did not exist in antiquity — only that, since Romans did not think in these categories, we will need to be both inventive and very careful if we hope to succeed in finding proof of its existence.[70] Nor do I mean to imply that moralists, medical writers and others did not know or failed to comment on adverse physical effects of excessive drinking: debilities mentioned ranged from simple headache to physical frailty and a shortened life.[71] Nor is it to suggest that the Romans could not distinguish between the *ebrius* and the *ebriosus* — between occasional drunkenness and a chronic condition: Seneca observes that he who is *ebrius* may be in this state for the first time, whereas the *ebriosus*, for his part, may be (at any given moment) *extra ebrietatem*.[72] But so far as I know no Roman medical writer took the further step of actually equating drunkenness with disease. Certainly the passage of Galen invoked in *The British Journal of Addiction* quite explicitly fails to make this equation; Galen says merely that 'this is what happens at the first stage of many diseases, as one can see occurring (also) in those who are drunk'.[73] Here the

---

[66] Aug. *Conf.* ix. 8.

[67] Aug. *Conf.* ix. 8 (*latentem morbum*); B.D. Shaw, 'The family in late antiquity: the experience of Augustine', *P&P* 115 (1987), 31.

[68] Shaw (see preceding note), 31, n. 120: 'It [i.e. the pervasive problem of excessive drinking] is, as always, a mode of behavior whose extent and effects are most difficult for the historian to measure'.

[69] Aug. *Conf.* vi. 2.

[70] For an example of a thoughtful approach to the complexities of these questions see J.C. Sournia, 'L'alcoolisme dans la Grèce antique', *Archéologie et Médecine* (= VIIèmes rencontres internationales d'archéologie et d'histoire d'Antibes) (Juan-les-Pins, 1987), 523-30 (= *A History of Alcoholism* (Blackwell, 1989)): short life expectancy prevented ancient medical recognition of most clinical indicators of chronic intoxication (links between cirrhosis and alcohol are a nineteenth-century discovery in Western medicine); related mental states pose formidable diagnostic problems across such historical distances (evidence for the chronic intoxication of Alexander the Great providing a case in point).

[71] Pliny, *HN* xiv. 70 (headache); xiv. 142 (pale face, baggy cheeks, bloodshot eyes, tremulous hands, fitful sleep at night); Sen. *Ep.* xcv. 16 (pallor, quivering of muscles soaked in wine, indigestion, emaciation, tottering and stumbling, jaundiced and discoloured complexion, twitching, giddiness, disturbed vision and hearing). Cf. also Macrob. *Sat.* vii. 6; Gal. Kühn xv, 162.

[72] Sen. *Ep.* lxxxiii. 11.

[73] Gal. vii K, 663-4 (= *de comate secundum Hippocratem*, ch. 4); cf. Kühn xiv, 540, for a similar contrast between drunkenness and disease.

contrast between the two conditions is explicit, and shows that Galen believed these to be quite different types of debility.

Is this, after all, so surprising? One of the clear gains of much recent anthropological research has been to show that in almost all cultures where drunkenness was frequent, highly esteemed, and actively sought, the association of drinking with what some, with a modern Western bias, have chosen to call 'alcoholism', is in fact extremely rare. The educated Roman élite conceived the 'problem' of a 'problem drinker' as first and foremost a problem of character, as moral weakness — which is why we find Roman jurists classifying the defect of a slave prone to excessive drinking not as physical, but as a mental or dispositional, failing.[74] Whether they were right to do so is quite another question — a question not solely for historians.[75]

---

[74] Ulpian, *Digest* xxi 1. 4.2, 14.4, 25.6.

[75] It is a pleasure to acknowledge the friendly aid of B.W. Frier, R. Kaster, L. Koenen, S. McCormack, M. Meckler, V. Nutton, J. Pinault, J. Porter and D. Shackleton Bailey. I am grateful also to J. Bodel and R.P. Saller, and to members of their NEH Summer Seminar on the Roman Family (American Academy in Rome, 1991) for helpful comments and suggestions.